Social
Psychology

ALFRED R.
LINDESMITH
Indiana University at Bloomington

ANSELM L.
STRAUSS
*University of California at
San Francisco*

NORMAN K.
DENZIN
University of Illinois at Urbana

Social Psychology

FIFTH EDITION

Holt, Rinehart and Winston

NEW YORK CHICAGO SAN FRANCISCO DALLAS
MONTREAL TORONTO LONDON SYDNEY

Designed by Joan Stoliar

Library of Congress Cataloging in Publication Data

Lindesmith, Alfred Ray, 1905–
  Social psychology.

  Bibliographies.
  Includes index.
  1. Social psychology. I. Strauss, Anselm L.,
joint author. II. Denzin, Norman K., joint author.
III. Title.
HM251.L477 1978   301.1   77-90837
ISBN 0-03-039861-4

Printed in the United States of America

890   039   987654321

Preface

THE FIFTH EDITION of *Social Psychology* extends the revisions of the previous edition. We have sought to clarify our symbolic interactionist point of view by more systematically comparing it with other social psychological perspectives. Yet, we feel that abstract statements on theory are unwarranted. Each of our chapters presents a symbolic interactionist analysis of the topic, or topics, at hand. The perspective cannot be divorced from its application to such substantive issues as scientific conduct, language acquisition, comparative psychology, childhood socialization, sex-identity training, moral careers, deviance, illness, aging, and death. Our revisions were aimed at more forcefully making this basic point.

Among the principle changes is found in Chapter 1, where we discuss science and social psychology and further develop our views on causal analysis and the statue of "variables" in the scientific method. We have renewed our emphasis on identity transformations that occur throughout the life cycle and we have reorganized our chapters to reflect this concern. Our discussion of deviants and deviant worlds has been shortened in order to give it a tighter theoretical focus. A new chapter on illness, pain, aging, and dying has been added, an addition that seemed called for because all human societies make, manage, and process these bodily related phenomena and a social psychological analysis is long overdue. William C. Cockerham's *Medical Sociology* (Englewood Cliffs, N.J.: Prentice-Hall, 1978) proved extremely useful in the preparation of this chapter, as were conversations with him.

We hope that this edition of *Social Psychology* communicates the excitement and understanding that comes from the application of symbolic interactionism to the study of human group life. We have presented what we regard as the basic implications of this, the most sociological of all social psychologies.

A.R.L. / A.L.S. / N.K.D.

Contents

PART ONE

Symbolic Interaction as Perspective and Method

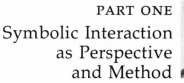

chapter *1* *Science and Social Psychology*　　　*3*

Science as Symbolic Activity　　4
The History of Science　　5
A Scientific Model: The Cause of Malaria　　9
Scientific Logic　　12
Inventing and Testing Theory　　20
Symbolic Interactionism in Social
　　Psychology　　30
Basic Considerations　　33
Ethnomethodology　　40
Theory, Research Methods, and the Study
　　of Interaction　　46
Summary　　47

chapter *2* *The Evolutionary Setting of Human
Behavior*　　　*52*

The Emergence of Humans and Culture　　53
The Evolution of Social Behavior　　55
Insect Societies　　58
The Behavior of Chimpanzees　　63
The Absence of Language among Lower
　　Animals　　70
Some Consequences of the Lack of
　　Language　　75
Summary　　79

chapter **3** *Symbolic Environments and Cognitive Structures*   *83*

     Symbolic Environments   84
     Social Worlds, Symbolic Coordinates, and
       Fictions   89
     The Categorical, or Language, Attitude   93
     Cognitive Structures and Cognitive
       Dissonance   99
     Summary   103

chapter **4** *Social Structure, Groups, and Language*   *107*

     Consensus and Human Groups   108
     The Group Bases of Language   109
     The Nature of Language: Signs and
       Symbols   115
     The Second Signaling System   117
     Symbolic Behavior as Shared Behavior   121
     Nonverbal Communication   126
     Summary   132

PART TWO
Social
Structure
and the Self

chapter 5 *Language Differentiation and the Learning Process* **139**

Forms of Language Behavior   140
Internalized Speech and Thought   146
Daydreaming and Dreaming   154
Metaphor, Analogy, and Flexibility of Thought   161
Images of Mobility   164
Humor, Interaction, and the Resources of Language   165
Language and the Structure of Thought   169
Internalized Audiences   173
Summary   175

chapter 6 *Perception, Memory, and Planning*   **178**

Social Patterning of Perception   179
Perception and Language   187
Human and Subhuman Perception   192
The Social Basis of Memory   196
Memory in Lower Animals   198
Human Remembering as a Symbolic Process   200
Historical Communication, Perception, and Memory   206
The Planning of Behavior   210
Summary   213

chapter 7 *Humans without Symbols: Restricted Communication*   **217**

Isolated Children   218
The Blind Deaf   219
The Mentally Retarded   222
Behavioral Disorders of Aphasia   226
The Social Isolation of the Schizophrene   235
Summary   238

Contents   ix

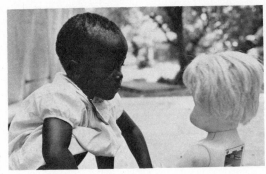

PART THREE
Life Cycle:
The Genesis of Self

chapter 8 *Motives, Activities, and Accounts* 245

Biologically Rooted Motives? 248
Need Psychology 255
Freudian Conceptions 258
The Marxian View 267
A Sociological Conception 269
Social Sources of Individual Motivation 275
Summary 279

chapter 9 *The Acquisition of Language and Concepts* 283

Instrumental Use of Gestures 284
Learning to Use and Comprehend Symbols 286
Declarative and Manipulative Functions of Language 290
Language Acquisition According to Chomsky 293
The Learning of Concepts 297
Reasoning and Child Development 303
Summary 308

chapter 10 *The Origins and Development of Self* 312

Socialization and Interaction 312
Development of Self-Awareness 315

Individuality and the Social Character of
    the Self   322
The Self in Early Childhood   329
Other Developmental Views: Freud, Erikson,
    Sullivan   329
Summary   348

chapter **11** *The Social Worlds of Childhood*   *351*

The Child's Egocentrism   352
A Critique of the Egocentric Perspec-
    tive   353
The Child's Network of Significant
    Others   356
Perspectives and the Generalized
    Other   360
The Nature of Objectivity   368
Differentiation of Basic Sex Roles   373
Summary   382

PART FOUR
Life Cycle:
Adult Transformations

chapter **12** *Self-Control, Social Control, and
Identity Transformation*   *389*

Voluntary Behavior   391
Interactional Loss of Self-Control   398
Hypnosis: The Ceding of Self-Control   403
Theories of Hypnosis   407

Institutionally Induced Changes in
   Self-Control   411
Coping Mechanisms   418
Summary   427

chapter *13* *Selves, Careers, and Social Worlds*   431

Careers   431
Membership in Social Worlds   437
Ideologies and Social Worlds   440
Reference Groups   445
Changing Worlds: Danger and Chal-
   lenge   450
Alienation and Modern Society   454
The Articulation of Implicated Selves   457
Summary   459

chapter *14* *Sexual Activity and Sexual
Identification*   464

The Evolutionary Picture   464
Hormones, Homosexuality, and Inver-
   sion   466
Sexual Identity and Self-Esteem   472
Falling In and Out of Love   476
Sexual Activities and Erotic Imagery   479
Sexual Politics: Meanings of the
   Sex Act   486
Abortion and Its Symbolism   489
Summary   491

chapter *15* *Deviance and Deviant Worlds*   495

Conceptions of Deviance   496
The Nature of Deviance   496
Deviant Careers and Social Worlds   503
Deviant Worlds and Individuals   505
Criminal Worlds   506
Drug Addiction and the Addict's
   World   512
The Homosexual   519

Political Worlds and Political
Deviancy   524
Individual Deviance   528
Summary   532

chapter *16* *Illness, Aging, and Dying*   *538*

Illness and Pain   539
Body Images, Disease, and Illness   545
The Social Worlds of the Old   547
Dying and Death   553
The Social Consequences of Death:
Mourning   558
The Meanings of Death   560
Summary   561

Index   *563*

PART ONE

Symbolic Interaction as Perspective and Method

Social Psychologist regard their discipline as an attempt to understand the thought, feeling, and behavior or influence by actual imagined or implied present of others (Gordon Allport) Refers to the fact that an individuals action often reflect an awareness that he or she is a part of a particular cultural, occupational or social group.

chapter 1

Science and
Social
Psychology

In this opening chapter we have two goals in mind: one is to introduce the reader in a general way to the field of social psychology; the other is to provide a brief description of the nature of science, using as our point of departure and model a relatively recent scientific achievement in the biological field—namely, the discovery of the cause of malaria at about the end of the nineteenth century. Sociologists commonly resort to the most advanced sciences, such as physics and chemistry, for their models. We have selected our example because it is simpler than those usually used, and because it is more directly relevant, it seems to us, to the kinds of problems and difficulties that arise when students of human behavior seek to achieve scientific status for their disciplines.

Social psychology, like other social sciences, aspires to be scientific, but like them its status as a genuine science is disputed and often denied. Certainly none of the social sciences can be said to have produced an organized, precise, structured body of reliable knowledge that compares with those of the advanced natural sciences. There are many who believe, indeed, that this is in fact not possible, that there is a basic indeterminacy or unpredictability in human behavior—perhaps even "free will"—which makes the search for a science of human behavior futile. During the last century and a quarter, for example, medical science has been revolutionized by the discovery of the causes of numerous diseases, but if we look for similar achievements in the search for the causes of complex forms of human social behavior, we do not find them. Instead of universal agreement (on the cause of a given disease, for example), there is widespread disagreement and dispute about the forms of human social behavior, and numerous types of theories that are inconsistent with each other and often contradictory are offered as explanations.

Social psychology is not an unambiguously defined field of study, and varied definitions of it have been given. Following the late pragmatic philosopher G. H. Mead, we may say in general that it concerns itself with the phases of social experience that derive from individuals' participation in the ongoing worlds of social groups, with their interactions with other people, and with the effects upon them of what is broadly designated as the cultural environment. The task of social psychology, as Simmel has said (42:14), is to identify the forms of social interaction that relate people to each other in everyday life and to investigate and analyze how people are affected by their social experiences. Human society has two basic aspects: on the one hand, it is conceived as a complex external structure involving people in relation to each other within a vast cultural environment; on the other hand, society also manifests itself within the individual. It is, in a sense, internalized by the person in the socialization process. These two aspects of society are different aspects of the same reality, and social psychologists devote their major attention to the latter, or individual, aspect.

Science as Symbolic Activity

We shall note in this book that the symbolizing capacities of humans mean that they live in symbolic environments. The world out there is not reacted to directly, but through the mediation of symbols. So, even if different groups live on the same physical terrain and under the same sky, it is not necessarily the same terrain or the same sky for all of them. The sky, for instance, can be the abode of a family of gods, the container for a hierarchy of seven ascending heavens, or the small segment of an expanding universe that is available to the naked eye from one small body called Earth. This idea of symbolic environments is obviously also pertinent to changing conceptions and emergent communities; the same terrain and sky—say, in and over the high Sierras—are, or were, symbolized and reacted to differently by scenery painters, mountain climbers, environmental geologists, and by the explorers and travelers of a century ago.

The above examples purposely include the idea of science because science too gives new and ever-changing conceptions of the physical universe. As one historian of science, Thomas Kuhn, has asserted (cor-

a model

rectly, we believe) in writing about scientific paradigms (or conceptual frameworks) (24:110):

> Examining the record of past research from the vantage point of contemporary historiography, the historian of science may be tempted to exclaim that when paradigms change, the world itself changes with them. Led by a new paradigm, scientists adopt new instruments and look in new places. Even more important, during revolutions scientists see new and different things when looking with familiar instruments in places they have looked before. It is rather as if the professional community had suddenly been transported to another planet where familiar objects are seen in a different light and are joined by unfamiliar ones as well. Of course, nothing of quite that sort does occur: there is no geographical transplantation; outside the laboratory everyday affairs usually continue as before. Nevertheless, paradigm changes do cause scientists to see the world of their research-engagement differently. In so far as their only recourse to that world is through what they see and do, we may want to say that after a (scientific) revolution scientists are responding to a different world.

Of course, the scientists in any given field or specialty have very complex versions of the reality which they thus seek to conceptualize. Some of those conceptualizations are unknown even to educated laymen, while others have been so revolutionary or so dramatic or so well publicized that even relatively uneducated people have some crude notion of the conceptualization. It is sometimes asserted that what is most visible to the layman is not the scientist's important formulations but their secondary, side products; that is, applied science. While the latter is appreciated, what nurtures it—pure scientific activity—is overlooked, underestimated, or quite misconstrued. While there is some truth to this assertion, it is safe to say that in important respects the twentieth century's physical and biological universe is, for the layman, appreciably different from that of the preceding centuries. Even the most scientifically innocent can grasp the ideas that an examination of the moon close up might yield some clues as to the origin and age of earth, that stars might have life cycles, and that the universe might be either expanding or contracting—and someday we might know which!

In the pages that follow, science will be discussed with primary emphasis on two matters: its relation to changing symbolic environments, and its aspects as a conceptualizing activity.

The History of Science

THE EMERGENCE OF MODERN SCIENCE

Modern science as a specialized institution and form of human symbolic activity appeared on the historical scene in approximately 1600 and is associated particularly with the famous investigations of Galileo. Its emergence is often referred to as the "Galilean revolution" because it signaled the rejection of an old tradition dominated in Europe by religious

Galileo, a founder of modern physical science. (*New York Public Library Picture Collection*)

philosophers and theologians and by the doctrines of Aristotle that had long been imbedded in the teachings of the Church. Prior to this approximate date, what we now call scientific thinking was not sharply differentiated from other types of intellectual activity, and there was no really separate and distinct literature, logic, method, point of view, or tradition that characterized what we, in retrospect, now regard as significant contributions to the early development of the scientific view. Modern science as a specialized social institution with its own particular organization and sense of community, with its own methods and its own logic, developed rapidly during the 1600s with the organization of the first scientific associations, stimulated by the accomplishments of a long list of famous scientific giants, such as Galileo, Harvey, Descartes, Newton, and others. Since that time science has, of course, become a basic social institution that has revolutionized social life and thought throughout most of the world.

Prior to about 1500, the flow of ideas in Europe, where modern science was born, was mainly from the East into Europe, as European scholars began to pay increasingly serious attention to the writings of the ancient Greeks, whose works reached them either through Latin translations or from Arabic sources. During this renaissance period, the influence of religious dogmas and the authority of the Church diminished, as did the authority of Aristotelian doctrine and that of other ancients. A new skepticism, a new willingness to entertain novel ideas, and a new courage in challenging authoritarianism in general made its appearance.

In the middle 1500s, for example, Copernicus proposed what was essentially the modern view of the solar system, a view that had been proposed many centuries earlier by Aristarchus of ancient Greece and rejected there by Aristotle. Such was the power of dogma and authority that it took a century and more before the Copernican conception was at all widely accepted.

The all-too-brief comments above indicate that modern science did not come into being suddenly in one fell swoop, but was preceded by a long earlier evolution that made it possible. The writings of the ancient Greeks are prime examples.

While the ancient Greeks are given credit for many important prescientific and scientific ideas, Greek science did not become science in the modern sense, although one may say that it was a near miss. The Greeks are said to have invented logic, and from them we inherited the phonetic alphabet, which revolutionized communication and made Greece perhaps the first significantly literate society. The Greeks glorified "Logos," the intellectual processes, and they glorified logical discourse, but they never really hit upon the idea of an expanding system of knowledge and theory geared to direct observation, with experiment as its test. They also never succeeded in using their knowledge to harness nature as we have done through the creation of an elaborate technology. Prestige seems to have been associated primarily with the skillful and persuasive use of words and mathematical symbols, rather than with the direct, systematic confrontation with evidence. Perhaps this may have been connected with the existence of slavery at that time, which led the Greek intellectual aristocrats to think of the hard, messy kind of labor involved in much research as something beneath them, something for slaves to do.

At any rate, Greek science did not take firm root, and after its golden era a couple of centuries before the birth of Christ, it went into decline. Noting this decline during the first centuries of the Christian era, Singer observes (43:152):

> Nature had not been harnessed as we have harnessed her. Science was a way of looking at the world rather than of dealing with the world. And as a way of looking at the world—a way of life—positive knowledge, that is, science, was a failure. The world was a thing that man could neither enjoy nor master nor study. A new light was sought and found. In its glare the old wisdom became foolishness and the old foolishness, wisdom. Weary of questions, men embraced at last and gladly the promises of faith.

As we have already indicated, European intellectuals did not really begin to build upon or accept the Greek scientific achievements until approximately 1500. Since Greek learning lost its impetus and creativity in the early centuries of the Christian era, this raises the question as to what happened to it in the intervening centuries during the Dark Ages of Europe.

THE
ARABIAN
PERIOD

The answer to the above query is that, apart from the Greek influence that was preserved and perpetuated by the Church, especially by the incorporation of Aristotelianism into Christian dogma, Greek learning was kept alive and added to by the Arabs, who translated many of the Greek documents into Arabic. During the period from about 900 to 1200 A.D. there was especially intense intellectual activity within the Arabic world, and a number of cities within the Arab empire became famous centers of learning, where scholars met and had access to the best libraries then in existence. When, after several centuries, European interest in the East was stimulated (as, for example, by the Crusades), European scholars more and more used materials and ideas made accessible to them through Arabic sources. This process added greatly to the ferment of ideas in Europe which was the basis and source of the emergence there of modern science.

PRECONDITIONS
OF SCIENCE

To appreciate more fully that modern science is in fact a social institution deeply rooted in society and dependent and responsive to developments within it, some of the earliest social developments prior to the flowering of ancient Greek civilization should be noted. Over a period of several thousand years the human populations had greatly increased, and when the first great civilizations came into being people began to live together in relatively large numbers in cities. The prior development of agricultural arts and technologies, such as the cultivation of grain and the domestication of animals, made a settled agricultural life possible and also, by making the production of food easier and more efficient, created the possibility of social classes, including a leisure class that devoted itself to intellectual, religious, and artistic pursuits.

Commerce and trade developed between the peoples and empires of the ancient world, promoting the collection, recording, and transmission of information and ideas from one place to another. Numerical and writing systems were invented and improved as the centuries passed. Observations were made concerning all sorts of natural phenomena, such as, for example, the apparent movement of the stars, planets, and the sun and moon. A remarkably accurate calendar was devised by the ancient Babylonians. The art of shaping metals for use in warfare and in other pursuits was gradually improved. As various empires, city-states, and kingdoms evolved during this period, they found that trade was absolutely vital to them, for example, as a means of producing the metals needed to forge effective weapons for warding off invaders and political enemies. Transportation of materials and of people by land and by sea promoted exploration, fostered the exchange of ideas and the spread of inventions, and stimulated the curiosity of those with intellectual natures. Of particular importance, of course, was the gradual perfection of written languages and numerical systems, which made it possible to record observations and happenings and laid the foundations for the beginnings of mathematical reasoning and of logic.

The classical civilization of Greece thus did not burst into bloom in a vacuum, but was instead the product of a long historical evolution, dating from the time when our human ancestors ceased to be hunters and nomads and adopted instead a settled, agricultural style of life. The Greeks, like all civilizations before and after, depended upon prior cultural, political, and technological accomplishments and built upon them.

A Scientific Model: The Cause of Malaria

As an example, or model, of the successful solution of a scientific problem, we take a simple example from the biological sciences—namely, the discovery of the cause of malaria. This model has the advantages of being widely known and being relatively simple and from a natural science field that is not so advanced and so far removed from the social sciences as nuclear physics is, for example. At the same time, many basic principles of scientific logic are exemplified. We mention physics because social scientists often draw their models from it. The model proposed here has additional advantages in that it suggests modes of analysis and problem solving that seem applicable to human behavior.

We will first describe how the explanation of malaria was discovered and then indicate some of the implications that this example has concerning various aspects of scientific method. Because this must be an abbreviated presentation, we will confine ourselves rather strictly to points that are either implicitly or explicitly involved in our example. John Dewey, incidentally, used the same example to illustrate the nature of scientific logic. (12:433–36)

The literal meaning of the word *malaria* is "bad air," and it is a reflection of early theories which attributed this disease and others to polluted atmosphere, putrid miasmas, exhalations from swamps and stagnant waters, or simply to night air. Malaria was a serious scourge in ancient times and was described by Hippocrates in the fifth century B.C. as well as by early Chinese, Arabic, and Roman writers. Before the time of Christ, the connection between the disease and stagnant water was noted and drainage was utilized as one preventive measure along with a host of others. It was also suggested that mosquitoes might have some-

Dr. Ronald Ross, who proved
that mosquitoes transmit malaria, with his wife, assistants,
and bird cages in Calcutta in
1898. (*New York Public Library
Picture Collection*)

thing to do with spreading the disease, but many other theories were
also proposed and malaria was often confused with a number of other
diseases. Long before the cause of malaria was discovered at the end of
the nineteenth century, the disease was treated with the bark of a tree
that contained quinine.

The cause of malaria today seems to many to be such a simple,
taken-for-granted fact that it should be observed that about two decades
of research effort by many scientists in various nations were involved in
its discovery. About two hundred years earlier a pioneer in microscopic
observation, van Leeuwenhoek, observed and described bacteria, but
little attention was given to his observations for many years thereafter,
until, in the second half of the nineteenth century the sciences of bacteri-
ology and immunology were established by such men as Pasteur, Koch,
and Lister. During this half century the microorganisms involved in a
number of plant and animal diseases were identified and studied, and
the role of insects in transmitting diseases became known. The guilt of
the mosquito with respect to disease other than malaria was established
before the crucial research on malaria was done.

The discovery of the cause of malaria began in 1880 when a French physician described a malarial parasite obtained from the blood of one of his patients. Italian investigators later demonstrated that the disease could be transmitted from human to human by infected blood, and in the 1890s British and Italian scientists suggested the mosquito (anopheles) as the transmitter of the disease. By 1900 it had been established that this theory was correct, by demonstrating that the disease was acquired only from the bite of an infected mosquito, and that persons protected from this mosquito did not contract the disease even in regions where malaria was rife. The biological cycles of the parasite had been traced out in sufficient detail to explain such matters as why quinine was an effective remedy, why the bite of an infected anopheles mosquito did not transmit the disease until days after the mosquito had become infected, and why other kinds of mosquitoes than the anopheles did not transmit the disease.

There are four subtypes of the malarial parasite, which is known as plasmodium, each of which has its own characteristic pattern of biological changes as it passes from its primary host, the mosquito, to its secondary host, man. In the mosquito the parasite undergoes sexual reproduction in the mosquito's stomach and, after a variable period of days, spores or seeds produced in the walls of the mosquito's stomach enter its salivary glands and are injected thereafter, along with saliva, into the bodies of future victims. It is only when this occurs that the insect becomes capable of spreading the disease.

When injected into the human skin by the mosquito, the "sporozoites" migrate to the liver where they grow and multiply asexually. Again, after a period of time, they begin to release, periodically, broods of new parasites called merozoites, which enter the blood stream and invade the red blood corpuscles. Inside these corpuscles they multiply until the corpuscle ruptures and releases a cluster of new parasites that invade other corpuscles to repeat the cycle.

When an anopheles mosquito draws some of the blood of a malarial victim into its stomach along with parasites, a small percentage of the parasites (known as gametocytes) are not digested and it is these that reproduce sexually inside the mosquito's stomach as we have indicated. There are about two hundred kinds of anopheles mosquitoes, some sixty or so of which transmit malaria. Other kinds of mosquitoes do not transmit the disease because when they ingest the parasites they digest all of them.

Repeated attacks of malaria may confer immunity of varying degrees, but this immunity is specific, not only with respect to the four species of plasmodium, but also with respect to the numerous strains within each. A person immune to one strain may be reinfected by another. In addition to man, monkeys, birds, reptiles, and some other mammals are susceptible to malaria.

Malaria is not ordinarily fatal, but it tends to recur because some of the parasites are able to hibernate in the liver for as long as twenty to thirty years. In some instances persons may have in their blood malarial gametocytes which die if they are not sucked up by a mosquito but which do not attack the red corpuscles or produce the disease. Such persons can transmit malaria even though they themselves do not have it. Death from malaria may result from anemia produced by destruction of red corpuscles, from excessive fever, or from clogging of blood vessels in vital bodily parts.

It needs to be noted that the story of the cycles of biologic change that the malarial parasite goes through in its two hosts has only been sketched here in an incomplete form. It has been noted that it moves from stomach, to salivary glands, to skin, to liver, to blood stream, changing in size, appearance, and form as it does so. We have also noted that the symptoms of the disease vary greatly from case to case, depending on a wide variety of factors, such as the individual's condition, the species or strain of the parasite, degrees of immunity, and others. The onset of malaria is still sometimes not recognized at once but may be definitely established by microscopic examination of a blood sample. Counting the number of parasites in a given unit of blood provides a rough indication of the severity of the attack.

Scientific Logic

THE NATURE OF CAUSAL PROCESSES

Using our example as a point of departure, we may first note that the theory of the cause of malaria that was demonstrated to be correct at the end of the nineteenth century is now accepted as an established fact. Ordinary laymen speak of malaria as a disease with a known cause, and while it may be affected by a wide variety of factors in its severity and incidence, it is ordinarily said to have only one cause—there is only one way in which the typical pattern of symptoms is produced. There are many other diseases that have been similarly analyzed and explained; there are others, like cancer, that are not understood and whose causes are unknown. While it is said today that there are about thirty or so substances that produce or cause cancer in humans or in lower animals, the term "cause" is here used in a popular and statistical sense only, not in the same sense in which this term has been traditionally used in modern science. Thus, while there may be some thirty substances that sometimes cause cancer in a loose sense, it is only too obvious to all, layman and scientist alike, that cancer is not understood today and that its cause has not been established with a certainty that is at all comparable to that of malaria. Unlike the cancer situation, the cause of malaria is always present when the disease exists, and the disease cannot occur when it is absent. Moreover, in the case of malaria there is, in addition to the *invariability* of the relation between cause and effect, the element of *uniqueness* of the relationship; the cause of malaria produces malaria only. It does not produce any other disease.

To make sense of the above, it is necessary to conceive of cause as a process, not as a thing, a factor, an event, or as a variable. Only if this is done does it make sense to say that any disease has a single cause. If one chooses to designate as "causes" all of the things, events, factors, and variables that are involved in a disease, the situation becomes hopelessly complex. For example, if one considered the vast numbers of such items in the causation of malaria—there are so many of them at the submolecular level alone, and so many of them are not understood—it would be necessary to say that the cause of malaria was unknown and could only be known when the science of biology had reached perfection and there was nothing more to be learned.

The idea that cause must be conceived as a process is not original with us, nor is it confined to biological sciences. John Dewey, for example, after using malaria as an example just as we have, remarked of scientific induction generally: "The integral role of determination of modes of interaction in scientific method involves processes to which the name causation is given." (12:440) Even more explicitly, the authors of a contemporary textbook on diseases and disease processes caution the student reader (45:248).

> The key word is *process*. In the Introduction . . . disease was described as dysfunction. Going one step further, it becomes evident that *dysfunction* is also a *process*. In his study of pathophysiology the student should keep in mind the question, What process or processes within the body have resulted in the expression of clinical disease? By always posing this question, the student may always avoid developing shallow, mechanical notions about the nature of illness.

Almost an identical caution is applicable in our field. Finally, Margenau, a professor of physics and natural philosophy at Yale, concludes concerning causes: "A partial cause may be a thing or an event, whereas a total cause is always a stage in a process." (29:425)

Following the leads suggested by Dewey and Margenau, we may describe a cause as a two-stage process in which the first stage is called *cause* and the second, *effect*, and in which the first stage leads to or produces the second in a series of interconnected and complex occurrences. A causal explanation of a phenomenon, be it a form of behavior, a disease, or a physical event, involves two problems. The first of these is the discovery or identification of the cause or causal process; the second is the description and explanation, insofar as this is possible, of precisely how the alleged cause operates to produce the effect. It should be emphasized that the discovery of a presently unknown causal process is not easy because of the fact that science concerns itself largely with causal processes that are not directly and easily observable. In the case of malaria, for example, the parasite that is instrumental in producing the disease is invisible to the naked eye—its identification and the tracing of its role in the disease required the prior invention of the microscope and the systematic investigation of microbes. On the other hand, there has never been any kind of scientific mystery involved in identifying the causal agent involved when a person is poisoned by the bite of a deadly snake, since the snake is highly visible and the effects of its venom appear quickly. In the case of other kinds of phenomena, such as physical phenomena, the identification of causal processes may require a restructuring of reality and the invention of new concepts, as exemplified by modern studies of motion and gravitational fields. At other times, causal processes are difficult of access either because they occur in the interior of an organism or at a subatomic, submolecular, or even a submicroscopic level.

The second phase of causal explanation is also difficult in many instances, for much the same reasons as those cited above. A causal process like that involved in disease may consist of a series of interrelated events, or what might be called a complex causal chain operating over a fairly extended period of time. A person infected with malaria may exhibit no symptoms for a substantial period of time. The difficulties involved in providing a full explanation and description of exactly what goes on during this period of incubation are demonstrated by the fact that there is considerable research on malaria still going on today, more than seventy years after the cause of the disease was discovered.

It is of interest, if one thinks of cause and effect as a continuous process, to note that an effective means of interrupting this process in the case of malaria was known in Europe about 250 years before the disease itself was understood. By using the drug quinine, extracted from the South American quinchona tree, Europeans were able to interrupt the disease process, either in its initial or its later stage. In the former case, one speaks of preventing the disease; in the latter, of curing it. Public interest in the search for presently unknown causes of disease rests upon the realization that when the cause of a disease is known, the possibilities of successful intervention to prevent or cure it are likely to be greatly increased.

SCIENTIFIC GENERALIZATION The causal generalization in our example was of the following form: "If A, then and then only, B," where A is the causal process and B is the malaria that it produces—the effect. This type of generalization is called a *universal* because it says something about all the members of a class— that is, all instances of malaria. A contrasting type of proposition is one that applies only to some of the instances as, for example, when we say that malaria is *sometimes* fatal. The latter are called *particular* propositions. We have indicated that there is no one single item, condition, factor, or influence which, by itself, produces malaria, but that there is one single unitary causal process that does. It is itself quite complex, involving many factors, items, and conditions in a series of interactions.

There is much variability in the world—so much, indeed, that one may say that no two things are ever exactly alike, whether they be physical objects, organisms, or persons. In the social sciences this point is often emphasized by the assertion of the uniqueness of individuals and the claim that this variability fatally handicaps the search for generalizations. If we turn to the case of malaria, we note great variability, some of which falls into types that are easily accounted for (for example, by species and strains of the causal agent); some of it, however, is a relatively simple expression of what one may perhaps describe as the natural tendency of things to vary. It is safe to say that no two cases of malaria are ever exactly the same. How then has it been possible to attribute malaria to a single causal process present in every case?

Generalization is possible because, while things differ and vary, there are also similarities among them. The generalization about the cause of malaria, which began as a theory and is now accepted as a fact, deals with features of the disease which are recurrent and common but does not deny the existence of differences. It is necessary to distinguish between what may be called the *essential similarities* upon which scientific definitions and theories focus and the *nonessential differences* between instances which are always there. A similar consideration applies to the various factors and conditions that influence this disease. Some are necessary; others may be present or absent when the disease occurs. A cause, or causal process, in contrast is both *necessary* and *sufficient* in that it is always present and guarantees the effect. A necessary condition only makes it possible. Thus, to get malaria one must be a creature of a certain type, but most of these creatures do not contract the disease. Similarly, the parasite is necessary, but not in itself sufficient to produce the disease.

An interesting logical problem raised by our example is that of accounting for our confidence that all of the countless instances of malaria that must have existed prior to the discovery of the cause of the disease were caused in the same way as at present. After all, none of these instances was ever examined to determine whether or not such an assumption was valid. And how can we be confident that this is the way malaria will be produced in the future?

The fact that a scientific generalization is often stated in the form of a universal does not mean that it claims to be an absolute truth. The term merely describes the form of the assertion. If we say that all dogs have three legs, this is a universal, even though it is patently false. If we say some dogs are brown, this is true but is not a universal, simply because it applies only to some dogs and not to all of them.

The role of universals in scientific generalization is closely linked to their logical form, for by making the claim of being applicable to all instances they focus scientific attention on possible exceptions. When unambiguous exceptions to such a generalization are found, they discredit the theory which they contradict and stimulate the search for a better one. The exceptional instance, in short, is the growing point of science. Theories of a nonuniversal, or "particular," or statistical nature do not serve this function. If, for example, it had been proposed in the early nineteenth century that poverty was the cause of malaria, since most of its victims were poor, this latter statement would have been true but of little significance, for everyone knew that rich persons also sometimes contracted the disease. A theory of this sort admits the exceptions in advance and deprives them of the crucial importance that they ordinarily have in scientific work. A false universal is thus of greater importance than a valid proposition that is nonuniversal, simply because the search for exceptions that it invites stimulates attempts to improve or replace it with a better one.

As Thomas Kuhn has observed, whenever the implications of a general theory are followed up by researchers in the processes of "normal" science, discrepancies tend to arise, either within the structure of theory or between the theory and the evidence. As this kind of embarrassing evidence mounts up it tends to generate, in an evolutionary process, a crisis which can only be resolved by what Kuhn calls a scientific revolution. The revolution is ushered into being by scientific geniuses who invent new theoretical schemes or paradigms to handle the embarrassing evidence or to resolve logical inconsistencies relating to the old schemes.

The progress of science is based on ways of conceptualizing reality that foster problems connected with achieving logical consistency within the structure of current theory, and on attempts to invent improved theories that take full account of accumulating evidence. The resolution of a given difficulty tends to generate new ones, and the real world always seems to be less tidy and more complex than the theories designed to explain it.

CONCEPTIONS AND DEFINITIONS OF REALITY We have up to this point dealt primarily with modes of causal analysis and generalization and types of theories that have been proposed concerning phenomena in the natural world. We need now to turn our attention to the fact that successful scientific analysis ordinarily presupposes and requires new ways of viewing—new ways of classifying and defining—the objects of inquiry. Just as scientific findings produce new views of the world, so also do new ideas of the nature of the world precede scientific developments.

As an example, we remind the reader that Hippocrates, who wrote about and practiced medicine in the fourth century B.C., is still honored and remembered today for his contributions to medical science. Why, then, did Greek medicine not continue to evolve and improve in the centuries that followed? Part of the answer to this question is certainly found in the Greek conceptions of health and the nature of the human body that prevailed at the time. Health was thought to involve a proper balance between the four elements (earth, air, fire, and water) and their main properties, which were said to be hot, cold, dry, and moist. Corresponding to these were the four bodily "humors": blood, phlegm, yellow bile, and black bile. The four humors, the theory held, were stirred and kept at the correct mixture by something called the "pneuma," or vital heat operating in the heart. At this time the fact that blood circulates in the body was unknown, and there was only the vaguest idea of bodily structures and organs and their functions. Moreover, diseases were not sharply differentiated, since all supposedly arose from an improper mixture of the humors. Scientific research and progress obviously required the abandonment of these concepts. In later centuries, during the Christian era, these concepts of the Greeks were commonly discarded in favor of the theory that disease was either an expression of the wrath of God or the malice of the Devil, to be cured by such means as worship and prayer or by pilgrimages to shrines and holy places in order to seek miracle cures.

When events and their elements are not correctly explained and the causes of phenomena are unknown, we tend to be uncertain or ignorant of what they are and how they should be classified. Thus, before the cause of malaria was known, malaria was commonly confused with other diseases; indeed, fever itself was regarded as a disease and attributed to many causes. Yellow fever was one of the diseases with which malaria was commonly confused. A fascinating historical account of a yellow fever epidemic in Philadelphia in 1793, by the historian J. H. Powell (37), effectively illustrates how prevailing misconceptions of the world may prevent even intelligent people from learning from their experiences with it.

The 1793 plague of yellow fever occurred more than one hundred years before the cause of this disease was understood and the mosquito's role revealed. It was introduced by emigrants from Santo Domingo, where there was an epidemic. When the Philadelphia epidemic began, it was attributed to a wide variety of causes and treated in numerous ways. There was a hot debate on what the disease in fact was. Benjamin Rush, a famous early American physician, called it "yellow fever" and argued that all fevers were variations of a single disease to be treated in the same way, by violent purging and by copious bleeding. Other physician colleagues disputed Rush's ideas, arguing that different fevers were different diseases, that the epidemic was simply an especially severe form of influenza or some other common ailment, that Rush's treatment did more harm than good, and so on. Rush at first contended that the epidemic was triggered by atmospheric pollution from a cargo of rotting coffee at the docks. Other medical authorities of the prestigious College of Physicians of the American Philosophical Society contended that it was a contagion spread by the emigrants from Santo Domingo, while another group said it was due to something connected with the Philadelphia climate and with polluted air. Everybody noticed the unusually dense swarms of mosquitoes but considered them effects or signs of the polluted atmosphere, conceived also to be the cause of the epidemic. No one blamed the mosquitoes for the epidemic.

Ironically, a person who signed only his initials to his comments wrote to one of the newspapers about the unusual prevalence of mosquitoes. He described how these insects multiplied in the rain barrels in which water was being stored by residents during the summer's drought. He indicated how this could be prevented by putting a small quantity of oil on the water, a technique discovered by accident. No particular attention was given to his remarks, and he himself did not blame the mosquito for the yellow fever. When Rush described the disease that was killing many of his friends and that he himself contracted, he observed that one of its symptoms was a kind of rash consisting of small, red, irritated, itching spots, particularly on the arms, "resembling moscheto [sic] bites." That they might actually have been mosquito bites apparently never entered his mind, and this insect emerged from the epidemic with its image as an annoying but essentially harmless pest unchanged.

Obviously, the people of Philadelphia in 1793 were living in a symbolic environment that was very different from ours today. As knowledge concerning diseases has increased, they have been redefined, regrouped, reclassified, and the world from which they emerge has been reconceived. Techniques of treatment and prevention used in the 1793 epidemic of yellow fever, such as bleeding, purging, smoking tobacco, applying vinegar to household articles, eating garlic, covering the floors of one's house with an inch or two of dirt, or wearing a tar-soaked rope around one's neck—these are today recognized as either harmful, dangerous, or mainly futile. Once a disease is explained, there is a tendency to define the disease in terms of its cause. Thus, there is not likely to be much objection if malaria is defined as a disease caused by a parasite, and so on. In a sense such a definition is erroneous and incorrect because it is tautological, being true by definition. One can appreciate this point by considering how a disease is identified or defined when its cause or causes are unknown as is the case with cancer and with the so-called functional psychoses. In both cases we are not quite sure what we are talking about since all we can do is to describe and classify symptoms. Is cancer one disease or many? Are there identifiable and actual mental illnesses, or is there a myth of mental illness, as one psychiatrist at least argues?

For the social scientist the definitional process is of special importance, because many current concepts are very vaguely defined. And sociological concepts often tend to lump together obviously dissimilar forms of behavior or to distribute essentially similar forms in different categories. The sociologist's problem is something like that of the biologist's in the study of disease. Forms and instances of behavior that display essential, sociologically relevant similarities need to be isolated, unambiguously defined, and related to the causal processes, usually learning processes, that produce them. The prefabricated definitions that are provided us by our society and by common sense are not likely to serve the purpose, since they are loaded with logical inconsistencies and disparities. Commonsense definitions serve practical rather than intellectual purposes, although they are commonly the starting points of systematic inquiry.

Definitions are of various types. The most obvious are those that specify types of objects or forms of simple overt behavior so as to distinguish them from other similar types. Definitions may be arbitrary, as, for example, when one wishes to talk about heavy men as opposed to men who are not heavy, to distinguish between hot and cool weather, or between persons who are rich and those who are not. If a speaker tells an audience that when he or she speaks of the rich the reference is to people with annual incomes in excess of $50,000, the audience is not likely to object, because they will be able to understand what is said. Another speaker, however, may use a higher or lower figure to distinguish between rich and not-rich. The situation is very different in the case of definitions of another type, definitions that are the products of scientific research and that are embedded within a network of theory. An astronomer would probably object if a student defined planets as stars or vice versa, but not if the sun were called a star. When definitions are arbitrary, the question of whether they are true or false is irrelevant; the relevant question is primarily whether or not they are reasonable and useful in discussion. For the second type of definition considered above, the situation is different, and truth and falsity become relevant. The students who tell a professor that planets are stars, or that atoms are like tiny invisible grains of sand and the same as electrons, will be told that their statement is false and will be graded zero for their response.

Because scientists are concerned with a twofold problem of (1) generalizing about phenomena, and (2) defining and classifying phenomena in such a manner as to make generalization possible, they must be continuously alert to the possibility that failure to generalize may be the consequence of faulty definitions or classifications, or misconceptions of reality. In the process of scientific advance, the scientist's point of departure is the commonsense view, but as scientific knowledge increases, the gap between the two tends to increase and it becomes more and more difficult for the layperson to understand scientific language and concepts. Unintelligibility of discourse is not, however, a criterion of scientific achievement, since scientists write mainly for each other and not for the general public. Common sense itself may not be grasped by the layperson if it is expressed in jargon or "gobbledygook."

Inventing and Testing Theory

The explanation of phenomena that are presently not understood, our model suggests, requires the search for processes that are presently unknown and unidentified. The examination of instances of the problematic situation does not automatically make the causal process evident, no matter how many instances may be observed. It is not a question of determining which one of a multiplicity of already identified influences is the crucial one, but of discovering something new, a process not previously noticed. Causal processes are not simply lying around waiting for someone to link them with their effects; they must be uncovered and are usually subsurface.

There are no established rules as to how new theories are invented. Great scientists of the past have sometimes described the situations in which they hit upon new ideas, but little can be said of these except that they are varied. One theorist has said that his best ideas came to him when he was walking up a gentle slope; another was inspired as he watched the flames in a fireplace; Newton is reported to have been struck with the idea of gravitation as he watched an apple fall to the ground. Sometimes the new insight came in a sudden and totally unexpected flash of intuition. In all these cases, the persons who made the new discovery had been deeply preoccupied with a problem and had been laboring at it. Brilliant scientific advances are not made by ignorant or idle people, but by those who are immersed in the scientific tradition and acquainted with existing knowledge. Students who are interested in pursuing this line should examine books like *The Double Helix* by James Watson (47), a fascinating description of the way in which Watson and Crick succeeded in discovering the structure of the genetic molecule, an achievement that earned them the Nobel Prize.

Theories, once proposed, are tested, one may say, in two general ways. First, they must account for the specific problem with which they are concerned. The theory of malaria, for example, had to apply to that disease and to account for its symptoms. It was, of course, further corroborated in a practical way, by the reduction of the incidence of the disease through mosquito control and other measures that it suggested.

The second method of testing a theory involves the matter of how the theory relates logically to other theories and to existing knowledge. An isolated or ad hoc theory, invented to explain only a specific phenomenon, is not counted as scientific because it does not fit into a general structure. Also, no theory in any field can be accepted if it contradicts established truths or laws in other disciplines.

In the advanced sciences theories are ordered roughly in hierarchic structures ranging from the highly general and abstract ones to those which are very specific and concrete. Ideally, this structure should be such that all of its parts are logically interrelated and internally consistent with each other. No such perfect structure exists, but some disciplines come closer to it than others. Change in these structures is generated, as we have said, by cognitive dissonance which occurs when the exploration of specific theories of low generality generate embarrassing evidence that conflicts with traditional ways of thinking. This cognitive dissonance may tend to spread into the higher levels and to cast doubt on the adequacy of more general and fundamental principles which may then be revised.

Modern physical science is said to have originated in the seventeenth century with the work of Galileo because many of the ideas he proposed came to be accepted by scientists as valid and became an established and accepted first approximation of the nature of physical reality and of how it should be investigated and explained. In the sociological field no such first approximation exists. Although much is known about human beings and human behavior, there is only, at best, a vague and fragmentary beginning of consensus concerning fundamental principles and the proper methods of investigation and analysis. The social sciences on the whole are characterized by the existence of competing schools of thought which advocate conflicting theories of human behavior without being able to persuade or convert other schools to agree with them. In this sense, the social sciences resemble classical Greek science, in which new theories (even those that turned out to be valid), once proposed, were not generally accepted, but instead were simply debated and discussed. Thus, while Aristarchus proposed that the sun was the hub of our solar system, Aristotle disagreed, and the dispute was not resolved until about two thousand years later. Similarly, it was proposed in ancient times that mosquitoes probably had something to do with malaria, but this proposal did not achieve acceptance until centuries later.

QUANTIFICATION   We first note that neither malaria nor its cause was described quantitatively. It is often said that quantification is the essence of science and that scientific theories must be mathematical rather than merely verbal. Apart from the fact that mathematical theories, like all others, are verbal in that they consist of written or spoken propositions, it appears that the insistence on quantification has been overstated. There are many diseases with known causes, and none has been described or explained either statistically or quantitatively. There is presently an intensive search underway for the cause or causes of cancer and various types of theories have been proposed—none of them mathematical. However, the above assertions in no way deny the enormous importance and advantages of quantitative methods and measurement when these are appropriate to the nature of the data under consideration.

In view of the emphasis upon statistical methods in the social sciences, it should be noted that while modern Western science is said to have originated at about the beginning of the seventeenth century (1600), statistical science matured about three hundred years later. Galileo, for example, was definitely a mathematician, but he was not and could not have been a statistician. Statistics is actually one of many branches of mathematics, and hence, while statistics is mathematics, the latter covers much more than statistics.

In the study of diseases such as malaria and many others, the main application of statistical methods is probably in the study of epidemiology or disease rates. The case against cigarettes, for example, was made in a statistical form by demonstrating that the probability of lung cancer is increased by smoking. It should be observed that cigarette smoking is not called the cause of lung cancer, a valid point emphasized by the tobacco lobby. While some statisticians currently use the word *cause*, they use it in the diluted sense in which one may say that cigarette smoking causes cancer, but not in the way in which one describes the "cause" of malaria. The epidemiological study of malaria shows that malaria rates are highly correlated with poverty, and poverty might, from a commonsense viewpoint, be called one of its causes. This use of the term is clearly radically different from the way it is used in our example and employed in the scientific tradition.

Statistical methods, it is argued, entered into the natural sciences, such as physics, when the particles the physicist studied became too minute to be observed directly and had to be dealt with indirectly or in the aggregate. (14) In the biological sciences, statistical methods were sometimes adopted because many processes of living tissues and organisms could not be directly observed. From this point of view statistical method is regarded as a set of techniques for describing, and analyzing, the numerical attributes of aggregates and their interrelationships. The series is the unit of analysis, not the individual. The logic involved is that of statistical probability, not that of causal analysis as illustrated in the study of malaria.

When, as in physical science, it is possible to describe causal processes and the objects of investigation in precise numerical terms, an enormous advantage is attained. Small discrepancies between predicted numerical consequences of a theory and the actual ones have, for example, often contributed to the formulation of important new ideas, as was the case with Einstein's statement of relativity theory. However, in the behavioral and biological fields such precise measurements of phenomena and of causal processes are usually not possible. Quantification is then commonly achieved by the resort to statistical description of aggregates, which necessarily involves abandoning the search for causal processes of the type exemplified by the processes that produce diseases. Considering the vital role that the latter type of analysis plays in the advanced sciences, this is an unacceptable price to pay, and most biologists, and indeed most scientists, have not done so.

The social psychologist who is concerned with the causal analysis of complex social behavior and interactional processes must recognize that internal cortical activities or thinking processes must be considered as vital parts of the problem. This is less true of statistical studies in which the focus is on aggregates rather than on individuals, but even in this case investigators commonly feel constrained to explain their numerical findings by referring to theories about the behavior of individuals. Internal symbolic processes are obviously both complex and relatively inaccessible to close observation, a fact which poses a central issue for investigators. How are they to gain reliable information concerning these processes? The position sometimes taken that these processes are subjective is erroneous and unacceptable and amounts to giving up without trying. (See the discussion in Chapter 3.)

An obvious principle that guides all scientific inquiry is that no relevant data of any kind with a possible bearing on one's problem should be set aside or ignored. Another principle is that investigators must immerse themselves in their problem, familiarizing themselves in all possible ways with the objects of study, getting as close to them as they can so that they may observe directly whenever that is possible. Another principle is that of limited inquiry. No one, in a single inquiry, can hope to deal intensively and adequately with many theoretical issues at the same time. He or she must therefore deal with only one or, at most, a few issues at a time. This point is especially important in the study of human behavior, where little scientific consensus exists concerning the fundamentals and where most basic issues remain unresolved.

In the more advanced sciences, what we refer to here as the princi-

TECHNIQUES OF INVESTIGATION AND SOURCES OF DATA

ple of limited inquiry is commonly discussed in terms of the concept of a "closed system." A closed system may be regarded as the body of evidence, influences, and facts that may be relevant to a particular problem. What the nature of the facts, influences, and problems is depends upon the particular scientific field in which they are formulated. Biologists, for example, deal with biological problems and facts, not with those of other disciplines. Systems may be closed either empirically (as in a controlled laboratory experiment) or by logical devices that focus attention upon a specific issue, ruling out matters that are logically peripheral or irrelevant. Thus, in the search for the cause of malaria, investigators ignored a great deal of interesting information about the approximately twenty-five hundred species of mosquitoes that exist. Had they attempted to present all such data, they would probably never have gotten around to doing anything else. Instead, they operated within a closed system, the boundaries of which were defined by the problem they were trying to solve. The same type of consideration applies to behavioral research and it is simply nonsense to ask investigators to tell us everything about their subjects.

From the above considerations, an obvious source of information about what goes on in people's minds is what they say about it. The French scientist Fournié said, "Speech is the only window through which the scientist can view the cerebral life." And the psychologist Lashley observed that "the problems raised by the organization of language seem . . . to be characteristic of almost all other cerebral activity." (25:61) What people report on this matter, however, cannot be simply accepted as true, since people report in different ways to different people in different situations. They may also lie or systematically distort for a wide variety of reasons and motivations. When asked why they do the specific things that one is investigating, they very commonly do not really know, and the answers that they give, while they may be honest and sincere, fall far short of meeting scientific requirements and standards. All of this means not that one should refrain from talking with the subjects, but rather that one should talk a great deal with them and their associates in order to ferret out inconsistencies, distortions, gaps in knowledge, and the like. What one subject says may then be compared with what others say; what they say may be compared with what they do and, in general, related systematically to any other relevant evidence in a search for recurring patterns and common features that may suggest possible modes of explanation. Once a possible theory or hypothesis is formulated in a tentative manner, the nature of the inquiry is likely to change its focus. Investigators may, for example, find that the implications of their hypotheses suggest new questions to ask, new distinctions or concepts that need to be formulated, and new places to look for evidence. In particular, conscientious inquiry dictates that there should be search for evidence that may not fit the hypothesis from those sources or subjects that are most likely to provide such embarrassing data should the hypothesis be false.

In addition to the above, it should further be observed that once a tentative theory is under consideration, it will suggest relationships between the specific subject matter and other similar subject matters. A theory concerning some aspect of homosexual behavior and how it is acquired, for example, should certainly bear some kind of relationship to what is known about how heterosexual behavior is established. All of this, we repeat, seems to us to imply that a great deal of talking must be done with the subjects, and even that one may need to come back to them again and again with new queries.

The novelist and the dramatist commonly assume that they must familiarize themselves thoroughly with the personages and aspects of life which they seek to portray. They need to try to understand motivations, perspectives, ways of life. Very often, indeed, the presentation in a novel or on the stage has its roots in the biography of the writer or is a portrayal of his or her own experiences or recollections. This brings out a point that is equally applicable to the social psychologist, namely, that self-observation is a vital aspect of understanding other people. This kind of understanding needs to be sharply differentiated from the kind that follows from scientific explanation, but in the study of human behavior it is an indispensable preliminary to the latter. Social psychologists studying people must first become thoroughly acquainted with them, perhaps by the technique known as *participant observation*, before they turn to the task of theorizing about them. (11) They must, in short, note what others say and do and what they themselves say, do, and think, and they should seek to work themselves into the perspective or viewpoints of those whom they study. The symbolic interactionist has, in sociology, especially emphasized this approach.

We are not arguing here that this is the only way in which fruitful study of human interaction can be carried on; only that it is one important way and one that is often neglected. As we have said, no sources of data and no techniques of inquiry should be excluded. We do, however, regard as suspect those attempts to theorize about what makes human beings do and say what they do that are not derived from direct observation and experience with the subjects. For example, we doubt if a valid theory of criminality in individuals of a given type is ever likely to be formulated by a person who has never encountered or talked with a criminal. Similarly, one may question whether the investigator whose object of study is really numbers, or "social indicators," rather than the behavior indicated by the numbers, can be expected to discover causal processes involved in the latter. Similarly, the researcher-bureaucrat who directs a large-scale study of something with the actual research being done by low-echelon employees, is too far removed from the empirical world being investigated to be expected to contribute vital new insights into it, although he or she may add low-level descriptions to the literature.

Another vital methodological point is that techniques of inquiry should be adapted to problems and data, not the reverse. In other words, researchers should not permit their preference for a given method, the statistical method for example, to dictate the exclusion of data not readily handled statistically, and they should not ignore important questions or problems that are not amenable to statistical formulation. At another level, no researchers should assume that the techniques used by those who are currently seeking to unravel the complex mechanisms, processes, and interconnections that occur in different parts of the brain are the only ways to study human intelligence and mental activity. At the same time, social psychologists can ill afford to neglect either statistical or neurological studies when the findings of these studies are relevant to their interests.

Experimentation with human beings is sharply limited both by ethical considerations and, more basically, by the inherent incapability of controlling influences that exist within the subjects. (39) Experimenters, of course, can readily control the external laboratory situation in which they place their subjects, but it is extremely difficult to control or even find out what the subjects may be thinking about as they answer questions or apparently follow the instructions given them. In the natural sciences a distinction is commonly made between experiments as such and *crucial experiments,* which are definitive tests of one theory against another or others. It is the latter that are of decisive importance in the acceptance or rejection of theories. The state of theory in social psychology, coupled with the difficulties of controlled experimentation, has contributed to the remarkable scarcity of crucial experiments in this field.

On the other hand, the social psychologists have access to some kinds of information that the natural scientists do not. We have already emphasized one of these—talk. Physicists' objects of study do not talk back to them. Another such unique source is the historical one. In the present state of our knowledge, information of an historical nature is vital for the understanding of both individuals and societies. Scientific generalizations in the natural sciences are ordinarily ahistorical. Perhaps, if our knowledge of human beings were better than it is, we might be able to decide whether or not we want to associate with particular persons without reference to their biographies. As things are, it is of great relevance to know biographical data. Knowledge of the past, of an incomplete and fragmentary nature, is available in books and libraries, where one can, in a sense, listen to the talk of people of past ages so that one may even be able to project oneself into their perspectives and social worlds. As has been observed, most of the people who have ever lived are presently dead and therefore cannot be interviewed. Books enable us to establish a kind of one-way contact with some of these people.

Scholars, of course, rely heavily on libraries, and there are many kinds of scholarly activities in the area of human behavior that are appropriately carried out in them. However, if the object of study is one that implies naturalistic observation of human animals in their native habitat, the library may be a hazard. (17) The air-conditioned comfort of a convenient library may seduce ambitious scholars into skipping the arduous, time-consuming business of going out into the field to observe directly the phenomena they propose to write about. After all, the books not only describe the phenomenon but also present a variety of theories concerning it. Why then venture out to repeat observations that capable observers have already made? Why try to invent a new theory when there already are a dozen or two that seem plausible?

The fallacy in this procedure is that the world of books is different from the real world. There is nothing in libraries that can substitute for firsthand experience with an object of study, especially when this object consists of human behavior. A balance therefore needs to be struck between the library and the field. Firsthand contact with the real world can provide us with a standard of judgment when we move into a library and may immunize us against overly hasty commitment to prestigious theories handed down by great thinkers of the past. (17) It can also help us to realize that an oft-repeated statement in the literature may not reflect an important truth but may be a simple consequence of the fact that many scholars of the past have copied from the same source.

Apropos of a tendency to speak somewhat contemptuously of mere library research, we should always keep in mind that all research of any kind must, if it is to have significance, be reported, recorded, and stored—usually in libraries. The hard-nosed empiricist who sometimes disparages those who spend more time with books than he or she thinks they should sometimes seems to imply that when his or her own investigations are completed, written up, and deposited in libraries no one ought to read them. Actually, of course, work in libraries is an indispensable and vital source of data in the scientific enterprise. Social psychologists who propose what they regard as an important new idea or theory solely on the basis of their own research or observations without consulting the library have neglected an important part of their duties. When they do go to the library they may find that their new idea is an old one that has been explored and debated for decades, perhaps one first suggested by Aristotle. Sociologist Wirth has quipped that what is commonly taken for originality is usually simple ignorance of the contents of libraries. On the other hand, someone who is struggling to explore the implications of an idea that is really new is likely to find the library a gold mine of additional information that he or she could not possibly have collected independently. In any genuinely scientific tradition, investigators can scarcely even begin their research without first acquainting themselves with the state of knowledge in the area they have chosen to explore. When they report on their own findings, by the same token, they are expected to relate them to the previous findings of others. All of this implies library work.

We return to the problem of understanding the seemingly inaccessible internal psychological or symbolic activities which nearly everyone realizes play a central role in the determination of behavior. This type of problem is not actually a new one for scientists, but is as old as science itself. When events of importance are known to occur beyond the range of observation, scientists have always tried to comprehend them intellectually by inference. Sometimes it has turned out that new technologies have brought things within the orbit of direct observation which were once thought to be beyond its range. For millennia, humans have looked at the moon from a distance of more than two hundred thousand miles and have drawn inferences about it which turned out to be astonishingly accurate when a human actually set foot on the moon. Similar things have happened in the study of the human body, of microorganisms, and of the minute invisible particles that occupy the attention of nuclear physicists. As Einstein and Infeld observe in a book entitled *The Evolution of Physics* (14:31):

> In our endeavor to understand reality we are somewhat like a man trying to understand the mechanisms of a closed watch. He sees the face and the moving hands, even hears its ticking, but he has no way of opening the case. If he is ingenious he may form some picture of a mechanism which could be responsible for all the things he observes, but he may never be quite sure his picture is the only one which could explain his observations. He will never be able to compare his picture with the real mechanism and he cannot imagine the possibility or the meaning of such a comparison.

The inferential process through which one tries to get at and comprehend inaccessible things or events has been designated as one of *triangulation.* (11:16–17) What this means in the natural sciences is that various lines of evidence are taken into account in the inferential process. When these diverse types of data all seem to point to the same conclusion, it is often possible to form reasonably clear, plausible, or even very precise conceptions of the inaccessible objects or processes.

Applying the triangulation idea to the study of human mental processes, one may get various kinds of evidence concerning them. For example, one source is what people report and what they do; other sources are the manner in which people report in different contexts and the signs that they give off unwittingly which may tell more than the words they use. Another source is the life history of the person, or part of it, both as seen by him or her and by others; another source is the observations made of the person by his or her associates. As we have indicated, the overt actions of people occur in a context of meanings within which mental processes also occur—a point that emphasizes the necessity of relating them to external events and which also brings the observers themselves into the formula. This has been very well expressed by Sullivan in a discussion of the psychiatrist as participant observer (50:19):

> The fact is that we cannot make any sense of, for example, the motor movements of another person except on the basis of behavior that is meaningful to us—that is, on the basis of what we have experienced, done ourselves, or seen done under circumstances in which its purpose, its motivation, or at least the intentions behind it were communicated to us. Without this past background, the observer cannot deduce, by sheer intellectual operations, the meaning of the staggering array of human acts.

When evidence from these various lines seems to converge and be mutually reinforcing and consistent, then, as Sullivan indicates, observers who are properly qualified by their own experience and their knowledge of themselves may be able to make very shrewd inferences about what kinds of processes are actually going on in another person's mind. In fact, while the inferential approach is less secure than that of direct observation, it also has its triumphs, as for example when an observant outsider informs a person of things going on inside his or her head of which he or she was totally unaware until they were called to his or her attention.

Another possibility that social psychologists should keep in mind is that apart from the kind of research that they and their colleagues do, there are many other disciplines with interests that overlap their own from which enlightenment may come. Unfortunately there is a tendency, created by the organizational structures of universities, for scholars not to keep up on the literature in other fields—indeed, it is difficult for them to do so. The triangulation process also applies here at the interdisciplinary level and with special force. In the writing of this book, for example, we have been impressed by findings reported by biologists studying the human brain, as well as by anthropologists, linguists, philosophers, and psychologists.

A final point that should perhaps be made is that those aspects of human experience which are genuinely subjective do not come within scientific jurisdiction at all. This is because, by a proper definition of this much abused term, subjective aspects of experience remain the private possessions of unique individuals and are incommunicable. Scientific knowledge is always in the form of propositions derived from communication and consensus within a scientific community. Knowledge, in short, is consensually validated experience; subjective experience is something else. The scientific mode of discourse is a public process from which purely personal or idiosyncratic aspects are systematically excluded because they interfere with objectivity and hence distort inquiry. In the study of social interaction this poses a particularly difficult and important problem because the investigators are themselves social beings and part and parcel of what they are studying. The detachment that is indispensable in objective inquiry is achieved only by much greater effort than that needed in achieving a similarly objective stance with respect to the phenomena of astronomy or physics, for example.

Symbolic Interactionism in Social Psychology

The point of view held by the authors has become known as that of *symbolic interactionism,* having been given that name in 1937 by Herbert Blumer. (4) He used this term to characterize the work and thought of a group of distinguished scholars that included the pragmatic philosophers George Herbert Mead, William James, John Dewey, Charles Peirce, and the sociologists W. I. Thomas, Robert Park, and Charles Horton Cooley. Particularly influential within this group was Mead at the University of Chicago. He stressed as central the ideas that "mind" and "self" are not things but forms of activity and relationships that emerge from, and are products of, social interaction. Through the use of shared *significant symbols,* individuals become capable of taking the viewpoints of others toward themselves and thus become objects within their own thought processes. In other words, they engage in reflexive behavior: they become self-conscious and conscious of consciousness; they become both participants in and observers or spectators of the interactions in which they are involved.

An often quoted statement within this group of scholars was that if things are defined as real they are real in their consequences. As this assertion implies, symbolic interactionists stress the idea that humans live in social and intellectual worlds of their own creation. Out of the almost limitless variety of forms of interaction that are made possible by language and the complex interaction it fosters within a complex social structure, new ideas and actions constantly appear and new objects of thought are created. The very term "symbolic interactionism" carries the implication of "process" rather than of "thing" or "object." In this point of view, the key concepts are interpreted as processes: *self, mind, consciousness, interaction, objectivity, language* are examples.

Since this entire book is aimed at expounding the viewpoint that we are discussing here, our present consideration of it will be brief. We believe that symbolic interactionism provides the theoretical underpinnings of a sociological social psychology concerned primarily with activities that are uniquely human as they are exhibited in social interaction, structure, and institutions. The fundamental source of explanatory theories of complex human behavior must be sought, we think, in the study of human beings as the prime communicating animals.

Some critics of symbolic interactionism think of it as a "school of thought" which is propagated by the wholly loyal disciples of its founding fathers. (21) We reject this conception for several reasons. In the first place, many of the ideas emphasized in the pages that follow have become commonplace and are widely accepted among professional sociologists working in a great many specialty areas. These assumptions have, in recent years, increasingly been drawn from the body of ideas and concepts with which we are concerned. We believe that the term *symbolic interactionism* does *not* refer to a somewhat specialized or esoteric "school" but instead has become an integral part of sociology itself.

ISSUES AND CONTROVERSIES

We must add that persons who, to some degree or another, profess general adherence to the interactionist viewpoint (including critics) have widely different interpretations of the perspective and its implications. Some, for example, believe that to say human behavior is decisively influenced by communication, language, and internal symbolic processes commits one to the exploration of "subjective" phenomena—which cannot be handled rigorously in accord with the traditional standards of science. Opposing this view are those who reject the subjective-objective dichotomy. They insist that mental processes, like all human behavior, involve the physical organism and its nervous system as indispensable participating and interrelated elements. They argue that this behavior should not be dismissed from scientific study just because current methods and theories are inadequate to study it; rather, they say that one should directly confront the human organism's active organization of its own behavior and develop better ways of coping with this phenomenon.

Some interpret the symbolic interactionist perspective as requiring the use of "soft," qualitative data, as opposed to "hard," quantitative statistical data, but many interactionists are quite committed to the statistical method. There is nothing inherent in the perspective that commits its practitioners to one method, or body, or type of data over another. This issue has been exacerbated in the controversy over whether interactionists take a determinate or indeterminate view of human interaction. Some interactionists, however, contend that human activity is inherently emergent and indeterminate, hence not entirely open to fixed quantitative statistical modes of inquiry. Others use such modes to better elaborate and trace out the implications of the interactionist perspective.

Also, we should note that not only is symbolic interactionism not the only "sociological social psychology" possible, as at least one textbook demonstrates (40), but symbolic interactionists by no means agree either on priority of theoretical issues or even on all their sustaining assumptions. For instance, some believe that the general position is broad enough to include *exchange theory* (30) or to permit genuine rapprochement with certain types of psychiatric theory. (41) Others, including ourselves, are very critical or skeptical of those possibilities, while yet believing that the general position should—as indicated later in this chapter—be very open to the findings and suggestions of compatible positions.

Often it is argued that symbolic interactionists, with their commitment to study individuals and interaction, contribute little or nothing to the understanding of organizations or to society as a whole. Often too this criticism is couched in terms of a micro-macro (small-scale, large-scale) emphasis. It fails to take into account the interactionists' assertion that organizations and societies are made up of the interactions of their respective members. This criticism continues in the form of an attack on the interactionists' supposed inability to handle larger interactive units, as well as the power arrangements that link those units to one another. This leads to the erroneous view that institutional, group, and governmental affairs can be studied "on their own level," without reference to the individual participants and their interactions.

Another contention, that interactionists are compelled by their very methods of investigation (participant observation, especially) to become champions of outcasts, underdogs, and little people in general, is contradicted by the opposite contention that all social scientists who enjoy comfortable and easy living in our capitalistic system are thereby committed to the establishment view and hence are really on the side of the "fat cats." (18) In our opinion, there is nothing intrinsic to the interactionist perspective that makes it politically conservative or liberal. In a fundamental sense, however, symbolic interactionism is a radical approach for it charges scientific practitioners to gain firsthand knowledge about the empirical world before they begin formulating evaluations and theories about that world. In our judgment few other approaches to human behavior put as much stress on this point. We are troubled by those who formulate grandiose theories about human behavior and its control on the basis of intimate knowledge of the laboratory behavior of rats, pigeons, and monkeys, or by those who seek to generalize about the behavior of human beings whom they have never bothered to meet, observe, or talk to. Finally, of course, genuinely scientific questions can only be resolved on the basis of reasoned evaluation of evidence without any reference whatsoever to political considerations.

The issue of politics and the political persuasions of symbolic interactionists lead directly into the question of relevancy: that is, does their perspective contribute anything to the problems of human societies? Can it, for example, offer scientifically grounded suggestions concerning the control and amelioration of such diverse social problems as drug addiction, crime, youthful unrest, marital discord, rioting and looting, corruption, the political abuse of power and authority, death and disease, abuse of children, old age and senility, and of public opinion and its control? Or does the interactionist perspective lead to yet another sterile academic enterprise, which on occasion titillates the general public or arouses interest among a few intellectuals? To those who claim it is irrelevant for the analysis of practical issues, we would respond that we find it is hard to conceive of any situation involving policy issues that could not be better handled with greater firsthand knowledge of the materials with which one is dealing. One sociologist who recently visited China remarked acidly that its revolution had been accomplished without the benefit either of Western social theory or the social sciences. The best answer to him is that revolutions may be accomplished without knowledge of the social sciences, but the myriad problems of industrialized, modern nations certainly might be better managed with the help of social science, including social psychological knowledge.

Basic Considerations

It is assumed in this book that human behavior provides the primary data with which social psychology deals, and that the explanation of any particular form of behavior requires that its relations to other types be traced and demonstrated. Thus a given kind of behavior is explained in terms of its interrelationships with other kinds of behavior and not in terms of "forces," "drives," or any other impetus which lies outside the behavioral field or which is inferred from behavior. In accordance with this principle we reject the idea that behavior is "caused" by psychological states, desires, motives, states of consciousness, or unconscious motives when these are taken to refer to forces which "make" things happen. From our point of view, terms such as these are only ways of naming various kinds of activity and have no special explanatory value. We believe, for example, that it is entirely fallacious to explain the existence of science in terms of a "rational faculty" or innate "reason." It is much more plausible to look at reason, not as a force or faculty, but as a complex and highly evolved form of symbolic activity which has emerged gradually as an historical product from other, simpler types of behavior. Similarly, conscience should not be thought of as a psychic force mysteriously implanted in man but as a special form of regulatory behavior by means of which other activities are inhibited or facilitated.

BEHAVIORISM
AND MIND-BODY
DUALISM

Psychologists who belong to the behaviorist school have emphasized ideas similar to those just stated and on the basis of them have either rejected or redefined many of the old terms of the "psychology of consciousness." Practically all of the terms used by lay persons to refer to what they call "mental phenomena," such as mind, idea, insight, imagination, reason, consciousness, understanding, and many others, have been conceived as activities rather than as entities or faculties, or have been dropped entirely as useful concepts. When we say this we mean that the words listed are, in effect, treated by behaviorists as though they were verbs rather than nouns; and the behavior is then usually described in as precise and unambiguous a way as possible. As we shall see later, behaviorists have tended to define these mentalistic terms by means of behavior which can be elicited from lower animals in the experimental setting and have tended to reject them entirely when this cannot be done. (26:5–52)

It is not our purpose to launch into a critique of behaviorism at this point but only to indicate that we start out with some of the same assumptions but reach different conclusions. We believe that psychological behaviorists have unduly restricted their perspective by not taking a sufficiently broad view of behavior. They have paid too much attention to gross bodily movement and to lower animals and have thus come to ignore language behavior or to treat it as a minor matter. It is our contention that mentalistic terms like consciousness, conception, reason, and the like need to be related to language behavior and conceived of as forms or aspects of symbolic behavior.

The implication of this for social psychology is that in order to explain why people do what they do we must know how they think. The chief source of information about how people think is what they say. These conclusions, however, are not of the type which behaviorist psychologists endorse. In addition to the usual tendency of behaviorists to ignore language, to treat it as a minor factor in behavior, or even to refuse to regard it as genuine behavior, they also try to avoid dealing with behavior which cannot be directly observed. The internal symbolic processes which constitute mental activity are admittedly not accessible to direct observation, and for this reason, among others, they are neglected by the behaviorists. Evidence of mental activity in human beings is usually secured through introspection or from verbal testimony; but the lower animals most often utilized in experimental work do not give verbal reports or engage in introspection. Moreover, evidence so obtained is difficult to interpret. Nevertheless, if it is agreed that human thought is a vital feature of human behavior, no evidence of any kind concerning it should be passed over or neglected.

The behaviorists have been reacting against a long tradition going back to the ancient Greeks which has been termed *mind-body dualism.* It consists of viewing body and mind as separate and radically different kinds of reality. The body is physically real and tangible, while the mind is viewed as intangible, nonmaterial, and separate from the body. Once this separation is made, two separate vocabularies are employed to deal with each realm, and nonsensical questions such as, "Which is more important, the mind or the body?" or "How can the mind influence the body?" may be asked. Our view of this position is also flatly and strongly negative. *We shall repeatedly indicate that mental activity is simply that activity of the human organism in which the central nervous system plays a central role.* G. H. Mead (31:1–2), whom we cited earlier in our definition of the field of social psychology, argued that the activities of the human central nervous system are basic to the genesis, existence, and organization of social experience and social behavior. Following Mead, we reject the narrow behaviorism of many psychologies which appear to rest on the mind-body dualism position.

Sometimes the behaviorist becomes a biological determinist by seeking explanations of behavior in the biological mechanism involved. A common expression of this tendency is to refer to the nervous system or to neural mechanisms to explain certain acts or kinds of behavior. Laypersons may, for example, say that their "nerves are on edge," or "frayed," or that they are "nervously exhausted." Neurologists and physiologists sometimes account for behavior which they observe by reference to some supposed neural or physiological process. Explanations of this type are called *reductionistic* because they tend to reduce behavioral problems to the biological level.

REDUCTIONISM AND ATOMISM

The term *atomism* is closely related to that of reductionism. It refers to the attempt to discover what things are like by taking them apart. The assumption is that "the whole is equal to the sum of its parts." The history of physicists' attempts to unravel the nature of matter is the prime example of the fruitfulness of this conception. The idea was proposed by the Greeks that all matter consisted of very small indivisible particles. The search for those ultimate atoms or building blocks of the universe has not turned out as anticipated, but it has given us modern nuclear physics.

Sociologists ordinarily are opposed to the reductionist and atomistic positions. They oppose the contentions of the reductionist that human behavior can be understood and explained in terms of physiological, neurological, anatomic, chemical, or physical concepts. They contend instead that at each level of scientific concern, phenomena are and must be explained by reference to other phenomena at the same level. Chemical phenomena are explainable by reference to other chemical phenomena, and so on. Social behavior, it is therefore contended, must similarly be analyzed and explained on its own level.

Sociologists ordinarily also reject the atomistic approach. They argue that a whole is definitely more than the sum of its parts. For example, a group may act as a unit and this involves, besides a number of individuals, a structured system of relationships among members and with other groups. Thus, a nation continues to exist although all of its specific members ultimately will die. Conversely, a group may vanish or die without any of its members doing so.

For reasons of this kind, and perhaps with a reference to the fact that even in some branches of physics the atomistic position has given way to field theory or holistic theory, the social scientist opposes reductionism and atomism in the study of social behavior. It is admitted, even sometimes stressed, that physical, biochemical, physiological, and neurological processes are involved in all behavior. Consideration of such influences cannot account for behavior, although it does contribute to understanding the physical and biological substrata that make the behavior possible. A football game, for example, could be described within the framework of mechanics as a number of objects varying in mass moving in irregular paths at certain velocities and colliding frequently. Needless to say, fans would scarcely enjoy reading such an account, nor would anyone feel that it dealt with the essentials of the game.

EXCHANGE THEORY.   In the last decade, *exchange theory*—another general position developed especially by sociologists—has gained some adherents. It has even gained the approval of some sociological social psychologists (30), who have found it compatible with their own conceptions of social psychology and human behavior. We disagree strongly with that assessment. We shall consider it here in more detail than the other positions just discussed because sociologists are more involved with its development.

As one critic of exchange theory has remarked: "The first difficulty one faces in trying to review exchange theory is that there is relatively little agreement among sociologists either on the definition of exchange theory or on the works which are supposed to be examples of it." (20:91) However, its most cited and influential works are by George Homans (21) and by Peter Blau (3). Homans, who had early rejected functionalism in a dialogue mostly with Talcott Parsons when developing his version of exchange theory, turned to behavioral psychology—mainly drawn from B. F. Skinner—and to elementary economics. He sees both perspectives as envisaging "human behavior as a function of its payoff: in amount and kind it depends on the amount and kind of reward and punishment it fetches." (21:13) And when what it fetches is the behavior of someone else, then one can refer to this "as an exchange of activity," which occurs between at least two people. It is exchange because rewards and punishments are being meted out.

In approaching the study and explanation of social exchange, Homans relies on general propositions borrowed from conditioning theory and from elementary economics. The following are examples of such propositions. (21:33–37; 20:92) The stimulus proposition: "If in the past the occurrence of a particular stimulus, or set of stimuli, has been the occasion in which a person's activity has been rewarded, then the more similar the present stimuli are to the past ones, the more likely the person is to perform the activity, or some similar activity, now." The success proposition: "The more often a person's activity is rewarded, the more likely he is to perform the activity." The deprivation-satiation proposition: "The more often in the recent past a person has received a particular reward, the less valuable any further unit of that reward becomes to him." In his book, Homans uses these kinds of propositions to explain the more specific findings of studies of interaction and group behavior—what he calls "elementary social behavior." He does not, however, merely apply the propositions drawn from neighboring disciplines, but necessarily elaborates them, since he deals with "social" behavior of considerable, although not the highest, complexity.

Blau goes further and turns his attentions to larger social structures and to indirect exchanges. (3:2) In a review of this book, Heath (20) attempts to pull together some of Blau's major propositions, and for convenience we shall quote a few to give the flavor of Blau's approach. (He, too, in drawing explicitly on the work of Homans, also relies on economics and conditioning psychology.) The examples of propositions are:

1. The desire for social rewards leads men to enter into exchange relationships with one another.
2. Reciprocal social exchanges create trust and social bonds among men.
3. Unilateral services create power and status differences.
4. Power differences make organization possible.
5. The fair exercise of power evokes social approval and the unfair exercise of power evokes social disapproval.
6. If subordinates collectively agree that their superior exercises power generously, they will legitimate his power.
7. Legitimate power is required for stable organization.
8. If subordinates collectively experience unfair exercise of power, an opposition movement will develop.

In general, Blau's analysis moves from analyzing simple social relationships in terms of direct exchange processes, to showing how complex social structures develop as networks of exchange become increasingly indirect.

Exchange theory, as exemplified by Homans and Blau, has been criticized on various grounds (10, 38): for example, that Homans's work is very limited concerning any analysis of larger social organizations; that the content of both books is very speculative; that many if not most of their propositions are really untestable; that their approach is too "psychologistic" for the understanding of sociological phenomena. We would agree with those criticisms but would add, more specifically, the following remarks. The formulations border on tautologies; they are based on generalizations derived from the study of infrahumans and hence do not take into account human symbolic abilities. The reliance on rewards and punishments reflects simply one more variation of need and drive-reductionistic psychology, whose striking inadequacies we shall criticize in Chapter 8. The reliance on elementary economics—a presentation that most economists would reject—reflects a focus on aggregate analysis, which will not get us very far either in understanding individuals or the complex social processes in which they participate. Aside from its assumption of rewards and punishments, the basic notion of "exchange" is amazingly simplistic, as contrasted with the full range of interactions that take place among humans. If the concept of exchange is to be greatly extended—to negotiation, coercion, competition, persuasion, and the like—then analysis needs to be done in terms of those and many other emergent kinds of distinctions, rather than foreclosed from the beginning by a preordained type of scheme. (7, 48) In general, the simplistic and foreordained character of exchange theory renders it quite speculative and relatively uninteresting. It certainly cannot handle convincingly most of the phenomena that will be discussed in this text and, indeed, does not even purport to do so. The attempt to wed it with a symbolic interactionist approach is, we believe, fruitless.

We say this because of the deficiencies of exchange theory and because of the genuine incompatibilities between it and the approach developed here. However, not all symbolic interactionists would agree with us. In a recent attempt to assimilate exchange theory with symbolic interactionism, Peter Singelmann (43) contends that there are "convergences" between the two approaches in four major areas. First, both "assume the operation of constructive mental processes when actors act toward their environment." Second, "exchange theory implies processes akin to G. H. Mead's 'self' and 'generalized other' in the sense that interaction in exchange requires persons imaginatively to assume the roles of others and view themselves in terms of the conceptions of others." Third, "in both perspectives social organization is viewed as emerging from constructed individual acts 'fitted' to one another." Fourth, in both, "social dynamics is conceived in dialectic terms, arising out of contradictions between micro- and macro- processes and inherent tendencies in social organization toward inconsistency, conflict and change." We shall say something at the end of this chapter about some of the assumptions which most social psychological approaches make in common, and

Singelmann is quite right in maintaining that exchange theory and symbolic interactionism share something. What they do not share, we believe, are just those assumptions and stances which make the crucial difference.

The organization of American universities into separate departments has the effect of making it unnecessary for persons in one specialty to read much of what is published by those in another, even when the subject matters overlap or are interrelated. Similar considerations apply to research that is reported in languages other than English. It is partly for reasons of this sort that many sociological social psychologists tend to be unaware of research and ideas directly relevant to their own when they are published by persons in other disciplines or in foreign languages. This stricture applies also to the present authors. Fundamental ideas of the sort that are advanced in this book have been advanced and translated into empirical research in a number of areas with which American sociologists are not too well acquainted. The work of Soviet psychologists will be cited to make our point. A RELATED RESEARCH TRADITION

A line of thought in the Soviet Union originating from the works of Ivan Pavlov (23) takes its point of departure from this internationally known psychologist's description of the *second signal system,* or language. This, he suggested, has far-reaching effects upon all higher levels of human behavior. Led by L. Vygotsky (51) and A. Luria (27, 28), this idea has been elaborated in a variety of experiments and research enterprises by numerous Soviet behavioral scientists whose findings are largely available only in the Russian language. From the works of Luria and Vygotsky, cited in later chapters, it is evident that their general theoretical orientation is in many respects very close to that of G. H. Mead and to ours. One point of difference is that the ideas of self and interaction, which are often taken to be virtually the whole of symbolic interactionist theory, are relatively undeveloped in the Russian literature.

Because Pavlov's conception of the conditioned reflex (derived from his experimental work with dogs) has been applied and extended by many investigators to include all behavior, including complex human social behavior, Pavlov's idea of the second signaling system is of special interest to us. Contrary to the views of many who have in a general way regarded themselves as his followers, Pavlov himself rejected the idea that human social behavior may be accounted for in terms of the same mechanisms that are found in animals. He argued as we do that in the evolution of humans new levels of behavioral integration and new principles of nervous activity were introduced by the invention of speech, or language. The following quotations from Pavlov's later work make this quite clear (28:262, 590–91):

When the development of the animal world reached the stage of man, an extremely important addition was made to the mechanisms of nervous activity. In the animal, reality is signalized almost exclusively by stimulations and the traces they leave in the cerebral hemispheres, which come directly to the special cells of the visual, auditory, or other receptors of the organisms. This is what we, too, possess as impressions, sensations, and notions of the world around us, both the natural and the social—with the exception of the words heard or seen. This is the first system of signals of reality common to man and animals. But speech constitutes a second signaling system of reality which is peculiarly ours, being the signal of the first signals. . . . It is precisely speech that has made us human. . . .

In the final analysis, all complex relations in man have passed into the second signaling system. Verbal and abstract thinking has been elaborated in us. The second signaling system is the most constant and ancient regulator of human relations. But there is nothing of the kind in animals. Their entire higher nervous activity, with its supreme manifestations, is included in the first signal system. In man the second signal system acts on the first signal system in two ways: in the first place by inhibition which is greatly developed in it, [and] . . . in the second place by its positive activity. . . . Such relations cannot exist in animals.

That Pavlov's position was not too far removed from that of Mead and the symbolic interactionists is further indicated by the fact that Pavlov (28:32), like Mead, rejected mind-body dualism and conceived of language as the bridge between the so-called subjective and objective worlds: "Ultimately these new signals began to denote everything taken in by human beings directly from the outer, as well as from the inner world; they were used not only in mutual intercourse, but also in self-communion."

Following Pavlov's lead, Luria (27, 28) and other Soviet psychologists (51) developed the view that the higher mental functions in humans are "social in origin," and the "complex products of sociohistoric development." Luria (27:32) remarks that from the very beginning the child's mental processes are influenced by a world of objects created by the work of society and by the people with whom he or she interacts. In addition, the child must master ". . . the existing language system and, with its aid, profit from the experience of other generations. This contact becomes the decisive factor in his future mental development, the decisive condition for the formation of the higher mental functions distinguishing man from animals." While the concept of self is not explicitly elaborated, Soviet psychologists place great stress on the extraordinary degree of self-regulatory behavior in human beings and have been deeply concerned with the nature of voluntary behavior.

Ethno-methodology

In this context we should note that current formulations derived from the phenomenological perspectives of Husserl, Schutz, and Gurwitsch have become incorporated into the works of such scholars as Berger and Luck-mann (2) and into that loosely formulated school of thought known as *ethnomethodology*. (1, 13, 16, 19, 32, 33, 54) Central to this line of thought are the following assumptions. First, human behavior is to be ap-proached subjectively from the standpoint of the phenomenological real-ity of individual actors. Second, there are as many phenomenological realities, or social worlds of experience, as there are individuals produc-ing such worlds. Third, social action and social order are seen as prob-lematic, yet taken-for-granted, productions. Society does not just exist. It has to be produced by interacting individuals. Fourth, in the course of interacting with themselves and others, individuals suspend many com-monsense assumptions and act "as if" they understand one another, when in fact they may be talking past each other. Fifth, these taken-for-granted assumptions embody the very essence of social interaction and social order. It is the task of the ethnomethodologist to uncover these as-sumptions and to show how they are routinely acted on or deliberately suspended. While it is beyond the scope of this chapter to detail fully this approach, we may note that the recent work in psycholinguistics and sociolinguistics reflects the commitment to studying human behavior from the standpoint of native actors. Theorists such as Cicourel (6) are endeavoring to discover and chart the deep and superficial structural rules that native actors consciously and unconsciously employ in the or-ganization of their behavior. Others (49) carefully study everyday con-versations for what they reveal about the underlying dynamics of broader social structures.

A central figure in this line of thought has been Harold Garfinkel, along with a number of students and colleagues who have worked with him in recent years at various campuses of the University of California system. Harvey Sacks, David Sudnow, Aaron Cicourel, Egon Bittner, Jack Douglas, Edward Rose, Don Zimmerman, D. Lawrence Wieder, Hugh Mehan, Huston Wood, and others have actively promoted what they regard as the distinctly radical or unique features of eth-nomethodology. The historical evolution of this perspective has been charted in a number of publications, including Attwell (1), Coser (9), Douglas (13), Garfinkel (16), Sudnow (49), and Mullins (35). It has achieved such prominence that the 1974 issue of the American Sociologi-cal Association's *Guide to Graduate Training in the United States* lists it as a distinct specialty within the discipline. Whether it represents a passing fad or an enduring addition to the sociological tradition remains to be determined.

The word *ethnomethodology* is used to describe what the practi-tioners of this approach see as the unique features of their perspective. *Ethno,* borrowed from the Greek, means race, culture, people and is com-monly used in forming compound words. For Garfinkel and his associates ethnomethodology refers to the practices of an observer who attempts to discover the methods that ordinary people use when they formulate definitions of the situation. An ethnomethodological investigation involves at least three steps. First the observers suspend the assumption that social situations are governed by sets of rules; that is, they withhold judgment on the functions that roles, norms, rules, or culture may have in any particular setting. The second step is to observe how lay persons and sociologists alike describe and explain what it is that they do. The third step requires treating these explanations as appearances produced so as to project the image that rules have been followed. The ethnomethodologist assumes that individuals produce accounts or explanations for their behavior which fit everyday conceptions of what that behavior was all about. Zimmerman and Wieder (13:289) say that the ethnomethodologist "is concerned with how members of society go about the task of *seeing, describing,* and *explaining* order in the world in which they live."

The aim of such investigations is to discover the formal properties of everyday, commonplace actions, and the method demands that the researcher look at behavior from "within" actual situations. In an article entitled "What Is Ethnomethodology?" this view of research activity is developed (16:3):

> Whenever a member is required to demonstrate that an account analyzes an actual situation, he invariably makes use of such practices of "et cetera," "unless," and "let it pass" to demonstrate the rationality of his achieve-

A taken-for-granted reality? (*Freda Leinwand*)

ment . . . Much therefore of what is actually reported is not mentioned
. . . In short, recognizable sense, or fact, or methodic character, or impersonality, or objectivity of accounts are not independent of the socially
organized occasions of their use.

For Garfinkel and other ethnomethodologists, all social interaction,
whether it be medical students taking exams, husbands talking with
their wives, students making purchases in stores, psychiatrists classifying mental patients, coroners deciding whether or not a death was a
suicide, workers managing clients in halfway houses, or interviewers
talking with mothers about their birth control practices, involves individuals producing, describing, and explaining each other's accounts of
their actions.

In one study Garfinkel instructed students to engage an acquaintance or friend in conversation and then to press the person to clarify his
or her remarks. Garfinkel presents the following case (16:43):

On Friday my husband and I were watching television. My husband remarked that he was tired. I asked, "How are you tired? Physically, mentally, or just bored?"

(S) I don't know, I guess physically, mainly.
(E) You mean that your muscles ache or your bones?
(S) I guess so. Don't be so technical.
(After more watching)
(S) All of these old movies have the same kind of old iron bedstead in
them.
(E) What do you mean? Do you mean all old movies or some of them, or
just the ones you have seen?
(S) What's the matter with you? You know what I mean.
(E) I wish you would be more specific.
(S) You know what I mean! Drop dead!

Garfinkel argues that people refuse to permit one another to understand what they are really talking about. They anticipate that others will
understand them and for this reason everyday conversations have a
vague, ambiguous tone. They rest on a body of background assumptions
taken for granted by the participants with each assuming that others take
for granted what he or she does. Thus the husband in the above example
assumed that his wife *knew* what he meant when he said he was tired.

Ethnomethodologists claim that they are concerned with the study of a
phenomenon that has received little attention within the intellectual confines of traditional sociological perspectives. Their interest in "the eluci-
dation of how accounts or descriptions of an event . . . are produced in
interaction in such a way that they achieve some situated methodological
status" (54:10) is taken to be a radical departure from traditional sociology. Furthermore,

EVALUATION OF
ETHNO-
METHODOLOGY

> Ethnomethodologists claim that the objective and constraining social structures of the world are constituted by "social structuring activities" (variously called "practices," "methods," "procedures," "reality work"). Ethnomethodology says that sociology ignores these structuring activities when they measure the degree of association between variables. One way of reading ethnomethodology is to see it countering this omission: ethnomethodologists study the social structuring activities that assemble social structures. (32:14)

These structuring activities are not reduced to the psychological realities of solitary individuals. In fact, the ethnomethodologist shows no interest in probing the subsective individual or social experiences of the person. Following Garfinkel's lead (16), they study social phenomena that are "available in embodied, sensuous, human activity, in talk and actions. Though we may disagree on other matters, that principle binds ethnomethodologists." (32:15) Garfinkel states the principle as follows:

> . . . there is no reason to look under the skull, since there is nothing of interest to be found there but the brains. The "skin" of the person will be left intact. Instead, questions will be confined to the operations that can be performed upon events that are "scenic" to the person. (32:17)

Ethnomethodologists have been criticized on a number of issues. Some critics claim that ethnomethodologists produce research that is trivial and trite. (9) Others argue that its focus on the mundane, taken-for-granted features of everyday life produces an ahistorical and amoral vision of human group life. (18) The cult, or sect-like features of the movement have also been criticized. (9) In their concern for the systematic study of everyday life, they have neglected to isolate, through a conceptual framework, the recurring features of interaction that any sociologist could examine and study. They have refused to define what they mean by everyday life. Nor have they specified those properties of everyday life that are taken-for-granted. A symbolic interactionist would study selves, situations, social objects, social relationships, and rules of conduct as these processes are fitted together during the course of any interaction sequence. Ethnomethodologists have gone no further than to state that their study would focus on talk, activity, and events that are "scenic" to the person. What are those events? What does "scenic" mean? How is talk to be studied?

A general reluctance to probe the subjective, and at times private, side of social experience severely delimits the social psychologist's field of study and excludes from analysis an aspect of the social act that G. H. Mead and many symbolic interactionists have taken to be critical in their research.

Ethnomethodology is termed a radical perspective (not in the political sense) because it directs sociological attention to a neglected area—

the everyday, commonsensical actions and interactions of laypersons and scientists as they produce the appearances of an existing social order.

The theoretical underpinnings of this perspective are largely phenomenological. Its practitioners are concerned with the perspectives of individuals and with viewing the world through the person's own expressions of it. They suspend the assumption that a real outside world exists and argue that social order is fostered and managed. Their methodology demands that people be studied in natural settings and promotes respect for the individual. We applaud both of these emphases.

The ethnomethodological movement has produced a fresh, healthy, questioning outlook concerning many taken-for-granted views of social behavior and the proper methods for studying it. It has also produced a considerable amount of philosophical fog. To a substantial degree it appears to be an understandable revolt against current statistical methods and common assumptions concerning the nature of a science of human behavior, and, indeed, whether such a science is possible or desirable. Persons who count themselves adherents of this school often give widely different interpretations of it. Many outsiders trying to understand it complain that they become more confused the longer they try. In time, perhaps, the issues raised may become more clear as ethnomethodologists make and publish more empirical studies which illustrate or demonstrate what their basic assumptions mean when translated into research actions. In this form the movement is likely to become more communicable than the philosophical position itself seems to be.

We are inclined to agree with the ethnomethodologists if we are right in thinking that they are in revolt against conceptions of scientific method of much of the sociological establishment and against the late, overwhelming dominance of what has been called the "Statistical Mafia" or the "IBM Lobby." That is one of the reasons for including in this edition a chapter on science, which departs in what we hope is an important and meaningful way from the usual discussions of models and variables, and which does not at the same time seek to divorce sociology from scientific traditions.

We are puzzled, on the other hand, by assertions such as that by Speier (13:190) that the major contributions of so-called ethnomethodologists to the history of modern sociology is in the discovery or emphasis on the "centrality of talk in the everyday organization of human activity." Speier goes on to argue that the sluggishness of sociology in recognizing this fact was, with the exception of Goffman, first noted by Garfinkel in 1967. We doubt this and suspect that this point was noted and recorded at least by the time of the ancient Greeks, but we would not go as far as one critic who allegedly said that ethnomethodology provides a "blinding glimpse of the obvious."

We quarrel with some versions of the ethnomethodological perspective on additional grounds. While the accounts that individuals give for their actions certainly are to be taken seriously, these accounts can in no way be regarded as the final or ultimate data for any sociological theory. Indeed, individuals seldom fully know why they acted the way they did in a particular situation, and groups of individuals who have engaged in the same behaviors, perhaps the use of heroin, will seldom give the same explanation of their behavior. As Mead noted, often it is only after they have acted that humans give plausible retrospective accounts of their behaviors, and even these do not qualify as scientific explanations. To study objectively a social phenomenon requires a commitment to acquire a close, working familiarity with those individuals whom one is investigating. While we endorse a respectful stance toward the perspectives of those whom we study, we regard these perspectives as problematic data that require further ordering and analysis.

Ethnomethodologists come close to renouncing the basic goals of science. Their commitment to revealing how persons construct, or structure, definitions of situations has become a goal, or end, in and of itself. They argue that it is futile to attempt to generalize, and they occupy themselves instead with the classification and description of their subjects' views.

Theory, Research Methods, and the Study of Interaction

Sociologists sometimes maintain that hypotheses which cannot be tested are ipso facto unscientific and worthless. Applying this view to all theory leads some social psychologists to adopt the view that the proper questions to be asked concerning human behavior are those that can be answered with available research techniques. This assumption often produces the view that the most important questions are those that can be most easily answered. Views of this sort lead to what C. W. Mills has called the "trivialization of research" (34) in which elaborate techniques of research and analysis, often mathematical in nature, are employed to answer questions that scarcely seem to matter, or to establish the validity of truisms and platitudes.

Our own position is that the important questions concerning human social behavior are probably those that are hardest to answer and also hardest to formulate. Hence, the emphasis in this book is on basic ideas and problems.

Sociologists of the symbolic interactionist persuasion have been most directly concerned with elaborating, applying, and examining that part of the approach which pertains to such concepts as socialization, self, language, interaction, deviance, small groups, social relationships, social objects, and social worlds. They have produced a substantial body of research literature to which specific references will be made later. Less attention has been given to a refinement of the general position itself. A disproportionate amount of sociological research has been concerned with the way in which the concept of role may be used in the description and analysis of social structure, rather than in accounting for the behavior of specific persons. Sometimes a preoccupation with the testing of Meadian theory is combined with the adoption of simplistic assumptions about the nature of human beings that are grossly incongruent with the symbolic interactionist position.

We think of social psychology as being primarily concerned with the conduct of persons as individuals rather than as members of aggregates. From this point of view it appears that the popularity of statistical methods, which are peculiarly appropriate ways of describing aggregate or average behavior, has caused sociologists to grasp the interactionist position (especially the writings of G. H. Mead) only dimly and partially. They sometimes select from it a few ideas that are especially amenable to statistical handling and ignore or slight the remainder. This procedure often produces the impression of rigidity and has a static quality that does not do justice to the dynamic nature of social relations viewed as process rather than as structure. (46, 47)

Because social behavior consists of events and not of structure, our explanations of the behavior, like explanations of physical events, must be couched in terms of process or sequences of interconnected processes. Many sociologists who focus on structure think of explanations in terms of variables rather than of processes, or of statistical associations between variables rather than of interconnected processes. Such analysis, in terms of attributes rather than interaction, communication, or process, almost inevitably makes it hard for those committed to it to see interaction as such. The symbolic interactionist position is inherently concerned, as the term itself indicates, with the analysis of process.

Summary

In summary, we can note that *all* social psychologies (of whatever theoretical variety) are concerned with the relationship between persons and groups or larger forms of social organization. All of the theories which have been discussed in this chapter share the following common assumptions. *First,* humans learn from experience. *Second,* humans are symbol-producing and symbol-using organisms. This sets them apart, in one sense, from infrahuman organisms. *Third,* human behavior is influenced by the presence of others. *Fourth,* humans are capable of maintaining some control and consistency in their own actions. *Fifth,* human behavior is constantly changing and adapting to new situations. *Sixth,* some behaviors and influences are more significant than others. *Seventh,* human behavior is lawfully produced; that is, human behavior can be objectively recorded, described, predicted, and explained. In short, all social psychologies employ some version of the scientific method.

Despite these shared assumptions, each position tends also to rely primarily on different kinds of research methods. Psychoanalysts employ in-depth interviewing, self-reports, dream and fantasy analysis. Psychological social psychologists rely very much on laboratory and field experimentation as well as on psychological tests and questionnaires. Symbolic interactionists attempt to study persons in their natural locales and primarily use field observation, open-ended interviewing, life-history construction, and unobtrusive methods. (11)

In this text, we develop a view of human behavior which stresses that humans are social and symbol-using organisms. We attempt to cross the boundaries of sociology, anthropology, psychology, political science, and history, and to utilize any and all data that elaborate our theoretical perspective. Our fundamental concern is to account for the structured regularity and irregularity of human conduct, and we assume that even deviance and deviant behavior are lawfully and predictably organized.

References   1. Attwell, Paul, "Ethnomethodology since Garfinkel," *Theory and Society,* vol. 1 (Summer 1974), pp. 179–210.
2. Berger, Peter, and Thomas Luckman, *The Social Construction of Reality.* Garden City, N.Y.: Doubleday, 1966.
3. Blau, Peter, *Exchange and Power in Social Life.* New York: Wiley, 1964.
4. Blumer, Herbert, *Symbolic Interactionism.* Englewood Cliffs, N.J.: Prentice-Hall, 1969.
5. Brown, Roger, *Social Psychology.* New York: Macmillan, 1964.
6. Cicourel, Aaron, *Cognitive Sociology.* New York: The Free Press, 1974.
7. Coleman, James S., "Loss of Power," *American Sociological Review,* vol. 38 (February 1973), pp. 1–17.
8. Cooley, C. H., *Human Nature and the Social Order.* New York: Charles Scribner's Sons, 1902.
9. Coser, Lewis A., "Presidential Address: Two Methods in Search of a Substance," *American Sociological Review,* vol. 40 (December 1975), pp. 691–700.
10. Davis, J., and K. Boulding, "Two Critiques of Homans' *Social Behavior,*" *American Journal of Sociology,* vol. 67 (1962), pp. 454–61.
11. Denzin, Norman K., *The Research Act.* 2nd ed. New York: McGraw-Hill, 1978.
12. Dewey, John, *Logic: The Theory of Inquiry.* New York: Holt, Rinehart and Winston, 1938.
13. Douglas, J. D. (ed.), *Understanding Everyday Life.* Chicago: Aldine, 1970.
14. Einstein, Albert, and Leopold Infeld, *The Evolution of Physics.* New York: Simon & Schuster, 1961. (First published, 1938.)

15. Freud, Sigmund, *The Basic Writings of Sigmund Freud,* trans. and ed. with an Introduction by A. A. Brill. New York: Random House, 1938.
16. Garfinkel, Harold, *Studies in Ethnomethodology.* Englewood Cliffs, N.J.: Prentice-Hall, 1967.
17. Glaser, Barney G., and Anselm Strauss, *The Discovery of Grounded Theory.* Chicago: Aldine, 1967.
18. Gouldner, Alvin, *The Coming Crisis of Western Sociology.* New York: Basic Books, 1970.
19. Heap, James L., and Phillip Roth, "On Phenomenological Sociology," *American Sociological Review,* vol. 38 (June 1973), pp. 354–67.
20. Heath, Anthony, "Review Article: *Exchange Theory,*" *British Journal of Political Science,* vol. 1 (1971), pp. 90–119.
21. Homans, George C., *Social Behavior: Its Elementary Forms.* New York: Harcourt Brace Jovanovich, 1961.
22. Huber, Joan, "Symbolic Interaction as a Pragmatic Perspective: The Bias of Emergent Theory," *American Sociological Review,* vol. 38 (April 1973), pp. 274–84.
23. Koshtoyants, K. S. (ed.), *I. P. Pavlov: Selected Works.* Moscow: Foreign Language Publications, 1955.
24. Kuhn, Thomas S., *The Structure of Scientific Revolutions.* Chicago: University of Chicago Press, 1970.
25. Laver, John, "The Production of Speech," in John Lyons (ed.), *New Horizons in Linguistics.* Baltimore: Penguin Books, 1972, pp. 53–75.
26. Lazarsfeld, Paul F., *Qualitative Analysis: Historical and Critical Essays.* Boston: Allyn and Bacon, 1972.
27. Luria, A. R., *Higher Cortical Functions in Man,* trans. by Basil Haigh. New York: Basic Books, 1966.
28. ———, *The Nature of Human Conflicts: An Objective Study of Disorganization and Control of Human Behavior.* New York: Grove Press, 1960.
29. Margenau, Henry, *The Nature of Physical Reality: A Philosophy of Modern Physics.* New York: McGraw-Hill, 1950.
30. McCall, George J., and J. L. Simmons, *Identities and Interactions.* New York: The Free Press, 1966.
31. Mead, George Herbert, *Mind, Self and Society.* Chicago: University of Chicago Press, 1934.
32. Mehan, Hugh, and Huston Wood, "De-Secting Ethnomethodology," *American Sociologist,* vol. 11 (February 1976), pp. 13–21.
33. ———, *The Reality of Ethnomethodology.* New York: Wiley, 1975.
34. Mills, C. W. *The Sociological Imagination.* New York: Oxford University Press, 1959.
35. Mullins, N., *Theories and Theory Groups in Contemporary American Sociology.* New York: Harper & Row, 1973.
36. Parsons, Talcott, "Psychology and Sociology," in John Gillin (ed.), *For a Science and Social Man.* New York: Macmillan, 1954, pp. 67–101.
37. Powell, J. H., *Bring Out Your Dead: The Great Plague of Yellow Fever in Philadelphia in 1793.* New York: Time-Life Books, 1965.
38. Robson, R., "The Present State of Theory in Sociology," in I. Lakatos and A. Musgrove (eds.), *Problems in the Philosophy of Science.* Amsterdam: North-Holland, 1968.
39. Rosenthal, Robert, *Experimental Effects in Behavioral Research.* New York: Appleton-Century-Crofts, 1966.
40. Secord, Paul F., and Carl W. Backman, *Social Psychology.* New York: McGraw-Hill, 1964.

41. Shibutani, T., *Social and Personality: An Interactionist Approach to Social Psychology*. Englewood Cliffs, N.J.: Prentice-Hall, 1961.
42. Simmel, Georg, *The Sociology of Georg Simmel*, trans. by Kurt Wolff. New York: The Free Press, 1950.
43. Singelmann, Peter, "Exchange as Symbolic Interaction: Convergence between Two Theoretical Perspectives," *American Sociological Review*, vol. 37 (August 1972), pp. 414–24.
44. Singer, Charles, *The History of Scientific Ideas to 1900*. New York: Oxford University Press, 1959.
45. Snively, W. D., Jr., and Donna R. Beshear, *Textbook of Pathophysiology*. Philadelphia: Lippincott, 1972.
46. Strauss, Anselm L. (ed.), *George Herbert Mead on Social Psychology*. Chicago: University of Chicago Press, 1964.
47. ———, *Mirrors and Masks*. San Francisco: Sociology Press, 1969.
48. ———, *Negotiations*. In manuscript, 1976.
49. Sudnow, David (ed.), *Studies in Social Interaction*. New York: The Free Press, 1972.
50. Sullivan, H. S., *The Psychiatric Interview*. New York: W. W. Norton, 1954.
51. Vygotsky, L. S., *Thought and Language*, ed. and trans. by E. Hanfmann and G. Vaker. Cambridge, Mass.: M.I.T. Press, 1962.
52. Watson, James D., *The Double Helix: A Personal Account of the Discovery of the Structure of DNA*. New York: Atheneum, 1968.
53. Wrightsman, Lawrence S., *Social Psychology in the Seventies*. Monterey, Calif.: Brooks/Cole, 1972.
54. Zimmerman, Don H., "A Reply to Professor Coser," *American Sociologist*, vol. 11 (February 1976), pp. 4–13.

Selected Readings

BERGER, PETER, and THOMAS LUCKMANN, *The Social Construction of Reality*. Garden City, N.Y.: Doubleday, 1966.

Presents a lucid and informative treatment of a phenomenological and interactionist view of individuals and social structures.

BLUMER, HERBERT, *Symbolic Interactionism*. Englewood Cliffs, N.J.: Prentice-Hall, 1969.

This collection of papers offers a comprehensive review of Blumer's analysis of theory and method as seen from the interactionist perspective. Blumer has been the one sociologist most influential in defining the essential and unique implications of this viewpoint for the sociological community.

COLEMAN, JAMES S., "Loss of Power," *American Sociological Review*, vol. 38 (February 1973), pp. 1–17.

A highly intriguing analysis of the relationship between the commitments persons make to social relationships and the costs they incur thereby. A significant advance beyond conventional exchange theory.

COSER, LEWIS A. (ed.), *The Idea of Social Structure: Papers in Honor of Robert K. Merton*. New York: Harcourt Brace Jovanovich, 1975.

This collection of essays represents attempts to articulate a social psychology based on a structural conception of sociology.

GOFFMAN, ERVING, *Frame Analysis*. New York: Harper & Row, 1974.

This difficult book introduces the student to the work of a prominent contemporary symbolic interactionist.

HOMANS, GEORGE C., *Social Behavior: Its Elementary Forms* (rev. ed.). New York: Harcourt Brace Jovanovich, 1974.

The reader is encouraged to examine this book and reach his or her own conclusions concerning the usefulness of an exchange theory for social psychology.

MILLS, C. W., *The Sociological Imagination*. New York: Oxford University Press, 1959.

Mills offers a critique of the sociological enterprise that is still relevant today. We concur with most, if not all, of his evaluations of contemporary sociology. The social psychology presented in this book is, in part, a reflection of his influence on the discipline.

STONE, GREGORY P., and HARVEY A. FARBERMAN (eds.), *Social Psychology through Symbolic Interaction*. Waltham, Mass.: Ginn-Blaisdell, 1970.

This book contains the basic essays in the symbolic interactionist tradition and should be examined in conjunction with the works of George Herbert Mead.

STRAUSS, ANSELM L. (ed.), *George Herbert Mead on Social Psychology*. Chicago: University of Chicago Press, 1964.

The readings in this volume present the main elements of Mead's view of self, interaction, and society.

chapter 2

The Evolutionary Setting of Human Behavior

A brief consideration of the behavior of a lower species will indicate some of the major differences between it and various kinds of human behavior. It will also call attention both to simpler forms of interaction and simpler modes of communication that foreshadow and form the basis of human cultural evolution.

The behavior of all animals (including human beings) is social in some degree; even among the lowest species, organisms stimulate one another and may live in some sort of group. Social groups as we know them require organization, psychological unity, a communication system, and a division of labor, however simple, whereby group members cooperate toward group goals. Another type of group, exemplified by a mass of people waiting for a train, is known as an *aggregate,* or an *assemblage;* members of the aggregate, whether it is composed of human beings or animals, do not act concertedly toward group goals or like members of social groups; they do affect one another's behavior, thereby making the behavior social to a limited degree. An aggregate is thus not a genuine social group because it involves only the most rudimentary social relations and lacks most of the features of social groups noted above.

While the emphasis in our discussion will be placed upon the evolution of forms of behavior, it is well to remember that cultural evolution presupposes and depends upon a prior biological evolution. The evolution of the human brain has been, of course, of central significance. Specialists in this area generally emphasize that the assumption of an upright posture was of critical importance in the evolution of humans because it freed the hands for the making and manipulation of tools and for other fine manipulative behavior. This, in turn, changed survival conditions and helped to produce the changes in cranial size and structure that distinguish Homo sapiens from the human-apes thought to have been our immediate predecessors. The human brain is not simply a relatively larger one than that of monkeys and other primates; it is also qualitatively and structurally different. For example, the areas associated with the thumb (and with control of the hands in general), language, speech, and with higher mental functions are proportionately much more elaborate and specialized. As will be indicated in our discussion of aphasia, in the brain of the ape there is no counterpart to the specialized left-hemisphere language center characteristic of right-handed humans. The bibliography at the end of the chapter includes a number of significant discussions of these biological aspects of the evolutionary story that constitute necessary preconditions for the evolution of culture and the development of language. (6, 7, 16, 26, 30, 32, 40, 42)

The Emergence of Humans and Culture

Geologists divide geological time into eras, periods, and epochs, beginning with the appearance of the earth perhaps four to seven billion years ago. The major eras are the Archeozoic, Proterozoic, Paleozoic, Mesozoic, and Cenozoic, the most recent. Some mammalian forms of life began to appear more than one hundred million years ago in the late Mesozoic era, and all the rest, including humans, evolved during the Cenozoic era, which consists of about the last sixty-three million years. The Quaternary period of the Cenozoic era covers about the last million years, and it is subdivided into the Pleistocene (glacial) and post-Pleistocene epochs.

Primitive forms of humans are thought to have appeared between one and two million years ago and an early form of modern humans made its appearance perhaps a quarter of a million years ago. For a period of several hundred thousand years, premodern humans (Homo erectus) and archaic types of modern humans (Homo sapiens) evolved physically, becoming taller and larger, and developing larger and larger brains. At the end of this, the Pleistocene or glacial epoch, more than twelve thousand years ago, Homo erectus and earlier forms of Homo sapiens had disappeared and been replaced by modern humans essentially like those of today with respect to physical appearance and intellectual potential. It is estimated that in 10,000 B.C., when the ice of the last glaciation had melted, there were fewer than one million human beings on earth. By 6000 B.C. the number is estimated at about five million, by 5000 B.C. at about ten million, and the estimated human population at about the time of Christ was a quarter billion. (44)

People of the New Stone Age (Neolithic), beginning perhaps about 10,000 B.C., gave this age its name by grinding and polishing and generally improving their stone tools. More important, they domesticated animals and plants, learned to plant seeds, to irrigate and harvest crops, and to store and transport foods, liquids, and goods. They invented the wheel and the plow and began to build houses. In contrast to humans of the Old Stone (Paleolithic) Age, those of the Neolithic Age began to live in settled, agriculturally supported, communities of considerable size, where they established cities and relatively large political units. These favored places were invariably river valleys such as those of the Tigris, Euphrates, and Nile. It was there that the first great ancient civilizations of Egypt, Sumeria, and Babylonia came into being. It is said that the city of Jericho has been continuously occupied since 7865 B.C. (plus or minus 160 years, by modern methods of dating). (6:143)

In these ancient civilizations writing was invented, number systems were developed, elaborate religious beliefs were formulated, and trade and commerce flourished. Very accurate observations of the skies led to the invention of the calendar and to the beginnings of astronomy. The calendar is a uniquely human invention. It serves as a device for bringing time and its passage into the social organization of societies. Through their calendar, human groups attach themselves to their past, and the calendar serves as a vehicle for gaining control over the future. Ceremonial calendars, which mark a yearly round of sacred and secular holidays, serve to set groups off from one another. In Egypt the pyramids were built between four and five thousand years ago, and in Babylonia, the Hammurabi code of law was promulgated about thirty-seven hundred years ago. Schools of a restricted sort were established in ancient Sumer and Egypt. In Greece during the fourth century B.C. Plato established an academy in which he taught advanced geometry, astronomy, music, literature, history, law, politics, and ethics.

In the chronology of human physical and cultural evolution, it is significant to note that while the former no doubt sets the stage for cultural evolution by providing us with our human brain and physical form, the two forms of evolution seem to be unrelated after that point. Cultural evolution or change has, in recent times, accelerated at a geometric rate without any further significant evolutionary changes in the biological equipment of humans.

We turn next to different "levels" of organisms and behavior. To begin with, just where to draw the line between the social and nonsocial in the interorganismic contact of the very lowest animals is an indeterminate matter. H. S. Jennings (17), the well-known student of protozoa, has confessed that in his younger days he concluded that aggregates of infusoria exhibited no social characteristics; he was reprimanded later by a critic who noted that the reactions he had described actually were social relations of the protozoan kind. Although the one-celled animal requires no other to aid it in performing its vital functions, it does, nevertheless, on occasion gather together with others of its kind. Dense aggregates may be produced by convergence toward a source of light or by movement against a current. These are aggregates in the literal sense of the term; there is no division of labor, no cooperative activity.

In the lower species, W. Allee (2:147) has pointed out that the mere crowding of organisms of the same species produces beneficial results: the animals multiply faster, eat more, and enjoy better chances of survival under adverse conditions. Some animals learn more rapidly in the presence of others. Allee hesitates to call the simpler aggregates "cooperative," and he refers to them as showing "automatic mutual interdependence." He and others have remarked that various "integrative levels" are reached by different species aggregations. The existence of a simple form of group organization is shown by the synchronous behavior engendered in densely clustered insects by the transmission of tactile stimuli from one individual insect to another. Touch one individual and all react almost immediately.

Although it is certain that various forms of group organization exist among the lower species, biologists find it no easy matter to classify one as more complex or more social than another if the forms are not very similar. Allee, for example, speaks of small but real differences of group organization (1:158):

> We are confronted with a gradual development of real differences without being able to put a finger with surety on any one clearly defined break in the continuity. The slow accumulation of more and more social tendencies leads finally by small steps to something that is apparently different. If we disregard the intermediate stages, the differences may appear pronounced,

but if we focus on these intermediates, it will be only for the sake of convenience that we interrupt the connecting chain of events at some comparatively conspicuous link and arbitrarily make this the dividing point, when one is needed, between the more and the less social.

This statement brings out two aspects of evolution: one is the continuity of species and the other is the notion of distinct "levels" or the emergence of new properties. The latter has been stated in this way (36:245):

> The principle of levels has come into current usage through a recognition of important differences in the complexity, the degree of development, and the interdependent organization of behavior functions through the animal series. The evidently superior properties that appear on a new level of organization are not to be explained as due to a new kind of energy or new vital properties, but as functional properties arising from a new system of organization which differs in given ways from "lower" and "higher" systems.

The "levels" concept thus assumes the existence of continuity and of similarity among species but stresses also the emergence of new properties of organization. The differences in levels have to do with *what kinds of processes and capacities are available* to an animal and its species mates in adapting to their environments." (37:57) Ants and bees live in organized colonies and operate at higher levels of capacity than do sponges or protozoa that live as individuals or in aggregates. Different animal aggregations reach the same general ends—such as providing food and shelter—but the organization of the aggregate, and the processes through which ends are attained, may be very dissimilar.

Interestingly enough, extreme complexity in group organization may exist together with relatively low level of capacity and operation. Some species of army ants engage in highly complex and successful expeditions in search of food. As many as thirty thousand ants may move in a column more than fifteen yards wide. The swarm continues to move as a body for some hours after it starts, but eventually divides into two or more subswarms. Despite the seeming complexity of these maneuvers, it turns out that the capacities of the individual ants are very limited and that the collective action is based on fairly simple responses to chemical and tactile stimulation. It is the "heterogeneous forest environment" that leads to the building up of the complicated swarm, for under simpler laboratory conditions no such organized behavior occurs and the "ants will run for days in an endless circular column. . . ." (37:59)

ANTHRO-
POMORPHISM
AND MORGAN'S
CANON
The concept of behavioral levels leads us to be on our guard against anthropomorphizing. *Anthropomorphism* (from the Greek *anthropos,* "man," and *morphe,* "form") means the projection of human traits upon things not human, and it is a fallacy to be guarded against in studying the lower animals. We are especially given to making the anthropomor-

phic mistake when the behavior of an animal or species seems to resemble human behavior (for example, when a pet dog does something for which it is usually punished and is then spoken of as feeling guilty or looking ashamed).

In a certain sense, however, the human vocabulary must always be anthropomorphic. Suppose one makes a statement as simple as the following: "The chimpanzee placed the box so that by standing on it, he could reach the banana." Surely this sentence does not mean that the chimpanzee has verbally formulated his purpose within the framework of English or any other language, as might be assumed by a too-literal reader. We should remember that although we apply human words to the actions of animals, the animals themselves do not.

It is not only in common speech that animal behavior is described and accounted for in human terms. Many years ago a comparative psychologist, Lloyd Morgan, attacked the then general propensity of both laypersons and scholars to find resemblances between the mental processes of human beings and those of lower animals. He enunciated a canon that has been quoted with general approval ever since by comparative psychologists (28:53):

> In no case may we interpret an action as the outcome of the exercise of a higher psychical faculty, if it can be interpreted as the outcome of the exercise of one which stands lower in the psychological scale.

At the time that Morgan was writing, it was customary to prove similarities between animals and human beings by narrating anecdotes. The anecdotal method has long since disappeared from scholarly writing, but there are numerous references to animal reasoning, generalization, hypotheses, concepts, dominance, leadership, purpose, goals, neuroses, communication, and cooperation. The terms are often used within quotation marks to indicate that the reader is not supposed to take the analogy to human behavior too seriously; that many writers and readers do take the analogies seriously, there is little doubt. Schneirla, who has attacked this kind of anthropomorphic writing, suggests that a distinction be drawn between the *description* of behavior and its causal *explanation*. We may, perhaps, speak loosely of protective behavior, food-getting, and courtship in various species, but a genuine causal description of the behavior will make clear that several processes are involved. Whereas, for example, intent and exchange of information and sentiment are involved in human courtship, none need be imputed to various of the lower species when they engage in sexual activity.

We believe that the concept of levels of behavior is a particularly fruitful one because it focuses attention both on the continuity of species and upon the differences among them. It makes mandatory that concepts and hypotheses concerning the behavior of any species be inductively derived from the study of that particular species—rather than, as is common, by extrapolation to lower species of the principles derived from mammalian investigation, or by the explanation of human behavior in terms of principles derived from lower mammalian types (*zoomorphism*). Morgan, advocating this same view at the turn of the century, said cogently (28:282–83):

> When the doctrine of evolution was winning its way to acceptance, it was natural that its advocates should employ every means at their command to strengthen their position and to emphasize the continuity underlying diversity of aspect. But now that the position is secure, and continuity is generally admitted, it seems desirable to mark off, by restriction of the range of the use of terms we employ, the stages of differentiation.

A comparative psychology based upon this principle would be of great significance to social psychologists.

The sections that follow describe the behavior of species far removed from each other—insects and great apes. The apes are just below humans in the phylogenetic series. The "social insects" have one of the most conspicuously organized group lives known below the level of humans. As the symbolic life, and especially language, is of such import in humans, communication among insects and apes will be of special interest to us.

Insect Societies

ORGANIZED INSECT GROUPS
Entomologists have studied certain "social insects," including bees, wasps, termites, and ants. Members of these species, unlike most others, are born, live, and die as members of *societies*, or communities.

These insect groupings are often complex and highly organized, involving the cooperative and systematic efforts of great numbers of individual insects. Ant communities, for example, may consist of thousands of members, each of whom carries on specialized activities: breeding, nursing, childrearing, providing communal rations, feeding other members, engaging in group warfare, cultivating fungi as food, bequeathing "real estate" to the young, working on "engineering" projects, and "training" other insects to be docile slaves.

Such communal activities are possible only because members of the insect society are able to cooperate with one another. The care of eggs and larvae by "nurses" illustrates the cooperative and coordinated nature of activity among ants (27:154–55, 167):

> The eggs soon develop into minute larvae, fragile and helpless things that need close and constant care to preserve them. . . . From the beginning and throughout their growth . . . they must be fed and cared for. Their care is always a first consideration. . . . The nurses continually hover over them. They lick them as a cat does her kittens. The larvae learn to perk up

their weak black heads and open their mouths, into which the nurses place food and drink. . . . For the most part, nurse ants take up and go through their duties in a business-like way. It is done thoroughly, and does not cease until the larvae have spun up around them their silken cocoons. Nor then; for these cocoons are constantly watched, cleaned, and cared for, and when the time comes for the young imago to escape, it is aided by the scissors-like jaws of the nurses, whose obstetrical services are aided by the efforts of the out-coming nymph.

In any insect community there exist physical differences among the individual members. Indeed, although ant communities consist mainly of the same sex (female), physical differentiation among ants is often very striking. This differentiation involves differential functions, each physical type being suited by nature for certain communal activities, and absolutely or relatively unsuited for others. The anatomical structure of a queen ant is very dissimilar to that of a worker, and her activities and social functions are correspondingly different; soldier ants, which are physically unlike queens and workers, engage in still different activities. All three ant types are genuine specialists. Bee and termite communities are similarly organized along biological lines. **DIVISION OF LABOR AND BIOLOGICAL DIFFERENTIATION**

Members of ant and other insect communities acquire their physiological structure through hereditary transmission. Wheeler, a recognized American authority on the species, believes that ants have undergone no important structural modification for approximately fifty-five to sixty-five million years and that ant activities today are virtually identical with those carried on millions of years ago.

The physiological structure of the insect not only determines its behavior but results in activity that is largely automatic. Entomologists have described ant behavior as composed of: (1) reflexes, (2) instincts (chains or series of reflexes), and (3) modifiable behavior. Modifiable, or learned, behavior is not automatic or stereotyped, but varies according to the demands of the environment. (50:507) The point is that the behavior of each insect is largely determined by its biological structure and by its individual experiences. Learned behavior, however, is of limited importance in the organization of the insect group, *because it is not transmitted from one generation to the next.* The learning dies with the insect whose possession it is; each insect must learn for itself anew.

By contrast to human beings (whose societies are organized largely in terms of codes, laws, customs, folkways, and symbolic understandings, and whose children must learn these in order to participate properly in the community), the capacity to learn "seems to be secondary in the early adjustment of new [insect] individuals. Its functions may be largely held to a generalized approach to the colony chemical, established through early feeding." (35:69) By the latter point, Schneirla has reference to the fact that insects recognize other insects of the same species because of learning. This learning takes place so early that it appears to be automatic or instinctive, although it is not. A mixed colony of ants can be formed if ants of different species are put together immediately after they emerge from their cocoons.

The preponderance of biological factors in the insect social pattern may be emphasized by terming such a pattern *biosocial;* that of the psychological or learning factors in the human pattern, by terming it *psychosocial.* (35:69)

THE NATURE OF INSECT COMMUNICATION

Although insects possess neither speaking nor hearing organs comparable to those of human beings, communication of a sort does take place among them by means of certain sensory organs. Sounds are produced by several methods: by wing vibrations, through breathing tubes, and by the friction of one part of the body against another. Gestures are made by body movements. The antennae of insects are also used as sensitive instruments by which excitement, discovery, and similar "emotions" are transmitted. Ants are said to congregate swiftly around a bit of food found by one of their number because the finder produces sound through the friction of one part of its body against another. The sounds are produced involuntarily in response to the smell of the food.

Such communication is necessary to all insect life, even among the most solitary, as some sort of sign behavior is required if individual insects are to mate. Where there are familial relationships, as between the female and her offspring, sensitivity to signs is more apparent. A biologist has suggested the important connection between elaborate insect communication and nest-building. As food must be brought back, colony members must follow one another's trails, danger signals must be responded to, and many other cooperative actions must be engaged in.

Such communication among ants—and among other social insects— should not be confused with articulate and symbol-using human communication. The language of humans consists of articulated systems of sounds—codified, conventionalized sets of symbols. Careful studies of bees, ants, termites, and other insects have not revealed the slightest shred of evidence suggesting the existence of symbolic communication among them. Moreover, although techniques of communication among young insects apparently require a simple initial process of learning, that process is in no way comparable to the complex one by which human infants acquire the use of language. The basic character of insect communication is so different from the symbolic communication of humans that Schneirla (34:391) suggests that we "use a term such as *social transmission* for interindividual arousal in insects, reserving the term *com-*

munication for higher levels on which a conceptual process of social transmission is demonstrable."

An example of modes of communication between insects is furnished by an investigation of mosquitoes. In 1878, Hiram Maxim noted that the whine of a hotel dynamo attracted large numbers of male mosquitoes but few females. No one paid attention to this observation until relatively recently when it was discovered that mosquitoes communicate by sound and that when two cages, one containing male and the other female mosquitoes, are placed within several feet of each other the males all congregate on the side nearest the females, even when sheets are draped over the cages and the transmission of all scent is prevented. (43) The two Cornell scientists who discovered this have used the knowledge by setting up electrified cages in which loudspeakers amplify the mosquitoes' buzz five hundred thousand times. Mosquitoes fly to the cages from miles around, only to be electrocuted there.

It was found that each variety of mosquito has a characteristic pair of sounds, both emitted by the female. One of these is the "love call," which attracts males of the same variety within hearing distance of the call; the other is a "lust call," which signalizes to other females the discovery of a source of blood. (The female mosquito is the disease carrier and biter, because she must have blood to complete the process of fertilizing her eggs. The male is strictly vegetarian, living on nectar and fruit juices.) The use of both love calls and lust calls on the amplifiers thus attracts both male and female mosquitoes. It was found that more than 90 percent of the mosquitoes in a vicinity respond to the sounds unless they are too loud, in which case they repel. It is believed that the mosquitoes' antennae act as receivers for sound. The mosquitoes of Florida and those of West Africa are attuned to different frequencies and hence do not "understand" each other.

A more complicated form of communication exists among bees, and relates to the manner in which a bee signalizes to the rest of the hive the discovery of a source of honey. Knowledge of this is derived mainly from the remarkable studies of K. von Frisch (45, 46), a German investigator who specialized in the study of bees. Von Frisch found that when a bee discovers a rich source of food about fifty to one hundred yards from the hive, she at once becomes excited and liberates there a characteristic odor. When the bee returns to the hive she gives some of the nectar or syrup that she has collected to other bees and then starts a "round dance," circling alternately to the right and to the left. Other bees are excited by the dance and move in close and touch the dancer with their antennae. During pauses in the dance they are given droplets of nectar that have been regurgitated by the dancer. One by one these bees then leave the dance to fly about at random near the hive until they find the food source. This food source is identified by the clues furnished to them by

K. van Frisch has investigated complicated communication among bees whereby an individual may transmit to other members the location of a food source. Such behavior is, however, neither culturally transmitted from generation to generation nor is it culturally changeable, as a human language. (*Treat Davidson from National Audubon Society*)

the dancer. This interesting communicative process is more complex than similar behavior of the ant, which simply leaves an odor trail to the food source.

Because bees collect nectar and pollen from sources as much as a mile or more from the hive, the round dance with its taste and odor cues is not adequate to indicate food sources at the longer distances. Hence, when the distance exceeds fifty to one hundred yards, varying by species, the dance of the returning bee is a different one, a short straight run on the honeycomb during which the abdomen is waggled from side to side tracing a figure eight. When the distances become greater the speed of the dance is reduced. It was long thought that "estimated flying time" to the objective was indicated solely in this manner. The speed of the dance not only appeared to be roughly proportional to the distance, but it also became somewhat slower when there was a strong head wind on the way to the feeding place. Recent research has shown that the dancing bees emit trains of sound that are closely correlated in duration with distance to be traversed. (48, 49) These sounds are evidently attended to in the darkness of the hive by other bees that follow the dancer with their feelers. The direction of the source is indicated in relation to the position of the sun by the direction of the bee's straight run on the comb that hangs vertically in the hive. A downward run means away from the sun; an upward run means toward it. Bees attending the dancer are so well guided by the messages that they rarely make errors of more than about ten degrees in direction. Bees also are able to make adjustments to the changing position of the sun during the course of the day.

In other research, von Frisch (47) has reported on what he has called "dialects" in bee communication. He is careful to note that in using this expression he is speaking metaphorically. When he extended his observations to other varieties of honeybees he found that different varieties had somewhat different types of dances with varying rhythms so that when two different varieties were placed in the same hive they misinterpreted each other's signals and would, for example, go too far or not far enough to look for the indicated food source. Some types insist on doing their dance only on the horizontal, while others will do it on either a vertical or horizontal plane. In any case, the patterns of signaling are stereotypes and innate in each variety so that a newly hatched and totally inexperienced bee "understands" at once the signals of others of its kind.

It is unnecessary to indicate here the arguments for denying that honeybees possess language in the human sense. It is sufficient to note that this is not claimed even by those who study insect communication. They note that the transmission of the behavior from generation to generation is a purely biological process and that the system of communication used is determined by membership in a species, not by membership in a language community or culture. After a careful observation of various kinds of insect communication, Schneirla said (35:64): "There is no evidence . . . that it is symbolic in the sense that human words are symbolic. Rather, the insect forms are derived from biological processes characteristic of the species and are fixed in nature rather than culturally changeable."

The Behavior of Chimpanzees

The great apes, who of all the animals stand closest to us on the evolutionary ladder, offer perhaps the most interesting comparison with human beings, for they are unquestionably more intelligent than our usual house pets or farm animals. The great apes that have been most thoroughly studied are the chimpanzees. We shall attempt to show, first, what sociable animals they are. In describing his behavior, we shall use language that will bring out his seemingly human qualities. We shall then point to his limitations, which emerge when we compare him with the more complex human being.

GROUP SOLIDARITY. "It is hardly an exaggeration to say that a chimpanzee kept in solitude is not a real chimpanzee at all." (20:293) This statement indicates the extraordinary extent to which chimpanzees are influenced by the presence of other chimpanzees. When forcibly removed from his companions or his group, this great ape "cries, screams, rages, and struggles desperately to escape and return to his fellows. Such

THE SOCIAL BEHAVIOR OF CHIMPANZEES

behavior may last for hours. All the bodily functions may be more or less upset. Food may be persistently refused, and depression may follow the emotional orgy." (53:45) The chimpanzee will in these circumstances even risk his life in an effort to return to his group. When he rejoins it, there is great rejoicing, and the one who had been isolated displays the deepest excitement.

A chimpanzee locked alone in a cage will stretch his hands out through the bars toward his companions, wave and call to them, or push various objects through the bars in their direction. If the isolated animal's cries are audible and his gestures visible to the others, they may embrace him through the bars of the cage and otherwise give evidence of what seems to be human sympathy for their unhappy fellow. But if they cannot hear him or see him, they show no awareness of his absence. If one of their number is taken away because of illness or death, there is usually no evidence that the others grieve for their missing companion or even know that he is no longer in their midst.

Chimpanzees have a characteristic cry of distress. When this cry is emitted in connection with some action taken by the human investigator, other chimpanzees tend to rally to the support of their companion and threaten or actually attack the offender. Sometimes it is difficult to train the animals when they are in a group because of this danger of attack, particularly when the chimpanzees are adults.

COOPERATIVE BEHAVIOR.   Investigators have noted numerous instances of cooperative activity among chimpanzees in the solution of problems. Each of two apes was individually trained to pull on a rope. Then a box of food was placed a short distance from a cage containing the two animals. Two ropes were attached to the box, and the rope-ends were left inside the cage. One of the chimpanzees, when he found himself unable to move the box by pulling on one of the ropes, solicited help from the other animal. He did this by such activities as pulling him toward the bars and placing his companion's hands on the second rope. Pulling in unison, the two chimpanzees succeeded in bringing the box close enough to reach for, grasp, and eat the food it contained.

Köhler has amusingly described what may be called a cooperative joke. A group of chimpanzees eating bread in a cage one day grew fond of teasing some chickens. The fowl would approach the cage, and the chimpanzees would offer them a piece of bread. The moment the chickens were about to peck at it, the bread would be withdrawn. One of Köhler's animals on his own initiative shared his piece with the chickens, watching them with an air of genial detachment. Sometimes while this was going on, another chimpanzee would poke a stick or a piece of wire at the chickens. Having hit upon this scheme, the two animals would then continue the game: one of them luring the chicken to the bars of the cage by holding out bread toward them, the other manipulating the stick or wire.

FADS AND ORNAMENTATION.　　Köhler also describes behavior among captive chimpanzees that bears a striking resemblance to human interest in fads and ornamentation. Thus, some chimpanzees inside a cage pushed straws through the bars, holding them among some ants just outside. When a straw was covered with ants it was withdrawn, the ants were eaten, and the performance then repeated. Other chimpanzees adopted this activity as a kind of sport. Several of the animals might be seen seated like fishermen in the yard alongside a path used by ants. Each of the chimpanzees held a straw that he lowered into the path and pulled up when it was covered with ants. After a time they evidently wearied of this game; they gave it up and turned to something else—for example, digging in the ground with a stick or jumping with a pole.

The chimpanzees' use of ornaments involved walking about with a rag, a bit of rope, some grass, or a bundle of twigs on them, or with strings dangling over their ears and around their faces. Köhler describes this as an almost daily occurrence and notes that the chimpanzees derived some kind of satisfaction from it. He also describes how the animals became interested in what we may perhaps call chimpanzee art. They smeared a white, paintlike substance over objects in their cages and sometimes over themselves. Like some young children, they did this deliberately and rather methodically, and apparently with some obscure kind of enjoyment.

RESPONSE TO MIRRORS.　　When Köhler first allowed Sultan to look at himself in a mirror, that gifted chimpanzee extended his hand with the palm turned inward (the typical chimpanzee gesture of greeting to a comrade). When the mirror was given to the animals they all appeared eager to obtain it, snatching it from one another and peering curiously into the glass surface. One female chimpanzee finally captured it, took it away from the others, and proceeded to examine it carefully, making repeated efforts to grasp or touch the chimpanzee that seemed to be peering at her from the mirror.

The animals began to pay attention to their reflections in shiny objects, in pieces of metal, and the like. They could sometimes be observed standing for relatively long periods of time over a pool, watching their reflections, grimacing, and swaying back and forth.

ECONOMIC BEHAVIOR.　　In an ingenious experiment (52), chimpanzees were trained to insert poker chips of various colors into a slot machine. A blue chip yielded two grapes; a white chip, one; and a brass chip, none. The animals were also shown how to obtain chips by performing work on a different machine. They learned to operate both machines, developed a preference for blue as against white chips, and preferred both over the brass ones. When denied access to the "chimp-o-mat," they learned to hold on to their "money" for a time. When shown a chip, they often responded to it by extending their lips and smacking them as they did when they were offered grapes.

BEHAVIOR TOWARD HUMAN BEINGS.   On one occasion Köhler inadvertently ran a splinter into his finger. He called it to the attention of a chimpanzee. The animal immediately assumed the mien and expression characteristically assumed in mutual skin grooming among apes: he examined the wound, placed two fingernails on each side of the splinter, and skillfully squeezed it out. Then he examined the finger very closely and allowed his hand to drop as though he were satisfied with a job well done.

Other interesting instances of quasi-human behavior toward people have been reported. Investigators have noted repeatedly that apes in captivity make sexual advances toward human beings as well as toward other animals, such as dogs. Some visitors have been greeted with something suspiciously like a "Bronx cheer." Sultan, Köhler's chimpanzee "genius," tried to enforce disciplinary action in Köhler's absence. Frequently, apes that have been scolded or punished seem to ask their human master for forgiveness by whimpering and throwing their arms around the master's neck.

Chimpanzees often display what may be characterized as a willingness to accept a human being as one of them. Köhler, for example, describes his participation in a chimpanzee dance around a pole. The apes seemed to relish his part in their sport and showed obvious "disappointment" when he withdrew. It is also notable that chimpanzees—particularly, it would seem, the adult females—show a kind of special and "benevolent" interest in human children.

LIMITATIONS OF CHIMPANZEES   When we consider the collective achievements of civilized humans, we are overwhelmingly impressed by the vast gulf between them and the apes. Chimpanzees do not weep. Although they have various ways of indicating pleasure, they do not laugh. Nor do they seem to have the slightest appreciation of human laughter; they tend to respond to it with bewilderment or rage. One could go on almost indefinitely enumerating specific kinds of human behavior that are beyond the ape. It is not so easy, however, to determine the exact sources of the chimpanzees' limitations or to define the precise limits of their accomplishments. This is a problem whose solution depends upon further experimental and observational investigation of animals. Here we can indicate only some of the

Chimpanzees have been trained to display rudimentary "economic" behavior. Here Lana inserts a poker chip into the "chimp-o-mat" to obtain milk, Coke, or a piece of apple. (*J. P. Lafont/Sygma*)

```
WHYT SS 14:59
PLEA MACH MAKE SLYD .OK; 15:00
WHYT SS 15:01
OPEN .WS 15:01
PLEA MACH GIVE MILK .OK; 15:01
WHYT .WS 15:04
PLEA MACH GIVE PIEC   OF   COKE .WS 15:04
SS 15:04
PLEA MACH GIVE PIEC   OF   APPL .OK; 15:11
.WS 15:12
PLEA MACH GIVE PIEC   OF   APPL .OK; 15:12
SS 15:12
PLEA MACH GIVE PIEC   OF   APPL .OK; 15:12
SS 15:13
WHYT OPEN .WS 15:13
PLEA MACH GIVE PIEC   OF   APPL .OK; 15:13
```

main types of differences between human and subhuman behavior that are to a degree substantiated by the work of comparative psychologists.

ANIMALS ARE LIMITED TO THE "HERE" AND "NOW." All subhuman behavior is sharply, although not absolutely, limited to the immediate, concrete situation. This limitation is one of time and space. Thus, Köhler states that a major difference between humans and chimpanzees is that the time in which the chimpanzees live stretches back and forth only a little way. The ability of chimpanzees to solve problems appears to be determined principally, Köhler says, by their "optical apprehension of the situation." Sticks and other instruments are most readily used as tools when they are in the immediate proximity of the problem situation. If they are moved away from it—as, for example, to the rear of the cage or into an adjoining room or corridor—the apes virtually cease to perceive them as potential tools, even though they may be perfectly familiar with these items and see them daily. Similarly, as we have noted, a group of chimpanzees may react violently when one of their number is removed, particularly if he cries out or struggles. But once the animal has been taken out of sight and hearing, the group appears to forget about him almost at once, although the solitary animal continues for some time to seek the company of his fellows.

The assertion that animals are limited to the "here" and "now" requires some qualification: the limitation is not absolute, nor does it warrant overemphasis. Thus, if chimpanzees in a cage see bananas buried in the sand outside and are not allowed out of the cage until the next day, when they are released they run quickly to the approximate spot to search for the buried fruit. Other experiments clearly indicate that delayed responses of this type are well within the range of the chimpanzee's abilities. Moreover, a chimpanzee separated from a human being to whom he has become accustomed will give unmistakable signs of recognition when he sees him or her again after months of separation. But, by and large, one may regard chimpanzees as limited to the "here" and "now."

WORKING TOGETHER BUT NOT IN COMMON.   That there are very distinct limits to cooperation among chimpanzees is evident from a highly significant experiment. Several animals were trained individually to build structures consisting of three boxes placed upon one another in order to obtain bananas hung up out of reach. Later, when the animals were given the same problem to solve collectively, each one proceeded to build as though he were alone. Thus, a chimpanzee in search of a second box would appropriate one already being used by another animal and become involved in a fight for its possession. When only two of the boxes were placed upon each other, a few of the animals usually attempted to climb the uncompleted structure simultaneously, thus upsetting it and necessitating a fresh start. Constant fighting and repeated failures to complete the three-box structure eventually exhausted all the animals but one. This chimpanzee then completed the structure and obtained the prize without permitting the others to share it. Repetition of this experiment always produced the same results with the same animal outlasting the others and winning the reward.

The vain attempts of four chimpanzees to build a three-box structure are described by Köhler as "building together but not in common." We may understand what he means if we compare the building activities of the chimpanzees with those of humans. Obviously, if each worker on the job sought to build for himself or herself without regard to the activities of fellow workers, the results would hardly be satisfactory. The activities of workers are organized and coordinated according to a plan or a blueprint that is passed around from one to the other, discussed by them, and at least generally understood by all of them. In other words, each worker subordinates individual activity to the purpose or plan that they all have in common. By virtue of possessing this common plan, each worker can and often must engage in an activity different from that of his or her fellows, but each worker will and must contribute to the final result.

Keeping the foregoing illustration in mind, we may say by way of contrast that the cooperative behavior of lower animals is determined by inherited mechanisms rather than by goals and plans collectively comprehended. The sex act may be taken as an illustration of this type of unlearned cooperative behavior. Apart from such an instinctive response, however, it is exceedingly difficult to train a number of animals to work cooperatively on any but the simplest project. If the task requires each animal to do only what he would do if he were working alone, an apparently cooperative solution may be reached. Two chimpanzees may, for example, team up to lift or pull an object that is too heavy for either to manage alone. But when the project requires that the animals learn to perform dissimilar but coordinated tasks (as in building a tower with boxes in order to obtain suspended fruit) they fail because success would require some degree of verbal formulation of purposes and plans, and apes cannot make verbal formulations. We shall see soon the further consequences of this inability.

Although chimpanzees can use various kinds of objects as tools and can even construct certain types of tools, they show almost no tendency to store the tools for future use or to transport them systematically from place to place. Moreover, chimpanzees show practically no disposition to store or hoard food against future contingencies. At this point one may note that other animals, especially certain insects, do store and transport food in very complex and systematic ways. Such behavior, however, does not have to be learned; it is biologically determined.

THE USE OF TOOLS

Chimpanzees have what seems to be an "innate destructive impulse," Yerkes states, that expresses itself in their tendency to break down into its constitutent elements any complex object made up of various movable or removable parts. Chimpanzees explore, pull, poke, and otherwise manipulate the object; they do not rest until it has been taken apart and the pieces strewn about. In this respect they are like small children. When chimpanzees do actually construct a tool—for example, by fitting two sticks together to make one long one—their action seems remarkable because it contrasts so sharply with their usual mode of behavior.

Moreover, unless they are continuously trained, there is a strong tendency for the animals soon to slough off most of the new behavior they have learned in the experimental training situation. As Köhler says:

If one is able to produce a—very temporary—type of behavior which is not congenial to the chimpanzee's instincts, it will soon be necessary to use compulsion if he is to keep it. And the slightest relaxation of that compulsion will be followed by a "reversion to type."

Yerkes exclaimed over the remarkable manner in which the chimpanzees of his laboratory colony learned certain human activities. Thus, when push-button drinking fountains were installed in their cages, only some animals were shown how to use them. The others learned from watching their fellows. Yerkes also observed that each generation became more tractable as experimental animals, certain of the activities required by the experiments being passed on from ape to ape "by imitative process" and from one generation to the next "by social tradition." These effects mentioned by Yerkes are the result of constant contact with human beings, and with an environment arranged by human beings. If the entire colony were returned to its native habitat, in a very short time probably few if any traces of human influence would remain; a new generation would not profit from the older generation's contact with civilization. This is particularly so, as drinking fountains, hammers, keys, and the like are not usually found in the ape's native environment. It is clear too that such transmission as may occur among trained chimpanzees is not the result of language communication as humans know it.

The Absence of Language among Lower Animals

Apes never learn to speak like human beings. Little success has been achieved in training them to imitate the sounds of human speech, although many investigators have tried. Relevant to this point are the reports of two experiments in which young chimpanzees were reared for a time in the homes of psychologists (14, 19). The Kelloggs (19) report that they were entirely unable to train their chimpanzee, Gua, to utter any words or to imitate human speech. The Hayeses (14), on the other hand, report that their animal, Vicki, acquired a vocabulary of three words—"mama," "papa," and "cup." From a demonstration witnessed by the authors, it was clear that the imitation was so crude that the sounds could hardly be identified, and could be called words only by a stretch of the imagination. It was also clear that Vicki used them in a mechanical and uncomprehending manner.

Psychologists continue to be preoccupied with the attempt to teach language to apes. Allen and Beatrice Gardner (10) have taught a chimpanzee to communicate in the American Sign Language, while Ann and David Premack recently taught one of their chimpanzees, Sarah, a vocabulary of about 130 "words" which consisted of brightly colored plastic shapes that could be readily placed in various combinations ("sentences?") on a magnetized language board. (29) These recent endeavors do not seem to us to have created a new situation or to have in any way discredited the idea that humans are the only animals capable of learning a language. They have, however, once more demonstrated the remarkable capabilities of one of our closest and most captivating primate relatives.

The Premacks (29) trained their chimp Sarah by rewarding her when she chose the right plastic "symbols" in a given context. For example, in order to obtain and eat a banana, she was required to put the plastic "word" for banana on the language board. In later phases of her learning, the plastic symbols were combined to form "sentences," as for example, "Give apple Sarah." When Sarah did this correctly she was given a piece of apple. Sarah was also taught the names of various trainers who wore their plastic symbol-names on string necklaces. On one occasion when she put on the board, "Give apple Gussie," the trainer promptly gave the apple to another chimp named Gussie—and Sarah never again made the same mistake. In the more advanced phases of her training, Sarah became able, as the Premacks said, to make complex assertions and judgments such as the following: "Sarah take apple, if/then Mary give chocolate Sarah," "Red color of apple," and "Red no color of banana." She was able to match the plastic word for apple with a real apple, and the plastic name for Mary (a trainer) with a picture of Mary.

The authors cautiously conclude that "Sarah had managed to learn a code, a simple language that nevertheless included some of the characteristic features of natural language." (29:99) They warn against asking from Sarah what one would require of an adult, but argue that Sarah holds her own in language ability when compared with a two-year-old child. The Premacks are able to say that Sarah has a language, because their definition of language is too broad. They use it to refer to systems of communication in general, viewing human languages as particular "albeit, remarkably refined forms of language." (29:92) *They have thus conferred language upon chimpanzees by the very nature of their definition.*

Closer consideration of the highly interesting accomplishments of Sarah casts doubt even on the Premack comparison of Sarah with an ordinary two-year-old child. For example, children even at this early age use their language to talk with each other, while Sarah talked only with human beings. In contrast to how children acquire vocabularies (see Chapter 12), Sarah acquired her vocabulary exclusively or mainly in a laborious learning process, motivated by material rewards. While the Premacks say that Sarah mastered about 130 words, they also observe that her level of reliability was about 75 percent to 80 percent. This raises the question as to how well humans, even two-year-olds, would be able to communicate if, in the process, they said approximately the opposite of what they intended to about 20 to 25 percent of the time. One may further wonder how much a colony of chimps in their natural habitat, all trained to Sarah's level and equipped with plastic words and language boards, would be likely to use this language.

In general, as we have already indicated, it seems improbable that the work of the Premacks and Gardners will result in any need to revise the belief that humans are the only animals capable of learning a language. The significance of this work is more likely to be felt in other areas, such as those that attempt to specify the basic points of difference that exist between human language and the lower-order system of communication. An anthropologist, G. W. Hewes, has recently reviewed this material in connection with a proposal he has made concerning the possible origin of human language. (15) In the process of doing so, however, it seems clear that Hewes is not overly impressed with the idea that at least two chimpanzees in the world now have language, although they cannot talk to each other, since each uses a different one. While Sarah uses plastic symbols, the Gardners' chimp Washoe was trained by them to use the American Sign Language. We are more impressed by the ingenuity and creativity of the teachers than we are by that of their pupils.

Who is imitating whom? Although at least two chimps in the world now have language, the ingenuity and creativity of the teachers are more impressive than that of the students. (*Magnum*)

Apes, of course, emit characteristic sounds of their own, but these do not constitute language in a genuine sense. This may easily be shown by considering three features of so-called ape language. First, the sounds are unlearned. This point has been proved conclusively by Boutan (5), who raised an ape wholly isolated from other apes from birth until its fifth year. It uttered the same cries as those made by other apes. Second, the sounds emitted by apes, as various investigators have noted, are "subjective": that is, they merely express emotions; they do not designate or describe objects. In the words of one writer (21:85): "Chimpanzees can exclaim *kha* or *nga* over their food just as humans delightedly cry *yum-yum*, but they cannot say *banana, today.*" Their cries of enthusiasm are responses to an immediate situation: such cries "cannot be used between meals to talk over the merits of the feast." And third, ape sounds do not constitute a system of symbols. Yerkes has summarized this lack of system (53:189–90):

> Certainly chimpanzees communicate effectively with one another by sounds, gestures, facial and bodily expression, postures, and visible attitudes which function as meaningful signs. Symbols probably are rare and play a subordinate, if significant, role in their linguistic expression. Therefore, the composite language of the chimpanzee differs greatly from our own. They, for example, have no system, or even assemblage, of sounds which may properly be termed speech, and nothing remotely like a written language.

The sounds emitted by apes, or by any other animal, clearly do not constitute systematized animal languages similar to human languages. Neither may one refer to animal sounds as words, for if one does, one is forced to recognize that human children also communicate their needs to one another and to their elders by means of cries—cries as natural for them as are chimpanzee cries to the chimpanzee. One would thus be led to say that children have language before they learn a language, and that they speak words immediately after birth. It is more in accord with accepted usage to restrict the term "language" to such conventionalized systems of sounds or words as those designated as the English, French, German, Spanish, and other languages. All such systems have to be learned, and they vary by communities, rather than by species.

The biologist J. Bierens de Haan has clearly and conclusively summarized the arguments against the possible existence of unknown animal languages. He notes, first of all, that human language has six characteristics (4:249):

> . . . The sounds used in it are *vocal, articulate,* and have some *conventional meaning,* they *indicate something,* are uttered with the *intention* of communicating something to somebody else, and are *joined* together to form new combinations, so that phrases of various and different content are formed.

Bierens de Haan reasons that animals possess at best "pseudo-languages," since human language is of a decisively different order. We may summarize the evidence he offers for this judgment and invite the reader to compare this analysis with that of linguist Hockett presented in Chapter 5:

1. *Vocal*. The great majority of animals—including most of the vertebrates—are mute.
2. *Articulate*. Syllables are joined together. This is impossible when sounds are produced by organs other than the mouth. Among the higher animals that possess voices, there is generally no joining together of syllables. Humans combine syllables into words.
3. *Conventional meaning*. There is, with few exceptions, no direct relation between meaning and the nature of the sound. Even among the higher animals, sounds are innate and typical of the whole species.
4. *Indication*. With the aid of conventional meaning it becomes possible to indicate something—an object, situation, and so forth. Among the animals, sounds do not name objects or situations, but express "sentiments" and "emotions."
5. *Intention*. Animal sounds are generally uttered without reference to other beings. Although not made with intent to influence others, these sounds may be responded to by other animals.
6. *Joined together to form new combinations*. Combining words into phrases does not occur among animals; only humans do this.

We do not assert that there is no communication among the infrahuman species. Quite the contrary. It is obvious even to the superficial observer that there is such communication. If communication is erroneously equated with language, then it is necessary to attribute language behavior to many lower species. But equating communication with language does violence to the usual meanings attached to these words and neglects the fact that there are many forms, or levels, of communication and that language is only one of these. If it is contended that lower animals have language like that of humans, it becomes necessary to explain the absence of behavioral effects of this fact upon them as compared to the many profound effects of language on human behavior.

Just as there is no doubt of the existence of communication among the lower animals, there is also, it seems to us, no doubt that humans are the only animals capable of language. Recent success in teaching chimps sign language and the use of plastic symbols does not challenge this conclusion. We shall be concerned with the nature of language behavior in the next chapter, but we may anticipate our discussion of it here by noting briefly that conversation is the fundamental form of linguistic intercommunication. Any intelligent person, given the proper training, can learn to converse with any other person on earth. However, one cannot converse with lower animals. Despite this fact, it should also be constantly kept in mind that as one ascends the evolutionary scale, sign behavior and communication become increasingly subtle.

Some Consequences of the Lack of Language

The fundamental difference between human and animal behavior, basic to and in a sense determining all other differences, is that humans can talk and animals cannot. Human possession of language symbols and our ability to produce them voluntarily enables us to overcome the time and space limits in which, as we have noted, subhuman organisms may be said to be enclosed. Indeed, it may be more accurate to say that the possession of language has enabled human beings to "invent" time and space—past, present, and future. Humans have the capacity to respond to events that took place hundreds or even thousands of years ago, to predict or conceive future events, and to imagine objects and events that are remote in space or entirely nonexistent. This capacity involves nothing more mysterious than the ability to formulate propositions and to make statements about such objects and events, and in turn to be influenced by those propositions and statements.

As Köhler significantly remarks (20:277), chimpanzees' reactions to a situation are determined by their "optical apprehension" of that situation. Similarly, one may also say that the crucial difference is not that animals lack purposes but that they do not make or formulate propositions about their purposes. It is this fact, coupled with the ape's inability to make verbal responses to the physical environment, that probably accounts for the animal's failure to store food and tools or to transport them systematically for future use. The same may perhaps be said of what we described above as the tendency of chimpanzees to destroy complex objects rather than to preserve them, as they may react impulsively to features of those objects that momentarily attract their attention.

It is sometimes said that animals also have concepts in the sense that they can be trained, for example, to discriminate between triangles and circles, responding positively to one and negatively to the other. Experimental proof of this is in a sense unnecessary, as it is perfectly obvious that the lower animals are capable of such discriminations. They make them constantly when reacting differentially to other species, to sex differences, and to food as opposed to what is not edible. One does not ordinarily say, because of this, that animals have conceptions of sexual differentiation or of themselves as members of species. Closer examination of experimental findings invariably reveals that the animal alleged to have the concept of triangularity, for example, or the ability to count to three, actually acts only in a special situation, and then only as a consequence of laborious training and repetition. Rats have been trained to leap against the one of three doors on which there are two marks rather than one or three marks. An unwary observer may conclude from this that the rat had learned to count to three. However, if the sizes and widths of the marks are varied so that large, heavy marks are mixed with small, light ones, the rat becomes confused and must be retrained in the new situation. The animal that is supposed to possess an idea of triangularity is similarly confused if a minute corner is cut off one of the tips, thereby converting the triangle into a trapezoid, or if one of the sides is slightly curved.

Experiments with concept formation in the lower animals have not been carried to the point where the essential idea, or *connotation*, of the concept is grasped, free from involvement in a particular concrete situation. When the child learns to understand the number 2, for example, the number becomes a positional point between 1 and 3 in an infinite series, and has no necessary reference to anything of a concrete nature. No one who teaches geometry would agree that a student who could sort out only triangles and circles had an intellectual grasp of triangularity and circularity. If this claim were made, one would be unable to explain what happens when the child learns about these matters in the way required to get high grades in his or her geometry examination.

An essential feature of the human concept is that it involves a general formulation and an explicit focal awareness of essentials. This means that concepts are both exact and communicable, and that individuals are able to specify to themselves, and therefore to others, the exact features of the situation to which they are responding. Also, as our earlier discussion indicated, the fact that concepts form parts of a system of communicable ideas means that as abstract ideas they may be moved about, manipulated, applied to new situations, and made to interact with other ideas. Different conceptual systems may also be applied to the same situation as one shifts perspectives. None of these features is noticeable in the so-called concepts formed by animals.

We shall be concerned more or less throughout this book with human behavior that is not duplicated, although it is sometimes foreshadowed, in the behavior of lower animals. The extent and significance of the range of behavior opened up by language can be suggested by referring to religion, morality, science, philosophy, and art; by noting the immense volume of printed matter in the world; or by calling attention to the existence in human beings of reflective self-consciousness, conscience, reason, imagination, and conceptual thought.

The differences between humans and the lower animals may be summarized by saying that the lower animals do not have a culture. The term *culture* is generally used to refer to behavior patterns including beliefs, values, and ideas, that are the shared possession of groups and that are symbolically transmitted. A culture also includes artifacts or products that are handed down in a physical sense, but whose significance resides in their relationships with human behavior. As language is both an integral part of culture and the indispensable vehicle for its transmission, the assertion that animals do not possess it is a far-reaching one for comparative psychology.

Although one may say that the lower animals are able to communicate with one another and that they exhibit a surprising range of social behavior, in the sense that they form aggregates at many levels, they do not reach the level of sociality that is embodied in conventional symbols and the shared, or common, purposes of humans. Even among the anthropoids, the significance of the behavior that the young learn from adults is limited, and animals reared in relative isolation from their own kind are not much handicapped or changed thereby. It should, however, be noted that young chimps deprived of their real mothers and provided with substitutes made of terrycloth are considerably retarded in their later sexual development. (11, 12) As the term *social* has been used in this context, it is clearly a broader term than *cultural,* as it refers to interstimulation of acting organisms in general. It should be remarked that *social* is sometimes used in a more restricted sense to apply only to interpersonal relations. In this latter sense, too, it is not identical with *cultural,* as there are many aspects of interpersonal relationships that are learned but that are not transmitted from generation to generation as part of the cultural heritage.

ANIMAL AND HUMAN GROUPS

The absence of language in the lower species is intimately connected with the size and nature of animal groupings. As we shall see later, the complex, large-scale cooperative enterprises in which humans are continuously engaged are made possible by interlocking sets of systems of communication and transportation. The latter are themselves extremely complex instances of cooperative endeavor, linking as they do virtually all the nations and peoples of the world so that, for example, information may be disseminated throughout the world in a matter of minutes. The complexity of this intercommunication process and the varied array of physical apparatus, establishments, and agencies involved in the transmission, analysis, and storage of information is in turn directly linked with the complexity of the human mind.

In contrast to humans, lower animals form fewer and simpler groups that are limited by the means of communication, locomotion, and other factors inherent in the biological nature of each species. Animal groups are invariably actual physical aggregates that can be directly perceived. Their structure, size, and movements tend to be determined by influences such as those connected with availability of food, climatic conditions, sexual expression and reproduction, and protection against predators. While one can point to certain similarities between animal and primitive human groups—such as the allocation of social functions according to sex, age, and territoriality—anthropologist Marshall D. Sahlins (33:198) observes that there is not a single trait of human society "even in its most rudimentary state that is in both form and functioning a direct survival of some specific trait of primate social behavior." Needless to say, there are no libraries, telephones, computers, newspapers, schools, jet airplanes, television sets, or any other external apparatus of communication and transport in the worlds of lower animals.

If we try to visualize a human being living in an animal's world and limited to the kinds of experience available to that particular species, we can readily comprehend that interaction at such a level would neither generate nor sustain the complex intellectual functions that we take for granted. Lest we permit considerations of this sort unduly to inflate our sense of importance as the highest form of life, we should remember that the present complexity of our social environment and of our mental processes is the result of a long and laborious evolutionary process extending back tens of thousands of years before the beginnings of recorded history. This evolutionary process may be thought of as originating at the remote and hypothetical point in time when the cultural aspects of the evolutionary process began to be differentiated from the physical aspects, or perhaps when the first language was invented.(32)

During the nineteenth century, when the evolutionary doctrine was being formulated, Alfred Russell Wallace, puzzled over mankind's place in the evolutionary scheme, observed that "natural selection could only have endowed the savage with a brain a little superior to that of the ape, whereas he actually possesses one but very little inferior to that of the average member of our learned society." (8:606) In a book devoted entirely to field studies of the behavior of primates in their natural habitats, Jarvis Bastian suggested that the solution to this puzzle "is very much tied up with the nature and uses of man's languages." (8:606) Elsewhere in the same volume, Peter Marler (8:584), concerning himself with the change from genetic control of vocal behavior as seen in the apes to transmission by a learned tradition, remarked that "only by the study of primate social systems in the natural state, still exposed to the kinds of selective forces that shaped the early history of man, can one hope to discover why this all-important change first came about. . . ."

Another type of animal that has received considerable publicity in recent years is the dolphin, or porpoise. (18, 22) The adaptability of this creature has been amply demonstrated, but the rash suggestions that it can talk and that it has a language are obvious examples of the way in which enthusiasm about the accomplishments of a given animal leads people to endow it with human qualities. It has been remarked that while humans may have some success in communicating with dolphins in "dolphin language," dolphins will probably have difficulty communicating with us in human language.

In this chapter we have briefly sketched the chronology of human evolution, noting that after a certain point in time, biological and cultural evolution cease to be closely correlated. The enormous acceleration of cultural evolution in recent times is linked with language and especially with the invention of writing. The social and communicative behavior of a number of subhuman species, especially of chimpanzees, is considered in comparison with that of human beings.

The study of subhuman behavior has two general purposes for the social psychologist. First, it provides a picture of response mechanisms and adaptive devices that generally increase in complexity, sensitivity, and variability as one ascends the evolutionary scale to humans. The social insects live in societies based on principles altogether different from those that form the foundations of human groups; and these principles are instructive chiefly in a negative way, showing us what human behavior is not, rather than what it is. The second main purpose in studying subhuman behavior is to bring into sharper focus the differences among organisms of various degrees of complexity. As the organisms develop to more complex and more specialized levels, new behavioral possibilities and properties emerge. These new behavioral possibilities and properties, if they are to be investigated as such, must be conceived of as related to the previous possibilities and properties from which they have evolved. This does not mean, however, that they are to be identified with that from which they have been evolved.

With reference to understanding human social behavior, the study of subhuman organisms enables us to form tentative conceptions of (1) similarities (common features) of human and subhuman behavior, and (2) differences (unique elements) that distinguish human behavior from that of other living forms. We must not neglect to give adequate attention to both of these two aspects. Experimental and comparative psychologists frequently stress the similarities and underplay or altogether disregard the differences between humans and other animals; theologians and philosophers, on the other hand, often stress the differences to the point of failing to recognize that humans are, after all, animals themselves.

Social scientists are concerned largely with political, economic, legal, moral, religious, and other specific forms of behavior that are found almost exclusively in human beings living in groups. They are concerned, in other words, with analyzing the unique phases of human behavior; therefore it is inevitable that they should seek explanations of this behavior in terms of something that human beings have and that other organisms lack. Such expressions as culture, cultural heritage, mores, institutions, traditions, laws, politics, economics, philosophy, religion, science, art, literature, and mathematics all point to unique attributes of human behavior. These differences between humans and apes cannot be logically explained by referring to things that human beings and animals have in common.

Social psychology as the study of the influence of groups on the behavior of individuals is, in a sense, merely a part of the broader comparative study of species, each of which presents its own particular problems, but all of which share certain attributes in the sense that they are all living forms. It is unnecessary to insist either that only the differences be investigated and emphasized or that exclusive attention be focused on the similarities. It is understandable that such disciplines as economics, political science, and sociology, dealing as they do with behavior which is for the most part not found except in human society, should not directly concern themselves with subhuman behavior. As social psychology is in a way a part of comparative psychology, it must concern itself to some degree with the behavior of lower animals in order to understand the evolutionary emergence of civilization, culture, reason, and intelligence.

References

1. Allee, W., *Animal Aggregations: A Study in General Sociology.* Chicago: University of Chicago Press, 1931.
2. ———, *Cooperation among Animals* (rev. ed.). New York: Abelard-Schuman, 1931.
3. Altmann, S. A. (ed.), *Social Communication in Primates.* Chicago: University of Chicago Press, 1966.
4. Bierens de Haan, J., "Animal Language in Its Relation to That of Man," *Biological Review,* vol. 4 (1929), pp. 249–68.
5. Boutan, L., "Le Pseudo-language: Observations Effectuées sur un Anthropoide: Le Gibbon," *Actes de la Société Linné de Bordeaux,* vol. 16 (1913), pp. 5–77.
6. Coon, Carleton, *The Story of Man.* New York: Knopf, 1965.
7. Critchley, M., "The Evolution of Man's Capacity for Language," in Sol Tax (ed.), *Evolution after Darwin,* vol. 2. Chicago: University of Chicago Press, 1960, pp. 289–308.
8. DeVore, I. (ed.), *Primate Behavior: Field Studies of Monkeys and Apes.* New York: Holt, Rinehart and Winston, 1965.
9. Eisley, Loren, *Darwin's Century: Evolution and the Men Who Discovered It.* Garden City, N.Y.: Doubleday, 1958.
10. Gardner, Beatrice, and R. Allen Gardner, "Teaching Sign Language to a Chimpanzee," *Science,* vol. 165 (1969), pp. 664–72.
11. Harlow, H. F., "The Nature of Love," *American Psychologist,* vol. 13 (1958), pp. 673–85.
12. ———, and M. Harlow, "Social Deprivation in Monkeys," *Scientific American,* vol. 207 (1962), pp. 136–46.
13. Hawkes, Jacquetta, *The First Great Civilizations: Life in Mesopotamia, The Indus Valley, and Egypt.* New York: Knopf, 1973.
14. Hayes, C., *The Ape in Our House.* New York: Harper & Row, 1951.

15. Hewes, G. W., "Primate Communication and the Gestural Origin of Language," *Current Anthropology,* vol. 14, nos. 1–2 (February–April 1973), pp. 5–12.
16. Huxley, J., *Man Stands Alone.* New York: Harper & Row, 1941.
17. Jennings, H. S., "The Transition from the Individual to the Social Level," in J. Cattell (ed.), *Biological Symposia,* vol. 8 (1942), pp. 105–19.
18. Kellogg, W. N., *Porpoises and Sonar.* Chicago: University of Chicago Press, 1961.
19. ———, and L. A. Kellogg, *The Ape and the Child.* New York: McGraw-Hill, 1933.
20. Köhler, Wolfgang, *The Mentality of Apes.* New York: Harcourt Brace Jovanovich, 1926.
21. Langer, S. K., *Philosophy in a New Key.* Baltimore: Penguin Books, 1948.
22. Lilly, J. C., *Man and Dolphin.* Garden City, N.Y.: Doubleday, 1961.
23. Lindauer, M., *Communication among Social Bees.* Cambridge, Mass.: Harvard University Press, 1961.
24. Maier, N. R. F., and T. C. Schneirla, *Principles of Animal Psychology.* New York: Dover Publications, 1964.
25. Marshall, J. C., "The Biology of Communication in Man and Animals," in John Lyons (ed.), *New Horizons in Linguistics.* Baltimore: Penguin Books, 1970, pp. 229–41.
26. Mayr, E., "The Emergence of Evolutionary Novelties," in Sol Tax (ed.), *The Evolution of Life,* vol. 1. Chicago: University of Chicago Press, 1960, pp. 349–80.
27. McCook, N. C., *Ant Communities.* New York: Harper & Row, 1909.
28. Morgan, L., *Introduction to Comparative Psychology.* New York: Young Scott Books, 1894.
29. Premack, Ann J., and David Premack, "Teaching Language to an Ape," *Scientific American,* vol. 227, no. 4 (October 1972), pp. 92–99.
30. Révész, G. A. *The Human Hand: A Psychological Study,* trans. by J. Cohen. London: Routledge & Kegan Paul, 1958.
31. ———, "The Language of Animals," *Journal of General Psychology,* vol. 30 (1944), pp. 117–47.
32. ———, *Origins and Prehistory of Language.* New York: Philosophical Library, 1956.
33. Sahlins, M. D., "The Social Life of Monkeys, Apes, and Primitive Men," in Morton H. Fried (ed.), *Readings in Anthropology,* vol. 2. New York: Macmillan, 1959, pp. 186–99.
34. Schneirla, T., "Animal Behavior and Human Relations," in M. Sherif and C. Sherif (eds.), *Groups in Harmony and Tension.* New York: Harper & Row, 1953.
35. ———, "The Concept of Levels in the Study of Social Phenomena," in M. Sherif and C. Sherif (eds.), *Groups in Harmony and Tension.* New York: Harper & Row, 1953, pp. 54–75.
36. ———, "Levels in the Psychological Capacities of Animals," in R. Sellars (ed.), *Philosophy for the Future.* New York: Macmillan, 1949.
37. ———, "Problems in the Biopsychology of Social Organization," *Journal of Abnormal and Social Psychology,* vol. 41 (1946), pp. 390–98.
38. Schrier, A. M., H. F. Harlow, and F. Stollnitz (eds.), *Behavior of Nonhuman Primates.* New York: Academic Press, 1965.
39. Sjoberg, Gideon, "The Origin and Evolution of Cities," *Scientific American,* vol. 213, no. 3 (September 1965), pp. 55–63.

40. Spuhler, J. N. (ed.), *The Evolution of Man's Capacity for Culture*. Detroit: Wayne State University Press, 1959.
41. Stollnitz, Fred, and Allen M. Schrier (eds.), *Behavior of Nonhuman Primates*, vols. 3–4. New York: Academic Press, 1971.
42. Tax, S., and C. Callender, *Evolution after Darwin*. Chicago: University of Chicago Press, 1960.
43. *The New York Times*, July 11, 1954, p. 19.
44. Tomer, A., *We Are Not the First*. New York: G. P. Putnam's Sons, 1971.
45. Von Frisch, Karl, *Bees: Their Vision, Chemical Sense, and Language*. Ithaca, N.Y.: Cornell University Press, 1950.
46. ———, *The Dancing Bees*. New York: Harcourt Brace Jovanovich, 1955.
47. ———, "Dialects in the Language of the Bees," *Scientific American*, vol. 207 (August 1962), pp. 79–87.
48. Wenner, A. M., "Sound Communication in Honeybees," *Scientific American*, vol. 210 (April 1964), pp. 116–24.
49. ———, "Sound Production during the Waggle Dance of the Honey Bee," *Animal Behavior*, vol. 10 (1962), pp. 79–95.
50. Wheeler, W. M., *Ants*. New York: Columbia University Press, 1910.
51. White, L. A., "On the Use of Tools in Primates," *Journal of Comparative Psychology*, vol. 34 (1942), pp. 369–374.
52. Wolfe, J. B., "Effectiveness of Token Reward for Chimpanzees," *Comparative Psychology Monographs*, vol. 12, no. 5 (1936).
53. Yerkes, R. M., and A. W. Yerkes, *The Great Apes: A Study of Anthropoid Life*. New Haven: Yale University Press, 1945.

Selected Readings

COON, CARLETON, *The Story of Man*. New York: Knopf, 1965.

An account of the origin of humans and civilization by a recognized authority. New archeological finds and new techniques continue to lead to new interpretations and insights in this area.

KÖHLER, WOLFGANG, *The Mentality of Apes*. New York: Harcourt Brace Jovanovich, 1926.

The author's study might also be described as one of participant observation, and it remains one of the most absorbing classic accounts of the behavior of chimpanzees.

STOLLNITZ, FRED, AND ALLEN H. SCHRIER (eds.), *Behavior of Nonhuman Primates*, vols. 3–4. New York: Academic Press, 1971.

This work presents some of the newer research on primates, including studies of them in their native habitats and attempts to teach them language.

VON FRISCH, KARL, *The Dancing Bees*. New York: Harcourt Brace Jovanovich, 1955.

The author devoted his life to the study of bees. The Nazis viewed his work as sufficiently important to make him an exception in their program of anti-Semitism.

chapter 3

Symbolic Environments and Cognitive Structures

In the preceding chapter we sketched in a broad outline the story of humankind's physical and early cultural evolution and indicated some of what appear to be the basic differences between humans and the lower animals. The argument will now be extended by noting that with the acquisition of language and conceptual thought, human reactions to the external social and physical worlds have become increasingly indirect. These reactions are increasingly affected by *ideas* that represent to humans an unknown and unknowable ultimate reality. Language, by enabling humans to be observers of their own actions, objects in their own thought processes, adds new dimensions to the simple and more direct consciousness of lower animals. It also ushers into awareness a private, incommunicable aspect of experience, commonly described as "subjective." We shall also explore some of the general characteristics of the ideas, perspectives, or cognitive structures which are provided ready-made by one's society. We conclude with a consideration of what we think of as a special, categorical attitude which the use of language engenders and with a brief consideration of a current theory that emphasizes the consequences of cognitive dissonance and cognitive development.

Symbolic
Environments

Humans, as we noted in Chapter 2, live in a symbolic environment because (1) they are responding directly to symbols, and (2) their relationships to the external world are indirect and organized by means of symbols. As Cassirer has aptly stated (7:25):

> Man lives in a symbolic universe, . . . [He does not] confront reality immediately; he cannot see it, as it were, face to face. . . . Instead of dealing with things themselves man is in a sense constantly conversing with himself. He has so enveloped himself in linguistic forms . . . that he cannot see or know anything except by the interposition of this artificial medium.

The symbolic environment may be thought of as a substitute environment, but it is important to note that this environment is not a mere reproduction or reflection of the external world. Some believe, indeed, that the "real" external world can never be known "for what it is." What humans know of it, they know by virtue of their particular sensory equipment and their particular and very socialized experience of it. The world in which human beings live and act is, in a sense, "constructed" by them in terms of the requirements of human conduct. That humans are able to invent symbolic structures and be affected by them introduces new dimensions and new levels of interaction into the relations of humans to humans, of humans to the external world, and of humans to themselves.

We may represent the two types of relationships with the environment as in the illustration on page 85.

The two types of environment discussed here may be illustrated by contrasting the relations of primitive and civilized humans to microbes. Primitive humans are generally unaware of the existence of microbes and thus have no symbols with which to designate, describe, and comprehend them. Nevertheless, microbes influence them and may even cause death. We may therefore say that microbes form a part of the nonsymbolic environment of primitive humans but that they do not appear or are not represented in their symbolic environment. They are not, as Mead (28) would have said, "social objects."

By contrast, civilized humans are aware of the existence of microbes and are able to formulate very elaborate statements about them. Microbes today constitute a part of, or are represented in, our symbolic environment. This fact is undoubtedly of great significance. To have symbols for microbes means to be aware or conscious of them, to comprehend them. It also means that microbes may possibly be controlled and subordinated to human purposes. That civilized humans are able to make statements about these forms of life, which are invisible to the naked eye, is thus a matter of the utmost intellectual and practical importance. We may add that human conceptions of the world are rarely static

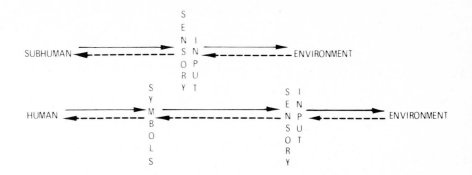

or unchanging. Thus, microbes have become linked by biologists in new and complex ways with each other, with viruses, cells, and with physiological and genetic processes.

Humans also use language to describe themselves, devising terms and concepts for the human body and its parts and finding various means of describing processes that go on within the body. Humans, in short, become objects to themselves; they become conscious of their own thought processes and of consciousness itself. They learn not only to make and to be influenced by statements about their physical world; they also learn to formulate verbal propositions about themselves and to be influenced by them. Insofar as humans are aware of their own responses, those responses become part of the human environment too.

The human environment, therefore, does not consist merely of natural and external events and processes. It also includes the symbols by means of which humans name, classify, and form conceptions of things as well as of the world of ideas and values. These symbols are products of group living. They reflect the fact that the members of groups—in the process of intercommunication and adaptation—devise linguistic schemes for classifying, describing, and responding to persons, objects, and events. These schemes form part of the social heritage and are the most significant aspects of the human environment. It is not just a matter of complexity that is involved (as the astronomer's world is more complex than that of most lay stargazers) but quite literally that the world is differently constructed by different groups. *In a certain sense, most of this text is an illustration not only of that point but of how those different constructions affect interaction between particular groups of human beings.*

From the foregoing discussions an important point emerges: namely, that human beings engage in activity while simultaneously observing their own actions. They are able, speaking metaphorically, to assume a more or less detached, uninvolved position concerning episodes in

HUMANS AS ACTORS AND OBSERVERS

A child being taught self-reflectiveness.
(*Suzanne Szasz/Photo Researchers, Inc.*)

which they are in fact involved. It is as though human beings, acting out parts on the stage, were also sitting in the audience watching their own performance and evaluating it as it unfolds. In certain situations these two roles interfere with each other, and people tend to switch from one role to the other. They may, for example, become so absorbed in what they are doing that they fail in their observer role and do what they had not intended to do or what they later regret. On the other hand, they may, in their role as observers, become so preoccupied in watching their own performance, or that of the others involved in the real-life drama, that they distract themselves in their role as actors and forget their lines or miss their cues.

This aspect of human behavior (which we shall refer to repeatedly in this book) arises from the fact that humans live largely within a symbolic environment of their own creation. It may be described in general terms by saying that humans become both subjects and objects, that they become conscious of consciousness, that through their conceptualizations they establish a kind of distance between themselves and their own experiences of the real world. This distance, or detachment, enables them to deal conceptually with their own experiences and gives them a new dimension by making them objects within their own thought processes. Presumably lower animals are incapable of this activity; they may be conscious, but they are not conscious of their own consciousnesses. They obviously have experiences of a direct sort but are unable to be the observer with respect to their own actions. It is for such reasons that a distinction is made between the one-dimensional consciousness of lower animals and the two- or more-dimensional consciousness of humans, which is often called *reflexive self-consciousness* or, more simply, *self-reflexiveness* (see Chapter 1).

It has been said that human beings live simultaneously in three kinds of worlds: the real world of things and events; a subjective, private world; and a symbolic or cultural world of shared beliefs, accepted ideas, and *objective* knowledge which are distilled from experience and observation and transmitted via language. SUBJECTIVE AND OBJECTIVE REALITY

Concerning the first of these worlds, that of reality as it really is or as it might be seen by an all-knowing God, little need be said here, although philosophers have had a great deal to say about it. As physical beings we are a part of this reality whether we understand it or not, deny it or not, and no matter how imperfectly we understand it. This world is assumed to exist independently of our intellectual grasp of it.

The second, the private subjective realm, is one in which we are alone. All of our experiences have a unique personal reference in the sense that they are ours and no one else's and that we alone have direct access to and awareness of them. This is true regardless of whether the experience is artistic, religious, or of any other kind.

The third realm is the cultural one of belief, ideology, ideas, knowledge, theories, and logic. It has the appearance of objectivity because—as we shall note more fully in the next section—it is communicated and shared within groups which act toward the presumed real world of objects, people, and events in terms of it. The cultural world really is created through what we may call "a process of consensual validation of experiences," which in their origin are inherently subjective; that is, unique experiences of unique individuals. The connection between "objective knowledge" of the real world and the real world itself is always problematic, as Henri Poincaré, the famous French mathematician and scientist, indicated by posing the question: What would happen if an omniscient being were to appear on earth and go about from one scientist to another telling them the absolute final *Truth* about the problems they were investigating? Poincaré's own answer was that nothing would happen because the scientists would be unable to comprehend what they were told. Indeed, one might wonder whether the omniscient being would be able to state the absolute truth in any presently existing language, or able to stay out of jail or a mental institution long enough to complete the mission.

The term *subjective* is commonly misused to designate events that transpire in the heads or brains of humans and presumably of other animals as well. These events, however, can no more be called subjective than those that presumably occur in the interior of the sun. Both types of event occur in a real, material world; those in the human brain are material events that involve a substratum of complex interlocking neural, chemical, and electrical occurrences that use up energy. It is therefore erroneous to call mental processes subjective merely because they are internal and relatively inaccessible to observation, just as are those inside the sun.

Clearly, subjective means something other than simple inaccessibility. What it actually refers to must be, not the material occurrences themselves, but some aspect of how these occurrences are perceived or grasped by the organism. What our analysis suggests is that the term refers to the communicability of experiences; there are aspects of all experience which escape the communication network and which cannot be fully shared with others because they are the peculiarly private property of unique individuals. This aspect of experience can properly be designated as subjective. We may, for example, readily tell another person that we have a toothache, and because he or she has had similar experiences, he or she readily understands what we are saying. Nevertheless, the toothache remains our personal experience and that of no one else. This latter aspect is the private, or subjective, part of the experience. It is difficult to describe or even talk about, because it is essentially incommunicable. We know that it is there, "in ourselves," by introspection and infer that it can also be present in others, but beyond that we are able to do little else than advise other people that they will not understand all of what we are trying to say unless they have had exactly the same experience themselves. How, for example, does it feel to die? We suppose there is only one obvious way to find this out for oneself. In matters of this kind, the languages of poetry and art come closer to communicating than does the precise, didactic language of science.

It is thus meaningless to assert that falling in love is a subjective kind of experience, since there are no other kinds. By the same token, it is equally meaningless to claim that weighing an object is an objective experience. The difference between these two types of experience is simply that the latter is more readily transmitted to others than the former. The terms in which both are conceived, perceived, and communicated are intimately related to the symbolic coordinates of the speaker's world. We turn next to that topic.

Social Worlds, Symbolic Coordinates, and Fictions

The idea of a symbolic environment also implies that all humans live in what may be termed *social worlds*. These can be thought of as groupings of individuals who are bound together through networks of communication—whether the members are geographically proximate or not—and through the sharing of important symbols. Groups also share common or similar perspectives on reality. For very simple societies, as described classically by anthropologists, one might think of the society as equivalent to a single social world, whose members have essentially a single organized outlook on reality. But as Tomatsu Shibutani notes (35: 128–37): "Modern mass societies . . . are made up of a bewildering variety of social worlds. . . . Each . . . is a cultural area, the boundaries of which are set neither by territory nor formal group memberships but by the limits of effective communication." In short, a country or nation is not the equivalent of society—there are many societies, many social worlds, within each nation; and people may have membership in international communities (such as the community of biologists or Jehovah's Witnesses) regardless of where they live. (We discuss social worlds more fully in Chapters 11 and 13.)

The members of social worlds conceive of reality in terms of certain basic *symbolic coordinates*. To grasp the notion of "symbolic coordinates," we might think of the early Christians' ideas of reality following from their interpretations of the teachings of Jesus—ideas linked with concepts of God and his son and the implications of those concepts. Then compare this view of reality, say, with that of the modern atheist who accepts a strictly materialistic, "scientific" view of the universe, or compare both with the Nazis' conceptions during the 1930s. One philosopher has suggested that perspectives on reality can be represented by quite different metaphors: a prison, a battlefield, a stage, a garden, and so on. Each metaphor has different implications as to how reality is conceptually organized. Each metaphor also has perspectives, too, on what space looks like and what time feels like—indeed what time periods (past, present, future) are most important or how they relate to each other. The basic items concerning all these are what we mean when we refer to the social coordinates of a given social world.

From the standpoint of the individual, the symbolic environment that he or she thinks of as "reality" itself seems like an objective "thing." Berger and Luckmann have phrased this in terms similar to ours (1:21, 22–23):

> I apprehend the reality of everyday life as an ordered reality. Its phenomena are prearranged in patterns that seem to be independent of my appre-

hension of them and that impose themselves upon the latter. The reality of everyday life appears already objectified, that is, constituted by an order of objects that have been designated *as* objects before my appearance on the scene. The language used in everyday life continuously provides me with the necessary objectifications and posits the order within which these make sense and within which everyday life has meaning for me. I live in a place that is geographically designated; I employ tools . . . which are designated in the technical vocabulary of my society; I live within a web of human relationships . . . which are also ordered by means of vocabulary. In this manner language marks the co-ordinates of my life in society and fills that life with meaningful objects.

Berger and Luckmann add that this reality presents itself to the individual as a world which he or she shares with others. And—a very important point—this "reality" is taken for granted *as* reality. "It does not require verification over and beyond its simple presence. It is simply *there*, as self-evident. . . ."

The reality, the symbolic coordinates and symbolizations, may be regarded by later generations as outmoded, mistaken, misguided, dead wrong, or dreadfully immoral. Rather obviously, the same judgments can be made by contemporaries. Insofar as the members of one social world are concerned with the views and actions of people from other social worlds, they will take corrective action: this can be argumentative, rhetorical, persuasive, or it can be directly coercive, giving rise to fights, imprisonment, or warfare.

PREJUDICES
AND
STEREOTYPES

Social scientists and students of language have mistakenly referred to the "incorrect" symbols of others as *fictions*. A striking contemporary example is that of the commonly held ideas of race. Whatever scientists may say about the pitfalls attending the classification of humans by biological characteristics, certain socially important classifications of race still exist. Just as humans classify objects into categories and act toward them on the basis of class membership, so they classify other humans into racial groupings and behave toward them on the basis of presumed racial membership. The ways in which one perceives other humans as black or white are as much part of social heritage as the words *Negro*, *black*, and *white*. The same individual may be classified differently in different places on the earth's surface or in different social groups in the same place, and behavior toward him or her will vary accordingly. In the United States many people believe that any person with "one drop of black blood" is a black person. In Brazil this same person would not be called a Negro or a black, nor be treated as such. The person would be classified as a white even though his or her ancestry were known. (See Chapter 13.)

In the United States people have held attitudes about black blood that are truly nonsensical. Since it is customary in America to regard anyone as a black if he or she has any "black blood," "mulattoes" are described as "blacks having some white blood" and never as "whites having some black blood." During World War II "black blood" and "white blood" were sometimes kept in separate blood banks. The idea underlying this practice seems to be that if white people receive a transfusion of "black blood" then their skin color may change, or they may be said to have "black blood" in their veins. It is sometimes supposed that this might affect the individuals or their progeny.

As indicated, these conceptions are logically absurd. In the first place, the blood of a pregnant woman does not flow through the vessels of the unborn child. Hence, we are never actually justified in saying that we have our parents' blood in our veins. Moreover, there is no difference between black and white blood; all blood types are found in both "races." Neither the physical nor the mental traits of parents or their future off-spring can conceivably be affected by blood transfusion. Popular thinking about these matters is based on certain misconceptions—the scientist would say—about the nature of races, blood, and heredity. It is widely believed that a person with one black grandparent has 25 percent black blood and 75 percent white blood; that octoroons have ⅛ black blood; and so on. These and similar notions form an essential part of the repertory of popular American thought and attitude, although certainly not for all white or black Americans today. The ideas have no foundation whatever in biology; indeed, scientific evidence points to the essential biological unity of all human types. Not only are all blood types common to all racial groupings, but the human organism is so uniform throughout the world that for experimental work in physiology and anatomy, the "race" to which the subject "belongs" is a matter of indifference. But as long as the members of some social world regard other persons as belonging to a genuine race, then they will act toward them accordingly.

Another term that is similar to *fictions* (especially racial ones) is *stereotypes*. Sociologists have long and customarily used the term to refer to certain oversimplified, fixed, and usually fallacious conceptions which people hold about other people. Etymologically, the first part of the term is derived from the Greek word *steros*, meaning solid, firm, hard. Historically, it is derived—at least in American technical usage—from a book on public opinion by Walter Lippmann, who used it to refer to "the pictures in our heads." (27) Lippmann asserted that because people approach facts with preestablished classifications, they do not see the facts clearly or in unbiased fashion. "For the most part, we do not first see and then define, we define first and then see." (27) There is stereotyped imagery of races, nationalities, national groups, occupational groups, social classes, and the sexes. But it is in the racial area that stereotypes have most often been studied. It has been found, for example, that our movies, radio and television programs, and popular literature have rarely portrayed blacks in any role other than that of servant or low-class person, although the practice is changing. These are the roles that fit the old white stereotypes of blacks. Similarly, stereotypes influence the depiction of females in the mass media. Women have traditionally been cast only as wives and mothers in situation comedies and television commercials.

Most Americans have had no opportunity to meet, or even to see, members of many different nationalities or ethnic groups in the United States. Yet a number of investigators who have tested college students over the last two or three decades have found that the preferential ranking of these groups is consistent and uniform. The following groups are ranked in order of diminishing acceptability: (1) Americans, Canadians, and English; (2) French, Norwegians, Germans, Swedes, and other Northern Europeans; (3) Southern European peoples; (4) Jews; and at the bottom are (5) blacks, Turks, Chinese, and Hindus.

The only persons who did not rank the ethnic and nationality groups in the usual order were either members of minority ethnic groups or radical political groups. The members of ethnic groupings that normally ranked low tended to move their own groups to positions at the top. Politically radical students showed much less ethnic prejudice than the average student because their political philosophy includes the belief that all ethnic groups are equal.

Once formed, the stereotype tends to persist even in the face of contradictory evidence and experience. It seems that direct contact with a race does not lead people to see that exceptions to stereotypes are not really exceptions. So long as one classifies certain persons as belonging to a group or race and attributes certain characteristics to the group in general, those who do not have these characteristics are dismissed as exceptions to, or deviations from, the norm; and we are told that "exceptions prove the rule." The standard or rule, as we have already seen, is what the group is supposed to be "by nature."

The notion of stereotype has been useful for the social psychologist in investigation of intergroup hostility, but it is not really a special and distinct concept. It provides an effective means of calling attention to erroneous and oversimplified concepts which people have of other people. By their very nature, all classifications are selective responses to a complex environment, and thus are necessarily somewhat simplifed versions of reality. Stereotypes often are strongly tinged with emotion, but this is also true of many other conceptions. Likewise, as classifications are embedded in systems, many of them resist easy change even when confronted with contradictory evidence. (The selective character of perception, as we shall see in Chapter 6, helps account for this impermeability to experience.)

Some students of language phenomena advocate that such fictions—*all* fictions—should be eliminated from the language, as they refer to nothing actual and are socially harmful. "No other animal produces verbal monsters in his head and projects them upon the world outside his head." (10:14) Such a proposal, of course, demonstrates a radical misconception of the nature of language and associated forms of symbolization.

The Categorical, or Language, Attitude

We organize or adjust our behavior toward things and persons by means of symbols, and these symbols come to embody a plan of action. "A category . . . constitutes a point of view, a schedule, a program, a heading or caption, an orientation." (13:237) Thus if one hunter shouts to another, "A duck!" the second hunter immediately looks into the air and makes the appropriate preparations for shooting at a bird on the wing. If the first hunter shouts, "Rabbit!" his partner responds in a different manner. Language symbols do not merely stand for something else. They also indicate the significance of things for human behavior, and they organize behavior toward the thing symbolized.

Some writers have gone beyond this and have pointed to a general attitude toward the world that is implicit in the very use of language and therefore common to all those who use language. They have called this general attitude the *categorical attitude*. In its simplest terms it may be described as the realization that (1) things can be named and talked about; (2) events and objects may be grouped or classified; and (3) by naming and classifying the features of our environment, new modes of behavior, as well as new possibilities of manipulating that environment, are brought into existence.

Children give their first evidence of acquiring this attitude when they learn that everything has a name: they soon exasperate their parents by persistent questions: "What's this?" "What's that?" They ask for names and at first are satisfied with mere names, as they identify the name with the things named. They have acquired a dim, initial appreciation of the importance of language symbols. Later, when they begin to ask, "Why?" children exhibit a second and more mature phase of the categorical attitude. (We shall discuss childhood learning in detail in Chapter 9.)

We may illustrate the adult categorical attitude by means of an analogy. Let us suppose that a boy who has lived all his life in an isolated rural section of Africa is suddenly placed in the middle of Johannesburg. He sees large numbers of people hurrying past, hears a chaotic jumble of sounds, and sees a bewildering array of buildings, billboards, neon

"What is it?" (*Magnum*)

signs, trucks, buses, automobiles, and other objects. The people he encounters respond to him in ways that utterly confuse him. He does not
know what to do or say or where to go. The city to him is merely an immense buzzing confusion.

We may compare this boy's view of Johannesburg with the view of
the world that a man without language would have. As one lives longer
in a large city and grows accustomed to it, "things" gradually become
classified or categorized. Most of the sounds that assail the ear are
disregarded as irrelevant, simply forming part of the roar of the city. The
countless motor vehicles are ignored; they are hazards that one must
consider in crossing a street. The newcomer is astounded by the sky-
scrapers, but soon grows used to them and thereafter may scarcely ever
look at them. The attitude of a city resident may be compared with the
attitude that humans acquire toward the world in general through their
use of language symbols. Things have been organized into systems or categories in terms of their significance for one's behavior.

CONCEPTS AND   The terms "concepts" and "categories" will be used almost synony-
CATEGORIES   mously here, although they have different connotations that should be
borne in mind. *Concept* has a broader meaning which includes

"categories" as a special kind of concept. To have a concept of something means to be able to picture it, to describe or represent it to oneself or another, or to grasp it intellectually. A concept is a way of thinking about something; this means that it is also usually a way of talking about it. Conceptual thought is communicable thought. Concepts of classes or types may be called *categories*. It is through the use of such categories of classification that we are able to group things together and able to distinguish one type of thing from another and, ultimately, to see the world as orderly. Indeed, without categories one could not think at all in a sophisticated human sense. There is an expression, "categories of thought," that refers to basic concepts (such as those of space, time, substance, and motion) that are regarded as fundamental in human reasoning about the material world.

We have indicated that the categorical attitude impels human beings to group things into classes. By categorizing or conceptualizing our experiences we are able to analyze them and to respond selectively to some aspects of experience while ignoring others. Through the use of categories and concepts we are able to picture the world as relatively stable, predictable, and orderly, and to find unity in its limitless diversity.

An example will indicate the connection between concepts and the language attitude. There is a certain type of animal that we designate as a "cow." When we use the word *cow*, we refer to all the cows in the world and also, in a sense, to all the cows that have ever existed or ever will exist. But no two of these animals are ever exactly alike. Cows vary greatly in size, color, and disposition. Nevertheless, we lump them all together, disregarding the differences among them. By so doing we identify them, thus indicating to ourselves and others their significance for human beings. By means of the concept "cow," we have created unity out of diversity and multiplicity. There are millions of cows, but one single concept may refer to all of them.

Still another implication of the categorical attitude then follows. When we see objects, we see them not only as concrete entities, but also as representatives of the classes to which they belong. Every time we see and recognize an animal as a "cow" we bring into the picture, in an implicit or indirect way, all the other cows in the world that we cannot see and have never seen. It is for these reasons that language concepts are called "universals."

One should not make the mistake of supposing that any given object can be classified in only one way. It may be placed in a number of different categories according to the way in which it is being viewed or used. Thus, it may be classified in a series of classes on an ascending scale of abstractness so that each is more inclusive than those that precede it and less inclusive than those that follow it. The more abstract the classification, the fewer and more general are the criteria of classification.

Conversely, the more concrete the classification the more numerous and specific are the criteria. For example, a particular cow may be classified on an ascending scale of abstractness as follows: Farmer Jones's cow, cow, mammal, animal, living form, material object. Cows may also be classified as four-legged creatures, objects weighing in excess of one hundred pounds, edible animals, economic assets, sources of milk, livestock, and so on. Each classification carries its own connotation of point of view and potential use. None of them is "natural," or inherent in the nature of the world, although some are obviously more effective than others for certain purposes.

To complicate matters still further, a cow may also be viewed as a composite, not a unitary, object. To a butcher it may be made up of sirloin, porterhouse, T-bone, and other cuts of edible meat. A biochemist, a physiologist, and an anatomist would each describe and classify the cow's components in wholly different ways. Farmer Jones himself might very well think of his cow as something compounded mainly of hay, corn, grass, water, and a little salt.

Dale, discussing the child's growing understanding of the concept

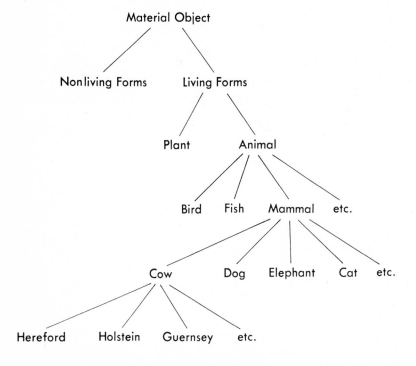

ASCENDING: increasing abstractness.
DESCENDING: increasing concreteness.

A child and father discussing an everyday concept. What is a lawnmower? (*Joel Gordon*)

of "dog," has made much the same series of points that we have indicated in discussing cows (12:31):

> One of the child's earliest learnings is the name for the shaggy thing that barks. It is called *Rover*. Next he learns that *Rover* is like *Sport* and *Shep*, and finally that things that look and act like them are called *dogs*. Once he has the *dog* classification, he may move in either or both of two directions in further classification. He may learn that there are terriers, St. Bernards, shepherds, and poodles; and then subdivide terriers into wire-haired, rat, Boston, and so forth. He can also go in the direction of more general classification—a dog is a quadruped, an animal, a vertebrate, or a mammal. If he continues, he may arrive at classifications used by the zoologist, involving abstractions that are extensive, precise, and increasingly complex. There are, of course, a variety of other paths that criss-cross the two chief directions . . . indicated, in the course of which his concept of *dog* grows richer.

Symbolic Environments and Cognitive Structures   97

That humans have concepts and categories with which to classify, subclassify, and cross-classify the objects of their environments is thus a fact of great importance. Our concepts and categories give us flexibility of point of view and a multiplicity of perspectives, enabling us to see connections among things in ways that otherwise would be impossible. They also enable us to think of things in terms of their constituent parts rather than as undifferentiated wholes or as total situations. They are therefore indispensable tools in any analytical procedure. All this implies that concepts alter our behavior in the direction of making it more discriminatory, more selective, and flexible (that is, more intelligent).

MEANING AND GENERALIZATIONS Some students of human behavior do not use the term "meaning" because they object to its implication. The term is often thought of as a metaphysical essence that resides in symbols, in a person's brain, or in objects themselves. We must emphasize that in this book we use *meaning* in a behavioral sense. *The meaning of an object or a word is determined by the responses that are made to it: that is, meaning is a relationship and not an essence.*

It is easy to slip into the fallacy of locating the meanings of words in the words themselves. But meanings arise, as noted previously, out of group activities, and they come to stand for relationships between actors and objects. Our position has been stated precisely and clearly by Lee (25:74), who says that language

> . . . is not a system of names for passively sensed objects and relations already existing in the outer world; but neither does it fit experience into predetermined molds. It is a creative process in which the individual has an agentive function; it is part of a field which contains, in addition, the world of physical reality, the sensing and thinking individual, and the experienced reality. In this way each word, each grammatical formation, is not an empty label to be applied; it has meaning, not because meaning has been arbitrarily assigned to it, but because it contains the meaning of the concrete situation in which it participates and has participated, and which it has helped create.

Thus, a concept implies a unitary mode of action; it enables people to act in the same way toward a variety of objects. There are many types of food, for example, but once a substance has been identified as belonging to the food category, a common mode of behavior toward it is established. Thus every class concept is also a generalization, as it "generalizes" behavior toward everything included within its boundaries. To the invention of generalizations there is no end; as long as group activity continues and experiences are undergone, new meanings will be discovered and transmitted among members of the group.

Symbols, or conventional signs carrying meanings upon which there is consensus, are from their very nature open to manipulation. *Signs* operate upon signs as in algebra, mathematics, or in argument. Concepts breed new concepts as they are manipulated in the handling of problem situations. In group action, differences of opinion and position which are expressed in conversation and debate produce new perspectives and new meanings.

We may imagine that the activities of lower animals make for the appearance of new meanings in their lives, as when a pet dog is taught a new trick; but these meanings cannot be communicated or shared and hence do not compare with the world of ideas opened up by language. Symbols enable humans to escape the narrow confines of the immediate natural world and to participate in the artistic, religious, moral, and scientific worlds created by their contemporaries and ancestors (6:41):

> Without symbolism the life of man would be . . . confined within the limits of his biological needs and his practical interests; it could find no access to the "ideal" world which is opened to him from different sides by religion, art, philosophy, science.

Cognitive Structures and Cognitive Dissonance

As has been stressed in our discussion of the categorical attitude, fictions, and stereotypes, human beings are strongly disposed to want to have labels and explanations to apply to the significant aspects of their environment, and they tend to be uneasy when these are not available. Labels and explanations constitute cognitive structures that range from the simplest to the highly abstract and systematic ones of modern science. All individuals have their own set of cognitions, which includes all of their beliefs and attitudes concerning the nature of the world, their society, the groups to which they belong, other people, and themselves and their own actions.

Theorists who write about human behavior have observed that people often hold contradictory beliefs, that they say or think one thing and do another. Criminals are an example; they know what is right, but deliberately do what is wrong. To use the language of a currently popular theory, a "dissonance" (or conflict) is set up among the criminal's cognitive items, beliefs, or bits of information. On the one hand, they know their acts were wrong; on the other hand, they know they did it, and they may be psychologically torn about the discrepancy. The internal conflict that is set up by this type of dissonance is often discussed in terms of conscience, guilt, and rationalization.

The term *cognitive dissonance* was introduced by Leon Festinger, a psychologist, to describe psychological incompatibilities between two or more items of knowledge or attitudes of the individual. Cognitive dissonance exists when an individual possesses two cognitions which contradict one another. The concept cognition refers to the thoughts, beliefs, and behaviors of the individual. A basic assumption of this perspective is that a state of dissonance is so psychologically unpleasant that individuals are motivated to reduce any condition of dissonance. Dissonance can be depicted as follows:

$$\text{Dissonance} = \frac{\text{Importance} \times \text{Number of Dissonant Cognitions}}{\text{Importance} \times \text{Number of Consonant Cognitions}}$$

The magnitude of dissonance increases as the number of dissonant cognitions increases in proportion to the number of consonant, or favorable, cognitions.

Dissonance may be reduced by decreasing the importance of the dissonant cognitions, or by decreasing the importance of the consonant cognitions that produce the individual's state of dissonance.

Festinger's theory assumes that such incompatibility or dissonance creates tension in individuals and motivates them to do something to eliminate or reduce the dissonance, such as changing their behavior or beliefs. "Cognitive dissonance is a motivating state of affairs. Just as hunger impels a person to eat, so does dissonance impel a person to change his opinions or his behavior." (15:3) By definition, no tension is likely to be set up by dissonance that individuals themselves do not perceive. Sociologists, and especially those of the symbolic interaction tradition, have long insisted that the investigation of most sociological problems requires that investigators grasp and describe the viewpoints of their subjects. In this process, sociologists have routinely commented on a variety of types of cognitive dissonance.

Dissonance theory, as formulated by Festinger (16), is a variation of another psychological theory of attitude change, Heider's *balance theory*. Heider (19) proposed that individuals are led to maintain a balanced state between their own attitudes, the attitudes of another individual, and their jointly held view of a common object. Balanced states exist when all three relations are positive; that is, when individuals A and B agree on their definition of object O. Unbalanced states exist when persons A and B disagree on their definitions of one another or of object O.

The merit of Festinger's work is that it brought one problem connected with handling symbolic influences on human behavior into sharper focus and made it a subject of empirical research. It is but one of a number of "attitude consistency" theories; Heider's being the first. Osgood and Tannenbaum (30) have produced an extension of Heider's perspective which they call *congruity theory*. This formulation suggests that individuals change their positions in line with their previous commitments. Persons always change their attitudes when incongruity ex-

Students taking an exam. Self-reflectiveness and cognitive dissonance? (*Alain Nogues/Sygma*)

ists. This formulation is quite close to Festinger's. Brehm (4) has offered an extension of the theory of cognitive dissonance which is called *reactance theory*. Brehm argues that when an individual's access to a desired object is restricted, the object becomes more favorable and the person reacts in an attempt to regain that object.

Popularization of the term cognitive dissonance has served to call attention to an aspect of human beliefs that has long been noted and that is, indeed, fairly obvious. Among university students, for example, it is well known that as one attends classes in various disciplines, one often feels constrained to accept, or at least verbally to repeat, conflicting and inconsistent views presented by different professors or contained in as-

Symbolic Environments and Cognitive Structures 101

signed readings. To the professors, on the other hand, it has long been obvious that many students scarcely notice the cognitive dissonance that these conflicting interpretations of the world embody. A student, they notice, may sometimes remark in class that what the professor says does not correspond with things he or she was taught in other classes, but most students probably do not even realize this. Instructors commonly observe that in examinations and papers, harried students often contradict themselves in consecutive sentences or paragraphs without noticing it: their motivations often are totally unrelated to cognitive dissonance but are instead focused on passing the course with a satisfactory grade and on doing whatever seems appropriate to this end.

The cognitive dissonance theory is perhaps more in the nature of a concept than a theory. As one social psychologist has remarked (14:134–35):

> Probably no other science abounds with as many unwarranted usages of the term "theory," for examples, role theory, reference group theory, cognitive theory. . . . These theories in actuality are often conglomerations of imprecisely formulated concepts.

Or as Gordon DiRenzo has wondered, "Is balance theory [the generic term covering several variants, including Festinger's] a theory in the proper sense of that term, a set of deductions from other theories, a conceptual orientation, a heuristic device, or a methodological tool of another type?" (14:1–22)

At most, the cognitive dissonance theory is of a very limited scope and has no applicability to wide ranges of problems connected with many aspects of social interaction. It does not present a general theory of the nature of human behavior, and it focuses on a sharply restricted range of behavior. To its credit, it has stimulated considerable research concerning the reactions to dissonance on the part of those who notice or perceive it. We have ourselves utilized the concept in Chapter 1 to indicate that the progress of science may be viewed as the result of the attempts of the scientific community to resolve logical problems created by discrepancies and inconsistencies between accepted theories or between theories and the evidence.

Nevertheless, it should be noted that this research on cognitive dissonance has been subjected to severe criticism which has cast doubt on its empirical basis and on the precision of its concepts, as well as on its applicability "in more sociologically complex contexts." (9) There are many influences besides sheer dissonance that need to be taken into account in considering matters of this kind. In a complex pluralistic world that is poorly understood, persons are simultaneously involved in many kinds of situations or roles, so that dissonance is often not noticed or is disregarded by them. Dissonances are often multiple and so numerous as

to become unmanageable. Often, perhaps usually, we simply note dissonance and live with it without bothering about it, especially if the
groups to which we belong support us. Recognized inconsistency may
be neutralized by compartmentalization as, for example, when a devout
Sunday churchgoer and true believer (on Sundays) in the Christian
ethic engages in unethical or illegal practices during the rest of the week.
In some situations, dissonance may be sought rather than avoided, as,
for example, by an artist seeking creative stimulation. Other questions
may be asked: What happens to the dissonance problem when it is considered from the group or societal perspective? Do groups have such
problems, and what strategies do they use to cope with them? Do persons who notice dissonance sometimes seek the help of others in dealing
with it, and what difference does this make? How are people and groups
made aware of a particular dissonance when it has existed for many decades without being given any serious attention by them, as in the case
of the discrepancy between American ideals of equality and the treatment accorded blacks?

Cognitive dissonance thus seems to be a much more complicated
matter than this particular tradition suggests. The theory needs to be
considered within a broader context of ideas and incorporated within a
broader theoretical structure, if it is to deal adequately with the wide
range of problems suggested by it and with the many individual variations hidden in the averages that describe aggregates.

We are inclined, therefore, to be highly skeptical of these various
attitude consistency formulations. They assume that humans are in a
constant state of change and that their attitudes are invariably in flux.
We favor a more stable view of the human's symbolic realities. These
theories appear to ignore the fact that humans can in fact suspend judgment about a position and that central to this process are the dialogues
persons carry on with themselves. Attitude consistency theory ignores
the place of the self in everyday interpersonal relationships. Shifts or
changes in the self and symbolic world of the person are often difficult to
accomplish. The psychologist George Kelly (22:9) has remarked: "It may
take a major act of psychotherapy or experience to get him [the individ-
ual] to adjust his construction system to a point where the new and more
precise construct can be incorporated." This fact is scarcely recognized in
the theories we have just reviewed.

Summary

The reactions of human beings to their surroundings are mediated ones.
They are not based on reality as such, but rather on ideas of that reality
expressed mainly by means of linguistic symbols. Hence the symbolic
environments of humans, the names, concepts, categories, stereo-

types—in short, the cognitions—by means of which they seek to understand the world and in terms of which they act, are social products. The acquisition of language habits generates the motivation to name, classify, and explain the significant aspects of one's environment. Such naming and explanation sometimes create incompatibilities between cognitive items. Recognition of this has led to the formulation of the idea that there is a general human desire to reduce or eliminate such cognitive dissonances. The limitations of the cognitive dissonance model were noted.

References

1. Berger, Peter, and Thomas Luckmann, *The Social Construction of Reality*. Garden City, N.Y.: Doubleday, 1966.
2. Berkowitz, L. (ed.), *Advances in Experimental Social Psychology*, vol. 1. New York: Academic Press, 1964.
3. Blumer, Herbert, "Social Problems as Collective Behavior," *Social Problems*, vol. 18 (1971), pp. 298–306.
4. Brehm, J. W., *A Theory of Psychological Reactance*. New York: Academic Press, 1966.
5. Brehm, J., and A. Cohen, *Explorations in Cognitive Dissonance*. New York: Wiley, 1962.
6. Brown, Roger, *Words and Things*. New York: The Free Press, 1958.
7. Cassirer, E., *An Essay on Man*. New Haven: Yale University Press, 1944.
8. ———, *The Philosophy of Symbolic Forms*. 3 vols. New Haven, Conn.: Yale University Press, 1953–1957.
9. Chapanis, N. P., and A. Chapanis, "Cognitive Dissonance: Five Years Later," *Psychological Bulletin*, vol. 61 (1964), pp. 1–22.
10. Chase, Stuart, *The Tyranny of Words*. New York: Harcourt Brace Jovanovich, 1938.
11. Church, Joseph, *Language and the Discovery of Reality*. New York: Random House, 1961.
12. Dale, E., *Audio Visual Methods in Teaching* (rev. ed.). New York: Holt, Rinehart and Winston, 1954.
13. Dewey, J., *Logic: The Theory of Inquiry*. New York: Holt, Rinehart and Winston, 1938.
14. DiRenzo, Gordon, Review of Harold Taylor, "Balance in Small Groups," *American Sociological Review*, vol. 36 (1971), pp. 134–35.
15. Festinger, L., "Cognitive Dissonance," *Scientific American*, vol. 207 (1962), pp. 1–9.
16. ———, *A Theory of Cognitive Dissonance*. New York: Harper & Row, 1957.
17. Fishberg, M., *The Jews*. New York: Charles Scribner's Sons, 1911, pp. 21–178.
18. Gumperz, J., and D. Hymes (eds.), "The Ethnography of Communication," *American Anthropologist*, vol. 66, no. 2 (1964).
19. Heider, Fritz, *The Psychology of Interpersonal Relations*. New York: Wiley, 1958.
20. Hymes, D. (ed.), *Language in Culture and Society*. New York: Harper & Row, 1964.

21. Jordan, Winthrop, *White over Black*. Chapel Hill, N.C.: University of North Carolina Press, 1968.
22. Kelley, George A., *A Theory of Personality: The Psychology of Personal Constructs*. New York: W. W. Norton, 1963.
23. de Laguna, G. M., *Speech: Its Function and Development*. New Haven: Yale University Press, 1927.
24. Langer, S. K., *Philosophy in a New Key*. Baltimore: Penguin Books, 1948.
25. Lee, D., "Symbolization and Value," in L. Byson et al. (eds.), *Symbols and Values: An Initial Study*. New York: Harper & Row, 1954, pp. 73–85.
26. Lewis, M. M., *Language in Society*. New York: Social Science Research Council, 1948.
27. Lippmann, Walter, *Public Opinion*. New York: Harcourt Brace Jovanovich, 1922.
28. Mead, G. H., *Mind, Self, and Society*. Chicago: University of Chicago Press, 1934.
29. Morris, C., *Signs, Language and Behavior*. Englewood Cliffs, N.J.: Prentice-Hall, 1946.
30. Osgood, C. E., and P. H. Tannenbaum, "The Principle of Congruity in the Prediction of Attitude Change," *Psychological Review*, vol. 62 (1955), pp. 42–55.
31. Riezler, K., *Man: Mutable and Immutable*. Chicago: Henry Regnery, 1950.
32. Rosenblueth, Arturo, *Mind and Brain: A Philosophy of Science*. Cambridge, Mass.: M.I.T. Press, 1970.
33. Scheffler, Israel, *Science and Subjectivity*. Indianapolis: Bobbs-Merrill, 1967.
34. Shibutani, T., *Improvised News: A Sociological Study of Rumor*. Indianapolis: Bobbs-Merrill, 1966.
35. ———, "Reference Groups and Social Control," in Arnold Rose (ed.), *Human Behavior and Social Process*. Boston: Houghton Mifflin, 1962, pp. 128–37.
36. Taylor, Harold, *Balance in Small Groups*. New York: Van Nostrand Reinhold, 1970.
37. Triandis, Harry C., "Cultural Influences upon Cognitive Processes," in L. Berkowitz (ed.), *Advances in Experimental Social Psychology*, vol. 1. New York: Academic Press, 1964.
38. Zajonc, R., "The Concepts of Balance, Congruity, and Dissonance," *Public Opinion Quarterly*, vol. 24 (1960), pp. 280–96.

Selected Readings

CASSIRER, E., *An Essay on Man*. New Haven: Yale University Press, 1944.
This work by an eminent German philosopher presents a view that pertains directly to the materials of this chapter. Those interested in his approach should read his more elaborate work, *The Philosophy of Symbolic Forms*.

CHASE, STUART, *The Tyranny of Words*. New York: Harcourt Brace Jovanovich, 1938.
A popular writer of the past attacks the shortcomings of linguistic communication by describing the many ways in which we are misled by words.

LIPPMANN, WALTER, *Public Opinion*. New York: Harcourt Brace Jovanovich, 1922.
A noted commentator who popularized the term *stereotype* discusses the pictures of political reality that people have in their heads.

ROSENBLUETH, ARTURO, *Mind and Brain: A Philosophy of Science*. Cambridge, Mass.: M.I.T. Press, 1970.

A neurophysiologist considers mind-brain relationships, presenting his views about the scientific meaning properly attached to such terms as *objective, subjective, conscious,* and *unconscious* mental processes.

chapter *4*

Social Structure, Groups, and Language

*T*he *symbolic* interactionist perspective demands an immediate and direct focus on various forms of symbolizing activity. Chief among them and certainly central to an understanding of human conduct is language. But language can be, and has been, considered from many different points of view: grammarians have studied its grammar; linguists, its forms and mechanics; anthropologists, its variations from one culture to another; sociologists and historians, its changes across time. Physiologists have noted its anatomical sources, and philosophers have speculated upon its reputed origins and initial development. As social psychologists, we are interested primarily in studying language as a very general form of human behavior and in considering its relationships to other behavior. In a sense everything in this text, in one way or another, is germane to that relationship. In this chapter, however, we shall consider only two general aspects of human language: its relation to group life and its nature. The emphasis on group life is both a necessity and a virtue—a necessity because all languages are rooted in groups, and a virtue because groups are at the very center of the interests of sociological social psychologists.

Consensus and Human Groups

Since coordinated group activity presupposes communication, shared goals, and perspectives, it is obvious that the formation of groups engaging in the complex types of activities which human groups necessarily do, and that involve the physical separation of their members, are consequences of linguistic communication. Membership is essentially not a physical matter, but rather a question of how people think, how they conceptualize their social worlds and themselves, and how they relate themselves to others through the communication circuits available to them.

It is for such reasons that, while lower animals form groups primarily by congregating within a restricted space, human social groups cover a much wider range, including some whose members are scattered over great space, sometimes indeed all over the world, and who do not and cannot congregate in one place. Memberships in relatively simple types of groups, like a married pair, a household, or, in the animal world, a litter, flock, pack, or herd, is mainly a matter of physical presence. On the other hand, human participation in large, physically scattered groups, sometimes called *abstract collectivities*, may at times be difficult to specify, since membership is not determined by any easily observable criteria but by how the person thinks. What, for example, determines whether one is a Christian, a communist, a member of the middle class, a liberal? There are, of course, physical aggregations or categories of people that are not viewed as social groups. A collection of individuals riding a train or all red-haired people or women wearing blue slacks provide examples of aggregates that do not qualify as functioning social groups.

Communication among members of social groups and the sense of belonging to a group may vary greatly. In an audience, for example, there may be little direct communication among its members. In a *primary group*—to use Charles Horton Cooley's term—such as the family, communication is on an intimate face-to-face basis. A sense of intimacy, solidarity, and "we-ness" characterizes primary groups. In more formal groups and associations, however, communication often takes the form of written correspondence, telephone calls, or highly formal notices and announcements disseminated from a central office. These may be supplemented by annual conferences attended ordinarily by a relatively small proportion of the total membership or by small seminars of very exclusive groups.

The primary group—characterized by a sense of intimacy, solidarity, and "we-ness"—is usually the unit within which individuals learn their native language, as well as vocabularies for conceptualizing their own worth. (*Bob Adelman*)

The Group Bases of Language

The study of primitive cultures by anthropologists demonstrates that all human societies have languages. While there are hundreds of different languages in the world, and often numerous dialects within each, linguistic behavior as such is universal. Differences among languages are very apparent, as any traveler to a foreign land can attest. What is not so apparent, although equally true, is that the language of every human society is complex, intricate, and systematic—the carrier of a great wealth of experience and attitude. "The mechanics of significant understanding between human beings," writes the linguist Edward Sapir, "are as sure

Although baby-talk speech may be fairly complex, the child must employ accepted linguistic forms to be understood by adults outside of the family. Here a child resorts to a nonverbal gesture to communicate to an adult. (*Rohn Engh/Photo Researchers, Inc.*)

and complex and rich in overtones in one society as in another." (41:78) Every existing language contains at least five thousand words. As examples of primitive language complexity we might note that in the speech of the Abipones, a South American Indian tribe, the verb can take more than four hundred endings to indicate mood, person, and tense; and in some Australian aboriginal tongues dual, triple, and even quadruple forms of nouns are in use. (19:401–15) Sapir has perhaps overstated the case for the equal complexity of all languages; but no linguist would deny that speech is highly developed the world over. It is for this reason that one writer has referred to language as mankind's "fundamental institution." (25)

LANGUAGE AS PART OF THE SOCIAL HERITAGE
The social heritage of any society consists of its traditional ways of acting, believing, and speaking. This social heritage—often referred to as *culture*—is distinct from the biological heritage. The latter is transmitted from parents to infant by way of parental genes in the chromosomes. The genes determine such physical characteristics as hair color and eye color. A basic difference between biological and social heritage is that the latter is never passed on biologically from parent to child; the child must ac-

quire the social heritage through some process of learning. This simple and obvious fact is both an advantage and a disadvantage: the latter because transmission by learning is fallible and imperfect; the former because, being fallible and imperfect, it provides for the possibility of rapid evolutionary change.

Traditional ways of acting, thinking, speaking, and handling the language vary widely from country to country and from place to place within the same country. The language of a given nation or segment of it is part and parcel of its social heritage: for example, Muslims, Christians, and Jews who have lived in close contiguity in Baghdad for hundreds of years nevertheless speak three quite different versions of Arabic. Like other traditional ways, language is passed down from generation to generation nonbiologically. Newborn babies are unable to speak their parents' tongue, nor do they acquire the ability to do so as a result of later bodily maturation. They must learn word order, pronunciation, and—if they learn to write—spelling and punctuation.

It is clear that the language learned by children is not primarily their language so much as it is that of their society and of their primary group. Adults have linguistic standards to which the child must conform. Although different individuals may set unique distinctions of pronunciation, enunciation, and meaning upon established ways of speaking and writing, nevertheless there is a common core to all these individual treatments. Language is a group product that, like every other part of the social heritage, must be learned (25:195):

> The child playing in the sand invents a word for the pebbles that fill its hand. The new word is "pocos." Does society adopt this word . . . ? Not at all. Society has an expression of its own for the designation of pebbles, and it does not look with favor on the exercise of further inventive genius. So the child's word "pocos" lingers for a time in the tolerant memory of the immediate family and then passes into oblivion.

Many children invent a baby-talk speech of some complexity which the parents learn, participating for a while in a bizarre linguistic game. But if growing children are to be understood by persons outside the family, if they are to become an adjusted member of society, they must eventually employ generally accepted linguistic forms. (See Chapter 9.)

Indeed, marked individual deviation from the accepted language meets with disapproval. To be sure, a certain amount of latitude is allowed; Americans do not all pronounce, enunciate, or construct sentences identically. But one must not stray too far from certain linguistic patterns. Generally speaking, a future tense cannot be substituted for a past tense to indicate something that has happened. In the United States, American word order must be used; German word order is scarcely permissible. In France, inflection and intonation must approach a common French standard; they must not be appreciably American or Chinese.

Marked deviation from the community's linguistic norm will fall stridently upon the ears of one's friends and associates; they are likely to respond with expressions of displeasure, distaste, snobbery, amusement, or ridicule. Deviants may even be punished: witness how "bad" grammar may deprive a person of vocational opportunities or prevent college students from passing freshman English.

The meanings of correct American speech in the world of the immigrant have been beautifully recaptured by the writer Alfred Kazin (26:22):

> A "refined," "correct," "nice" English was required of us at school that we did not naturally speak, and that our teachers could never be quite sure we would keep. This English was peculiarly the ladder of advancement. Every future young lawyer was known by it. . . . It was bright and clear and polished. We were expected to show it off like a new pair of shoes. When the teacher sharply called a question out, then your name, you were expected to leap up, face the class, and eject those new words fluently off the tongue.

Reactions to the violation of linguistic rules are in no way different from reactions to transgression of other customs and rules. Linguistic ways are public property and must not be grossly violated. And like other items of the social heritage, language may be utilized by individuals and turned to private ends; it may be made to fit the pattern of unique personalities. But individuals must operate within a framework of what is and what is not deemed permissible. Language is essentially a group product, the outcome of the common experiences of members of social groups.

SPECIAL LANGUAGES The social character of language may be underscored by noting what linguists term *special languages* (47:249):

> By the term "special language" we mean a language which is employed only by groups of individuals placed in special circumstances. The language of the law is a case in point. In the exercise of their profession lawyers employ a language very far removed from that of ordinary speech; it is a special legal language. Another example can be found in ecclesiastical language. A special language is often used in addressing the Deity. . . . All forms of slang are special languages. Students, artisans, and thieves all use a language of their own. . . . They all have this in common . . . when their structure is examined they are found to be the outcome of a common tendency to adapt the language to the functions of a particular group.

Just as each society has a native tongue of its own, each subsection of a given society, each social world, has some special lingo, slang, or word usages of its own. Medical students, for example, have to learn anatomical and medical terms; students of this textbook must know some sociological and psychological terminology; each generation of high school and college students uses a distinct slang of its own generation;

Park Avenue society speaks an English somewhat different from the speech of the slum districts. Thousands of vocations, businesses, and recreational groupings have their special vocabularies which the newcomer has to acquire and use correctly in order to be "on the inside." This insularity of speech sometimes allows insiders to convey information to one another in the presence of outsiders.

Each special language is based upon and utilizes the framework of the larger society's language. Yet persons who are outside the group that employs a special language are made aware of being strangers to the ways of that group when they encounter its distinctive vocabulary. All of us have probably undergone experiences in which we felt a stranger to some group in our own society because we did not possess the key to its language. A civilian among soldiers is a case in point.

Many terms in a special language are of a shorthand variety, designed to save time. Others are coined in order to make more precise references than the ordinary vocabulary permits. Some terms function in less instrumental senses; they further group solidarity in that when members use the terms, they are strongly reminded of their membership in the group.

It has often been said that the history and interests of a people are reflected to an astonishing degree in their language. Many interesting examples of this mirroring of interests can be found. The English have a language rich in nuances and expressions for the sea; Eskimos make minute distinctions among numerous kinds of snow and snowfall. (19:115) Klineberg comments on the Arabs' concern with the camel (27:50):

LANGUAGE AND GROUP EXPERIENCES

> There are said to be about six thousand names connected in some way with "camel," including words derived from the camel and attributes associated with it. These include, for instance, names and classes of camels according to function—milk camels, riding camels, marriage camels, slaughter camels, and so forth; names of breeds of different degrees of nobility of lineage, derivation from different lands, and so forth; names of camels in groups, as several, a considerable number, innumerable, and with reference to their objectives—grazing, conveying a caravan, war expedition, and so forth; as many as fifty words for pregnant camels, states of pregnancy, stage at which movement of the foetus is first felt, mothers who suckle and those who do not, those near delivery, and so forth.

The special languages of the subgroups in any society provide us with illustrations of this mirroring of interests by language. The idioms and vernacular of sociologists, physicians, soldiers, journalists, bankers, college students, office workers, and football players all reflect their respective dominant interests and concerns.

Language is also the carrier and the embodiment of features of the environment that group members feel to be important. Words employed by people designate, refer to, and select aspects of the world relevant to their lives. "For not everything in the world has a name. . . . Language singles out for specification only those features which are, in a peculiar sense, *common* to the social group." (28:272) As Lewis says (30:224):

> Among the Solomon Islanders . . . there are nine distinct names for the cocoanut, signifying stages in its growth, but no word corresponding to our general term "cocoanut." On the other hand, they have only one word which covers all four meals of the day—breakfast, dinner, tea, supper—but no special name for each of these. It is of practical importance to them to distinguish the nine stages of the cocoanut but not to discriminate between "dinner" and "tea." . . . *A concept is a means of preserving distinctions which are of practical importance in the life of a community.*

Examples taken from the argot of the confidence man will illustrate concretely how the members of a group develop concepts that refer to matters of group interest. The confidence man is a criminal who lives by his wits and his tongue; his stock in trade is to relieve people of their money by deceiving them. This is done by persuading the victim to invest money in what is, in reality, a fake enterprise. Here are some terms in the confidence man's vocabulary (35:269–96):

> *Mark:* A victim, or intended victim. Synonyms for mark are apple, Bates, egg, fink, John Bates, Mr. Bates, savage, chump.
> *To put the mark up:* To locate a good prospective mark.
> *Tow:* A bank roll.
> *To rumble:* To excite a mark's suspicion.
> *The send:* The stage in a big con-game at which the mark is sent home for a large amount of money.
> *To sting:* To take a mark's money.
> *Touch:* The money taken from a mark.
> *To tear off:* To cheat one's partner out of his share of a touch.

In this sense we can argue that all social groups develop concepts or categories that refer to major or dominant statuses and positions in the life cycle. They are likely to have words designating sex, age, and marital and economic status, and they may have complex vocabularies indicating one's position in the kinship structure of that group. The socialization of children into the ways of the group requires that they learn that group's particular language. Furthermore, we can note in passing that a group's standing in the broader society is, in part, reflected in the degree to which their private or peculiar languages are spoken by the members of that society.

Thus black standard English is seldom spoken by other, white, school-age children, and central phrases from Hebrew have seldom become incorporated in our national vocabulary. Colonializing nations have long recognized that language control leads to group control. The

British, for example, were quite skilled in making the English language "the" language for the countries they controlled. The Portuguese followed a similar pattern, as did the Spanish. As a group or a nation gains control over its own fate, one of its first actions is to require the learning of this "native" language. Indeed, it may insist on conducting all public business in that language and in the process ban from its schools the languages of its prior oppressor.

The Nature of Language: Signs and Symbols

Classifying and analyzing symbols are exceedingly complex and controversial tasks. Generally acceptable concepts and a stable working vocabulary have not yet been achieved, although various attempts have been made to provide them. Recognizing the difficulty of the problem and the possibilities of confusion, we shall present a greatly simplified account and confine ourselves to making only a few fundamental distinctions.

In the first place, it should be noted that the nervous system is a complex communication system in which some of the messages, at least, function as signs. On the other hand, some are more in the nature of built-in mechanical connections that function in an automatic and virtually mechanical way below the level of awareness. The autonomic nervous system especially exemplifies this. This portion of the system is primarily involved in the regulation and coordination of bodily functions and processes of which we are ordinarily unaware. The messages transmitted in this portion of our total nervous system may be compared to the way in which a thermostat regulates the temperature in a room, that is, in a mechanical rather than a representational manner. Nervous impulses that can be said to perform a representational or sign function are those that are received and processed in the cerebral cortex and that inform the organism of external objects and events and coordinate behavior with respect to them. Sometimes, of course, and especially when something goes wrong inside of us, we respond to messages from within our own bodies, interpreting them as signs that we are ill, for example, and need to see a doctor. Nervous impulses or messages that qualify as signs are commonly accompanied by awareness, but this is not always the case by any means.

All living creatures learn to respond to cues in their environment. Inevitably, some stimuli come to stand for other stimuli. "The sound of a gong or a whistle, itself entirely unrelated to the process of eating, causes a dog to expect food, if in past experience this sound has always preceded dinner; it is a sign . . . of his food." (29:23) The dog learns also to respond to visual cues (a stick), to movements (the raising of a hand), to odors (that of a cat), and so on. Such learning of cues has been called "conditioning" by psychologists, and in the laboratories they have conditioned many animals to respond to "substitute stimuli." The world of any animal (human or subhuman) is full of such cues, and behavior is largely to be accounted for in terms of responses to them. Hereafter we shall refer to *learned cues* as "signs."

We may think of sign behavior as running a gamut from the very simple to the very complex. It ranges from the most elementary forms of conditioning to the most complex verbal behavior. Between these two poles there exists a wide range of sign situations. A simple sign response may be produced in an animal by repeatedly sounding a buzzer and always feeding him immediately thereafter. This situation may be made more complex in various ways, such as by delaying the reward, by introducing the factor of punishment, by giving the animal multiple-choice problems, or by requiring him to respond to two simultaneous signs. Thus, an animal may be taught to obtain food by pressing a lever; later he may be taught that pressing the lever will yield the usual reward only when a green light is on, and not when a red light is glowing. Experimental psychologists who study the conditioning processes in animals can investigate only the nonverbal sector of the sign range because there is no verbal sign behavior among subhuman animals.

All psychological behavior probably involves sign behavior at some level. Indeed it might be more correct to say, as some psychologists have, that psychological behavior is sign behavior. To elaborate on this point, let us consider a fairly simple psychological act—the perception of a box. If we ask a physiological psychologist to describe what happens when the box is perceived, he or she will begin by noting that light reflected from the box reaches the eyes. From that point on, the account will be concerned entirely with descriptions of how the light impinges on the retina of the eye, how the retina is connected with the central nervous system, and how impulses pass through the nerves. The act of seeing is described as occurring entirely inside of us. The process of seeing is, in short, a representational or sign process in which the things that occur within us represent or function as signs of the real box. When the account is concluded, we are unenlightened as to why we see the box outside of us, and why we see it as a box and not as an image of our retina or as something in our heads.

Among human beings there is a tremendous range of sign behavior, from the simple thought processes of the illiterate and the retarded to the complex thinking of the genius. Almost any object, act, occurrence, or quality may function as a sign of something else. The red glow of wood or metal indicates that it is hot; a gesture may reveal anger; a cross is a symbol of religious affiliation or sentiment; a red light is a warning of danger; a falling barometer forecasts a change of weather; a pointer on a dial tells aviators how high they are flying; and so on, endlessly. Words are our most versatile signs, for by means of them we can talk of anything to which they refer, whether it is before us or not, and whether it is in the past, future, or only in our imagination.

From such illustrations it will be seen that signs are related to the thing signified in a variety of ways. The relationship of the falling barometer to the impending change of weather is different from the relationship between the cross and the affiliation or sentiment to which it refers, and both of these differ from the relationship between words and their meanings. Signs of the type represented by the cross have been called *icons;* those represented by things like the barometer, *indexes.* One should note that what is signified may be even more varied in nature than signs; besides referring to all kinds of real acts, events, and objects, signs may also indicate nonexistent things which can only be imagined, and they may also indicate other signs.

The Second Signaling System

A further complication must be added by noting that signs may be classified as *conventional* or *natural,* and in other ways as well. A *natural sign* is a movement, sound, smell, gesture, or any other stimulus that is perceived regularly to precede or be connected with something else. The natural sign and what it indicates occur together in the same space-time framework, and both are thus parts of a concrete situation. For example, the dog that follows the rabbit's trail connects the scent with the actual rabbit because he has learned that the two go together. By contrast, the *conventional sign* derives its meaning from social consensus and is "movable," or arbitrary, in the sense that different signs (for example, in different languages) may mean the same thing, and that the sign (for example, a word) may be used in situations in which the object referred to is not present. Conventional signs are relative to social groups or language communities in which the same signs are interpreted in the same ways by a plurality of persons.

Natural signs are not "natural" in the sense that they occur only in nature. They also may be human artifacts such as the psychologist setting up a sequence of buzzes (food in a dog's experience) or the lines in a spectrum being taken as evidence of the presence of certain elements. Similarly, the click of a Geiger counter is a natural sign of the passage of an electron. Symbolic analysis enables humans to notice and respond to much more subtle cues than the natural signs which the lower animals are able to master.

Another and perhaps better way of expressing the ideas developed in the preceding paragraphs is to indicate that signs may represent other signs; for example, when we use the word *box* to refer to the visual data relayed to our central nervous system when confronted with a boxlike object. For lower animals these sensory experiences are natural signs of an external but unnamed object. When we call the object a "box," this word functions as a *second-order sign* to designate the sensory experiences which in their turn are *first-order,* or relatively direct, signs of the actual boxlike object before our eyes. It has been argued that an essential difference between what we have called natural signs and conventional signs or symbols is that the latter are always at least second-order signs, which are related only indirectly to physical reality through the mediation of *lower-order signs* (that is, sensory experiences or natural signs). This idea was succinctly expressed by Pavlov, as we have indicated elsewhere, by calling the simple sensory cues the *first signaling system,* and referring to language and speech as the *second signaling system.*

While it is commonly said that signs function in the place of the objects they represent, it should be kept in mind that the word *box* is not the box itself and that the light reflected from the box (which enables us to see it) is also not the box itself. When we see the box, we respond to the light waves that it reflects; when we name it, we respond to the sound waves that constitute the spoken word. All organisms respond to the external world not as it really is but in accordance with the information they have about it. They respond to signs that *represent* external objects. While the organism's information may be adequate for its specific behavioral needs, it is always highly schematic, incomplete, and inaccurate when judged, for example, by the standards of the physicist. The latter does not claim to be able to tell us what the world is "really" like but only tries to indicate how it may be represented or conceived. (37:3–5)

In the diagram below, the fact that there are no arrows linking

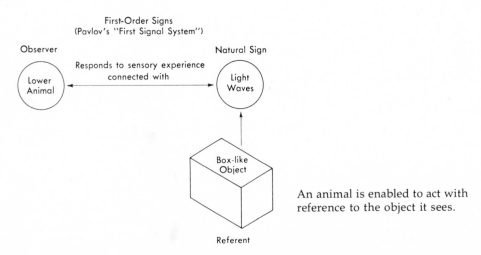

First-Order Signs
(Pavlov's "First Signal System")

Observer   Natural Sign

Lower Animal ◄— Responds to sensory experience connected with —► Light Waves

Box-like Object

An animal is enabled to act with reference to the object it sees.

Referent

the box directly with the observer indicates that the observer, in a very profound sense, never can have any direct communication with a box as it really is, whatever that may mean. All of his or her contacts with it are indirect, mediated, and shaped by the nature of the sense organs and the sensory input from it, be it visual or tactile. Lower animals with different kinds of eyes, for example, may see objects without color or in simplified color schemes, while others attend primarily to movement and evidently perceive stationary objects only vaguely.

The problems of determining what the precise effects of symbolic behavior are and the differences between human and animal behavior may thus be thought of as the study of the interrelationships of different levels or systems of sign behavior. One of the obvious basic consequences of the existence of second-order signs such as words is that they make sensory experience a subject of discourse and an object of reflective thought and analysis, thus establishing the behavioral foundations for all of the higher cortical functions in humans. Being human social inventions, they are basic to human society.

As Luria, the Soviet psychologist (34:9), has observed:

> Language, which mediates human perception, results in extremely complex operations: the analysis and synthesis of incoming information, the perceptual ordering of the world, and the encoding of impressions into systems. Thus words—the basic linguistic units—carry not only meaning but also the fundamental units of consciousness reflecting the external world.

In this book we designate all conventional signs by the term *symbols,* recognizing that the characteristic forms of human symbolic activity have to do with language or are derived from it. Three important characteristics of language symbols that distinguish them from other kinds of signs may be briefly summarized:

1. They constitute symbol systems so that the meaning of any single symbol cannot be grasped in isolation but must always be understood within the system. For example: "wife" is intelligible only in terms of a wider linkage of symbols like "husband," "marriage," and the like.
2. Language symbols, as we shall show, are inherently social in character and meaning. They evoke from the person who produces or uses them the same or similar responses as those elicited from the persons to whom they are directed. If communication is faulty or if the speaker talks past the listener, the words do not function as symbols.
3. They can be produced voluntarily even when the external events or objects to which they refer are absent or nonexistent. We may thus say that although people carry their symbolic systems around with them, the fact that one makes assertions about an object does not prove that the object is present or even that it exists.

We should not, however, make the mistake of thinking of language merely as a system of words, as a combination of phonemes, or as the contents of a dictionary. Language is, first of all, a form of behavior. It is

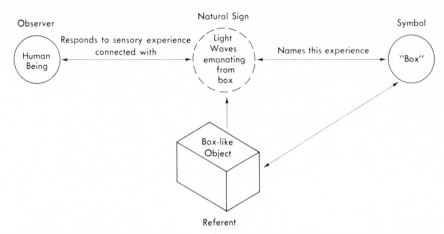

Second-Order Signs
(Pavlov's Second Signal System)

Observer — Human Being — Responds to sensory experience connected with — Natural Sign (Light Waves emanating from box) — Names this experience — Symbol ("Box")

Box-like Object

Referent

A human being is enabled to act toward, use, remember, imagine, and conceptualize boxes and to reason, talk, and plan about them with other human beings.

not merely a system of symbols, but is the activity of using and interpreting symbols. Speech is often said to be the most primitive and ancient form of language behavior, but speech is meaningless unless it is addressed to an understanding listener. Hence, we may say that conversation is the essential and original form of language, noting not only that language behavior originates in cooperative social action but that it *is* such action. This is why parrots are not given credit for language behavior, even though they may produce words.

Conceived of in this manner, language becomes at once more significant and more complicated. The act of listening and comprehending, for example, does not itself involve an act of speaking, but only appropriate response to the other's verbalizations. The response evoked by the other's utterances may be a bodily act or it may be a covert or internal response, perhaps leading to a reversal of roles in which the listener becomes the speaker and vice versa.

Conventional signs or symbols are not necessarily linguistic, as a brief reference to such cultural items as flags, rings, pins, crosses, uniforms, insignia, art objects, monuments, and music will make clear. However, all nonlinguistic symbols of this sort, as well as all ceremony and ritual, have meanings based on group consensus and are deposits of collective experience; hence they fall into the general category of conventional signs. If we return for a moment to the triadic relationships of observer, sign, and thing signified, the added element that appears in conventional signs is this: instead of a single observer we have a group or a community that interprets the sign in the same way and gives to it its meaning. It is for this reason that conventional signs, unlike natural signs, always involve a group reference and the matter of communicability.

It should not be assumed that human beings operate exclusively on the level of linguistic symbols, although that is their most characteristic mode of behavior, or that this symbolic behavior is itself a single, unified process: it falls into many different types which in their turn represent a graded scale from the most simple to the most complex. The use of proper names is an example of a very simple symbolic process, as the person's name refers only to a single object and can be fairly adequately defined by pointing. The use of a class name such as "human being" is more complex because the name refers to many objects and involves differentiation between "human" and "nonhuman." The use of such terms as "tautology," "contradiction," "truth," "generalization," and "abstraction" is still more complicated because these symbols refer to other symbols and to the manner in which they are interrelated. The manipulations of abstract orders of symbols by mathematicians, logicians, philosophers, and other scholars are among the most complex kinds of symbolic behavior.

Analyzing language from the viewpoint of modern linguistics, Charles F. Hockett (20:574) has enumerated key properties of language as follows: (1) *duality*, or the combination of a relatively small number of basic sounds, meaningless in themselves, in a relatively large number of meaningful words (for example, the three words, "tack," "cat," and "act," which are composed of three sounds in different combinations); (2) *productivity*, which refers to the fact that words may be combined in completely new ways to say something that has never been said before and nevertheless be understood; (3) *arbitrariness* of linkage between symbol and what is signified, a feature that removes the limits on what can be talked about; (4) *interchangeability*, which has reference to the ability of speakers of a language to reproduce any linguistic message that they can understand, and is closely associated with the fact that speakers hear what they themselves say; (5) *specialization*, or the sharp functional distinctions between words even poorly pronounced, in contrast, for example, to the gradations of anger expressed by raising one's voice; (6.) *displacement*, or the ability to talk of things remote in time and place from where the talking occurs; and (7) *cultural transmission* or transmission by learning rather than transmission through the genes.

Symbolic Behavior as Shared Behavior

Let us suppose that a dozen dogs have been conditioned so that whenever a buzzer sounds each produces saliva and otherwise behaves as though he anticipated being fed. Then suppose that all twelve dogs are together in one room and that the buzzer is sounded. Presumably, all would respond in the same way to the same stimulus. Can we not say that all of them are responding as a group to a sign which all understand in the same way? To answer this question, let us compare such a situation with that existing in an Eskimo settlement where the food supply is running low. A hunting party sets out to kill seals to replenish the food supply. Can we say that the Eskimos, like the dozen dogs described above, are making similar responses to the same stimulus, and that therefore the two types of activity are the same?

A moment's reflection will show that there is a fundamental difference between these two situations. Through intercommunication the Eskimos respond as a group, acting collectively rather than individually. Their behavior is shared; that of the dogs is not. Each member of the

Gestures, which may seem very "natural" to those who use them, show great variety of meaning cross-culturally. The meaning of such gestural symbols are conventionally defined by the social group.

Eskimo community grasps the common purpose. In terms of that common purpose, which each understands and knows the others understand, they respond not in the same way but in different ways in order to attain the common goal. Some members of the settlement stay at home and prepare to take care of the kill; others form the hunting party within which all may play different but coordinated roles. It is no accident that the Greek word *symbola*, from which our English word "symbol" is derived, referred to "the two halves of a broken stick or coin which were kept as tokens of a contract. Thus the word came to mean an item, such as a word, employed as an instrument of communication." (33:83)

The shared character of language may be emphasized by noting how conventional gestures are utilized and understood. Gestures—such as shaking hands in greeting, showing affection by kissing, and waving good-bye—all seem very "natural" to Americans. Yet these acts do not seem natural at all to the people of some other countries and societies. A

Palaung woman in Southeast Asia said, after several Englishmen had heartily shaken her hand: "I suppose that they mean to be kind, but what a strange custom. I am very glad that it is only my hand that they wish to shake and not my head!" (19:121) Most human gestures are highly conventionalized and stylized, taking on their meaning through cultural definition. The identical gesture may stand for very different meanings in different lands; conversely, different gestures may stand for the same meanings. Only if both persons—the one who makes the gesture and the one who sees the gesture—attach the same significance to it can there be communication between them. An "outsider" will attach the wrong meaning (or no meaning) to the gesture; hence communication will be impaired.

The following cross-cultural mixture of gestures representing "greeting," quoted from Hiller, serves to illustrate the shared and conventional character of human gestures (19:101–02, 119):

> Among the Wanyika, people meet by grasping hands and pressing their thumbs together; dwellers in the region of the Niger join their right hands and separate them with a pull so that a snapping noise is made by thumb and fingers. The handshake of the Arab seems to be a scuffle in which each tries to raise to his lips the hand of the other. The Ainus draw their hands from the shoulders and down the arms to the fingertips of the person greeted, or they rub their hands together. . . . Polynesians stroke their own faces with the other person's hands. . . . The Fuegians in saluting friends hug "like the grip of a bear." Some peoples greet by placing one arm around the neck of the person saluted and chucking him under the chin, or encircling his neck with their arms. . . . [Among the Ainus a distinction is made] in the manner of greeting appropriate for men and women . . . men rub their hands together, raise them to the forehead (palms up), and then rub the upper lip with the first finger of the right hand. . . . In some Eskimo tribes . . . the courteous way of greeting a stranger is to lick one's own hands, draw them first over one's own face and then over that of the visitor. . . . Among the Polynesians, Malays, Burmese, Mongols, the Lapps, and others—a usual salute is that of smelling each other's cheeks.

Even gestures of assent, dissent, and beckoning—which most Americans probably feel to be among the most natural and nonconventional gestures—are conventionally defined. Hiller (19:103–04) goes on to note that inhabitants of the Admiralty Islands express a decided negative reaction by making a quick stroke of the nose with a finger of the right hand. If the reaction is doubtful the finger is rubbed slowly across the nose. To beckon a person the hand is held half erect with the palm forward, moving in the direction of the person addressed. On the other hand the beckon approach for the Bahima of eastern Africa involves a reversal of the palm in a manner that would indicate repulsion for an American. The Niam-Niam of central Africa wave their arms when they beckon.

The natives of New Zealand indicate assent by head elevation and with the chin, instead of by nodding as Americans do. Turks show negation by throwing the head back and then by making a clucking noise with the tongue. This would be quite foreign to an American. Such gestures would have either no meaning or the wrong meaning to us. As outsiders of these societies, we do not share the gestural symbols of these peoples.

If often happens that two persons become involved in an argument in which both use the same words, but the words have different meanings for each person. When this occurs, a genuine interchange of ideas does not take place, as each individual makes remarks inappropriate to the meanings that the other has in mind. They talk past each other and grow angry at what each feels to be the other's stupidity. If the two parties do not become aware that they are using words in different ways, communication is seriously impeded or made impossible; this can be termed *pseudo-communication*.

PSEUDO-
COMMUNICATION

    If, however, the disputants grow aware of the different meanings possessed by common terms, their discussion often develops into a consideration of proper linguistic usage. Thus, it is apparent that the citizens of the United States and the Soviet Union use the word *democracy* in different senses. Once this fact is appreciated it becomes necessary to distinguish between "American democracy" and "Soviet democracy," if communication is to take place. Unless there is agreement as to the meanings of terms, persons who believe they are discussing the same things may actually be talking about different things.

Up to this point we have been discussing language symbols as symbols whose sole function is to refer to objects or to designate meanings. Thus if someone says "We are having lovely weather," we have treated such a statement as an indication by one person to another that the sun is shining and that it is pleasant outside. Obviously, however, this statement may mean something entirely different. Speakers may be in a social situation in which they are expected to talk whether or not they feel they have anything to say. As all the people present are at least generally aware of the weather that day, there is really no point in saying anything about it; nevertheless, all are likely to feel more at ease if there is conversation. Here the purpose is not to tell people something they do not already know but rather, by uttering certain sounds, to give evidence of good will and sociability. Hiller has called this kind of conversation "social ritual." Language so used may be termed "expressive" rather than "representational." Another example of purely expressive speech is swearing—although swearing *at* someone usually also involves some

EXPRESSIVE
VERBAL
BEHAVIOR

communication. Gossiping, too, is primarily expressive communication. Words used expressively cannot be understood by referring to the dictionary; they can be understood only as conventionalized ways of giving vent to certain feelings. Thus, the nervous woman at a tea talks about the weather; an angry man swears; two persons greet each other by saying, "Hello!" or "How do you do!" In these situations the function of language, it is sometimes said, is not so much communication as expression—but of course, some meaning is definitely being communicated.

The expressive use of language may seem to be very much the same as the use of sounds made in certain situations by chimpanzees or dogs. But there is a difference. The dog's growl is a biologically natural sound for him to make, but "hello" and other expressive human sounds are conventionalized forms of utterance. No doubt in certain situations all human beings tend toward expressive verbal behavior, but the vocalizations vary immensely from society to society and are socially defined. Thus, we may say that expressive human speech, although on a lower symbolic and cognitive level than speech designating and describing objects, is nevertheless on a higher level than the expressive utterances of animals. Chimpanzees, for example, can no more be taught to say "hello" appropriately than to use the word "papa" correctly. (See Chapter 2.)

In Chapter 7 we shall discuss *aphasia*, the loss of power to use language symbols. Studies of aphasia and other speech disorders offer experimental evidence that expressive speech is more primitive than representative speech. Aphasics whose powers of speech are nearly gone and who cannot name even the most familiar objects in their everyday environment, nevertheless usually retain the ability to swear and to exclaim. (17) Most students of aphasia believe that when ability to use language symbols disintegrates, it is logical to expect the most complex forms of language behavior to disappear before the simplest ones do.

Nonverbal Communication

It is sometimes emphasized by those who dispute the importance which we attach to language behavior that much communication between people occurs on a nonverbal level without speech, or spoken language. The preceding section on gestures provides one example, but there are many others.

The communication, for example, may be by touch, as in romantic attachments of a past era, when young people were expected to go through a rather long preliminary period of dating during which they first became acquainted with each other through verbal communication. At a certain point, if everything seemed to be going well and if he was encouraged to do so by the young woman, the man was supposed to

Communication between persons may take place on a nonverbal level. A particularly rich form of nonverbal behavior is that communicated by touch. (*E. Trina Lipton*)

clasp her hand. Then if she responded positively by squeezing, there followed a predictable period of handholding and mutual squeezing and stroking, leading to a new gambit—the first kiss. Assuming a positive response from the young lady, the young man would next put his arm around her waist and there would follow a series of warmer and closer embraces along with kissing and considerable body contact, leading to breast manipulation, then to genital manipulation, and sometimes to the culminating act. Marriage hastens this general process and, alas, often standardizes it. In any case, gestures and "tactile communications" take precedence over verbal ones, or if verbal, they are expressive rather than representational. There is not, as a rule, a babel of conversation in cars parked in lovers' lane.

This process of steps or gambits was generally quite exactly prescribed, as was the order in which they were to be taken. "There is usually a well-established code for these communications, with degree of intimacy of direct tactual contacts." (13:209) The boy who omitted a step or two or changed their order was likely to be regarded as "fast," while one who was unable to read the signs given by his partner to signal the next step was viewed as "slow." As the process moved along, other senses besides the tactile—such as taste and smell—entered into the interaction.

To be systematic about nonverbal communication, one should make at least the following distinctions. To begin with, words themselves may be used expressively so as to designate additional or contradictory meanings in addition to their "actual" meanings. Thus Pittinger and Smith remind us that words can be drawled or clipped, can be spoken loudly or softly, with a raised or lowered pitch, with a spread or squeezed register, with a rasp or with openness, and with increasing or decreasing tempo. (40:61–78) There is also *body language,* involving various parts of the body. Body language is, however, a grossly undifferentiated term. As commonly used, it refers to several different kinds of phenomena. It can include gestures (made in the empty air or against someone else's body). These gestures may be in place of words or can accompany verbal language. They may be highly stylized, or they may be idiosyncratic, but they are likely to be readable to anyone from the same general social background. There is also a class of highly stylized gestures like salutes or nose thumbing. Finally, there is a kind of iconic sign language connected with the body, consisting of the messages flashed by one's posture, grooming, hair styles, facial expression, eye movements, and the like.

Most of these nonverbal gestures or body movements are certainly not natural signs. If a person involuntarily squirms in pain or moves restlessly in hot weather, we might speak of these movements as uncontaminated by symbolism, but it is difficult to do so with most other body movements. The words of Birdwhistle, one of the most sophisticated researchers in the area of *kinesics* (nonverbal communication), are highly instructive (4:182–83):

> Early in the investigation of body movement patterning, I had had to deal with that deceptively transparent set of phenomena commonly called *gestures*. A considerable body of ethnographic data was extant demonstrating that these varied from culture to culture. An even larger body of philosophical and psychological literature maintained that these could be understood as "signs" as distinct from less transparent or easily translatable "symbols." Examination of these phenomena in context, however, soon revealed that this was at best a dubious interpretation of their activity or function.

What Birdwhistle is getting at, of course, is that gestures are no less "conventional signs" (in our teminology) than are words themselves. As he says, gestures "are incapable of standing alone." One must know the interactional context in which the gesture is made. "A 'salute,' for example, depending upon the integrally associated total body or facial behavior, may convey a range of messages from ridicule and rebellion to subservience or respect." The same is true of a smile, a wink, a wave, or a bow. "To call these 'signals' is to indicate a specificity such behavior lacks in actual practice." (4:183)

One proviso needs to be added to Birdwhistle's general point, and that is the real possibility that there are a few cross-cultural facial expressions of emotion. Research by Ekman (9; 10:151–58) and Eibl-Eibesfeldt (8) gives evidence that similar facial expressions are used across cultures for expressing happiness, sadness, anger, fear, surprise, and disgust. Ekman notes, however, that "universals in facial expressions of emotion can be explained from a number of nonexclusive viewpoints as being due to innate neural programs or living experiences common to human development regardless of culture"—and notes also that future research is needed to determine this matter. Ekman severely criticizes an extreme view like LaBarre's that "there is no 'natural' language of emotional gesture," because it does not distinguish facial gestures from facial expressions of emotion. Ekman does admit readily, however, that many facial gestures are independent of facial expressions of emotion and that these "may well be culturally variable." But we should note that this discussion deals only with facial expressions as they express rather basic emotions—as compared with all other gestures which may stand for less basic matters and even for finely differentiated emotions like love of country or embarrassment over a spouse's behavior.

Let us now return to Birdwhistle's point about the conventional-sign aspects of gestures. He illustrates this in an interesting description of the various types of gestures, which he calls *markers,* that accompany verbal communication. He notes that such markers may be used to indicate the specific person or persons referred to when pronouns such as he, she, and them are used. The markers in such cases may be slight movements of the head, a finger, a hand, or the eyes in the direction of the persons referred to. When the reference is to I, me, us, or we, the gestural markers are different. Also, the markers indicating future events are likely to be different from those used in speaking of past occurrences. Verbal communication concerning such words as *in, behind, on top of* ("area markers"), or *quickly, slowly, lightly, roughly* ("manner markers") is also accompanied by characteristically patterned gestures. Such markers sometimes replace speech rather than merely accompanying it, as, for example, when one is in the dentist's chair and unable to talk but wishes to tell the dentist to "take it easy."

All of the above is relatively simple in comparison to what Birdwhistle calls the total body language used when one woman tells another about the intricacies of dressmaking. The concept of gestural markers, he says, is not sufficient to describe the various processes involved. He adds that he is inclined to view all of the latter "as examples of derived communicational systems," derived, that is, from prior verbal communication. This brings us to our next points, which pertain to interaction.

The ways in which nonverbal communication as interaction occurs may be schematically represented by indicating whether or not the messages are transmitted or received knowingly or unknowingly.

	Receiving		Sending
		Knowingly	Unknowingly
Unknowingly			
Knowingly			

Examples may readily be found for all four cells. Thus, a speaker who arouses the hostility of an audience may feel a vague sense of discomfort and unease without knowing why. The members of the audience, on the other hand, may, without consciously doing so, lean back in their seats with folded arms and expressionless faces. In this case, the message is transmitted unintentionally and received without clear awareness. Some of the research on nonverbal communication falls within this unknowingly-unknowingly cell.

To illustrate another of the four possibilities: there is a story about one of the authors who, at a class reunion at his university which he attended with his wife, met a woman who had been his classmate many years earlier. She told him that during her student days she had tried for a full year to attract his attention, a fact of which he was totally unaware. In this case, the messages were deliberately sent but were not grasped by the person to whom they were directed, and indeed, they may not really have been received at all. The opposite situation (unknowing-knowing) can be illustrated by the situation wherein someone becomes irritated but is unaware that this irritation is apparent to bystanders, who easily read his or her gestures and facial expressions. The last situation, where both sender and receiver are quite aware, hardly needs illustration, but we might note that a particularly pleasant example from the theater is the elaborate but shared—and hence perfectly understood—facial and body movements made by a skilled mime like Marcel Marceau. This French artist can be perfectly understood by Americans because he draws upon social situations and gestures that are cross-cultural. On the other hand, some of the limitations of miming, because of cultural differences, are suggested by an American student of French culture, Laurence Wylie, who participated, along with men and women from many countries, in a Parisian school of mime. He remarked that when Americans were required to act out what happens when fire meets water, rubber meets glass, and glass meets steel, "they could not prevent themselves from getting involved in the idea of winning a contest. They became a street gang defending its territory." (50:2)

In sending those messages, the Americans were drawing not only on national imagery but undoubtedly on what Ekman would call wittingly sent and culturally shared "emblems" and "illustrators." When emblems are used, the receivers usually not only know the message but also that it was deliberately sent to them. Such emblems are most often used

A skilled mime like Marcel Marceau can communicate complex situations nonverbally by the use of stylized cross-cultural gestures. Many gestures, however, do not carry the same meaning from culture to culture. Hence, Marceau's gestures might be meaningless to a native of Bali. (© *Max Waldman distributed by Magnum Photos, Inc.*)

when verbal discourse is prevented by agreement (as in miming), by external circumstances, or by distance. Thus, there might be an emblem for sleeping, like moving the head into a lateral position, perpendicular to the body, while bringing both hands below the head to represent a pillow. According to Ekman, many messages are emblematic in more than one culture, but often "a different movement is used in each culture." To represent suicide, in the United States one places a finger at his or her temple, the hand arranged like a gun; in New Guinea, the emblem to represent hanging is to grab the throat with an open hand and push up; in Japan, one plunges the fist into the stomach to represent hari-kari, or draws an index finger across the neck to represent throat-slitting.

Ekman's illustrators seem essentially the same as Birdwhistle's markers; they are "used with awareness and intentionality, although . . . usually in peripheral, not focal, awareness." (11:358–9) In reference to hand gestures, Ekman distinguishes the following types of illustrators (11:360):

batons: movements which accent or emphasize a particular word or phase.
ideographs: movements which sketch the path or direction of thought.
deictic movements: pointing to an object, place, or event.
spatial movements: depicting a spatial relationship.
rhythmic movements: depicting the rhythm or pacing of an event.
kinetographs: depicting a bodily action, or some nonhuman physical action.
pictographs: drawing a picture in the air of the shape of the referent.

These illustrators are intended to explain further what has been said verbally. They are socially learned and culturally derived. Their interactive function—and that of emblems too—are suggested by Ekman's finding that they are hardly ever used when the person is totally alone, or not actually communicating with someone. We would also note that American Sign Language (ASL), which is taught to the deaf, represents an attempt to standardize a nonverbal gestural system. Every letter in the English alphabet is given a different gestural configuration.

Our own interactional scheme—the four cells—does not take into account either the misreading or the failure to receive an intended message, or the simple failure to recognize that there is anything to read, like the professor so involved in his or her subject that he or she is oblivious to students' impatience after the bell has sounded. These interactions too, albeit nonverbal, fall within the realm of the symbolic, of "communication." Without shared understandings from prior verbal communication or from participation in common culture, nonverbal communication would be primitive, indeed.

Erving Goffman and Gregory P. Stone are two American sociologists who have repeatedly called attention to the role of gestures and appearances in everyday interaction. In his book, *The Presentation of Self in Everyday Life,* Goffman has referred to the ways in which individuals "give" and "give off" information about themselves when in the presence of others. The information they give off is often unintentional and is transmitted by gestures, or by appearances such as the manner of dress the person has chosen for the occasion. Stone has developed this point by suggesting that one's "social appearance" is central to one's presentation of self and to one's influence over the reactions of others.

Summary Concern with human groups is a central focus of sociology. Groups differ widely in size, duration, and complexity. Individuals who are born into groups or join them must learn the appropriate behavior and beliefs for each. A basic characteristic of human groups is that they exist because of and through communication, especially spoken and written language. Language is always a group product, and it is both an intrinsic part of the social heritage and the mechanism by means of which this heritage is transmitted from one generation to the next. Language is universal among all human groups, although each separate group tends to develop a special language of its own as an expression of its particular points of view, interests, and way of life. Psychological activity is essentially *sign behavior* and ranges in complexity from the simple direct responses of lower animals to the higher thought processes of human beings. *Signs* are classified as *natural* and *conventional*, the latter being called *symbols*. The basic type of human symbolic activity is the process of conversing, whether between persons or as thought, "within" one person's head. We cannot stress too much that the meanings of symbols arise in interaction and are thus a group contribution. *Symbolic behavior*, whether language activity or something else, is shared behavior from which common goals and understandings arise.

References

1. Argyle, Michael, *Social Interaction*. Chicago: Aldine, 1969. (Especially, pp. 91–126.)
2. Bernstein, Basil, *Class, Codes, and Control*, vol. 1. London: Routledge & Kegan Paul, 1973.
3. Birdwhistle, Ray, *Kinesics and Context*. Philadelphia: University of Pennsylvania Press, 1970.
4. ———, "Some Relations between American Kinesics and Spoken American English," in Alfred G. Smith (ed.), *Communication and Culture*. New York: Holt, Rinehart and Winston, 1966, pp. 182–89.
5. Cassirer, E., *The Philosophy of Symbolic Forms*. 3 vols. New Haven: Yale University Press, 1953–1957.
6. Cherry, Colin, *On Human Communication*. New York: Wiley, 1957.
7. Diamond, A. C., *The History and Origin of Language*. New York: Philosophical Library, 1959.
8. Eibl-Eibesfeldt, I., *Ethology*. New York: Holt, Rinehart and Winston, 1970.
9. Ekman, Paul (ed.), *Darwin and Facial Expression*. New York: Academic Press, 1973.
10. ———, "Universal Facial Expressions of Emotion," *California Mental Health Research Digest*, vol. 8 (1970), pp. 151–58.
11. Ekman, Paul, and Wallace Friesen, "Hand Movements," *Journal of Communication*, vol. 22 (1972), pp. 353–74.
12. Fishman, Joshua (ed.), *Readings in the Sociology of Language*. The Hague: Mouton, 1968.
13. Frank, Lawrence K., "Tactile Communication," in Alfred G. Smith (ed.), *Communication and Culture*. New York: Holt, Rinehart and Winston, 1966, pp. 199–208.
14. Giglioli, Pier P. (ed.), *Language and Social Context: Selected Readings*. Baltimore: Penguin Books, 1972.
15. Gumperz, John, "Linguistics and Social Interaction in Two Communities," *American Anthropologist*, vol. 66 (1964), pp. 137–54.
16. Hall, Edward, *The Hidden Dimension*. Garden City, N.Y.: Anchor Books, 1969.

17. Head, H., *Aphasia and Kindred Disorders of Speech*. New York: Macmillan, 1926.
18. Hertzler, J. O., *A Sociology of Language*. New York: Random House, 1961.
19. Hiller, E. T., *Principles of Sociology*. New York: Harper & Row, 1933.
20. Hockett, Charles F., *A Course in Modern Linguistics*. New York: Macmillan, 1965.
21. ——, "The Origin of Speech," *Scientific American*, vol. 203 (September 1960), pp. 88–96.
22. Hymes, D. H., *Language in Culture and Society*. New York: Harper & Row, 1964.
23. ——, "Toward Ethnographics of Communication: The Analysis of Communicative Events," in Pier P. Giglioli (ed.), *Language and Social Context: Selected Readings*. Baltimore: Penguin Books, 1972, pp. 21–44.
24. Hymes, D. H., and J. Gumperz, *Directions in Sociolinguistics*. New York: Holt, Rinehart and Winston, 1969.
25. Judd, C. H., *The Psychology of Social Institutions*. New York: Macmillan, 1926.
26. Kazin, A., *A Walker in the City*. New York: Harcourt Brace Jovanovich, 1951.
27. Klineberg, O., *Social Psychology* (rev. ed.). Holt, Rinehart and Winston, 1954.
28. de Laguana, G. M., *Speech: Its Function and Development*. New Haven: Yale University Press, 1927.
29. Langer, S. K., *Philosophy in a New Key*. Baltimore: Penguin Books, 1948.
30. Lewis, M. M., *Language in Society*. New York: Social Science Research Council, 1948.
31. Lieberson, Stanley (ed.), *Explorations in Sociolinguistics*. Indiana Research Center for the Language Sciences, Bloomington, Ind.: Indiana University Press, 1967.
32. ——, *Language and Ethnic Relations in Canada*. New York: Wiley, 1970.
33. Lorimer, F., *The Growth of Reason*. New York: Harcourt Brace Jovanovich, 1929.
34. Luria, A. R., *Cognitive Development: Its Cultural and Social Foundations* (trans. by Martin Lopez-Morillas and Lynn Solotaroff, ed. by Michael Cole). Cambridge, Mass.: Harvard University Press, 1976.
35. Maurer, D., *The Big Con*. Indianapolis: Bobbs-Merrill, 1940.
36. Mead, G. H., *Mind, Self, and Society*. Chicago: University of Chicago Press, 1934.
37. Miller, George A., *Language and Communication*. New York: McGraw-Hill, 1963.
38. Morris, C., *Signs, Language, and Behavior*. Englewood Cliffs, N.J.: Prentice-Hall, 1946.
39. Park, R. E., "Reflections on Communication and Culture," *American Journal of Sociology*, vol. 44 (1948), pp. 187–205.
40. Pittinger, R. E., and H. L. Smith, "A Basis for Some Contributions of Linguistics to Psychiatry," *Psychiatry*, vol. 20 (1967), pp. 61–78.
41. Sapir, E., "Communication," *Encyclopedia of the Social Sciences*, vol. 2 (1942), pp. 78–81.
42. Shibutani, T., *Society and Personality*. Englewood Cliffs, N.J.: Prentice-Hall, 1961.
43. Skinner, B. F., *Verbal Behavior*. New York: Appleton-Century-Crofts, 1957.
44. Smith, Alfred G. (ed.), *Communication and Culture: Readings in the Code of Human Interaction*. New York: Holt, Rinehart and Winston, 1966.
45. Sommer, Robert, *Personal Space*. Englewood Cliffs, N.J.: Prentice-Hall, 1969.
46. Strauss, Anselm L., *Mirrors and Masks*. San Francisco: Sociology Press, 1969.

47. Vendryes, J., *Language*. New York: Alfred A. Knopf, 1925.
48. Watson, O. M., *Proxemic Behavior: A Cross-Cultural Study*. The Hague: Mouton, 1970.
49. White, L., "The Symbol: The Origin and Basis of Human Behavior," *Philosophy of Science*, vol. 7 (1940), pp. 451–63.
50. Wylie, Laurence, as reported in an interview in *The San Francisco Chronicle*, July 8, 1973, p. 2.

BIRDWHISTLE, RAY, *Kinesics and Context*. Philadelphia: University of Pennsylvania Press, 1970.

Selected Readings

A detailed and systematic consideration by an authority in the field of nonverbal aspects of oral interaction.

EKMAN, PAUL (ed.), *Darwin and Facial Expression*. New York: Academic Press, 1973.

A consideration of the facial expressions of emotion in relation to Darwin's theories and observations on this subject.

GIGLIOLI, PIER P. (ed.), *Language and Social Context: Selected Readings*. Baltimore: Penguin Books, 1972.

A varied and illuminating collection of articles by British and American writers on the role of linguistic practices in personal and group interaction.

LIEBERSON, STANLEY, *Language and Ethnic Relations in Canada*. New York: Wiley, 1970.

A consideration of the nature and social consequences of language and cultural differences with particular attention given to the relations between the English and French communities of Canada.

SOMMER, ROBERT, *Personal Space*. Englewood Cliffs, N.J.: Prentice-Hall, 1969.

An interesting analysis of the implications of the fact that people stake out personal spatial claims for themselves and react in characteristic ways to what they see as an invasion of their territory or space.

PART TWO

Social Structure and the Self

chapter 5

Language
Differentiation
and the Learning
Process

In Part One we presented the basic assumptions of symbolic interactionism on the field of social psychology. Its relevance for the understanding of scientific conduct, biological and cultural evolution, symbolic
environments, and language behavior were developed. In Part Two we
take up the relationship between social structure and the self, treating
the effects of symbolic systems—which are themselves products of social
groups and social structures—upon the organization of human, self-
directed behavior.

In this chapter we shall be concerned with ways in which the symbolic process becomes increasingly complex and differentiated, and with
some of the consequences that follow when language processes are internalized. (See also Chapter 9.) Complex mental functions in their
uniquely human aspects come to be increasingly organized and even
dominated by symbolic factors. As language processes are internalized,
their influence spreads to virtually the whole range of behavior, and
complex activities not found in lower forms of life make their appearance. Human perception, memory, reason, and multiple levels of
thought arise within the social environment and cannot be understood
apart from the complex communication networks and patterns of interaction in which they are embedded. We will also suggest that humor, an

aspect of behavior commonly neglected by social psychologists, may be connected with, or a consequence of, the invention of languages and that there exists a variety of modes of discourse that portray reality in widely different ways to different audiences.

Forms of Language Behavior

BASIC LANGUAGE PROCESSES

As children gradually acquire mastery of their group's language, they learn to use it in increasingly complex ways and in a greater variety of situations. Besides learning to understand and speak it, they also learn to read and write it and to think with it. Each of these activities is a part of the symbolic process that is language behavior, but each in some degree develops separately and differently, presenting special problems and adding its own potentialities for the evolution of human personality and human society. Taken together, the various parts of the symbolic process make it possible for organisms to be transformed into self-conscious and self-regulating social beings.

SPEECH FOR OTHERS AND SPEECH FOR ONESELF.   For some time after they have begun to speak, children make little distinction between

James Aycock/National Park Service

Dev O'Neill

P. Almasy for WHO

E. Trina Lipto

words that they address to themselves and those that they address to others. After a time, however, they learn to adopt their remarks to the exigencies of the social situation. They become aware of the responses of others to the remarks they make, and therefore begin to adapt them to the requirements of intelligible communication. The child's development in this respect is usually a fairly continuous one in the direction of increasing clarity and adequacy.

Much of children's early speech is not directed at others for purposes of communication, but is more in the nature of self-expression or self-stimulation. They not only talk aloud to their parents, but also talk to themselves as they play alone. At this early stage the things they say to themselves and those they say to others are very much the same.

As children grow older, they continue to talk to themselves, but when they are in the presence of others, they do not usually do so aloud. The things they say to themselves become sharply differentiated from what they say to others as inner and outer speech become increasingly distinct and differentiated. Outer speech continues this course of elaboration and differentiation as children learn that they must speak in one way to adults and in another to their peers, in one way to their parents, and in other ways to other adults. They learn to adapt their outer speech in increasingly complex ways to situations and to people as they become increasingly aware of the complexities of their social environment.

A collage of conventional American symbols: "America the Powerful"

National Park Service

National Park Service

They learn that what one says to people varies according to whether they are old or young, male or female, acquaintances or strangers, white or black, friends or enemies, well dressed or poorly dressed, rich or poor, powerful or humble. Situations too become differentiated. Some are public and impersonal, others intimate and private. The endless elaboration and differentiation of outer speech, depending upon audience and situation, also reacts upon and changes the nature of inner speech.

The communication process is further complicated by the fact that, as it matures and becomes sophisticated, a wide variety of subliminal and subvocal processes come into play. The mere words that are exchanged in conversation may sometimes be of little significance in themselves because the real substance of the communication is carried by intonation, facial expression, gestures, or other nonverbal signs. These may be deliberate or they may simply be emitted without awareness. Understanding between people may sometimes be more effectively obtained by a caress, a pat on the hand, a smile, or a facial expression than by paragraphs of talk. (40) What one says to another may be contradicted by the way in which it is said or by other clues of which one is unaware (as when a male writes a ten-page letter to his lover to tell her that their love is finished). Silence in answer to a question may answer it more succinctly than words. Particularly in exchanges that are charged with great emotional significance (where the issues are delicate and the personal risks substantial), it is necessary for the participants to be sensitive to the nonverbal aspects of communication and to the intentions, motives, and reactions of the other that are not announced in the words he or she utters. Silence may speak more loudly than words.

LISTENING AND COMPREHENDING.   Conversation is a very complex activity, as each participant is engaged almost simultaneously in a number of distinct processes. Thus while A speaks to B, B listens to A. But B is also busily engaged in formulating the remarks that he or she intends to make as soon as A stops speaking. B also may be commenting to him- or herself upon what A is saying. Some of these comments may not even be explicitly formulated, and generally they will not be uttered aloud. Thus, B may silently remark that A is stupid or confused or dishonest; but, when his or her turn to speak comes, these comments are suppressed in favor of others that meet the conversational requirements of courteous social intercourse. To complicate matters still further, A not only speaks to B; A also listens to what he or she is saying to B—correcting, revising, retracting, and evaluating as he or she goes along. Both A and B alternate between listening to their own speech and to the speech of the other. The remarks made by each are called forth by and adapted to remarks made by the other as each assesses the other's intentions and motives. Each is thus involved both as a participant and as an observer.

Comprehension of the speech of someone else presupposes mastery of the language and is itself the counterpart of speech. The words of the other person act as stimuli that produce in the listener an internal symbolic process that constitutes the act of comprehending. When we listen attentively to another person, our own word schemes are not directly involved, as we temporarily cede control to the other. Speech and the comprehension of speech are not so much different processes as they are different phases of the same process. None of us can meaningfully communicate linguistically with others unless we ourselves comprehend our own remarks. Conversely, we do not adequately comprehend the ideas of others until we are able to formulate them for ourselves. The crucial test of human comprehension of a word is the individual's ability to use the word correctly; that is, to be able to evoke on the part of the listener the same response it evokes for the speaker.

As we will see in our later discussion of aphasia, if we shift our attention to the neurological and physiological levels and ask what goes on in the brains of two persons engaged in conversation, the situation becomes infinitely more complicated. While some of these internal processes have been roughly identified, a great many others have not been. It is altogether impossible, for example, to provide a meaningful description in neurological and physiological terms of the simplest conversational episode or to distinguish one type from another. While thought, speech, and conversation unquestionably require the participation of various neurological and physiological mechanisms and processes, they are not identical with them and must be viewed in a broader sociohistorical perspective. (26) Nevertheless, sociologists, psychologists, and

"Stinging a mark" (see the discussion on p. 114). (*Culver Pictures*)

other behavioral scientists share a profound joint interest with biological scientists in the nature of the functioning of the human brain.

Although it is often held that dogs and other animals "comprehend" things said to them, the standard of comprehension is not the same as that applied to human beings. Parents, for example, do not assume from isolated correct responses that their children understand correctly all the words directed at them. The child is subjected to another and more crucial test; he or she must be able to use the words correctly, not just once or twice, but in a wide variety of situations and in various combinations. If we keep in mind that *the fundamental prototype of language behavior is conversation,* we shall not become confused by the fact that lower animals, such as dogs, seem to be able to comprehend verbal cues. As we have seen, children show a similar subverbal comprehension before they have learned to speak.

WRITING AND THE LITERATE TRADITION. It is virtually impossible to exaggerate the importance of the invention of written symbols in the evolution of culture. Primitive writing systems developed very early in the evolution of the ancient civilizations, arising out of the practical necessities and problems that arose when human beings first began to live together in large permanent settlements and to form political units. The very term *civilization* implies the existence of literacy, political organization, and city life. Cultures that lack writing are called *primitive* or preliterate. Without writing, history gives way to myth and legend and organized intellectual activity is severely limited. Without writing there could be no mathematics, algebra, science, or any of the other numerous disciplines incorporated within the literate tradition. In preliterate societies, customs, practices, and beliefs are passed down through the generations essentially through long chains of person-to-person conversations. This method of transmission is sharply limited in the kinds of information that can be transmitted, and it also tends to distort the past because of the tendency of people everywhere to reinterpret and understand the past in terms of the present. (17)

Writing probably began in the ancient civilizations in the form of pictures or drawings to represent external objects, persons, and animals; marks were used to indicate numbers. From the latter, various types of number systems were invented and elaborated; from the former, the modern alphabet was created primarily by the Phoenicians and the Greeks during the first millennium B.C. The earliest writing systems were ordinarily very cumbersome, hard to master, and restricted to very small elite segments of the population. It is important to note that the emergence of a phonetic alphabet not only made it much easier to become literate but also radically altered the function of writing. This function was at first that of representing the world by means of pictures or simplified drawings. In contrast, the alphabet permits us to describe and record the sounds that people make when they speak, regardless of what they talk about. It took several thousand years, after the first appearance of primitive forms of writing, for humans to develop the modern phonetic alphabet.

As we have indicated, writing was initially a response to the practical necessities created by the development of commerce, trade, agriculture, and organized government. The earliest writers wrote laboriously on stone or clay. The Egyptians later learned to write on papyrus, and paper was first produced about A.D. 200 in China from whence its production and use was acquired centuries later by the rest of the civilized world. The art of paper-making was introduced into Europe in the twelfth century A.D. by the Arabs, and in 1452, Gutenberg is credited with the invention of the printing press. These technological advances added revolutionary new dimensions and possibilities to the social and intellectual significance of writing and of literacy.

The invention of writing has another and more subtle intellectual implication in that it converts language and the thoughts it expresses into material objects in the external environment. Oral speech, in contrast, consists only of sounds or events which occur and vanish except as they may be remembered by individuals. Recorded speech or writing invites sustained attention and analysis, both with respect to the structure

Cave drawings, an instance of writing from ancient civilization. (*Hubertus Kanus—Rapho/Photo Researchers, Inc.*)

of language and the structure of thought. Writing also enormously facilitates thinking as one readily realizes if one tries to imagine what mathematics would be like without it. Because of writing, talk about talk and thinking about thought are stimulated and greatly facilitated.

In view of the preceding discussion one may indicate that it is probably no accident that the flowering of Greek civilization during the first millennium B.C. was preceded by the adoption of the modern phonetic alphabet and accompanied by an expansion of literacy in Greek society. (17) It is also probably not altogether a coincidence that the Greeks invented logic, cultivated rational discourse, speculated on human nature and the nature of the world, practiced mathematical reasoning, and wrote plays and poetry.

The development of writing in a society creates a complex literate tradition that, more than anything else, contributes to an accelerated rate of cultural evolution, to the accumulation of knowledge, and the development of science and technology. With writing, recorded history begins and a new sense of the past emerges. New modes of symbolic operation become possible and new conceptions of the world, of humans, and of the past and the present emerge. The literate tradition does not displace the oral tradition but rather supplements it. Writing differs drastically from oral communication or conversation in that: (1) it is not supplemented by the wide variety of nonverbal signs that routinely accompany conversations; and (2) what is written acquires an objective public character which ordinary conversation does not have. Writing is thus a much purer example of linguistic communication than oral communication usually is, and by the same token, it is intellectually more exacting. Thoughts tend to evolve and change as one attempts to represent them on paper and sometimes, indeed, they may simply evaporate.

As we have said, the oral and literate traditions coexist in modern societies. They also interact with each other, and items pass from one to the other. The oral tradition is the carrier of what is called "practical common sense," while the literature is represented by what is learned from books and advanced training and education. There is often conflict between the two traditions. No one in our society can avoid the influence of the oral, but it is quite easy to minimize that of the literate tradition.

Internalized Speech and Thought

FROM EGOCENTRIC SPEECH TO THOUGHT.   Some have observed that from the ages of about three to seven years the speech that growing children redirect at themselves becomes more and more abbreviated and to outsiders less and less intelligible. (See Chapters 10 and 11 for a critique of this formulation.) Their self-directed remarks may become increasingly truncated. They use various abbreviating devices (for example, the subject of the sentence tends to be omitted because it is implicitly understood).

It is interesting to ask what happens to the egocentric speech of children. It does not simply disappear without leaving any trace but gradually becomes internalized. What begins as external egocentric speaking eventually goes underground. In the process it is transformed. It ceases to be speaking in a literal sense and becomes thinking.

Ingenious experiments have enabled L. Vygotsky (41:29–52) to discover and describe some features of the gradual transformation. His evidence indicates that the internal speech of adults retains many of the characteristics of childish egocentric speech. It is, for example, very abbreviated, much concerned with self, often highly fragmentary and disjointed, and filled with irrelevancies. The egocentric speech of the children, it should be emphasized, is not mere verbal play; like the adult thought which grows out of it, it serves an adaptive function. Thus, if children are alone or in a very noisy room, or if they think they are not being understood, their egocentric utterances diminish. However, when they are faced with problems, both their references to self and assertions of their own ego increase in number. Speaking aloud apparently helps them solve problems by "thinking them through" aloud. Also, some adults think aloud.

The process which transforms external language into thought may be nicely illustrated by referring to the manner in which people learn to count. Children at first count aloud, touch, or point with hands or head to the objects that they are counting. If they are prevented from pointing or saying anything, they are usually unable to count at all. They begin also by counting similar objects, for their counting depends on external features and overt processes which to the adult are not at all essential. As children grow to adulthood, the external props are discarded one by one. They learn to count dissimilar objects. It becomes unnecessary for them to point, and later it becomes unnecessary for them to count aloud. They may continue to move their lips and count inaudibly to themselves, but eventually this external activity also may disappear. Young children's initial dependence upon external props and upon more primitive activities reappears when they tackle more difficult mathematical problems. For example, the following are instances of how a child in the fourth grade adds "by counting." (23:207)

$$
\begin{array}{cccc}
6 & 5 & 7 & 6 \\
8 & 7 & 3 & 8 \\
\hline
14 & 12 & 10 & 14
\end{array}
$$

For the person who has some facility at mathematics, the very awareness of number-words may vanish, so that mathematical thought often appears to proceed without any dependence upon language symbols.

A very similar process of internalization is involved in learning to read properly. Here, as in learning to count, children begin by reading aloud, progress to reading inaudibly to themselves, and end by following a sequence of ideas with relatively little attention paid to specific words.

THE DUALISTIC ERROR.   There is a strong inclination on the part of many persons to conceive of thinking as independent of the more overt forms of language behavior that precede it and make it possible. Laypersons are not the only ones who commit this dualistic error. As Vygotsky has written (41:29):

> The fundamental error of most investigations in thinking and speech, the fault which was responsible for their futility, consisted in regarding thought and word as two independent and isolated elements.

Language behavior is erroneously supposed to have a material or behavioristic basis, whereas thinking is regarded as something separate, distinct, and of a purely "mental" or "spiritual" character—in short, disembodied. The "mental powers" involved in thinking are thought of as seeking external means of expressing themselves, and language becomes merely their external agent or tool. Language is then said to be "a vehicle for the transmission of ideas"; it is a way of transferring the ideas occurring in the mind of one person to the mind of someone else. Thus the indissoluble unity of language and characteristically human thought is destroyed, and placed outside the realm of empirical research. This separation of language and thought is a more specific instance of the tendency in Western thought to dichotomize "mind" and "body" and—in less secular terms—"soul" and "body."

ARE LANGUAGE AND THOUGHT IDENTICAL? While it is generally agreed that language and thought are interconnected processes and forms of human behavior, the matter of specifying the precise nature of the interrelationship is very much of a moot point among philosophers and scholars. We cannot enter into the detailed arguments that are advanced on this question by numerous schools of thought except to indicate that they exist, and that they constitute a considerable body of literature.

As a rough working conception suitable to the limited purposes of this discussion, we propose that language behavior and thinking could be pictured as two intersecting circles with considerable overlap, as follows:

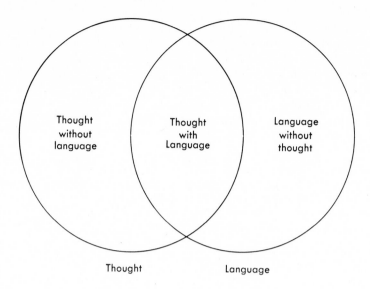

This scheme oversimplifies and to some extent misrepresents the situation, but it does seem to make the points that thinking processes of some sort go on in lower animals and in infants, and that language behavior may sometimes be relatively mechanical in nature and have little or no communicative significance. We think that the idea of the behaviorist John Watson, that thinking is simply talking to oneself, is a considerable overstatement, and that the opposite position, that thinking and talking are two radically separate and independent kinds of activity, is definitely and demonstrably false. In the case of socialized human beings, we postulate that there are levels of psychological activity (similar to those in the lower animals) that do not enter into explicit awareness; Freudian psychologists place a heavy emphasis upon this type of subliminal thinking. On the other hand, it also seems plausible to assume that in some of its most complex manifestations, thinking may occur in some sense without language, and transcend the limitations of existing language structures. Without the latter assumption, it would be difficult to make sense of human creativity. It seems evident that the creative drive of human imagination and inventiveness constantly tends to outrun the capabilities of existing formal symbolic devices. As a result, new forms of language, mathematics, and other notational or coding systems are constantly being produced.

Symbols do not and cannot represent the real world completely and exactly, nor can they convey the full content of human experience. There is much that slips through the net. If thinking were completely confined within the limits imposed by language there would be no way of accounting for the progressive expansion of knowledge and the emergence of new ideas.

Consideration of the thought processes employed by creative artists is instructive at this juncture. Do painters or musicians have to use language as they paint or compose? Do sculptors use language as they shape a stone figure with a live model before them? From the subjective reports of artists and musicians, it is clear that they may manipulate musical and artistic symbols with or without verbally formulating their means and ends to themselves. When artists are asked what a given picture "means" they often reply in what seems to be gibberish, or they refuse to talk at all, simply saying that the picture should speak for itself. The symbols that they create and use are nondiscursive and nonlinguistic; they cannot very well be translated into verbal symbols. Such nondiscursive thought is naively believed by some to be purely recreational and easy when compared with the strenuous thinking of the scientist or mathematician. J. Dewey, among others, has countered with the following (9:45–46):

> The idea that the artist does not think as intently and penetratingly as a scientific inquirer is absurd. A painter . . . has to see each particular connection of doing and undergoing in relation to the whole that he desires to produce. To apprehend such relations is to think, and is one of the most exacting modes of thought. . . . Any idea that ignores the necessary role of intelligence in production of works of art is based upon identification of thinking with use of one special kind of material, verbal signs and words. To think effectively in terms of relations of qualities is as severe a demand upon thought as to think in terms of symbols, verbal and mathematical.

Because artists work directly with other than language symbols, we should not be misled into thinking that language is irrelevant to their thought processes. The ideas that artists seek to represent in their work are, in a broad sense, the products of their social experience; they have been communicated to them from their social environment. Their conception and perceptions of the world are also socially conditioned. A striking historical example is afforded by the pictures drawn by the illustrators who accompanied explorers like Captain Cook on their voyages during the eighteenth century. They were supposed to make accurate drawings of flora, fauna, geological formations, and the natives whom they encountered. Their depictions of the natives often strike the modern eye as ludicrous, because the natives are drawn in classic European artistic poses and sometimes even look like Europeans. They were also romanticized or given other projected attributes. By contrast, the foliage and even the natives' houses are generally more accurately drawn, suggesting that they could be more accurately perceived and conveyed to audiences because less of a conceptual screen intervened between the artist's eyes and the objects of their inspection.

A dance in Otaheite: stylized communication. Note the European features of the participants as drawn by a member of Captain Cook's expedition. (*Globe Photos*)

Painters of the abstract expressionistic school have sometimes been pictured as throwing pots or globs of paint on their canvasses and letting nature, the laws of motion, and the forces of gravity produce the artistic forms. If painting were no more than this, there would clearly be nothing to prevent an imbecile, or a chimpanzee, from being regarded as an artist. This point has been wittily underlined by the famous composer Paul Hindemith, who noted that in a book published in 1751 by the English musician William Hayes, *The Art of Composing Music by a Method Entirely New, Suited to the Meanest Capacity,* musicianship was satirized by suggesting the following advice: "Take a brush with stiff bristles . . . dip it into an inkwell, and by scraping the bristles with the finger, spatter with one sweep a whole composition onto the staff paper." As Hindemith caustically adds (19:142): "You have only to add stems, bar lines, slurs, and so forth to make the opus ready for immediate performance." We might add that it is hard to imagine an aphasic as an artist and equally difficult for most people to view paintings by chimpanzees as serious art. When archeologists uncover artistic products in prehistoric remains, they regard them as evidence of a relatively complex social environment and culture.

The Soviet psychologist L. Vygotsky represented the interrelationships of language and thought by two intersecting circles as we have done. He went on to say (40:125, 153):

> Thought is not merely expressed in words; it comes into existence through
> them. Every thought tends to connect something else, to establish a rela-

An abstract expressionist painter
contemplates his work. (*E. Trina
Lipton*)

tionship between things. Every thought moves, grows and develops, fulfills a function, solves a problem. . . .

The relation between thought and word is a living process; thought is
born through words. A word devoid of thought is a dead thing, and
thought unembodied in words remains a shadow. The connection between
them, however, is not a preformed and constant one. It emerges in the
course of development and itself evolves.

It is of interest that Vygotsky's ideas and the research conducted by
him and his followers (26) takes its point of departure from an aspect of
Pavlov's thinking that has received little attention in the United States—
that is, his description of language as the second signal system. (See
Chapter 4.) Soviet psychologists and physiologists led by Vygotsky and
Luria have reported on the results of extensive observation and experimentation concerned with the relationship between complex mental and
cortical processes and language behavior. The conclusions reached are
practically identical with the theoretical perspective developed in our
book. Luria and F. Yudovich have stated their ideas about the signifi-

cance of the point of view that links complex mental activity with language and the processes of social interaction (26:15):

> Perception and attention, memory and imagination, consciousness and action, cease to be regarded as simple, external, innate mental "properties." They begin to be understood as the product of complex social forms of the child's mental process; as complex "systems of functions" which appear as a result of the development of the child's activity in the process of intercourse; as complex reflective acts in the content of which speech is included, which, using Pavlov's terminology, are realized with the close participation of the two signal systems—the first signal system being concerned with directly perceived stimuli, the second with systems of verbal elaboration.
>
> Only by understanding that the sources of all complex mental processes do not lie in depths of the soul, but are to be found in complex forms of human social life and in the child's communication with people surrounding him, can we finally outgrow the prejudices which have been rooted for centuries in psychological science.

A similar position has been developed by the Americans H. Werner and B. Kaplan. (44)

In our discussion of aphasia in Chapter 8 we note that these patients can perform acts of direct reference but not acts of symbolic reference—in other words, they characteristically fail to organize their activities on the highest level of abstraction. Such simple dichotomies as "concrete attitude" and "abstract attitude" or "direct reference" and "symbolic reference" do little more than suggest the immense range of sign behavior, from the simplest to the most complex. No human thinks systematically, logically, and on the highest planes of abstraction about all matters, nor do all matters require abstract thought. Some may never learn to think consistently at the highest levels (that is, similar matters may be dealt with on varying levels of abstraction). Various classifications of sign behavior and thought have been suggested as preliminary to investigation of the full range of thought. Dewey and Bentley (11:16) offer a tentative hierarchy. The idea that thinking covers a range of sign behavior is likely to be a fruitful one. Study of this range is a task for the future. In the meantime, it is worth asking what are its implications for our understanding of such related mental processes as daydreaming or fantasy. These processes, unlike *thinking* (which involves conscious and reflexive attempts to enter into the activities of another individual), represent, as Singer (34:3) suggests,

> a shift of attention *away* from some primary physical or mental task we have set for ourselves, or *away* from directly looking at or listening to something in the external environment, *toward* an unfolding sequence of private responses made to some internal stimulus.

The inner processes that the daydreamer attends to involve "pictures in the mind's eye" which may anticipate future experiences in which the thinker will take part, or the pictures may recall past experiences of some significance to the person. We may regard daydreaming as a normal mental process.

Daydreaming and Dreaming

It is common, however, in psychological writing to make a distinction between objective, or rational, thought and autistic, or fantasy, thought. The former is supposed to be more or less impersonal, systematic, objective, and logical; the latter is supposed to occur because it satisfies the subjective wishes and desires of the person and so is more or less irrational, illogical, and out of touch with reality.

The assumption that fantasying or daydreaming is a process apart from rational or systematic thinking is associated with the belief that daydreamers substitute the satisfactions of the daydream for those denied them (temporarily or permanently) by the exigencies of actual life. Often it is said that they derive three main types of satisfactions: compensation, escape, and release. Compensatory daydreams allow the person imaginatively to attain goals that are otherwise unattainable. The Cinderella legend has its counterpart in the fantasies of anyone who wishes for something he or she cannot get. The second type, daydreams of escape, occur under such conditions as drudgery, anxiety, boredom, hardship, and fear. The fantasies temporarily transport the dreamer into more pleasant surroundings. Daydreams of release function as safety valves by allowing the individual to dissipate anger, hatred, resentment, irritation, or jealousy in a harmless imaginary form.

Although fantasy is supposed to serve the three functions of escape, compensation, and release, it is not an easy matter to prove that these are its only or its main functions. It is difficult to determine the function of a given daydream merely by examining its content. Even if one knows a great deal about the personality and background of the daydreamer, the fantasy activity may still not fit into any of the three conventional categories.

The attempt to uncover the function of daydreams is based upon the assumption that fantasying is something special and apart from rational thinking. It is assumed that it must yield special satisfactions or it would not occur. Hence, daydreaming is supposed to occur mainly in connection with situations of stress, anxiety, boredom, and the like. This is underscored further by the vivid and elaborate fantasies of the psychotic, and the excessive daydreaming of maladjusted people. However, a closer scrutiny of daydreaming (without previous commitment to a dichotomization of "reality-thinking" and a substitute for it) brings some other relevant matters into focus.

During many of their bouts of daydreaming, normal adults know perfectly well that they are daydreaming, and they will sometimes set

Social Structure and the Self

aside certain times of the day to engage in this often pleasant activity. Young children, some have remarked, have difficulty in distinguishing between reality and fancy; they sometimes get them quite confounded in their discourse, to the amusement or exasperation of their elders. The requirements of adult life make it necessary eventually for the child to draw a fairly strict line between fact and imagination. The severe psychoses and the condition of senility cause their victims to lose the ability to make this clear separation, at least in their less normal moments. In the psychotic, various types of fantasying seem to constitute "thinking" and "reasoning." These commonplace observations do not lead to a separation of fantasying and reasoning but suggest, not prove, quite the opposite—namely, that fantasying is a type of reasoning.

As fantasying is not a single process but embraces many types of covert activity, we may, speaking more strictly, say that reasoning of various kinds may occur when anyone fantasies. The fantasy life of very young children may be one of their dominant lives or the only life they know. They have not yet been sufficiently socialized into correcting their perspectives by checking them against the facts or comparing them with the views of other persons. Severe psychotics do not, for the most part, operate with *consensual validation* (public verification) in mind; the various types of fantasying in which they engage constitute their modes of handling social relationships and responding to the physical world. Maladjusted persons get, we sometimes say, "absorbed in their fantasy life." This is the way they meet the impinging world. Normal adults, although they know the difference between reality and fancy and between public knowledge and private secret, are not constrained to reason only in socially sanctioned and verifiable modes or in systematic or rational ways. It is well known that even scientists present their findings and check them for public appraisal in systematic ways, but that their guiding ideas may have occurred to them through processes that are like reveries.

A *stream of consciousness* or of *associations* is likely to be a peculiarly rich mixture of covert mental processes. Visual and auditory images, subverbal comments, daydreaming dramas, recollection, reseeing of past scenes, self-judgments, internal dialogue, and many more elements jostle each other. Even a daydream that happens to have a fairly tight plot or progression may have intrusions in the form of the daydreamer's comments or judgments. A certain amount of control may be exerted over daydreams by repeating and reviving them. Many daydreams appear to be of short duration and fragmentary, and are preceded and followed by conscious and rational thought processes. Like the latter, the fantasying may be absorbing enough to exclude external stimuli that might otherwise impinge upon the awareness of the person (or the stimuli may break the line of reasoning or fantasying). It is easier to daydream when other people are not around to break the reverie, but this is perhaps true for any kind of thinking except that which depends upon immediate reciprocal stimulation and verification.

Some writers, for example R. Faris, have contended that it is "more plausible to consider it [daydreaming] as preparation for hypothetical activity than as consummation." (12:100) This is certainly one of the functions of all thinking, and there is little reason to deny that it is the function of much fantasying. A point that should be especially noted is that interaction between humans is dramatic in character, and thus a dramatic imagery is required for both actual and imaginary participation in it. For example, a man is preparing for such interaction when he pictures to himself various ways of getting well acquainted with a woman who attracts him. In order to imagine the play of gestures and to judge the effects of conversational lines, he plays out various dramas in his imagination. Out of these a plan or at least a preparatory act may emerge.

It is indeed a moot point whether persons about to enter knowingly upon a new status, or about to embark upon any enterprise involving new interpersonal relationships, can initiate their lines of behavior without daydreaming of themselves in their new role. Cues for actual behavior seem sometimes to be derived from this kind of thinking, which is also intertwined with less pictorial reasoning. Anticipatory fantasying may even occur in an overt or shared form, as when husband and wife plan an exciting trip or anticipate the birth of a child. The preparatory functions of fantasying—rather than the merely wish-fulfilling functions—can be suggested by the experience of emigrants who imagine what the new land is going to look like and what is going to happen to them there. Visionaries, utopians, and leaders of social movements do not merely plan, organize, and execute. *Dreamer* is a word to be applied to them literally. In order that the symbolism of a movement may recruit members and help retain them, it must be kept vivid and rich. Retrospective fantasying may occur when an individual reconstructs a particular pleasurable act. Indeed, as we suggest in Chapter 14, the sexual act may be grounded in retrospective and prospective fantasy.

Like other forms of thinking, fantasying may turn toward the past. It is true that one may help eradicate shame and other unpleasant feelings by refurbishing a past conversation or incident in daydreams. But it is also characteristic of human beings to seek explanations of the past and to "rethink" incidents and discover new meanings in them. Some of this reinterpretation and reconstruction presumably goes on in the form of reverie. Processes of reverie abound in times of personal crisis when individuals are questioning themselves about where they are going and must consequently consider where they have been.

These processes are also implicit in any thinking or imagining in which people seek to establish relationships with real or imaginary persons. Some people clearly do get pleasure out of imagining meeting movie stars or other celebrities, and they may daydream long conversations occurring in such improbable situations. This kind of fantasying may not merely be pleasurable; it may transform the individuals in their own eyes. Such shifts of self-conception may occur even though the dreamers are aware that they are fantasying. Another kind of vision is that sought by Eastern mystics who fast in order to have an elaborate reverie, or series of reveries, in which sacred animals and gods appear. Here there is social sanction both for the vision and its life-long effects upon the individuals, and perhaps upon their social group. This last example suggests also the close connection between ritual and reverie. Ritual, when it is not merely routine, represents a collective acting out of hallowed dramatic sequences, and these, like reverie, may orient one for future conduct. In S. K. Langer's felicitous phrasing (25:128):

> [Rituals] are part of man's ceaseless quest for conception and orientation. They embody his dawning motives of power and will, of death and victory, they give active and impressive form to his demoniac forms and ideals. Ritual is the most primitive reflection of serious thought, a slow deposit, as it were, of people's imaginative insight into life.

Seen in such wider contexts, fantasy processes are multiple in kind and function, and are orienting as well as wish-fulfilling.

Most of the literature on autistic thought and fantasying behavior has been produced by psychiatrists and clinical psychologists who are impressed with the great amount and truly fantastic quality of the reveries of their patients. This latter fact, combined with certain witting and unwitting assumptions about the nature of humans and their relationship to reality that are made by many psychiatrists and psychologists, leads to an undue stress upon the crippling or merely compensatory effects of fantasy life. Excessive fantasying does not lead to maladjustment but may be a symptom of it.

Another type of mental activity is dreaming. The meaning of dreaming **DREAMING** and of particular dreams has long intrigued and sometimes worried humans, for books on dreams go back as far as the second century A.D. There is a type of literature called "dream books"; these purport to offer guidance in the interpretations of dreams by supplying the meanings of dream sequences and events, usually in terms of predictions for the future of the dreamer. Eating cheese in a dream, for instance, may be said to portend good fortune. The symbols interpreted in dream books are universal, in the sense that anyone eating is in for happy times. These questions of what specific dreams "mean" and whether a universal symbolism exists have had a lively treatment at the hands of scientists during the past century, largely in the fields of psychiatry and psychoanalysis. Social psychologists appear to be much less interested in dreaming, presumably because they do not utilize dreams for obtaining insights into the mental and emotional processes of patients; but dreaming is an interesting, and perhaps important, psychological phenomenon in its own right.

There are many studies of dreaming that deal with physiological correlates, duration, speech, and frequency of occurrence of types of imagery (visual, auditory), as well as with the dream imagery of the blind or the deaf-blind, with sex and age differences, with types of dreams, and the like. The literature of psychiatry is replete with examinations of the meanings of dream symbols and with the roles of certain kinds of dreams in the lives of certain types of neurotics. Despite the considerable bulk of this literature, both empirical and theoretical, the nature and significance of dreaming are areas of dispute.

By far the most influential theory of dreaming is that of Freud. Freud's dream theory is part of a much wider and very elaborate theoretical system concerning the psychological nature of humans in general. For our purposes, we need stress here only a few of the chief features of his views on dreams. Various wishes are said to threaten to disturb the sleeper's rest, and dreams perform the function of seeming to fulfill these wishes. Usually the wishes are unacceptable in the sense that the person does not care to admit that he or she has them. Hence they tend to be excluded from consciousness, or *repressed,* during waking hours. In sleep they appear in dreams, but in disguised forms, since even during sleep the person's psychic mechanisms are operating. The obvious, or *manifest,* content of the dream is an expression of its *latent,* or real, meanings. Freud writes that "we have got to turn the manifest dream into the latent dream, and we have to show how the latter became the former, in the life of the dreamer." (16:19) Through the technique of evoking the patient's free associations, or nonlogical linkages, the patient and analyst eventually arrive at an interpretation of latent content and a knowledge of the connections between this and the manifest content.

The transformation in the dream of latent content into manifest content is termed *dream work,* and it proceeds through a process termed *secondary elaboration*—that is, the person *attempts* to give a rational account of his or her otherwise unaccountable and unfathomable dream. Dream work is an example of primitive modes of operation, which are characteristically unconscious. These modes are not rational and objective, and furthermore, they do not involve logical connections between propositions. Their hallmark is associations or nonlogical linkages. Freud termed this type of mental functioning *the primary process,* and the sharply contrasted logical type he considered to be a *secondary process.* The primary process of mental functioning manifested in the dream is *regression.* The

Social Structure and the Self

reason that dreams are visual is that there is censorship of undesirable wishes and of *instinctive impulses* which causes these wishes and impulses to emerge in disguised forms. "On account of the . . . process of regression ideas are turned into visual pictures in the dream; the latent dream-thoughts are . . . dramatized and illustrated." (16:31) Some associations which appear in the dream are not unique to the dreamer but are universal or at least very common.

Freud pointed out that there were certain possible objections to his wish-fulfillment theory of dreams in the form of contradictory data. Persons who had had serious traumas reexperience these in their dreams. Freud questions what possible satisfaction of impulse can be had by this painful experience. Likewise, the reappearance in dreams of exceedingly unpleasant incidents from early childhood causes pain to the dreamer. Freud tentatively accounts for this partly contradictory evidence by stating that (18):

> The sleeper has to dream, because the nightly relaxation of repression allows the upward thrust of the traumatic fixation to become active; but sometimes his dream-work, which endeavors to change the memory traces of the traumatic event into a wish-fulfillment, fails to operate.

The Freudian theory of dreams has been considerably amended by Thomas French, an American psychoanalyst. He has contended that the mode of mental functioning exemplified in the dream is neither Freud's secondary process nor primary process (15):

> In fact, it is not associative thinking at all . . . but rather thinking in terms of a practical grasp of real situations: "If I act upon this wish, then I must expect such and such consequences. Shall I renounce the wish or suffer the consequences? Or is some compromise possible?" The dream's solution may not be very good from the point of view of waking life, but it is always intelligible, once we grasp the nature of the conflict.

French sees dreaming as very much like ordinary processes of practical thought, which generally are neither overly logical nor verbally formulated. He rejects the associational psychology which was prevalent in Freud's day, and suggests that the connections between specific latent and manifest meanings are related to dreamers' attempts to reconcile their conflicting wishes. In French's account we should note particularly that although the notion of wishes is retained, the nature and functioning of dreaming are conceived of very differently.

The psychoanalytic conception of dreaming as wish fulfillment has been attacked repeatedly. Faris, for instance, contends that dreaming is an effort to solve problems, although the nocturnal effort is far less efficient than those of waking life. (12:101–04) A more systematic attack has been launched by C. Hall (18), who argues that dream symbols are not disguised, but are merely representations of ideas: "Dreaming is pictorialized thinking; the conceptual is more perceptual. . . . A dream symbol is an image, usually a visual image, of an object, activity, or scene; the referent for the symbol is a conception." Since different persons may have different conceptions of "woman," for instance, the dream symbols for woman vary accordingly. Hall, who has counted 102 symbols for the male organ in psychoanalytic writing, concludes that "since the referent is not an object, person, or activity, but a conception, the 102 different phallic symbols represent 102 ways of conceiving of the male genitals." (18) The dreamer may, of course, hold different conceptions, and hence he or she may utilize different symbols referring to these conceptions. Dream symbols, consequently, are not universal, although they may be widespread in a given culture. Hall's criticism of Freud seems to stem mainly from two objections: (1) that Freud's "disguise" theory of dream symbolization makes of sleep a more active period than seems likely on the basis of studies and observation; (2) that Freud's associational psychology is "passé."

H. Sullivan, a thoughtful psychiatrist whose views we shall encounter again, in his turn criticized any account of dreaming as cognition on the grounds that dreamers cannot help distorting their reports of what happened during their dreams. The point is that there is an impassable barrier between the covert process of dreaming and the verbal formulations of waking life. Even if dreamers wish to remember the exact details of their dreams, they cannot (37:343):

> People who feel that they should analyze . . . a dream . . . into what it stands for, seem to me to be in exactly the state of mind of the person who says to a child of two-and-a-half, "You ought to show more respect for your mother because God on Mt. Sinai said to Moses, 'Honor thy father and thy mother.'" . . . the psychiatrist is dealing with the type of referential operation which is *not* in the syntaxic [verbal] mode, and one merely stultifies himself . . . by trying to make this kind of report syntaxic.

For Sullivan, dreaming is like other mental processes which go on in waking life but outside of awareness, and which have to do with the avoidance of severe anxiety. During sleep, people have less need to defend themselves against anxiety-arousing events, so that dreaming functions to guard against anxiety during sleep and (symbolically) to satisfy needs unslaked during the day. No regression is imputed to dreaming by Sullivan, and he is chary of interpreting symbols in any but a purely personal context. We must note, in Freud's defense, that he, too, was sensitive to the fact that dreamers could never have direct access to their own dreams. His concept of secondary elaboration referred to this fact.

These alternative treatments of dreaming suggest something of the controversy surrounding the topic. Is dreaming like logical reasoning—that is, practical, everyday thinking—or is it vastly different? Is it problem solving, or wish fulfilling? Are the symbols unique to individuals or groups, or are many of them universal? We shall not attempt to mediate in this free-for-all. However, because we reject many of the Freudian assumptions about motivation generally (and will make this explicit in Chapter 8), we do reject the views that dreams are disguises for unsanctioned and unconscious instinctual impulses and wishes and that there is unvarying correspondence between a given manifest content and the latent content of a dream. In our view, the living organism, even when asleep or unconscious, is engaged in covert symbolic processes. The processes involved in dreaming are on "lower levels" than those involved in self-conscious rational thought, particularly when the latter is being prepared for public appraisal. It seems unlikely that the modes of sign manipulation employed in dreaming should differ very much, if at all, from those employed in waking hours, particularly when the person is at a very low point of self-awareness.

As for the reporting of dreams, we would agree with Sullivan as to the great difficulty, or even the impossibility, of reporting dreams accurately; and we would add that no one can possibly remember a dream without converting the dream sequence into words and so distorting and probably oversimplifying it. An important aspect of dreaming, for the social psychologist, is that a dream, like any other private experience, can be responded to by self-conscious persons afterward. They may be ashamed of themselves for dreaming what they did, or they may be pleased; they may accept their analysts' view or that of some other person, including a fortune teller or the author of a dream book; and, as with all other interpretations, they may change their mind about it at a later time.

Metaphor, Analogy, and Flexibility of Thought

Events and objects can be viewed and classified in many different ways. One may make a game of this by trying to see some common object—an apple, for example—from as many different perspectives as possible. Besides thinking of it as an edible fruit one may imagine it as a ball, a Christmas tree or table decoration, a magical object, a pupil's gift to a teacher. Each of these ideas leads us to look at the apple from a different perspective and to act as if it were what we assume it to be or what we use it for. This ability to switch perspectives and to regard the same event or object in many different contexts is uniquely human.

When something is treated linguistically as if it were or might possibly be something else we speak of employing *simile* or *metaphor*. So a novelist might describe a helicopter hovering over an airfield as if it were an insect. Metaphorical language is not merely poetic, not simply a colorful embellishment, but is necessary to communication. If it is said that a party was "like a funeral" or that a man's speech was "like the braying of an ass," it is understood that the analogy is to be taken descriptively, not literally—for example, that policemen are "pigs." Metaphors are often used in humor and satire: for example, in the occupational lingo of funeral directors the person in charge of cremation is called a "chef." And during the Watergate hearings of 1973, one columnist described how Dick Tracy (the great fictional detective) had been called into the White House the previous year to handle matters threatening our national security and then had engaged in all the activities now under investigation—bugging, burglarizing, and political "dirty tricks." Then, at the end of the columnist's story, it is revealed that Dick Tracy is the President himself.

According to the German linguist P. Wegener (25:111–15), all discourse involves a context which is well known to speaker and listener, and also a novel element. To express the latter, the speaker will utilize a metaphor or analogy—if precise descriptive terms do not already exist—and the context tells the listener that the analogy is not to be taken at face value. It is impossible to strip explicit or implicit metaphor from speech, for many novel elements cannot easily be handled with extant vocabulary. So the speaker must hint, suggest, and evoke. The same is true of speech to oneself. In other words, *analogy* is at the heart of new perspectives, new orientations, vision, and advance in thought.

However colorful and "concrete" metaphors and similes appear to be, they betray a process of abstraction at work. As Langer (25:113) has pointed out, a word like *run*, when used in connection with rumors, brooks, and competition for political office, has nothing to do with leg action. She suggests that originally all the usages of the verb were probably metaphorical, but now "we take the word itself to mean *that which all its applications have in common*, namely, *describing a course.*" Wegener has termed such a word a "faded metaphor"; he hypothesizes that "before language had any faded words to denote logical subjects, it could not render a situation by any other means than a demonstrative indication of it in present experience." We need not necessarily agree with Wegener's account of the development of language to see that abstraction rests in some part upon analogy. "The spontaneous similes of language are our first record of *similarities* perceived," Langer writes. But *analogical thinking* is integral to abstract cogitation of even the most abstract and systematic sort. Of course, it is used constantly in developing new political and social positions and in justifying them. A good example is the thinking that lay behind the formation of a black community theater as part of the general thrust of blacks toward achieving heightened self-pride in an ordinarily devastating and intrusive white America. The head of this theater is quoted in *The New Yorker* as saying (3:62):

Our job has always been to show black people who they are, where they are and what condition they are in. . . . We take the view that a community heals itself from within. There are many sources of healing within the community, and theater is one of them . . . what we do here is like putting a stethoscope to the ears and attaching it to the community body. Some people don't like what they hear, but hearing what's there is the first step toward becoming healthy.

We are properly advised against taking an analogy too literally, as in relying upon analogy in order to prove a point in an argument. "The great danger of analogy is that a *similarity* is taken as evidence of an *identity*." (4:128) However, as the famous economist John Maynard Keynes argued, one must always generalize by analogy from a sample of a class to the entire class, because in many respects each instance is unique and there is no absolute identity of all instances in the class.

Significantly, new shifts in perspectives are heralded by new analogies or metaphors. When the world was conceived of as round rather than as built on the order of a pancake, the new conception led to a restructuring of behavior and social relationships. An extensive new vocabulary is built as a result of acting upon a new abstraction. Those who adhere to old ones will variously greet the new with ridicule, anger, retaliation, and sometimes with the accusation that the new is in bad taste, as in matters of esthetics. As Burke (4:136) has remarked, the universe can be sliced like a cheese, "and when one has chosen his own pattern of slicing, he finds that other men's cuts fall at the wrong places." Action based upon new analogies thus challenges loyalties and the deepest self-involvements of humans. Women's-liberation images of men as exploiters and imprisoners of females throughout the ages have enraged many men, even when the metaphors have been amended by the adjective "unconscious." To comprehend how powerful a generator of passion and action a dramatically coined metaphor can be—for all parties concerned, whether they agree or disagree—we have only to think of the imagery of the *Communist Manifesto:* "Workers of the world unite, strike off the chains which bind you."

Keynes's point, as well as our previous discussions of the nature of categories, makes clear that all abstraction and all generalization is inevitably an oversimplification of reality. Hence all analogies, however fruitful they have been, will be questioned sooner or later. Action based upon a given analogy will not do justice to the claims and rights of some individuals, and eventually the latter will sense this and create their own alternative perspectives. We see this in sectarian splits, in the initiation of social movements, and in the formation of new groups designed to meet newly generated demands. The attack on an old metaphor is not always made with slam-bang directness. As the old can be qualified gradually, it often happens that alterations in social relationships and structures, and even in scientific theory, are made almost imperceptibly until someone signalizes the really new point of arrival by coining a phrase for it like "manifest destiny" in the nineteenth century or "the American century" in the twentieth century.

The danger and necessity of analogy are the danger and necessity of language itself. No classification covers all qualities of the objects it embraces. Yet without classification and metaphor there would be limited flexibility of behavior, and our attention would be focused fairly directly upon immediate situations. The danger and fruitfulness of metaphor can be epitomized by a strategy, actually an old and necessary technique often used by the philosopher John Dewey. Dewey would take two sharply opposed philosophical positions and show that from yet another and "transcending" position, the opponents were really rivals on the banks of the same local stream. In turn, we can be sure that Dewey's position will be lumped with many that he attacked. From a historical perspective, the positions of even the bitterest opponents often appear to be much closer than the rivals would have thought possible.

Images of Mobility

Our general point of view and some of the points to be discussed are excellently summarized in the following statement by C. W. Mills (29:677):

> It is only by utilizing the symbols common to his group that a thinker can think and communicate. . . . By acquiring the categories of a language, we acquire the structured "ways" of a group, and along with the language, the value-implicates of those "ways." Our behavior and perception, our logic and thought, come within the control ambit of a system of language. A vocabulary is not merely a string of words; imminent within it are societal textures—institutional and political coordinates. Back of a vocabulary lie sets of collective action.

A good example of Mills's coordinates and of the allied vocabularies is the way Americans talk and write about the mobility of ethnic groups. The reader might try to identify the groups that are likely to take one or more of the following positions, concerning the fate, function, and nature of the various ethnic groups that make up American society. (3:81)

> (1) Each immigrant group tends to come in at the bottom of the ladder, and then rises; this tendency has helped to keep America an open society. *But,* despite the waves of migration and the obvious rise of various ethnic individuals, the society is not really open—especially at the top. (2) America is, in essence, a melting pot where each immigrant group becomes Americanized, accepting American ideals and values including those of democracy, where every man has a chance to rise. *But* the so-called melting pot is a myth; people mostly rise only within their own ethnic circles. (3) Some immigrant groups are natively more endowed than others; therefore some will

rise and others will not rise very much. *But* persons, not groups, are mobile; mostly it is individuals who rise regardless of ethnic origin. (4) Some groups are so pushy that they threaten others' standard of living—especially that of the original immigrants (natives) or older (especially Protestant) immigrant groups. *But* the natives no longer contribute much—are no longer vital—to the country and will or should be displaced by more vibrant, more successful (urban or urbane) descendants of recent immigrants. (5) By the third generation, the children are quite Americanized—do not suffer from the marginality of the second generation—and subscribe to American ideals of success. *But* the third generation is more relaxed than the second, and need not be so mobile, or so obviously mobile, as the second. (6) Just like every other ethnic group, Negroes should rise through their own individual hard work, or through ethnic (black) political power. *But* Negroes are not like other ethnic groups because they were slaves and therefore not really immigrants; so they need a hand up the social ladder by federal or other agencies.

Humor, Interaction, and the Resources of Language

It is sometimes claimed that humans are the only animals who talk, weep, and laugh. We should take that statement with a bit of skepticism, since animals certainly exhibit playful behavior, and chimpanzees, at least, seem to engage in practical jokes. Yet, as Wolfenstein (46:11) observes, "humor is a distinctively human achievement: among living things only human beings laugh." Whether humans learned to laugh before they learned to talk may be an open question, but there is little doubt that once they developed language they probably laughed and joked a great deal more. Even in the face of disaster, humans satirize their oppressors and may make bitter jokes at their own plight. Humor, in the form of jokes, puns, and witticisms, has often been compared to dreams. (16, 46) Like dreams, jokes have latent meaning; they also, like dreams, disguise hostile emotions and may reflect underlying definitions of the sect or of social relationships. In humor, people may reflect their responses to problematic situations. A dramatic example is that of the criminal who was being led to execution on a Monday morning and who remarked: "Well, this is a good beginning for the week." (46:212)

There are so many forms of humor that one can hardly begin to list them: satire, irony, gallows humor, ethnic jokes, sex jokes, puns, slips of the tongue, misprints, spoonerisms, "in jokes," black humor, jibes. Whatever its form, humor usually draws directly on the resources of language. That is so even when the humor is gestural—as in takeoffs—and does not involve actual speech.

To say that humor depends on the resources of language means much more than merely the fact that words and sentences are used to create humor; it also presupposes a common universe of discourse and shared experiences. To take the most obvious example: understanding the prevalent types of humor of a foreign country is one of the last and most difficult accomplishments of newcomers to its culture. What they do understand quickly, of course, is humor about those matters which they share with its citizens. But the subtleties and styles of a country's humor depend very much on the intricacies of its social relationships and the linkages of its social groups. On the other hand, certain jokes, such as sex jokes, are more readily transferable from country to country—although even in this case they tend to carry a particular cultural stamp or style. This is illustrated by the contrast between British and American styles which often leads Americans to think the British lack a sense of humor—to the amazement of the latter.

Insofar as a universe of discourse is widely shared, the audience of a given bit of humor can be quite huge: for instance, jokes about leading politicians. Every informed Englishman during the days of Gladstone and Disraeli understood the following exchange between the two men. Gladstone said Disraeli would either be executed on the scaffold or die of a loathsome disease, whereupon Disraeli replied this depended on whether he embraced Gladstone's principles or his mistress. During the Watergate affair, jokes about the White House and the President had wide currency. They included remarks like: "Nixon has taken crime off the streets and put it in the White House where he can keep an eye on it"; and "Truth is such a valuable commodity that officials have used it very sparingly." Certain political jokes, however, are culturally and historically restricted. Consider the following: At the time of the Watergate investigation, Richard Nixon dreams that he is telling Abe Lincoln of his troubles. He asks Lincoln's advice as to how to get them off his mind. "Have you thought of going to the theatre?" Lincoln asks.

Today in industrialized countries one finds that frequent and widespread humorous references are made to machines, especially to computers, which "are taking over from humans." A very good source of laughter, sure to amuse virtually everyone, are those occasional typographical errors and slips of the tongue—a missed *r* in an advertisement for a shirt sale, or the apology of a newspaper for having inadvertently referred to "defective Clancy of the police force" rather than to "detective Clancy of the police farce." In countries undergoing the squeeze of inflation, bitterly tinged humorous commentary is bound to be current, like that about President Nixon's attempt—after three previous "phases" of attempts to control inflation—to check rising prices by imposing new but very limited controls, this last attempt being popularly labeled as "phase three and a half."

Certain types of puns and other sayings can be understood and used by citizens of very different backgrounds, again because they can

A family laughs. The primary group as a context for humor. (*E. Trina Lipton*)

share certain general perspectives. For instance, the conundrum: "What did the ram say as he fell off the cliff?" Answer, "I didn't see that damned ewe turn." Other examples are the boners of children—"The equator is a menagerie lion running around the middle of the earth," or "A volcano is a place where you go up and look over the rim and see the Creator smoking." There are some errors of students—the remark in an essay about a storm at sea that "nothing could be heard above the roar of the wind and the waves except that of the sailors working on the wenches." Limericks, of course, enjoy cross-cultural appreciation—there is one that suggests that even animals to some extent share in this humor: "There was a young lady from Niger, Who smiled as she rode on a tiger, They came back from the ride, With the lady inside, And the smile on the face of the tiger."

The phenomenon of "in jokes" exists because the universe of discourse, the shared communication, is limited in scope. For example, a black comedian during the days of the civil rights movement told the following jokes to a white liberal audience. They understood the first to be a cutting satire on themselves, but clearly many did not quite understand the second. The first joke: "A black friend of mine is running a 'rent-a-nigger service' for white liberals who need one for a cocktail party." The second joke was about a black who sneaked down to a supermarket, where he surreptitiously bought a watermelon, stowing it in a small valise. When he got home he ate it with quick delight but with the window blinds of his house pulled down. The counter-joke told by racists is:

"How do you bring a race riot to an end? By dropping a load of watermelons into the crowd."

In jokes are always related to some social world—be it racial, sexual, ethnic, occupational, or recreational. Each social world has its particular stock jokes, humorous sayings, and fabled humorous stories about personages, social types, or important concerns in that world. For example, golf: a newcomer to the game, looking for his ball that strayed in the midst of trees and underbrush, rises with the ball in his hand and says to his partner: "Here's the ball, now where's the course?" Collectors' worlds are replete with humorous and sometimes sardonic stories about ignorant collectors who get "taken" by purchasing fakes. A book about a famous counterfeiter of fraudulent modern paintings, supposedly by artists such as Matisse and Picasso, was read with high good humor by many a participant in the art world, and autobiographies by art and antique dealers tell many a comic story at the expense of culturally ignorant but wealthy customers. An art dealer named Duveen once told how he sought to get Henry Ford's business by publishing a beautiful catalogue of salable objects in his gallery just for Ford, but Ford only remarked that now that he had the book he didn't need any pictures. These examples also illustrate that the comic side of things seen from "inside" a world is very varied. It can be about outsiders, clients , and newcomers, but also about its heroes and villains, about ordinary events or key happenings and important activities: "A professor with two children baptized one and kept the other as a control group." People who participate in ethnic worlds are likely to enjoy a host of jokes and jibes not only at their own expense but at the expense of other ethnic groups. The same is true of religious and sectarian worlds. (A non-Baptist protestant once remarked that what was wrong with most Baptists of his acquaintance was that they hadn't been held under water long enough.) In every social world and society certain topics are also relatively taboo, out of bounds for humorous purposes—like God, Jesus, and the Pope. People may tell taboo jokes in one social setting and not in another. Women, for example, are more likely to share sex jokes with each other than with men—and vice versa.

If one reviews the examples of humor just given, it is apparent that their effectiveness as humor depends not merely on language as a body of words but language as sets of meanings—and the interaction which sustains their meanings. The persistence and pervasiveness of humor—as well as its many forms—suggest that in the face of taboos and threats, it is a vital and basic form of human behavior. The few social psychologists, psychiatrists, and philosophers who have sought to analyze humor as a phenomenon have tended to restrict their foci to the so-called functions of humor, or simply have classified its forms, or have attempted to account for all of humor by remarkably overgeneralized theories. The conditions for and the consequences of telling jokes, laughing at slips of speech, creating irony, and other settings for humor are multitudinous; no simplified theory could possibly account for them all. For the social psychologist the important future task is to get humor back into the interactional picture as an essential and important part of human behavior.

Language and the Structure of Thought

Rather obviously, the content of a person's thought is affected by his or her social environment. The form or manner of his or her thinking is similarly influenced. E. Sapir, making a point akin to that made earlier concerning symbolic environments, suggests the very great importance that particular languages have for the construction of thought and environments. He says (32):

> Human beings do not live in an objective world alone . . . but are very much at the mercy of the particular language which has become a medium of expression for their society. It is quite an illusion to imagine that one adjusts to reality essentially without the use of language and that language is merely an incidental means of solving specific problems of communication or reflection . . . the "real world" is to a large extent unconsciously built up on the language habits of the group. No two languages are ever sufficiently similar to be considered as representing the same social reality. The worlds in which different societies live are distinct worlds, not merely the same worlds with different labels attached.

The influences of language structure upon the structure of thought are illustrated by the difficulties of translators. The translation of other languages into English involves more than merely finding equivalent words; the translator is faced with the problem of conveying meanings and nuances of meaning that may be practically impossible to express in English. The translation of non-European languages into English is difficult because the modes of thought are likely to be still more divergent from ours than are those of peoples living within the general European tradition. Differences between Chinese and American thinking are suggested by the following quotation (5:27):

> Chinese poets seldom talk about one thing in terms of another. . . . If a metaphor is used, it is metaphor directly relating to the theme, not something borrowed from the ends of the earth. . . . For our Western taste, used as we are to the operatic in poetry, that is, the spectacular or shocking effect produced by some unusual analogy or metaphor, the substance of Chinese poems seems often mild or trivial.

The following newspaper account suggests some of the difficulties of conscientious translators when they attempt to interpret English expressions for the Chinese (38):

Some of the great difficulties among the diplomats sitting around the international table here [at the United Nations] arise from the differences in languages, alphabets, and, consequently, ways of thinking; and in no tongue is more ingenuity required for accurate, precise translation than Chinese.

The Chinese ideograph script is one of the world's oldest written media, but the talk at Lake Success is so brimful of new ideas, new concepts and new words that, to translate even the basic Charter itself into Chinese, it was necessary to devise almost 2000 new combinations of characters.

A perfect example of the troubles faced here by Chinese translators is the word "uranium," which has a persistent way of cropping up with a decision to call the atomic base "U-metal." That, however, only started their headaches.

The symbol for "U" was found in the Chinese word for grapefruit, which in literal translation is the "U-tree." What was just as disturbing, from a purist point of view, was the discovery that the symbol for metal was contained in the first part of the word for "bell," which literally translated meant "metal boy."

After some cudgeling of brains, however, the calligraphers came up with the proposal to shave off the "tree" part of the "U-tree" character, discard the "boy" part of the "bell" character, and then in the best manner of diplomatic compromise, join the severed remains to form a new symbol: "U-metal" or, as we would say, uranium.

Although new words may be added to a language with relative ease, the basic structure of a language is highly stable and resists change. Most people who speak a given language are unaware of its structure as something that differs from the structures of other language systems. Consequently, the uniform modes of thought imposed upon them by their native tongue are not recognized or taken into consideration as such, but are accepted as part of the "real nature of the world" or as among the elements of "common sense."

Since most Americans are acquainted only with the general family of Indo-European languages, they are likely to view skeptically the contention that thinking is not essentially the same the world over. They know that the content of thought varies from group to group. Nevertheless, they are likely to believe that the form of all "correct" thinking is always and everywhere the same. The divergent modes of thought of other peoples—which actually do exist—are thus often regarded merely as varieties of error.

It would be very interesting and revealing to know what effect the English language may have on our thinking processes. It is probably impossible for anyone operating within the framework of our language to become aware of the influences it exerts upon him or her without first being acquainted with other languages, preferably non-European ones. For this reason, we shall illustrate our point with materials from the Navaho Indian language, which is quite different from our own. (24:194):

[Navaho language] delights in sharply defined categories. It likes, so to speak, to file things away in neat little packages. It favors always the concrete and particular, with little scope for abstractions. It directs attention to some features of every situation, such as the minute distinctions as to direction and type of activity. It ignores others to which English gives a place. Navaho focuses interest upon doing—upon verbs as opposed to nouns or adjectives. . . . The important point is that striking divergences in manner of thinking are crystallized in and perpetuated by the forms of Navaho grammar. Take an example of a commonplace physical event: rain. Whites can and do report their perception of this event in a variety of ways: "It has started to rain"; "It is raining"; "It has stopped raining." The Navaho people can, of course, convey these same ideas—but they cannot convey them without finer specifications. To give only a few instances of the sorts of discrimination the Navaho must make before he reports his experiences; he uses one verb form if he himself is aware of the actual inception of the rain storm, another if he has reason to believe that the rain has been falling for some time in his locality before the occurrence struck his attention. One form must be employed if rain is general round about within the range of vision; another if, though it is raining about, the storm is plainly on the move. Similarly, the Navaho must invariably distinguish between the ceasing of rainfall (generally) and the stopping of rain in a particular vicinity because the rain clouds have been driven off by the wind. The [Navaho] people take the consistent noticing and reporting of such differences . . . as much for granted as the rising of the sun.

The author goes on to point out that Navaho is a very literal language which gives concreteness and specificity to everything that is said. The result is that Navaho thought contrasts with English thought by being much more exact and particular. This is illustrated by the way in which the Navaho express the meaning conveyed by the English verb "to go." The German language distinguishes between two ways of going in two verbs—*gehen* and *fahren*—the first, for example, indicating that one walked, and the second denoting that one drove by automobile or was transported by a train. The Navaho go much further by specifying precisely whether the journey was made on foot, or by horseback, wagon, auto, plane, or train; they also indicate whether they are starting to go, going alone, returning from somewhere, or arriving at a point; and, if they make a trip astride a horse, different verb forms indicate whether it was at a walk, a trot, or a gallop. (24:197–201).

The study of non-European languages makes it evident that there are different modes of reasoning. Every human being is introduced, as a child, to a system or systems of language embodying certain peculiar and nonuniversal conceptual distinctions. Thus, the child is inducted into traditions of thinking, traditions consisting not only of certain kinds of ideas but of certain ways of thinking. The point is made particularly clear by a consideration of time divisions. If certain temporal distinctions are not made by one's language, one cannot think in terms of them. Behavior can scarcely be organized, systematized, arranged, defined, regulated, or coordinated in terms of temporal categories of which the person is unaware. While our own language (43:126–29)

> . . . always expresses tense with perfect definiteness there are languages . . . which are incapable of doing so. . . . in Samoyedic [Siberian] only two temporal forms of the verb are recognized . . . one of these . . . signifying present and future . . . the other indicating the past. . . . The minute temporal distinctions which we recognize as "present," "present perfect," "past," "past perfect," "past future," "future," "future perfect," and "past perfect" are impossible in these languages.
>
> A number of languages clearly reveal the efforts which have been made to render intelligible the elusive and abstract nature of time by interpreting it in terms of space. . . . [In Sudan language for example] the locations in space are crudely expressed by means of body-part words, and these spatial expressions then serve as indicators of time . . . here the fundamental intuition of time is quite different from that to which we are accustomed. . . .
>
> [For] some people future and past fuse linguistically into what might be called a "not-now" . . . in Schambala [African] the same word designates the distant past as well as the distant future. For them there exists only a "today" and a "not today."

Other critical categories (such as those of number, action, and quality) also differ in various languages.

Since the language which people use is largely an inheritance from previous generations, the modes of thought that it conveys are also derived from the past. This has its disadvantages as well as its advantages, for the experiences of past generations are not comparable to those of later ones. The errors of the past are tenacious because they become embedded in the language and popular thought, so much so that they become unquestioned assumptions. Scientific progress often depends upon freeing oneself from the implications of popular speech. Note, for example, the sayings that the sun rises in the east, and that members of a race are related to each other by blood. Symbolic logicians make analyses of speech through its logical forms so that the contradictory and ambiguous qualities of sentence forms can be avoided. Recognizing all this, Sapir reminds us that "language is at one and the same time helping and retarding us in our exploration of experience." (32:11)

In setting forth the general hypothesis that language profoundly influences the forms of thought, we are not saying that a given language rigidly determines the form of thought of the society in which it is spoken. But language so thoroughly interpenetrates the modes of experiencing that at the very least it limits the possibilities of perception and of thinking.

During recent years, anthropologists who take a position close to our own have begun to develop what has been termed *componential analysis*. This is a sophisticated linguistic analysis undertaken in an effort to avoid projecting the enthnographer's modes of cognition and perception on to his or her subjects, and instead attempting to discover *their* modes. Charles Frake, one of the leading exponents of this view, expresses the position in terminology that should ring familiarly to our readers (14:54):

> A successful strategy for writing productive ethnographies must tap the cognitive world of one's informants. It must discover those features of objects and events which they regard as significant for defining concepts, formulating propositions, and making decisions. The conception of an ethnography requires that the units by which the data of observation are segmented, ordered, and interrelated be delimited and defined according to contrasts inherent in the data themselves and not according to prior notions of pertinent descriptive categories.

Frake then points out that anthropologists customarily do what he suggests when they study kinship systems. No ethnographers describe social relations in an alien society by referring to the doings of uncles, aunts, and cousins. However, when they describe pots and pans, trees, shrubs, and other features of the environment, they customarily do so "solely in terms of categories projected from the investigator's culture." Frake suggests that if the investigator were to follow the sensible strategy used when studying kinship, "then the problem of describing a tangible object such as a plant may become rather more complex than the relatively simple task of defining contrasts between categories of kinsmen." Why? Because the plant world is frequently differentiated in the amazingly complex ways that we have noted. Frake gives the example of a Philippine rain forest agricultural society whose members "exhaustively partition their plant world into more than 1600 categories."

What Frake suggests ethnographers should do is by no means an easy task, but the componential analysts believe that it must be done. That task is not necessarily much easier when investigators are studying a group within their own nation if that group's symbolic worlds are markedly different from their own. These anthropologists would probably agree with us that investigators cannot simply stop with penetrating the symbolic worlds of their subjects; as social scientists, they must develop their explanations *after* grasping these other worlds.

Internalized Audiences

Thinking goes on in the form of a symbolic process, an inner conversation; hence thought, like speech, is formulated in terms of the requirements of communicability. More specifically, this means that thinkers, like speakers, have in mind an audience to which they adapt the formulations of their thought. This audience may at times assume the form of particular persons whose imagined responses are taken into account, or it may assume the form of a conception of "people in general." At other times, the imagined audience may be represented merely by abstract rules, principles, or standards. These may be considered the equivalent of an audience, because they derive their authority from social consensus.

All reasoning involves processes of self-criticism, judgment, appreciation, and control. Socially transmitted traditions of thought determine, among other things, which problems are important and which are unimportant, which questions are crucial and which are trivial, which solutions are to be rejected out of hand and which ones are to be judged acceptable, and so on.

The fact that thinking is a symbolic process means that thinkers can view and criticize their thought processes only from the standpoint (that is, according to the norms) of particular social groups, because symbols are group products. To reason "correctly" means to conform to the canons of thought and to the conceptions of right thinking that prevail within a given circle. To be "right" always means "right from some point of view."

It is worth noting that no complex society has only one way of reasoning: various types of discourse representing different modes of thinking and of viewing the world exist simultaneously. Among the types of discourse that exist within our own society we may mention the poetic, philosophical, dramatic, scientific, mystic, and religious. Each type implies a unique approach to human experience, and each has its own criteria of validity and relevance. Scientists, for example, cultivate systematic doubt and believe only what empirical evidence forces them to believe. By contrast, the poetic approach requires what Coleridge called a "suspension of disbelief" (that is, a willingness to accept presented illusions as reality). Scientifically minded people who are troubled because poets do not define their terms as they go along seek to apply the standards of one type of discourse to another type to which they bear no relation.

These different types of discourse, corresponding to different frames of reference, imply the utilization of different internalized audiences. For example, the modes of reasoning acceptable in poetic circles are significantly different from those of the scientists, and those of the latter are not deemed appropriate in the area of religious and moral beliefs. As individuals move from one activity to another (for example, from the laboratory to the home or the church) they change their frames of reference and their standards of proof, validity, and relevance. For individuals, the importance of any given audience varies according to how relevant they consider its opinion to be; thus, the opinions of the scientist's wife concerning his theories, if she is not a scientist herself, are likely to have less influence upon him than her opinions of his table manners.

It is important also to note that these different modes of discourse pertain not only to thought itself but to overt behavior, and hence to interaction. The formation and organization of some American communes during the late 1960s and early 1970s were predicated on mystic ideas of "community" and "communal living." Such mystic discourse is immensely different in style and leads to quite different kinds of action than, say, that depicted by James Watson in his narrative description of the division of labor and competition among biological scientists involved in the discovery of the structure of the genetic molecules.

Summary

In the course of learning a language, we internalize it. In the process, the language is progressively differentiated into a variety of forms, linked with more and more aspects of behavior, and used in increasingly discriminating ways. The internalization of language, which begins as the acquisition of a motor skill, ultimately creates what are called "the higher mental functions." The invention of writing has profoundly affected cultural evolution and the psychic life of individuals. Apart from the external, or public, use of language, the more personal, or egocentric, use of symbols contributes to the development of personality and enriches inner life (for example, in fantasy). Language has a structure, and it is a group, or social, product. It is therefore plausible and expected that the thinking activities of persons, permeated as they are by the influence of language, will be influenced by its structure and by the social environment that nurtures it. This is seen not only in daydreams, but in fantasies, and perhaps in dreams and jokes as well. The thinking and reasoning of individuals reflect the nature of their group associations and are generally oriented toward them. Within various universes of discourse the realities of human experience are expressed in a variety of ways.

References

1. Bernstein, B., "Elaborated and Restricted Codes: Their Social Origins and Some Consequences," in J. Gumperz and D. Hymes (eds.), "The Ethnography of Communication," *American Anthropologist*, vol. 66, no. 2 (1964), pp. 55–69.
2. Bleuler, E., "Autistic Thinking," *American Journal of Insanity*, vol. 69 (1913), pp. 55–69.
3. Bullins, Ed, "Profiles: Dramatist," *The New Yorker*, June 16, 1973, p. 62.
4. Burke, Kenneth, *Permanence and Change*. New York: New Republic Press, 1936.
5. Bynner, W., *The Jade Mountain*. New York: Knopf, 1929.
6. Carroll, John, and J. B. Casagrande, "The Function of Language Classifications in Behavior," in E. Maccoby et al. (eds.), *Readings in Social Psychology*, 3d ed. New York: Holt, Rinehart and Winston, 1958, pp. 18–31.

7. Chomsky, N., *Language and the Mind*. New York: Harcourt Brace Jovanovich, 1968.

8. Cipolla, C., *Literacy and Development in the West*. Baltimore: Penguin Books, 1969.

9. Dewey, John, *Art as Experience*. New York: Minton, Balch and Company, 1934.

10. ———, *Logic: The Theory of Inquiry*. New York: Holt, Rinehart and Winston, 1938.

11. ———, and A. F. Bentley, *Knowing and the Known*. Beacon, N.Y.: Beacon House, 1949.

12. Faris, Robert E. L., *Social Psychology*. New York: Ronald Press, 1952.

13. Fishman, J., "A Systematization of the Whorfian Hypothesis," *Behavioral Science*, vol. 5 (1950), pp. 323–39.

14. Frake, Charles, "Cultural Ecology and Ethnology," *American Anthropologist*, vol. 64 (1962), pp. 53–59.

15. French, T., "Dreams and Rational Behavior," in F. Alexander and H. Ross (eds.), *Dynamic Psychiatry*. Chicago: University of Chicago Press, 1952, pp. 35–39.

16. Freud, Sigmund, *New Introductory Lectures on Psychoanalysis*. New York: W. W. Norton, 1933.

17. Goody, J., and I. Watt, "The Consequences of Literacy," in Pier P. Giglioli (ed.), *Language and Social Context*. Baltimore: Penguin Books, 1972, pp. 311–57.

18. Hall, C. S., "A Cognitive Theory of Dream Symbols," *Journal of General Psychology*, vol. 48 (1953), pp. 169–86.

19. Hindemith, Paul, *A Composer's World*. Garden City, N.Y.: Doubleday, 1961.

20. Hoijer, H. (ed.), *Language in Culture*. Chicago: University of Chicago Press, 1954.

21. ———, "The Relation of Language to Culture," in A. Kroeber (ed.), *Anthropology Today*. Chicago: University of Chicago Press, 1954, pp. 554–73.

22. Hymes, D., "Directions in Ethnolinguistic Theory," in A. K. Romney and R. G. D'Andrade (eds.), "Transcultural Studies in Cognition," *American Anthropologist*, vol. 66 (1964), pp. 6–56.

23. Judd, C. H., *Educational Psychology*. Boston: Houghton Mifflin, 1939.

24. Kluckhohn, C., and D. Leighton, *The Navaho*. Cambridge, Mass.: Harvard University Press, 1946.

25. Langer, S. K., *Philosophy in a New Key*. Baltimore: Penguin Books, 1948.

26. Luria, A. R., and F. Yudovich, *Speech and the Development of Mental Processes in the Child: An Experimental Investigation*. London: Staples Press, 1959.

27. Masson-Oursel, P., *Comparative Philosophy*. New York: Harcourt Brace Jovanovich, 1926.

28. Merton, R. K., "Sociology of Knowledge," in G. D. Gurvitch and W. E. Moore (eds.), *Twentieth-Century Sociology*. New York: Philosophical Library, 1945.

29. Mills, C. W., "Language, Logic, and Culture," *American Sociological Review*, vol. 4 (1939), pp. 670–80.

30. Rapaport, D., *The Organization and Pathology of Thought*. New York: Columbia University Press, 1951.

31. Sapir, E., "The Status of Linguistics as a Science," in D. G. Mandelbaum (ed.), *Selected Writings in Language, Culture, and Personality*. Berkeley: University of California Press, 1949.

32. ———, "Time Perspective in Aboriginal American Culture: A Study in

Method," in D. G. Mandelbaum (ed.), *Selected Writings in Language, Culture, and Personality*. Berkeley: University of California Press, 1949.

33. Scheerer, M., "Cognitive Theory," in G. Lindzey (ed.), *Handbook of Social Psychology*. Reading, Mass.: Addison-Wesley, 1954, pp. 41–42.

34. Singer, Jerome L., *The Inner World of Daydreaming*. New York: Harper & Row, 1975.

35. Strauss, Anselm L., *The Contexts of Social Mobility*. Chicago: Aldine, 1971.

36. ———, *Mirrors and Masks*. San Francisco: Sociology Press, 1969.

37. Sullivan, H. S., *The Interpersonal Theory of Psychiatry*. New York: W. W. Norton, 1953.

38. *New York Times*, February 9, 1948, pp. 1, 3.

39. Vinacke, W. E., *The Psychology of Thinking*. New York: McGraw-Hill, 1953.

40. Vygotsky, L., *Thought and Language*, ed. and trans. by Eugenia Haufmann and Gertrude Vakar. Cambridge, Mass.: M.I.T. Press, 1962.

41. ———, "Thought and Speech," *Psychiatry*, vol. 2 (1939), pp. 29–52.

42. ———, and A. R. Luria, "The Fate and Function of Egocentric Speech," *Proceedings and Papers*, Ninth International Congress of Psychology, Princeton, N.J.: Princeton University Press, 1930, pp. 464–65.

43. Werkmeister, W. H., *A Philosophy of Science*. New York: Harper & Row, 1940.

44. Werner, H., and B. Kaplan, *Symbol Formation: An Organismic-Developmental Approach to Language and Expression of Thought*. New York: Wiley, 1963.

45. Whorf, B. L., *Language, Thought, and Reality*, ed. by J. B. Carroll. Cambridge, Mass.: M.I.T. Press, 1956.

46. Wolfenstein, Martha, *Children's Humor*. Glencoe, Ill.: The Free Press, 1954.

Selected Readings

CHOMSKY, N., *Language and the Mind*. New York: Harcourt Brace Jovanovich, 1968.
A presentation, by an eminent student of linguistics, of a controversial view of the relation between thought and language.

GOODY, J., AND I. WATT, "The Consequences of Literacy," in Pier P. Giglioli (ed.), *Language and Social Context*. Baltimore: Penguin Books, 1972, pp. 311–57.
A highly illuminating consideration of the significance of literacy and of the contrast between the oral and literate traditions. Special attention is given to the possible connections among the invention and diffusion of the modern phonetic alphabet, the spread of literacy, and the flowering of ancient Greek civilization.

MILLS, C. W., "Language, Logic, and Culture," *American Sociological Review*, vol. 4 (1939), pp. 670–80.
A succinct and important statement by a well-known American sociologist that makes the same point we have made—that human thought is decisively influenced by the language and perspectives of social groups.

VYGOTSKY, L., *Thought and Language*, ed. and trans. by Eugenia Haufmann and Gertrude Vakar. Cambridge, Mass.: M.I.T. Press, 1962.
A brief but impressive statement by an influential Soviet psychologist on the nature of language and thought and their interrelationship, along with critical comments on the theories of Piaget.

chapter 6

Perception, Memory, and Planning

I*n this* chapter we shall explore the language and group foundations of human perception, memory, and planning. The temporal foundations of human action—as seen in those behaviors that are directed to the past, the present, and the future—will be examined. In this context we shall consider some of the so-called higher mental processes. It is pertinent to remind the reader of Pavlov's distinction between the first and second signal systems which we have already touched upon in Chapter 4. We noted that sensory input or stimulation is transmitted to the brain in the form of "messages" that are coded in terms of impulse frequency. These messages serve a representational function when they are processed in the central nervous system so as to orient the organism within its environment. In other words, sensory input from seeing, touching, hearing, tasting, and smelling provides both human and nonhuman organisms with *signs*, or *cues*, representing the environments of these organisms. This is what Pavlov called the first signal system.

At the neurological level, what Pavlov referred to as the second signal system consists of the new or additional neural circuits established in the central nervous system when human beings acquire language. These new neural patterns are established largely within the left, or dominant, hemisphere of the brain in those areas in which the most complex and

Social Structure and the Self

least understood regulatory and integrative processes linked with voluntary behavior and consciousness are believed to take place. The processes involved are viewed as second-order signs or symbols, since they represent the lower-order sign processes involved in simple sensory experience. Since these language-derived sign processes of the second signal system merge with, absorb, or dominate many of the lower-order neural patterns, and since the second signal system is social in nature and origin, the existence of the latter has the effect of making many of the psychological activities of human beings subject to social influences transmitted symbolically in a communication or interactional process. The phenomenon of hypnotism is a striking example of this point. It should be noted, however, that many internal neural functions of a mechanical, unconscious, and involuntary sort remain beyond the reach of social and voluntary control.

The internal symbolic activities considered in this chapter are only some of those that might be examined and, in other parts of this book, we have dealt with the other consequences that follow from the internalization of language. *Memory, perception,* and *planning* are conveniently grouped together because they are responses to the past, present, and future. When one considers how these three functions differ in human and nonhuman subjects, the enormous importance of language internalization should become evident.

Perception and memory, considered here as symbolic activities, have often been viewed as though they were mechanical, while planning as such is usually not thought of as a separate activity. Thus, visual perception has been treated as though it were a process of photographing, and the human visual apparatus has been treated as though it were a camera. What is ignored by this view is that the past experiences of the organism influence its perceptions and that cameras do not have experiences, desires, aspirations, or attitudes. The same mechanical approach has been used in an effort to reduce human emotions to purely physiological functions located in the viscera or in some part of the brain. Memory has been treated in a similar manner; it has been conceived of as a mechanical record akin to the "memory" attributed by some to electronic calculating machines. Although this has shed light on some aspects of remembering, it has not clarified other important aspects.

Social Patterning of Perception

The term *perception* refers to the ways in which organisms respond to the stimuli picked up by their sense organs. It used to be thought of as something analogous to such mechanical processes as photographing an

SELECTIVITY IN PERCEPTION

object or recording sound on a record. That analogy to a mechanical sequence is inadequate, however, since it ignores the fact that perception is influenced by interests, needs, and past experiences. The analogy also does not take into account the fact that the total volume of physical stimuli reaching us both from sources within our body and in the environment is so great that most of them obviously must be ignored and therefore can neither function as cues nor enter significantly into the determination of behavior. Physical illness sometimes reminds us painfully of some of the multitudinous processes that normally go on inside of us without our being aware of them. The hypochondriac is the illustration par excellence of preoccupation with stimuli originating in bodily processes. Ordinary healthful living requires that we be highly selective in the stimuli to which we pay attention and, at the same time, that whole ranges of stimuli be consigned to the background and ignored. We shall return to this point.

Response to environmental cues constitutes the reality orientation of the organism. The data which are supplied by the sense organs and the receptor nerves are interpreted and acted upon as signs of the nature, location, size, movement, and quality of objects and occurrences. The degree and nature of inner elaboration or "interpretation" of experience varies among species and among individuals. It reaches its peak in human beings in whom the elaboration may be very great, and in whom it assumes a symbolic form. Individuals' reports of what they perceive, and their ideas of what they see or hear, include matters of inference, interpretation, and judgment—in short they do not discriminate between what may be called direct perception, or physical stimulus, and the meaningful elaboration of the perception that occurs when it is classified, named, analyzed, and judged (3:31):

> On the face of it, to perceive anything is one of the simplest and most immediate, as it is one of the most fundamental, of all human cognitive reactions. Yet . . . it is exceedingly complex. . . . Inextricably mingled with it are imagining, valuing, and the beginnings of judgment.

This point is demonstrated graphically in a study by W. Hudson. (30) He showed some pictures to white and African experimental subjects; some were attending school and others had not been to school. His pictures were constructed so that they could be seen self-evidently as either two- or three-dimensional. For the most part, the subjects who were attending school saw the picture as three-dimensional, while the others saw the pictures as two-dimensional. Some degree of education apparently is a necessary condition for seeing pictures in three dimensions.

It is easy to assume that some simple perceptions are much less complex than they are. Studies of congenitally blind people whose sight has been restored through surgery indicate that considerable learning is required before color and simple geometric figures can be distinguished visually. M. Von Senden (56:31–32) reports one patient who, after thirteen days of training in discriminating a triangle from a square:

> could not report their form without counting corners one after another . . . and yet it seems the recognition process was beginning already to be automatic so that some day the judgment "square" would be given with simple vision, which would then easily lead to the belief that form was always simultaneously given.

Similar results have been obtained by A. Riesen (45:107–08) with chimpanzees that were reared in darkness. D. Hebb also reports parallel findings for rats. (26) Data of this kind suggest that learning to perceive involves interpretation of physical stimuli. Meanings are not inherent in the latter, but must grow out of experience.

Stimuli viewed as purely physical events are presented to us by our environment and are not changed in any way by being named, classified, or interpreted. Stimuli become cues, however, when attention is paid to them or when they are responded to. The individual learns to select and interpret the stimuli relevant to his or her actions and interests and to ignore others or take them for granted. Children at first pay attention only to the grosser aspects of physical stimulation; their perceptions are undifferentiated. For adults, on the other hand, J. Gibson has said (21:120–38):

> The experience aroused by any given array of stimulation is only a small fraction of the potential experiences which might be aroused by it. The number of discriminations which are theoretically possible at any one time is enormous, but only a few are realized. . . . His [the adult's] momentary perception is differentiated, but schematic. What he specifies and distinguishes are only the objects and properties which support his momentary course of action or to which, as we say, he pays attention.

It is easy, but fallacious, to conceive of perception as a single, passive act, as if an organism looks out upon an environment and receives impressions of it through the sense organs. This *copy conception* was attacked by Dewey (13, 14) and others who stressed that perceiving is part of a larger organization of activity. Some persons do sit idly and allow stimuli to flow in upon them, but usually they are engaged in some sort of activity. What is noted and how it is interpreted in turn affect the course of action. As the action enters new phases, new kinds of cues are sought and evaluated. Lines of activity are typically intermittent and extend over periods of time, as, for example, when an individual is engaged in buying a house, planning for a vacation, or making a garden. When a given line of behavior is temporarily suspended, we have time to ruminate over the past and to anticipate the future. Both past and future may influence our perceptions when we resume the earlier activity. Perceiving as part of the larger pattern of activity is necessarily focused toward the future, even though it occurs in the present. As Ittelson and Cantril, following Dewey's general position, say (31:27):

> Perception certainly seems to be of the world as it is right now, or, perhaps, as it was a few minutes ago. Indeed, the definition of perception frequently appears in psychology texts as "the awareness of immediately present objects." . . . [But] While present and past are involved in the perceptual process, the chief time-orientation in perceiving is toward the future. The primary function of perception . . . is prediction of the future.

The facts are that perception is selective; that motivation and needs sensitize one to specific stimuli or sometimes lead to distorted perception; that stimuli are often misinterpreted; and that perceptions of the same situation may vary from individual to individual. But these facts should not cause one to ignore the further fact that reality sets limits to perception. People who persistently see nonexistent objects like pink elephants or who hear voices when no one is speaking are out of touch with reality; they are hallucinating. Perception is, therefore, not arbitrary, but is limited by what is actually present in the environment. None of us can live in the real world if we see only what suits us.

Learning to perceive causes behavior to become more discriminating, more flexible, with respect to environmental reality. It does not, however, free behavior from reality. Admittedly, the complications introduced into the perceptual processes when they become linked with high-order conceptualizations and symbolic systems (such as one's conceptions of self) increase the probabilities of distortion and error. The perceptions of the lower animal or the child are probably less subject to error than those of the sophisticated adult.

Selectivity of perception is especially marked in social interaction in which the person's self-esteem is at stake. Psychiatrists and clinical psychologists have long noted the human tendency to ignore or misperceive things that would be damaging to their egos if correctly noted. The psychiatrist H. S. Sullivan coined the expression *selective inattention* for this process in which "we fail to recognize the actual import of a good many things which we see, hear, think, do, and say, not because there is anything the matter with our zones of interaction with others, but because the process of inferential analysis is opposed by the self system." (53:374) Some experimental studies by psychologists have shown how perceptions are distorted because of the perceiver's needs and motives; and this work supports, if it does not greatly amplify, the observations of psychiatrists and other trained observers. Some years ago Henry Triandis, in summarizing work on "cultural influences on perception," suggested that members of given societies may see object A rather than object B, when presented with both, "because of (1) the greater meaning of A than B . . . ; (2) the higher frequency of occurrence of A relative to B; and (3) the more pleasant associations with A than B." Therefore, he

Selective inattention: who sees this office as disorganized? (*Uzzle/Magnum*)

concludes, "cultural experience may enhance the availability of a category and depress another." (54:13)

The same point is supported by research on cross-cultural differences pertaining to perception of optical illusions. Thus, M. Segall and his associates studied 1878 subjects from fourteen non-European cultures and from three European cultures. The experimenters used versions of the Muller-Lyer, The Sander Parallelogram, and the Horizontal–Vertical illusion. Their "results strongly support the hypothesis that the perception of space involves, to an important extent, the acquisition of habits of perceptual inference." (50:14) For instance, Europeans experience the first two illusions much more sharply than do non-Europeans, but experience the Horizontal-Vertical illusion less sharply.

Social or, as Triandis says, cultural influences affect perception in a very marked way. Laymen, of course, have noticed this phenomenon. The poet Carl Sandburg (48) made the point effectively in a poem entitled "Elephants Are Different to Different People," as shown in the excerpt below: **SOCIAL FACTORS IN PERCEPTION**

> Wilson and Pilcer and Snack stood before the zoo elephant. Wilson said, "What is its name? Is it from Asia or Africa: Who feeds it? Is it a he or a she? How old is it? Do they have twins? How much does it cost to feed? How much does it weigh? If it dies how much will another one cost? If it dies what will they use the bones, the fat, and the hide for? What use is it besides to look at?"

Pilcer didn't have any questions; he was murmuring to himself, "It's a house by itself, walls and windows, the ears came from tall cornfields, by God; the architect of those legs was a workman, by God; he stands like a bridge out across deep water; the face is sad and the eyes are kind; I know elephants are good to babies."

Snack looked up and down and at last said to himself, "He's a tough son-of-a-gun outside and I'll bet he's got a strong heart. I'll bet he's strong as a copper-riveted boiler inside. . . ."

Three men saw the elephant three ways. . . .

One might object that each man saw the same elephant but interpreted it differently; but interpretation is involved in all acts of perception.

A real-estate broker looking at a house is not likely to observe the same details as will an artist, a fire-insurance agent, or an architect. When viewing a landscape, artists will perceive details and relationships of line, space, light, and color that escape ordinary "seeing." What is selected and emphasized in perceiving is connected with the observer's perspective, with his or her value system, interests, needs, and the like. Perception, clearly, is dependent upon previous experience, interests, and concern. These in turn are related to such factors as the perceiver's occupation, class, and age—in short, to his or her social background.

PERCEPTUAL DISCRIMINATIONS VARY FROM GROUP TO GROUP. Group influences on perception are well illustrated by an experiment devised by James Bagby to show possible differences in perceptions between Mexicans and Americans. His subjects were asked to look at ten pairs of slides through a stereoscope. On one side of each slide Bagby used pictures showing, for instance, a matador, a dark-haired girl, or a peon; on the other side he used similar objects, but ones familiar to most Americans: a baseball player, a blond girl, and a farmer. The pictures were also similar in contour, texture, and distribution of light and shadow. In general, both the Mexicans and the Americans saw objects that were familiar to them. (2)

Differences of background and point of view may also lead to the discrimination of differences in skin color. In our Southern states, people customarily make a very fine distinction between who is "white" and who is "black"; hence, most Southerners of either "race" are very conscious of skin color. Yet in other parts of the world (such as the Arab countries) where there is a great variety of skin color, people seem to be quite color blind to such differences. Arabs probably know that such differences exist, but as these do not have the social significance for them that they have for us, Arabs fail to observe them closely or to see them as we do. Similarly, people have long noticed that after associating with black colleagues they see them as individuals and actually fail to notice skin color, although they may notice each individual's speech or mannerisms or clothes.

Social Structure and the Self

To continue this theme of perception and color, an anthropologist (35) has noted concerning the color perceptions of natives of New Guinea that "their color classifications are so different that they see yellow, olive-green, blue-green, gray, and lavender as variations of one color." More recent research with Zuni and Navaho subjects has demonstrated that they use different categories for color than do English-speaking people. (28:92–105).

One study reports probability distributions for the comparative color responses plotted against a continuum of colors. In a color range marked by the numbers twenty-five to forty, the probability that English-speaking people will say "green" is extremely high, and their reaction times are very short. The Navaho, however, have four terms that refer to this color range—the terms correspond to our brown-green, blue-green, green-yellow, and purple-green—and their reaction times are much longer in this "green" range than in other ranges on the complete color continuum. (36) It is striking that bilingual Navahos use color categories that differ from those used by Navahos who speak no English. S. Ervin, who studied this, concluded that (16:240):

> In the domain where one language had a single high probability name and the other had none, the high probability term and its translation dominated in bilinguals in both languages. Where the two languages differed in the boundary between two categories, both of which have translational terms, the bilingual's dominant language determined his boundary in both languages. Where a category in one language covered the domain of two categories in the other language, the boundary point in the latter language was variable and reflected the degree of learning in that language.

PERCEPTUAL INTERFERENCES.   Preoccupation with a given point of view or perspective often completely prevents a person from perceiving facts or relationships that are relevant to some other problem or point of view. Darwin once remarked that when he was a young man he walked over a plot of ground searching for evidence to prove a geological theory. Many years later while idly retracing his steps he saw details that had earlier escaped him completely because at that time he had been looking for something else. Darwin commented that the previously unobserved objects were now no less plain to his eye than the ravages of a fire would have been. This sort of experience is frequent in scientific work. Similarly, Mark Twain wrote that after he had become a Mississippi River pilot he rarely perceived the beauties of the river and its banks—he then saw them only in terms of snags, dangerous or favorable currents, proper or improper distances from shore, and the like.

A study making the same point was published by the German psychologist M. Zillig. (60:206–07) She had several popular and several unpopular students perform calisthenic exercises before a class. The popular students had been instructed to make mistakes, and the unpopular students had been trained so as to make no mistakes. At the end of the exercises the audience was asked to vote on which group had done the exercises correctly. The vote was in favor of the popular pupils. After checking with the children through conversation, the investigator concluded that the voting reflected differences that were actually seen.

NONVISUAL PERCEPTIONS.   Other forms of perceiving (hearing, for example) are also influenced by social factors. Differences in musical taste among groups and among individuals with different social backgrounds are striking. Thus, anthropologist H. Roberts notes (46:95):

> My own experience with primitive peoples—Negro, Polynesian, Indian—has shown that it would be extremely unlikely that minute tone differences would . . . be heard, not because of any inherent inability, for in directions in which their interest and welfare lie the hearing of such people is as acute as any, but because their attention has never been directed toward fine distinctions in scale tones, except sporadically in the attempt to copy an admired instrument exactly. They hear delicate nuances of intonation in speech, especially where tone in language has become important to meaning through certain trends of development. They distinguish minute forest sounds where differences convey so much that is vital to them. . . . But these are all in the line of specially developed interests.

However, we do not have to go so far afield. The music of numerous composers, including Mozart and Beethoven, was harshly judged when first played but has been appreciated by later generations who apparently hear very different things in the music. As Triandis remarks (54:16), "On the question of aesthetic judgment involving visual or auditory materials, there is little doubt that culture is a most powerful determinant. . . ."

The point can be brought home in another way. Westerners listening to Balinese music may be enchanted by it, but they can scarcely hear its more subtle nuances without special training. Repeated listening, although it will probably result in their "hearing more," will hardly allow them to bridge the gap between Balinese and Western culture and tastes. Of course, speaking of social rather than cultural differences, a musically educated American will hear things in the music of a modern composer like Stockhausen that will be missed by one who is not musically educated or is accustomed to hearing only older music.

Differences in food tastes are also instances of the social determination of nonvisual perception as illustrated by the food preferences of the cannibal, the Moslem aversion to pork, or the American aversion to roasted caterpillars. It is significant that as the generations succeed each other—becoming somewhat different social beings—eating habits also change accordingly. Today Americans of every ethnic background are eating various kinds of food—from sushi to fish and chips—formerly associated exclusively with certain nationalities.

As for touch—another nonvisual form of perception—a literature of social criticism has contended that, because of their Puritan heritage, Americans have an undeveloped sense of touch, that they are afraid of their bodies. Explicit programs and directives are offered to correct this situation and to help people get rid of the inhibitions they are said to have concerning bodily pleasures and communication with others through touch. This movement is part of a larger movement that emphasizes ideological criticism of bureaucratic, affluent American ways of life and it is concerned with emergent new conceptions of community, intimacy, and communal life.

Perception and Language

VERBAL SYMBOLS ORGANIZE PERCEPTIONS.   We have noted that human beings act toward objects in the light of their classification of them. Categorizing is an integral part of most acts of human (as opposed to animal and infant) perception. An object is perceived characteristically, not as an isolated item but as a member of some class. Actually, we see class representatives, not bare and unnamed isolated objects. Glance around the room, making note of what you "see." Do you not see class representatives such as walls, books, pencil, chair, and flowers? Linguistic classification is not external or incidental to such perceiving but is an integral part of it. What we term "perceiving" involves linguistic distinctions, for objects cannot be perceived as class members unless the observer's language has already designated these classes or enables him or her to invent new categories. As J. Gibson says (21:136):

> The factor which makes for the socializing of perception in human organisms, we may suspect, is the process of word-making. Presumably, since only human beings make words, only human beings show the phenomenon of a cultural stereotyping of their percepts. . . . The phenomenal world of a language community is partly determined by its language, that is, people see what they have words for. A promising explanation of this fact is that the entities of stimulation that get identified, the variables that get discriminated and abstracted, are very much determined by the verbal responses which accompany perceptual and motor activity. Words tend to fix or freeze the objects and qualities which become differentiated out of the stimulus flux; words tend to determine a man's repertory of perceptions. . . . Since people must reach a kind of consensus of mind-reactions in order to communicate, they tend to reach a consensus of individual perceptions.

The linguistic character of even rather simple adult perception is shown in a study by L. Carmichael. (10) Visual outline drawings were presented to subjects, and as the drawing was shown, a word characterizing it was spoken by the investigator. Thus ☼ was called either

"sun" or "ship's wheel." Reproduction of the outline drawing shortly afterward (from memory) varied according to the word spoken. Carmichael attributed this variation to certain processes initiated by the word that affected perception of the drawing.

F. Bartlett's (3) careful work indicates also how linguistic elements influence perception. Subjects briefly shown the figure ⊠ sometimes thought the rectangle was completely drawn in. In such a figure as ▭, naming was of great importance in helping to shape perception. Subjects looking at this figure who saw "picture frames" perceived an object that looked like ▭ or ▭. The figure ⚓ was called a "pickax" by one observer and reproduced with pointed prongs; another person called it a "turf cutter" and drew it with a rounded blade. Several persons called it an "anchor" and exaggerated the size of the ring on the top. Only one person correctly perceived the pointed blade; he had seen it as a prehistoric battle-ax. Bartlett notes that if a figure seemed odd, disconnected, or unfamiliar it was usually seen in terms of an analogy—that is, in terms of the identity of a known object. He concludes that "a great amount of what is said to be perceived is in fact inferred."

A commonsense maxim holds that, in general, "people see what they are looking for." This is not always true by any means, but the phrase indicates that verbal frames of reference organize perceptual responses. A person's perceiving is likely to follow along the lines of familiarities and expectations. The illustrations taken from the work of Bartlett and Carmichael demonstrate this very well, as does the existence of some types of "suggestion." Thus, when Binet (43:173) showed subjects "a series of lines of gradually increasing length, but with occasional 'catches' where the lines did not lengthen as expected . . . not one of his forty-five pupils completely escaped the suggestion of increase in length in all lines." This kind of suggestion can be accounted for very simply by supposing that Binet's subjects were *set* to see successively longer lines.

During World War II American flyers were taught to recognize various types of aircraft. Gibson describes the role of language in this process (21:129–30):

> Before training, the forty novel objects looked more or less alike. Americans
> did not confuse airplanes with birds as Fiji Islanders might have done, but

they confused them with one another; that is, the forty objects looked like only two or three different objects. After training, however, they all looked different. Correspondingly, at the outset the forty objects elicited only a few specific responses and at the end they aroused forty different responses. The responses, of course, were *names*. They were identifying reactions in the sense that there was only one reaction for one object. Similarly, before training a student could make a drawing which represented only a generalized airplane; after training he could make forty different drawings. Presumably he could visualize forty different shapes. Before training only a few properties or qualities of the objects could be observed, but in the end many properties could be seen. The evidence for this is that *adjectives* could be applied, and judgment of more or less could be made with respect to a given adjective. . . . The learning exhibited other interesting phenomena; for instance, the experiments on drawing silhouettes indicated that one kind of constant error was a stereotyping or caricaturing of the shape.

COMPLEX SOCIAL PERCEPTIONS.   If simple perception such as that studied by Carmichael and Bartlett involves naming, analogy, and inference, it may be assumed that more complex acts of perceiving will involve more complex uses of language. By way of illustration, let us consider what is involved when a teacher observes a student cheating on a quiz. Does the teacher actually "see" the cheating? In a literal sense this is impossible. All he or she can see is the student glancing at a neighbor's paper or looking about the room. The actions of the student appear furtive and guilty to the teacher in the examination setting because he or she attributes to the student certain motives or intentions. The teacher cannot see these motives or intentions, but if they are lacking, no cheating has taken place. Concepts of "fairness" and "breaking the rules" are also involved, as well as notions about what acts are taboo during a quiz period. Our most characteristic acts of perceiving occur on this moderately complex level. In order for such phenomena as embarrassment, irony, and humor to be perceived at all, a common background of social experiences among the participants is necessary.

We may illustrate the point further with a cross-cultural example. Among the Murngin, a primitive Australian tribe, respect is expressed by every man to his mother-in-law by strict avoidance, so that if the mother-in-law is seen coming down the path, both he and she must avert their eyes and turn aside. By this act the man is indicating his respect for her position. An American observer might perceive this act on at least three increasingly complicated levels. On one level the observer might see only a man and a middle-aged woman walking toward each other, then turning aside and not looking in each other's direction. The second level, assuming the observer knows only how the two persons are related to each other, would involve seeing the son-in-law and the mother-in-law avoiding each other and refraining from looking at each other. The observer would not know what was being expressed—shyness, guilt, hatred, mutual punishment, or fear. The third, and most complex, level would involve a comparatively thorough knowledge of Murngin family relationships, including recognition of the meaning of "avoidance for respect." In this instance the observer would "see" the son-in-law paying respect to his mother-in-law by respectfully "avoiding" her.

COMPLEX PERCEPTIONS AND CODABILITY.   It will be remembered that Solomon Islanders have a complex and detailed perception of coconuts, that the Eskimos make fine discriminatory classifications of snow, and that Arabs have many words for camel (including fifty that describe various stages of the pregnancy of camels). These fine discriminations, as we have remarked, make it possible for those who make those discriminations also to make the associated perceptual distinctions. It can be argued that without the linguistic distinctions, people can still make the same perceptual distinctions (for instance, Brown has argued that Americans distinguish as many kinds of snow as Eskimos). (8:455) But the Eskimos' categories have what has been termed *high codability*. High codability means that the classes of things to be talked about have established single names permitting the members of a language community to respond quickly and consistently from one situation to another, both to the names and the things. Such terms are especially useful in communicating perceptual distinctions, and probably in making them.

All this is consonant with materials we have already discussed showing the influence of differential language structures on thought. If a language virtually prescribes the indication of a physical feature (a large stomach, bald headedness, or medium stature) as does Nootka grammar whenever one speaks about these objects, then assuredly perceptual discriminations are affected. As Kluckhohn concluded in a summary of the literature on such matters: "The facts compel agreement that languages differ in their categories and as to what distinctions it is obligatory to make. . . ." (35:895–910)

Possibly, there may sometimes even be a linkage between social structure, norms, and specific categorical distinctions. For instance, the Pawnee Indians have an identical word for mother's brother's wife, ego's wife, and the sisters of ego's wife. Lounsbury's study showed that an adolescent Pawnee is first to have sexual intercourse with his mother's brother's wife; when he marries, he may have intercourse with his wife's sisters. "The designation of all these women by a single kinship term is consistent with these customs, though such correspondence between category content and social structure is itself arbitrary and may occur in one culture but not in another." (54:20) Social structural considerations may easily be seen to affect category content, hence perception in our society. We have only to recall the discussion of special languages to realize that categorical distinctions made by some groups are related not only to efficiency and pertinent interests but to the moral judgments they make about types of persons.

Studies of children support the view that perception is a learned way of responding in which verbal elements play a vital role. Because the child has not yet fully internalized the adult's symbols, so he or she does not perceive the world in an adult fashion. LIMITATIONS OF CHILDREN'S PERCEPTIONS

Luria's experiments with children under eight years of age support this view. (39) When presented with a rectangle of four blocks and asked whether they see odd or even, children reply "even." When presented with an incomplete rectangle of five blocks, the number is seen as "odd." But offer the child a complete rectangle consisting of nine blocks, and, unlike an adult, he or she will say "even." If then a tenth block is added to make an irregular figure, the child will say "odd." In this and other instances the child's seeing is not quite equivalent to adult seeing, because the child's language distinctions are different and fewer. Children see odd and even in terms of regular and irregular shapes rather than in terms of number.

Because they must learn distinctions made by adults, children must reach a certain age before they can perceive given events, relationships, and objects. Thus, infants do not recognize pictures as pictures until they are able to speak: seeing a "picture" involves seeing an object as a member of the category "picture." Similarly, because they lack the ap-

In counting the total number of squares in the figure at left, young children count the middle twice. In counting the total number of squares in the figure at the right, they make the same sort of error. (From A. Luria, "The Problem of the Cultural Behavior of the Child," *Journal of Genetic Psychology*, vol. no. 35 (1928).

propriate linguistic discriminations, young children are unable to perceive subtle relationships between adults, such as flirtation and irony. As they grow older and acquire additional and subtler linguistic meaning—as their categories become richer and more inclusive—youngsters' perceptions of such events become increasingly keen (and frequently embarrassing). There is little doubt that after the second or third year the child's perception, like that of the adult, is fused with and made possible by the utilization of language. We shall have more to say of children's perception later, in the discussion of socialization.

Human and Subhuman Perception

We have been maintaining that human perception characteristically depends upon seeing objects as class representatives and therefore depends upon language. A corollary of this is that animals do not perceive objects as members of named classes. Are there any data for this subsidiary contention, apart from the evidence that animals do not possess language systems?

Leaving the great apes aside for the moment, we may accurately say that the lower animals see objects as parts of concrete perceptual situations. As one author (5:38) notes: "in general [animals] react to a whole situation and often show a curious incapacity out of such a complex to isolate fragments that must be of great importance to them and are unable to recognize these fragments in other complexes." As an instance of this phenomenon we may note the curious perceptions of the cuttlefish, *Octopus vulgaris*. This animal immediately seizes and eats a crab that it perceives moving across the sandy bottom, but does not recognize a crab dangled on a string before its eyes. It may even attempt to remove the dangling crab by directing a jet of water upon it. When the same crab is allowed to crawl on the bottom, the octopus immediately seizes the prey. The octopus does not see the crab as a crab; it does not see it as an object detachable from its normal surroundings. (5:40)

One of the neatest sets of experiments bearing upon perception in lower animals was performed by Kirkman on black-headed gulls. Russell's descriptions of Kirkman's results is so pertinent to our discussion that it is worth quoting at length (47:182–83):

> If the bird is broody and the egg is in the nest and intact, it will be incubated. Many other objects, very roughly resembling the egg in size and smoothness of contour, but not necessarily in appearance, will, if placed in the nest, be treated as *functionally equivalent* to the egg, that is, they will be brooded. If a gull returning to its nest finds one of its eggs with a gaping hole in it, made by some marauding gull intent on sucking, it will forthwith complete the sucking of the contents, even though the embryo be far advanced. Generally speaking, for the gull an egg with a conspicuous hole in its side, whether its own egg or another's, whether inside its nest or

outside, is "something to be sucked"; it has food valence. An intact egg in another bird's nest has similar food valence.

If an egg, its own or another's, is placed close to the nest of a sitting bird, it will roll it back into the nest—it is "something to be retrieved." Later experiments by Kirkman demonstrate that the gull may also roll into the nest various egg-shaped or other-shaped objects, which are treated as functionally equivalent to the egg.

The egg or egg-equivalent however loses its "retrieving" valence if it is more than a certain distance from the nest. For every black-headed gull there is a maximum distance from the centre of the nest, be it one foot, one and one-half feet, or more, beyond which the egg or eggs put outside are completely ignored. They cease to exist for the bird. It may walk over by them several times in the course of an hour or more and yet be blind to them; they have become "just part of the landscape."

It is clear from these experiments that the valence of an egg changes according to the psychological situation; we may infer also that for the gull there is no such thing as "an egg," but merely something, which according to the circumstances is to be incubated, or retrieved, or eaten. The "egg" may be ignored entirely; it may pass out of the perceptual field, be treated as part of the neutral background. If the gull could form concepts and use words, it would have no concept of "an egg," and no word for it, but would have separate words for the egg-object in different situations. For us "an egg" is recognizable as such in all situations, it is a continuing object, retaining its identity; not so for the bird.

A predominantly situational kind of perception may be characteristic of the lower orders of animals, but what of those animals closest to humans on the evolutionary ladder? Some experimentation has been done upon the visual and auditory perceptions of chimpanzees. Their hearing is about like ours except that a higher range of tones is heard over and above the usual human range. It has also been established (59:101) that chimpanzees can discriminate and respond suitably "to differences in three dimensions of color stimuli: hue, saturation, and intensity; to differences in the shape, size, and surface appearance of solid objects; to distinguish, recognize, and otherwise react appropriately to plane figures and pictorially represented objects." (An ape has been known to extend his arm in greeting to a photograph of himself, thus suggesting recognition of a fellow ape.)

However, we should note carefully an experiment carried out by Yerkes which suggests that radical differences exist between simian and human perception. In each of four corners of a room Yerkes placed a small wooden box with a hinged lid. (59:104–06) The boxes were identical except in color: each was differently painted. An ape was allowed to watch his breakfast being placed "ostentatiously" in one of the boxes. The lid was then closed; the animal was led from the room for five minutes, then confronted again with the four boxes. The boxes may or may not have been shifted about in his absence. Yerkes states that the apes always chose the box that happened to be in the position of the box in which the breakfast had been placed. Such incorrect responses tended to persist, accompanied by "increasing disturbance," when the experiment was repeated. Yerkes reasoned that the animals chose the boxes purely by spatial location, so he varied the boxes according to pronounced differences of shape, size, color, and brightness. The chimpanzees still continued to choose by position instead of by physical characteristics of the boxes. Yerkes's conclusions dovetail neatly with the point we are trying to make (59:105–6):

> The experiment proved conclusively that apes naturally depend upon the general visual configuration of their surroundings instead of on some single aspect such as size, shape, or color.
>
> It may not be amiss to ask how the ape's behavior in this experiment may be translated into human experience. Confronted with the experimental problem which was presented to the animals, we might initially have difficulty because of casual or careless observation. But the chances are that a single error, if we really were highly motivated in the experiment, would stir us to careful examination of the situation and that in our second trial and thereafter we should recognize and identify the food-containing box, not by its location in the room or its surroundings, but instead by its distinguishing characteristic, color. The chances are that we should promptly come to respond in the experiment by depending on the verbal symbol, green for instance, appropriate to the box in which we had seen the food placed, for it is by the use of such symbolic processes that we are able to represent and hold in mind objects no longer present to our senses.
>
> It seems doubtful that our chimpanzee subjects at the outset even noticed the color of the food box. Why should they, since the definite location and spatial relations of the right box to the other features of the room might be expected to serve as cues for correct response? When, quite unbelievably, these customary cues proved to be inadequate or misleading, it obviously was next to impossible for the ape to discover the single dependable clue . . . and to hold it in mind. Perhaps, after all, the latter point is the critical one, for unless the significant feature of the food box is both attended to and held in mind during the interval of delay, correct response can occur only by chance.

Recently, apes have been trained to perceive in ways seemingly comparable to those of humans. When rewards are placed under red-painted objects, the animal learns eventually to look only under red objects, regardless of the shape, texture, and material composition of the object and regardless of the particular shade of red, or how the red is combined with the other colors on the object.

One cannot, however, conclude that apes are able to see as human beings do. The animals have to be carefully trained, step by step, before they can discriminate in such a fashion; they do not ordinarily do so. There is thus no reason to conclude that an ape can be said to possess the concept of "redness." The possession of the concept implies the ability to respond selectively to the quality of redness in new situations and combinations, and to relate it to the multitude of matters associated with redness—such as wavelengths, the spectrum, "red Russia," stop lights, warning signals, blood, and so forth.

PREJUDICE, BIAS, AND TASTE, AND THEIR BASIS IN "NAMING"

We have already suggested that people often do not perceive certain food combinations as "belonging together." Their perception of what belongs together depends, of course, upon processes of naming and labeling: "condiments" such as mustard and pickles do not go with "desserts" such as ice cream and cake. The same phenomenon of classifying objects underlies rejections and acceptances, taboos and preferences, in areas other than that of food taste.

Thus, during World War II, nude or seminude Melanesian women were often within sight of American fighting men. Yet, for the most part, the soldiers were not tempted to make sexual advances. As one veteran stated: "They didn't look attractive to us; they weren't 'white' enough in color or features. Now the Polynesian women!" During the same years, a Southern student expressed much the same view when she refused to believe it possible for a white person actually to fall in love with a black.

The field of artistic judgments and art criticism is an especially rich one in which to explore the linguistic categories underlying perceptions. The philosopher John Dewey (12:298–325) has complained that many critics approach paintings with prejudgments concerning what is "great" and "poor" art. These prejudgments are based upon standards derived from the study of painters already acknowledged to be "great." Consequently, most of the important artistic innovations are likely to be condemned as outrageous, and their creators as incompetent or even vulgar. The history of every art form is, in fact, replete with the blunders of critics. Dewey terms this kind of criticism *judicial criticism* because the painting is judged not in terms of the given artist's purposes but in terms of the purposes of some other artist or set of artists.

A discerning observer may note that many casual museum-goers judge pictures in precisely this fashion, although their perceptions are less sophisticated than those of professional critics. Naïve persons are unable to see much in the painting because their artistic categories are underdeveloped. Instead of looking for *plastic values* (such as color, light, space, brushwork, and other technical items), they focus their attention upon relatively irrelevant aspects of the picture, such as age, price, story, photographic likeness, and reputation of the artist. Consequently, abstract painting may be misconstrued because it does not represent, nor is it intended to represent, anything that is recognizable or real. Similarly, medieval painting may be disliked because it "always deals with religious subjects, which don't interest me in the least." We have seen one woman turn away in bewilderment and revulsion after looking in vain for the mandolin in an abstract Picasso painting labeled "Woman with a

Raw vision: Picasso's "Woman
with a Mandolin"
(*Charles Uht*)

Mandolin." The major point to be noted about biased perception is the
intimate fusion of inference and "raw vision." We see in biased fashion
because we enter the perceptual situation with preformed expectations.
To this extent we are all more or less biased, although one may be aware
of his or her own prejudices. Also, it is worth noting in passing a point
that we shall discuss more fully later, that our prejudices and biases are
immensely influenced by the specific communication networks in which
we participate. That participation brings particular objects to the forefront of our attention, and our judgments about those objects are formed
in frequent communication with significant others.

The Social Basis of Memory

Perceiving involves the response to or interpretation of signs in the form
of sensory stimulation resulting from the organism's contacts with the
external environment or arising within the organism. *Remembering* is a

response to signs of past experiences, which in some form or other are preserved within the organism. In the one case the sign bridges a spatial gap, in the other a temporal gap. Thus, remembering, like perceiving, is a complex form of sign behavior. Like perception, memory is profoundly influenced by the communicating we do in the groups to which we belong.

CONTENT OF MEMORY.   An illustration of how memory is affected by group membership is a story told about a number of Swazi chiefs from South Africa. The chiefs visited England, and after returning home discovered that their most vivid memory was that of a British policeman regulating traffic with uplifted hand. The vividness of this particular memory was related to the Swazi custom of greeting one another with the same gesture.

Bartlett (3), who has studied remembering among these people, writes that they have the reputation among their neighbors of possessing excellent memories. After testing the memories of several representative Swazi, he concluded that this reputation was unfounded; but he later discovered that Swazi memories connected with cattle and cattle raising were almost phenomenal. As Bartlett explains, cattle raising is a central concern of Swazi society. Mark Twain, writing of Mississippi River steamboat pilots of the early nineteenth century, notes a similar phenomenon. A pilot had to recall thousands of items about the river—its curves, banks, sandbars, currents, snags, and depths. "But if you asked that same man at noon what he had had for breakfast, it would be ten chances to one that he could not tell you." (55:100) Twain's comment pertains to occupational interests and their effect on remembering, while Bartlett's pertains to cultural influences. Another good instance of the latter is provided by a study carried out by Goodman. She used the same story with Japanese children and American middle-class urban children who were in the fifth and sixth grades, and compared their remembrances of the story with results reported by Nadel for Nupa and Yoruba (African) children. The following sentence was embedded in the story: "God will punish him." Fifty percent of the Nupa children recalled this sentence as did 25 percent of the Yoruba, and 17 percent of the Americans. Only 6 percent of the Japanese children, who were the least religious of the four groups, recalled the sentence. (54:14)

It is common knowledge that an individual's interests are a good key to what he or she will remember. If a woman is inclined to gossip, she is likely to remember gossip tidbits, although her memory for other items may be far from superlative. People who like poetry may be able to recite dozens of stanzas yet fail to remember algebraic proofs or the names of people whom they have met. Numerous small boys in the United States astound their elders with their ability to remember the batting averages of favorite baseball players. These same boys may be the despair of their teachers because of deficient memory in classroom work.

A series of studies has pointed clearly to the role of social factors in remembering. Zillig (34:219) presented subjects of both sexes with favorable and unfavorable statements about women. A week later the subjects were tested to see how many statements could be recalled. The women revealed a tendency to remember more of the favorable statements, the men to recall the unfavorable ones. Levine and Murphy (38) studied the memories of pro-Soviet and anti-Soviet subjects for pro-Soviet and anti-Soviet reading materials. They concluded that the forgetting or retaining of these materials is affected by the individual's attitude toward communism. Wood (58) asked subjects with favorable and unfavorable attitudes toward blacks to read an article describing differences between blacks and whites. The subjects were then asked to write abstracts of the article. They omitted and distorted items in accordance with their attitudes. When similarly biased subjects read and rewrote these abstracts, the omissions and distortions were even greater than in the first abstracting. In a later study, E. Jones and J. Aneshansel asked prosegregationist and antisegregationist students at Duke University to learn a series of antisegregationist statements. Each group was divided into half; then one half was told that the statements could well be used as counter-arguments for prosegregation, while the other half was merely asked to read the statements. The results showed that "prosegregationists learn the statements *better* . . . when a subsequent debate is anticipated"; otherwise, the antisegregationists learned better. (32) Edwards (15) concluded that his subjects' political attitudes were linked with their varying degrees of recognition of items covered in a previously presented speech on the New Deal.

Probably most persons could point to instances in their own lives where certain vivid memories were linked with interest and attitude. The studies cited above demonstrate that even run-of-the-mill memories are dependent upon perspective and interest. As our examples and the various studies cited above show, perspective and interest are not merely individual matters, but are much affected by group membership and the kinds of communication that flow among the members. The circumstances involved in those situations where one's self is transformed will also be remembered. (See Chapter 12.)

Memory in Lower Animals

Acts of remembering are linked with social backgrounds and are intimately related to human utilization of symbols. Animals do remember, but theirs is a relatively primitive level of performance. The deficiencies of their memories, from the human point of view, may be pointed up by a series of experiments.

Suppose that a banana is buried in the ground before the eyes of a chimpanzee, and then the animal is led away to bed. The next morning when he is taken back to the yard he will remember the location of the buried banana. Now let us contrast this successful performance with a less successful one. A chimpanzee is taught to expect food in a box standing to the left of a similar box when a red light is glowing. When a green light is glowing, the food is in the other box. If the red light is turned on and then switched off and the chimpanzee is prevented from going to the box at once, he loses his ability to select the correct one (the one with the food). A delay of very short duration, perhaps a minute or two, has this effect.

We can find a ready explanation for his failure if we remember that the ape responds to natural signs but not to symbols. The ape can remember—we sometimes say "recognize"—the hiding place of the banana because he is in the presence of signs that stand for its burial; that is, he can see the spot in the yard where it was buried. Similarly, the ape can associate the box on the left with a glowing red light. But when the sign is absent, as when the light goes out, he cannot remember. If he could keep repeating to himself "red light, left box, red light, left box" then he could remember correctly in the absence of the light.

Human beings do this constantly, as anyone who takes the trouble to analyze the experience of following directions will soon realize. Humans do not even have to keep repeating the symbols unless the directions are fairly complicated. They would not in a delayed-response experiment have to keep saying to themselves "red light, left box." Comparative psychologists have discovered that the various animal species can remember for varying lengths of time in the absence of signs, but no animal except humans can remember for more than a few minutes. Humans can remember for years, provided that they have the requisite symbols and are motivated to remember. This is explained by humans' possession and use of language forms.

We have already seen in our earlier discussion of levels of behavior that even the lowest organisms have memories of a sort. The one-celled animal that becomes conditioned to light or warmth, the bee that finds its way back to the hive, the dog that responds correctly to his master's commands and signals—all these animals are furnishing examples of the operation of "memory." Another memory process of a relatively low order that is found in both humans and lower animals is the *kinesthetic,* or body, memory involved in remembering a bodily skill long after one has ceased to practice it. It would be as foolish to deny memory in the lower animals as it would be to deny that human memory is of an immensely higher order. Some feats of memory by animals seem remarkable—the dog that recognizes his absent master after five years, the cat that finds its way home from some miles away—but they are in no way dependent on language symbols. More remarkable yet are the annual bird migrations over thousands of miles; but even these, however impressive they may seem to us as acts of remembering, are not based on some humanlike language. Biologists are still puzzled as to how most of those migrations are carried out. Their puzzlement and their attempts to discover the genuine mechanisms of what seems like marvelous memory, human style, are eloquent testimony that subhuman remembering, as indicated earlier, actually operates on a different level.

Human Remembering as a Symbolic Process

REMEMBERING DEPENDS UPON CATEGORIZATION.   Humans without language would be, like the animals, tied down to concrete situations. They would have no conceptions either of history or of a personal past. Upon reflection, it becomes clear that much of our remembering revolves around memorable events, holidays, and dates. We cast back "in our memories" to last summer, to last Friday, to the weekend before last, to the day we entered college, or to our sixteenth birthday. We often recollect by means of such notational devices. If we are asked where we spent last Thanksgiving and what we did, the task of recalling is made relatively easy. If, on the other hand, we are asked what we did last November 6 (unless that is some memorable date, such as a birthday), recollection is likely to be either weak or totally absent.

To hear a melody and recognize vaguely that one has heard it somewhere does not perhaps clearly depend upon language. However, to say to oneself, "How does the first movement of Beethoven's Fifth Symphony go?" and then by an act of "concentration" to call up themes from that movement, is clearly dependent upon a linguistic framework. Music is so closely linked with language that attention could not be kept focused upon that symphony and that movement if the linguistic framework were missing. Similarly, if one asks, "What is the color of my house back home?" it is by virtue of language that one can call up that house and name its color. Without language categories, such an act of remembrance would be impossible. Again, we are asked to meet a friend for lunch at twelve o'clock in such and such a restaurant, and at a quarter of twelve we remember our engagement. Could we have remembered without the aid of the appropriate names—time categories—which we verbalize to ourselves, perhaps repeatedly, or which we actually write down on a memo pad? Moreover, how would we remember the past or keep appointments in the future without our systems of time notation?

The psychology of legal testimony supplies an interesting instance of the organization of memory around verbal plans or labels. People may erroneously remember details as having happened, provided that the details fit into a frame of reference. An instance of this is provided by early litigations over patents on the telephone (33:354):

> Certain people in a little town . . . gave at a second court-hearing testimony totally different from that which they had given several years earlier at the first hearing. The first testimony was vague and uncertain. In the interval between the two hearings the major subject of discussion in the town had been the apparatus in question. At the second court hearing the people recounted as fully established facts incidents which had apparently been generated by their discussions.

Studies of distortion in the transmission of rumors show the same sort of inaccurate remembering. As it is passed from one person to another, the content of the rumor undergoes alteration, according to how the transmitting person hears and remembers the rumor—both activities depending upon the person's frame of reference. (1)

Not only does society provide the linguistic and other devices used by the individual in registering an event, recalling, identifying, and placing it, but human memory has other important social dimensions as well. French psychologists and sociologists, particularly, have elaborated the idea that the things people remember form interlaced and mutually reinforcing systems organized around group situations. Thus, Halbwachs (24) noted that the student's memory of a given professor, and the course he or she took with him, is different from the professor's recollection of the student and the course. The student's memory is generally much more precise, Halbwachs deduces, because his or her experiences are part of a unique group situation shared with others. Professors, on the other hand, experience each class and the individuals in it primarily as one of a series of similar situations occurring in their professional activity. They have met successive classes in the same room, or in very similar rooms; class follows class, and, as the professors have no special group framework for each of them, they retain only the haziest ideas of what they did, what happened, who was present in any of the classes, or in which buildings and rooms they were held.

Most of our memories, Halbwachs observes, are organized in this way within a framework provided by the group to which we now belong and by those to which we have belonged. When we are within a given group (for example, our families) over a period of time, the members talk about past experiences and keep them fresh in our minds. Familiar faces and old haunts become linked with memories of past events. When we leave the group for a long time or permanently, the memories fade along with the faces, places, and names until only a bare skeleton or almost nothing remains. If we return after many years to the old group and the old environment the memories are revived, although they are not the same. As we remember and reconstruct the past, according to Halb-wachs, we project ourselves into a group framework and use it to revive and organize past experiences. This argument is used to explain the tendency for memories of experiences in temporary groups—for example, the kind formed on board an ocean liner—to shrink and disappear very quickly. This is especially true if no lasting relationships are established and if one does not again meet any of the persons involved. Human memory, Halbwachs contends, is therefore *collective*, or social, in nature. We are able to think of memory as individual only because we overlook or take for granted its group connections.

SOME EXPERIMENTAL EVIDENCE.   These examples of remembering are quite commonsense ones, although they represent valid evidence. Experimental investigations with both children and adults direct our attention to the linguistic foundation that underlies complicated acts of remembering as well. Bartlett, whose work we have already mentioned, has concluded that remembering is based upon initial acts of perceiving which in turn are notably affected by linguistic representations. He observes that memory is dependent upon *schemata;* that is, upon a system of labeling. (3) Munn, in a survey of research done upon memory in children (42), notes that the superiority of two-year-olds over one-year-olds depends at least in part upon linguistic factors; the memory of the older children is aided by their possession of names for colors and knowledge of letters, figures, and words.

A Soviet psychologist, Luria, after conducting a series of ingenious experiments upon children, also states that language is essential for the more complex adult forms of remembering. His investigations are so conclusive as to warrant including a digest of them here (39:497–98):

> A child who can hardly memorize five or six words of the series is asked to commit them to memory, with the aid of the pictures laid out on the table. Not one of the pictures actually reproduces the word in question, and the task can be performed only if the child connects in one structure the word with one of the pictures. Such mastering of association can be acquired, but by no means by all the children. Older children can learn to reproduce by this method, twenty-five to thirty words after one reading, while their natural memory could fix five or six at most. Moreover, the connecting links were established with extraordinary subtlety. Thus in order to remember the word "spade" the child chose a picture of chickens picking up grain "because they picked it just as the spade digs the earth"; for the word "theater" the child chose the picture of a crab on the seashore "because the crab looks at the pebbles in the sea, and they are just as pretty as a theater."
>
> In the process of play a child was given orally a series of ten figures to memorize; and asked to repeat them in the given order. The child found usually that he could not memorize the series. Then we gave him some material—paper, strings, chips, playing-blocks, pins, hailshot—and asked him

to use it for memorizing these ten figures. It was a question of his some-how utilizing the material to invent some system of writing.

The younger and backward children were unable to invent, to memorize with the aid of the material. The functional application of the material is not clear to them; it has nothing to do with the task given. On the other hand, pre-school children, who have attained a higher stage of development, utilize the material for memorizing. The child guesses the possibility of utilizing, say, paper for the purpose and begins to use a method invented by himself. This is usually some system of quantitative marks: a child makes marks on the paper corresponding in number to the figure stated (six times for the figure 6, twice for the figure 2), or else tears off the corresponding number of bits or makes a corresponding number of knots on a piece of string. When the child thus passes from simple, natural memory to artificial means of memorizing, the task of memorizing ten or even fifteen figures became easy. Simple natural memory was replaced by a system of signs and their subsequent reading, and the maximum of work was usually shifted from recollection to a recognition of series.

The invention does not take place at once. At first he guesses he must make marks, but does not guess how to make them distinguishable. Thus he tears off bits of paper and puts them in a heap; or he makes knots but leaves no intervals between them to denote figures. Obviously when he tries to reproduce them he finds himself helpless. Then, after some fruitless efforts, he usually guesses that his notes must assume a different shape; he differentiates his marks in little heaps, in groups.

Set the same problem to a schoolboy of the first or second year of study and you witness something very different. A child who has mastered the writing of letters and figures will not attempt to invent a new system of signs, but will apply the ready-made system of writing. The symbols represented will have the common feature of integral symbols, and not be a mere quantitative inscription representing the number. Thus a pre-school child inscribes by laying aside in heaps the corresponding number of hailshot; a schoolboy, on the other hand, tries to lay them in the shape of a figure. It is extraordinary how the older children always represent figures in that way, in spite of difficulties. Given material such as strings, chips, pins, out of which they attempt to form figures although it would have been easier to adopt the system of knots and scoring-stick marks; it is interesting to note that if you forbid them to represent figures you will make them quite helpless to cope with the task. We have hardly ever seen among children of these school groups any instances of reversion to the method of quantitative counting so characteristic of pre-school children.

In a recently reported experiment, Luria showed children aged one year and four months to one year and six months an inverted cup and an inverted tumbler. When they saw a coin placed under one and were told "The coin is under the cup—find the coin," they could do so. But when they were simply told this, a number of them could only grasp both containers; they got the idea only after constant repetition of the command. If the command was changed from cup to tumbler, very few did not continue to look under the cup. Children a bit older solved this last task, but if the changed instructions were delayed even by ten seconds, many did not succeed, but continued instead to look under the wrong object.

Equally impressive results bearing on language and recall were demonstrated with two- to three-year-olds who were asked to press a ball whenever a red light flashed, but not to press it when a blue light flashed. Most failed to perform correctly; they got so excited by both signals that after a few times the blue light also called forth their responses. When the flashes were accompanied by correct commands ("press" and "don't press"), the children responded successfully. Asked to give *themselves* the verbal commands, however, they either stopped pressing completely or pressed the ball for both lights. Only older children were able to line up their own commands with their motor responses. Shortly after that (in a manner that touched upon children's passage from egocentric speech to thought), even audible commands become unnecessary for successful performance; the children become able to think silently. (40)

AMNESIA FOR CHILDHOOD MEMORIES. Why is it that there is such a dearth of recollections of childhood experiences, and a virtually total amnesia for the period of infancy? Some writers have hypothesized that repression of memories takes place. This is an unsatisfactory explanation, since it neither accounts for the forgetting of pleasant happenings nor for the complete absence of memory of the earliest experiences of a fully sentient infant.

Schachtel (49) has argued that infants or young children live in a world of feeling and fantasy in which their experiences are such that they quite literally cannot be formulated in words. Hence they cannot be recollected, for infants lack symbolic means to retain them and adults do not have the proper mentality to recapture them later. Schachtel lays great stress upon the stereotyped, abstract, and schematic character of adult language that transforms growing children in socializing them and renders them in a sense unfit to be a child even in remembrance. We need not adopt Schachtel's nostalgic attitude toward the richness and vitality of childhood imagery, but his emphasis upon the crucial import of symbolic structures for remembrance is important. Infants, lacking these symbolic structures, have nothing to record them with so that they can recapture them later.

A subsidiary, but also important, point is that the transformations of children during the course of their socialization make recollection difficult or impossible. The Luria experiment has suggested this same conclusion. In a study of the development of children's concepts of money, one of the authors (52) found that it was unusual for the children to recollect any of the concepts held at earlier ages. In fact, they rejected notions once firmly believed with no awareness that they had once accepted them—rejected them with ridicule, laughter, and incredulity. This is precisely what one would expect if it is assumed that development implies

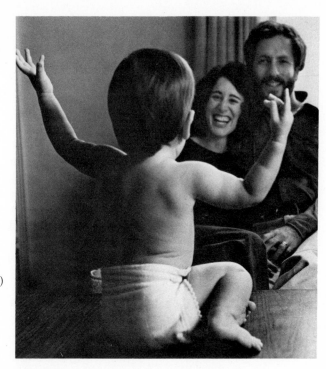

Who will remember this experience?
(*Hella Hammid/Photo Researchers, Inc.*)

genuine transformation of behavioral organization. In his studies of children, Piaget also has observed that when children are asked where they learned their most recent conceptions, they often remark, "I have always known that."

Halbwachs (23) has suggested that although certain childhood memories can be recaptured, at least in a gross sense, certain others cannot because perspectives have changed. For example, one can often remember the name of a book read as a child, conjuring up the look of the print and some of the imagery of the pictures and possibly even recapturing some of the overtones of the feeling experienced while reading the book. (However, it takes a rare person, like the novelist Marcel Proust, to recapture feeling.) But, as Halbwachs shrewdly notes, it is literally impossible to divest oneself of the experiences of the intervening years so as to feel exactly as one did when reading the book as a child. He remarks that the effort to recapture feelings poses the same problem as the effort to recapture the spirit of preceding periods in history. We may add that even a Proust, dredging up minute and poignant details of his childhood, gives only the illusion of an accurate recollection. Recollection is active, not passive. Proust's *Remembrance of Things Past* is an artistic and artful reconstruction, a creative act, not the record set down by a passive watcher as his memories file by like a parade. Adults, moving along through the life cycle to new perspectives and abandoning old ones, can be expected to find it difficult to recapture any but the grossest or most static, if poignant, moments of their past.

Historical Communication, Perception, and Memory

As perceiving and remembering are selective, and selectivity is socially influenced, it pays to examine some relationships between those activities and durable networks of communication. Some groups, organizations, and social structures persist for a long time. This means that memories of past events and dead personages are passed along from generation to generation; but not without reinterpretation by each generation, as it receives and transmits this heritage. The evidence for the above assertion is plentiful, though necessarily the evidence is historical rather than experimental or contemporary. We shall discuss several instances of collective heritage, using each to emphasize a different facet of collective remembering and perceiving.

A relatively simple instance is the common garden variety of remembrance that most of us have about the relations between American Indians and white Americans during the nineteenth century. Unless we have heard or read specifically to the contrary, we tend to believe the mass media's version of *How the West Was Won*. Indians tend even to be equated with the West! A more complete version would include the idea that rarely have a group of natives been so completely swept clean off their land and with such cruelty. Our individual memories of these events are nonexistent, so our views of this past, and to a large extent our views of Indians today, are rooted in our induction into channels of communication represented mainly by the mass media. Since European children also may read the same stories and see the same movies, they, too, may be inducted into the standard set of legends. Various Europeans have described this induction. (22:18, 32–33) Recently, some Indians have been trying—probably not very successfully, since collective memories are tenacious—to refashion Americans' conceptions of the past relations of whites with Indians.

With more passion and perhaps more face-to-face interaction, most Southern whites have images both of what the "War Between the States" was like and what followed directly thereafter during the Reconstruction period. The present generation has heard about these events from their parents through folk tradition. Southerners who were not born in the South have been inducted into the intense communication about these events through friends and acquaintances, perhaps from teachers, as well as through the various mass media that circulate in the South. Indeed, some of the nonnatives may have sharper and more passionately held

"How the West was won." Whose version? (*Culver Pictures*)

images than Southerners whose forefathers fought in the Civil War. These collective memories have helped to shape the subsequent course of events in the South and in the North also. Attempting to answer this legendary tradition, black historians have done firsthand research that shows that both popular and scholarly historians (mostly Southern whites) have often made errors in fact and in interpretation. (18) More recent emphasis on black pride and other attempts to counter the destructive effects of being black in a white-dominated society have also sought to rectify the remarkably inaccurate history of race relations in the United States.

We need not attribute deliberate distortion to historians, press, or ordinary conversationalists as they reshape the past through their interpretations of it. Quite enough distortion occurs through the selective processes of perceiving, remembering, and retelling without the necessity of our assuming deliberate manipulation, although assuredly falsification of history often does occur. The selective processes can be seen at work in "house organ history," whether it is a history of a corporation, a voluntary organization, a religious denomination, a city, or a profession. These accounts are almost certain to be "slanted" in the direction of self-aggrandizement, if only because those who write the histories are either biased in the direction of "progress," or have seen events from a particular position, or both. A typical instance is how medical historians, some of whom are excellent scholars, write about the history of medicine. Readers who wish information on the economics or organizational and social structures relevant to medical discoveries ordinarily cannot find much data, and what they find tends either to be oversimplified or considerably erroneous. The same can be said for professional histories and historical records written by prominent persons (for instance, the history of American nursing has largely been written by "nursing leaders" and their students, who passed down their view of the profession's chronology from their particular perspectives). (11)

Continuity of the legendary tradition of any group is broken when the communication channels either disintegrate or are captured by people who wish to change the information transmitted by those channels. The latter strategy is illustrated by what happens when authoritarian governments begin to beam different interpretations of national history over the mass media, blocking out as completely as possible all competing versions of the past. The disintegration of communication channels generally means either the disappearance of the communication-bearing group itself, or the disappearance of persons who acted as key transmitting agents for the old days. Another possibility is the transformation of the group itself so that in some sense the original group has disappeared, as happens with minority groups that become assimilated into the mainstream of a nation's life. Its members are likely to forget much of the ethnic heritage—such as foods, religious beliefs, and customs—whereas an embattled minority group, as in the Balkan countries, may persist for centuries with collective memories of its distant past as vivid as those of yesterday.

A new group, organization, or social structure may also appropriate as part of its functioning heritage various events and objects that either were forgotten and are now rediscovered, or which genuinely had little connection with its actual past. History is full of such events. The rediscovery by Renaissance scholars of the Greek past, and how this past was interpreted in contemporary terms, is one of the great stories of Western civilization. In turn, this story becomes part of *our* past—if we know about it. A contemporary instance of the same type of rediscovery is how Americans and Europeans are learning about the great pre-Greek civilizations that contributed to the rise of the Western world. The proliferation of best-selling archeological books is not to be overlooked, for they are sources for transmitting this information to new audiences. They are present as remarkably visible elements in the actual and conversational baggage of travelers in the Near East. In Israel, each new archeological discovery is front-page news and is avidly read about by almost everyone, as it is likely to have direct bearing on ancient Jewish history and symbolic bearing on the identities of Israeli citizens.

An even more striking and momentous contemporary instance of discovering the past is the search for national identity that is exhibited by newborn nations as they comb their tribal and regional pasts in an effort to get a national past of which they can be proud. As Everett Hughes remarked some years ago, it would be interesting to see what elements they would choose to incorporate into their national memories; and he was quite right. Many European nations, of course, went through a similar process during the last century. (25) The pasts they constructed and reconstructed are immensely relevant to the perceptions, memories, and actions of contemporary citizens. Stalin himself bowed to the persistence of older national memories when, during World War II, the question of the Soviet Union's survival was at stake. Communist symbols became minimized, and the older national symbols were reinstated into public favor. They had never really disappeared from the more private channels of communication.

Despite the heritage that individuals learn about through whatever communicative processes they engage in within various groups, organizations, and social structures, they are never automatons merely absorbing uncritically what they hear. As we repeatedly say or imply throughout this book, individuals selectively respond to the symbolic as well as to the physical world. Although we cannot understand any individuals unless we view them embedded in a historical context not of their own making, at the same time we must not forget that they have conceptions, however vague, of that past as it impinges on them. Thus, individuals will be memorializing it, rejecting it, re-creating it, cashing in on it, escaping it, or running from it; these are but a few of countless possibilities. Personal styles are built around such possibilities, as are those of emergent new groups. Thus the rejection of affluent America by some citizens—younger and college-educated especially—has meant a corresponding rejection of patriotic America and its historic memories. Hence segments or replicas of the flag were worn on shirts or as patches on the seat of pants, or the flag was displayed upside down. This reactive social movement, although expressed differently by different individuals, was so widespread as to cause much moral indignation among more upstanding citizens, who reaffirmed their historic and personal pasts with equally symbolic but countering gestures. The re-creation and memorialization of pasts—with appropriate updating and reinterpretation—is evidenced by the revival of nineteenth-century beards as well as by the wearing of old-fashioned clothing, including clothes of the frontier and Gold Rush styles. To the unsympathetic eye, people who dress and act in accordance with those styles seem all cut by the same standardized cookie cutter; to insiders, however, much individuality of style and behavior is being expressed.

The Planning of Behavior

As we have stressed repeatedly throughout this chapter, the human is a planning animal, making continual references to the past, the present, and the future. As the person moves through the present into the future, the past is recast and reformulated to fit the images of the future. This merger of the past and future in the present constitutes what G. H. Mead termed the *specious present*. That is, as we act in the present, we bring our previous actions to bear upon our anticipated actions in the next moment. These anticipations, in turn, shape our actions in the present. In the *specious present*, past, present, and future flow into a single temporal phase of experience. William James described this as the *stream of consciousness* of the person. In their plans, however ill-defined and vague, humans reveal an ability to take control over their own behavior so as to give it the semblance of organization and predictability. Plans, then, take many forms. They can be well-thought-out, written down, and made public, as when a president or head of state lays out a ten-year economic plan. They can refer to private affairs or public affairs, and they can refer to individual actions, to the actions of large collectivities, to the plans of families, or to the plans of two lovers. Persons vary in their ability to formulate plans. Young children, for instance, seldom have any control over when they will enter school, be taken on a vacation, or be permitted to open a savings account. Furthermore, persons vary in their power—legitimate or illegitimate, institutionalized or informal—to formulate plans. This ability and authority to make plans varies by one's location in the power networks that make up social groups and complex bureaucracies. We can also see that individuals' plans vary by where they see themselves in their overall moral career. The plans of the aged and the elderly, which reflect some attempt to control their last years of life during retirement, are quite different from those of a person just beginning a work career. Plans are always about the future, even when formulated in the present, for they refer to how individuals will organize their action in the next moment, day, year, or decade. Finally, we can note that some plans are hidden from others—embezzlers, for example, seldom make their plans known—while other plans are matters of public information—a phase of an economic anti-inflationary plan, for example. These aspects of plans, and the human's ability to plan, are not often considered in the social and psychological literature. By way of illustrating this conclusion, we will make brief reference to the stimulus-response view of planning as a form of human activity.

Having indicated that planning, perceiving, and remembering are interrelated intellectual processes of great complexity, we may approach
the matter in another way by reminding the reader of an older psychological model of behavior that stressed *S-R* (or *stimulus-response*) *bonds* as
something like the basic elements of all behavior. Stimuli were said to
"elicit," or cause, responses, and complex behavioral patterns were said
to consist simply of multitudes of such S-R bonds organized in
sequences and patterns. The model was largely derived from observing
lower animals.

This conception came under fire from other psychologists and
others interested in human behavior on the grounds, among others, that
it presented an overly mechanical view of human behavior, and that it
tended to ignore problems raised by the fact that, in human behavior in
particular, there is commonly or often a vast time gap between stimulus
and response—that is, a *delayed response*. It was suggested by critics that
one ought to know what was happening during this interval. It was observed that perhaps a basic and radical difference between lower animals
and humans was that the latter were capable of checking or inhibiting
their responses in order to gather further information and to allow time
for processing and evaluating them, and also to formulate plans for an
eventual response on the basis of anticipated consequences and contingencies and on their assessment of the stimulus situation. From this viewpoint, the most important parts of human behavior are precisely those
that the S-R model omits—namely, those events that transpire in the
time interval between the S and the R. It may well be argued that it is
during this interval that a given event or situation becomes a specific
stimulus by virtue of whether or not it is noticed at all, and, if noticed,
how it is interpreted. An automatic S-R connection is comparable to an
automatic electronic control device like a thermostat, but we do not say
of the latter that it has plans to keep our house warm in our absence,
although we might say that it is "programmed" to do just that. In this
case, it is the programmer, not the thermostat, that plans. We argue that
social scientists ought to focus on the programmer rather than on the
thermostat.

By virtue of their higher mental processes, then, humans can, on a
symbolic level, engage in true deliberation—which, as John Dewey notes
with his usual emphasis on behavior, is "a search for a *way* to act, not
for a final terminus." (14:193) Dewey also emphasizes, as we have, the
unified character of past, present, and future, reminding us that we
judge present "desires and habits" in terms of their probable consequences, with which knowledge is linked. (14:207) "We know . . . by
recollecting what we have observed, by using that recollection in constructive imaginative forecasts of the future, by using the thought of future consequences to tell the quality of the act now proposed."

PLANNING, FEEDBACK, AND PROBABILITIES

The process of deliberation referred to by Dewey is actually a much more complex and delicate practice than it may seem to be at first glance, especially when plans involve the presumed reactions of other people. One way of illustrating this point is by referring to what are called *self-fulfilling* and *self-negating* predictions. The former are exemplified by the person who seeks to make money in the stock market by following some of the well-known formulae disseminated in financial circles. If, for example, there are many investors who believe that stocks should be sold when stock averages behave in certain ways that are believed to constitute sell "signals," then stock prices will fall when the signal occurs, simply because there are enough people who heed the signal to force prices down. The self-negating prophecy, or prediction, is one which induces the person whose behavior has been predicted to prove that the prediction is wrong. Some years ago, before going barefooted was as common as it is now, a professor arguing before a class said that it was easy to predict human behavior and made his point by predicting that everyone would be wearing shoes and stockings at the next meeting of his class. At the next session of his class a number of students walked in barefooted to prove him wrong.

The above examples indicate some of the difficulties of planning and predicting that are introduced by the fact that people tend to seek information about the plans that others make concerning them and to alter their own accordingly. As activity proceeds, information concerning its effects and the reactions of others tends to flow back to the persons involved in what is called a *feedback* process. Feedback data are then interpreted and utilized to confirm, negate, or alter the ongoing course of action.

Another illustration from the legal field illustrates other aspects of planning. How do individuals decide whether or not they should take the risk of violating the law? Obviously, this may involve a very complex set of considerations, one of which is the probability of being caught. Suppose the question is that of driving an automobile when drunk. Two questions may be raised: (1) from police statistics, what are the objective probabilities that a drunken driver will be arrested?; (2) how does the person feel about his or her own chances of being caught? This is the difference between *objective* and *subjective* probability, and the two may be quite unrelated. Another similar example is provided by considering how people in big cities might plan their movements within it in relation to their estimates of the dangers of being victimized by a criminal. A further question is raised as to how such persons make their assessments of danger. Is it from the criminal statistics, from the reports of their friends and associates, from what they hear and see from the mass media, or do they simply draw on their imagination?

Because there is an inherent uncertainty about the future that in-

Social Structure and the Self

creases geometrically with time, probability judgments weigh heavily in virtually all planning. Sometimes this uncertainty may be dealt with by planning a series of lines of action in case the unexpected should happen. The thief, for example, expects not to be caught, but should he or she be caught, he or she takes along a sum of money to bribe the victim, the policeman, or some other official. If all of this fails, he or she may have made advance arrangements with a "fixer" who will perhaps be able to get the case dismissed. Respectable citizens do not face the same hazards that a thief does, but despite all the planning we may do, the uncertainty of the future is never eliminated.

Summary

The distinctive qualities of human mental activity are the consequences of humans' incorporation and use of language symbols. *Goal behavior* involves response to signs representing the future; *memory* is response to signs representing the past; and *perception* is response to signs representing the present environment. Skill in interpretation of and response to signs on any level is *intelligence*. *Reason* involves the interpretation and use of symbols and is the equivalent of conceptual thought. It is a peculiarly human activity.

Such complex mental functions as perceiving and remembering are examples of complex human sign behavior. Individual human beings take over language symbols as part of their repertoire of behavior. This incorporation of group-created conventional signs creates new complexities of response and makes human mental functions different from (and superior to) those of the lower animals. Mental processes in the lower animals parallel the higher functions in humans but are of a lower order of complexity, being based on simpler forms of sign behavior. Perception and memory in the lower animals are more closely tied to biological conditions than they are in humans. Unlike the lower animals, human beings are able to assimilate socially developed symbolic systems that transform their psychic life, add new dimensions to their behavior, and make it possible for them to profit from the experience of past generations and to anticipate and plan for the future in ways unparalleled in the rest of the animal world.

References

1. Allport, G., and L. Postman, "The Basic Psychology of Rumor," in T. Newcomb and E. L. Hartley (eds.), *Readings in Social Psychology*. New York: Holt, Rinehart and Winston, 1947, pp. 547–58.
2. Bagby, James, "A Cross-Cultural Study of Perceptual Preponderance in Bin-

ocular Rivalry," *Journal of Abnormal and Social Psychology*, vol. 54 (1947), pp. 331–34.

3. Bartlett, F. C., *Remembering*. New York: Cambridge University Press, 1932.

4. Bauer, Raymond, and Kenneth Gergen (eds.), *The Study of Policy Formation*. New York: The Free Press, 1968.

5. Bierens de Haan, J., *Animal Psychology for Biologists*. London: Hutchinson Publishing Group, 1929.

6. Blondel, C., *Introduction à la Psychologie Collective*. Paris: Librarie Armand Colin, 1928.

7. Brown, R., "Language and Categories," in J. Bruner et al., *A Study of Thinking*. New York: Wiley, 1956.

8. ———, and E. Lenneberg, "A Study in Language and Cognition," *Journal of Abnormal and Social Psychology*, vol. 49 (1954), pp. 454–62.

9. Bruner, J. S., and R. Tagiuri, "The Perception of People," in G. Lindsey (ed.), *Handbook of Social Psychology*, vol. 2. Cambridge, Mass.: Addison-Wesley, 1954.

10. Carmichael, L., H. P. Hogan, and A. A. Walter, "An Experimental Study of the Effect of Language on the Reproduction of Visually Perceived Form," *Journal of Experimental Psychology*, vol. 15 (1932), pp. 78–86.

11. Davis, Fred (ed.), *The Nursing Profession*. New York: Wiley, 1966.

12. Dewey, J., *Art as Experience*. New York: Minton, Balch and Company, 1934.

13. ———, *Experience and Nature*. La Salle, Ill.: Open Court Publishing Company, 1925.

14. ———, *Human Nature and Conduct*. New York: Holt, Rinehart and Winston, 1922.

15. Edwards, A. L., "Political Frames of Reference as a Factor Influencing Recognition," *Journal of Abnormal and Social Psychology*, vol. 36 (1941), pp. 34–50.

16. Ervin, S., "Semantic Shift in Bilingualism," *American Journal of Psychology*, vol. 74 (1961), pp. 233–41.

17. Frake, E., "The Ethnographic Study of Cognitive Systems," in T. Gladwin and W. Sturtevant (eds.), *Anthropology and Human Behavior*. Washington, D.C.: Anthropological Society of Washington, 1962.

18. Franklin, John H., *From Slavery to Freedom: A History of American Negroes*, 2d ed. New York: Knopf, 1956.

19. French, D., "The Relationship of Anthropology to Studies in Perception and Cognition," in S. Koch (ed.), *Psychology: A Study of a Science*. New York: McGraw-Hill, 1963.

20. Gans, Herbert, *People and Plans: Essays on Urban Problems and Solutions*. New York: Basic Books, 1968.

21. Gibson, J. J., "Social Perceptions and Perceptual Learning," in M. Sherif and D. Wilson, *Group Relations at the Crossroads*. New York: Harper & Row, 1953, pp. 120–38.

22. Grosz, George, *A Little Yes and a Big No*. New York: The Dial Press, 1946.

23. Halbwachs, M., *Les Cadres Sociaux de la Mémoire*. Paris: Librairie Félix Alcan, 1925.

24. ———, *La Mémoire Collective*. Paris: Presses Universitaires, 1950.

25. Hayes, Carleton, *Essays on Nationalism*. New York: Macmillan, 1926.

26. Hebb, D. O., *The Organization of Behavior*. New York: Wiley, 1949.

27. Heider, F., *The Psychology of Interpersonal Behavior*. New York: Wiley, 1958.

28. Hoijer, H., *Language and Culture*. Washington, D.C.: American Anthropological Association, 1954.

29. Horowitz, Irving (ed.), *The Use and Abuse of Social Science: Behavioral Science*

and National Policy Making. New Brunswick, N.J.: Rutgers University Press, 1971.

30. Hudson, W., "Pictorial Depth Perception in Subcultural Groups in Africa," *Journal of Social Psychology*, vol. 52 (1960), pp. 183–208.

31. Ittelson, W., and H. Cantril, *Perception: A Transactional Approach*. Garden City, N.Y.: Doubleday, 1954.

32. Jones, E., and J. Aneshansel, "The Learning and Utilization of Contravalent Material," *Journal of Abnormal and Social Psychology*, vol. 53 (1956), pp. 27–33.

33. Judd, C. H., *Educational Psychology*. Boston: Houghton Mifflin, 1939.

34. Kleinberg, O., *Social Psychology* (rev. ed.) New York: Holt, Rinehart and Winston, 1954.

35. Kluckhohn, C., "Notes on Some Anthropological Aspects of Communication," *American Anthropologist*, vol. 639 (1961), pp. 895–910.

36. Lander, H., S. Ervin, and A. Horowitz, "Navaho Color Categories," *Language*, vol. 36 (1960), pp. 368–82.

37. Lantz, DeLee, "Color Naming and Color Recognition." Unpublished Ph.D. dissertation, Harvard University, 1963.

38. Levine, L. M., and G. Murphy, "The Learning and Forgetting of Controversial Material," *Journal of Abnormal and Social Psychology*, vol. 138 (1943), pp. 507–17.

39. Luria, A. R., "The Problem of the Cultural Behavior of the Child," *Journal of Genetic Psychology*, vol. 35 (1928), pp. 493–504.

40. ———, "The Directive Function of Speech in Development and Dissolution," *Word*, vol. 15 (1959), pp. 341–65.

41. Mead, Margaret, "The Primitive Child," in C. Murchison (ed.), *Handbook of Child Psychology*. Worcester, Mass.: Clark University Press, 1933.

42. Munn, N., "Learning in Children," in L. Carmichael (ed.), *Manual of Child Psychology*. New York: Wiley, 1946, pp. 370–449.

43. Murphy, G., L. B. Murphy, and T. Newcomb, *Experimental Social Psychology*. New York: Harper & Row, 1937.

44. Pepitone, A., "Motivational Effects in Social Perception," *Human Relations*, vol. 1 (1950), pp. 57–76.

45. Riesen, A., "The Development of Visual Perception in Man and Chimpanzees," *Science*, vol. 106 (1947), pp. 107–8.

46. Roberts, H., "Melodic Composition and Scale Foundations in Primitive Music," *American Anthropologist*, vol. 34 (1932), p. 95.

47. Russell, E. S., *The Behavior of Animals*. London: Edward Arnold (Publishers) Ltd., 1938.

48. Sandburg, C., "Elephants Are Different to Different People," in L. Untermeyer (ed.), *A Critical Anthology: Modern American Poetry*. New York: Harcourt Brace Jovanovich, 1936, p. 249.

49. Schachtel, E., "On Memory and Childhood Amnesia,"*Psychiatry*, vol. 10 (1947), pp. 1–26.

50. Segall, M., D. Campbell, and M. J. Herskovits, *The Influence of Culture on Visual Perception*. Indianapolis: Bobbs-Merrill, 1964.

51. Sherif, M., *Psychology of Social Norms*. New York: Harper & Row, 1936.

52. Strauss, Anselm L., "The Development and Transformation of Monetary Meanings in the Child," *American Sociological Review*, vol. 17 (1952), pp. 275–86.

53. Sullivan, H. S., *The Interpersonal Theory of Psychiatry*. New York: W. W. Norton, 1953.

54. Triandis, H., "Cultural Influences on Cognitive Process," in L. Berkowitz (ed.), *Advances in Experimental Social Psychology.* New York: Academic Press, 1964, pp. 1–48.
55. Twain, Mark, *Life on the Mississippi.* New York: Bantam Books, 1946.
56. Von Senden, M., *Space and Sight,* trans. by P. Heath. New York: The Free Press, 1960.
57. Whorf, B. L., *Language, Thought, and Reality,* ed. by J. B. Carroll. Cambridge, Mass.: M.I.T. Press, 1956.
58. Wood, C., "An Analysis of Changes Occurring in Successive Stages of Abstracting." Unpublished Master's thesis, State University of Iowa, 1944.
59. Yerkes, R. M., *Chimpanzees: A Laboratory Colony.* New Haven: Yale University Press, 1943.
60. Zillig, M., "Einstellung und Aussage," *Zeitschrift für Psychologie,* vol. 106 (1928), pp. 58–106.

Selected Readings

BARTLETT, F. C., *Remembering.* New York: Cambridge University Press, 1932.
  A classic and important systematic discussion of memory.
SULLIVAN, H. S., *The Interpersonal Theory of Psychiatry.* New York: W. W. Norton, 1953.
  A highly illuminating and influential work that presents a broad view of the manner in which human perceptions of self and others evolve.
VON SENDEN, M., *Space and Sight,* trans. by P. Heath. New York: The Free Press, 1960.
  The author makes the point that one must learn how to interpret sensory experience and presents highly interesting data to support his position.
WHORF, B. L., *Language, Thought, and Reality,* ed. by J. B. Carroll. Cambridge, Mass.: M.I.T. Press, 1956.
  Presents the views of a distinguished student of linguistics concerning the influence of language on complex mental processes.
YERKES, R. M., *Chimpanzees: A Laboratory Colony.* New Haven: Yale University Press, 1943.
  Contains a wealth of material pertinent to the comparison of the mental processes of humans and primates.

chapter 7

Humans without Symbols: Restricted Communication

In preceding chapters we have stressed that without language we could not be the complex beings we are. The question that then arises is: What if we did not have language, and what if we could not produce and respond to symbols? There is no way of answering the question directly, as all societies and groups have always had systems of language and, of course, even children, whether deaf or retarded, become thoroughly human when they learn to communicate symbolically. No adult, once he or she has learned a language, can be deprived of this knowledge; hence there is no way, even if we wished to, to produce human beings without a language in order to see how they would act.

Although it is not possible to rear infants experimentally in a speechless environment or to destroy the language functions of adults deliberately, there have been certain unplanned occurrences that have produced conditions very roughly equivalent to those that would be required for such experiments. (Furthermore, as we shall show in Chapters 9, 10, and 11, it is possible to study the effects of language acquisition on the behavior of young children.) In this chapter we shall review several of these "natural experiments" for the light they shed, however indirectly, on what happens when language functions are missing or impaired. We shall consider such exceptional individuals as the mentally retarded, children reared in almost complete isolation, persons who are deaf and blind, and sufferers from two types of mental impairment, aphasia and schizophrenia. These are very different kinds of unusual human beings, but they all have one handicap in common that matters to us here; their language functioning is minimal or much impaired. Schizophrenic patients are marked by a regression in their use of normal modes of communication. Aphasics are characterized by the loss or disturbance of language responses. Some subnormal persons have never learned to speak, write, or otherwise communicate with facility. Children reared by human beings in isolation from society are rare, but a remarkable case has been studied. Finally, the condition of the deaf and blind is especially relevant to our inquiry, as is illustrated by Helen Keller's classic account of how she learned language. Each of these unfortunate natural occurrences illuminates a different aspect of the relation of language to behavior. Together they provide strong evidence of the importance of language by showing what happens to persons who lack language, to those who lose it, or those whose language ability is seriously impaired. These "natural experiments" will reveal how basic language is to the emergence and structure of the self.

Isolated Children

THE CASE OF ISABELLE   A significant case that illustrates the importance of language in the shaping of human behavior was reported by K. Davis. (8:432–37) A girl named Isabelle, an illegitimate child, had lived virtually alone with her deaf-mute mother in a single room until she was about six and one half years old. Her behavior was described as being almost "that of a wild animal, manifesting much fear and hostility. In lieu of speech she made only a strange croaking sound. In many ways she acted like an infant." It was said by a psychologist who examined her that "she was apparently utterly unaware of relationships of any kind." At first it was hard to know whether she was able to hear or not, because she was so unresponsive to sound. When tests established that she was not deaf, specialists working with her were inclined to believe that she was feebleminded and "wholly uneducable," and that it would be futile to attempt to teach her to speak. Her score on tests, even nonverbal ones, was exceedingly low. A Stanford-Binet test gave her a mental age of nineteen months, although her chronological age was more than four times greater, placing her in the low-grade feebleminded category.

In spite of pessimism regarding the outcome, Isabelle was subjected to systematic training. It was a week before she made her first attempt at vocalization, but in two months she was beginning to put sentences together. Nine months later she could write well, retell a story after hearing it, and recognize words and sentences on the printed page. Seven months later she possessed a vocabulary of between fifteen hundred and two thousand words. She had covered in two years the stages of learning that usually require six, and her IQ had tripled. When Davis reported on her she was fourteen years old, had passed the sixth grade in public school, and behaved like a normal child.

It is instructive to note that this child was not actually reared in isolation, but had the constant companionship of her deaf-mute mother who took care of her and from whom she learned gestures. As later events demonstrated that Isabelle was not mentally defective, it is probable that articulated, verbal speech was the crucial environmental factor that had been absent. It is virtually certain that if her mother had not been a deaf-mute, Isabelle's retardation would have been relatively slight and would not have attracted any special attention.

The alternative explanation is that her retardation was due merely to lack of stimulation of a nonverbal sort—that is, from lack of a multiplicity of "contacts"; however, this seems rather improbable. Observers sometimes have stressed the importance of the presence of other people in one's early social environment, without specifically recognizing that the presence of others is not in itself the crucial factor for the development of complex mental functioning. The person who grows up experiencing extremely restricted contacts with other persons need not be greatly retarded if the few persons with whom he or she does have contact are intelligent and articulate. On the other hand, deaf children, if given no special training, will be seriously retarded no matter how many adults surround them. Lack of opportunity to learn language behavior is the key to retarded mental development.

The Blind Deaf

Persons who are deaf, or deaf and blind, must have special training if they are to learn a language. Invaluable in this connection is the report by the noted blind and deaf woman, Helen Keller, who began to learn American Sign Language at the age of seven. The following is her own story, somewhat abridged, of her discovery of language (16:22–24):

> The most important day I remember in all my life is the one on which my teacher, Anne Mansfield Sullivan, came to me. I am filled with wonder when I consider the immeasurable contrast between the two lives which it connects. It was the third of March, 1887, three months before I was seven years old.
>
> The morning after my teacher came she led me into her room and gave me a doll. The little blind children at the Perkins Institution had sent it and Laura Bridgman had dressed it; but I did not know this until afterward. When I had played with it a little while Miss Sullivan slowly spelled into my hand the word "d-o-l-l." I was at once interested in this finger play and

Helen Keller with her teacher Anne Sullivan. In her autobiography Miss Keller describes the intellectual, emotional, and conceptual changes in her life as a result of language acquisition. (*Wide World Photos*)

tried to imitate it. When I finally succeeded in making the letters correctly I was flushed with childish pleasure and pride. Running downstairs to my mother I held up my hand and made the letters for doll. I did not know that I was spelling a word or even that words existed; I was simply making my fingers go in monkey-like imitation. In the days that followed I learned to spell in this uncomprehending way a great many words, among them *pin, hat, cup,* and a few verbs like *sit, stand,* and *walk.* But my teacher had been with me several weeks before I understood that everything has a name.

One day, while I was playing with my new doll, Miss Sullivan put my big rag doll into my lap also, spelled "d-o-l-l" and tried to make me understand that "d-o-l-l" applied to both. Earlier in the day we had had a tussle over the word "m-u-g" and "w-a-t-e-r." Miss Sullivan had tried to impress it upon me that "m-u-g" is *mug* and that "w-a-t-e-r" is *water,* but I persisted in confounding the two. In despair she had dropped the subject for the time, only to renew it at the first opportunity. I became impatient with her repeated attempts and, seizing the new doll, I dashed it upon the floor. I was keenly delighted when I felt the fragments of the broken doll at my feet. Neither sorrow nor regret followed my passionate outburst. I had not loved the doll. In the still, dark world in which I lived there was no strong sentiment or tenderness. I felt my teacher sweep the fragments to one side of the hearth, and I had a sense of satisfaction that the cause of my discomfort was removed. She brought me my hat, and I knew I was going out into the warm sunshine. This thought, if a wordless sensation may be called a thought, made me hop and skip with pleasure.

We walked down the path to the well-house, attracted by the fragrance of the honeysuckle with which it was covered. Some one was drawing water and my teacher placed my hand under the spout. As the cool stream

Social Structure and the Self

gushed over one hand she spelled into the other word *water*, first slowly, then rapidly. I stood still, my whole attention fixed upon the motions of her fingers. Suddenly I felt a misty consciousness as of something forgotten—a thrill of returning thought; and somehow the mystery of language was revealed to me. I knew then that "w-a-t-e-r" meant the wonderful cool something that was flowing over my hand. That living word awakened my soul, gave it light, hope, joy, set it free! There were barriers still, it is true, but barriers that could in time be swept away.

I left the well-house eager to learn. Everything had a name, and each name gave birth to a new thought. As we returned to the house every object I touched seemed to quiver with life. That was because I saw everything with a strange, new sight that had come to me. On entering the door I remembered the doll I had broken. I felt my way to the hearth and picked up the pieces. I tried vainly to put them together. Then my eyes filled with tears; for I realized what I had done, and for the first time I felt repentance and sorrow.

I learned a great many new words that day. I do not remember what they all were; but I do know that *mother, father, sister, teacher,* were among them—words that were to make the world blossom for me, "like Aaron's rod, with flowers." It would have been difficult to find a happier child than I was as I lay in my crib at the close of that eventful day and lived over the joys it had brought me, and for the first time longed for a new day to come.

It is extremely significant that Miss Keller describes the changes that language brought in her life as both an intellectual and emotional revolution. Not only did the acquisition of words give her an intellectual grasp of the world, but it also altered her attitudes toward things and people and toward herself. Indeed, her temperament appears to have been changed. Her memory of her first seven years was vague, and she even hesitates to apply the term "idea" or "thought" to her mental processes during that time. The transformation was, in short, not merely a superficial one attendant upon the acquisition of an additional motor skill; it was a fundamental and pervasive change that altered, and indeed revolutionized, her total personality and image of herself.

It is interesting to note that controversy developed over the question of whether Helen Keller had a right to, or could intelligently use, words of sight and sound. As she was both deaf and blind, how could she talk of colors or sounds? What could such words as "mirror," "reflect," "see," "loud," "flash of light, " and innumerable others possibly mean to her? What right did she have to talk about the "azure blue of the sky," the "green grass," the "deep blue pools of water," or the "sound of the human voice"? Influenced by the academic preconceptions of the time, some psychologists contended that she had no "right" to use such terms, as they must be meaningless to her.

Helen Keller emphatically maintained that she had to use such words and expressions because there were no substitutes for them if she wished to communicate with her felllows. She maintained, moreover, that she understood these expressions. The idea of the mirror held no difficulties for her because she understood the figurative meaning of "reflect." Such an expression as "I see" was understood and used correctly as in "I see my error," or "I see the point"; and she was able, by means of this sort of analogy, to grasp the meaning of "I see with my eyes." She compared her situation with that of a stranger on an island [with other people] where a language unknown to him is spoken. This stranger, she says, "must learn to see with their eyes to hear with their ears, to think their thoughts, to follow their ideals." (17:124)

Helen Keller also pointed out that ordinary people constantly talk about things they have never seen, sounds they have never heard, and feelings they have never felt. She might have called attention to the fact that color-blind persons speak of the green grass and the blue sky like the rest of us.

As between the theorist who asserts that words of color and sound can mean nothing to a deaf and blind person, and the deaf and blind person herself who insists that the words do have meaning for her and who uses them correctly, we feel compelled to accept the testimony of the latter. This is simply another instance of the way in which the thoughts, feelings, and speech of all persons, not only the deaf and the blind, are molded according to the patterns imposed by societies, languages, and social groups. It is not surprisng that the deaf and blind person should have conceptions and images of color. The language they have acquired permits them to see and hear.

Such a case as that of Helen Keller shows clearly that the use of symbolism in human life does not depend on any specific sensory data or exclusively on articulate language. Once people grasp the principle of symbolic activity, they may use a wide variety of substitute signs or cues in the organization of their behavior. The system of signs which we express in the audible sounds constituting the spoken English language may be translated into written symbols, into American Sign Language, into the system of dots and dashes of the Morse code, or into the intricate secret codes used in modern warfare. All of these external signs, when they are internalized in the thinking process, function in basically the same way as the spoken signs.

The Mentally Retarded

The mentally retarded are retarded in mental ability by reason of injury, disease, or constitutional deficiency. They are conventionally classified into various categories, and range from the severely retarded to the near-normal person. Subnormal individuals of the highest types can carry on simple conversation, but on lower levels almost no linguistic communication takes place.

There are thus different levels of sign behavior among the mentally deficient. These differences are revealed in different degrees of socialization, learning, and ability, and in performance on intelligence tests. They are also revealed in different capacities to organize behavior abstractly. An interesting inquiry along these lines was made by Werner. (33:175–76). He studied two groups of mentally retarded children, one group being more retarded than the other. The children were shown a screen in which there were four holes, and they were told that these holes were numbered 1,2,3,4. The investigator than pointed to the holes in a given order—for example, 1,3,2,4, or 4,2,1,3—and the children were asked to repeat the process. The more retarded children succeeded more often on this test than they did on another in which the holes were lighted up in various sequences and the children asked to indicate orally in what order they were lighted. The less retarded children did better on the second test than on the first. Werner interpreted these results as indicating that perception in the lower group is more personal and concrete, and that it becomes more abstract and impersonal with increasing mental ability. The gist of Werner's argument is that there are qualitatively different modes of mental organization among the retarded. Furthermore, Strauss and Werner (30) have shown differences of behavioral organization between those who are retarded because of injury to the brain and those whose deficiency is congenital in origin.

The retardation of the mentally deficient in the lowest categories is very much like that of blind and deaf individuals who have not been specially trained. Neither can enter into the stream of symbols that characterizes the human community. In the mentally retarded, a basically biological deficiency prevents the individuals from acquiring and manipulating symbols; in the blind deaf, it prevents them from learning, unless they are especially taught.

There is other evidence besides the kinds presented in this chapter on the destructive effects of social isolation or biological deficiency. Criminologists are familiar with the fact that in the early history of American prisons the "Pennsylvania system" sought to prevent the evil effects of association among prisoners by preventing them from communicating with each other. It was quickly observed by both American and European officials that this form of social isolation had very destructive effects upon personality. In extreme instances in which virtually complete isolation in solitary confinement was practiced, over a substantial period of time, derangement, mental deterioration, or suicide was the usual result. This scheme was quickly abandoned when its effects were noted, after having been adopted both here and in Europe with considerable enthusiasm and high hopes during the first half of the nineteenth century.

It is also said that seemingly senile people can and do show improvement when taken out of the back wards and given verbal and non-

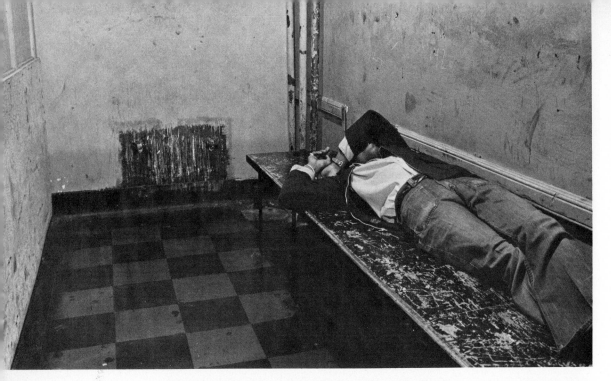

Social isolation may have destructive effects upon the personality and in severe cases may mimic the symptoms of mental retardation, senility, or various forms of aphasia. (*Eric Kroll/Taurus Photos*)

verbal contact with normal people. Also, many people classified as mentally retarded lead normal, functioning lives in their local communities. One of the authors of this text was told of a fifty-year-old male who, although classified as mentally retarded in childhood, was elected steward of his local teamsters' union. An exceptionally able young sociologist of our acquaintance, who is a Chicano, was believed by at least one of his public school teachers to be a retarded child because of his inept performance in public school.

For many decades, some people attributed a special instance of supposed or imputed mental retardation to the so-called inferior races, meaning, mostly, black people. This debate reached its apogee during the poverty program years of 1964 to 1968, when it was focused specifically on children reared in urban ghettos. While racially biased people argued passionately about the impossibility of raising the IQs of blacks through any kind of education, well-intentioned liberals—both white and black—admitted the existence of those lower IQs, or at least some lower level of mental functioning, but pinned their hopes on compensatory and other special educational programs which might counteract the crippling effects of a "culturally deprived" environment. Although deeply entwined with political issues, the scientific question was, and is,

Social Structure and the Self

whether black ghetto children are only less informed and less interested in matters important to educated whites, or whether their mental capacities really suffer because of an impoverished environment.

In our judgment, the research that exists demonstrates the former but certainly not the latter. The IQ tests clearly have been biased against the performance of these children. The kinds of data which are more impressive than school- or test-collected data are those obtained in natural settings, such as that obtained by the linguist William Labov and reported in his *Language in the Inner City*. (18:354–56) These data demonstrate—when analyzed with linguistic techniques—a very high-level mental functioning of ghetto adolescents. For example, their spontaneous narratives reveal both a progressive complexity with the increasing age of the storyteller and a very high level of verbal and mental ability in general. Labov concludes his book with the statement that: "It should be clear that black English vernacular is the vehicle of communication used by some of the most talented and effective speakers of the English language."

Again, Labov's analysis of the popular verbal game of "sounding," a form of ritual insulting, shows the adolescents engaging in a very complex interaction wherein they display both a considerable virtuosity of verbal skill and of mental agility. Comparisons, similes, allusions, and puns abound in this ritual game. For instance, one form is (18:297–353), "Your mother so . . . she . . . ." Here are a few examples:

> Your mother so skinny she could slip through a needle's eye.
>   Your mother's so skinny, about that skinny, she can get in a Cheerio and say, "Hula hoop! Hula hoop!"

Or, the similes get more complex and involve a "second subordination": "Your mother is so . . . that when she . . . she can . . . ." It is not easy to get all of this into one proposition in the heat of the moment during the fast verbal game. Thus, "Joe's mother was so dirty, when she get the rag to take a bath, the water went back down the drain." Not all children show the same aptitude in handling "constructions with this ability," but, in general, they certainly can perform quite capably. It is worth noting that not only are these collective interactions, but they represent a game. The characteristics attributed to mothers and other persons are purely fictional. Labov concludes—and his wording brings him close to our own understanding of the linkages among interaction, mental processes, and symbolic behavior—that "an understanding of ritual behavior must therefore be an important element in constructing a general theory of discourse." (18:353) Thus many individuals may be regarded as mentally retarded or uneducated simply because they do not speak the language of the dominant group in their society.

Behavioral Disorders of Aphasia

We shall use the term *aphasia* to refer in a general way to the loss or disturbance of language responses. Aphasia is often, but not necessarily, brought about by cerebral injury. Aphasic conditions may also be produced under hypnosis or by traumatic experiences. The loss of function may assume various forms, such as the inability to read, to write, or to name familiar objects.

The English neurologist Henry Head distinguished four main types of aphasic disorder: verbal, nominal, syntactic, and semantic aphasia. (13) We shall not concern ourselves with such subtypes of aphasic disorders other than to indicate that they exist and that the problem of classifying and naming them is a difficult one. Thus, the four types delineated by Head are not always easily distinguishable or sharply separated. The student should keep three points in mind: (1) *Aphasia* refers to a variety of disorders that have not yet been satisfactorily classified or uniformly labeled by all writers; (2) As these disorders vary in severity and in the type of linguistic activity affected, many aphasics are able to make significant statements about their own difficulties and experiences as aphasics. Of course, when the destruction of the language function is relatively complete, this is not possible; (3) The brain injuries that produce aphasia vary greatly in nature and severity and it is sometimes very difficult and often a matter of controversy to distinguish disabilities that are the consequences of loss of some part of the language function from those that are not.

Some idea of the nature and variety of speech-related disorders produced by brain injury may be obtained by considering some of the commonly used terms in this field. Some of these terms are: *agnosia, apraxia, alexia, amusia, acalculia,* and *agraphia.* (2, 22) *Agnosia* refers to the person's inability to recognize objects presented to him or her by the senses. Thus, persons who cannot recognize a familiar object by sight, but do so at once upon feeling it in their hands, are said to be afflicted by *visual agnosia.* The opposite situation, in which an object is recognized when it is seen but not when it is felt, is *tactile agnosia. Alexia* refers to difficulty in reading, and *agraphia* to difficulty in expressing one's thoughts in writing. *Amusia* refers to the inability to understand or appreciate music or to hum, whistle, or carry a tune; the term *acalculia* is used to designate disorder in processes of dealing with numbers. *Apraxia* designates difficulty in voluntarily formulating a general plan involving a series of purposive movements. By way of illustration, R. Brain (2:118) cites the case of an apraxic patient who could not relate himself spatially to his clothes and was therefore unable to get into them.

In a follow-up study after Head's work a team of British investigators, W. R. Russell and L. E. Espir (27), used wounded soldiers of World War II as subjects just as Head had used those of World War I. Russell and Espir note that in right-handed persons aphasia is ordinarily produced only by injury to the left hemisphere of the brain. By careful study of the location of the wounds they were able to indicate the brain area in which the language functions appear to be integrated. They observed that even small wounds in the center of this area can create disorder in all aspects of speech behavior and also can produce mental confusion. They called this type of disorder *central aphasia,* in contrast to other types produced by wounds that are nearer to the periphery of the language area. (27:170) Thus, a peripheral injury may make it impossible for individuals to express their thoughts aloud in words even though they may indicate by other means that they understand and that their inner thought processes are intact. This is often called *motor aphasia.* All of these disorders, and others not mentioned here, occur in a wide variety of combinations and are designated by a confusing array of special terms by different investigators.

Aphasia may occur in children as well as in adults. Its effects, however, are different; this difference may perhaps be accounted for in general terms by noting that adults possess a great many skills and behavior patterns that are originally acquired with the aid of language and that do not necessarily disappear with aphasia. In the child, on the other hand, a relatively minor or peripheral defect such as deafness may prevent the acquisition of language, and this in turn will prevent the child from acquiring the complex functions and patterns that must originally be learned with the aid of language mechanisms. It may also be observed in passing that deaf mutes who communicate with sign language may also suffer from aphasia.

Some of the most significant materials on aphasic thought are to be found in Head's work. The comments made by some of his patients are interesting and provide a certain amount of insight into their condition. One of them said (13:256):

> When I think of anything, everything seems to be rolling along. I can't hold it. . . . I can see what it is. I seem to see it myself, but I can't put it properly into words like you ought to. I can see what it is myself like. My mind won't stop at any one thing. They keep on rolling. Myself, I imagine when you're talking you're only thinking of what you're talking about. When I'm talking to anybody it seems a lot of things keep going by.

Another patient, attempting to explain the difficulty he had in finding his way about London, said, "You see it's like this: with me it's all in bits. I have to jump like this," marking a thick line between two points with a pencil, "like a man who jumps from one thing to the next. I can

see them but I can't express. Really it is that I haven't enough names."
(13:371)

A number of interesting comments by these patients indicate that images and the flow of imagery are profoundly affected by the loss of language that occurs in aphasia. Head always asked his patients to draw pictures, both from a model and from memory. One of the patients who had drawn a jug from a model could not do it from memory. He commented as follows (13:193):

> I was trying to see the glass bottle; the picture seemed to evade me. I knew it was a bottle, and I could describe the drawing. But when it came to seeing it as a picture, I was more or less nonplussed. I often seem to have got the picture, but it seemed to evade me.

When this patient was questioned further it became clear that he experienced images, but that they appeared to be unstable and could not be controlled or evoked at will. He said, "The more I try to make them come the more difficult it is to get in touch with them, as one might say." (13:195)

Head performed the following test with one of his patients. He rolled bits of paper into wads and had a contest with the patient to see who could toss the improvised balls more accurately into a basket placed some distance away. The aphasic proved more adept than Head. Then a screen was moved in front of the basket so that the basket was not visible, and the contest was repeated. This time Head did far better than the patient; the patient seemed to be at a loss as to what to do. He explained his difficulties (13:208):

> When I could see the basket I could follow the line of vision; when it was in the same place. . . . I'd seen the basket before you put the screen there; I knew you hadn't changed the position, but in some odd way I didn't feel perfectly confident in my own mind that it was in that position.

We noted in an earlier chapter that it is through the internalized use of language that human beings are able to imagine objects and events that are removed in time and space. This point is neatly corroborated in the study of aphasia for, as the preceding quotations show, the aphasic's flow of imagery is so disturbed that he is unable to visualize objects adequately when they are not immediately within his range of vision.

The inability of some aphasics to deal with objects that they cannot see or touch but must merely imagine is brought out in a curious manner by their inability to strike an imaginary match on an imaginary matchbox, to drive an imaginary nail with a nonexistent hammer, or to demonstrate with an empty glass how one drinks water. These same patients are able to strike actual matches, to drive actual nails, and to drink water from a glass when they are thirsty. Goldstein (10) described these and other inabilities of the aphasic as a regression from an abstract or categorical attitude toward the world to a more concrete attitude.

It is clear from the foregoing reports that aphasics appear to have lost a certain flexibility of orientation so that they no longer seem to be at home in the world. We may put this in descriptive terms by saying that aphasics are not self-starters. Because they cannot talk effectively to others or to themselves about things or persons that are not actually present, their whole inner life is impoverished and simplified, and their freedom of thought and action is largely lost. They are more or less at the mercy of the external stimuli that play upon them.

Aphasics are often able to function adequately or normally in simple concrete relations. But when they are required to act, as all persons constantly are, on the basis of long-range goals or abstract principles, or of merely remembered events, objects, or persons, they tend to fail. This limitation to the concrete present makes impossible much of the voluntary, or "creative," kind of human behavior. Aphasics are unable to make these verbal formulations; therefore their responses are piecemeal, unintegrated. They respond to each concrete situation as such; and when no immediate demand is made upon them, or when excessive demands are made, they tend to lapse into inactivity or anxiety, realizing that there is something wrong with their inner life.

K. Goldstein has shown how drastically aphasia affected the intimate social relations of one of his patients. The patient was a husband and father, and prior to his affliction he had been devoted to his family. During his stay at the hospital, however, he appeared to show neither concern nor interest in his absent family and became confused when any attempt was made to call his attention to them. A casual observer would have regarded him as callous and indifferent. Yet when he was sent to his home for brief visits he warmly displayed his former interest and devotion.

Goldstein concluded that this patient's "out of sight, out of mind" attitude toward his wife and family grew directly out of his inability to formulate his relationships to his family when it was physically absent. He could not imagine or conceive it adequately, and consequently he could not engage in internalized thinking about it. In short, when his wife and children were not visible to him he was unable to think of them, because he could not produce and manipulate the necessary verbal symbols.

In one of the most significant tests he administered to aphasics, Head required the patient, seated opposite and facing him, to imitate his movements. Head placed his left hand to his right ear, his right hand to his right eye, and so on. Then he repeated the tests while the patient observed and imitated these movements as they were reflected in a mirror.

The patients either had great difficulty with the first part of this test or they found it altogether impossible to imitate Head's movements, whereas they were generally able to imitate the movements correctly when they observed them in a mirror. The reason was not difficult to find. When the doctor and patient sat facing each other the patient could not imitate directly, but had to transpose directions (remembering that his left hand corresponded to the investigator's right hand, and so on). When Head's movements were reflected in the mirror, this act of transposition was unnecessary; all that was required was direct mechanical imitation.

In general terms, the significance of this simple but exceedingly effective test may be stated thus: it demonstrates that person's lacking language cannot project themselves into the point of view of another person. The patient is unable to guide his actions by imagining himself to be in some other position than the one in which he actually is. We may say that he is enclosed within his own point of view; that his point of view is, to use Piaget's term, *egocentric*. In a fundamental sense, normal adult social interaction rests upon the ability of persons to anticipate and appreciate the actual and possible reactions of other people—in short, to assume the role of another person. The loss of this ability in aphasia (in varying degrees, depending upon the severity of the disorder) thus provides powerful experimental and clinical evidence to support the thesis that language is the basic social and socializing institution.

DIRECT AND SYMBOLIC REFERENCE Head made a distinction between what he calls *acts of direct reference* and those that require some sort of *symbolic formulation* between the initiation and the completion of the act. This distinction is roughly equivalent to Goldstein's distinction between the "concrete" and the "abstract" (categorical) attitudes. (11) Acts of symbolic reference imply a complex adaptation involving the recognition of signs, logical symbols, or diagrams. Acts of direct reference are organized on a simpler level.

Aphasics generally function adequately in acts of direct reference but have trouble with, or are unable to carry out, acts of symbolic reference. The contrasts on the following page provide a few illustrations of the difference between the two classes of acts.

Practically all the activities that are listed are either completely beyond the reach of subhuman animals or can be taught to them only with great difficulty. The acts listed in the second column are especially difficult for very young children to execute; they are generally learned later in life than the corresponding acts listed in the first column.

Not all the types of behavior listed in the second column are beyond the capacity of all aphasics. There is considerable variation ac-

Acts of Direct Reference	Acts of Symbolic Reference
Imitating the movements of the investigator as reflected in a mirror.	Imitating the movements of the investigator seated opposite, facing him.
Shaving.	Gathering together in advance the necessary articles for shaving.
Selecting from a number of objects before him the duplicate of one placed in his hand out of sight.	Selecting from objects placed before him the duplicates of two or more objects placed in his hand out of sight.
Tossing ball into a basket that he can see before him.	Tossing a ball into a basket concealed behind a screen.
Exact matching of colored skeins of yarn.	Sorting and arranging colored skeins of yarn in a systematic way.
Pointing to familiar objects in his or her room.	Drawing a ground plan of his room that shows the location of familiar objects.
Swearing.	Giving the name of the Deity upon command.
Recognizing familiar streets and buildings of a city.	Following directions within a familiar city.
Repeating, fairly correctly, the numbers up to ten and sometimes beyond that if he is given a start.	Carrying out arithmetical operations, particularly those involving numbers of several digits.

cording to the severity of the disorder and the type of aphasia involved. Moreover, aphasics often learn over a period of time to perform some of the more complex acts listed above, although usually with difficulty, by resorting to more primitive methods than the ones ordinarily used by normal persons. Thus patients who cannot follow directions in a city may learn a route by sheer repetition and memorization of landmarks. Similarly, they may learn to make change properly by repetition and memorization rather than by calculation.

The data on aphasia indicate that introspective evidence of the role of language must be interpreted with caution. Just as other functions drop out of consciousness when they become automatic, so language may fade out of the picture when many apparently purely motor and other types of skills of which it is the basis are fully established. UNRELIABILITY OF INTROSPECTIVE EVIDENCE

    To illustrate our point, one may ask if the game of billiards requires or presupposes language ability. Offhand there would certainly seem to be no possible connection between the propulsion of billiard balls on a green table and the ability to talk. If we ask billiard players about the game, they tell us only that when they aim the cue they make a sort of geometrical calculation and have in their "mind's eye" a kind of geometrical image of the path which they wish the cue ball to take, striking first one and then the second of the two other balls involved. It would appear that language plays no part in this activity.

However, such introspective evidence is contradicted by the facts. Aphasics, even though they may have been skillful at billiards prior to the onset of aphasia, usually lose that skill along with their language ability. They report that they cannot visualize the three balls simultaneously and that they become confused. They do not know at what angle to strike the second ball and may even hit it on the wrong side.

Similarly, one would suppose from introspective evidence that the ability to draw a picture of a cow, let us say, is totally unconnected with language and thus would be unaffected in aphasia. This is not so, as we have reported above. It was Head's standard practice to ask his patients to draw pictures of familiar objects from memory. He requested an English army officer, for example, to sketch an elephant. Prior to his illness, this officer had spent many years in India and had once shown rather good amateur ability at drawing. Nevertheless, the drawing he produced was exceptionally poor. It lacked some essential parts, such as the trunk and tusks; some of the parts were in wrong relation to one another; and, in general, the whole picture was scarcely recognizable as an elephant. Later, when the bullet wound that had caused the aphasia had healed and the patient had recovered much of his language ability, he drew upon request a detailed drawing of an elephant. The drawings are reproduced on page 233.

These are but two of the many illustrations available. They point to the conclusion that language may play a vital role in an activity without the individual's introspective awareness of the fact.

LANGUAGE
IMPAIRMENT
AND THOUGHT

We have had a great deal to say about language and thought in past chapters, emphasizing that the latter cannot exist without the former. Thought without language is reduced to the level of the thinking, if we may call it such, that is characteristic of lower animals. Those who study aphasia sometimes erroneously conceive of thinking and language as two entirely distinct and separate processes. Thinking, speaking to others, and speaking to oneself are inextricably interrelated and interdependent processes. Head has compared the aphasic with someone in solitary confinement whose only contact with the outside world is a defective telephone. While this comparison is picturesque, it is incomplete. When asphasics try to talk to themselves to formulate their own thoughts they use the same defective telephone.

The neurologists who study speech-related functions in the brain

The upper drawing was made by a patient with severe aphasia. The same patient made the lower drawing after he had recovered most of his powers of speech. (From Henry Head, *Aphasia and Kindred Disorders* [1926]).

generally agree with W. R. Russell and L. E. Espir that in the brain speech cannot be separated from thought. The Soviet psychologist A. R. Luria (20:34), in a book on aphasic disorders, also comments: "The reorganization of mental activity by means of speech, and the incorporation of the system of speech connections into a large number of processes, hitherto direct in nature, are among the more important factors in the formation of the higher mental functions, whereby man, as distinct from animals, acquires consciousness and volition."

Aphasia and related disorders, in their almost bewildering variety of manifestations, serve to bring home to the normal person the enormous complexity of the language function and its interconnections with other processes. Russell and Espir observe that severe aphasia destroys the individual's capacity to enjoy reading a book. Aphasics may read slowly, absorb the meaning with difficulty, and lose the train of thought because the previous pages are inadequately stored or remembered. Russell and Espir note that there are a number of storage systems that aphasics must use in reading: (1) visual patterns acquired much earlier for the recognition of letters and words; (2) the associations that give meaning to the words; and (3) "the capacity to hold something of what he reads for long enough to correlate it with later pages." (27:145) These same writers observe that intelligence and personality are disorganized in severe aphasia. They add that some of the long-range effects of aphasia are loss of memory, difficulty in concentration, mental fatigability, irritability, and change of personality. "The scaffolding on which speech is developed," they add, "is built up in relation to hearing, vision, and the sensori-motor skill involved in uttering words." However, this scaffolding "is concerned with much more than speech for it seems to provide a basis for the psychological processes of thinking and learning." (27:170–71)

The normal human being finds it difficult to imagine how it feels to be an aphasic. There seems to be little in our experience that enables us to project ourselves, as it were, into the aphasic's position or to see and experience the impairment of thought that hinges upon his or her speech difficulties. We suggest that students play a verbal game with themselves in order to have a better notion of how it might feel to be an aphasic. Suppose that one makes believe that he or she is in a foreign land whose language he or she knows only moderately well. Conversation with others is necessarily reduced to rather simple and concrete levels, as considerable facility in the language would be required in order to exchange views on complicated, abstract, or philosophical matters. It is easier to talk, with the aid of gestures, about concrete objects that are present, such as the immediate scene and the weather. If an attempt is made to speak of events long past or far in the future or of objects out of sight; one's vocabulary proves insufficient. However, if one tries to carry on such a normal, slightly involved conversation, the effort is likely to prove exhausting. As an acquaintance of the authors once said:

> I went to bed exhausted every night from trying to speak German; particularly when I was with a lot of German people who were engaging in a crossfire of conversation. It was simply exhausting—after a while you felt you wanted to sit down and recuperate. And you felt absolutely frustrated and bottled up; you wonder if you're ever going to think a complex thought again in your life. You can ask for beer and coffee and potatoes, but when you have to discuss a complex feeling or reaction or analyze a political situ-

ation, you're simply stalled. You struggle to speak, but you're reduced to the level of your vocabulary.

Suppose that in addition to conversing with others in the foreign language, one also had to converse with oneself (that is, to think) using only this same restricted vocabulary. How difficult it would be to carry on internalized conversation that had any semblance of complexity!

Apropos of our imaginary verbal game, it is interesting to read the conclusion of an investigator who studied the imperfect English speech of two French children. (7) He noted that certain types of "breakdown" in their speech resembled the defects of aphasics. Breakdowns consisted of tendencies to simplify, to revert to more simple speech reactions, and to avoid speaking of abstract matters. Neither this nor our strenuous verbal game faithfully represents the situation of the aphasic, but both should give one an idea of the thinking impairments that arise from aphasic speech disorders.

The Social Isolation of the Schizophrene

SCHIZOPHRENIC THOUGHT

A large percentage of persons in almost any hospital for the mentally ill is likely to be classified as schizophrenic. Although schizophrenia is a broad category including a very heterogeneous group within its boundaries, psychiatrists are agreed that schizophrenes suffer impairment of thought processes and disturbances of social relationships.

Generally speaking, schizophrenes have lost contact with society. Their speech is often unintelligible, partly because they invent words and partly because they give many ordinary words a unique signification and combine them in unconventional ways. As their use of language tends to be individualistic, schizophrenes cannot carry on sustained normal communication with normal persons. "The schizophrenic becomes so used to his own language that he is no longer able to tell people what he thinks, even when he feels like doing so." (15,35) Indeed, schizophrenes may develop their own *private language* with its own unique set of meanings which are expressed in a disjointed, temporal fashion. Sentences, as commonly understood, are not utilized. Novel words may be repeated, over and over again. This private language may be unique to each schizophrene. (35:130)

Conversation with a schizophrene leaves one with the feeling that both he or she and you have been talking past each other. Only those persons who know him or her intimately, or who have deep insight into the nature of the disorder, can make much sense of his or her utterances. For the schizophrene, the "demarcation between the outer world and his ego is more or less suspended or modified in comparison with the normal." (10:23)

> The distinction between self and nonself . . . , the differentiation between a world of independent objects and one's attitudes and expectations concerning such objects, the distinction between the meanings one feels and seeks to convey and the semantic values of conventional words, the polarity between symbolic vehicles and objects . . . appear to break down, to varying degrees, in schizophrenic states. (34:254)

These features of schizophrenia are linked with and are indices of the impairment of intellectual processes. This impairment has been conceived of as a deterioration in normal ability to conceptualize and generalize. Goldstein (10:23) has concluded that schizophrenes give evidence of inability to reason abstractly. (Normal persons can assume both "concrete" and "abstract" attitudes.) E. Hanfmann and J. Kasanin (12:46–48) came to substantially the same conclusion from a comparative study of normal and schizophrenic persons. But they noted also that schizophrenes differ greatly in the degree of ability to reason abstractly, some showing little or no impairment. This might have been anticipated, in view of the heterogeneous character of the group psychiatrically classified as schizophrenics.

A psychologist, J. Hunt (14:10–19), has attacked the view that schizophrenes lack generalizing ability, believing this to be a hypothesis open to debate and lacking validation. A later study by Hanfmann and Kasanin (12) has a bearing on this question. They have listed five subcategories of schizophrenes arranged according to degree of intellectual impairment. Patients in one category suffer no discernible intellectual impairment, whereas patients in the other categories exhibit various degrees of it. This kind of refined classification suggests the direction that future research in this area is likely to take.

A study by H. Rashkis, J. Cushman, and C. Landis (26) throws additional light upon the controversy over the generalizing ability of schizophrenics. These investigators draw distinctions between "abstract," "complex," and "concrete" behavior (these, the reader may note, are in descending order). (26:70)

> *Abstract behavior* . . . the subject is actively able to grasp the essential aspects of a new situation, to behave in accordance with his attitude, and to account satisfactorily for his behavior. *Complex behavior* . . . the subject selected terms representing aspects of a possible situation without being able to account for his selection. *Concrete behavior* . . . the inability of the subject to grasp essential relationships, to arrange new material in a conceptual scheme, or to relate aspects of a new situation with regard to his own personal experience or sensory preference.

Subjects were given a sorting test. Only normal adults were able to sort on the highest, or abstract, level. Both schizophrenics and normal children (aged thirteen to fifteen years) could sort on the middle, or complex, level. It is interesting to note that paretics (syphilitic psychotics) were unable to attain any complexity or abstractness at all in their sorting; their behavior was entirely on the lowest, or concrete, level.

Few authors have maintained that schizophrenics actually revert to earlier modes of thinking as they retrace their development in reverse. Many researchers of schizophrenia believe that severe schizophrenes operate on a level of reasoning that is lower than the level on which they reasoned before they became severely disordered. However, the researchers maintain that recognizing this is something other than equating adult schizophrenic thought with childhood thought, either of schizophrenic or normal children. As H. Friedman has noted (9:96):

> This functional regression is not total: the schizophrene's perceptual functioning cannot be conceived of as being identical with that of the child; vestiges remain which reveal the efficacy of the individual's past, that is, the previous functioning on a higher developmental level. This is most clearly observed in the survival of a perceptual discreteness and plasticity of an order not attained by children, and in the variety of responses which point to a wider acquaintance with environmental stimuli.

Some observers think of schizophrenia as "regression." By this they mean that the patient loses the capacity to reason abstractly, and reverts to a lower (preadult) level of thought. The more severe the disorder becomes, the more his or her thinking regresses. This conception of a *peeling-off* or *lamination* process, as it has been termed, is based upon the assumption that the most complex thought processes appear in the developmental career of each person after and as a result of the appearance of simpler thought processes. Rather than explanations hinging on cognitive regression, schizophrenia might be better accounted for in terms of fundamental distortions in the communication process.

N. Cameron has given us an excellent summary description of the schizophrenic's plight, particularly with reference to communication (4:55–56):

> The continual interchange between a given person and those around him not only develops the social character of his language and thought, but also maintains it afterward at an adequate social level. For if this organization falls below the point of intelligibility where others can share it, and if it cannot then be amplified by other words, gestures, signs, or demonstrations, it can no longer function in communication . . . that is just what happens in schizophrenic disorganization. Social communication is gradually crowded out by fantasy; and the fantasy itself, because of its nonparticipation in and relation to action, becomes in turn less and less influenced by social patterns. The result is a progressive loss of organized thinking, and ultimately an incapacity for taking the role of others when this is necessary to enable one to share adequately in their attitudes and perspectives.

Summary The lack or loss of language has serious behavioral consequences. Isolated children and the blind deaf who do not learn a language fail to become socialized human beings; they exhibit the types of behavioral disabilities that the analyses in preceding chapters would lead us to expect. Investigations of aphasia and schizophrenia also seem to confirm the importance of language as the integrative agent in human behavior.

We must, however, make some qualifications and reservations. The data on isolated children are meager; the same is true of the material on the blind deaf. Moreover, the phenomena of aphasia and schizophrenia are very complex and subject to controversy. Further research may show some of our interpretations to be wrong; certainly such study will lead to qualifications and refinements. Nevertheless, present knowledge about these several phenomena supports the general thesis that complex mental responses involve complex use of language symbols. Loss or lack of symbols leads to incomplete or inadequate socialization and development of the self.

References

1. Agranowitz, A., and M. R. McKeown, *Aphasia Handbook for Adults and Children.* Springfield, Ill.: Charles C Thomas, Publisher, 1966.
2. Brain, R., *Speech Disorders: Aphasia, Apraxia, and Agnosia.* London: Butterworth, 1961.
3. Brownfield, C. A., *Isolation: Clinical and Experimental Approaches.* New York: Random House, 1966.
4. Cameron, N., "Reasoning, Regression, and Communication in Schizophrenics," *Psychological Monographs,* vol. 50, no. 1 (1938).
5. Carterette, E. C. (ed.), *Brain Function: Speech, Language, and Communication.* Berkeley: University of California Press, 1966.
6. Cassirer, E., *An Essay on Man.* New Haven: Yale University Press, 1944.
7. Crewdson, J., "Speech in an Imperfectly Learned Language," *British Journal of Psychology,* vol. 32 (1941), pp. 82–99.
8. Davis, K., "Final Note on a Case of Extreme Isolation," *American Journal of Sociology,* vol. 52 (1947), pp. 432–37.
9. Friedman, H., "Perceptual Regression in Schizophrenia: An Hypothesis Suggested by the Use of the Rorschach Test," *Journal of General Psychology,* vol. 81 (1952), pp. 93–98.
10. Goldstein, K., *Human Nature in the Light of Psychopathology.* Cambridge, Mass.: Harvard University Press, 1940.
11. ———, and M. Scheerer, "Abstract and Concrete Behavior: An Experimental Study with Special Tests," *Psychological Monographs,* vol. 53, no. 2 (1941).
12. Hanfmann, E., and J. Kasanin, "Conceptual Thinking in Schizophrenia," *Nervous and Mental Disease Monographs,* no. 67 (1942).
13. Head, H., *Aphasia and Kindred Disorders of Speech.* New York: Macmillan, 1926.
14. Hunt, J. McV. (ed.), *Personality and the Behavior Disorders.* New York: The Ronald Press, 1944.

15. Kasanin, J. (ed.), *Language and Thought in Schizophrenia.* Berkeley: University of California Press, 1944.
16. Keller, H., *The Story of My Life.* Garden City, N.Y.: Doubleday, 1917.
17. ———, *The World I Live In.* New York: Appleton-Century-Crofts, 1938.
18. Labov, William, *Language in the Inner City.* Philadelphia: University of Pennsylvania Press, 1972.
19. Lantz, DeLee, and E. H. Lenneberg, "Verbal Communication and Colour Memory in the Deaf and Hearing," in Parveen Adams (ed.), *Language and Thinking.* Baltimore: Penguin Books, 1972, pp. 58–76.
20. Luria, A. R. *Higher Cortical Functions in Man,* trans. by Basil Haigh. New York: Basic Books, 1966.
21. Mason, M., "Learning to Speak after Six and One-half Years of Silence," *Journal of Speech Disorders,* vol. 7 (1942), pp. 295–304.
22. Nielsen, J. M., *Agnosia, Apraxia, Aphasia: Their Value in Cerebral Localization,* 2d. ed. New York: Hefner Publishing Company, 1962.
23. Oléron, P., "Conceptual Thinking in the Deaf," in Parveen Adams (ed.), *Language and Thinking.* Baltimore: Penguin Books, 1972, pp. 43–49.
24. Osgood, C. E., and M. S. Miron (eds.), *Approaches to the Study of Aphasia: A Report on an Interdisciplinary Conference on Aphasia.* Urbana, Ill.: University of Illinois Press, 1963.
25. Penfield, W., and L. Roberts, *Speech and Brain Mechanisms.* Princeton, N.J.: Princeton University Press, 1959.
26. Rashkis, H., J. Cushman, and C. Landis, "A New Method for Studying Disorders of Conceptual Thinking," *Journal of Abnormal and Social Psychology,* vol. 41 (1946), pp. 70–74.
27. Russell, W. R., and L. E. Espir, *Traumatic Aphasia: A Study of Aphasia in War Wounds of the Brain.* New York: Oxford University Press, 1961.
28. Schuell, H., J. J. Jenkins, and E. Jiménez-Pabón, *Aphasia in Adults: Diagnosis, Prognosis, and Treatment.* New York: Harper & Row, 1964.
29. ———, *Differential Diagnosis of Aphasia with the Minnesota Test.* Minneapolis: University of Minnesota Press, 1965.
30. Strauss, A. A., and H. Werner, "Experimental Analysis of the Clinical Symptom 'Perseveration' in Mentally Retarded Children," *American Journal of Mental Deficiency,* vol. 47 (1942), pp. 185–88.
31. Templin, M. C., *The Development of Reasoning in Children with Normal and Defective Hearing.* Minneapolis: The University of Minnesota Press, 1950.
32. Weisenberg, T., and K. E. McBride, *Aphasia.* New York: The Commonwealth Fund, 1935.
33. Werner, H., *The Comparative Psychology of Mental Development.* New York: Harper & Row, 1940.
34. ———, and Bernard Kaplan, *Symbol Formation.* New York: Wiley, 1963.
35. Wolcott, Roy H., "Schizophrense: A Private Language," *Journal of Health and Human Behavior,* vol. 11 (1970), pp. 126–34.

Selected Readings

BRAIN, R., *Speech Disorders: Aphasia, Aphraxia, and Agnosia.* London: Butterworth, 1961.
An interesting and well-written account that provides a good overall view of the many varieties of language disorder and the problems and complexities of this area of research.

DAVIS, K., "Final Note on a Case of Extreme Isolation," *American Journal of Sociology*, vol. 52 (1947), pp. 432–37.
   A brief but quite detailed descriptive account of a case of isolation that attracted considerable attention and was unusually well investigated.
HEAD, H., *Aphasia and Kindred Disorders of Speech*. New York: Macmillan, 1926.
   A classical and influential study still well worth reading, especially for its discussion of the behavioral manifestations of aphasia and similar disorders.
KELLER, H., *The World I Live In*. New York: Appleton-Century-Crofts, 1938.
   Helen Keller was both deaf and blind. Her book provides insights as to how the world appears to or is conceived by such a person.
LURIA, A. R., *Higher Cortical Functions in Man*, trans. by Basil Haigh. New York: Basic Books, 1966.
   Luria, a Russian scientist who was strongly influenced by the Pavlovian idea of the "second signaling system," discusses the higher mental processes in relation to brain mechanisms.

PART THREE

Life Cycle: The Genesis of Self

chapter *8*

Motives, Activities, and Accounts

*I*n *Chapters 1* through 7 we discussed social structure and the self, stressing the point that language and symbolic systems connect persons to social groups and social worlds. A processual model was implied; with increased language differentiation, the person's cognitive world gains in complexity. In Part Three, we extend this processual model by examining the *life cycle* changes that accompany the genesis of self in childhood.

One of the especially perplexing aspects of the study of human beings arises from the fact that they, unlike any other objects of scientific study, have ideas of their own about why they act as they do. Consideration of what people say in explanation of their behavior inevitably leads to a consideration of motives and motivation. The concept of motivation is especially applicable to human behavior. It is less applicable to the lower animals, and when applied to them is usually translated into biological terms. It is, of course, entirely inapplicable to inorganic matter and plant life. In this chapter we shall be concerned with the concept of motivation as it is applied to human behavior, and we shall see that it poses some of the most difficult and controversial problems in the social sciences.

The issue of motives and motivation, as we shall show in this chapter, is often confused in the social and psychological sciences. It is useful

Gestures and motives: each anticipates the actions of the other. (*Mimi Forsyth from Monkmeyer Photo Service*)

at the outset to state one's position in this matter. We assume that the human organism is active from birth to death. Accordingly, activity per se is a constant factor across all human situations. The explanations for the direction, shape, and form that activity takes, however, are varied and variable. The explanations that persons give for their behavior we shall call *accounts,* and these accounts are often subsumed under what Mills termed *vocabularies of motive.* As humans act they may alter their reasons for acting. In this sense, accounts and motives are embedded in ongoing activity. This suggests that those who ask "What motivates human behavior?" or "What are the motivations for a particular action?" are asking erroneous and misleading questions. *Motives,* not *motivations,* are what concern us in the pages below. We turn first to common conceptions and misconceptions concerning these points.

When specific acts are explained in ordinary discourse, the explanations rest upon assumptions about behavior in general. Systems of philosophy also require that assumptions be made concerning the nature of behavior and its motives. In this connection, the problem of motivation is an old one; and it has been handled in many different ways. The various hedonistic philosophies have tended to conceive of the seeking of pleasure and the avoidance of pain as the bases of most action. Another approach has been to think of humans as motivated by certain powerful drives or combinations of drives, such as sex and hunger, love, self-interest, and self-preservation. The sources of the purposes which move human beings have been found also in supernatural beings or superordinate structures such as God, the state, the community, the economic system, or the class system.

Since human beings have a curiosity about and a deep interest in the "why" and "how" of behavior, every generation makes a fresh attack on the problem of motivation. Nevertheless, one is struck by the tenacity with which certain classical conceptions reappear in new guises. The terminology may be new, but the themes are not.

The imputation of motives to others is, of course, an integral aspect of human interaction. It is inconceivable that social life could exist if persons did not make guesses or assumptions about the purposes of others. The mark of human behavior, as opposed to animal behavior, is that it is organized around anticipation of others' responses to one's own actions. Anticipation involves assumptions as to how and why others will react. It also involves judgments about previous acts of others, as they have bearing upon their possible future acts. A knowledge of the purposes of others is the most effective basis for understanding what they are doing now and knowing what to expect from them in the future.

Incorrect assessment of such purposes has important consequences, since it may lead to embarrassment, misunderstanding, loss of money and time, or other even more unfortunate effects. When acts are familiar, traditional, routinized, the assessment of motivation is easy and taken for granted. No one raises questions about why people walk erect, build houses, or wear clothes, although the question of motivation is brought into sharp focus when they do not do these things. If the reasons for customary behavior are inquired after, usually by an outsider, the person who is questioned may be at a loss for an answer. In relatively homogeneous societies, the questioning of motives is relatively infrequent, because the bases of customary behavior are infrequently challenged. (20:175)

> There are societies . . . with little or no group-awareness of group incentives; they have few, or no, formulated ideals of conduct, and they do not attempt to bring their group incentives into the light of day in the guise of accepted motives. Their problems of group behavior are problems of *how* and not *why*. They learn how to behave in this or that contingency; and if ever they ask why—and they rarely ask this unless some [anthropologist] asks them—the answer is, This is how we have always behaved. The society is unified and integrated by the sharp clarity of its techniques coupled with the obscurity of its motives.

In heterogeneous societies, actions more frequently raise questions because the behavior is unfamiliar to some, or because it is performed in contexts which make it unclear. Then some guesswork, and sometimes some sleuthing, is called for on the part of the investigator. The difficulties of correct assessment are further increased by the fact that people very often do not clearly formulate to themselves the purposes of their actions and so can give little help to others who wish to understand them. There may also be several purposes, or levels of purposes, involved in the same act. The importance of clues to future behavior is further underlined by the existence of duplicity in interaction. The concealment of motives and the deliberate misleading of other persons is sometimes cultivated as an art, and appears to be necessary for smoothly functioning social relationships, even relationships among friends, lovers, and kin. "Nothing but the truth" would thoroughly disrupt human relations.

Biologically Rooted Motives?

The idea that human behavior has its roots in human biological nature and can be explained only in biological terms is commonly designated as *biological determinism*. The tendency to assume this position is enhanced by the relatively great prestige of, and progress in, the biological, as compared to the social, sciences. The biological determinist thinks of motives as nothing more than gross bodily conditions. For example, dehyrdration may be equated with thirst, or contractions of the stomach muscles, and low sugar content in the blood may be equated with hunger. There is no question that bodily conditions are connected with motivation and that they condition it in a variety of ways. However, it is an error to regard any gross physical condition as the entire motive or cause for any action. Bodily conditions, such as those ordinarily associated with thirst and hunger, are by themselves inadequate to incite goal-directed behavior until they have been interpreted in certain ways or until the organism has learned what action to take. Before this learning takes place, the gross physical condition of the organism leads, at most, to restless exploratory behavior of an undirected kind.

HUNGER The case against the view that biological conditions directly motivate particular acts can be made by discussing the phenomenon of hunger. Consider the varied acts associated with eating a meal. Persons with presumably similar physiological states of hunger may act very differently while eating, according to standards of etiquette prescribed by their country and their social class. The foods chosen are not linked directly with the organism's biological structure. Thus, Dutch and American people generally eat different items for breakfast. The Chinese avoid milk and milk products and Americans abhor snake meat, although milk is available in China and snakes in America and both foods are nourishing.

Life Cycle: The Genesis of Self

The social foundations of hunger: an American extended family sits down to a meal. (*Ray Ellis/Photo Researchers, Inc.*)

As for the duration of meals: the typical American emphasis on speedy breakfasts and lunches seems to be connected mainly with industrial and commercial practices rather than with biological needs, whereas long dinners are related to leisure time and sociability. Nor does the order in which foods are eaten—since it is not identical in all countries—seem to be explainable on biological grounds. Although Americans from long habituation may think sweet food necessary to round off a meal, certain other peoples do not find this so. And scarcely accountable for on biological grounds is the symbolism—social, religious, personal—surrounding the eating of meals. Thus, many whites will not eat with blacks, and vice versa; children, for practical purposes, may be excluded from dinner parties.

Physical need for food should be clearly distinguished from the verbalized desire for it. It is unwarranted to assume that a newborn infant experiences the physical need for food as anything more than a diffuse, undefined discomfort. Infants simply cry and their parents are likely to assume they need milk. After repeated feedings, infants begin to respond in a way which seems to suggest that they have learned to expect milk in a given situation. However, since infants do not know what milk is and cannot verbalize their need, it is erroneous to equate their attitude toward milk with that of adults. Only after they have learned to speak and understand the meanings of words can children be said to be hungry or to desire food in the same sense that adults do.

The word *hunger* is applied to all three of the following: (1) the sheer fact of biological need; (2) the subverbal appreciation of the connection between the eating of certain substances and relief from hunger distress; and (3) the conscious verbal formulation of interpretation of a felt biological need.

The first, or physiological, need for food is obviously unlearned, whereas the third, the interpretation of the need, sometimes does not correspond to biological facts: persons may express desire for food when they do not require it biologically, and vice versa. They may believe they have all the food they require, when actually their bodies are in a state of malnutrition because they eat inadequate foods. The biological need of

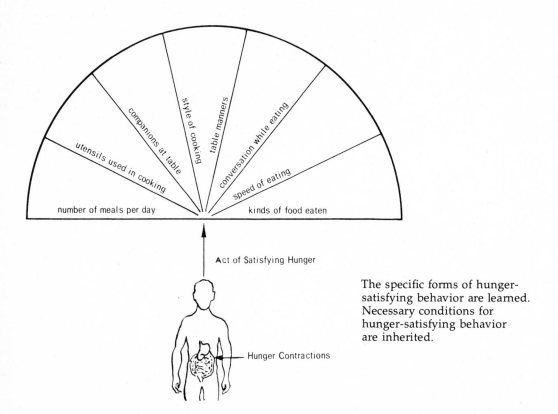

Act of Satisfying Hunger

Hunger Contractions

The specific forms of hunger-satisfying behavior are learned. Necessary conditions for hunger-satisfying behavior are inherited.

the organism for food may go unrecognized when the stomach is distended by nonnutritious substances. Through intravenous feedings the stomach may be temporarily bypassed altogether in the feeding process. In other words, physical need for food and verbalized desire for food are distinct and separate phenomena and are sometimes wholly unrelated.

There is, of course, no disputing the existence of a biological need for nourishment in all organisms, including humans. But there is a vast difference between acknowledging this need and assuming that specific human ways of satisfying it and thinking about it are simple consequences of biological conditions. As a matter of empirical fact, the average American child spends a great deal of time in learning the proper ways of satisfying his or her biological need for food. The necessity is biological, but the social behavior involved in satisfying it is not biological. The same may be said of other similar conditions imposed on us because we are biological organisms.

The learned character of hunger responses may be illustrated by reference to the upbringing of middle-class American children. They are taught innumerable lessons involving mashed vegetables, baby-food formulas, dessert, between-meal snacks, the use of silverware, proper table manners, and so on. Any parent who spends years teaching a child how and when to be hungry should not believe that hunger-satisfying activities among humans are chiefly biological.

Hunger for food is viewed so persistently as a gross biological matter that it is worthwhile to compare it with the hunger for drugs. Virtually all aspects which are pertinent to the present discussion of food hunger are pertinent to opium hunger too. In both, gross bodily conditions are necessary concomitants. The fallacy of viewing drug addiction as a purely physiological condition is easily perceived, however, primarily because drugs are not necessary to life and because the drug habit is generally acquired when the person is an adult or close to adulthood. (See Chapter 15.)

INSTINCTS

Few, if any, contemporary psychologists and physiologists postulate a direct or automatic connection between biological conditions and complex human action. However, many laypersons still do. The offering of general "instincts" as explanations of action is a variant of this position. Common speech and popular writing are replete with references to paternal, maternal, gambling, religious, and other instincts. During the latter part of the nineteenth century and the early years of the twentieth century, because of the influence of Darwin's work, it was standard practice in scholarly works to account for particular acts as expressions of generalized instinctual drives. It was usually also assumed that the behavior of lower forms of life was largely controlled by instincts.

Attempts by various psychologists and philosophers to draw up lists of "universal instincts" produced heated intellectual battles and hopeless disagreements. Some lists contained only one or two instincts, others as many as forty. One of the most ingenious theoretical schemes was devised by William McDougall (23), who suggested thirteen instincts, each paired with corresponding sentiments. They were: combative, parental, curiosity, food-seeking, repulsion, escape, gregariousness, self-assertion, submission, mating, acquisitiveness, constructiveness, and appeal. All sorts of complex behaviors were thought to be accounted for by naming the instincts involved in them. Sentiments were conceived of as more complex and composite in nature but as having instinctual bases, or possibly bases in several instincts. McDougall viewed the self-regarding sentiment as the most important, in the sense that it was believed to give unity to the personality. The sociologist Ellwood, after reviewing the scientific literature, concerning this question up to the mid-1920s noted that over 5,600 instincts had been identified.

As an exercise in understanding why instincts as explanatory concepts have been abandoned, let us consider two types of behavior: self-preservative and maternal. These were often believed to be motivated by their corresponding instincts. We have a right to ask three questions concerning each alleged instinct: (1) What is its physiological basis? (2) Does it clearly determine behavior? (3) Is it universal in the species?

The *instinct of self-preservation,* if it can be designated as such, must be an inheritable something, traceable to the structure of the organism. Yet physiologists have not unearthed any evidence of biological bases for an instinct of self-preservation. To contend that such an instinct exists is to confuse cause and effect. The instinct of self-preservation is not the cause of an organism's activity but merely a shorthand description of the activity. Perhaps, as Klineberg (17:119) has suggested, self-preservation is a kind of general label standing for a number of physiological drives such as thirst, hunger, and elimination.

We may also note the whimsical operation of an instinct that seems to work all the time for some individuals but sometimes fails to work for others. Japanese statesmen, at least before and shortly after World War II, in accordance with Japanese moral standards would commit suicide to save face; frustrated Americans and Europeans take their own lives; soldiers of all countries defy this supposedly deep-rooted instinct by obeying commands which mean virtually certain death. Unless one presupposes a still stronger instinct or set of instincts which negates self-preservation, its vagaries are difficult to account for.

An instinct that is perhaps worthy of more consideration is the *maternal instinct,* because a physiological basis for it can possibly be discovered. Investigation of the behavior of rats has disclosed that concern for offspring—as shown by the mother's behavior—begins to decline from

Life Cycle: The Genesis of Self

twelve to twenty days after parturition, generally disappearing by the twenty-fifth day. It is apparently tied up with gland relief, since maternal concern parallels the development and decline of lactation. Other physiological bases are suggested by the fact that maternal behavior may be induced in male rats by implanting anterior pituitary glands of females. (17:80)

Assuming, then, that typically maternal behavior in the human mother is rooted in her physiology, can her behavior be adequately explained on physiological (instinctive) grounds? Many feminists, of course, strongly reject the idea of a maternal instinct. Consider the following eccentricities of the instinct. Psychoanalysts have demonstrated the prevalence of child rejection by some American and Western European mothers. Apparently these parents do not act in typical maternal fashion: instead of fondling the baby, they ignore or wreak vengeance on it; instead of expending time, energy, and concern upon the growing child, they avoid, tantalize, or hate it.

Maternal behavior is exhibited by women who have never lactated and by little girls before the age of puberty. A mother's love for her children does not disappear when she becomes old and loses the physiological functions alleged to be the basis of mother love. A woman who has had her ovaries and uterus removed by surgery does not, of course, change her attitudes toward her children because of this operation. Further inconsistencies are the practice of abortion and infanticide. How can the instinct permit these acts? Above all, how can it permit female infanticide and discourage male infanticide in one society, and do exactly the reverse in another? Moreover, in many societies it is a common practice to give away children to other families who wish to adopt them, and apparently this is done without outraging motherly impulses.

There is a sense in which behavior of a newborn baby is instinctive. However, the use of the term in this connection is merely descriptive, not explanatory. The older instinct doctrine conceived of instincts as "forces," or causes of whole ranges of human reaction. When we describe the yawning, sneezing, and other similar automatic behavior of a newborn child as instinctive, it is understood that this is only a way of saying that the child does not have to be taught to do these things.

Instinct as an explanatory concept has not only been virtually abandoned in the study of human beings, but it has also proved inadequate to account for the behavior of lower forms as well. It is meaningless to label behavior as instinctive if no biological structures or physiological conditions can be shown to be linked with it. Careful investigation of lower species, as we suggested earlier, indicates that their behavior is not nearly so mechanical or automatic as popularly believed, and that even so-called "instinctive patterns of reaction" are always related to and dependent upon the environment in which they occur. It has also been suggested that behavior sometimes believed to be rigidly determined by inherited mechanisms may in fact be the result of early and rapid learning. (15:109–120) It is well known that there is no necessary one-to-one correspondence between organs and specific activity. *Biological structures should perhaps be thought of as necessary conditions which make certain types of behavior possible but do not determine or explain specific modes of response to the requirements of a changing environment.* For instance, it has been observed that (6:43–45):

> Every bee [worker] in the hive has during its lifetime to pass through all the different jobs. First, in the first ten days of their life, the young bees have the task to attend to the brood, to clean the cells in which the queen will deposit her eggs, to warm the developing brood by sitting on it, to feed the older larvae with honey and pollen from the store-cells, and, when eventually their own food glands have been developed, to feed the young larvae with the secretion of those glands. Then, in the second period, running from their tenth to twentieth day, they have other occupations, such as to take the food from the returning bees and bring it to the store-cells, to clean the hive, and, further, to build the comb when their wax-glands have fully developed, which happens between the tenth and the seventeenth day. Finally, in the third period, which runs from the twentieth day up to their death, which in summer occurs between the thirtieth and the thirty-fifth day, the bee works as a field-bee, collecting food. . . . There is a clear connection between the execution of the instinctive actions and bodily development. . . . Yet it would be wrong to believe that the appearance of all these instincts is determined by bodily development alone.

To demonstrate this last point, that the apparently automatic instinctive behavior of bees is not purely a consequence of bodily development, Bierens de Haan (6) cites an interesting experiment in which a population of bees was divided into two groups, one older than eighteen days and the other younger. Each group was thus deprived of bees that normally perform vital functions in ordinary colonies; the younger bees, for example, at first had no members that normally forage for food while the older bees lacked those that build comb and care for the young. The result eventually was not that the divided colony perished as one might anticipate from a rigid instinctivistic view, but that each of the divided colonies developed the occupational differentiation required for survival and some of the bees even exhibited biological changes enabling them to perform their unusual functions—for example, bees older than normal comb builders developed new wax glands. It was observed that bees that had been isolated from the colony during the first ten days of their life, when returned to the colony, first performed the activities they had missed during their period of isolation.

The outcome of this investigation has been a blurring of the dividing line between instinctive and learned behavior as the necessity of viewing organisms in their environmental situations has received more stress. The concept of instinct as a general unfolding drive or force has given way to a concept of it as a term describing limited segments of behavior in which learning appears to play little or no part.

Need Psychology

We have said that psychologists do not ordinarily claim that there is a direct connection between physiological states and complex behavior. Nevertheless, they have been reluctant to abandon the conception that social behavior is somehow rooted in biological bases. The concept of need, or drive, may be taken as an illustration. It is a frame of reference which is widely used in some form or other by many psychologists (36):

> [One] type of need is allied with bodily functions and is variously referred to as biological, biogenic, unlearned, primary, basic. Lists given by various authors do not agree in detail, but Sherif's in *An Outline of Social Psychology* [34] is representative. He lists such motives as hunger, thirst, sex, breathing, and evacuation. Then there are social needs—synonymous as sociogenic, secondary, psychogenic, acquired, and derived, etc.—which are recognized as due to learning. Some of these latter ends are suspected as deriving, often in devious and subtle ways, from the more basic biological needs. But more current writers believe that some if not the majority of social needs originate solely in social interaction. Since needs are learned, and since men learn to want, wish, aspire to, an almost infinite number of things, the numbers of social needs are tremendous, and vary from society to society and group to group. Most writers wisely refuse to enumerate all possible social needs, unlike their careful attempts to list biological needs.
>
> This kind of motivational scheme grew out of the conviction, or the suspicion, that the basic fact about the human being is his body, and that much of his behavior could be traced to its workings. The more sophisticated treatments eschew the attempt to trace most behavior to the body, but the biological skeleton usually shows through in such statements as: "We have to keep in mind that no matter how real and how absolute acquired motives are felt to be, they constitute the superstructure of human motivation." As the deprivation of biogenic needs (sleep, food, or water) begins to grow intense, the individual returns or regresses to the level "which is dominated by the biogenic needs, and the superstructure of the acquired motives is subject to collapse in various degrees."

Various criticisms may be made of this position. The concept of *primary biological need* is itself dubious. To begin with, a person may be unaware of a biological deprivation and so it may not eventuate in behavior: for example, an individual suffering from a vitamin deficiency caused by a poorly balanced diet may not realize that the deficiency exists. People dying of starvation are said not to feel hunger after the first few days. Persons who suffer oxygen deprivation at high altitudes, such as mountain climbers and aviators, do not feel a craving for oxygen, but simply lose their judgment and develop other symptoms such as slowness of movement and reaction and poor motor control. They must be taught to expect these effects and how to avoid them through the use of artificially supplied oxygen. (34:585) Physiological needs not based on any innate drive may also be learned, and they may lead to behavior which serves no good biological end. Examples of these "learned needs" are the drug addict's need for morphine and the alcoholic's craving for drink. In many writings the notion of biological needs is replaced by a scheme of social needs. These may include the need for achievement, the need for affiliation, or by the more general assertion that persons are drawn to those who have complementary needs.

No one denies that there are unlearned components in much human activity or that organisms must do certain things to survive. It is also clear that certain physiological lacks or deprivations may lead to attempts to relieve the accompanying distress. Reactions to such deprivation may also be random and ineffective unless the individual is taught to recognize the lack and what to do about it.

Admitting the importance of biological survival and well-being does not, however, justify the usual need psychology. Such terms as "primary" and "basic" are rhetorical devices for making human behavior seem to be grounded in a solid biological substratum. The intellectual security thus created is only an illusion which oversimplifies and misrepresents the nature of human goals.

The designation of biological needs as "primary" or "basic" and social needs as "secondary" or "derived" seems to imply two things: (1) that the social are less important, and (2) that they directly or indirectly stem from basic, more fundamental needs. The first point is merely an unproved postulate, and most social psychologists no longer rely upon it.

The idea that human beings are most effectively motivated in terms of their assumed basic biological needs has had some interesting social implications, the shortcomings of which have been demonstrated. It used to be argued, for example, that workers' hours could not be shortened or their pay raised because this would leave them unmotivated to do the necessary work of industry. It was felt that laborers would not know what to do with their spare time. (Needless to say, those who advanced such views did not apply these arguments to themselves.) As *Fortune Magazine* observes (33):

> . . . Now there is no doubt that, given more time off, some workers might drink too much, or beat their wives, or go insane watching daytime television. Others might work themselves to death in second jobs. But the $30-billion leisure market, the remarkable emergence, almost from nowhere, of a huge, new do-it-yourself market, and even the familiar Sunday-afternoon sight of cars crawling along bumper to bumper, suggest strongly that most American workers have a pretty good idea of what to do with their time off.

Although many social psychologists employ some variant of need psychology in theory and research, most of them today are probably willing to admit that most social needs arise on their own level and are not really expressions, however indirect, of primary needs. Many desires and aspirations associated with eating and sexual behavior, for example, are connected in only the most tenuous ways, if at all, with the primary drives with which they are linguistically connected.

There is an enormous range of behavior which can be accounted for only in terms of social structure. The needs involved are endless in number and are constantly increasing or changing. Each of the unique features of modern, urban, technological civilization has ushered in its appropriate and unique needs. Some cosmopolites feel a need to live in cities of more than a million people; others may have a specific need to live only in New York City or to live in the country even if they must work in the city.

The refinement of symbol manipulation has led to the needs for intelligence, for rationality, for explanations of natural phenomena and of one's own actions. The foreknowledge of old age and death creates the need for orienting oneself to these realities. The unanswerable questions that can be asked about the origin, ultimate meaning, and destiny of human beings have led to the development of the needs that are satisfied by religious and philosophical doctrines. The formulation of standards and values produces the corresponding desires to be loyal, honest, reliable, and virtuous. Practically every such human ambition, wish, or desire may be called a "need" without furthering the study of behavior at all. People need whatever they think they need.

In the past there have been attempts to classify social needs into a relatively few basic types. One such typology which was famous for many years among sociologists and others was Thomas and Znaniecki's four fundamental wishes: for security, response, new experience, and recognition. (40:72, 73) However, the classification of human behavior into categories corresponding to assumed needs, wishes, or drives does not at all explain the behavior. Thus, if a husband is said to be unfaithful to his wife because of the "wish for new experience" and another husband is faithful because of "the wish for security," we must still ask why one is unfaithful and the other is not. To label behavior in such terms is quite arbitrarily to impute to the individual abstract and unverifiable motives which are conceived of as the forces or causative agents behind the overt acts. A need as such is not directly perceived; all that can be observed is behavior itself. Hence, the need is first inferred from the act and then used to interpret and explain it. Such explanations are circular or tautological because they do nothing that cannot be accomplished by a simple description of the behavior.

In a striking passage, Allport has brought out both the difficulty of deciding among contending lists of basic motives and the reductionism implicit in them all (3:193):

Taking the case of Tolstoy, Adler would find the style of life adopted by Tolstoy to be a consequence of his compensatory striving for power, for health, or for personal integrity. . . . Freud might decide that the "simplification of life" was a mere ritual evolved to escape feelings of guilt derived from an unhallowed infantile love; or perhaps he would attribute it to a death wish. Rank would see it as a desire to return to the peaceful pre-natal life. . . . McDougall might attribute it to the combined effects of the propensities for submission and comfort. H. A. Murray might say that there was a need for submission and inviolacy . . . Any of these writers, to be sure, would admit that the original motive had become greatly extended both in the range of stimuli which provoke it and in its varieties of expression. But THE COMMON FACTOR IN ALL THESE EXPLANATIONS IS THE REDUCTION OF EVERY MOTIVE, HOWEVER ELABORATE AND INDIVIDUAL, TO A LIMITED NUMBER OF BASIC INTERESTS, SHARED BY ALL MEN, AND PRESUMABLY INNATE. . . . Not four wishes, nor eighteen propensities, not any and all combinations of these, even with their extensions and variations, seem adequate to account for the endless variety of goals sought by an endless variety of mortals. The concept of need as an explanatory device is hardly distinguishable from the old instinct schemes. However, it may confidently be predicted that this kind of explanation will be with us for many years to come, since the belief in the body's primacy is deeply rooted.

There are some special variants of need theory which, sometimes, also are evinced in human behavior: that is, a tendency toward equilibrium, avoiding cognitive dissonance, and achieving balance (as discussed earlier in another context). In the words of its founder, Leon Festinger: "The existence of dissonance, being psychologically uncomfortable, will motivate the person to try to reduce the dissonance and achieve consonance." (13:3) Another psychologist, Theodore Newcomb, has laid emphasis on a "strain toward symmetry or equilibrium." (29:393–404) And a prominent sociologist, George Homans (referred to in Chapter 1), has outlined a general theory of exchange which is based on the motivational principle that individuals tend to maximize the rewards and minimize the costs received from interacting with other individuals: that is, Homans is necessarily assuming an inborn tendency, or need for, the human organism to respond to rewards and costs—however social they may be in content. This is simply a disguised version of biological needs and their elaboration, through socialization, into social needs. (16) It is quite close to *psychological reductionism,* a position we earlier criticized.

Freudian Conceptions

Probably the most influential motivational scheme of this century is the Freudian. Some variant of it is utilized by most clinical psychologists and psychiatrists. Social workers, child psychologists, and anthropologists have often found it useful or acceptable, although sociologists far less so.

It was most popular in sociology between the years 1930 and 1939. Fragments of the Freudian terminology and conceptual scheme have also found their way into popular thought. It is difficult to set forth current Freudian ideas in a form that would be subscribed to by all Freudians, because there are considerable differences in viewpoint, formulation, and emphasis among them. Whatever these differences may be, there is a fair amount of agreement on a number of basic points and assumptions. (See also Chapter 11.)

Among the basic assumptions underlying the Freudian view of motivation are the ideas that all human behavior is motivated, that the explanation of any behavior requires that its motives be analyzed, that the energy sources of motives are biological in nature, that motives range from those which are entirely conscious to those which are altogether unconscious, that most important ones are either unconscious or partly so, and that the conflict of motivational forces plays a dominant role in personality development. The following statement of basic tenets by a noted psychoanalyst would probably elicit fairly general agreement. We are quoting at some length, since we are critical of this motivational system and therefore wish one of its proponents to state it for the reader (42:44–45): **SOME BASIC POINTS**

> Psychoanalysis . . . deals with mental forces acting in the same, divergent, or opposite directions and with their resultants. The forces . . . are subjected to what one could call the "integrative principle," which characterizes biologic processes—the organism and its structural parts form a coherent unity manifesting the tendency to preserve itself and to develop in determined ways. Thus the various needs and urges and impulses of the individual must be co-ordinated so as to lead to integrated conduct, which is necessary for his adaptation to the conditions of reality. Conflicts arise when two or more urges cannot be combined toward such behavior; and so emotional conflicts and their various consequences constitute the most important sources of knowledge of mental phenomena.
> To account for the varying degrees of intensity inherent in any mental experience, one must postulate a "charge of energy" which is correlated to nervous excitation. The consciously perceived mental energy corresponds to what one usually calls "interest." It invests every mental process and is discharged in feelings, affects, and emotions as well as in motor activity. . . . Following a general trend of biologic investigation, Freud approached the study of mental phenomena not only from a causal but also from a finalistic point of view. Everyone is directly aware of "aims" which he feels urged to pursue, though the source or the urge is not conscious. He is also aware that he must frequently achieve secondary aims in order to reach his conscious goal. An aim has an object. A simple example is the urge of hunger, the goal of which is to be satisfied and the object of which is food. . . . Freud was concerned with the classification of the basic instincts and drives. This approach led to problematic and controversial formulations and

also to a number of uncertainties which have required revision of many corollary concepts. . . . In his first formulation of a dualistic concept of the basic drives, Freud distinguished the self-preservative or *ego drives* from the race-preservative or *sexual drives*. . . . Freud included in the ego drives all self-interest, and he extended the concept of the sexual or erotic drives to comprise all interest in objects which did not serve the self-interest.

The dynamic force of the sexual drives in this broad sense was called "libido." The ego drives were considered to be empowered by a different energy which could not be transformed into libido. . . . [Later] Freud dropped his former dualism, recognizing that the self-preservative and constructive developmental urges were empowered by the same force which characterized sexuality in the broadest sense of the word. But opposite to this kind of energy (libido), which includes all kinds of constructive drives, he postulated a destructive drive tending to dissolution and death. This dualism asserted that in the organism there normally arises not only a kind of energy which is discharged into pleasurable, constructive, and integrated activities but also another kind, the discharge of which determines disintegration and destruction. . . . According to Freud, the two always appear mixed with each other. . . . Some analysts resort to other explanations to account for aggression and destruction. They point out that, since these tendencies are biologically necessary for defense and for acheiving security and satisfaction, they need not necessarily be derived from a hypothetical death instinct. . . . The ultimate motive behind every urge and wish which determines human behavior is discharge of tension. But homeostasis alone cannot account for all biologic phenomena with which the mental drives are associated; it is responsible merely for the maintenance and re-establishment of the same conditions—the status quo—in the organism. No growth, no development, no expansion and propagation can derive from homeostasis alone. . . . [Alexander has] introduced the "principle of surplus energy," and from it he derived certain biologic formulations and theories concerning eroticism, growth, development, and propagation. . . . Through this approach no classification of drives can be formulated; a distinction is made merely between those tendencies which comply with homeostasis alone . . . and those which result from the surplus energy and its discharge in various activities. The latter Alexander calls "erotic drives." According to this theory, the discharge of all surplus energy, by which homeostasis is re-established, is pleasurable. . . .

Repression is the most important psychodynamic phenomenon which Freud discovered in his earliest studies. . . . When a drive or memory . . . undergoes repression, it is . . . subjected to mental processes which are extraneous to the individual's conscious inner experiences, and, so long as it remains unconscious, it is inaccessible to introspection. . . . Repression is one of the dynamic defenses against drives and memories which cannot be controlled by the ego and which thus jeopardize its integration. . . . After undergoing repression, drives and memories . . . become subject to the patterns of mental functioning which characterize the "system unconscious" from which all drives . . . derive. This system is also called the "id." . . . To comprehend the phenomenon of repression and its implications, one must study it from a dynamic as well as from a structural and topographic view. The first considers the forces employed by the ego to maintain the exclusion of a repressed drive from the ego and from consciousness in spite of its pressure from the id . . . the latter concerns the localization of the process in the mental apparatus. It has been said that repression takes place between the system unconscious—the id—and the preconscious—the ego. These mental localities are not anatomically related to different portions of the brain, but are . . . different patterns of mental functioning which maintain a constant reciprocal relationship. . . . It is helpful to repeat that the preconscious and conscious mental phenomena are rooted in the unconscious system. Every drive and interest, every memory and representation of the "inner foreign country," originate in this system.

Thus, according to the Freudian position human hehavior is activated either by innate biological needs or by elaborations of them. Human culture is conceived of both as an agency which frustrates and disciplines primitive urges; and as a consequence of such frustration, the basic sources of energy are undirected and goalless and are channelized through cultural forms. Freud says (14:151):

> . . . Our civilization is built up at the cost of our sexual impulses which are inhibited by society, being partly repressed but partly, on the other hand, made use of for new aims. However proud we may be of our cultural achievements . . . it is by no means easy to satisfy the requirements of this civilization and to feel comfortable in its midst, because the restriction of the instincts which it involves lays a heavy psychological burden on our shoulders.

However complex the social proliferation of instinctual demands may be, these demands are nonetheless a "facade behind which the function of the underlying innate drives are hidden." (25:19)

Freudian emphasis on unconscious drives and motives involves a corollary skepticism concerning the purposes which people consciously assign to their acts. Psychoanalysts believe that not only is there much duplicity and concealment about motives, but most persons actually know very little about their own motivations. They also point to the difficulty of assessing the motives of others because one's own repressions and motivations get in the way. "The obstacle which one's own repressions constitute against understanding others can be appeciated if one realizes that the uniformity and harmony of the conscious mind are guaranteed by repressions." (1:20) In the training of psychoanalysts, great stress is placed upon the understanding of one's own motivations so that they will not be allowed to interfere with the effort to understand the patient.

The Freudian scheme of motivation applies to human behavior the *conservation of energy principle,* which holds that energy can neither be created nor destroyed. Repressed wishes carry energy charges and this energy must be discharged in some way or other. It cannot be destroyed. Hence the occurrence of such processes as *sublimation,* in which forbidden sexual impulses obtain indirect gratification through acceptable modes of behavior such as artistic creation, intellectual pursuits, simple labor, or other not obviously sexual outlets.

Some psychiatrists conceive of their professional task primarily as that of understanding the unique individuality of the patient. Others place a relatively greater stress upon generalizing about classes of individuals and types of behavior and seek to make psychoanalysis a generalizing science. Allport has designated these two ways of approaching behavior, respectively, as the *idiographic* and the *nomothetic*. (3:22) As to the generalizer's point of view, it is interesting to observe that the various individuals who engage in a given form of behavior (for example, heavy drinking) usually give a wide variety of contradictory reasons for doing so. For the Freudian who seeks to generalize about the particular form of behavior under scrutiny, the problem thus posed is resolved by searching for the underlying unconscious motives which the individuals themselves do not and cannot give.

The Freudian therapist attempts to give patients insight into their repressions and unconscious wishes. This is accomplished in the "prolonged interview" in which the patient tells the psychiatrist about himself or herself and the psychiatrist attempts to make the patient conscious of the real (or unconscious) sources of his or her behavior. Though Freudian theory places a very pronounced emphasis upon the primacy of the unconscious, Freudian therapy emphasizes consciousness as the primary agency through which personality integration is achieved.

EVALUATION The Freudian system is complex, and as we have stated, it has many variants. We will therefore content ourselves at this point by commenting critically upon those of its aspects which have to do most explicitly with motivation.

The idea that all human behavior and all cultural forms stem directly or indirectly from primal biological sources has already been critically examined in this chapter, and there is no need to repeat those remarks. We may add that Freudian theory is an especially elaborate form of a modified biological determinism. Despite the ample allowance that contemporary analysts often make for social or cultural factors, the theoretical scheme still presents an extremely oversimplified view of the relationship of men to groups. This is perhaps to be expected from the fact that this body of theory arose from therapeutic practice with individual patients, and that its main focus is still perhaps on therapy.

Because orthodox Freudian psychoanalysts think of society and its functions as growing out of individual biological urges, they are compelled to view the urges which derive from group life as entirely secondary. The sociologist's position is usually that groups by their very interaction generate new "needs"—that is, wishes, aspirations, ambitions, ideals, values, and goals—and that these needs constantly change and proliferate. This is a pervasive feature of group life and need not and cannot be explained in terms of primal urges. Individuals are born into or join groups which are already going concerns, often with long histories, and learn the appropriate motives for action in them. As groups change and develop new interests, individuals change with them, dropping old motives and acquiring new ones. The Freudian idea that culture is a dependent variable, that it merely reflects the psychology of the individual, does not square with history and has led to strained and improbable interpretations of many institutions and historic events— war, crime, social movements, marriage, drug addiction, the Nazi revolution, international affairs, and student demonstrations, for example. Freud himself set this pattern. The following statement about the origin of religion gives an idea of the flavor of some of these interpretive efforts: "Psychoanalysis . . . has traced the origin of religion to the helplessness of childhood, and its content to the persistence of the wishes and needs of childhood into maturity." (14:229)

One of the features of Freudian psychology which still is relatively popular, despite its stress upon instinctive drives, is that it does assign an important role to learning. The instincts that are recognized are only two in number, Life and Death, or Eros and Thanatos, and they are thought of mainly as energy sources having no implicit direction or goals. The direction, form, and content of the resultant pattern of behavior, as well as the objects toward which it is directed, are regarded as a matter of learning. In the actual acquisition of specific behavior, primary stress is placed upon the interaction between a child and his parents and siblings. Although the behavioristic psychologist and social scientist usually do not accept the whole Freudian scheme, some are receptive to the idea that organic drives become harnessed to social motives through a conditioning, or learning process.

At the heart of Freudian psychology lies *the energy postulate,* which involves the idea that individuals have fixed quantities of energy at their disposal. What this means is that all socially learned motives are merely transformations of basic urges and do not have autonomous status of their own. The energy postulate leads Freudians to assume further that motives acquired in adult life are merely complex permutations of old ones. As Piaget, criticizing Freud, says: "When there is transfer of feeling from one object to another, we must recognize that in addition to continuity there is construction of a new feeling through the integration schema." (30:186) Allport made much the same point when he insisted upon what he called the *functional autonomy of motives.* (3:190–212) By this he meant that a form of behavior, first performed as a means to a given end, may become an end in itself when the original purpose has long since disappeared. The error involved in the Freudian view of motivation is that of confusing historical continuity with functional continuity. The motives of acts being performed now obviously must be operative in the present. The fact that these motives have a history does not mean that they are determined by early childhood antecedents. Some analysts, heeding this type of criticism, qualify Freudian theory—in practice, at any rate—to place more stress upon current functioning.

The use of the concept of energy makes no distinctions between types of energy; for example, physical, psychological, moral, and intellectual energy are not distinguished. The inadequacy of this concept becomes obvious if we think for a moment of a person like Mahatma Gandhi, the great Indian leader. One of his most energetic and influential actions consisted of going on hunger strikes, thus depriving himself of all energy intake. Excess intake of energy often leads not to productive and creative activity, but to the deposit of fat and to general torpor.

Tempting as it may be to think in this way of human behavior, it should always be kept in mind that when we do so we are making use of an analogy—the energy postulate—borrowed from the physical sciences. It invariably turns out that such borrowings do violence to the subtle apects of human behavior.

One of the major objections to the Freudian system hinges on the conception of "the unconscious" and of unconscious motives. There is no question that people are often unable—or unwilling—to give adequate grounds for their acts or that there is much irrationality in human behavior. Considering the complexity of human interaction and personal life histories, individuals can hardly be expected to be able to account fully and accurately for their behavior and all its antecedents. This fact had been recognized for generations before Freud.

However, the Freudian view of unconscious functioning is open to question on a number of points. First, it exaggerates the extent of unconscious motivation. A great deal of human behavior certainly appears to be routine, standardized, planned, or otherwise rational. The Freudians have been accused, we think altogether rightly, of taking a dim view of the rational processes and of tending to seek for motivational complexities where they do not exist. In the hands of a novice, or as a parlor game, this can be a form of "motive-mongering." At best, such an analytic approach tends either to reduce complex phenomena to terms of individualistic motives or shies away from these phenomena, many of which, like the establishment of the United Nations, are of a conscious and planned character. When analysts write about a complicated social phenomenon such as crime, they invariably allow their theory to dictate the selection of cases in order that they may stress the irrational and unconscious. Their case studies of criminals, for example, focus on what might be called individualistic crime or the pathology of crime, such as sadistic murder, rape, and other sex offenses. Another criticism often made of the Freudian conception of the unconscious is that the term is so loosely used as to confuse issues. It may be used to indicate an experience which an individual has forgotten, or it may be used to designate an innate drive. It may be used to designate an experience that individuals have never had, in the sense that they failed to notice that certain things were happening. It may be used to designate simple ignorance about themselves and their acts, or it may refer to their failure to analyze their own behavior. Miller has listed sixteen different usages of the term and pointed out that the writers are not always explicit about how they are using it. (24:271–85)

An examination of any one portion of Freudian theory tends to lead one to a consideration of the whole system. However, we shall confine ourselves here to a few comments on the Freudian theories of repression, memory, and unconscious purposes.

One does not have to deny the existence of repression, or something like it, to quarrel with the Freudian interpretation of it. People certainly do sometimes bury memories so deeply that they are entirely unconscious of their existence; and they are often unaware of impulses and desires which influence them. As used in much of Freudian theory, however, the concept of repression is overextended, as when it is used to explain why persons do not recall experiences during infancy. The total volume of anyone's experience is so great and behavior is so complex that it seems inevitable that everyone should forget much and that none of us should be fully aware of the reasons for our actions. As Cameron and Magaret say: "We all learn to practice selectivity among our own reactions, to accept what fits in with our ideal picture of ourselves and to reject that which seems at variance with it." (9:13) H. S. Sullivan refers to *selective inattention*, which enables us to maintain our self-esteem by not noticing things that may threaten it. (38) The concept of repression calls attention to an important psychological process, but a satisfactory description of the process remains to be formulated.

Researchers seeking to check the theory that unpleasant experiences are more often forgotten than pleasant ones have found only a relatively slight tendency in this direction. As Faris says: "These studies . . . do not furnish crucial proof of any operation of repression. An efficient repressing mechanism should work better." (12:127) Since the differences noted are average group differences, it appears that some persons also have an opposite tendency to recall unpleasant experiences.

The Freudian conception of repression rests on a particular view of memory. "For Freud, the whole of the past is preserved in the unconscious . . . another conception of memory has been opposed to it, that of reconstruction-memory." (30:187) The latter concept, as we have stated in Chapter 6, interprets memory as a reconstructive act, dependent upon the nature and organization of the material and the linguistic categories available to the person. Forgetting is regarded as a very complex and not necessarily repressive process. It is clear that repression is often associated with anxiety and threats to self-esteem, but the precise nature of the connection is not clear.

A final point may be mentioned concerning unconscious motivations: by definition they are inaccessible to the individual. This means that evidence concerning their existence cannot be obtained by direct testimony, but their existence must be inferred from what the person says and does. Evidence of this sort is subject to interpretations that differ according to the school of thought followed by the interpreter. The acceptance or rejection by the patient of a specific interpretation in itself proves nothing concerning the correctness of the interpretation. Taken with other evidence, the patient's rejection of an imputed motive is often viewed as proof of its existence, just as is the patient's agreement with the analyst in other circumstances. We may even ask if a wholly unconscious motive can exist at all. As we have already indicated with respect to oxygen deprivation, a person may desperately need oxygen and be entirely unaware of it; as long as this is the case, no appropriate behavior to satisfy the need occurs, and thus the biological need can scarcely be called a motivational force. Vitamin deficiency, withdrawal symptoms connected with drugs, calcium deficiency, and many other similar conditions illustrate the same point. (Appropriate behavior is mobilized only through some sort of recognition or consciousness of the condition, and the corrective behavior may be inappropriate if the condition is misnamed—that is, if it is not recognized for what it is.) So-called unconscious motives should probably be called by some other name than "motives" to indicate that they are not like the ordinary conscious ones for which the term might well be reserved.

We have offered such a long and detailed analysis and criticism of the basic Freudian position on motivation because of its continuing influence upon contemporary thoughts. (We note, for example, that a revised version of Freudian thought has resurfaced in recent years in the statements of women's liberation groups who contend that Freud's theories have deprived them of certain sexual gratification.) There is no doubt that it has provided a needed corrective of rationalistic and static psychologies and suggested new depths and dimensions of behavior. It has fostered a well-warranted skepticism about easy explanations of behavior in terms of its face value. As S. K. Langer said (18): "The great contribution of Freud to the philosophy of mind has been the realization that human behavior . . . is a language; that every *move* is, at the same time, a *gesture*."

Another very influential motivational terminology in the contemporary world is that provided by Marxism. Most American social psychologists pay scant attention to it; although in some of the other social sciences— political science, for example—it is more influential. Also, among some younger sociologists there has been considerable reliance on, or stimulation from, Marxism. European social scientists give considerable attention to it, and, of course, in communist countries Marxist ideas of motivation are dominant. A brief general consideration of the Marxist view offers an interesting contrast to the Freudian scheme.

The Marxist social scientist conceives of the individual as the product of institutions, whereas the Freudian scheme considers institutions to be the product of individuals. The Marxist locates sources of motives in the social structure rather than in the individual. Like the Freudians, Marxists do not take seriously the expressed purposes of people, regarding them as mere surface manifestations or rationalizations of fundamental economic and class interests which may go unrecognized. In Marxist theory, these interests have nothing to do with primal biological urges but are thought of as arising from the social structure and its particular historic past.

The details of Marxist theory are involved. However, the major theme is that the source from which the important motivations flow is the economic system. An individual's position within the economic structure has a pervasive effect upon most of his or her thought and action. Since individuals share or have similar positions, they form different social classes and other somewhat less massive and important interest groups. The course of history is conceived of as the struggle for power among these groups.

According to this view, all thoughts, beliefs, philosophies, writings, art, and the like are determined by the basic economic facts of the society and reflect the position in the class structure of those who have formulated or created them. In Marxist terminology, mental products are *superstructure*. Marxists have used the term *ideology* to discredit their opponents' arguments and to suggest that these arguments are mere reflections of class interests. The Marxist use of the term "ideology" is not quite identical with the Freudians' use of the term "rationalization," since the former refers to a collective, or group, rationale. Since ideas are thought of as derived from class position, Marxists theoretically disparage as "idealistic" any psychology which attaches much importance to the motivational aspect of ideas, although they make practical use of this aspect in the political sphere.

The Marxist position is a radically environmentalistic one and hence comes into conflict with views stressing hereditary or biological factors in the determination of behavior. In the Soviet Union the anti-heredity bias is so strong that under Stalin it was a political issue, and there was danger in taking the opposite stand. Soviet writers—the non-dissident ones at least—are generally contemptuous of psychologies which place the mainsprings of human behavior in the individual organism, and Freudianism has been castigated as bourgeois and as evidence of the degeneracy and immorality of capitalist society. The Russian physiologist Pavlov, famous for his studies of conditioning in dogs, is held up as a worthy model in preference to Freud, as are Vygotsky and Luria.

The Marxist recognizes a difference between the real interests of a person or class and the perceived interests. Thus in the Marxist view the real interests of white-collar clerks may be identical with those of factory workers because both stand in opposition to an oppressing elite. However, white-collar workers usually ally themselves with their employers and thus, according to the Marxist, betray their own class interests. They do this because their eyes have not been opened to the way in which society really functions. In this sense they have a *false consciousness*. Marxists explain white-collar attitudes by reference to the special occupational position of this group of workers. They contend that only through Marxist analysis—that is, analysis in terms of class structure—can white-collar workers see their true position and recognize their affiliation with the working class. This distinction between real interests and perceived interests is paralleled by the Freudian dichotomy of unconscious and conscious motives. Like the Freudians, Marxists try to help their adherents to bring the real sources of their behavior into the open.

Marxist theory involves some ambiguity, as many critics have pointed out. It should be noted, however, that there is little specific in Marx or Engels that has directly guided the empirical research of contemporary Soviet social scientists. However, the theory of historical epochs, which predicts alterations in symbolic, cognitive skills, has guided the research of Luria, and earlier, that of Vygotsky. Aside from an emphasis on environmental forces and the specifics of the sociohistoric context, the writings of Marx have, as far as we know, produced ideology, not scientific growth and development. Paradoxically, however, "Marxist materialism" as reflected in the work of some Soviet psychologists turns out to be the approximate equivalent of American "behaviorism."

Although they profess to regard ideas as mere reflections of the basic economic facts of life, Marxists nevertheless use and manipulate ideas as powerful tools of action when they try to get people to acknowledge their real interests. In the practical political arena, Marxists have the greatest respect for the importance of ideas. More consistent with the theory is the belief that the basic economic changes following the seizure of power by a revolutionary elite will bring pervasive ideological changes.

There is a certain amount of significance and truth in the idea that occupation and class position are important sources of motivation. The Marxist theory is much too one-sided, but it has played an important historical role in social science by counteracting individualistic assumptions concerning the motives of humans. It has placed a needed emphasis upon institutionally derived loyalties and has called attention to economic interests, group allegiances, and intergroup conflicts as determinants of individual action.

A Sociological Conception

RATIONALIZATION AND INTERPRETATION

As we have seen, both Freudians and Marxists regard as suspect the verbal accounts which individuals give of their own purposes. The Marxists often regard such accounts as a cover-up of real economic motives or as evidence of ignorance. Freudians call them "rationalizations" and heavily discount them. Although they admit that some statements of purpose of a rational and conscious sort are in accord with reality, they are mainly concerned with irrational and unconscious motivations.

A technical definition of *rationalization* is that it "is a common technique by which the ego keeps certain tendencies repressed. . . . Emphasis upon the acceptable motivation allows the ego to keep the unacceptable repressed, since the selected motives can sufficiently explain the act in question." (1:13) It should be stressed that the psychoanalytic concept of rationalization implies that when acceptable motives are substituted for unacceptable ones, individuals are actually unable to think of the latter: when they deny their existence, they are not being dishonest or "kidding" themselves. In popular discourse, the term "rationalization" is usually taken to mean "giving socially acceptable but 'phony' reasons instead of the socially unacceptable but 'real' reasons for one's acts." Thus, a woman quarrels with her husband in the morning and throughout the day deals harshly with her daughter on the grounds that she needs discipline. This conception implies that the real reasons for one's acts are usually known, and hence tends to equate rationalization with dishonest or deluded thinking. It is a common belief that honest people do not rationalize or that they do so infrequently.

Strictly speaking, dishonesty has nothing to do with rationalization, for if a person deliberately makes false statements he or she is not really rationalizing at all but merely lying. A genuine rationalization is a formulation which the individual believes to be true even though it may be labeled self-deception by outside observers. The concept is probably used so widely by laypersons because it allows them to disregard or discredit the opinions of other people. As Burke has said (8:19–20):

> Much deep sympathy is required to distinguish our reasoning from another's rationalizing. . . . As people tend to round out their orientations verbally, we sometimes show our approval of their verbalizations by the term reasoning and disapproval by the term rationalizing. Thus these words also serve as question begging words.

The central sociological conception of rationalization is that people interpret their behavior and the entire situation in which it occurs either before the act or after the act—or both. Such interpretations sometimes represent distortions, however subtle, of the facts, so that one's face or self-esteem is preserved. Concerning the interpretations that are made after the act, note that they may have to do mainly either with "purpose"—that is, motive—or with "the objective situation" in which the act occurred. For example, suppose that a man shows cowardice when he is attacked or threatened at a party by another man. He may avoid the implications of cowardice, either in his own eyes or those of others, by a rationalization in terms of motives ("I didn't fight because I wanted to wait until a better moment to answer him"); or he may rationalize by interpreting and perhaps distorting the objective situation ("He had a number of friends there and they would have helped him"). Whether the interpretation after the act is chiefly concerned with purpose (of the self or of others) or with the objective situation, distortion or inaccuracy may creep in because of the person's self-involvement. In order to obtain a true or correct interpretation of an event or situation, one thus attempts to rule out all bias stemming from personal involvement and to base interpretation upon genuine evidence, so that if possible all disinterested observers may agree on "the facts." Procedure in courts of law is the classic example of a formalized, if not always successful, attempt to accomplish this. No sharp line can be drawn between a rationalization about a situation and a description of it, for it is difficult to rule out the influence of all personal interest and bias.

Scott and Lyman (32) have pointed out that these rationalizations, which they term *accounts*, are called forth when the social actor needs to explain unanticipated or untoward behavior—that is, problematic rather than accepted routine behavior, whether past, present, or future. They note that in general there are two types of accounts: *excuses* and *justifications*. They also usefully distinguish five linguistic styles that "frame the manner in which the account will be given" and that often indicate "the social circle in which it will be most appropriately employed." First, there is the *intimate style,* used among those who share deep, intense, personal relationships. There is a tendency to use single sounds or words, and jargon for the communication of ideas. An example which

Scott and Lyman give: a husband caresses his wife in bed but gets no endearing response; the wife just says, "pooped." Second, there is the *casual style,* used among peers, in-group members, and insiders: typically, words are omitted and slang is used. Thus among those who are regular users of hallucinogenic drugs, the question, "Why were you running about naked in the park?" might be answered, "I was on." Third, there is the *consultative style,* which ordinarily is used when the amount of knowledge available to one interactant is unknown or problematic to the others. In response to the questions: "Why are you smoking marijuana? Don't you know that it's dangerous?" the individual might reply, "I smoke marijuana because everybody who's read the LaGuardia Report knows it's not habit-forming." Fourth, there is the *formal style,* for groups perhaps larger than six persons, where listeners must await their turns to speak. The formal style typically occurs in bureaucratic organization, in the courtroom, and in organized meetings. Fifth, there is the *frozen style,* an extreme version employed among people required to interact while yet remaining strangers—for example, telephone operators speaking to customers and air pilots talking to the airport tower.

Scott and Lyman also emphasize that accounts may or may not be honored, so each person must learn a repertoire of proper accounts for appropriate audiences as well as proper styles of wording the accounts. When an account is not honored, it will most frequently be viewed as illegitimate or unreasonable.

In common experience many acts are interpreted more than once. Indeed, if the act is at all important, it may receive several interpretations, sometimes distributed over a number of years. Individuals are sometimes aware of this reinterpretation, but more often they are not. This kind of reseeing of the past we have already discussed as *reconstructive memory.* It should be apparent that a large proportion of the later interpretation is not at all concerned with the preservation of self-esteem—that is, it is not rationalization in the narrower, Freudian sense of the word.

Interpretations of an act may also be made before the act takes place. Such *preinterpretations* include an estimate of the situation in which behavior is called for—including the possible actions, intentions, and expectations held by others—and some judgment of how and why one proposes to act with regard to the situation. The *how* and *why* of the coming act have to do with persons' purposes; and if they should happen to phrase the matter aloud to someone else and explicitly to themselves, they will generally use the word *because* when referring to these purposes. For example, someone is asked what he is going to do next summer and answers, "Go to Europe." When asked, "Why?" or "Why next year?" he offers a statement that includes purpose: "Because I am getting to the age where I feel I can spend my savings and because I have never been there." The initial statement of purpose is likely to be somewhat condensed; if he is encouraged, the person may present his reason in more detail. "I have never been there" may be expanded to an explanation that he wants to go to Europe so that he, too, can talk about Paris when others speak of their experiences there.

Purpose, as we are using the term, is synonymous with motive; and Mills (26:904–13) has called statements about purpose *motivational statements,* whether offered to others or to self, since they are formulated, at least partially, in verbal terms. When others ask us to account for an act, either forthcoming or past, we usually give them a motivational statement so that they may understand the reasons or grounds for our act. The statement that we offer them may—but certainly need not—be quite false. We may couch it in terms that appear reasonable to them so as to "get by," or we may conceal our real motives for various other reasons. As Schwartz and Merten have remarked (31:294), "The ease with which people shift from what [Alfred] Schutz calls 'in order to' to the 'because of' motivational explanations gives the actor considerable latitude in the way he can construe his actions." This point was brought home to most Americans who watched the televised Watergate hearings in 1973.

MOTIVE AND CAUSE

Motive, as we are using it, should not be confused with *cause. Motive has a forward reference in time.* It is concerned with purpose and with the anticipated consequences of acts. *Causation has a backward reference:* it refers to antecedent processes, that is, those which immediately precede an event and which influence it decisively or determine it. (Motives are in a sense personal and private, whereas causes are general and public.) Causation applies to classes of events, and causal explanations are subject to public verification. The causation of human behavior is poorly understood, but it is known that much more than motives is involved.

Motives appear or are mobilized at the beginning of an act and indeed are a part of the act, since they persist throughout its course. They may, of course, change during the act by becoming more complicated or more simple; they may be joined by other motives; or they may even be replaced, particularly if the act has considerable duration. Hence, in describing any complicated event in a person's life, reference must be made to the purposes the individual had in mind. But in addition, a whole range of other conditions must be taken into account—namely, the motives of others and the material or objective situation. Individuals themselves are in a sense the final authority on their own purposes, since they know better than anyone else what they had in mind, even though the mechanisms of repression or rationalization may have operated to distort their knowledge of their actions. With respect to the objective situation, on the other hand, individuals usually cannot be well informed, since it is impossible for them to be in possession of all the information concerning their own nervous system, physiological state, and past experiences which might be relevant to an explanation of why they performed a specific act exactly as they did at exactly the time they did.

Before an action is completed, the purposes of the behavior are likely to loom large to the person engaged in it. After the action is completed, second thoughts often occur and the person may then wonder whether his or her reasons were as simple as they seemed. When asked to account for past actions, persons often give commonsense, causal explanations rather than motivational ones. For example, a husband may scold his wife at the breakfast table, believing at the time that he is scolding her because she has spoiled his coffee. He may later explain the quarrel by saying that neither he nor his wife had enough sleep the previous night.

Since motives appear at the beginning of acts or in preparation for action, and since each individual feels his or her own motives in a direct way, it is easy to understand how they have come to be viewed as causes of the behavior of which they are a part, and indeed as "forces" which "make" the behavior occur. It was a common practice in the earlier years of this century for sociologists to explain institutional and other cultural behavior in terms of the operation of wishes, desires, interests, needs, and other "social forces." However, the idea of causation no longer includes the conception of force in this sense at all. There are many different ideas of causation in the philosophy of science, but on this particular point there is rather general agreement.

The scientific concept of causation is, of course, a general feature of many scientific fields in which no problem of motivation exists. Indeed, in view of the instability and variability of human purposes, and in view of the fact that purposes are really part of behavior rather than mysterious forces lying behind it, motives are not so much explanations of behavior as they are behavioral problems, themselves requiring analysis and explanation. From this viewpoint, the problem of explaining such behavior as stealing, for example, includes the problem of accounting for the fact that people steal from so many different motives.

An example will help to clarify some of the points we have been making. Let us suppose that a company of American soldiers is ordered to advance in the face of strong enemy fire and that the order is obeyed. If we then try to answer the question of why the company advanced in terms of the motives of each soldier we become involved in a bewildering network. Perhaps no two soldiers have advanced for precisely the same reasons, and perhaps they may have advanced for almost opposite reasons. The problem of accounting for the fact that the company actually moves as a unit seems insoluble from this perspective.

Motives, Activities, and Accounts   273

From the standpoint of the army general who issued the order which was passed on till it finally reached the company commander, the individual motives of the men are of little significance in the total picture and are ignored at the moment of action. As the only requirement is that troops obey the orders and fight effectively, it is sufficient for the commander to know that motivations to advance exist in troops. It may be said of a reasonably well-organized and efficient army that it is ultimately the individual soldier's private and personal problem to seek and hold onto whatever rationalization he can find to help him do what he has to do in any case, although indoctrination procedures probably help him. Max Lerner made this point on the group level in a speech at the time of Hitler's rise when he asserted that the Balkan nations would surely have to surrender to the Nazis and that the only problem was what rationalization would be found for the surrender.

These examples point up the truism that people and groups may do the same things for different reasons and different things for the same reason. Since causal generalizations are based upon elements that are common to various instances of a given form of behavior, in problems like the above these generalizations cannot be stated in terms of motive. Psychoanalysts have attempted to meet this difficulty by looking for uniformity and common motivations on the unconscious level. What is suggested here is that the matter may be dealt with in another way, provided that one conceives of motive as something other than a specific determinant of behavior. It may be conceded that most significant human behavior is and must be motivated, but this is a far cry from contending that any given form of behavior must always be motivated in the same way.

The conception developed here may be further clarified by reemphasizing the fact that gross organic needs ordinarily do not lead to anything but random or restless behavior, and that they merely prepare the organism to respond when an appropriate situation appears and thus to learn rapidly. The ease with which the newly born infant is taught to nurse is a case in point. Organic needs do not automatically trigger behavioral responses which satisfy these needs, as we have seen in connection with oxygen deprivation and vitamin deficiency. K. S. Lashley (19:445–71) has made a similar point with respect to rats, noting that hunger does not have a motivational effect upon them in running a maze until they have learned to associate the maze with food. Organic needs become motivational, as a rule, only after the organism has learned to interpret them in certain ways and to associate certain objects or modes of behavior with the satisfaction of the need. In other words, physiological states in human beings give rise to purposes when they are harnessed in conceptual schemes. When this has happened, the drive-satisfying behavior may vary with the intensity of the physiological need

Soldiers: persons may do the same thing for different reasons. (*Richard Lawrence Stack from Black Star*)

(as it does within limits in the case of hunger) and may thus appear to depend directly on it, although this may not be the case. A physiological state of disequilibrium without direction or goals is not a motive—it is merely a biological condition.

Social Sources of Individual Motivation

As Mills (26) says, "Motives are of no value apart from delimited societal situations for which they are appropriate vocabularies. They must be situated. . . . Motives vary in content and character with historical epochs and societal structures." One implication of this statement is that although our motives generally appear to us as peculiarly personal and private, many of them are in fact learned from others and are in a sense furnished to us tailor-made by the society or the groups in which we live.

When one joins a group of long standing, he or she finds that the proper codes of conduct, including the ends and means of group activity, have been spelled out in considerable detail. They may even be formalized and embodied in written documents such as the Hippocratic oath, an oath of allegiance, or in constitutions, contracts, or codes. When persons leave groups and join new ones, they must learn new motivations. As Weber has pointed out in connection with work, for instance, "The motives which induce people to work vary with different social classes. . . . When a man changes rank, he switches from one set of motives to another." (41:316–17) Even when persons live rather stable lives, changing their group memberships very little, some of their motives nevertheless change with advancing age according to prevailing social definitions. Although the physical processes of aging are much alike in all cultures, the motivational adaptations to them are endlessly varied.

The above statements by Weber and by Mills, in short, point to a phenomenon of immense importance for the social psychologist. How a person sees his or her own behavior and how he or she may explain it to others, as well as how they may see it and interpret it to others—including him or her—is crucially important. It is important for understanding their interaction as well as for understanding their thoughts about themselves. But social psychologists cannot comprehend the full significance of this accounting and interacting and thinking unless they link them with both the personal biographies of the individuals and the social biographies of the groups to which they belong. This point relates very closely to our earlier discussions of the group contexts of language and thought as well as to the group and historical contexts for remembrance. Said another way—although the quote pertains to identity rather than to motives—"personal identity is meshed with group identity which itself rests upon an historical past." (37:173)

The fallacious commonsense imputation of motives has its academic counterpart. For example, psychoanalysts have reinterpreted the private lives of famous persons such as St. Augustine and Leonardo da Vinci in terms of twentieth-century sexual symbols. They thus ignore the fact that these historical characters viewed the conduct of others and themselves in very different terms than do people of our own era. Such scholarly interpretation is equivalent to translating other rationalizations into our own. Since human beings are interested in the lives of past generations, such translating is inevitable. The only corrective to a superficial handling of the past is an adequate understanding of the period under consideration through exhaustive examination of historical sources. The accuracy of the account should rest upon an understanding of the actual symbols available to the historical personages; it should not rest upon the degree to which their motives appear plausible to us in the light of our own motives at the present time.

It follows that individuals cannot express purposes or rationalize behavior in terms which they have not learned. One cannot motivate people to act by using terms outside their comprehension: one must appeal to purposes which they understand and which make sense to them.

Conversely, it is incorrect to impute rationalizations to an individual when these involve motivational terms which he or she does not possess. Nevertheless, such imputation is a common recourse when it is found to be impossible to assess behavior in one's own terms. There is almost always a tendency to explain other people's behavior in terms of one's own vocabulary of motives. This form of incorrect assessment is called *projection* and is seen in a crude form in most romantic historical novels. The characters, supposedly living a century or two ago, are made to rationalize their activities according to the symbols of the twentieth century. Likewise, in American movies, heroes and heroines dress in the clothes of other eras but act as if their incentives were those of twentieth-century Americans. But the projection of motives may take more subtle forms.

In contrast to this projection of the outsider's symbolic representations and in accordance with our view of the social contexts of individual motivation, two sociologists, Peter Berger and Thomas Luckmann (5:120), whose social psychological position is much the same as ours, have written about socialization into social worlds and the resulting internalization of their perspectives. They wrote that "internalization is the basis, first for an understanding of one's fellowmen and, second, for the apprehension of the world as a meaningful and social reality." They elaborate then "I not only 'understand' the other's momentary subjective processes, I 'understand' the world in which he lives, and that world becomes my own. . . . A nexus of motivations is established between us and extends into the future." In consequence, both "not only live in the same world" but "participate in each other's being."

Apropos of motives and explanation, Alan Blum and Peter McHugh (7:98–109), influenced by critical positivistic tendencies in ethnomethodology, have also severely criticized symbolic interactionist conceptualizations of motivation. They reject, as we do, the idea of motivation as simple "cause," but contend that symbolic interactionists accept the actor as "a research informant, whose report acquires analytic status because the actor is thought to be a privileged and exclusive source on questions of his motives." They argue that the researcher ought systematically to try to learn how a motivational statement is generated to begin with—how, for example, the actor is constrained to cite a reason at all; how it takes the form it does (giving a reason for, say, telling a joke); how it comes to be acceptable to the hearer as an answer. We believe that Blum and McHugh have badly misread the conceptualizations of motive and motivation by symbolic interactionists. However, they make an excellent point, provided one mutes their criticism, when they say that there is often an inadequate formulation of the "conditions" under which specific types of motivational statements are given, chosen from alternatives, offered or given to others, or accepted or rejected by those who give them as well as by others. This leads us into considerations touched on in the next section.

MOTIVES,
MORALE,
AND SOCIAL
STRUCTURE The stability and endurance of social groups or structures depends upon getting the members to carry out necessary lines of action. This means that persons must be motivated to perform these actions. When a structure recruits "from the inside," as when persons are born into it, the problem of motivation is handled early through the socialization of the young. But when members are recruited, as in an army or a vocation, the new member must be taught to act in accordance with the essential purposes of the body or group. Since many recruits join voluntarily, some learning of appropriate motivations starts beforehand; for example, future doctors learn something about the aims and aspirations of the medical profession long before they go to medical school. Involuntary membership may present the group with the problem of apathy or lack of enthusiasm, since the purposes of the organization may seem irrelevant to the new members, or they may even be antagonistic. These attitudes are exemplified by political apathy among citizens and "going AWOL" among soldiers. Insofar as good citizens and good soldiers decry unmotivated or badly motivated colleagues, they exemplify their own attachment to the long-range functions of the state and the army. Considerable variation in personal motivation may exist among the membership of any group, but in general, motivations must be geared in with, or at least not antagonistic to, the group purposes.

Social structures vary tremendously in the amount of latitude permitted to their membership in this regard; and the degree of latitude is related intimately to the nature of the structure. For instance, if an embattled religious sect is to survive, it must arrange matters so that group and individual motivations are virtually identical. The very existence of a revolutionary or radical political elite, such as the communist party leadership in a capitalist country (at least in earlier years when the party was revolutionary), also requires that individual and institutional motivations be closely intermeshed. The concept of "party discipline," as the communists use it, requires that individuals make the party's decisions and policies their own, regardless of how they may vary from week to week or how they may appear to the individuals personally. They are required to sacrifice personal comforts and immediate personal desires in the long-run interests of the party, and they are willing to do this because they identify their own essential interest with that of the party. A group characterized by this attitude is said to have a *high morale,* or *high solidarity.* This is equivalent to saying that even in the face of setbacks, the membership persists in pursuit of group aims, and, indeed, may thrive upon a certain amount of opposition or suppression, since this adversity supplies additional justification for revolutionary ardor. Self-interest and group interest coalesce so completely in groups of this kind, whether political or otherwise, that the person may sacrifice his or her own life for the good of the cause and may do so not only willingly but with elation.

Most organizations, of course, allow more latitude between individual and group purposes, and demand lesser degrees of allegiance and sacrifice. For these groups to function effectively it is necessary that there be a certain amount of consensus concerning matters relevant to group survival. Individuals may retain membership for a variety of reasons, some of them quite peripheral: for example, people belong to churches for business and social reasons as well as for religious ones.

In any society some parts of the total structure are generally recognized as more vital than others. There is a corresponding difference in the pressure upon individuals to conform to the controlling norms. People who "buck the system" because they do not value it or because they will not support the group endeavors are liable to severe punishment. Court martial, imprisonment, and so on are deterrents to deviance; but positive allegiances operate more efficiently.

When a social structure fails to elicit the minimal allegiance necessary for its proper functioning, then we speak of *poor morale,* or *low solidarity*. Presumably, there are different types of poor morale, depending on the kind of group structure, but essentially it comes down to a lack of effective coordination because of discrepant individual aims. To take the simplest case first, there may be so little consensus about group values and such diversity of individual purposes that the group cannot act in concert. A more complicated form of poor morale stems from discrepant definitions of group ends on different social levels represented in the group. Whenever the structure is complex, there is a problem of obtaining a working consensus shared by the various echelons. This condition can exist in a political party, an industrial corporation, a religious organization, or a university. Of course, some segments of the organization may have excellent morale, others poor morale, since they evaluate differently the way matters are progressing.

Summary

Motivation presents an old and thorny problem for the student of human behavior. The manner in which it is handled by social theorists is likely to determine the way in which they will deal with a great many other problems. Through the course of group interaction, individuals develop *accounts,* or linguistic explanations, of their behavior. These accounts are lodged in ongoing interaction. A common conception of motives, which we reject, gives them a biological base, as when hunger is identified with the contractions of the walls of the stomach and other bodily conditions. A biological condition by itself has little motivational significance, except as it is perceived or interpreted by the individual in whom it exists. The theory of instincts and need psychology are other biologically tinged views with a bearing on motivation. The influential Freudian conception of motivation, which emphasizes unconscious wishes and desires, has serious weaknesses arising mainly from the fact that no theory about the content of the "unconscious" can be proved because the unconscious is, by definition, virtually unknowable. Marxist theory presents an interesting comparison with that of Freud, for in the former the emphasis is placed upon unconscious economic, rather than sexual, motivations. A conception of motives held by symbolic interactionists treats them as essentially verbal in nature, as part of behavior, but as something other than causes of behavior. Knowledge of motives, in this conception, is used primarily to enable a person to project himself or herself into the outlook of another person; that is, for "understanding," rather than for "explaining," behavior. Motives are learned in social experience, vary from group to group, and are relative to a social context. A consideration of group morale, or solidarity, gives some indications of the way in which persons are motivated by their group identifications. The research implication of our discussion is that the accounts people offer for their own behavior, far from explaining it, themselves require analysis and explanation. Motives are social and interpersonal products. They emerge and may be observed in the interaction process. They are often "after the fact" explanations of human conduct.

References

1. Alexander, F., and H. Ross (eds.), "Development of the Fundamental Concepts of Psychoanalysis," in *Dynamic Psychiatry*. Chicago: University of Chicago Press, 1952.
2. ———, and W. Healey, *Roots of Crime*. New York: Knopf, 1935.
3. Allport, G. W., *Personality. A Psychological Interpretation*. New York: Holt, Rinehart and Winston, 1937.
4. Arnold, William, and David Levin (eds.), *Nebraska Symposium on Motivation, 1969*. Lincoln, Neb.: University of Nebraska Press, 1969.
5. Berger, Peter, and Thomas Luckmann, *The Social Construction of Reality*. Garden City, N.Y.: Doubleday, 1966.
6. Bierens de Haan, J. A., *Animal Psychology*. London: Hutchinson Publishing Group, 1946.
7. Blum, Alan, and Peter McHugh, "The Social Ascription of Motives," *American Sociological Review*, vol. 36 (1971), pp. 98–109.
8. Burke, Kenneth, *Permanence and Change*. New York: New Republic Press, 1936.
9. Cameron, N., and A. Magaret. *Behavior Pathology*. Boston: Houghton Mifflin, 1951.

10. De Charms, Richard, *Personal Causation: The Internal Affective Determinants of Behavior*. New York: Academic Press, 1968.

11. Eysenck, H. J., *Uses and Abuses of Psychology*. Baltimore: Penguin Books, 1953.

12. Faris, Robert E. L., *Social Psychology*. New York: The Ronald Press, 1952.

13. Festinger, Leon, *A Theory of Cognitive Dissonance*. New York: Harper & Row, 1957.

14. Freud, Sigmund, *New Introductory Lectures on Psychoanalysis*. W. W. Norton, 1933.

15. Hebb, D. O., *The Organization of Behavior*. New York: Wiley, 1949.

16. Homans, George C., *Social Behavior*. New York: Harcourt Brace Jovanovich, 1961.

17. Klineberg, O., *Social Psychology* (rev. ed.). New York: Holt, Rinehart and Winston, 1954.

18. Langer, S., *Philosophy in a New Key*. Baltimore: Penguin Books, 1948.

19. Lashley, K. S., "Experimental Analysis of Instinctive Behavior," *Psychological Review*, vol. 45 (1938), pp. 445–71.

20. Lewis, M. M., *Language in Society*. New York: Social Science Research Council, 1948.

21. Maslow, A. H., "The Instinctoid Nature of Basic Needs," *Journal of Personality*, vol. 22 (1954), pp. 340–41.

22. McClelland, David, and David Winter, *Motivating Human Behavior*. New York: The Free Press, 1969.

23. McDougall, William, *Outline of Psychology*. New York: Charles Scribner's Sons, 1923.

24. Miller, J. C., *Unconsciousness*. New York: Wiley, 1942.

25. Miller, N. E., and J. Dollard, *Social Learning and Imitation*. New Haven: Yale University Press, 1941.

26. Mills, C. W., "Situated Actions and Vocabularies of Motive," *American Sociological Review*, vol. 5 (1940), pp. 904–13.

27. Miyamoto, Frank, "Self, Motivation, and Symbolic Interactionist Theory," in T. Shibutani (ed.), *Human Nature and Collective Behavior*. Englewood Cliffs, N.J.: Prentice-Hall, 1970.

28. Montague, F. Ashley (ed.), *Man and Aggression*. New York: Oxford University Press, 1968.

29. Newcomb, Theodore, "An Approach to the Study of Communicative Acts," *Psychological Review*, vol. 60 (1953), pp. 393–404.

30. Piaget, J., *Play, Dreams, and Imitation in Childhood*. London: William Heinemann, 1951.

31. Schwartz, D., and G. Merten, "Participant Observation and the Discovery of Meaning," *Philosophy of Social Science*, vol. 1 (1971), pp. 290–95.

32. Scott, Marvin B., and Stanford M. Lyman, "Accounts," *American Sociological Review*, vol. 33 (December 1968), pp. 46–62.

33. Seligman, D., "The Four Day Week: How Soon?" *Fortune Magazine* (July 1954), p. 118.

34. Sherif, M., *An Outline of Social Psychology*. New York: Harper & Row, 1948.

35. Sorin, Gerald, "The New York Abolitionists: A Case Study of Political Radicalism," *Contributions in American History*, no. 11. Westport, Conn.: Greenwood Press, 1971.

36. Strauss, Anslem L., "Identification." Unpublished monograph.

37. ———, *Mirrors and Masks: The Search for Identity*. San Francisco: Sociology Press, 1969.

Motives, Activities, and Accounts   281

38. Sullivan, Harry Stack, *The Interpersonal Theory of Psychiatry*. New York: W. W. Norton, 1953.
39. Sutherland, Edwin H., *The Professional Thief*. Chicago: University of Chicago Press, 1937.
40. Thomas, W. I., and F. Znaniecki, *The Polish Peasant in Europe and America*, vol. 1. New York: Knopf, 1927.
41. Weber, M., paraphrased by K. Mannheim in *Ideology and Utopia*. New York: Harcourt Brace Jovanovich, 1936.
42. Weiss, E., "History of Metapsychological Concepts," in F. Alexander and A. Ross (eds.), *Dynamic Psychiatry*. Chicago: University of Chicago Press, 1952.

Selected Readings

ARNOLD, WILLIAM, and DAVID LEVIN (eds.), *Nebraska Symposium on Motivation, 1969*. Lincoln, Neb.: University of Nebraska Press, 1969.
A variety of viewpoints on this difficult problem.

BLUM, ALAN, and PETER MC HUGH, "The Social Ascription of Motives," *American Sociological Review*, vol. 36 (1971), pp. 98–109.
A systematic consideration of the relationships and differences between the motives recognized by persons and those socially attributed to them.

BURKE, K., *A Grammar of Motives*. Englewood Cliffs, N.J.: Prentice-Hall, 1945. (Especially, Part I)
A sensitive and sophisticated discussion by a literary critic of the linguistic nature of motives and of the functions of motivational accounts.

DE CHARMS, RICHARD, *Personal Causation: The Internal Affective Determinants of Behavior*. New York: Academic Press, 1968.
A highly interesting discussion of, and attempt to make sense of, such concepts as causation, motivation, the mind-body problem, the sense of individual freedom, and other related matters in the context of psychological theory.

MAC IVER, ROBERT M., *Social Causation*. Boston: Ginn and Company, 1942.
An extended and sophisticated presentation by an eminent sociologist of the concept of causation applied to social behavior.

chapter 9

The Acquisition of Language and Concepts

The learning of language is not merely a matter of mastering the mechanics of speech. The symbols that make up a language are concepts and represent ways of acting and thinking. Infants must learn to classify objects and to act appropriately toward them. They must also learn that some words refer to things that do not exist as material objects but only as ideas, abstractions, or relationships. To teach anyone the conventional meaning of a word is to teach him or her how to act or think with reference to the object or the concept to which the word refers. The meanings of words are not locked up in dictionaries but are found in people's acts. In this chapter we shall review the growing literature on language acquisition, paying particular attention to the speech patterns of young children. As language is acquired, the child develops the ability to be consciously self-aware, as we shall discuss in Chapter 10. Language acquisition is basic to the genesis of self in early childhood. The research and theory of Piaget, Vygotsky, and Chomsky will be discussed. We shall argue that the "universal" features of language usage may reflect "universal" characteristics of the primary group, and may not, as Chomsky has argued, be based on innate, inherited biological, or neurological, tendencies.

The child's learning of language is not merely an intellectual matter.

Language puts children in touch with their parents and peers in new and significant ways and initiates their acquisition of broader and more socialized perspectives. It introduces them to new pleasures and satisfactions and also creates a great many new needs and problems. Through learning a language children learn the rules and standards that regulate social relations and they develop ideas of morality and religious matters. Language is also the means whereby children are gradually prepared for and later inducted into the roles which they are destined to play and through which they learn to grasp the viewpoints and understand the feelings and sentiments of other persons. By means of language, they become aware of their own identity as a person and as a member of groups in which they seek status, security, and self-expression, and which, in turn, make demands upon them.

Since newborn babies cannot be aware of their caretakers' symbols, they remain for some time relatively unsocialized. Socialization begins even before infants begin to learn language, since they are responding to all kinds of stimuli. On the other hand, until they begin to comprehend and use conventional speech, their humanness is only partial. Children become socialized when they have acquired the ability to communicate with others and to influence and be influenced by them through the use of speech. This implies socially acceptable behavior toward named objects.

However, the learning of concepts one-by-one in piecemeal fashion is not enough, for concepts are interrelated. A word such as *spoon* refers to more than a piece of shaped metal, although "metal" and "shaped" are themselves complex concepts. The meanings of *spoon* (that is, modes of response toward it) are linked with and contingent upon a whole system of related meanings (for example, what foods are eaten with spoons, how spoons are handled, what they are made of, where they are placed as part of a table setting, and so on).

Just how the child passes over to a consistent and conventional use of words is a crucial problem for social psychology. We do not really know the full details of this transformation (from babbling and initial imitation to adult verbal behavior) in which the spoken word is used with a conventional meaning. We shall consider such materials as are available. (31, 45)

Instrumental Use of Gestures

Children make meaningful as well as sheerly expressive bodily movements long before they speak conventionally. Such gestures may be accompanied by vocalizations. At first these may not be understood by even extremely solicitous parents, but gradually their meanings are discovered so that an approximate interpretation is readily made. As late as the eighteenth month of life, babies communicate needs largely through gestures and expressive utterances rather than through actual words. *Neologisms,* or made-up words, may be used. (6, 49)

The infant's gestural communication gradually recedes and becomes secondary to his or her other gradually evolving vocal language. Some children are retarded linguistically because they develop an elaborate gesture "language" so well understood by their parents that there is neither incentive nor urgent necessity for learning genuine speech. Parental refusal to respond usually results in the abandonment of such a system of gestures.

The most important point to note about infants' use of gestures is that it is instrumental. They use gestures, although they are not aware that they are using them, to reach for something, to avoid something, or to call for something. Children's expressive bodily movements occur within a context of social relations; that is, people react to their gestures and children respond both to people and to their actions with still further gestures. Although at first children make expressive movements toward a brute physical environment, the responses of their parents soon transform their environment into a thoroughly social one in which their early expressive movements become endowed with a social significance.

The foregoing considerations suggest that language might best be viewed as a *conversation of gestures.* Language and speech behavior are processes that vary by context, speakers, listeners, and their intentions. Any language contains a set of rules, however implicitly organized and recognized, which governs the expression and interpretations given both to spoken utterances and nonverbal gestures. This view of language is crucial for the understanding of early childhood speech, for infants speak in a highly personal, often nonverbal language. Indeed, the family must be viewed as a complex language community. The child must master the language of all the family members before he or she can successfully take their perspectives in any speech encounter.

Children learn to speak before they learn to think (in a verbal sense), for their first utterances bear no meaning for them and are unlikely to have clear, conventionalized meaning for their caretakers. (50) Their verbal sounds begin to get attached to concrete objects and concrete movements. Initially, the young child may develop a complex "crying" vocabulary, as Roger Brown (8) has noted, with as many as seven different cries designating diverse states like happiness, pain, anger, discomfort, hunger, and frustration. Often a verbal utterance is combined with a particular nonverbal gesture. The sound "jeewish" (which the parent translates as "juice") may be accompanied by a pointing gesture to the refrigerator or to a container filled with juice. The child has elaborated the contextual meaning of his or her nonconsensual utterance with an unspoken gesture. While many have argued that the family is basically a monolithic speech community, our remarks suggest that each speaker in the family has his or her unique mode of speaking and gesturing. Each will have an unique style of pronunciation, accent, gesture, and particular patterns of intonation and resonance.

Learning to Use and Comprehend Symbols

BILINGUAL CHILDREN

Bossard and Boll (5:265) suggest that at least one of every five white Americans has grown up in a home where language other than English was dominant. Such persons may adopt a set of *protective devices* which aid them in the production of their speech acts. They may speak in a restrained fashion and attempt to be an inconspicuous speaker, seldom talking in "mixed linguistic" company. On the other hand, they may overcompensate and adopt a meticulous mode of talking. As bilingual children, they may develop a stigmatized view of self based on their linguistic status. This is especially so if they come from a disadvantaged ethnic or racial group which is stigmatized by the broader society. Labov (30) has gone so far as to argue that many American blacks speak a form of "nonstandard" English which gives them a distinct linguistic disadvantage in public schools.

If one of every five Americans comes from a bilingual family, the above remarks would suggest that indeed all Americans are socialized into multilingual speech communities—if nonverbal features of language are incorporated into the definition of "language." The problems of the bilingual child are simply more complex than those of the child who comes from a family where only standard English is spoken. Both kinds of child speakers, however, must learn complex sets of verbal and nonverbal languages.

LEARNING THE SPEECH ACT

The *speech act,* to paraphrase Searle (42:16), can be defined as the production of a set of sounds that are understandable to at least one other person. Such acts are the basic units of linguistic communication and may be verbal or nonverbal. The infant, of course, enters the world with no conception of the speech act and must be taught how to speak. Initially its utterances—the cry, the whimper, the giggle—are not attached or linked to an internal second signal system that would give a referent to the sound. In this context, it is useful to recollect Vygotsky's (50:17) distinction between vocal speech (verbal utterances) and inner speech (silent thought). Thought is "soundless" inner speech. The child's first speech acts are global, social utterances that (1) are understood by the

Life Cycle: The Genesis of Self

Young children (as well as adults) often combine a verbal utterance with a nonverbal gesture. This gesture elaborates the contexual meaning of a verbal utterance and illustrates the term "conversation of gestures." (*David S. Strickler from Monkmeyer Photo Service*)

recipients of the sounds but not by the child, (2) are undifferentiated sounds which, (3) are not attached to internal symbolic or categoric referents. As children acquire a speech act repertoire, their talk becomes increasingly egocentric, or self-centered, in nature. *Egocentric* utterances progressively merge with *sociocentric* formulations such that children are increasingly able to place themselves in the perspectives of others and to view action from their standpoints. *Sociocentric speech* is possible because of the emergence of inner speech, or thought. Vygotsky's remarks (50:19) summarize our position on this point.

Vygotsky's model can be contrasted to the proposals of Piaget. Vygotsky views speech as having a social origin that stands outside the infant. The infant's speech is first social in nature, then it becomes egocentric in nature. Egocentric speech progressively translates into inner thought and speech. Piaget, on the other hand, views the origins of speech and thought as first arising within the infant. His model works from the individual to society. Vygotsky's model works from the social

The Acquisition of Language and Concepts   287

environment to the individual. Thus, he reverses the more traditional psychological views of speech and thought development. Piaget's choice of the term *egocentric* to describe the child's thought was perhaps unfortunate. (See Chapter 13.)

For children to become credible and understood members of the family speech community they must relinquish their private, autistic speech for the differentiated symbol system consensually understood by all members of the family.

THE CHARACTERISTICS OF BABY TALK

We have noted that the child's speech acts tend to move from undifferentiated utterances to progressively refined categorical statements. In an intriguing study of baby talk in six languages, Charles A. Ferguson (16) has noted that baby-talk words are modifications of normal adult words; the child, for example, says "choo-choo" for train or "itty bitty" for little. Ferguson's research revealed the following features of this form of speech. First, baby-talk items consist of simple consonants, stops, and nasals, and only a few vowels. Second, there is a predominance of reduplication, or repetitions, of particular sounds. Third, in each of the six languages studied (Arabic, Marathi, Comanche, Gilyak, English, and Spanish) there was a typical morpheme form of talk. The most typical was a sound that began with a monosyllable and ended with a consonant. Given those cross-cultural commonalities, Ferguson maintains (16:110):

> In view of this similarity one is tempted to make the hypothesis that every language community provides a stock of baby-talk items which can serve as appropriate material for babies to imitate in creating their phonemes but which do not interfere with the normal words of the language and can gradually be discarded as real words emerge in the children's speech. . . . The baby-talk lexicon of a language community may thus play a special role in the linguistic development of its children.

Thus, by differentially rewarding, or through showing indifference, adults contribute to the child's progressive speech skills. They may encourage excessive baby talk or talk to the child in a more adult language. If the latter, then the use of baby talk will be at a minimum. However, it must be noted that the human's ability to make certain vocal sounds is a function of the speech apparatus itself, and certain sounds are easier to make than others. Furthermore, cultures vary in the kinds of sounds they emphasize. As a consequence, the character of the child's speech acts are to a certain degree conditioned or influenced by its physiological development—for example, the size of the tongue and the ability to move the lips or to bring the tongue to bear against the teeth, as when the "f" sound is made. The ease with which some sounds are produced may account for the remarkable similarity in baby talk across cultures that

Life Cycle: The Genesis of Self

Ferguson observed. All cultures, for example, had a word for mother, and it assumed the "ma-ma" form. The "m" sound is an easily produced sound. Thus, while American mothers may take some delight in their infant's first utterance of "ma-ma," this sound is really one of the most simple phonological sounds that the infant can make.

Indeed, the first word spoken by infants the world over is usually a syllable or repeated syllable such as "mama," "dada," "bebe," "nana," "wawa," or "papa." The word is expressive of either pleasurable or unpleasurable states. These syllabic phonetic forms become stabilized in the infant's speech with the help of delighted elders who pick out certain ones and repeat them to the baby until he or she uses them correctly.

The use of other words soon follows, especially when the infant somehow makes the momentous discovery that things have names. When children have managed to discover that every object has a name, they have taken a conspicuous step toward learning parental speech.

Besides discovering that things have names, children may also be said to discover that names have things—that is to say, that the words they learn correspond to aspects of the real world. In complex types of learning especially, the progression may be from words to things rather than the reverse. The fact that racial prejudice can be learned before contact with the racial group in question may be taken as an illustration of this point. The acquisition of a vocabulary sensitizes individuals to certain aspects of the environment which they may encounter later, and predisposes them to notice those which correspond with or confirm what they have previously learned through verbal communication alone. It is in this sense that we may say that the world is not made up of ready-made, discrete objects, events, and qualities waiting to be perceived and named, but is rather built up through collective experience and crystallized in linguistic forms. As learning proceeds, this type of movement from words to things tends to become more and more important.

Usually the infant's first words are employed as sentences rather than as single words. They do duty as one-word sentences. Analyzed merely as parts of speech, they are characteristically nouns or interjections. The infant, however, uses these words as complete, although by adult standards, crude sentences. Thus "mama" will have to be interpreted by parents in a variety of ways, depending upon the situation in which the word is spoken as well as the intonation and gesturing that accompany it. "Mama" may mean that the infant "wishes" the mother to come, or that he or she is hungry, or content, or that he or she sees the mother enter the room. "Ball" may mean "there is the ball," "where is the ball?" "I want the ball," and so forth. These earliest word-sentences cannot be understood out of context nor without noting associated inflection and gesture.

At this stage of their language development children possess words that have only a partly socialized meaning (that is, they have learned to employ words conventionally) with approximately the same meanings that their parents attribute to them. Their use of words is close enough to conventional adult usage so that from the context in which the word is spoken their parents are able to understand them.

Children are able to use words in an amazing variety of ways because they have not caught on to their full public meanings. As de Laguna has written (14:270):

> It is precisely because the words of the child are so indefinite in meaning, that they can serve such a variety of uses. . . . A child's word does not . . . designate an object *or* a property *or* an act; rather it signifies loosely and vaguely the object together with its interesting properties and the acts with which it is commonly associated in the life of the child. The emphasis may be now on one, now on another, of these aspects, according to the exigencies of the occasion on which it is used.

Adults, who are much more conscious of the "real" (conventional) meanings of words, cannot employ words so irresponsibly or so variously.

Children use these early words as a way of responding to a situation. A child does not merely name an object with a word (such as naming mama by using the word "mama"). "Mama" means "mama come here" or "I'm glad to see you," and so forth. As Lewis (31:91) has noted: ". . . when he speaks the sounds it is his way of dealing with the situation." The child's words are instruments; they are means of handling the environment. We shall see below how children progress rapidly to the point where words become very effective means for managing the environment and manipulating certain key environmental objects.

Declarative and Manipulative Functions of Language

We have previously noted the instrumental use of gestures and word-sentences; its implications now call for further analysis. The work of M. M. Lewis will be closely followed here, since in our judgment his is the most careful inquiry into this aspect of our problem.

Children use their early "conventional" words instrumentally in ways that are either *declarative* or *manipulative*. Declarative use involves drawing adult attention to some object. By uttering such words as *chair* or *doll*, the children direct adult attention to those objects. Manipulative use of words by children involves, in addition to drawing attention to some object, a demand that their needs with regard to that object be satisfied by the adult. For example, the word *cookie*, when used in manipulative fashion, is equivalent to a demand for aid in reaching the cookie

a cookie. The words *tick-tock,* used manipulatively, might
ʰow me your wrist watch."

 instrumental use of language, whether declarative or
ults in drawing other people within his or her circle of

... ᴛʜᴇ declarative use he attracts another's attention and so assures himself
of company. If he is delighted, the presence of another person enhances his
delight; if he is afraid the presence of another person alleviates his fear.
. . . In the manipulative use the child is again using the word as a social
instrument; this time as a means of securing the help of others in satisfying
his practical wants.

Even before infants learn any real words, they have used their own
vocalizations for declarative and manipulative purposes. But when they
learn real words, those two instrumental functions become more effective, because they enable children to point more precisely to the objects
which attract their attention.

A series of significant points is involved here. (1) Children's instrumental use of sounds has its roots in the children's past, and this instrumental use of sounds merges imperceptibly into their acquisition of
conventional speech. (2) Children's learning of conventional speech
rests upon their using it as an instrument; that is, upon their calling
adult attention to more specific objects and aspects of their environment
than was possible with their ambiguous baby vocalizations. (3) Finally,
children's gradual approach to conventional speech presupposes the cooperation of adults. If adults paid no attention whatsoever to them, or if
children could not use words as social instruments, it is difficult to imagine how they could ever learn conventional usage.

INITIAL USE OF WORDS IS INACCURATE.   When children discover adult
words, they do not employ them to specify precisely the same objects
that are referred to by adults. To put this into commonsense terms, children do not at first use adult words with their correct adult meanings. To
the adult, the child's application of words often seems haphazard and
frequently amusing.

Infants, in fact, apply sounds and home-made words to objects long
before they master adult words. It is out of these initial vocal references
that the infant's ability to use adult words correctly eventually develops.
Taine has given us an instructive description of how children begin to
apply vocalizations to the objects of their infantile world (49:254–56):

She was in the habit of seeing a little black dog belonging to the house,
which often barks, and it was to it that she first learnt to apply the word
oua-oua. Very quickly and with very little help she applied it to dogs of all
shapes and kinds that she saw in the streets and then . . . to the bronze

dog near the staircase. Better still, the day before yesterday when she saw a goat a month old that bleated, she said *oua-oua*. . . . *Cola* (chocolate) is one of the first sweetmeats that was given her and it is the one she likes the best. . . . Of herself and without or rather in spite of us she has extended the meaning of the word and applies it now to anything sweet; she says *cola* when sugar, tart, a grape, a peach, or a fig is given her. . . . In the same way the above mentioned little boy of twenty months used the word *teterre* (*pomme de terre*) to designate potatoes, meat, beans, almost everything good to eat except milk, which he called *lolo*. Perhaps to him *teterre* meant everything solid or half-solid that is good to eat. . . . Once more education produced an unexpected effect on her; the general character grasped by the child is not what we intended; we taught her the sound, she has invented the sense.

From this description it is clear that when children first apply learned words to objects, they do so with different meaning than does the adult. Although Taine thought he had taught his daughter the essential meanings of the word *baby*, he had not. Similarly, although the child applied the word *cola* to the correct object, she also applied it to other, incorrect objects. The child sometimes uses adult words to designate objects outside the adult definition, and sometimes he or she does not use the word to designate enough objects. "Some words he uses more widely than we do, others more narrowly." (32:210)

INACCURATE USAGE REFLECTS THE CHILD'S POINT OF VIEW.   Why is the child at first unable to grasp the correct adult meanings of a word? For an answer to this question we may refer to our discussion of language in Chapter 3, where we noted that the vocabulary utilized by any given society or social group necessarily reflects its interests and preoccupations. To state this in another way, the distinctions implicit in a society's words are distinctions that members of the society consider important and relevant.

It may be assumed that infants, before becoming overly influenced by human association, will make distinctions of importance to themselves. They choose features of their world that appear similar and group them together under an identical word. Where adults make a distinction between prunes and carrots—as fruit and vegetable—infants at first may use the same sound (say, "teterre") to pick out similar features of a solid-something which tastes good.

Children cannot very well group together the same objects as does an adult, for the latter sees the world from points of view derived from participation in certain social groups. Children have yet to acquire these standardized categories. Features of their environment that strike them as similar are features that grow out of their own experiences.

Thus, since chocolate tasted sweet, and peaches tasted sweet, and grapes tasted sweet, Taine's daughter called them all by the same name, small dogs, and later to his baby sister. Similarly, when an infant touches a rose, the infant's mother may carefully call it "rose," whereupon he or she is likely to apply "rose" to all flowers. The child's need to deal declaratively or manipulatively with an object—calling our attention to it, or to his or her needs with reference to it—often leads the child to make naïve and unique use of words.

The child's adoption of adult words is encouraged by the adult's readier response to conventional sounds than to the child's private vocalizations. The conventional sound proves to be a more efficient instrument for calling attention to an interesting object or to one's desires with regard to the object; hence the child has an incentive for appropriating the conventional sound.

Perhaps this is an instance of social pressure. But children, it should be noted, do not automatically conform to social pressure. Their choices and use of words are selective. Their experience determines the range and extension of words; the decision does not lie with the adult. For a time, children may stubbornly resist the adult's word, so that even after they are aware of the conventional word and have imitated it correctly, they may continue to use their own unique word form. Or they may alternate, sometimes using the adult word and sometimes their own. The conventional term has to be accepted by the child as the more efficient instrument of the two before he or she will finally adopt it.

Contemporaneously with and, undoubtedly, as a partial result of adult intervention, children learn to make increasingly adequate distinctions among classes of objects. For instance, they begin to discriminate between a solid-something eaten with a spoon (potato) and a solid-something eaten by hand (bread). The adult encourages the child to make such distinctions and helps to crystallize and fix them by supplying the necessary conventional words. Growing discrimination and adult intervention-cooperation go hand in hand; it is fruitless to inquire which contributes more. Both contributions are crucial to the gradual convergence of child and adult symbols. Children thus stand on the threshold of mastering their native language; they are becoming capable of employing voluntarily the symbols of the society to which they belong.

Language Acquisition According to Chomsky

The linguist McNeill has commented on the character of early childhood speech (35:34):

> At the age of about one, a normal child, not impaired by hearing loss or speech impediment, will begin to say words. By one-and-a-half or two

years, he will begin to form simple two and three word sentences. By four years, he will have mastered very nearly the entire complex and abstract structure of the English language. In slightly more than two years, therefore, children acquire full knowledge of the grammatical system of their native tongue. This stunning intellectual achievement is routinely performed by every preschool child, but what is known about the process underlying it?

Thus, by the age of four, children have acquired the major linguistic categories and meanings of their social groups. Children quickly become masters of their own behavior. That this linguistic ability appears so early in the developmental cycle is the subject of considerable controversy. Chomsky, a linguist whose writings have had a very great impact on other linguists and on psychologists, argues that language may be, in some sense, an innate ability. He makes this point quite explicit in the following passage. (10:59)

> . . . On the basis of the best information now available, it seems reasonable to suppose that a child cannot help constructing a particular kind of transformational grammar to account for the data presented to him, any more than he can control his perception of solid objects or his attention to line and angle. Thus it may well be that the general features of language structure reflect, not so much the course of one's experience, but rather the general character of one's capacity to acquire language—in the traditional sense one's innate ideas and innate principles.

The suggestion that innate ideas and principles, as part of a general capacity to acquire language, may be inherited, poses formidable difficulties if one tries to imagine how it might be translated into specific genetic mechanisms, as Piaget (39) has pointed out. However the problem is conceived, it should be formulated so as to bring it, theoretically at least, into the realm of empirical inquiry. The human brain and nervous system are without doubt amazingly complex structures that unquestionably play a central role in the easy acquisition of language in early childhood, but it is extraordinarily difficult to conceive of their being programmed with innate ideas and principles, or with what some call an underlying *language acquisition device* (*LAD*). It is possible that better understanding of the brain and its functions, coupled with further study of the nature of language and how it is learned, may take the mystery from this problem. Another point that might be made concerning those who, like Chomsky and McNeill, are so impressed by the child's ability to acquire language, *is that small and seemingly insignificant causes fairly commonly produce large and even revolutionary effects.* The invention of writing may be taken as an example. Spoken language had been in existence tens of thousands of years before the absurdly simple idea of a primitive form of writing came into practice. Those who participated in and contributed to the early evolution of writing would surely have been incredulous if they could have been told of the revolutionary consequences that were to follow from their invention. (See 8, 11, and 45.)

We ourselves adopt a "constructionist" view of language acquisition. From the moment of birth the infant is exposed to linguistic experiences, and these experiences are progressively adopted by the developing child. The regularity of speech behavior is contingent on the symbolic environment to which the child is exposed. In this respect we side with H. S. Sullivan (48:178–79), who suggests that:

> The learning of gestures, by which I include the learning of facial expressions, is manifested by the infant, certainly well before the twelfth month, in the learning of the rudiments, one might say, of verbal pantomime. And this learning is, in good measure, learning by trial-and-error approximation to human example. . . .

As the foregoing suggests, we need not resort to an innate, "deep-structure" interpretation of how language appears in the child's behavior. Sullivan's observations suggest that the infant is constantly involved in the process of mimicking the languages and sounds of the adult world. Sullivan's remarks can be framed in terms of two propositions. *"The more complex the linguistic community of the primary group, the more elaborate and complex will be the speech patterns of the young child."* And, again: *"The greater the complexity of this community, the more rapid will be the child's acquisition of speech."* These propositions are consistent with our earlier discussion of social isolation. If social behavior is not directed toward the child, his or her rate of social development will be correspondingly retarded or impeded. The basic similarities between languages (similarities that impress Chomsky), rather than being the result of inheritance, may simply be a reflection of the basic similarities of primary groups throughout the world. In the primary group, speech is acquired by infants, just as Charles Horton Cooley suggested that "human nature" is derived from this source.

THE SYNTAX OF THOUGHT AND SPEECH

Sounds, gestures, and thoughts are organized and made intelligible through the use of a set of syntactical rules that are specific to language communities. Written speech is governed by a set of rules that are quite precise and rigorously governed and studied by grammarians. Thought, on the other hand, has its own set of rules which may bear little relationship to the specifications governing the printed word. Finally, spoken vocal utterances are governed by another set of rules. Speakers, for example, develop their own styles of punctuation, exclamation, and interrogation.

Of concern in this context are the peculiarities of inner speech. Many students of early childhood thought and speech have erroneously judged the child's speech behavior from the standpoint of the syntax of formal, written utterances. Furthermore, when they claim that the child thinks "egocentrically," they are making that judgment on the basis of adults' thought and speech rules. There is no "thought rule" governing the organization of a thought, nor is there a rule concerning the prominence of the thinker's self in his or her own thoughts. We turn then to a further elaboration of *thought*, following Vygotsky's formulation. (50: 146–47) We note that (1) thought is truncated, abbreviated, and often abstracted from concrete experience; (2) its meaning is embedded in a larger context of perhaps unformulated thoughts; and (3) it is grounded in words that flow together. The word *love*, for instance, merges into a number of other images and experiences that are involved in the love relationship. Unlike vocal speech, thought does not fall into separate categories or units. We quote Vygotsky's remarks on this point: (50:150)

> When I wish to communicate the thought that today I saw a barefoot boy in a blue shirt running down the street, I do not see every item separately: the boy, the shirt, its blue color, his running, the absence of shoes. I conceive of all this in one thought, but I put it into separate words. A speaker often takes several minutes to disclose one thought. In his mind the whole thought is present at once, but in speech it has to be developed successively. A thought may be compared to a cloud shedding a shower of words.

Thus, as Vygotsky notes, there is no direct transition from thought to speech. The same relationship holds for the various transitions that move thoughts into printed or written sentences, sentences into paragraphs, and paragraphs into books. To understand another speaker's speech, "it is not sufficient to understand his words—we must understand his thought." (50:151) In other words, the subjective side of speech must be penetrated if listeners or readers are to comprehend and place themselves in the perspective of the utterer or the writer. One author (Hulett, 23) has noted that the message that is sent is seldom, if ever, the message that is received.

Rather early in the process of acquiring language symbols, children begin to use them to influence their own behavior. F. Lorimer has described an amusing instance of this (33:134–35):

> A child of about eighteen months was warned not to put her hand into a certain open chest and not to take out things in the chest. The inhibition was clearly established, but the original impulse was strong. For ten enormous minutes I watched with fascination the battle between the impulse and inhibition, as the little hand reached forward toward the things in the chest and withdrew to the verbal accompaniment "no, no, no!" uttered by the child herself. Then the battle subsided, called to a close by the distraction of other interests.

Such a self-command (the beginnings of what is commonly called "will power") derives from previous adult commands and prohibitions.

Children will eventually internalize their self-directed words so that they will say "no" to themselves silently, or will merely think the command. But at an early age, self-directed language is not completely internalized. Let us take another example: Ask young children to say how many pencils are lying on a table. They are likely to touch each pencil, counting aloud "one, two, three" as they touch. If you hold their hands, thereby preventing them from touching the pencils, they either cannot tell you the total number, or they will nod their heads in the direction of the pencils and count "one, two, three." Youngsters at play are often overheard giving themselves commands like "put this block there." As the child grows older, language becomes internalized so that counting, commanding, and expressing desires can be carried out silently. The external conversation of gestures-vocal-speech merges into inner thought, or into "the internal conversation of gestures."

The Learning of Concepts

Learning language, as we have stressed, requires that the child master systems of interrelated concepts. A number of investigators have studied how children's conceptions of time, space, movement, shape, weight, and numbers progressively become more sophisticated and differentiated. L. Ames (1), for example, has traced children's use of terms for time (day, minute, and so forth) as these become detached from concrete ac-

Asked his age, this boy's response displays how the external conversation of gestures-vocal-speech merges into inner thought. (*Freda Leinwand*)

tions and grow increasingly abstract and inclusive in scope. Studies of children's notions of social relationships, such as those bearing upon social class and race, also show, in a general way, how knowledge of these matters gradually becomes more discriminative and more systematic.

For instance, C. Stendler (46), in a study of American small-town children, found that awareness of social class differences develops slowly, passing through four states: (1) preawareness, (2) the beginning of awareness, (3) the acceptance of adult stereotypes of class, and (4) the recognition of individual differences among people, regardless of social class. Likewise, it has often been pointed out that young children are not attuned to racial differences, especially to their more subtle aspects. J. Moreno (36) has reported that when young schoolchildren were asked whom they would like to have sit beside them, there was no apparent color discrimination in the first three or four grades. Likewise, E. Horowitz and R. Horowitz (21), in a study of a small Tennessee community, noted that black and white children attempted to carry on friendships despite parental admonitions and injunctions. One of the chief causes of punishment for the white children was that they kept on being friendly to black children.

RACE
CONCEPTS

Let us pursue the matter of children's conceptions of race a little further. The topic is both interesting and of theoretical importance. All black children in the United States discover sooner or later that they are black. The consequences for these children are momentous, for they apply to the entire range of social relations and to virtually every facet of life. One would expect that if blacks must learn to be blacks (American style), the process could be studied empirically by investigating the skin color distinctions made by black children and the growth of their sense of identification.

Some years ago, a significant investigation was made along these lines. K. Clark and M. Clark (12), using groups of 119 Northern and 134 Southern children, studied conceptions of self and race. The children ranged from three to seven years of age. They were given four dolls that were identical, except that two were white with yellow hair and two were brown with black hair. The children were then asked to do the following:

1. Give me the doll that you like best.
2. Give me the doll that is a nice doll.
3. Give me the doll that looks bad.
4. Give me the doll that is a nice color.
5. Give me the doll that looks like a white child.
6. Give me the doll that looks like a colored child.
7. Give me the doll that looks like a Negro child.
8. Give me the doll that looks like you.

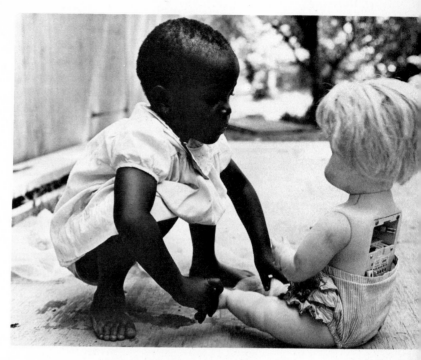

Children must learn racial identification as well as the social
meaning applied to racial
terms. Such distinctions are not
innate. (*Fujihira from
Monkmeyer Press Service*)

The responses of children to these requests yielded at least four points of interest. (1) There was confusion concerning self-identification. The confusion diminished with age and was greater among the light children than among the darker. (2) The children displayed greater facility in identifying skin color than in grasping the significance of the term "Negro." (3) There was consistent preference for the white dolls, which were often characterized as "nice," "of a nice color," and so on. This preference diminished with increasing age. (4) A negative attitude was displayed toward the dark dolls by children of all ages.

These responses demonstrate that racial identification—and all that it implies—must be learned. In learning to label oneself as a member of a racial group, one takes over a large part of the value systems of the larger society in which the learning takes place. It is significant that although black children grow up in black families, they nevertheless learn from their parents and other sources that whiteness is preferable to darkness. A study by M. Seeman (43) suggests, despite Moreno's (36) study, that many young children show their color biases in their choice of playmates, but that they have not yet verbalized their color preference as they will in later years. In his study of upper-class children, again done some years ago, E. F. Frazier noted that parents then often tried to shield their children from feelings of inferiority and self-abasement. (17:69) They went to great lengths to conceal from them their racial identity and its significance.

The manner in which the learning process is guided and integrated by verbal mechanisms is suggested by the responses of children to the words *Negro* and *colored* in requests six and seven in the Clarks' study. The children showed considerably more confusion with regard to the first term than they did to the second. For example, at the age of five, 30 percent responded incorrectly to "give me the doll that looks like a Negro child," whereas only 7 percent responded incorrectly when asked for the "colored doll." At the age of six, incorrect responses to "Negro" dropped to 17 percent, and at the age of seven, to 7 percent. This decrease with age suggests that learning about the significance of being a black may be accelerated by initial experiences in school.

In another study, R. L. Yokley (52) presented black children with a series of identical diagrammatic faces ranging in color from very dark brown to "white" flesh tones. He found that the very youngest had three classifications: Negro, colored, and white. "Negroes" were at the darkest end of the series and lived in Africa; American blacks were not "Negro," but "colored." The young children also made inflexible distinctions among these three classes of persons. No one who was of a given skin darkness could be anything but a Negro, and so on. Somewhat older children caught on to the equivalence of "Negro" and "colored," but also made a rigid separation by skin color of white and colored and Negro. Older children grasped the possibility that many white persons could be darker than some blacks. This confusion about skin color led some children to believe that they and some members of their families were white. The notion of a segregated school—which they all attended—was not grasped at first. This is easy to understand, since segregation, as a concept, is complex. Moreover, some children of "white" or light skin color attended the school.

Similar difficulties of identification and conceptualization are experienced by some white children. The point may be illustrated through two examples. R. Horowitz (22) presented pictures of white and black children to a group of preschool children. Children were asked to say which child in each picture was like himself or herself. The oldest white girl "who had expressed advanced and well-crystallized prejudices against Negroes" chose, in one picture, a black girl "because the latter had curls and she too had curls which were her pride and glory. Although accurately perceiving the racial nature of all the other pictures, she denied that this one was of a Negro child."

It is important to note that words or terms such as *Negro, colored,* and *black* carry no intrinsic meaning in and of themselves. Children must be taught the meanings of these words. That words such as *colored* or *Negro* or *lady* should carry racist or sexist connotations is indicative of the broader network of social relationships that make up the child's world. Thus, through the process of language socialization, adults pass on to children their stereotypes and preconceptions concerning members of other racial, ethnic, sexual, and work groupings. Illustrative of this fact is the following story related by Sherif. (44:352–53) Although the data are now over thirty years old, similar processes can be observed today. (See 30 and 13.)

> A little girl was told by her mother to call older women "ladies." One day the little girl answered the door and then ran to her mother saying that a lady wanted to see her. Her mother went to the door and when she returned she said, "That wasn't a lady, dear, that was a Negro. You mustn't call Negroes 'ladies.' "

In summary, we may note that there are two fundamental aspects or phases involved in the process of racial identification. The first is the basic recognition of the criteria of classification which one uses to place oneself and others in given categories. The second aspect follows the first; it involves the acquisition of the understandings and expectations associated with and implied by the classification. The classifications are not universal, either in all societies or in all groups in any one society. The particular racial and ethnic concepts learned in childhood vary with the groups in which the children have membership. (40)

Most studies of children's learning of concepts are of the very general kind described above. Emphasis is upon revealing what children of varying ages know about certain topics, rather than upon the exact tracing of stages and mechanics involved in the development of that knowledge. Our discussion of the nature of symbols and of concepts indicates that change in a given concept is clearly linked with the development of related concepts. As new classifications are found or learned, the child's old concepts are revised, qualified, or assimilated by the new ones. The refinement of concepts waits upon the development of related concepts. Later meanings are built upon and absorb earlier and simpler ones, although the children themselves do not usually recollect most of their earlier conceptions. Children at the same stages of conceptual development tend to commit similar types of errors.

These points can be illustrated by a consideration of some steps through which children pass when learning about money and its uses. (47) Concepts of numbers, coins, monetary transactions, and associated persons like customers and storekeepers are all related in systematic, if immature, ways for the young child. At the beginning, children play with money as with other objects, piling it and pushing it. They make no connection between buying and money. Money is a "penny." At around five and one half years of age, American children also recognize nickels, but cannot consistently match the silver coins put before them to test their discrimination. The child's preferences for coins are based on their

CONCEPTIONS OF MONEY

size or upon rote memory of relative significance. Money buys goods, but any coin buys anything. Primitive rules cover exchange; four coins are given for four pieces of candy. As the child sees it, both customer and storekeeper pay each other.

At about six and one half years, children begin to name all coins correctly and to recognize that nickels buy more than pennies and less than dimes. But a given coin buys only its exact equivalent, no more and no less; a nickel will not purchase a penny piece of candy. Money now has a more genuine function than formerly; it does not merely accompany each transaction, but in some sense makes it possible, since things are not merely bought—they are worth something.

The child may develop a finer sense of mathematics at this stage. A nickel cannot buy a ten-cent piece of candy—not merely because ten is not exactly five, but because it is more. How much more is yet unknown, for the child's mathematics is simply in terms of "more" or "less." In a vague way the child is beginning to sense that there is a connection between the amount of money paid by and to the customer. Money now buys services as well as objects, so that the storekeeper's employees—whose existence has now been recognized—can be paid. Storekeepers, who need money to buy things for their families and for their employees, now sell "to make money" rather than merely to service the customer.

Children at this age (about six and one half years) may also reason that customers must pay for the goods because simple taking of them means a loss to the storekeeper. Previously, they said one paid "just because," or because "you'd be punished" for taking goods. The owner of a store is still paid directly by a customer, and must actually sell in order to be paid. Something like absentee ownership is not grasped.

At about eight years of age children finally get the arithmetical details straight. Sales transactions are now impersonal, nonwhimsical, and arithmetically ordered. But it is not until almost a year later that certain other relationships become depersonalized. For instance, at the nine-year-old level, the child understands that a customer who is disliked nevertheless receives the same change as one who is well liked. The child also understands now that some of the customer's money goes to the manufacturer and some goes to the employee, and that the storekeeper gets some of the remainder. (But the contradiction in this notion is that owners are believed to sell goods for exactly the same price that they paid for them; to do otherwise would not be "fair.") Around the age of nine some children are vaguely aware that goods may, perhaps, be sold for more than cost, but moral considerations plus rigid application of change-making principles confuse the issue. It also occurs to some of the children that the owner pays proportionate amounts to him- or herself and to the employees: "He'd get about fifty dollars, his helpers twenty."

How many different connections among these words has a child learned by the time he or she is an adult?

Absentee ownership is beginning to appear as a concept. Finally, at about the age of ten, children grasp the concept of profit. They also finally understand that neither the customer nor the storekeeper gets the better of the bargain when the one gets change and the other is paid. It is not until about a year later that the possibility of shortchanging is seen.

Reasoning
and Child
Development

SENSORIMOTOR INTELLIGENCE.   It would be incorrect to maintain that babies and very young children do not give evidence of intelligent behavior, for even prior to the acquisition of language they are capable of primitive kinds of "mental" activity. We may term this activity, following J. Piaget (38), *sensorimotor*, because through touch, sight, and movement the infant locates and relates objects in space and time. Sensorimotor intelligence has nothing to do with language; it develops partly as a result of biological maturation and partly as a result of the child's experiences with objects. At a crude cognitive level, the infant begins to make distinctions between his or her own body and objects that are external to it.

At first, infants do not even realize that objects which have disappeared from their field of vision still exist. The objects do not have any temporal permanence. Thus, if one covers an object with a cloth while the five-month-old infant is reaching for it, he or she will cease reaching and lose interest. (38:37)

> The primitive world is not made up of permanent objects . . . but of moving perceptive pictures which return periodically into non-existence and come back again as a functional result of the proper action.

Nor does the young infant at first have any clear idea of objects in space. Through exploration of objects—rotating and touching them, seeing their various sides—he or she soon arrives at some elementary notions of space and of the permanence of objects.

The sensorimotor "reasoning" of infants eventually makes them vaguely aware of their body as one among many stable objects. This represents a considerable advance over their initial picture of the world as made up wholly of impermanent objects.

LOGIC IN CHILDREN.   Many child psychologists believe that "the child's reasoning processes at the age of six are [not] essentially different from his reasoning processes at the age of twelve or eighteen." (26:380) This belief involves several assumptions. First, children's logic is essentially the same as that of adults. Second, the more frequent errors committed by the child are a consequence of false premises rather than of inferior logic or inability to reason abstractly. Third, these false premises exist because the child has had inadequate experience with the given subject matter. Fourth, adults also, when confronted with unfamiliar subject matter, are likely to commit errors in logic and judgment. This belief in the general equivalence of child and adult reasoning can easily lead to a subtle form of anthropomorphism concerning the child. Our earlier discussion of the evolution of sign behavior implies that children should be expected to acquire mastery of the higher orders of symbolic activity only gradually. This becomes obvious if we consider some of the difficulties with logic which children encounter. Casual observation of the child's speech reveals some of these, but others are not apparent unless the child is trapped into revealing his or her thought process through clever questioning and verbal testing. Some of these deficiencies in logic can be illustrated in tabular form. We paraphrase Piaget. (38)

The ability to reason abstractly has a lengthy developmental history. The authors recently observed an episode in which a child could not describe correctly the kinship relations between his mother and his two maternal aunts, nor could he indicate how many sisters each had. When questioned about the matter in the absence of the women in question, he fell into the confusions and contradictions typical of a five-year-old. However, when all of the adults were seated at the table and he was asked how many sisters each had, he was able to give the correct answers. The effort that this task cost him was unmistakable. He looked fixedly at his mother, then turned and looked at her two sisters one by one, naming each as he did so. Then he repeated the same process for each of his two aunts. The child's behavior clearly represents a phase in learning to understand relationships. At the age of five years the child's comprehension of abstractions tends to be on a relatively low level—his comprehension is concrete rather than abstract, as Goldstein would say.

Life Cycle: The Genesis of Self

Difficulties in	Illustration
Classifying abstractly (generalizing)	Four trays, each holding a small wooden dog and one other object, are shown to the child. He is asked to name the common element (that is, the dog). Few children under four or five years of age could name it, could say "all trays have dogs."
Realizing that the class name is only a convenience	The young child believes the name is "in" the object, is inseparable from the object. For example, the sun's name is "in" the sun.
Understanding the relativity of relationships	The child maintains that a pebble is light, a boat is heavy. He does not realize that a pebble is light for him and heavy for the water in which it sinks, or that the boat is light for the water, but heavy for him. Another example: the child cannot grasp the following set of abstract relations. "Edith is lighter than Suzanne. Edith is darker than Lily. Which is darkest—Edith, Suzanne, or Lily?
Imagining the merely possible	Asked to suppose that the sun is really called the moon and vice versa the child is likely to argue that that is impossible, that it cannot be. Asked "If your brother is a year older than you, how old is he then," a child with no brother will protest that he has no brother.
Avoiding logical contradictions and inconsistencies	The child will maintain that big bodies are heavier than small ones, but that a small pebble is heavier than a large cork. He will state that rivers have strength because they flow, and a moment later maintain that rivers have no strength because they can't carry anything.
Understanding logical necessity	If asked why water goes down and smoke goes up, the child answers that heavy bodies fall and light ones rise. His answer is based not on logical necessity but on moral obligation. The object must rise or fall because it is morally obliged to, rather than because it is lighter or heavier than air.
Dealing simultaneously with several logically related matters	The child is asked the following question: "If the animal has long ears, it is a mule or a donkey; if it has a thick tail, it is a mule or a horse. Well, this animal has long ears and a thick tail. What is the animal?" The child cannot answer correctly. Example: "The animal can be a donkey because you say that if it has long ears it is either a donkey or a mule. But it can be a mule, for you say that if the animal has a thick tail it is either a mule or a horse."

The persons or objects must be physically before him if he is to solve even the simpler kinds of questions concerning their interrelations.

Here is an illustration of how children may apply what they learned in a relatively concrete situation to one in which a higher degree of abstraction is required. The child has learned, by purchases in stores, that the more pieces of gum were bought the more pennies were needed. He or she is then shown one stick of gum and asked what it costs—"one penny." Then the stick of gum is broken in halves in full view, and the question is repeated—"two cents." Another half is divided, and the answer is "three cents."

Piaget has analyzed the failures of children on certain tests dealing with concepts of space, number, movement, and the like. His technique is suggested by the following (38:133):

> To study the formation of classes we place about twenty beads in a box, the subject acknowledging that they are "all made of wood," so that they constitute a whole, B. Most of these beads are brown and constitute part A, and some are white, forming the complementary part A'. In order to determine whether the child is capable of understanding the operation A plus A' equals B, *i.e.*, the uniting of parts in a whole, we may put the following simple question: In this box (all the beads still being visible) which are there more of—wooden beads or brown beads, that is, A < B?

Piaget has suggested that there are four fairly clear stages in the learning of logical operations. For our purpose there is no need to describe these stages; but the import of his theory is that as children move from stage to stage, the organization of their behavior changes accordingly.

The very interesting experimentation carried out some years ago by L. S. Vygotsky has influenced American research and theory about child development. (50) One of Vygotsky's most general findings was that children reason according to *chain complexes*. This term means that in putting together objects that "belong" together, children do not use a consistent classificatory system, but instead use a succession of similarities (they look yellow, then they look blue); but the successive similarities have no constancy. J. Bruner and R. Oliver (9), influenced by both Piaget and Vygotsky, also concluded that children form chain complexes. Thus, children were offered words in pairs (for example, *peach* and *banana*) and then were asked in what ways those two objects were alike. Next, additional words were presented (*meat* and *potato*) and the children were then asked how all the words were alike. They gave answers such as that the banana and peach are yellow, the peach and potato are round, and the potato and meat are eaten together.

Roger Brown has questioned these kinds of experiments. (7:385–88) He agrees that children in such experiments tend to sort objects on a part-whole basis and to form chain complexes; also that they seldom are able to formulate rules that accurately describe the classes they form, and they do not fully understand the relation of class inclusion. He argues, however, that even adults cannot always give the rule describing their use of words; and while it is probably true that adults understand class-inclusion relations and children do not, knowledge of these relations actually is not required for referential use of a word, nor for most propositional purposes. He argues, therefore, that the "intellectual characteristic of children that seems most likely to be reliably characteristic and to have general implications for their understanding of words is their use of chain complexes." Brown cautions against supposing that because adults seldom reason with chain complexes in the experiments, that they also seldom do so in real-life solving of problems.

It seems clear that the evidence supports the assumption that there are genuine differences in the reasoning processes of children and adults. Obviously adults do not always reason according to strict canons of logic. Basil Bernstein (3) has argued that the lower classes think within a restricted, very particularistic linguistic code, whereas the middle classes employ an elaborated, abstract speech system. Exactly why social class membership should produce these variations is not fully explained by Bernstein. It is not even certain whether adults with relatively little education can reason as "abstractly" as they might if they were more highly educated. Interviewers who talk with persons from lower economic groups discover that they and their interviewees speak different languages; they may also discover that they think and talk more abstractly than do the interviewees, who handle their world more concretely. In one study, interviewers approached the people of a rural Arkansas town after a devastating tornado had destroyed much of the community. (41) Interviewers noticed characteristic differences in the ways in which people of different social status described the tornado. Middle-class or educated persons were more able to give a detached, impersonal account of what had happened than were members of the lower classes. Accounts by the latter groups tended to be personal and to be based on the individuals' own experiences. Perhaps because of limited social experience, they seemed unable to give a clear, general account of what had happened or to take into consideration the experiences of others. Their descriptions were more concrete and personal than those of higher social classes.

THE REASONING OF ADULTS

From the point of view of the middle-class interviewer trying to determine what actually happened, the descriptions given by middle-class people seemed much more enlightening. They were more systematic and generalized and were easier for the interviewer to obtain. Lower-class persons often seemed to lack a generalized framework within which they might organize their ideas of what had happened.

B. Kaplan (28), who explored differences in modes of thought in relation to degree of education, has also concluded that the less-educated rely more on *concrete symbolism* than the well educated, and that their thought processes are "less differentiated." Other studies support this general conclusion. While this discussion has taken us away from our primary focus on children's reasoning, these studies are clearly pertinent to the general idea involved.

Summary In the child's acquisition of language from his or her earliest babblings and simplest vocalizations to the final convergence with adult speech, the progression is from the instrumental use of words, word-sentences, and gestures to the more complicated forms of speech. Ways of speaking are intimately connected with ways of thinking, and we have emphasized the ways in which the child's assimilation of language is related to self-control and to the development of logical thought. The rules governing speech are much different from those that control thought. The growth of logical comprehension in the child is illustrated by the manner in which black children acquire concepts of race and the way in which children's ideas of money and the process of exchange are developed. One's patterns of speaking and thinking reflect one's location in the social structure. There is need for much further study of the relationship between language behavior and socialization. On the whole, this has been a neglected research area, but it is a field deserving of serious social psychological attention.

References 1. Ames, L., "The Development of Sense of Time in the Young Child," *Journal of Genetic Psychology*, vol. 68 (1948), pp. 97–125.
2. Bellugi, U., and R. Brown (eds.), "The Acquisition of Language: Report of the Fourth Conference Sponsored by the Committee on Intellective Processes Research of the Social Science Research Council," *Society for Research in Child Development*, vol. 29, no. 1. Chicago: University of Chicago Press, 1964.
3. Bernstein, B., "Elaborated and Restricted Codes: Their Social Origins and Some Consequences," in J. Gumperz and D. Hymes (eds.), "The Ethnography of Communication," *American Anthropologist*, vol. 66, no. 2 (1964), pp. 55–69.
4. ———, "Some Sociological Determinants of Perception," *British Journal of Sociology*, vol. 9 (1958), pp. 150–58.

5. Bossard, James H. S., and Eleanor S. Boll, *The Sociology of Child Development*, 3d ed. New York: Harper & Row, 1960.
6. Brown, R., *Psycholinguistics*. New York: The Free Press, 1970.
7. ———, *Social Psychology*. New York: The Free Press, 1965.
8. ———, *Words and Things*. New York: The Free Press, 1958.
9. Bruner, J., and R. Oliver, "The Development of Equivalence Transformations in Children," in J. Wright and J. Kagan (eds.), "Basic Cognitive Processes in Children," *Society for Research in Child Development*, vol. 28. Chicago: University of Chicago Press, 1963.
10. Chomsky, N., *Aspects of the Theory of Syntax*. Cambridge, Mass.: M.I.T. Press, 1965.
11. Cicourel, Aaron V., "Basic and Normative Rules in the Negotiation of Status and Role," in David Sudnow (ed.), *Studies in Social Interaction*. New York: The Free Press, 1972, pp. 229–58.
12. Clark, K., and M. Clark, "Racial Identification and Preference in Negro Children," in G. E. Swanson, T. M. Newcomb, and E. L. Hartley, (eds.), *Readings in Social Psychology* (rev. ed.). New York: Holt, Rinehart and Winston, 1952, pp. 551–60.
13. Conn, J. H., and L. Kanner, "Children's Awareness of Sex Differences," *Journal of Child Psychiatry*, vol. 1 (1947), pp. 3–57.
14. de Laguna, G. M., *Speech: Its Function and Development*. New Haven: Yale University Press, 1927.
15. Ervin, S. M., and W. R. Miller, "Language Development," in the *National Society for the Study of Education* (62nd Yearbook). Chicago: University of Chicago Press, 1963.
16. Ferguson, Charles A., "Baby Talk in Six Languages," *American Anthropologist*, vol. 66, part 2 (December 1964), pp. 103–14.
17. Frazier, E. F., "The Role of the Family," in *Negro Youth at the Crossways*. Washington, D. C.: American Council on Education, 1940, pp. 39–69.
18. Freidson, E., "Adult Discount: An Aspect of Children's Changing Taste," *Child Development*, vol. 24 (1953), pp. 39–49.
19. Havighurst, R. J., and B. L. Neugarten, *American Indian and White Children: A Sociopsychological Investigation*. Chicago: University of Chicago Press, 1955.
20. Hoggart, R., *The Uses of Literacy*. London: Chatto & Windus, 1957.
21. Horowitz, E., "The Development of Attitudes toward the Negro," *Archives of Psychology*, vol. 2, no. 194 (1936).
22. Horowitz, R., "A Pictorial Method for the Study of Self-Identification in Preschool Children," *Journal of Genetic Psychology*, vol. 62 (1943), pp. 135–48.
23. Hulett, J. E., Jr., "Communication and Social Order: The Search for a Theory," *Audio-Visual Communication Review*, vol. 12 (1964), pp. 458–68.
24. Hymes, Dell, "Toward Ethnographies of Communication: The Analysis of Communicative Forms," in Pier Paolo Giglioli (ed.), *Language and Social Context*. Baltimore: Penguin Books, 1972, pp. 21–44.
25. Inhelder, B., and J. Piaget, *The Growth of Logical Thinking*. New York: Basic Books, 1958.
26. Jersild, A., *Child Psychology* (3rd ed.). Englewood Cliffs, N.J.: Prentice-Hall, 1947.
27. Kagan, J., and J. C. Wright (eds.), "Basic Cognitive Processes in Children," *Society for Research in Child Development*, vol. 28, no. 2. Chicago: University of Chicago Press, 1963.
28. Kaplan, B., unpublished study, Clark University.

29. Kessen, W., and C. Kuhlman (eds.), "Thought in the Young Child," *Society for Research in Child Development,* vol. 27, no. 2. Chicago: University of Chicago Press, 1962.

30. Labov, William, et al., *A Study of the Non-Standard English of Negro and Puerto Rican Speakers in New York City.* Washington, D.C.: Office of Education, 1968.

31. Lewis, M. M., *How Children Learn to Speak.* New York: Basic Books, 1959.

32. ———, *Infant Speech.* New York: Harcourt Brace Jovanovich, 1936.

33. Lorimer, F., *The Growth of Reason.* New York: Harcourt Brace Jovanovich, 1929.

34. McCarthy, D., in L. Carmichael (ed.), *Manual of Child Psychology.* New York: Wiley, 1946, pp. 476–581.

35. McNeill, D., "The Creation of Language," *Discovery,* vol. 27 (July 1966), pp. 34–38.

36. Moreno, J., *Who Shall Survive?* Washington, D.C.: Nervous and Mental Disease Publishing Company, 1934.

37. Piaget, J., "Principle Factors Determining Intellectual Evolution from Childhood to Adult Life," in *Factors Determining Human Behavior.* Cambridge, Mass.: Harvard University Press, 1937, pp. 32–48.

38. ———, *The Psychology of Intelligence.* London: Routledge & Kegan Paul, 1950.

39. ———, *Structuralism.* New York: Basic Books, 1970.

40. Radke, M., H. Trager, and H. Davis, "Social Perception and Attitudes of Children," *Genetic Psychology Monographs,* vol. 40 (1949), pp. 327–447.

41. Schatzman, L., and A. Strauss, "Social Class and Modes of Communication," *American Journal of Sociology,* vol. 60 (1955), pp. 329–38.

42. Searle, John R., *Speech Acts.* New York: Cambridge University Press, 1970.

43. Seeman, M., "Skin Color Values in Three All-Negro Classes," *American Sociological Review,* vol. 11 (1946), pp. 315–21.

44. Sherif, M., *An Outline of Social Psychology.* New York: Harper & Row, 1948.

45. Slobin, Dan I., *Psycholinguistics.* Glenview, Ill.: Scott Foresman and Company, 1971.

46. Stendler, C., *Children of Brasstown.* Urbana, Ill.: University of Illinois Press, 1949.

47. Strauss, A. L., "The Development and Transformation of Monetary Meanings in the Child," *American Sociological Review,* vol. 17 (1952), pp. 275–86.

48. Sullivan, H. S., *The Interpersonal Theory of Psychiatry.* New York: W. W. Norton, 1953.

49. Taine, H., "Note on the Acquisition of Language by Children and in the Human Species," *Mind,* vol. 2 (1877), pp. 251–53.

50. Vygotsky, L. S., *Thought and Language.* Cambridge, Mass.: M.I.T. Press, 1962.

51. Wallach, M., "Research on Children's Thinking," in the *National Society for the Study of Education* (62nd Yearbook). Chicago: University of Chicago Press, 1963.

52. Yokley, R. L., *The Development of Racial Concepts in Negro Children.* Unpublished Ph.D. dissertation, Indiana University, 1952.

BROWN, R., *Psycholinguistics*. New York: The Free Press, 1970.

This is an important collection of papers by an eminent linguist and social psychologist who cogently reviews the theories of Chomsky and presents his own highly original research on the "first" language of young children.

CHOMSKY, N., *Aspects of the Theory of Syntax*. Cambridge, Mass.: M.I.T. Press, 1965.

The controversial theory of language acquisition and language competence of this linguist is sketched in this volume.

PIAGET, J., *Structuralism*. New York: Basic Books, 1970.

Piaget offers a critical review of currently popular theories of language behavior.

SEARLE, J., *Speech Acts*. New York: Cambridge University Press, 1970.

A philosopher offers a cogent "social interactionist" perspective on speech behavior.

chapter *10*

The Origins and Development of Self

Consistent with our symbolic interactionist orientation, we hold that any theory of socialization and interaction must ultimately consider the question of how the newborn human becomes a self-conscious participant in the interaction process. In this chapter, we review the social conditions that give rise to the development of self in early childhood. We conclude with a discussion of various developmental theories, including those of the psychiatrist Harry Stack Sullivan, who in our judgment offers the most coherent interactional treatment of the rise of self-consciousness in the human organism that is currently available. Chapter 11 will extend our analysis, focusing on the social worlds of early childhood. We begin now with a general view of socialization and interaction.

Socialization and Interaction

Human beings have to develop self-control and a sense of self; the newborn infant is born with no sense of self, other, or social situation. The cardinal task of the child's caretaker is to transform this socially neutral infant into a symbolically functioning human being. The child enters an ongoing world of social interaction that is presented through the symbolic and behavioral actions of its most immediate caretakers, typically those persons who make up the primary group of the family. Assuming there are no organic or neurological deficiencies, the object called "child" possesses at birth the necessary equipment to become social and self-conscious. (35, 48)

We assume that the child immediately after birth is exposed to the necessary interactional experiences that will eventually become incorporated into his or her behavioral repertoires. In short, before socialization can occur, the child must be exposed to face-to-face interaction. Once interaction begins, every succeeding exchange between the child and the mother can be viewed as an instance of socialization. Should interaction cease, or be deflected for a period of time, the child will symbolically regress to an earlier level of development. (See our earlier discussion of social isolation.) The research on maternal deprivation, pioneered by John Bowlby and his associates in the mid 1950s, clearly revealed that those infants in orphanages who were not exposed to face-to-face interaction rapidly began to lose weight, and many were so understimulated, interactionally, that they began dying at the ages of three and four. (8)

CHILDHOOD AS STATUS PASSAGE: CHILDREN AS OPTIONAL OBJECTS

We must make clear, however, that there is nothing intrinsic to the object called "child" that makes it more or less human. Accordingly, depending on the actions taken toward it, different types of selves will be produced. When a society does not have a status called "childhood," "children" will, in a sociological sense, actually not be produced; consequently, childlike behavior as it is known in current scientific theory will not be found in those societies and social groups that have no conception of childhood. (20) It would be expected that their children would be permitted to engage in the behaviors normally reserved for adults only. They would own property, exercise political power, make sexual contracts, and engage in the vices of that group. (26, 45)

A group's stance toward the desirability and inevitability of childhood will determine whether or not that group produces children. Six categories are suggested. Childhood may be viewed as desirable or undesirable (as is claimed to be the case for the Parisian French, by Wolfenstein). (46) Next, childhood may be regarded as inevitable, optional, or it may not exist. Middle-income Americans regard childhood as desirable and inevitable. The French (according to Wolfenstein) view it as undesirable and inevitable and think one should move through it as rapidly as possible. The American Amish view it is as optional and desirable, although for those studied by Kuhn (25) it ceased to exist after the age of two. The Balinese have no period called childhood and immediately transform their children into adults. (28)

The Origins and Development of Self   313

Those groups which view childhood as undesirable produce adults at a much faster rate than do those who define it as desirable. This suggests that distinct cultures of childhood and adulthood will exist in those groups which prolong entry into the adult's world. Thus, while we would argue that "child-like" behavior as it is known in current scientific theory will not be found in those societies and social groups that have no conception of childhood, nonetheless we contend that the steps or phases by which the self develops are universal in nature. Their specific contents will vary from group to group, but the forms are universal. With the foregoing reservations and points in mind, we can turn to a discussion of the self and its emergence in early childhood. We must first treat the general place of the concept called "self" in the literature of social science.

THE CONCEPT "SELF"

Some such concept as *self* or *ego* is essential to any account of human social nature or the socialization process. Human beings characteristically act with self-awareness, exercise self-control, exhibit conscience and guilt, and in the great crises of life make decisions with reference to some imagery of what they are, what they have been, and what they hope to be. The wider social community enters the person through its language, which in turn, furnishes the foundations for the self.

It is obviously easier to say that concepts of identity or self are necessary in analyses of group and individual behavior than to write with clarity about the nature and functioning of self. Philosophic thought has long wrestled with the relationships of subject and object, knower and known, and the general relationships of self and the objective world. The literature of these relationships is exceedingly complex and abstract. Psychology, which broke away from philosophy partly as a reaction against such abstruse speculation, also reacted against the very idea of self as a scientific concept. It was argued on methodological grounds that the so-called self of humans was like their soul; it could not be investigated by reliable scientific methods and therefore had no claim to consideration by scientists. On theoretical grounds, it was banished as a mentalistic construct and relegated to the ash can along with faculties, humors, and other outmoded concepts. It was also argued that stimuli and responses and their relationships could be studied without bothering about whether human beings have selves.

Proponents of the "self" idea have gained the advantage in the controversy in the last few decades. The concept was never entirely rejected in all fields of psychology; it was granted some validity, particularly in child and social psychology. Then, with the increase of the influence of psychoanalytic theory upon studies of personality and in the psychological clinic, there has come a revival of interest in problems of self. During the last two decades there has been a considerable amount of research involving or focused on the idea of self. One reason for this has been a growing discontent with theorizing about self, which is done without some empirical base in research; another reason has been a growing awareness that the concept has implications that can guide significant research provided those implications are followed through. Our own view is that some of the most significant research is that which focuses on implications of the self-concept. We tend to concur with Theodore Newcomb and his colleagues (31:142) that the original emphasis on the self as a product of social interaction has been reinforced rather than altered by the more recent investigations. As they say, now we "know much more about the psychological processes by which children learn to perceive themselves, but the earlier conclusion that the self is a social product has scarcely changed at all."

Development of Self-Awareness

Observers of child behavior have long noted that the child develops a kind of crude self-awareness within two or three years; and that it takes many more years before full adult self-awareness comes into being. The abilities to think of oneself as an object and to have feelings about oneself evolve throughout the childhood years. The observation that self-awareness has a gradual development misled many philosophers as well as laypersons into thinking of this development as a biological process. It was assumed that infants lacked self-awareness because they were physically incapable of experiencing it. Bodily maturation was supposed to provide the capacity to conceive the self. Self-consciousness, in other words, was seen essentially as a natural outgrowth of innate physical endowments. Although this hypothesis was completely disproved by studies made in the nineteenth century (40:156–78), it is easy to see how it could have been formulated. [5] Now, however, there is general agreement that socialization, over and beyond mere biological maturation, is essential to the development of self-consciousness. Deprived of human association, the biologically developing infant could scarcely develop a sense of self. (8, 37)

The infant at first has no conception of what belongs to his or her body and what does not but seems rapidly to develop several patterns (30:207):

BODY AWARENESS AND BODY DISPLAY

> At six or eight months he has certainly formed no clear notion of himself. He does not even know the boundaries of his own body. Each hand wandering over the bedspread for things which can be brought into the mouth discovers the other hand and each triumphantly lifts the other into his mouth; he draws his thumb from his mouth to wave it at a stranger, then

cries because the thumb has gone away. He pulls at his toes until they hurt and does not know what is wrong.

This is not to say that others in the immediate environment of the neonate do not make social judgments about the child's body and its relative degrees of perceived attractiveness. The neonate enters the world with a physical body which, given the presence of others, is constantly on display and under evaluation. At the outset the infant passively enters into the display rituals that surround the presentation and inspection of its body. At this early age the child lacks any ability to adorn, dress, or systematically manipulate its own body. As a sense of self is grasped, the child more actively controls these ritual elements of self-presentation.

Slowly, infants learn the boundaries of their own being and learn to make distinctions between what is part of their body and what is part of something else. M. W. Shinn has described two incidents in this process (41:143):

> The 181st day her hand came into contact with her ear; she became at once very serious, and felt it and pulled it hard; losing it, she felt around her cheek for it, but when her mother put her hand back, she became interested in the cheek and wished to keep on feeling that. . . . To the end of the year, she would . . . feel over her head, neck, hair, and ears, the hair she discovered in the eight month, 222nd day, while feeling for her ear, and felt it over and pulled it with great curiosity.

This lack of differentiation between body and surrounding environment is merely a specific illustration of the infant's generally blurred perceiving. (33:236–37) Piaget has used the term *indissociation* to describe this undifferentiated perception.

If the case of the blind child is considered, the following findings emerge (39:1032):

> While the environment of the blind child may fade in and out of his awareness, his own body remains constant. The child may be unable to experience the impact which his manipulations have on the toy which he holds, but he can experience the impact which he has upon his own body . . . his own body becomes the vehicle for feedback.

In comparison with the sighted child, "the blind child explores his own body whereas his sighted counterpart" can more directly explore his environment as well as his body. (39:1032)

This lack of differentiation, as we discussed in Chapter 9, exists because the child has yet to acquire the necessary linguistic skills which permit him or her to differentiate self from others. To have a sense of self—to be able to objectify his or her own activity and separate it from that of others—the child must be able to see him- or herself as a distinct object and realize that the self is not the same as the material-body self. Further, as Mead argued, the child must be able to see him- or herself from the perspectives of others. (27) The genesis of self involves an awareness that other perspectives outside of the child's direct control exist and must be taken account of. The child's knowledge of self is contingent on a separation of self from others.

Central to the creation of the self as a social object is an identification of that object which will be termed as self. Identification, as Stone (42), Strauss (43), and Allport (1) have argued, involves naming. Once an object has been named and identified, it can be acted toward. This is true for children, as well as for any other object, whether it is a chair, a cigarette, or a scientific theory. For children to acquire a sense of self, they must be named and singled out from other objects. They must be labeled as distinct objects. Such an identification permits a differentiation from other persons or selves. As Allport (1:115) has argued, the most important linguistic aid becomes the personal name. Rituals of a rather elaborate order surround the selection of first and middle names for children by many American parents. Rossi (36) has shown that kinship, generational, and religious processes enter into the selection of names for newborn children. Similar events have been observed in other countries. Thus, Young and Willmott (47) have shown that lower-class London families also employ rather complicated rules in the selection of names for their children.

NAMING THE OBJECT CALLED "CHILD"

Allport has commented on names and the emergence of a separation of material-body self from the social self (1:115): "By hearing his name repeatedly the child gradually sees himself as a distinct and recurrent point of reference. The name acquires significance for him in the second year of life. With it comes awareness of independent status in the social group."

Even after infants learn to distinguish between their bodies and the world, they do not have full self-awareness. The child continues for several years to have difficulty in properly locating processes that go on "within his or her own mind" and in keeping them separated from external processes. Thus, Piaget (33) noted that if the child were asked: "Where is the dream when you dream?" he or she would say that it is "in the room" or "beside the bed." Asked by Piaget where the name of the sun is located, children usually answered that it was very high in the sky. Conversely, they attributed to words qualities signified by the objects or events. Thus the word *elephant* was declared to be a very "strong" word in comparison to *mouse*. Children, of course, also project human attributes on to various animate and inanimate objects. They may believe, for example, that fish eat three meals a day; that if a pin is poked

CONFUSION OF "SELF" WITH "NONSELF"

into a tree, the tree feels it; that it hurts a rock to be broken by a hammer. They assume that all persons are like themselves, that animals are like humans, and that inanimate objects are alive. They may even identify themselves with material things.

Young children have a particularly difficult time learning to use personal pronouns correctly. Their initial use of *I, me, mine,* and *you* may be confused and inaccurate. They hear their mother use the word *you* toward themselves and will address themselves as *you* instead of *I.* They may speak of themselves in the third person instead of the first person; for example, "Donnie wants that." (2:161): "The two-year-old often confuses quite sadly the first, second and third persons. He may be overheard to say to himself, 'You be careful, William get hurt. NO! I won't get hurt.' He is first, second and third person all at the same time."

Cooley has suggested that young children misuse pronouns because they cannot directly imitate them. Ordinary words, such as *apple* or *doll,* can be easily imitated, whereas words like *you* or *I* have to be reinterpreted by the child rather than copied directly. (12:200) Actually, as we have seen, children at first do not imitate such words as *apple* or *doll* very directly. However, they have their chief difficulties with relationship terms such as *brother, father, I,* and *you,* since during their early years they are unaware of perspectives other than their own.

Increasing accuracy in the use of pronouns shows children's maturing conception of their own existence and individuality. This is reflected also by the acquisition of new pronouns. Before the age of five, first-person pronouns in the plural (*we, us, ours*) appear very infrequently in the children's vocabulary. They increase as children grow older and become more conscious of their own participation in groups.

Read Bain (4:767–75), following Cooley's lead, studied his young daughter's acquisition of pronouns. The first pronoun appeared at the age of fifteen months, but she did not systematically employ it until the age of twenty months. By the age of two years and nine months she was using seventy-one proper nouns (persons) and fourteen pronouns (*I, me, my, mine, myself, we, us, your, something, it, both, any, none*). By the age of ten months and twenty days, she was answering to the question, "Where's Sheila?" with "She-e! She-e!" Although she also had a term for mother and father, she did not make these designations until the age of one year.

THE LOOKING-GLASS SELF There is a close connection between self-awareness and imagining how one looks to other persons. As an illustration, we may consider what is properly termed *self-consciousness.* Almost every one of us has been placed in a situation in which we felt an acutely heightened sense of self; that is, in which we were extremely conscious of our existence and ap-

Early childhood self-awareness and a mother's eye (*E. Trina Lipton*)

pearance. Consider, for example, a student making his first speech in a public-speaking class. He perspires, fidgets, feels tense, and may even have "butterflies in his stomach." Although he may be on good terms with everyone in his audience, he concentrates on such thoughts as: "What are they thinking of me?" "How do I look?" "What kind of impression am I making?" Nor does our imaginary, fright-stricken student have to face an audience to feel acutely self-conscious; he need only think of facing the audience to experience some of the same symptoms. "Mike-fright" has been known to happen to radio speakers before a "dead" microphone. *Self-consciousness* is an extreme example of being self-conscious; it illustrates very well the connection between self-awareness and imagining what one looks like to others.

Cooley, when he coined the phrase *the looking-glass self*, had this connection in mind. His analysis is worth quoting (11:184):

> As we see . . . our face, figure, and dress in the glass, and are interested in them because they are ours, and pleased or otherwise with them according to as they do or do not answer to what we should like them to be; so in imagination we perceive in another's mind some thought of our appearance, manners, aims, deeds, character, friends, and so on, and are variously affected by it.
>
> A self-idea of this sort seems to have three principal elements: the imagination of our appearance to the other person; the imagination of his judgment of that appearance; and some sort of self-feeling such as pride or mortification. The comparison with a looking-glass hardly suggests the second element, the imagined judgment, which is quite essential.

The Origins and Development of Self   319

This emotional-affective response of self-feeling, which appears when persons present themselves in front of others, is not present in the early stages of self-awareness.

As we have noted, newborn infants lack the ability to visualize themselves through the eyes of others. They are not born with this ability: they must acquire it through learning, and essential to this is language acquisition, which permits children to take the roles of other individuals.

LEARNING TO TAKE THE ROLE OF THE OTHER

Language is necessary to the development of self-awareness. Many writers have recognized this relationship and expressed it in various ways. Some have suggested the importance of linguistic anchorages like address, salutations, and property. Others have regarded parental use of the child's name as an important factor. Still others have assumed that the use of pronouns by both the child and his or her elders helps fix the child's idea of self-reference. But none of these views is as concrete or as convincing as that of G. H. Mead. (27)

Mead notes that among the most significant adult vocalizations, from the standpoint of children, are those that have to do with themselves. These are picked up, imitated, and gradually incorporated in the evolving system of signals, or cues, which children use to stimulate themselves. They hear their name repeated over and over by others who accompany it with appropriate gestures and activities to indicate what it means. The remarks that they are able to remember and to repeat to themselves gradually increase in complexity: at first they can use only simple words, then groups of words, and later simple sentences. Finally, they become capable of rehearsing in their imagination, entire conversations in which they have been involved. They learn to ascribe motives to their actions and become concerned over the reactions of others to their behavior. As the person converses with himself or herself, an inner dialogue can be observed. The person takes, or assumes, the attitude of another person and judges that attitude in terms of his or her own response to the situation at hand. Mead described this as an exchange between the "I" (the person) and the "me" (the reflected attitudes of the other).

Through this process of self-stimulation, children learn to think of themselves as persons, with personal points of view, feelings, ambitions, and goals. Such recognition of themselves as persons necessarily means that they recognize or conceive of themselves along lines similar to the conceptions that others have of them. In this inner forum, this personal rehearsal and dramatization of roles, young individuals learn to apply symbols to themselves and to their own behavior. As Mead has pointed out, young children are characteristically less adept on the "me" side.

Life Cycle: The Genesis of Self

They respond directly to stimuli, but do not have the means, or have in-adequate means, of taking the other's attitude.

In the course of responding to themselves, children (1) develop an awareness of their own responses, (2) learn something of their conse-quences, and (3) achieve a certain objectivity about them. Fundamental in the process is the medium of language. Individuals become aware of objects, as we have noted before, when they are able to name and clas-sify them. Similarly, they become aware of themselves when they learn to apply symbols to themselves and to their acts.

To the necessity of symbolization for the realization of selfhood, there ought to be added an emphasis upon the turmoil that may accom-pany this development of self-symbolizing. This was succinctly noted by Baldwin, writing around the turn of the century. (5) He pointed to the fact that self-conceptions depend upon assessments of others' perspec-tives toward one, and since wrong assessments as well as correct ones are made, children cannot learn about themselves without some turmoil. In the writings of Freud and other psychoanalysts, this point is raised to a central theme. Children identify closely with one of their parents, take over some of the parent's moral perspectives, and apply these to their own behavior. But the identification is fraught with peril and the in-ternalization of parental views may result in a harsh control over basic attitudes.

A mirror and a reflected self: Who am I?
(*Marion Faller from Monkmeyer Press Service*)

Individuality and the Social Character of the Self

The preceding discussion indicates that the self is a social product. It is a consequence of the individual's incorporation within his or her own emerging sense of self of a social process, which involves ongoing conversations between the "I" and the "me." Indeed, in a sense, the self is just this process of intraindividual communication. Selves do not exist except in a symbolic or social environment from which they cannot be separated. Intraindividual communication is only a part of the total communication network, which extends also to relations between individuals and between the individuals and groups. The very idea of an isolated self as an atomistic unit is an error. Symbolic behavior, as we have shown in earlier chapters, is shared behavior. "Self" therefore implies "others" and is inseparable from them. The meanings of the symbols by which selves are organized are contributed by the responses of others. The fact that a self always seems to belong to an autonomous biological organism should not cause one to neglect the fact that it is built upon a social foundation and that it continues to draw its sustenance from its roots in social relations. As Mead (27:164) has said: "No hard-and-fast line can be drawn between our own selves and the selves of others, since our own selves exist only insofar as the selves of others exist."

However, a commonsense idea of individuality runs counter to this. It is thought that because persons have unique bodies and somewhat unique experiences, they are quite autonomous products. There is no need to deny individuality in affirming the basic social nature of self. As Cooley (12) has said, the use of the word "I"—which of course expresses individuality—would be inconceivable in the absence of an audience to address or to exert power over. But in an even more subtle sense, the social nature of the self necessarily implies, rather than denies, individuality. The *generalized other,* the organized community of attitudes to which the person responds, the "me," is not a mere importation into the person; it is an assimilation attended, as remarked before, with anguish, anxiety, concern, and care. In a report of a series of observations of his young daughter, Cooley contended that a sense of appropriation was crucial to the development of a sense of self. He pointed to the early and passionate use of pronouns like "mine" and "my." In a limited way Cooley was getting at a much larger point—namely, that people are not compliant automatons. Psychiatrists base tedious methods of psychotherapy on the knowledge that you cannot just tell patients about themselves—they must learn it for themselves and pretty much at their own rate of speed. The conceptions that people have of their bodies, their actions, and their pasts are not mere reflections of the perspectives of others. They are amalgams of these perspectives—many of them originally discordant and some of them discovered by the person, rather than taught him or her directly. Perspectives on self derived from significant others are like any other perspectives in that they are not adopted *in toto* or retained entirely on faith. All perspectives are tested and tried out in action. They are appropriated and possessed.

The use of such expressions in common speech as "self-consciousness," "I hate myself," "I hurt myself," "I am a problem to myself," and "I will be here myself" are indications of the self in action. However, popular usage of self-words is often inconsistent and confusing, particularly because the self sometimes is identified with body and sometimes is not. *Self* has both an objective and a subjective reference. The use of the term *self* as a noun seems to imply the existence of a corresponding entity or object. This, however, is an erroneous conception—as erroneous as it would be to think of *speed* in the same manner. Both terms refer to events and relationships, rather than to entities having a definite location in space. It is for reasons of this kind that the self or ego has been described as a "grammatical illusion." THE NATURE OF SELF

If the self is thought of as a thing, it is reified; that is, it is either conceived of as the body, or is thought of as an entity somewhere within the body. It is common the world over to refer, at least poetically, to some part of the body that is especially favored because it is the seat of selfhood (perhaps particularly the heart, the eyes, the breath, and the brain). E. Horowitz (22) has reported some amusing answers by subjects to a request that they locate their selves. They named such varied zones as head, face, brain, eyes, heart, chest, lungs, teeth, hands, and genitals. C. Kluckhohn and H. A. Murray's (23:9) definition of the personality as "the organization of all the integrative (regnant) processes in the brain" is a sophisticated example in technical literature of the tendency to locate the self in a part of the body.

In order to have a self, one must first have a body. Hence some psychologists have spoken of the "physical self" as apart from "the social self." Little is gained by this, since we already have a word to designate the body, namely *body*. The self is not in the body as a physical part; neither is it a spiritual or mystical entity located somewhere or everywhere in the organism. Yet the body is implicated in the very notion of self. Without stating what the self is, we may yet note briefly some relationship between body and self.

People perceive and evaluate their body, its parts, and its functioning much as they perceive and evaluate other objects and events. They also have, as our discussion in later pages will show, conceptions of the inner environment that contribute to their evaluation of themselves as persons. They may believe that they have a weak heart and plan their life accordingly. By virtue of private experiences with their physique and the comments of others on it, they come to have special notions of how much work or how much joy they can get out of their body and what its limitations are. They develop ideas about their appearance and pass judgments upon it. Consequently, they may come to "hate themselves" because they believe their body is ugly, despite the fact that their judgment may not be shared by others. Conceptualizations of the body may enter into self-regard in very oblique and complex ways, as when a man hates himself because he finds he cannot control his actions. We speak then of "shame," or sometimes of "susceptibility to temptation." The body may be used as an instrument against self, as when one commits suicide; or it may be mortified as a sign of guilt, submission, or holiness. In short, appraisals of the body enter intimately into action and are subtle indicators of self-regard. But this body appraisal is symbolic in nature. It comes from interaction with others and is thus a social product.

THE SELF AS ORGANIZATION

A DEFINITION.   It will be pointed out in Chapter 13 how persons' conceptions of themselves serve to evoke and organize appropriate responses and, as part of the same process, to inhibit other responses. Such conceptions have a much greater effect in the control of behavior than a simple verbal command or a single inhibiting response. *In the same way, at a higher level of integration, one may think of self as (1) a set of more or less consistent and stable responses on a conceptual level that (2) exercises a regulatory function over other responses of the same organism at lower levels.*

This definition of self does not imply that the self is a "motivating force." It is not the ultimate vital source of behavior and energy. Neither is it a suprabehavioral court to which all behavior is somehow mysteriously referred. Dualistic notions of this kind often pervade popular thinking about human behavior and are also found in scientific literature.

The self is an organization or integration of behavior imposed upon individuals by themselves and by societal expectations and demands. Social requirements and pressures impose limitations upon the degree of inconsistency tolerated in the behavior of individuals and impel the person to eliminate or reconcile such inconsistencies. The organization and integration of lines of activity that appear to the outsider as contradictory or inconsistent are essential parts of what is referred to as the self. For the person, they merge together in the conversations between the "I" and the "me." Clearly, persons have multiple "I's" and multiple "me's."

CHANGES IN SELF AND SELF-INVOLVEMENT.   An important aspect of self is that it changes with time through the course of one's life. At the points in their lives when old patterns are breaking up under the impact of disjunctive experiences, persons may feel at odds with themselves until a new integration or rationale is achieved. (See Chapters 12 and 13, where we also discuss the collapse of social worlds.) However, throughout life there runs a thread of continuity contributed by name and constancy of personal identity. Individuals assimilate experiences, identifying them as their own and accepting responsibility for the actions identified as theirs. The symbolism of "keeping a good name" suggests some of this. Persons who try to escape their pasts change their names, give false histories, and try to forget or disown their early experiences. Such disassociation of self from self is not easy, although it can in some measure be achieved. In certain rare instances it seems that persons may have two fairly separate identities, so that in one of them the person has little or no memory of the other. Such cases are now and then reported in the newspapers, and others have been described in the psychological literature.

The self, as we have defined it, does not enter significantly into all behavior but is differentially involved in various acts; at one extreme, involvement is very slight. Psychological experiments dealing with "level of aspiration" have shown that when involvement in a task is increased (that is, when the individual is appropriately motivated), performance is improved or changed. In many involuntary and automatic activities, little of the self is implicated, although even in these the action may have significance of which individuals are not themselves aware. Moreover, an automatic action, like tapping the table with your fingers, may acquire significance if it is singled out for attention or criticism by other persons so that it takes on meaning for you yourself.

SELF AND SELF-CONTROL.   Self-control is usually thought of in connection with self-awareness; for example, we speak of persons controlling their appetites or curbing their passions. We ought to note, however, that regulatory functioning is not necessarily accompanied by acute self-consciousness. For example, a driver may pilot a car quite skillfully for many minutes while engaged in conversation or sunk deep in thought. Any physical skill tends to assume an automatic character, although when it is first acquired it is at the forefront of attention. Some skills may become the basis of self-esteem, as in persons who use them professionally or competitively, so that they continue to be at the center of attention in a somewhat different way.

THE MECHANISM OF SELF-CONTROL.   Self-regulation is inseparable from social control. The language mechanisms by which self-control is exerted are derived from social sources, and the regulatory process itself occurs largely in the form of internalized conversation. Mead has paid some attention to this process. He distinguished two phases of internalized conversation, the "I" and the "me." They may be made clear by means of a simple illustration. Let us suppose that a man walks into a bank and finds himself in a position where he can make off, without fear of detection, with a large sum of money. We shall suppose that our hypothetical man is not above temptation in this particular situation. Something like the following (in the form of an inaudible and greatly abbreviated conservation) might take place:

Phase One—"I"	Phase Two—"Me"
I could use that money.	But it's stealing.
So what! Everyone steals if they have a chance to.	You know it isn't so.
I could get a new car.	No. Better be honest
No chance of getting caught.	Dishonest.
Banks make lots of money; they won't feel it.	Isn't right to take it. Isn't theirs either.

If he is above temptation, Phase One does not exist and the conversation does not occur.

The actual process of conversing internally does not go on in terms of complete sentences or in terms of words alone, but rather as a kind of mental tug-of-war between conflicting impulses interspersed with visual and auditory images and daydreams, and accompanied by corresponding feelings. Such conversations are not necessarily short, nor do they always take place in a single episode. The battle against a particular temptation may be a sporadic and long one that is brought alive periodically by external circumstances.

Much of our thinking, particularly when we are dealing with difficult or problematic situations of a moral or volitional kind, involves these two general phases of conversation. Mead called Phase One the "I" and Phase Two the "me." The "me" in his scheme represents internalized group standards; or, said another way, the "me" is the community in the individual. To Mead, the "I" represented impulses which, in a sense, are supervised by the "me," either being squashed as they get underway or afterward, or diverted into acceptable channels.

The widespread popular conception that the impulses of the "I" always require supervision and are of a negative and unsocialized character requires considerable qualification. Impulses may be perfectly socialized but, nevertheless, judged inappropriate to the situation after a brief consideration. Such judgments are continually being made, since life is anything but routine. Control is not necessarily a matter of stemming ignoble temptation or putting the lid on passions; it may be quite the reverse, as when one checks overgenerous impulses in favor of other considerations. Furthermore, control may be positive in the sense that we have to urge ourselves to do things, the urging representing the regulatory side of our action. A sharp line ought not to be drawn between negative and positive self-control, since lines of action necessarily involve both the eliciting of certain responses and the negation of others. Puritanical traditions emphasize the repressive aspects of control and disregard the fact that the "I" may become socialized and need not be an expression of the brutish side of human nature.

Social control is not based exclusively, and certainly not primarily, upon coercion. Neither can effective group action be based upon the continuous direct surveillance of individuals. If this were not true, humans would revert to sheer brutality and opportunism whenever they were out of sight or earshot of other persons, or whenever the chances of detection were slight. Orderly social controls are based on contract, obligation, trust, and responsibility. Even limited alliances involve these.

Theories of human nature that postulate opposition between individual and society picture society as a kind of policeman watching over the individual. Self-interest is thought of either as being in opposition to collective interest or as utilizing the latter to gain its primary ends. This is a misconception of the nature and function of ethical codes and of the requirements of group life. Compliance with community norms and with contractual obligations is not only a requirement of effective collective action but is a necessity for the creation and fulfillment of individual aspirations. There is no natural opposition of humans and society. S. E. Asch made a similar point when he suggested that the accentuation of self is often a response to social failure (3:320–21):

> When the possibilities of entering into appropriate relations with others are barred, the ego turns its potentialities for care upon itself. Avarice, greed, and ruthless ambition often are the answer the ego gives when it fails to find in the surroundings the opportunity for its outgrowing needs.

CONSCIENCE, GUILT, AND SHAME.   Internal control in moral matters is referred to as *conscience*. What is regarded as right and wrong varies widely among societies, among groups, and even from situation to situation within a homogeneous population. Also, as N. Cameron and A. Magaret (9:285) point out, "The behavior which one man views within an ethical context of 'right' and 'wrong' may be for his neighbor a matter of expediency, taste, or arbitrary cultural control." Naïve judgments are sometimes made about another person's acts because the varied content of consciences is not taken into account. Sometimes conscience is identified with religious precepts. Religion and morality are frequently so closely intertwined that a coalescence of ethical and religious teaching seems part of the natural order of things. However, in some societies large areas of morality lie outside the religious sphere.

In Western theological writing and in commonsense thinking, transgressions of the dictates of conscience are associated with guilt. One stands alone before his or her God—or conscience—and suffers remorse for what he or she has done or left undone. The subtleties of guilt and self-judgment and the means of expiation hardly need be dwelt upon. However, some anthropologists, including R. Benedict (7), have argued that in some countries or societies guilt is not an invariable accompaniment of wrong-doing. It is argued that there are "shame cultures" as well as "guilt cultures," and that in the former remorse is less a controlling mechanism than fear or shame because of what other people may think of the wrongdoing. The Japanese, according to Benedict, are said to react with shame in many situations in which we would feel guilt. It has been hypothesized that certain modes of childhood training result in the predominance of guilt; such a mode exists when parents (rather than governesses and nurses) rear the child and chastise the child, rather than calling on gods or bogeymen to do so. In so doing, they themselves are the models that the child is taught to emulate. Such direct relations of parent and child cause the child to assimilate the standards of his or her parents early and to feel guilty when violating them. On the other hand, when children are not directly reared by their parents, they come to view their parents' standards more as externally imposed rules, the violation of which causes more shame than guilt.

The differentiation of shame and guilt has been criticized by J. J. Honigmann (21:291–94) as difficult to put to the test. He noted "the lack of satisfactory, operational criteria by which to verify the existence of either guilt or shame. . . . The identification of guilt or shame remains too much a matter of intuition." He also suggested that within the same society, or even within the same social class, ways of handling children may vary so much that some persons may react primarily with shame and others with guilt. A more basic criticism of the general hypothesis is that although it is valuable, it oversimplfies matters. Shame cultures were first noted because their members appeared to react quite differently from Westerners in the face of certain moral dilemmas. But the more inclusive point is that in different societies people learn to regulate behavior and to atone for failure in different ways. As we have pointed out in earlier chapters, modes of thinking vary from society to society and from group to group. Moral conceptions vary correspondingly. Modes of emotional expression also have social sources, and emotional reactions vary widely. Hence, it is very unlikely that the polar shame-guilt hypothesis takes the entire range into account. It is also possible that an explanation solely or mainly in terms of particular kinds of relations in childhood is too narrow to account for cultural variations in this respect.

The child does not enter the world with a sense of self. The self develops out of the matrix of experiences to which the child is exposed. The foregoing sections have implicitly presented a number of notions central to a social psychological theory of self-development. We shall next review the work of Cooley and Mead, contrast it with the psychosexual formulations of Freud and Erikson, and conclude with an appreciative statement of H. S. Sullivan's *The Interpersonal Theory of Psychiatry*.

Mead and Cooley presented views of early childhood that could be termed interactional and developmental. They argued that the self emerged in three sequential phases. For Mead these phases were termed *play, the game,* and *the generalized other*. In each phase the child was progressively better able to differentiate self from other. In the play phase of self-development, the child was seen as unable to take more than one role at a time. In the game stage, multiple roles could be segregated but they could not, as in the generalized other phase, be combined into a consistent symbolic perspective. The generalized other describes persons' interpretations of their experience with others who make up their world. They need not be an actual group per se. In the generalized other stage of self-development, individuals were capable of standing over and against the outside community and capable of clearly seeing themselves in terms of the moral and symbolic expressions of others. This is what Mead meant by the terms "I" and "me." The "I" component of the self described the individual's distinctly personal views of self, whereas the "me" referred—in Sullivan's terms—to the "considered and reflected appraisals" of others. The self, for Mead and Cooley, reflected constant interaction between (1) the individual's definitions of situations, and (2) the definitions reflected to the individual by others. Cooley located the emergence of the self in the primary group of the family. *Self-feeling* was basic to his theory. Mead, on the other hand, argued that the genesis of self was based, not on self-feeling per se, but upon the child's ability to *reflexively* respond to the attitude of the other.

COOLEY AND
MEAD

While Mead and Cooley saw self-reflexivity as a problematic element in every interactional episode, other theorists take a more deterministic view. We term them the *psychosexual developmentalists*. The two most prominent theorists in this tradition are Freud and Erikson. Each, in a

Other
Developmental
Views:
Freud,
Erikson,
Sullivan

somewhat different fashion, stressed age, sex, and family experiences as crucially determining variables in the emergence of the self and personality. Each adopted a relatively fixed sequence of stages through which the infant must pass on the way to adulthood. Each assumed that processes internal to the organism significantly entered into the developmental process. We turn first to Freud, whose work is still highly influential in the fields of psychiatry and clinical psychology. (See also our earlier discussion in Chapter 8.)

FREUDIAN
DEVELOPMENTAL
THEORY

The general Freudian thesis of personality development has been concisely stated by Benedek (6:100):

> The integration of the *sexual drive* from its pre-genital sources to the *genital primacy* and to functional maturity is the axis around which the organization of the personality takes place. From the point of view of personality development, the process of interaction is the same in both sexes. Men and women alike reach their psychosexual maturity through the reconcilation of the sexual drive with the superego and through the adjustment of sexuality to all other functions of the personality. . . . *The sexual drive is organized differently in men and women, in order to serve specific functions in procreation.*

In our presentation of Freudian developmental theory, we shall rely mainly on Benedek's summarization. It should be remembered that there is some divergence of opinion among Freudian psychoanalysts and others who subscribe to the general outline as Benedek gives it. She herself indicates some of the points of divergence.

THE STAGES

The early developmental history of the child is described in terms of the dominance of certain sensitive, or *erotogenic,* zones, such as the oral, anal, and genital regions. Infants' earliest libidinal pleasures are connected mainly with their mouths. They suck at their mother's breast and their own fingers, and they also use their mouths to explore and test the objects they encounter in the external world. The oral phase of development occupies approximately the first year. The psychoanalyst Abraham distinguishes two phases of this stage: the *passive-receptive,* in which children merely have things done for them, and the *active-incorporative,* in which children are able to reach actively for objects. During the oral period, if the infant's instinctual needs are not adequately met, insecurity, anxiety, and conflict develop. Throughout this period, children are "narcissistic," deriving most of their gratification from themselves and their own bodies, with little reference to external objects. However, children during this time are learning what causes them pain and which of their actions bring disapproval and withdrawal of love. The differentiation of id and ego has begun, as children begin to establish relationships with their mother and with objects.

In the second phase, the anus becomes the dominant erotogenic zone. "Its double function—retention and elimination—becomes the center of interest and the source of pleasure." (6:71) Toilet training then becomes critical. Parents, in a fashion that depends on their cultural and personal backgrounds, attempt to teach the child sphincter control. By this time the child understands adults well enough so that he or she can cooperate with or resist them, depending upon the kinds of relationships that have been established. "Toilet training," Benedek says, "is the ego's first conscious struggle for mastery over an id impulse." (6:72) The mother's approval is balanced against the instinctual pleasure of soiling. When the mastery of the impulse becomes a goal in itself, a new phase begins. The ego, even in the absence of the mother, resists the id impulse. This represents a big forward step in building personality structure. One of its immediate results is that the child is now vulnerable to threats from id impulses which may break through against the controlling ego. This conflict also represents a clash between the *pleasure principle* and the *reality principle*. The former, in the service of the id, strives for immediate gratification; the latter postpones immediate gratification for later gratification through a mastery of the reality situation.

The particular method of toilet training employed is important, since it causes the child to react in certain ways. Thus, oversevere training seems punitive to the child and may lead him or her to rebel and become hostile toward the mother. This creates a vicious circle as the mother reacts to this rebellion. When sphincter control is secure, the conflict situation diminishes and the child is ready for the next step. During the anal period, differences in learning between the sexes begin to appear. Benedek remarks that mothers generally recognize that girls are more easily trained than boys. This is because the girl identifies with the mother more readily, whereas in boys a good relationship with the mother is merely preliminary to self-assertion and eventual identification with the father. The roots of competitive behavior are said to lie in the achievement of sphincter control. A British analyst, Jones, even stated that the model for competitive behavior among men derived from boyish competition in urinating.

The third general stage is called *oedipal,* or *phallic,* because the child's sexual urges, originally directed toward his own body, now become intensified and directed toward the parent of the opposite sex. For obvious reasons, boys become aware of genital gratifications earlier than girls. The mother is the object of the boy's first heterosexual interest. The girl's development is slower and more complex. Her sexuality remains more diffusely located in sensations of the skin and in motor coordination rather than focusing on the genitals. As we noted in Chapter 8,

Freud postulated that the sight of the male genitals arouses "penis envy" in the girl, and that this is instrumental in breaking the girl's attachment to her mother and directing her erotic impulses toward the father and eventually to other males. Freud believed penis envy to be the key to feminine psychology. (This is one of the points at which some analysts disagreed with Freud.) In any case, the girl is said to turn toward the father, thus arousing an instinctual conflict between attraction to the father and the potential loss of gratification of needs by the mother. However, sometimes after lengthy conflict and vacillation, the girl develops her own kind of oedipus complex—the *electra complex*. The boy's oedipal development is more direct, yet there is a crucial conflict associated with it. The boy is in competition with his father for the mother, but cannot win. Although he cannot actually consummate his urges, he feels guilty and "expects retaliation to be directed toward the organ from which he receives pleasure. The fear of castration—mutilation—develops in varying intensity, even if a threat of physical punishment was never uttered." (6:82) Fear of castration brings about ambivalence toward the father. The boy tries to please him by identification with him in nonsexual areas of behavior and tends also to idealize him. Identification with the father leads to internalization of the father's moral code, although the working out of the oedipus complex, and the associated development of a mature superego, takes many years. In the meantime, genital urges may find expression in masturbation or other substitute activities and attachments. Benedek also lists various ego defenses against sexual tendencies which help to repress and resolve the oedipus complex. These include the intellectualizing of curiosity about sex, development of infantile sexual theories, denial of sexuality in the parents, and identification with the opposite sex. The latter is a defense against the dangerous heterosexual urge. This is known as a "negative oedipus complex" and is usually temporary, since it is not a feasible solution of the sexual problem. The various phases of the resolution of the oedipus complex do not occur in a fixed time sequence but may occur more or less simultaneously.

During the oedipal period, the structure of the personality becomes much more complex and differentiated. The superego is developing and is in conflict with the id. The ego is now undertaking the function of mediating between (1) the id and the superego, and (2) the id and reality. At this stage, the ego represses the sexual tendencies, thus initiating the latency period.

The beginning of the latency period coincides in our society more or less with the beginning of school. "The desexualization of the child's interest enables him to comply with environmental requirements and thus to expand in mental and social growth." (6:88) The basic biological tendencies of giving and taking, retaining and eliminating, and other tendencies from the anal and oral stages continue to develop into more

Life Cycle: The Genesis of Self

complex forms. Oral receptive pleasure continues in the form of pleasure in the reception of material and spiritual gifts. During latency, children learn how to share. Aggressive incorporation appears in the form of envy, jealousy, and maliciousness. Passion for collecting betrays the retentive tendency. Boys characteristically collect masculine objects (for example, stones, strings, keys) and girls accumulate feminine objects (for example, beads and dolls). If either sex evinces much interest in the wrong kind of objects, this is an index of bisexuality. The existence of the latency period as a biologically determined stage is another point upon which all Freudians do not agree.

The next phase is brought about by the onset of puberty and is coterminous with adolescence. The physical maturation which occurs in this period reawakens latent conflicts and the ego must again master them. Girls, for example, become sensitive to the changes in their bodies and may become ashamed or shy. In both sexes, attempts are made to master sexuality through repression, a technique which was successful in the earlier oedipal stage. As the sexual drive becomes more urgent, "all the available resources of sublimation are mobilized, and expansion of interests and achievements is generated." (6:97) Safe ego gratification is afforded by these interests. Yet "the ego . . . cannot withstand for long the pressure of the instinctual impulses; the defenses yield and the instinctual tension is released." (6:97) During adolescence, also, the child discovers new values and ideals and appraises those of his or her parents, thus reactivating the old conflict with them: the boy quarrels more with his father, the girl with her mother. As the child becomes more independent of the parents, the superego becomes less rigid and a new and more complex level of personality integration is reached. Sexual maturity requires a personality which accepts both the sexual drives and the social regulation of them.

The systematic account of development offered by Freudians ends at about this point. Later events tend to be interpreted as a working out, in relation to an adult environment and advancing age, of earlier genetic occurrences. This account of development must be viewed as an ideal, or average normal, picture. Children, it is said, vary in the rates at which they pass through some or all of the phases; some experience one or more phases only in dreams or fantasies. Sometimes part of a phase may be repeated as a consequence of regression, which is in turn a consequence of disappointments. Adolescence is such an especially tortuous process that some analysts refer to the "normal psychopathology" of the period. It is also noted that some individuals do not go through adolescence to the final stage but remain fixated at earlier points, and that if the process goes awry, libidinal urges may find expressions in a wide variety of curious or abnormal ways.

By way of criticism of this account, we can do no better than to quote
Benedek herself to show what is left out of it. In discussing the anal
stage, she comments briefly on the development of speech during the
second and third years (6:74):

> It is in another area of maturation that the child learns to speak. . . . This
> complex process is considered to be the result of the progressing matura-
> tion of the speech apparatus and of intellectual accomplishments and is,
> therefore, not usually discussed in connection with the psychodynamic
> aspects of personality development.

She touches briefly upon initial learning of words and sentences and
notes how the child "has stored in his mind symbols related to . . experiences" that occur before the development of language and that these
experiences and symbols may never reach the level of verbalization, but
may form the content of the unconscious. (6:76) This is virtually all that
is said of language behavior. The separation of "emotional experience"
from cognition, which is implied in the above quotation from Benedek,
is characteristic of psychoanalytic thinking. It stems from the classical
tripartite distinction between cognition, conation, and affect (intelligence, will, and emotion). Those who make this distinction neglect
the fact that emotional experiences do not exist as pure states, but are
shot through with cognitive elements. The fiction of the separation of intellectual development and personality development can be maintained
only if one disregards or vastly underrates the role of language in the organization of behavior, including emotional behavior.

A second major criticism is that a *genetic fallacy* is persistently
maintained when the last event in a chronological series is identified
with the first. Benedek's frequent use of the term "model" (as in the
suggestion that urinary competition provides the model for all later male
competition) is an illustration. The attribution of sexuality to both newborn infants and adults is another. Some analysts have themselves made
note of the resulting confusion, and have differed with Freud on this
point. The same type of fallacious genetic reasoning is evident in the
conception of the biologically rooted drive as the theme which unites all
processes throughout the developmental sequence. Although learning is
given an important place, its primary function is seen as the harnessing
of the id drives in socially acceptable ways. The genetic approach of
Freudian analysts gives their explanations a narrative character. If they
are asked why two persons whose childhood experiences appear to be
substantially the same turn out very differently as adults, the analysts'
answers will frequently consist of two biographical narratives.

A third difficulty arises from the general character of analytic theory
itself, which makes it difficult or impossible to subject it to empirical
tests at crucial points. In a recent review of psychological studies of

children, Koch has pointed out that there is virtually no evidence of a nonclinical sort on which to base an evaluation of psychosexual stages. (24:22) With respect to some minor points, it has been possible to check the implications of the analytic account. Through checking, for example, the existence of the latency period, the validity of the concepts of sublimation and repression, and the oedipus complex itself, as described by Freud, have been made questionable. Anthropologists, through the use of comparative data, have raised serious doubts of the alleged universality of some of the central factors in the developmental process, such as Freud's concepts of the superego and oedipal attachments. The assumption that development is virtually over, except for minor variations, when adulthood is reached, appears questionable to sociologists. (See Chapters 12 and 13.)

On the other hand, despite the many objections that have been raised concerning it, Freudian developmental theory has some clear-cut virtues. The very fact that it is a general theory concerning areas of human behavior which are vital to self-esteem makes it significant and challenging. It at least proposes explanations for many forms of behavior which are ordinarily passed over in silence by other psychological systems. Analytic theory has also performed the function of calling attention to the subtlety of human interaction and to the existence of concealed factors which subjects themselves are unable to report. It has sought to isolate and analyze crucial experiences in the life of the child and has described, with much clinical detail, various significant processes, such as identification with parents and other mechanisms of interaction and ego defense. Close contact with patients provides the analyst with a continuous flow of clinical data which is of great value to anyone interested in childhood development, regardless of how it may be interpreted.

Another Freudian approach to developmental stages which has gained a wide audience in recent years is that proposed by Erik H. Erikson. (15, 16, 17, 18, 19)

ERIKSON'S MODEL OF DEVELOPMENTAL STAGES

Although his background is that of a psychoanalyst trained in the Freudian tradition, Erikson's experiences while doing research among American Indians and in treating patients in the United States have led him to still another approach to developmental stages. His scheme has gained great popularity, principally among child and adolescent psychiatrists and among clinical psychologists, many enthusiasts taking it as a rather definitive picture of developmental reality. Erikson himself apparently meant it only as a suggestive guide. We shall not outline this scheme in any detail, for basically, we believe, it is not very different in some important assumptions from the Freudian one.

Erikson rethought Freud's theory of infantile sexuality, developed a diagram that emphasizes the step-by-step (or progressive) nature of the mind's development, and stressed the ways (or modes) that the body's sensitive zones (openings, organs) work. (10:75) He linked this with a sequence of social experiences, emphasizing critical periods that the child must manage, either doing well or failing in some degree. (10:137) Later he added additional stages and developmental tasks, eight of each in all. Erikson does not regard these stages and tasks as rigidly sequential, but remarks (10:138):

> If the chart . . . lists a series of conflicts or crises, we do not consider all development a series of crises. Development proceeds "by critical steps—critical being a characteristic of turning points, of moments of decision between progress and regression, integration and retardation."

In a sense, the developmental tasks run all through the adult years, perhaps in any individual never being accomplished for once and for all.

An interactionist must view such a scheme as not remarkably different from the Freudian, to which Erikson was reacting. Thus, there still is a very great emphasis on psychosexual linkages, and despite the disclaimers, it attempts to give very much of a "stage" picture of development. The earlier stages, in which the family is very much implicated, receive much more emphasis and are discussed in greater detail than the later, or adult, years. And Erikson focuses considerably—understandably, since he is a psychoanalyst—on psychic health: hence the abilities to become trustful, autonomous, industrious, and to become truly able to exhibit initiative and to share intimate relations are crucial. There is nothing "wrong" with emphasizing such matters, but this kind of focus on psychic health tends unduly to restrict the scheme for more wide-sweeping social psychological purposes. Certainly it tends to restrict focus—despite Erikson's own interest in historical matters and in famous figures like Gandhi and Luther—to individuals rather than to interlocking social biographies.

The point is underscored by the largely clinical use to which Erikson's chart and writings have been put. A painful example is given by Charlotte Green Schwartz and Merton J. Kahne (38), who document how

ERIKSON'S DEVELOPMENTAL MODEL

Developmental Stage	Identity Crisis
viii. maturity	ego integrity versus despair
vii. adulthood	generality versus stagnation
vi. young adulthood	intimacy versus role confusion
v. puberty and adolescence	identity versus role confusion
iv. latency	industry versus inferiority
iii. locomotor-genital	initiative versus guilt
ii. muscularity-anal	autonomy versus shame, doubt
i. oral sensory	basic trust versus mistrust

Life Cycle: The Genesis of Self

college psychiatrists have picked up Erikson's scheme and applied it faithfully to college students as a "real" explanation of adolescence. Consequently, when the campuses felt the effects of the events of the 1960s, beginning with the civil rights movement, college psychiatrists simply translated students' memberships in all the emergent social movements into Eriksonian language. The scheme allowed them to discount the students' complex memberships and commitments to political movements, and, we may add, almost totally allowed them to misread the students' participations in a variety of other social worlds. Indeed, most recently Parsons (32), in his efforts to elaborate the Freudian and Eriksonian schemes, has suggested that between adolescence and early maturity is a clearly discernible developmental stage which he terms "studentry." In this sense, Erikson's scheme may be restricted to only certain classes of individuals. Finally, with his emphasis on sequential *identity crises* in adolescence, Erikson often gives less attention to the transformations in self which occur in middle and late adulthood. The foundations of these identity crises are also not fully clear. They, too, may be relevant only to certain groups of individuals.

We turn now to the developmental scheme of Harry Stack Sullivan. His approach, in our judgment, overcomes many of the flaws of Freud and Erikson.

SULLIVAN'S DEVELOPMENTAL THEORIES

Theorists who do not subscribe to the central tenets of the Freudian position are disposed to locate the critical junctures in development at other points and to ascribe somewhat different significances to them. This is true even of formulations that focus exclusively on children. One of the most systematic and thoughtful accounts of personality development, and one which differs in important ways from the Freudian position, is that of Sullivan. Like Freud, Sullivan developed his position mainly out of his experience with psychiatric patients. Through his close association with anthropologists and other social scientists, he came to place more emphasis on the social environment than Freud had. He repudiated much of the Freudian vocabulary and developed one of his own. The *interpersonal theory* of psychiatry he formulated has found expression in an influential journal and has also been disseminated through the work of his students. Perhaps because of the great difficulty of communicating with schizophrenes, he early became concerned with the nature of communication. Sapir, who markedly influenced Sullivan's thinking on communication, was a pioneer anthropological linguist. The roles in development which Sullivan ascribes to communicative processes and the cultural milieu give his work special significance for the social scientist. Our discussion of his position will be based primarily on Sullivan's posthumously published lectures. (44)

For Sullivan, the avoidance of severe anxiety is central to human behavior, and he argued that a *self-system* starts to develop in infancy as a protection against overmuch anxiety. The process of *selective inattention* was mentioned in this connection. Sullivan formulated several other concepts that require elaboration before an account of his developmental stages will make much sense to the reader.

From the first moments of life, infants are in interaction with adults, mainly of course with their mothers, who are concerned particularly with satisfying the infant's initial bodily needs. The mother, too, has needs, which in turn are met by her general activity in caring for the child. Sullivan thus says that the situation is *integrated* insofar as it is meaningful for both organisms. In adults, a mutually satisfying friendly conversation would be an illustration of an integrated situation. Situations may be *resolved* when the needs are met. There is then no longer any reason for continuing the immediate interaction unless new bases immediately arise. Situations *disintegrate* when they are terminated before they are resolved. Anxiety may play a large role here: it arises, for example, when one makes friendly overtures to a desirable person and is rebuffed.

There are, according to Sullivan, three modes, or types, of experience: the *prototaxic, parataxic,* and *syntaxic.* These terms refer to the manner in which experience is registered and to the nature and degree of inner elaboration which it is accorded. In the *prototaxic mode* there is an absolute minimum of inner elaboration, and experience consists mainly of discrete series of momentary states which can neither be recalled nor discussed. The *syntaxic mode,* in contrast, involves a maximum of inner organization and elaboration, and because it is fully encompassed by symbolic formulation and is logically ordered, it can be discussed and completely communicated to others. The *parataxic mode* of experience lies between the other two. In it, experience is partially organized or organized in a quasi-logical manner, but there are also elements of which the individual is unaware. (44:29)

The child's earliest experiences are in the *prototaxic mode,* but he or she quickly progresses to the parataxic as soon as he or she begins to make sense out of the environment and notes certain interconnections and simple sequences. Lower animals also are capable of reaching the parataxic level, according to Sullivan. The syntaxic mode begins to appear with the learning of language and is hence confined to human beings, although Sullivan takes pains to emphasize that it is rarely possible for us to express all aspects of an experience in words. Roughly, one may say that the three modes represent the incommunicable or ineffable (prototaxic), the partially communicable (parataxic), and the wholly communicable (syntaxic). This scheme allows a considerable place for unconscious behavior without positing an "unconscious mind" or instinctual urges as the mainsprings of behavior.

Sullivan's treatment of needs, as we shall see, is a fluid one. The infant quickly develops new needs in addition to the initial bodily ones, both through experience and maturation. Needs appear chronologically, some not until several years have passed. Thus the sexual drive, or, as he terms it, the *lust dynamism,* does not arise until puberty. (Here Sullivan explicitly departs from Freud, who views the sexual drives as present from birth.) The various needs are given sophisticated treatment and are not regarded as inner forces. Apart from elementary biological needs of the infant, most of the needs with which Sullivan is concerned arise in interpersonal interaction and do not have to do with biological matters. Needs come to be satisfied in highly complex ways through interaction. Much satisfaction, Sullivan holds, must take place through *sublimation—* that is, by indirect means. This is because the initial means adopted are met with reactions by significant others which arouse anxiety in the person.

Sullivan's designation of stages is itself a clue to important differences STAGES between his position and that of orthodox Freudian psychoanalysts. *Sullivan distinguished seven stages of personality development: infancy, childhood, the juvenile era, preadolescence, adolescence, late adolescence, and adulthood.* (44:33–34)

Infancy extends from birth to the appearance of speech. *Childhood* covers the period from the onset of articulate speech to the appearance of a need to have playmates. The *juvenile era* covers the period of grammar school through, as a result of maturation, the desire for an intimate relationship with a companion of the same sex. *Preadolescence* ends with the display of sexual awareness and the desire for an intimate of the opposite sex. *Adolescence,* which varies from culture to culture, ends when the individual has developed some social relationship and pattern of activity which fulfills his or her lust, or desire, for sexual activity. *Late adolescence* extends the individual's attempts to form a socially acceptable pattern of intimacy and sexual behavior. At *adulthood* the person enters into a love relationship (which may or may not satisfy the person's sexual desires). During this era the person establishes a relationship with another person who is regarded as a significant other. That person becomes highly important to the individual and his or her concerns may take precedence over the individual's own view of his or her life situation.

Sullivan's account of *infancy* and *childhood* covers much of the same ground that has been covered in those chapters of this text that deal with the development of language, thought, and self. He emphasizes the role

Preadolescence sexual friendships and social frustrations. (*Michael Heron from Monkmeyer Press Service*)

of anxiety in the origin of the self-system. The Freudian concepts of the ego, id, and superego are not included, and there is no discussion of instinctual drives or of the oedipus complex. In childhood, along with the gradual learning of the syntaxic use of language, children may also use language as an anxiety-reducing instrument, as when they verbally disown certain of their actions—"I didn't do that, it was my hand," or "I did it. I am sorry." Parents' demands for apologies and explanations further this use. During childhood the need for tenderness, which appeared during infancy, is manifested and elaborated in the desire for play and physical contact with others, particularly the mother. If the mother is consistently unable to respond with tenderness, children may be compelled to sublimate the need or they may give it up. Like other observers, Sullivan remarks upon the fact that children learn to deceive adults and so escape rebuff and anxiety. Sullivan is constantly concerned with inadequate means of handling issues that may be taken by the child, and at this point notes a number of inappropriate modes of concealment which may lead to trouble later. One of them is the use of *verbalisms,* or *rationalizations,* to ward off punishment.

Vicious cycles of malevolent development may start through interaction of the sort that occurs when the mother continually disparages the father and explains the child's behavior by saying he is like his father. This may establish the conviction in the child that he is detestable and

Life Cycle: The Genesis of Self

unworthy and must expect always to be treated badly. Such an unfortunate turn of events may "very easily prevent a great deal of profit from subsequent developmental experiences. . . . There is literally a slowing down of healthy socialization." (44:217) Important in Sullivan's thought is the idea that any developmental mishap may prevent and slow up the learning process. The arrest of development is not a static thing, for the person continues to change and develop; however, "the freedom and velocity of the constructive change are very markedly reduced." (44:218)

In *late childhood* children become more aware of their identity as a male or female and begin to adopt appropriate behavior. Their knowledge of other cultural perspectives also broadens. Like Piaget, Sullivan emphasizes the necessity, imposed by the requirements of others, for the child to begin to distinguish between reality and fantasy (autism, or autistic thought). Toward the end of this period, children have learned to sort out that which they must conceal from that which they can talk about because it will make sense to adults.

Even when malevolent or other inappropriate personality organization has developed, the transition to the next stage introduces a real possibility for correction. Sullivan is impressed by the amount of change that can occur "as one passes over one of these more-or-less determin-

Two friends on the way to school. (*Hella Hammid from Rapho/Photo Researchers, Inc.*)

The Origins and Development of Self   341

able thresholds of a developmental era." (44:227) This means that children are, to some extent, given the choice of a fresh start, although the older they grow the more they become the heirs of their own past.

The juvenile era begins at about the time the child starts to school. School plays a key role in various ways. Many more "authority figures" appear on the child's horizon—teachers, playground bullies, traffic policemen, and other parents—and he or she has to learn to live with all of them. By the end of this era, authority figures, including the parents, are being compared with one another as persons. The parents are no longer regarded as the most perfect people on earth, nor are they any longer endowed with omniscience. At the beginning of the era, children typically begin to desire contact and play with other children; this sociability is in contrast to the greater egocentricity of younger children. Hence, schoolchildren are open to tremendous influence from their peers. They learn that their peers have points of view, and they discover how many perspectives there are. Through their interaction with their peers, some of it brutal and antagonistic, they learn a great deal about how to handle themselves without suffering unduly from anxiety. They must face the possibility of ostracism. Toward the end of the period, especially, they begin to be sensitive to their reputation, that is, their general self-conception deriving from juvenile groups. Sullivan notes that mobility of the parents may be disastrous by causing children to continue to be strangers as they go from one school to another.

The juvenile era is given tremendous weight by Sullivan as a determinant of future development. It is "the time when the world begins to be really complicated by the presence of other people." (44:232) Through rough-and-ready interaction with these new people, children's misconceptions of self are corrected and they acquire a wider grasp of selfhood and their place in the community. If they are fortunate in their development, they emerge with an "orientation in living," that is, an idea of how to satisfy their needs without arousing too much anxiety. (44:244) This represents their first and most important socialization experience. If they have not learned this, they are in for trouble. They may, for example, use the technique of disparaging others as a protective device: this is equivalent to saying "I am not as bad as the other swine." This does not give a secure base to a sense of personal worth.

Preadolescence is ushered in by an interest in a new type of personal relationship: friendship with a person of the same sex. This is quite different from previous relationships, for it turns upon intimacy and collaboration in satisfying each other's expressed needs. (44:248)

> Because one draws so close to another, because one is newly capable of seeing oneself through the other's eyes, the preadolescent phase . . . is especially significant in correcting autistic, fantastic ideas about oneself or others.

Participation in preadolescent gangs has a similar desirable effect. The need for chums arises both as a result of interpersonal development and of maturation. Sullivan emphasizes the great therapeutic effects of these preadolescent intimacies in saving persons from previous unfortunate courses.

However, the preadolescent period is also an era of danger because of differences in rates of development among friends. Children reach puberty at different ages; the variation within the same sex may be as much as three or four years. Hence, some preadolescents lag behind the others. Some still require intimate chumship when the others no longer do, or one child may not yet need these intimate relationships when most of his or her peers do and so later may have to establish such relations with a much younger or much older person.

The early stage of adolescence is defined "as extending from the eruption of true genital interest, felt as lust, to the patterning of sexual behavior which is the beginning of the last phase of adolescence." (44:263) Sullivan thinks of lust as the last of the maturation needs and draws a sharp line between it and the need for intimacy. *The need for intimacy* starts much earlier and has an independent development. At the onset of adolescence there is a significant change in the object of intimacy. *If there has been no very serious warp in development, the child begins to seek increasing intimacy with a member of the other sex,* the pattern of intimacy being much like that of preadolescence. In America the fulfillment of this need faces serious obstacles, since it runs into the sex taboos. The obstacle which prevents access to intimacy leads to *reverie* and *fantasy,* and in the gang, children may engage in discussion pertaining to it. The discussion of "who's who and what's what" in the heterosexual world is of great profit for those of the gang who are already in the adolescent stage.

In adolescence, life becomes tremendously complicated by the elaboration of potentially conflicting needs. The appearance of lust—a very powerful need—adds greatly to the problems of the period. There may be collision between the requirements of lust and the maintenance of self-esteem. Genital urges may create acute self-doubts, puzzlement, embarrassment, and other unpleasant reactions. Because of the way sex is viewed in Western society, the desire for sexual activity often clashes with a sense of security in interpersonal relations. This is true in adolescence and in later life as well. Intimacy and lust requirements may also conflict with each other. A common manifestation of this conflict is the separation of persons into two mutually exclusive classes: those who can only satisfy one's lust, and those who can only satisfy the need for intimacy and friendship. The distinction between "good women" and "bad women," "sexy girls" and "good girls," conveys this idea. (44:269–70)

Thus satisfying one's lust must be at considerable expense to one's self-esteem, since the bad girls are unworthy and not really people in the sense that good girls are. . . . The trouble . . . is that lust is a part of personality, and no one can get very far at completing his personality development in this way.

The shift in the sex of the desired object of intimacy may also clash with security needs. For instance, the parents may disparage and ridicule the adolescent's interest in the opposite sex. The parents may be jealous, may not wish the child to grow up too fast, or may fear sexual accidents. The various collisions of needs may lead in this stage to homosexual play, but more usually produce autosexual behavior, that is, masturbation.

Sullivan points out (44:271–72) that the "number of wretched experiences connected with adolescents' first heterosexual attempts is legion, and the experiences are sometimes very expensive to further maturation of personality." They may be destructive to self-esteem and may erect permanent barriers to satisfactory heterosexual consummations.

Several unhappy long-term outcomes include the following: there are people who feel pursued by the opposite sex and expend a great deal of energy trying to avoid them. Lust may be disassociated from consciousness and may be expressed only in fantasies. Lack of potency may be connected with failure to resolve the lust-intimacy problem. In some persons, the appearance of lust may be accompanied by the continuation of intimacy needs on the preadolescent level, leading to transient or persisting homosexual tendencies, with the genital drive handled in a variety of ways—homosexual reverie, homosexual relations, autoeroticism. In some persons, lust may mature, although they remain chronically juvenile. The Don Juan type or lady's man, and on the feminine side the persistent "tease," are often chronic juveniles, according to Sullivan. These people have a need to be envied by others of their sex, and hence often boast of their conquests.

Sullivan indicates the extreme diversity of alternatives which face the adolescent. He or she has to discover (44:297) "what he likes in the way of genital behavior and how to fit it into the rest of life. That is an achievement of no mean magnitude." The range of alternatives is demonstrated by showing that there are about forty-five patterns of behavior that are "reasonably probable." Sullivan reaches this figure by setting up classifications of intimacy, kinds of objects of lust, and types of sexual activity.

Late adolescence is for Sullivan the period when the mode of sexual activity is decided upon. In addition he lays stress upon the great growth of experience in the syntaxic mode of communication. Through formal education and work experience, persons acquire greater insight into their own and others' behavior and may develop enormously in knowledge and maturity. Many adults, because of their developmental heritage, are greatly restricted in what they can learn from a potentially enlightening environment (44:306): "Large aspects of living are, as it were, taboo—one avoids them." As to truly mature persons, Sullivan confesses that psychiatrists have very little to say, since they do not meet them in their offices as patients. With the progress of patients toward maturity, the psychiatrist loses sight of them. (44:310)

Sullivan's view has much in common with the Freudian conception. In both there is considerable attention given to unconscious features of behavior, and both focus attention on the dynamic interplay of personal relations. Both have a place for bodily maturation and posit a close relationship between this maturation and the development of personality. They are also alike in that they are mainly derived from clinical experience with adults rather than from a firsthand, intensive study of children. One further point of similarity is that both more or less terminate their systematic accounts of development at the threshold of adult life. The differences between the two conceptions will become apparent as we review some of the main general features of Sullivan's scheme. **EVALUATION**

Sullivan's account provides an important place for needs which arise sequentially. Sex appears late, rather than early, as in Freud's account, and is not given supreme priority. Many of the important needs arise from interpersonal relations rather than biological bases.

Those needs that are of biological origin, such as the infant's need for "tenderness," quickly become transformed as they are felt and interpreted and as they enter into progressively more complex interpersonal patterns. Even what Sullivan calls "lust," with its obvious biological concomitants, is of this nature. The needs which arise in interpersonal relations, although associated with biological maturation, are essentially consequences of the developing complexity of the communicative processes and the self-system. Instinct is not inevitably in conflict with society—indeed, Sullivan explicitly rejects the instinct theory and the id concept which makes humans essentially evil beings held in check by social proscriptions. The "unconscious mind" in which Freud located the instinctual impulses does not appear as such in Sullivan's theory, although he makes ample provision for the unwitting aspects of behavior.

The crucial experiences of each period are specified pretty clearly by Sullivan and in such a form that empirical testing of his views is possible. He presented his position as a tentative one, recognizing the need for empirical validation. He acknowledged that a great many of these critical experiences, and even the stages themselves, might vary from culture to culture. The role of various adults as representatives of culture, rather than as unique personalities, is always recognized and often specified. Like other writers, Sullivan has emphasized the important fact that the differential rates of biological and experiential development of children may crucially affect personality development. His treatment of some of these consequences, as in his discussion of the transition to adolescence, shows great insight. Following a line of thought which has generally taken hold in recent years, he also emphasizes the uselessness and possible danger in training children before they can assimilate the training experience.

The scheme is genuinely developmental in the sense that no genetic fallacy is introduced. No stage is in any way a repetition of a preceding one, and in each stage genuinely new behavior emerges. A tremendous possibility of change is acknowledged by Sullivan, particularly during transitions into new stages.

So-called arrests of development are not viewed by Sullivan as "fixations" or "regressions." The capacity to learn from experience is greatly reduced by such arrests, but change and development go on. This change is not conceived of as merely a new form of an old personality organization, but as a genuine, if unfortunate, innovation.

A central concept in Sullivan's system is that of *consensual validation,* by which he means the manner in which the meanings of symbols and the validity of ideas, including ideas of self, are confirmed in the process of communicating with others. (This is the same idea that has been discussed in numerous other places in this text.) Sullivan notes that symbols do not carry meaning, but evoke it in user and listener, and that consensual validation makes symbols precise and powerful instruments in handling both people and ideas. Through his emphasis on the effects of the communication process upon the developing personality, Sullivan introduces a social dimension into the very center of individuality. This is in line with his explicitly stated idea that the scientific analysis of interpersonal relations requires a *field theory* rather than an elementaristic or atomistic approach. Sullivan's main contribution has not been in the analysis of what he called the *syntaxic mode,* or public communication, but in his more discriminating treatment of the "unconscious." He has reinterpreted the unconscious as a distortion of the communication process through such mechanisms as (1) selective inattention, (2) dissociation, (3) misinterpretation, and (4) masking processes. Cottrell and Gallagher have said of Sullivan (13:23–24):

> Sullivan attempts to show the influences within a given culture which channelize awareness. . . . If we accept [G.] Mead's analysis of the way in which meaning emerges from an incorporated verbal structure of rights and duties, Sullivan's work suggests an important amendment. The meaning that is borne by verbal interchange in interpersonal relations can be completely distorted by the dissociated elements which are at work to set the tone and color of the situation.

Our criticism of Sullivan's developmental scheme is based mainly on what it leaves out rather than what is included. The omissions can be attributed in part to Sullivan's explicit psychiatric interests and in part, possibly, to the scantiness of his actual writings. The gravest omission is the lack of consideration of personality change after the initiation of adulthood. By implication, the importance of such change is suggested, but it is not discussed. The consequence of this is that such influences as the following are left out: the influence of occupational status and other adult statuses; the shifting of age memberships, including the effect of children on parents; adaptations to the approach of death; the handling of slow or abrupt changes of statuses of many kinds. The sociologists Cottrell and Foote, who are admirers of Sullivan, have also commented upon Sullivan's tendency to emphasize early patterns to the exclusion of later experiences. They remark that, according to the logic of his own position, this should not be done. (29:193)

> If the maintenance of certain characteristic patterns of interpersonal behavior depend for their support on significant others, then to alter the composition of any person's community of significant others is the most direct and drastic way of altering his "personality."

The developmental account itself, insofar as it deals with children, must be amplified, as Sullivan himself recognized. It can be extended, of course, by actual investigation of children. Cultural variation as well as variation by sex, and the general influence of social structures, must be more extensively taken into account. A wider range of psychological processes also needs to be included.

One major reservation about the account itself is justified. Sullivan makes anxiety virtually central to—actually, the basic motive of—human behavior. No one should, of course, deny its great importance. Despite his great sophistication about the ramifications of anxiety and the associated needs for security and intimacy, Sullivan's treatment of this central concept is very like that of the older motivational theories. In his defense, it should be said that he was very tentative about the centrality of anxiety (44:8):

> In discussing the concept of anxiety, I am not attempting to give you the last word; it may, within ten years, be demonstrated that this concept is quite inadequate, and a better one will take its place.

The research on children that has been done in the last two decades by anthropologists and sociologists considerably amplifies our knowledge of cultural variations in child-rearing and child development. However, this research does not—except as it accepts and details the psychoanalytic developmental account—provide an overall systematic developmental theory; Sullivan's does.

Summary In this chapter we have surveyed recent research bearing on the process of self-development. The human infant enters the world with no self-conception. Exposure to interaction produces the socialization experiences that progressively mold and build an emerging self-conception. The self is not a part of the physical body, but is rather a set of symbolic indications that individuals make to themselves on the basis of their interpersonal experiences with others. The formulations of C. H. Cooley and G. H. Mead were reviewed and contrasted with the developmental schemes of Freud, Erikson, and H. S. Sullivan. Of the Freudian models, Sullivan's was found to be the most satisfactory. Freud's original scheme lacked any systematic view of the self and Erikson's formulations stressed individual crises that must be surmounted if a "healthy" personality is to form. Both Freud and Erikson heavily stressed sexual experiences, and Freud posited that the sexual drive was the major motivating force for the human organism. Sullivan's theory, on the other hand, located the origins of the self in interpersonal relationships. Thus, his views extended the statements of Cooley and Mead and presented testable hypotheses which can be subjected to empirical examination. This fact, by itself, makes Sullivan's theory much more attractive than either that of Freud or Erikson.

References

1. Allport, Gordon W., *Pattern and Growth in Personality*. New York: Holt, Rinehart and Winston, 1961.
2. ———, *Personality*. New York: Holt, Rinehart and Winston, 1937.
3. Asch, S. E., *Social Psychology*. Englewood Cliffs, N.J.: Prentice-Hall, 1952.
4. Bain, Read, "The Self- and Other Words of a Child," *American Journal of Sociology*, vol. 41 (May 1936), pp. 767–75.
5. Baldwin, J. M., *Social and Ethical Interpretations in Mental Development*. New York: Macmillan, 1897.
6. Benedek, T., "Personality Development," in F. Alexander and H. Ross (eds.), *Dynamic Psychiatry*. Chicago: University of Chicago Press, 1952.
7. Benedict, R., *The Chrysanthemum and the Sword*. Boston: Houghton Mifflin, 1946.
8. Bowlby, John, *Child Care and the Growth of Love*. Baltimore: Penguin Books, 1953.
9. Cameron, N., and A. Magaret, *Behavioral Pathology*. Boston: Houghton Mifflin, 1951.
10. Coles, Robert, *Erik H. Erikson*. Boston: Little, Brown, 1972.
11. Cooley, C. H., *Human Nature and the Social Order*. New York: Charles Scribner's Sons, 1902.
12. ———, "A Study of the Early Use of Self-Words by a Child," in *Sociological Theory and Social Research*. New York: Holt, Rinehart and Winston, 1930.
13. Cottrell, L., and R. Gallagher, "Developments in Social Psychology, 1930–1940," in *Sociometry Monographs*, no. 1. Beacon, N.Y.: Beacon House, 1941.

Life Cycle: The Genesis of Self

14. Cressey, Paul G., *The Taxi-Dance Hall Girl Changes Her Name*. Chicago: University of Chicago Press, 1932.
15. Erikson, Erik H. (ed.), *The Challenge of Youth*. Garden City, N.Y.: Doubleday, 1965.
16. ———, *Childhood and Society*. New York: W. W. Norton, 1950.
17. ———, *Gandhi's Truth*. New York: W. W. Norton, 1969.
18. ———, "Identity and the Life Cycle," in George S. Klein (ed.), *Psychological Issues*. New York: International Universities Press, 1959.
19. ———, *Young Man Luther*. New York: W. W. Norton, 1962.
20. Goodman, Mary Ellen, *The Culture of Childhood*. New York: Teachers College Press, Columbia University, 1970.
21. Honigmann, J. J., *Culture and Personality*. New York: Harper & Row, 1954.
22. Horowitz, E., "Spatial Localization of the Self," *Journal of Social Psychology*, vol. 6 (1936), pp. 379–87.
23. Kluckhohn, C., and H. A. Murray (eds.), *Personality in Nature, Society, and Culture*. New York: Knopf, 1948.
24. Koch, H. L., "Child Psychology," *Annual Review of Psychology*, vol. 5 (1954), pp. 1–26.
25. Kuhn, Manford H., "Factors in Personality: Socio-cultural Determinants as Seen through the Amish," in Francis L. K. Hsu (ed.), *Aspects of Culture and Personality*. New York: Abelard-Schuman, 1954, pp. 43–60.
26. Linton, Ralph, "Age and Sex Categories," *American Sociological Review*, vol. 7 (October 1942), pp. 589–603.
27. Mead, George Herbert, *Mind, Self and Society*. Chicago: University of Chicago Press, 1934.
28. Mead, Margaret, "Children and Ritual in Bali," in Margaret Mead and Martha Wolfenstein (eds.), *Childhood in Contemporary Cultures*. Chicago: University of Chicago Press, 1955, pp. 40–51.
29. Mullahy, P. (ed.), *The Contributions of H. S. Sullivan: A Symposium*. New York: Hermitage House, 1952.
30. Murphy, G., L. Murphy, and T. Newcomb, *Experimental Social Psychology*, New York: Harper & Row, 1937.
31. Newcomb, T., Ralph Turner, and Philip Converse, *Social Psychology*. New York: Holt, Rinehart and Winston, 1965.
32. Parsons, Talcott, and Gerald M. Platt, "Age, Social Structure and Socialization in Higher Education," *Sociology of Education*, vol. 43 (Winter 1970), pp. 1–37.
33. Piaget, Jean, *The Child's Conception of the World*. Totowa, N.J.: Littlefield, Adams and Company, 1967. (First published, 1929.)
34. Rainwater, Lee, *Behind Ghetto Walls*. Chicago: Aldine, 1970.
35. Richardson, Stephen A., "The Effect of Physical Disability on the Socialization of the Child," in David A. Goslin (ed.), *Handbook of Socialization Theory and Research*. Skokie, Ill.: Rand McNally, 1969, pp. 1047–64.
36. Rossi, Alice, "Naming Children in Middle Class Families," *American Sociological Review*, vol. 30 (August 1965), pp. 499–513.
37. Schaffer, H. R., *The Growth of Sociability*. Baltimore: Penguin Books, 1971.
38. Schwartz, Charlotte Green, and Merton J. Kahne, *Conflict and Contradiction in Psychiatry: The Evolution of a Professional Sub-speciality*. Mimeographed, 1973.
39. Scott, Robert A., "The Socialization of Blind Children," in David A. Goslin (ed.), *Handbook of Socialization Theory and Research*. Skokie, Ill.: Rand McNally, 1969, pp. 1025–45.

40. Sherif, M., and H. Cantril, *The Psychology of Ego-Involvement*. New York: Wiley, 1947.
41. Shinn, M. W., "Notes on the Development of a Child," *Education*, vol. 1 (1891), pp. 140–45.
42. Stone, Gregory P., "Appearance and the Self," in Arnold M. Rose (ed.), *Human Behavior and Social Processes*. Boston: Houghton Mifflin, 1962, pp. 86–118.
43. Strauss, Anselm L., *Mirrors and Masks*. San Francisco: Sociology Press, 1969. (First published in 1959.)
44. Sullivan, Harry Stack, *The Interpersonal Theory of Psychiatry*. New York: W. W. Norton, 1953.
45. Van Gennep, Arnold, *The Rites of Passage*, trans. by Monika B. Vizedom and Gabrielle L. Caffee. Chicago: University of Chicago Press, 1960.
46. Wolfenstein, Martha, "French Parents Take Their Children to the Park," in Margaret Mead and Martha Wolfenstein (eds.), *Childhood in Contemporary Cultures*. Chicago: University of Chicago Press, 1955, pp. 99–117.
47. Young, Michael, and Peter Willmott, *Family and Kinship in East London*. London: Routledge & Kegan Paul, 1957.
48. Zigler, Edward F., and Susan Harter, "The Socialization of the Mentally Retarded," in David A. Goslin (ed.), *Handbook of Socialization Theory and Research*. Skokie, Ill.: Rand McNally, 1969, pp. 1065–1102.

Selected Readings

ERIKSON, ERIK H., *Childhood and Society*. New York: W. W. Norton, 1950.
Contains a treatment of the author's well-known child developmental stages and presents the research on children which led to his theoretical modification of Freud.

FREUD, SIGMUND, *The Basic Writings of Sigmund Freud*, trans. and ed. with an Introduction by A. A. Brill. New York: Random House, 1938.
Contains all of the basic elements of Freud's theory, including *Psychopathology of Everyday Life*, *Totem and Taboo*, and *The Interpretation of Dreams*.

MEAD, GEORGE HERBERT, *Mind, Self, and Society*. Chicago: University of Chicago Press, 1934.
Contains the most important essays by Mead on the emergence of self out of interaction.

SULLIVAN, HARRY STACK, *The Interpersonal Theory of Psychiatry*. New York: W. W. Norton, 1953.
This book presents the most comprehensive picture of Sullivan's developmental theory. Students are encouraged to explore these readings by Erikson, Freud, Mead, and Sullivan and to draw their own conclusions concerning which theory is most viable for an understanding of the emergence of self in childhood and adolescence.

chapter 11

The
Social Worlds
of Childhood

*A*major consequence of children's linguistic socialization is, of course, that they become involved in increasingly larger systems of social relationships. The acquisition of the verbal and nonverbal languages that make up the family speech community permit children to become more adept participants in complex social situations. As they become increasingly more self-reflexive, they are able to stand outside their own behavior and to view it from the stances of others; they begin to move from the *play* stage of social awareness to the *game* and *generalized other* modes of social interaction. In this chapter, we examine the complex social worlds that make up childhood. Social worlds—to remind the reader—consist of groupings of persons bound together by networks of communication and common understandings. Often widely distributed in geographical space, members of the same social world share similar views of reality. The social worlds of childhood embed children in common interactive experiences with significant others. Like members of other social worlds, children come to develop their own patterned ways of thinking and acting. We examine these patterns in this chapter. We shall employ a developmental, or sequential, model of analysis to lay bare the underlying processes that make the child a more competent interactant. One of the more popular theories which has gained increasing interest in recent years is that of the Swiss psychologist, Jean Piaget. While we have drawn upon his work in earlier chapters, we shall depart here from his specific developmental scheme and offer a set of criticisms of his perspective. In the last section we discuss sex role socialization.

The Child's Egocentrism

In a series of books, Piaget (40, 41, 42, 43, 44, 45, 46, 47, 48, 49, 50) has documented what he has called the *egocentric* character of childish thought. The entire intellectual development of children—from the time at which they can speak with relative adequacy to the point at which they acquire an approximately adult view of themselves and the world—is described as a gradual process of overcoming this initial egocentric tendency. It is perhaps unfortunate that Piaget selected the term *egocentric* to describe the child's early thought patterns; for it implies that such thought is not social in nature and origin, although it decidedly is. James F. Markey, in his long-ignored work *The Symbolic Process and Its Integration in Children,* suggested that Piaget's "encumbrance with the psychoanalyst's conception of . . . autistic . . . thought . . . permits him to ignore its essential aspects." [33:152]

Children are at first enclosed in their own point of view and see all things from within it. They are, as Markey noted, the centers of that universe. Their perceptions and judgments tend to be absolute or egocentric, because they are unaware of any other points of view and perceptions. Thus, Piaget points out that most young children of five or so believe quite firmly that the sun and moon follow them as they walk about. At this age, children are not troubled by the logical difficulties that would confront adults. They do not attempt to account for the many sudden changes in direction of the movement of moon and sun, or to account for the way in which these bodies may appear to other people who are moving in various other directions. Their conviction arises from their own perception of movement. Because perspectives other than their own are not taken into account, children's own perceptions appear absolute—the only possible ones.

Another illustration is furnished by the child's difficulty in making proper use of such terms as "brother" and "sister." Thus, John and Paul are brothers aged four and five, respectively. If we ask Paul how many brothers he has, he may say "One" or he may say "Two, counting me." If he has decided that he is not his own brother, and is asked how many brothers his brother John has, he usually denies that John has any. By questioning Paul we may sometimes induce him to say that there are either one, two, or three brothers in his family.

Paul's confusion over the significance of the term "brother" arises because the word refers to different persons when he and John use it. Paul is fairly clear about the fact that John is his brother. But because he views the situation absolutely rather than relatively, he becomes confused when required to take any point of view other than his own. He cannot view the family of which he is a part from John's standpoint.

The following is another illustration of the young child's egocentricity (49:32–48):

> What will happen when it is a question of imagining distant objects, and of coordinating the perspectives of different observers? . . . The child is placed opposite a small model of three mountains, and given a certain number of colored pictures of these mountains; he is then asked which of the pictures show the mountains from the positions occupied successively by a doll on the mountains in the model. The function of age in this development of these reactions is very clear. The little ones do not understand that the observer sees the same mountains quite differently from different points of view, and hence they consider their own perspective absolute. But the older ones discover the relativity necessary to objectivity after a number of systematic errors due to the difficulty of coordinating the relationships in question.

The egocentrism of young children is also reflected in their play activities. M. B. Parten (39:263) has asserted that "since the young children lack the power of expressing themselves with language, they have difficulty in playing in cooperative groups." Young children playing in the sandpile usually do not really play together, although they are fond of playing in company; older children, however, are likely to play together cooperatively. Another investigator, K. Bridges (2:72), has noted that "two-year-olds usually play or work by themselves with little reference to others except to claim their toys or otherwise interfere with them. . . . Older children engage more often in group play than younger ones and seldom play alone." These and other investigators have asserted that as children grow older they learn to play cooperatively; and that in the earlier years, although children may like to play in the presence of others, they do not in a genuine sense play *with* them. Because children do not at first grasp the roles of others, and because they lack an adequate time perspective, they tend to act in terms of short-range egocentric goals. Their ideas of fair play and of the "rules," it is asserted, are inadequate or absolute.

A Critique of the Egocentric Perspective

Vygotsky has remarked that psychology owes a great debt to Piaget, for he revolutionized the study of children. Vygotsky observes (54:9):

> Like many other great discoveries, Piaget's idea is simple to the point of seeming self-evident. It had already been expressed in the words of Rousseau, which Piaget himself quoted, that the child is not a miniature adult and his mind not the mind of an adult on a small scale.

Piaget assumes that the child is unlike the adult and this difference sets the tone for early egocentric thought. It is on this point, and others to be elaborated below, that we part company with Piaget. As we have argued earlier, there is ordinarily little, if anything, intrinsic to the human organism which upon birth will make it more or less responsive to the symbolic environment to which it is exposed. In short, we argue for a model of social development that begins from ongoing social worlds of experience, not from traits and attributes that the infant brings into the world at birth.

This point warrants elaboration. Piaget isolates three modes of thought: *autistic, egocentric,* and *rational.* As Vygotsky (54:13) notes, Piaget's conception of development is psychoanalytic in origin for it assumes the child is initially autistic and will change to rational thought only after a long and arduous process of socialization. Furthermore, Piaget repeatedly implies or asserts that autism and egocentrism are tied to the child's psychic nature and are impervious to social experience. He repeatedly asserts that until the age of seven or eight real social life does not exist among children. They engage in open monologue conversations; they are incapable of placing themselves in the perspective of others; they are essentially self-centered and egocentric in nature.

We reject the two assumptions that underly this formulation. First, there is nothing intrinsic to age that makes a seven- or eight-year-old child more or less egocentric. Second, the degree of egocentric thought present in the child's behavior repertoire will be a direct function of the complexity of his or her social environment. Consequently, thought and its complexity are *not* a function of organic and psychic factors but are inextricably bound up in the world of social experience. In short, thought is a product of social interaction. To argue otherwise, as Piaget does, is to construct a psychologistic, not a sociological model of thought and development. Piaget assumes, then, that thought moves from inner, autistic experiences to outer, sociocentric utterances which are mediated by a lengthy period of egocentric thought. As outlined in Chapter 9, in our discussion of the Chomsky formulations, our model of linguistic development assumes that thought follows vocal utterances, that initial utterances are global and nonspecific in nature, and that thought and speech progressively merge into one.

We wish to make two more points concerning egocentric speech. First, we concur with Vygotsky that egocentric speech quickly joins with inner thought. Furthermore, egocentric, or self-centered, speech and thought always involve the utilization of a social perspective. The dialogue between the "I" and the "me" is a social process. Egocentrism, or the primacy of the "I" over the "me," is always a matter of degree and is not as clear-cut as Piaget's work would imply. But more importantly, the presence of egocentric speech in the young child can be taken as evidence that the self as a distinct object is starting to emerge in the child's thought patterns; this is Markey's point also. The presence of pronouns in the three-year-old child's vocabulary is unequivocal proof that a linguistic conception of self as actor is forming. In this sense we wish to reverse the usual meanings of egocentric and argue that (1) all individuals are egocentric from someone else's perspective, and (2) young children who think and talk egocentrically are in essence separating themselves from others, however unsuccessfully, and in that process are making distinct objects of themselves.

The following excerpts from one of the author's studies (8:299–300) in a preschool will underscore the above position.

Two girls are standing below the large doll house inside the preschool.

FIRST GIRL: "They're people up there." (Points to three girls playing upstairs.)
SECOND GIRL: "Shall we go up there?"
FIRST GIRL: "No, they'll say 'you can't come up here.'"

A three-year-old girl has just finished working at the painting table. She gets up and goes across the room to get a book. An instructor confronts her:

INSTRUCTOR: "Are you through painting? Don't you want to hang up your painting?"
GIRL: "No, I don't want to!"
INSTRUCTOR: "Don't you really?"
GIRL: "No." (Shakes her head and walks off.)
INSTRUCTOR: "I'll do it for you." (Grimaces.)

These examples reveal that young children, at least in preschools, use personal and impersonal pronouns with ease, and in direct reference to ongoing activity systems. There are few elements of egocentric thought in either episode. The examples also suggest that the children were capable of placing themselves in one another's perspective and of formulating lines of action on the basis of that role-taking process.

It would be expected that the more familiar the situation to the children, the more reflexive and accurate they would be in separating themselves from the selves of other individuals. In those worlds which children control—sectors of preschools, their own bedrooms, and playrooms—greater levels of reflexivity will be observed. *The argument to this point can be quickly summarized. The child actor is a sophisticated interactant. Many theories of child development gloss over children's interactional skills either by studying them in unfamiliar test-taking situations, or by focusing on solitary individuals without attempting to catch them in moments of serious play.* Too many students of early child development, as Markey observed in 1928, have failed to check their findings out in nonlaboratory settings. The situation has not changed significantly since 1928. Piaget's view of the egocentric child may hold for those children whom he observed in his institute, but our position is that if left to their own devices, and if exposed to a sufficiently rich and complex interactional environment, three- and four-year-old children will act in ways that are essentially adultlike. Perhaps the point can be underlined with one more field observation done by another author of this book. A very alert four-and-one-half-year-old child was observed making quite adultlike remarks in which she made clear distinctions of "mine" and "mummy's." A few minutes later, watching her mother turn the pages of a book of art reproductions, she "dropped" to the level of pointing at objects and naming them ("tiger," "mother," "baby"). Later in the afternoon, she tried to explain to the author that her mother and she had looked for his parked car—where they thought he would be but was not—and did it not have something blue in it (a coat)? And several minutes later, when the author said, "Let's go get your parents," she objected that they were not her parents, but her "mummy and daddy"—denying that she knew what "parents" meant! Interviewed á la Piaget about what was a "mummy" and a "daddy," and how did they get to be that (and was the author without children a daddy?), her thought processes perfectly fitted Piaget's descriptions of children of that age. They gained that status by passing the age of seven—which she counted up to—and becoming grown-up, then became "daddy" or "mummy."

The Child's Network of Significant Others

Infants, as Mead and Cooley observed, are born into an ongoing network of interconnected social worlds. These are filled with individuals who will later become their *significant others*. That is, these people will stand in some position of influence and authority over the children, and they will come to view those people as influential in the organization of their own behavior.

Six categories of significant others can be identified. The child is likely to confront and interact with his or her various significant others at predictable times and in predictable places. The first class of significant others are those termed *sociolegal*, and they are the child's parents or guardians, his or her siblings, and other members of the kinship system. The second class of significant others are *socio-others*, drawn from the sociability network that surrounds the primary group of the family. These individuals assume fictional "kinship" in the family and may be called "aunts" and "uncles." Baby-sitters also fall in this category. Third are the *coequal*, or *compeer*, significant others. These may include siblings, but more importantly, playmates and children in the neigh-

A child with significant others.
(*Suzanne Szasz/Photo Researchers, Inc.*)

borhood and at school who come to assume a high degree of socializing influence over the child. By the age of three or four, compeers may rival parents and other sociolegal significant others in their influence over the child. Certainly by the first grade, and by seven or eight, he or she may have moved nearly entirely into a peer-oriented world of social control.

The fourth class of significant others are *child care experts*. These persons have attained some legitimate authority over child care and child evaluation. Pediatricians, physicians, child psychologists, and psychiatrists, teachers, lawyers, politicians, professors, presidents, and social workers dictate and shape the broader process by which a society produces its children. A fifth class of child caretakers and significant others is drawn from the mass media. *Media others* enter the child's world through television, the radio, record players, the movie theatre, storybooks, and nursery rhymes. These others may view themselves as experts on childhood; but more importantly they staff and populate the child's world of fantasy and entertainment. Captain Kangaroo, Mr. Rogers, and the Big Bird and the Cookie Monster on "Sesame Street" represent such fictive and real others who daily enter the child's world of interaction. Media others may have more contact with the child than do

The Social Worlds of Childhood   357

any of the above classes of individuals. A typical American television station, for example, programs up to seven hours of children's television six days a week. Recent research (7) indicates that four- to six-year-olds may watch up to four hours of television a day. This exceeds the interactive experiences they may have with one or both of their parents.

The last major class of significant others comes from the world of public places. *Public place others* include policemen, firemen, mailmen, clerks and strangers in stores, and individuals normally met by the children or their caretakers when in the public arena. These others fall into a residual category and their influence on the child is likely to be specific to particular situations or services. These six categories of significant others constitute what may be termed the child's interactive world. The two most important categories of significant others will be drawn from the sociolegal and compeer sectors of the child's social world. These persons make up the child's primary group and they provide the sources of self-worth and self-awareness that the child first experiences. They are, as M. Kuhn argued, *orientational significant others.* They shape conceptions of self, provide vocabularies of motive, furnish symbolic environments, and promote a sense of "we-ness" and solidarity. Depending on the stances that these others take toward the children, their rate of social development and their lingerings within the egocentric mode of thought will be hastened or retarded. We turn next to the decline in egocentrism in early childhood.

THE DECLINE OF EGOCENTRISM
As a consequence of entering into more extensive and complex social relations children become increasingly and more systematically aware of the points of view of other persons. They learn that these are often at variance with their own and that they must be taken into account. The young boy learns that though he has a brother, his brother also has a brother (himself); that a pebble is light in weight from one point of view but heavy from another point of view; that an object may be to the left of one object but at the same time to the right of another. Children's thinking becomes increasingly relativistic. They then come to realize that the sun follows neither them nor anyone else. They learn to conceive of it as the center of a solar system and think of the earth as one of several spherical bodies revolving about the sun. When they have achieved this mature point of view, we may say that they have, in a sense, synthesized virtually all conceivable views of the sun as a physical object and can assume the perspective of anyone in any location with respect to it. The age of transition, learning to grasp other points of view—learning to become nonegocentric—is placed by Piaget at approximately seven, but some English and American investigators have challenged this. In accordance with our own position, as stated earlier, presumably the age of

transition besides being different in different individuals also varies from society to society, from social world to social world. Presumably a young child might remain relatively egocentric in some respects and achieve somewhat greater social awareness in others. The important point is not the exact age at which egocentricity disappears, but that the disappearance is gradual. Of equal importance is children's *interactional age,* which is the amount of time they have spent in exposure to a given social experience. *Chronological age,* as such, is often superseded by interactional age. Hence, rates of cognitive development cannot be predicted simply on the basis of how old a child is.

    G. H. Mead has described graphically how children playfully imitate the roles of elders or associates and thus gradually develop an ability to see objects, other persons, and themselves from a nonegocentric standpoint. Mead emphasizes what Piaget merely noted in passing, namely, that language is basic in the development of the ability to play roles (34:150–51, 364–65):

> [There are] countless forms of play in which the child assumes the roles of the adults about him. . . . In the play of young children, even when they

Numerous forms of play-acting display the increasing ability of the child to take the role of the other. (*Burke Uzzle;* © *1969 Magnum Photos*)

play together, there is abundant evidence of the child's taking different roles in the process; and a solitary child will keep up the process of stimulating himself by his vocal gestures [spoken words] to act in different roles almost indefinitely. . . . A child plays at being a mother, at being a teacher, at being a policeman; that is, it is taking different roles. . . . He has a set of stimuli which call out in himself the sort of responses they call out in others. He takes this group of responses and organizes them into a certain whole.

The children's playing at being persons other than themselves is paralleled in actual life in their interactions with parents and playmates. One of the theories of play is that it is a preparation for later adult activity wherein individuals apply the skills that they have acquired. (7) Thus the standards of fair play and the proper attitude toward defeat in competition are often said to be learned on the gridiron or on the "playing fields of Eton." No doubt it is from considerations of this kind that the widespread absorption of children (and adults) in comic strips and comic books concerns and alarms some who feel that constant identifications with comic-strip characters of doubtful virtue may lead the children to emulate these fictional "heroes." Without accepting this position, one may recognize that this kind of play activity and fantasizing gives the child a repertoire of roles and practice in switching from one to the other.

The initial role taking of young children (placing themselves in the perspectives of another person) is simple and limited, involving only limited and brief fragments of behavior and the imitation of a few specific persons. As the child's circle of acquaintanceship is enlarged, as his or her mastery of communication develops, and as his or her real roles multiply in number and become more complex, the role-taking processes become more complicated. (38)

Perspectives and the Generalized Other

When children have developed the ability to grasp the role or attitude of one other person at a time, they are on the road to becoming social beings. However, before they can participate in organized adult activity, children must be able systematically to conceive their own role from the standpoint of all other participants. An illustration will help to make this clear.

Suppose that a group of Air Force men is on a bombing mission. Each man has a definite, assigned general role that involves certain duties and obligations. Each man has a clear conception of his general role, as he imagines it from the points of view of all the others. He also has a clear picture of how his own role fits in with the role of each of the other men.

Mead asserts that, by contrast, the very young child is able to take

Life Cycle: The Genesis of Self

the role of only one other person at a time. From this simple kind of role taking, the child eventually develops the ability (1) to take the roles of others in the situation, (2) to organize these roles into an integrated whole, and (3) to view his or her own behavior from this standpoint. Mead's suggestion of how this learning takes place is as follows (34:151–52, 154):

> If we contrast play with . . . an organized game, we note the essential difference that the child who plays in a game must be ready to take the attitude of everyone else involved in that game, and that these different roles must have a definite relationship to each other. . . . In a game where a number of individuals are involved . . . they do not all have to be present in [his] consciousness at the same time, but at some moments he has to have three or four individuals present in his own attitude.

Through their participation in organized games, in play, and in other activities, children learn to take the role of the participants and grasp the fact that the roles of others are intertwined. At the same time, they begin to see how their own activity within the situation looks from the standpoint of the others. They see their own actions as part of a whole pattern of group activity.

Mead has coined a term for this organization of the roles of others; he calls it the *generalized other*. He used this expression because it means that one is taking the related roles of all the other participants rather than the role of just one other person. This concept of the generalized other applies to the organized roles of participants within any defined situation.

The term *generalized other* does not refer to an actual group of people, but rather to a conception or an interpretation that persons derive from their experiences. They then regulate their behavior in terms of these supposed opinions and attitudes of others. They stand outside their own behavior and view it from the perspective of these others. They imagine what people would say "if they knew" or what they will say "when they know." The term "people" may not have any specific reference to actual persons but may merely represent the child's conception of abstract moral standards. These standards widen as role playing becomes more generalized. Internal "I"-"me" conversations become increasingly more complex.

We would disagree with Mead's views only on one important point. Young children will be found, if one observes them closely, to be taking the role of multiple others (mother and father, for example) quite nicely in some situations but regressing in other situations to Mead's "able to take only one person at a time." Some children do the former quite easily. Mead's points about their increasing ability to do that, along with the general direction of their development, seem accurate enough.

As children's conceptualizing ability approaches the adult standard, their concepts become more numerous and the interrelationships of those concepts become more complex. Children's ability to play roles and to be different persons, and to understand the actions and motives of others develops in a parallel course.

The earlier role conceptions of children are, from the adults' viewpoint, rather curious and often amusing, although in their own way they represent a primitive if incorrect systematization of how roles, or behavioral expectations vary for different individuals. Thus, very young children know there are storekeepers and customers, but they think that the customer buys goods and both customer and storekeeper pay each other. Only the customer buys goods; the storekeeper never does. Monetary activity is confined to buying and selling. Although one storekeeper may help another sell, the distinction between owner and employer is unclear

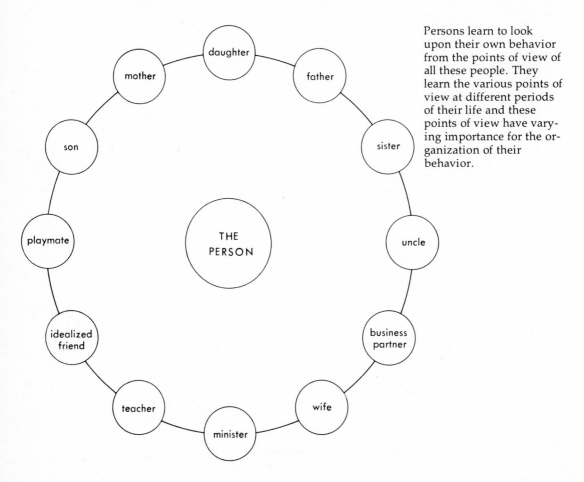

Persons learn to look upon their own behavior from the points of view of all these people. They learn the various points of view at different periods of their life and these points of view have varying importance for the organization of their behavior.

Life Cycle: The Genesis of Self

and is not involved in the buying-selling transactions. There are no other roles such as that of manufacturer. (52:278)

The work of E. Hartley and his associates (16) shows that the young child is unable to organize certain perspectives properly. Thus, a young child can conceive of a mother only from one perspective, and deny that mothers can play other roles (that of a salesperson, for example). Older children widen the positions from which role players are viewed until they are able to conceive of any individual as momentarily or permanently playing one role but potentially capable of playing many others. The inflexibility of the very young child, who, like Gertrude Stein, may insist that a mother is a mother is a mother, represents an inability to slide in imagination from perspective to perspective or to organize perspectives into a more inclusive whole.

Hartley's discussion is deficient in that it does not bring out the fact that the young child who cannot conceive of the mother as a salesperson nevertheless can conceive of her as a daughter or her grandmother. Children can do this because in their immature systematization of role concepts, certain roles seem compatible with each other while others do not.

At one step of concept development, children will deny that two roles are compatible; later, having grasped their relationship, they will agree that they go together. Thus, they will at a young age deny that a teacher can be a storekeeper or vice versa, because each belongs to a different world. Later the child agrees that a teacher could be a storekeeper "after school," but still denies that a storekeeper can be a customer. Still later he or she sees that a storekeeper can buy in a store and still in a general sense be a storekeeper. He or she does not yet perceive that the storekeeper must be a customer of manufacturers.

Much of children's early learning about role relationships occurs in concrete situations in which the roles are played out before their eyes. However, most role relationships are rather abstract. Even those relationships that seem most concrete and visible—for example, those between a teacher and a pupil—involve much more than is visible on the surface. Greater maturity and breadth of experience are necessary before the child can be expected to understand the subtler aspects of such relationships.

THE GENERALIZED OTHER AND MORAL BEHAVIOR

That generalized others are learned conceptions has two important implications: (1) children do not acquire moral views automatically or mechanically, and (2) even persons belonging to the same groups cannot have identical generalized others. Children are rewarded, punished, and exhorted so that they will conform to adult expectations. However, every parent knows that learning is not a rubber-stamp process and that one cannot mechanically or forcibly inculcate adult ideas into a child.

The concept of the generalized other has been mildly criticized by C. W. Mills (36:672) on the grounds that it implies too great homogeneity and does not take into account the multiplicity and heterogeneity of modern societies. It is argued that the generalized other of a given person is always relative to particular groups and persons and that not all participants in a given social act have equal influence. A person is said by Mills to build up his or her moral and intellectual standards only in terms of significant other persons rather than all others in the situation. There is obvious truth in this. The standards of the criminal, for example, do not enter into the generalized other of the law-abiding citizen except to reinforce them by negative example. Even significant others are significant in different ways and to different degrees. A student's intellectual orientation may be described in a gross way by relating it to a specific university, a specific subject, and a specific department. Closer scrutiny may reveal, however, that really decisive influence has been exercised by certain professors, or perhaps by one professor. The same may be said of moral standards, which are perhaps most usually acquired from parents. The mother's and father's influence upon the child may be very different, and in some cases, neither of them may exercise the dominant influence—that is, the child may acquire moral conceptions from peers, from a well-liked teacher, or from someone else. (See also the discussion of child development as conceived by Freud and Sullivan in Chapter 10.)

SOCIAL STRUCTURE, MEMBERSHIP, AND SELF-CONCEPTION As children become adults, self-conceptions undergo a variety of patterned types of changes and become increasingly anchored in the groups and broader societal structure in which they participate. Manford Kuhn (29:30) has developed this point in a study in which people of various ages were asked to make twenty statements in answer to the question, "Who am I?" It was noted that children's answers to the question tended to scatter over a wide range and to focus on particular, individualistic, or idiosyncratic aspects of their lives. With increasing age, the conceptions of personal identity funneled into the kinds of broad social categories that also are employed to describe the social structure. Adults identified themselves more often by occupation, class, marital status, sex, age, race, religion, and other similar criteria. Thus, when a very young child who has lost his parents in a crowd is asked who he is, he may be able to supply his first name and a variety of irrelevant information that does not give much help to those who are trying to return him to his parents.

Two examples from Kuhn's study will underline the point. A fourth-grade girl replying to the question, "Who am I," wrote a series of negative statements about her behavior, obviously reflecting parental discipline and admonition: "I boss too much. I get mad at my sisters. I am a show off. I interrupt too much. I waste time. Sometimes I am a bad sport. I fiddle around. I am careless at times. I forget."

In contrast, the response of a university senior included the following items among others: "I am of the female sex. My age is 20. I am from (city and state). I have two parents. My home is happy. I am happy. I am of the middle class. I am a (sorority name). I am in the Waves Officer School. I am an adjusted person. I am a (department major). I attend church." It is apparent that the latter series tells us much about the person's position in society, whereas the former series tells us about almost nothing except the parental discipline imposed upon a fourth-grade child.

As children are processed through the educational system and drop out of it at various stages to assume adult responsibilities, they are distributed in a variety of jobs, places, and positions. This process of distribution is complex but not haphazard. It is regulated in a general way with respect to occupation by the number of job opportunities existing in each field and by price mechanisms that offer differential economic rewards for different occupations in rough proportion to the balance of supply and demand.

In order for a job, rank, office, or any other status to exert a pervasive and decisive influence upon a person, it must in some way become linked with his or her self-conception and with the networks of social relationships that make up his or her social worlds. At the heart of this linking of self-regard and social position is a fateful commitment to doing well as "that kind of person." A civilian soldier is not insulted by being told that he is not a soldier, but a professional military man is. The latter's behavior is largely oriented around his being a soldier. It is, therefore, a matter of some importance to him to believe that he is a good one, in a good army, preferably one of the "best soldiers in the best damned army in the world."

We say that a person's commitment to central statuses, or those roles that are important to him or her as a person, is fateful because failure to uphold the standards will be read by the individual as failure and will cause him or her to feel guilty or ashamed, to lose self-respect, and to make efforts at redemption. When conception of self is based on a simple central status, all other statuses tend to become subordinate to this one and to be judged by reference to it. To continue with the example of the professional military man, he will tend to judge many nonmilitary phases of his life in terms of the bearing they have or are likely to have upon his military career. The higher his status the greater will be the demands of his profession on him for more total commitment, and the greater will be the probability that this commitment will eclipse or take precedence over any others. In discussing morale, we have already seen that certain social organizations demand almost total devotion and allegiance of members, even to the exclusion of familial and other roles that may cut athwart the group purposes. Even family roles may become impossible to maintain or may become subordinate to and subtly colored by more essential loyalties.

MORALITY AND OBJECTIVITY In an interesting study, E. Lerner (30:546) asked children between the ages of eight and twelve the following question: "Is it worse to tell a lie to your father or to your mother?" Typical reasons given for naming the father were "because he can punish harder" and "because you can't get away with it with him." Those who thought it worse to lie to one's mother reasoned in such terms as "she is sweeter" and "she is the best friend you have."

Murphy, Murphy, and Newcomb, in commenting upon Lerner's study, remark that (37:546):

> Moral judgments . . . are clearly *not* simply assimilated readymade from the preceding generation, but are reworked in terms of the child's needs and degrees of identification with, and respect for, other individuals. . . . Many moral judgments of children are in violent conflict with those of their parents and, indeed, of the whole social world around them, if a line of conduct close to their own needs is involved. The parent who has tried to teach the small child that caterpillars, bugs, spiders, and other "pests" must all be exterminated knows that even when the whole world backs him up the child may protest that the destruction of some tiny animal friend is wrong, and that in fairy stories, despite the universal condemnation of the wolf or the tiger, the child may alarm the parent by wholeheartedly assuming the wolf's point of view. Thus Boeck found a dependable stimulus for protest or tears to lie in the destruction of the wolf at the end of the Red Riding Hood story. . . . The moral responses . . . depend not only on the world of culture, but on the individual's own needs.

The needs to which these three authors refer are, of course, not simply biological ones, but the outgrowths of social experience. It should be self-evident that just as the needs of any two children are not identical, so their moral experiences cannot be the same.

Studies of the development of children's moral ideas and judgments demonstrate in part that the child moves from predominantly egocentric to increasingly relativistic moral standards. Piaget (46) has analyzed this aspect of childhood. In his study of lower-class children of Geneva, Switzerland, he discerned a series of transformations in their moral conceptions. The young Genevan up to four or five years of age is characterized by "moral realism." Right is right and wrong is wrong: if a person does wrong, he or she should be punished regardless of motives. Later the child realizes that moral rules are not objectively real but reflect group values. This realization is based upon the recognition of multiple perspectives. Geneva children remain at this stage until nine or ten. Then a

Life Cycle: The Genesis of Self

third level is reached at which the rules are allowed to be altered by considerations of equity; for example, a lame boy may be given a head start in a race. Piaget believes he has demonstrated that the child's conception of moral rules changes from the belief that rules are absolute to the knowledge that they are agreed upon. Other studies of children support Piaget's conclusions (30, 51).

Studies like those made by E. Macaulay and S. Watkins (31) also point to the gradual growth of wider moral meanings. Children were asked to make a list of the most wicked things they could think of. Their answers showed that up to nine years of age the children's moral conceptions are rather definite and concrete and are formulated in terms of their own personal relations. After this age moral conceptions appeared to grow more generalized. Stealing and fighting in general were beginning to be regarded as wrong at age nine. From the age of eleven years, conceptions began to show the influence of conventional adult notions of sin, although only the children in late adolescence wrote of such sins of the spirit as hypocrisy and selfishness. As Murphy, Murphy, and Newcomb have noted about the elementary-grade child (37:650): "Abstract conceptions of justice and 'fairness' are not yet very clear. 'Ideals' and general rules of the institution have little weight."

Piaget's specific explanation for the direction of moral development is dubious. He hypothesized that the early conceptions of moral rules are absolutistic because of the authoritarian relations that exist between parent and child; and that conceptions grow more relativistic, general, and systematic as cooperative relationships spring up between the child and others, particularly his or her peers. Neither does it seem adequate to explain the growth of moral conceptions merely as a consequence of reward and punishment or of learning from specific direct experiences "to recognize a common element in a variety of situations." (12:438) Conceptions of roles and of rules grow side by side. Built into role conceptions are the justifications and canons appropriate to the roles. When children are young, their moral standards lack relativity and generality because they cannot grasp the fuller meaning of acts as seen from wider perspectives. It is therefore worthwhile to distinguish between the full and general comprehension of moral values and the learning of a specific rule.

These remarks are supported by some imaginative research reported by Lawrence Kohlberg, a psychologist who has been stimulated by both Piaget and Mead. (25, 26, 27) To children varying in age from seven to seventeen, Kohlberg (3:405; 25:18–19) posed stories that embodied moral dilemmas. For instance:

> In Europe, a woman was near death from a special kind of cancer. There was one drug that the doctors thought might save her. It was a form of radium that a druggist in the same town had recently discovered. The drug

was expensive to make, but the druggist was charging ten times what the drug cost him to make. He paid $200 for the radium and charged $2000 for a small dose of the drug. The sick woman's husband, Heinz, went to everyone he knew to borrow the money, but he could only get together about $1000, which is half of what it cost. He told the druggist that his wife was dying, and asked him to sell it cheaper or let him pay later. But the druggist said, "No, I discovered the drug and I'm going to make money from it." So Heinz got desperate and broke into the man's store to steal the drug for his wife. Should the husband have done that? Why?

Such dilemmas can be resolved by subordinating a rule of law or authority to a higher principle. Kohlberg's results concerning moral judgment are much more complex than Piaget's. He found six stages of development and distinguished thirty aspects of morality. His evidence does not support Piaget's conclusions about the origins of absolutism (authoritarian relations) or the sources of relativism (peer group cooperation). Kohlberg studied children as old as seventeen, and found that developmental stages continue through the entire age range. In the sixth stage children judge their conduct in accordance with their own internal standards, doing right to satisfy their own conscience. Although an operating conscience exists earlier, only considerably later do children explain conduct to themselves in terms of their conscience.

Roger Brown comments on Kohlberg's findings, and they are comments with which we agree. He remarks that to speak a language the speaker must have a system of general rules, and so also must a person in order to act morally. But parents "do not provide lessons in what to do if your wife needs a medicine you cannot afford or in how to resolve the conflicts that may arise in a bombing raid. We have no rote answers to Kohlberg's dilemmas." (3:407) Such dilemmas can only be resolved by reference to general rules. Brown's comments are in accord with our previous contention that it is worthwhile to distinguish between the learning of specific rules and the comprehension of general moral values.

The Nature of Objectivity

Just as the actions of people appear in different perspectives, so also do physical events and objects. These different perspectives cannot be called "roles," as this term has been defined, but they are points of view of other persons. If a person were unable to conceive of other, wider perspectives than those provided by immediate sensory impressions, he or she would be unable to form any realistic conception of the physical world or to appreciate the accomplishments of science. Thus, no atoms are visible to the naked eye and few have ever been seen, even through microscopes. A person who depended only on direct experience would deny their existence. An objective view of the physical world requires that the various aspects presented by objects in different situations and

Life Cycle: The Genesis of Self

combinations be synthesized into broader conceptions that will permit various observers to agree on essential, publicly verifiable facts. To achieve such objectivity, one must do something closely akin to what has been called taking the role of the generalized other; one must combine or synthesize divergent and conflicting views into an overall view that harmonizes them.

The point may be reinforced by recalling a simple illustration that Piaget has provided. (40) He noted, as we have seen, that children often believe that the sun and the moon follow them when they walk. As soon as children are able to communicate such ideas and become concerned with avoiding contradiction, they must necessarily discover that this notion leads to logical absurdities. The moon cannot follow everyone without moving in different directions at the same time. Discussion and controversy over matters of this kind eventually lead to the realization of apparent (illusory) motion and finally to the idea of relative motion. Advanced general conceptions of motion, as the word "general" indicates, take account of apparent motion.

A simpler illustration of the way in which divergent viewpoints are reconciled is provided by the finish of a close race. Viewed from different angles, different contenders seem to have won. If this were the whole story the question of the winner would always remain a matter of personal opinion and of controversy. By agreement, however, it is recognized that these different perspectives depend on the different positions of the observers; and so the decision is based on how the race looks to those persons who are exactly on the finish line. In horse races the camera that photographs the finish simultaneously from both sides is the final arbiter in case of doubt, and if it fails to indicate a single winner, the race is declared a tie.

The fact that truth appears to be relative to the position of the observer is systematically taken into account in the physical sciences. A. P. Ushenko (53), for example, has discussed what he calls *perspectival truth*. He indicates that what is true in one perspective may be false in another, and that the contradiction is resolved by incorporating limited perspectives into broader and more inclusive ones.

The acceptance by laypersons of the scientist's view of the physical world is largely an act of faith. The scientists are the layperson's significant others who probe the mysteries of the physical world, performing complicated experiments and erecting structures of concepts and mathematical symbols far beyond the layperson's power of comprehension. The layperson's faith is justified, he or she argues, by the results which everyone can see. A religious person, on the other hand, may take a very different view, rejecting the materialism and one-sidedness of science and seeing the physical world and science itself primarily as evidence of the working out of a divine plan. The significant others in this concep-

Different perspectives depend on the position of the observer. (*Wide World Photos*)

tion are religious and moral leaders. There are, of course, many different philosophical positions with respect to the nature of the physical world, each claiming priority over all the others.

The ability to take into account the view of other persons and to assume their roles is fundamental to the achievement of objectivity in thinking. Thinking objectively also requires that individuals become aware of the mechanisms of their own thought. In order to discount biases, to make allowance for the uniqueness of one's own views, and to examine critically one's own conclusions, the individual must be able to make comparisons and relative judgments. This is impossible so long as there is no awareness of the existence of other possible views.

Another indispensable requirement for objective thinking, as Mead noted, is individuals' ability to make a sharp separation between processes that go on only in their own minds and those that are outside and independent of the person. Lacking this ability, they project their own human sentiments and desires upon the outside world. The complete separation of what comes from inside of us and that which is independent and outside of us is actually exceedingly difficult; perhaps, in a strict sense, it is impossible. Our evidence of the external world is derived from our sense organs, and the symbols and ideas which we use to represent the external world are human creations. The whole broad sweep of intellectual history reveals a persistent tendency to confuse names with things, to ignore things that are not named, to assume that there must be things where there are names, and generally to confuse objects of thought with actual objects and events. This tendency has been progressively reduced, but not by any means eliminated, through research in the natural sciences and in the study of humans and through an increasing sophistication of logical and philosophical thought. The child, for example, at first thinks of external objects and events in terms of the necessities and compulsions felt in his or her own life. Clouds, stones, trees, and other objects are endowed with human qualities. The child talks to toys and to animals as though they might answer. This projection of human qualities upon nonhuman objects is known as *anthropomorphism*. It is a striking characteristic of childish thought and also occurs in much adult thinking. *Geocentrism*—the belief that the earth is the center and the hub of the universe—is a similar error; it arises from the inability of people to view the solar system from the standpoint of an outside observer. Another fallacy of the same type is *ethnocentrism*—the tendency to judge other groups by the standards and customs of one's own group. To understand an alien culture one must place oneself in the role of a member of that culture.

Here again a study of the role-playing inadequacies of young children is pertinent. Lerner (30:260) notes that:

> [The] lack of perspective is clearly indicated in the entirely spontaneous manner in which the child is prone to judge or compare members of other groups (out-groups) in terms of a quite unconscious attitude of superiority or, in general, as a matter of distinctly absolute valuations. The socialization of this sociocentric self is indicated, in turn, in terms of a progressively increasing conscious realization of these centripetal tendencies.

Lerner asked questions designed to uncover familial, school, and communal variants of ethnocentrism (which he calls "sociocentrism"). For example, "A boy here in Geneva told me that boys in X (another town known to the subject) tell more lies, while a boy in X told me just the opposite; who is right, why?" Here are two sets of answers, the first exhibiting sociocentrism, the second exhibiting a more sophisticated relativism. (We would note that the age differences recorded by Lerner probably reflect different interactive, not age-determined, experiences.)

> 7 years, 0 months: Who is right? *The boy from Geneva because in Geneva they don't tell lies.* And in X? *They do.* Why? *Because they are better brought up.*
> 7 years, 7 months: Who is right? *The boy who says that in X they are liars and that in Geneva they are not almost all liars.* Why? *In X they do nothing but tell lies, but not in Geneva.*

11 years, 1 month: *Both of them wrong because they shouldn't say bad things about other people. Because they also tell lies . . . I don't know, I've never been there.*

12 years, 3 months: *But, no, it's the same thing all over: they lie as much as they do here. And we lie as often as they do.*

Any kind of organized group activity presupposes at least a minimum of agreement or consensus. Objectivity develops from the attempt to resolve conflicting views. Apropos of this point, Murphy (37:738) and his associates have reviewed studies of how groups resolve group problems. They conclude that whenever the thinking of the whole group is better than that of its individual members, this is due in part to (1) the larger number of ways of looking at the problem; (2) the larger number of suggestions for a solution; (3) the larger number of effective criticisms of each proposed plan; and (4) the patent need to accept social criticism and not be "bullheaded" (as people working alone frequently are). By progressively freeing themselves from the biases and limitations of their own unique points of view, people are able to assume progressively broader and more detached perspectives. They become capable of agreeing, to a certain extent, upon the "facts" of the case.

The work of the scientist illustrates particularly well the way in which objective knowledge arises from the clash of divergent points of view. Scientific investigation requires the ability to imagine how one's work will appear to the critical eyes of other scientists. Theories, techniques, and findings must all be subjected to examination and rechecking by others before they are accepted. The exact conditions under which experiments and observations are made must be reported so that the same steps can be followed by other investigators. Scientists, in short, must be adept at role taking. They must be first-rate critics of their own work. The respect that Charles Darwin commanded as a scientist was due in considerable part to the thorough self-criticism to which he subjected his work. He attempted to anticipate all possible objections and counterarguments and patiently answered them. Consequently, as each of his books was published, his scientific audience had considerable assurance that its contents were solidly grounded. Of course, even Darwin's findings were not accepted until other biologists had rechecked his observations and experiments; nor were all of his conclusions found to be valid.

UNDERSTANDING
THE ROLES
OF OTHERS

Much misunderstanding arises among people when they are unable to appreciate each other's roles. Individuals' ability to understand the behavior of others is limited by the range of their acquaintance with forms of behavior like their own or with which they are familiar. "Average" persons readily appreciate the motives and views of other people who

Life Cycle: The Genesis of Self

are like themselves. Furthermore, they are likely to have some grasp of the behavior of persons who are somewhat different from themselves because they have talked to or read about them. Beyond this, however, there are roles that they may be almost entirely unable to comprehend, such as those of "foreigners" or persons outside the boundaries of Western civilization. Consider, for example, the average American housewife grappling with the fact that a Toda woman of southern India may have as many as three husbands at a time.

In a complex and closely connected world society such as ours, it is vitally important for people to appreciate the existence of many types of roles and perspectives other than their own. Conflicts among nations, religious groups, and subgroups within nations arise from a lack of such understanding. Because of an absence of adequate intercommunication, people do not grasp one another's motives and ways of acting. The chief means of broadening the understanding of people are indirect ones such as those involved in learning a foreign language, reading books, and studying anthropology.

Instead of recognizing our failures to understand the acts of others, we usually misinterpret those acts. We assume that people are playing roles within our own system of values and symbols, and we interpret their behavior in terms of our symbols instead of theirs. To choose an example close to the experience of most college students: parents misinterpret many acts of their teen-age children. The real meanings of these acts are not grasped because parents are outsiders to the adolescent age group and to the adolescent world. Conversely, children often misinterpret their parents' acts because of the failure to grasp the meanings of adult behavior. Misinterpretations are not always harmless and amusing. In a multigrouped society, misjudgments of roles often have serious results, as both interracial and international relations testify. This fact is nowhere more evident than in the area of sex-role socialization, the next topic to which we turn. (In this context the reader should also consult Chapter 14.)

Differentiation of Basic Sex Roles

No society fails to embody in its practices and language the fundamental biological distinction between the sexes. Many societies recognize still further categories, which include men who act like women and women who act like men. These in-between persons are sometimes taken for granted, sometimes looked upon as biological abnormalities. Scientists and sophisticated laypersons recognize also another intermediate hermaphroditic class of persons who at birth have some of the genital apparatus, and perhaps physical traits, of both sexes. (11)

Regardless of these intermediate classes, we may take for granted that humans universally recognize the existence of polar biological types: that is, men and women. It is easy to understand why the incorrect assumption is frequently made that infants "naturally" know to which sex they belong. Every child must not only (1) learn the meanings of "male" and "female" but also (2) classify himself or herself with both or neither.

This poses a problem. How do children learn to identify themselves as members of one or the other sex? The reader who looks for a detailed and exact answer to this question will be disappointed, for pertinent scientific data are rather meager. However, the larger outlines of the process of sex identification are clear enough.

RECOGNITION OF SEX DIFFERENCES
When young children begin to learn sex distinctions, they employ criteria which betray rudimentary conceptions of the differences between men and women. These criteria vary according to opportunities available to children for observing and conversing about sex behavior. In the United States such experiences vary widely according to social class, social worlds, conditions of housing, number of siblings in the family, sibling position, moral philosophies of the parents, and other relevant factors.

In an outstanding study, Conn and Kanner (5) have analyzed the criteria which children use to differentiate the sexes. Although their sampling is deficient—the study covers children ranging from four to twelve years of age, of many social classes—it offers valuable hints about the learning of sex differences.

One of the items which the children mentioned most frequently as a sign of sex membership was clothing. Their data indicate that this sign is learned, accepted for a time, and then discarded. (5:13) A few children under the age of seven equated sex differences with differences of attire, apparently recognizing no other distinctions. Clothing was most important for children ages nine to ten. When asked if there would be any difference between undressed boys and girls, these young children were "either puzzled by the questions, or declared categorically that removal of clothes made a distinction impossible." (5:13) Apropos of this finding is a story involving a five-year-old acquaintance of the authors who attended a party at which children of both sexes bathed in the nude. When asked how many boys and how many girls were at the party, she answered: "I couldn't tell because they had their clothes off."

Hair was frequently mentioned as a differentiating characteristic of the sexes. (5:13) Many children thought that differences of hair styles are inherent—though helped along by scissors and the barber. As another young acquaintance of the authors confidently asserted: "Boys have straight hair and girls have curly hair." Differences of urination posture were mentioned spontaneously by forty-four children. Although

Life Cycle: The Genesis of Self

breasts were generally recognized as belonging only to women, they were not spontaneously mentioned by the children as distinguishing features. "There were so many other things closer to the children's interest and immediate awareness." (5:17) Only nine of the two hundred children spontaneously included this distinguishing sign. The method used by the investigators is not open to the charge that children did not mention breasts because of inhibiting taboos.

An interesting finding is that (1) older children spontaneously mention other criteria such as shape of the face, complexion, hands, strength, and gait; but that (2) children below certain ages did not mention these criteria. The investigators conclude that many younger children do not possess the requisite language necessary to see these sex differences. Their summarizing table is below. (5:16)

Difference	Youngest Age of Naming
Hair	4
Clothes	5
Eyes	5
Hands	5
Face	6
Complexion	7
Hands and feet	8
Figure	8
Strength	8
Gait	9

That the child has learned to identify persons correctly as male or female does not mean that he or she has gained an adult conception of sex differences. The meanings of "male" and "female," like those of other symbols, cannot be fully grasped by youngsters. Children have neither the requisite experiences nor, in the case of the youngest of them, the mentality necessary to understand adult concepts of sex contrasts.

On the learning of sex differences, Conn and Kanner (5) present helpful data. Older children from urban centers generally recognized and mentioned genital difference between the sexes, but did not always realize that such differences also characterized animals. Consequently, varying conceptions of sex differences were offered. A common notion was that all animals of the same species were of the same sex: for example, all cats are females and all dogs are males. Other criteria for classifying animals were used: for example, some children regarded ribbons as a distinguishing sign and other children regarded names as evidence of sex. Farm children, of course, are likely to be more sophisticated about the sex of animals.

Involved in adult conceptions of sex differences is an awareness of the sex act and its conventional socialized meanings. In some countries and classes, children may be allowed to engage in sex play with others of their own age and have frequent opportunities to witness adult coitus. These conditions prevail among the Trobriand Islanders, a South Sea people. Consequently, this part of the adult symbolization is learned earlier than it is by many American children. The Conn and Kanner figures, which seem relatively trustworthy, indicate that only a small proportion of a total of two hundred children under twelve years of age had knowledge of the existence of coitus. There are, however, no grounds for assuming that even these relatively sophisticated children had adult concepts of the act. We must note that the Conn and Kanner research is now over thirty years old. While their study is a landmark investigation, it must be regarded with some caution: for recent changes in the sexual arena (see Chapter 14) are likely to produce earlier awareness on the part of children in the realm of sexual behavior and sex role identification. More sensitive research on this topic is called for.

The point is brought home vividly by Richard Wright's (57:36) account of how, at the age of six, in a bar where he had insisted on hanging around, he had been taught numerous sexual terms and obscenities. Two or three years later, he unwittingly enraged his grandmother when, after his bath, she was scrubbing ". . . my anus. My mind was in a sort of daze, midway between daydreaming and thinking." Before Wright knew it, "words—words whose meaning I did not fully know—had slipped out of my mouth. 'When you get through, kiss back there.' . . . Granny became terribly still, then she pushed me violently from her." Later still, Wright was playing in front of a neighboring house with another child when an older girl said, "They gonna make a lotta money in there today. . . ." Richard asked why, and the girl asked if he didn't know what they were selling in there. " 'They don't sell nothing in there,' I said. 'Aw, you just a baby,' she said slapping her dingy palm through the air at me in a contemptuous gesture."

The institutions that any society assembles for the production and rearing of children differentially stress sex role attributes as they structure the socialization process. (1) This is particularly evident in the education arena, wherein males and females are segregated in bathroom and physical education activities. Perhaps more critical are the lessons in sex role socialization young children receive in preschool and day care centers. Bathroom interactions in nursery schools may provide occasions for conversations about anatomical differences between the sexes. The bathroom becomes a "social place." One observer in the Columbia University Nursery School noted that "As the children grow more efficient in taking care of themselves, many interesting conversations are carried on

Life Cycle: The Genesis of Self

[there]. And, the teacher often adds bits of information in response to natural questions." This observation was made in 1929. Observers such as Joffe (22:467–75) and Henry (18) have noted that many preschools are explicitly organized so as to set males and females against one another. Teachers expressly value and reward appropriate "male" and "female" behavior and can be seen to discourage "female" behavior on the part of males and aggressive "male-like" behavior on the part of little girls. One of the authors observed a preschool teacher in a racially mixed middle-class preschool repeatedly embarrass a four-year-old male who insisted on dressing each day in the garments of a newly wed bride. Joffe reports the following episode drawn from a parent-cooperative nursery in Berkeley, California, in the spring of 1970 (22:470):

> L. and N. have been arguing over the use of a spade. N. pushes L. and L. responds by delivering a solid punch to N.'s chest. A mother who has witnessed the scene says to the observer (within hearing of L.), "Did you see the punch L. gave N? He really can take care of himself like a man."

Young children find that they are rewarded when they act on preferred sex role stereotypes. They often bring "sexual rhetorics" into their games. Joffe observed the following exchange between two girls and a boy (22:472): "C. and two other girls are playing on top of a large structure in the yard. A. (male) comes over and C. screams, 'Girls only!' to which A. screams back, 'No, boys only!' "

Phrases such as "My, your hair looks nice today," or "Oh, what a pretty dress you have on," inform young females that they will be positively addressed and identified if they look nice. To look nice is to be dressed nicely and to have one's hair and other physical features properly in order. Thus, by the early age of three, young children begin to assign to themselves and others quite specific self-identities with sexual dimensions.

The meanings associated with sexual activities must be learned by children. They do not in any significant degree invent them; nor do they acquire them through biological endowment or maturation. They may not understand the full adult significance of many sexual words and acts until they are well into adolescence, or later.

LEARNING THE MEANINGS OF SEXUAL BEHAVIOR

Although humans everywhere recognize the existence of sexual excitement, coitus, masturbation, sex organs, and the like, they nevertheless take dissimilar attitudes toward these objects, acts, and events. Words convey or mirror attitudes: that is, they have meanings. The child—whether American or Japanese or Marquesan, upper or lower class, boy or girl, rural or urban—when he or she learns words, learns also the conventional points of view which they express.

Kinsey (23) asserted that there were at the time of his study differential American class attitudes toward the meaning of sexual behavior; we shall summarize a few:

Event or Object	Upper Classes	Lower Classes
"Heavy Petting"	Part of the sex act or a substitute for it.	Not much practiced. As a substitute for the sex act, a perversion.
"Clitoris"	Many recognize its function in sexual foreplay as exciting to female. A function emphasized in widely read marriage manuals.	Word not in common use, nor any equivalent for it, since few know the organ exists. This is true particularly of males, but also to a lesser degree of females.
"Foreplay"	Widely regarded as an important preliminary to coitus.	Generally not considered important.
"Positions"	Some sophistication about possible variations.	Only one position is natural: the "American one."

MOTIVATION AND LEARNING

As we might expect, Kinsey found that sexual vocabularies varied tremendously by region, class, race, age, and other groupings. These differences of vocabulary, of course, mirror differences of attitude and constitute important data for anyone interested in understanding, explaining, and predicting human sex behavior. When the child learns these idiomatic terms he or she also internalizes the meanings they express. American middle-class parents recognize this fact implicitly, since they teach their children euphemistic expressions for sex organs and sex acts rather than the "vulgar" terms children will pick up later from others of their own age. Public use of technical sex terminology is permissible, whereas the use of corresponding "Anglo-Saxon monosyllables" is taboo. Although the one-syllable words refer to the same objects and events, they convey very different attitudes. Because words evoke attitudes, such Anglo-Saxon terms have been considered inappropriate in public discussion, but this taboo has been considerably relaxed in recent years.

Anthropologists agree that, although great variations in sexual codes exist, no society sanctions all aspects of all sex behavior and every society frowns upon and forbids certain sex acts. These taboos rest upon basic assumptions concerning the nature of the world, of humans, and of the sexes and their relations. As generations succeed one another—at least in our Western world—they develop different philosophies of sex and partly reject the standards of previous generations. Each new generation in turn sets up new standards and taboos which it believes to be improvements on the old ones. This process of substituting one set of mores for another is likely to be called "emancipation" by young people and "immorality" by their elders. It should not be assumed that this process of change over the generations means progress toward a sexual utopia in which everyone will be completely emancipated. Indeed, the very term "emancipated" is meaningless. What is more, sexual codes have a tendency to move back and forth, to change from relative laxity to relative stringency and vice versa in pendulum-like fashion. Changes in the styles of women's and men's clothing, for example, have often reflected quite clearly some of these changes in sexual attitudes.

We are concerned in this chapter with the worlds in which children live and with noting that with respect to sexual matters as in other areas of behavior, the child's world tends to change as adult sexual practices and ideas change. For the most part, however, change occurs more slowly in the child's world than it does in some segments of the adult population, especially those that attract the attention of the media because of their radical views and practices in the sexual field. For some time adult talk has been becoming more open and frank on sexual matters, but the strong resistance to sexual education for the young by significant portions of the population suggests that many children continue to be brought up in the older traditional ways. It would be a mistake to assume that explicit discussion and representation of sexual matters in the literate tradition as exemplified, for example, by a recent long-term bestseller by Comfort (4), will at once have profound effects on young children of parents who are relatively unimpressed by the literate tradition. It is also too soon to speculate on the effects that the women's liberation movement, the "pill," and other contemporary innovations are likely to have on the child's world. A woman student of one of the authors recently told him about having been a member of the drug culture, but she went on to say that that was now all behind her, that she now had a child to take care of, and that she certainly did not want her child to follow her path. The same, we think, is often true in the sexual field. In Chapter 14 there is a fuller discussion of other issues in the sexual field that are of interest to social psychologists.

Laypersons and even students of child behavior frequently make the mistake of anthropomorphism; they project adult attitudes and conceptions onto the child, or regard children's ideas and modes of thought and behavior as curious forms of error. This tendency to interpret the behavior of children with concepts derived from and appropriate to adults is also noticeable in the study of the child's sex behavior.

The fallacy is aggravated by the use of the same terms in describing child and adult behavior, or by employing such hazily defined terms as

MISCONCEPTIONS OF CHILD BEHAVIOR

"libido" and "sexual." While the popularization of psychoanalytic theories and concepts has undoubtedly swept away many of the puritanical and mid-Victorian misconceptions about children, it has sometimes opened the way to errors of another kind. Thus, when one states that the infant masturbates, it is usually assumed that infant and adult masturbation are equivalent acts—a very dubious assumption, indeed. The rebellion against the reluctance of past generations to face sexual facts has led to an excess of zeal in discovering sexuality in the behavior of children. *It must be emphasized that children live in a world of their own; they have their own concepts, their own ways of acting, and their own perspectives.* It is just as erroneous to judge children's behavior by adult standards or to read adult motives into it as it is to measure African Bantu behavior by adult American standards.

To describe the behavior of lower animals in human terms leads almost inevitably, as we have seen, to anthropomorphism. Similar strictures apply to descriptions of the behavior of the human child. One has no more right to attribute sophisticated sexual ideas and concepts to the behavior of infants than to attribute them to chimpanzees and dogs.

Here are extreme examples of this type of error. Isaacs (21:160)

The behavior of children should not be judged by adult standards; nor should adult motives be read into such behavior. (*Jerome Wexler/Photo Researchers, Inc.*)

Life Cycle: The Genesis of Self

writes: "Penelope and Tommy were playing 'mummy and daddy' and Tommy insisted upon being the mummy." The boy's act is interpreted as an attempt to quiet his fear of castration—yet no data are presented regarding the actual state of the child's sexual knowledge or how he may have obtained it. The child analyst Klein (24:42–46) provides an even more flagrant example. Her patient was a three-year-old boy. Between the ages of eighteen and twenty months, he slept in the same room with his parents and thus had occasional opportunities to witness coitus, if one can stretch the meaning of the word "witness." The child is therefore, writes Klein, fearfully jealous of his father, feels inferior because of his own lack of physical potency, fears that his mother was hurt by coitus, wishes to smash his father's genitals, wishes to kill his father, and so forth. How can such complex ideas be attributed to young children?

Other child psychologists and psychoanalysts have been much more circumspect in their interpretations. Cognizant of the social origins and learned nature of sexual behavior, many psychoanalysts have pointed out weaknesses in Freud's theory that feminine character may be largely explained in terms of "penis envy" (see Chapter 10) and reactions to it. According to this theory, which Freud reiterated in one of his last books, when the young girl discovers that every boy has a penis she is disappointed and shocked at her own lack of the same organ. (See Chapter 10.) Hence she develops a sense of inferiority or penis envy. The traits of character she develops in her childhood and adult years are, according to Freud, the consequences of her attempt to adjust to her sense of inferiority. But the sociologist is inclined to note that reactions of this type are associated with the patriarchal organization of Western European society—that is, a society in which men and masculine values are relatively dominant. This patriarchal situation, however, is by no means universal, even in Western society.

Disinterested investigation of girls' reactions to the discovery of genital differences, such as that by Conn and Kanner (5:444–88) shows beyond question that girls do not always respond with penis envy. It is true that some girls exhibit envious feelings, but most do not. Instead they accept these differences in a matter-of-fact manner or react with amusement. In the light of the learned character of such behavior, one would not expect all girls to react identically. Freud's overstatement of the case should lead us to be wary of equating children's sexual responses with those of their elders.

By word or act, punishment or reward, and through the various media of communication, the young boy and girl learn the sex behavior associated with their roles; they learn to avoid those acts which will evoke reactions of ridicule, disgust, or anger. The taboos are internalized in children to the extent that they become angry and ashamed if they break them.

Summary   The world of early childhood is made up of a complex set of *significant others* who take part in the process of socializing children into the complicated areas of causal understanding about the physical world, as well as into the more intricate topics of morality and sex role behavior. Children quickly relinquish an egocentric conception of their surrounding world and replace that biased view with a more relativistic perspective that is grounded in the multiple perspectives of their generalized others. Children enter the world with no knowledge of sex role differences. Through their interactive experiences with peers and parents and other adults, they soon develop sophisticated images of proper "male" and "female" behavior. A society's institutions of education take on the major assignment of teaching children what these differences between the "sexes" are.

References   1. Aries, Phillipe, *Centuries of Childhood*. New York: Random House, 1962.
2. Bridges, K., *The Social and Emotional Level of the Preschool Child*. London: Routledge & Kegan Paul, 1931.
3. Brown, R., *Social Psychology*. New York: The Free Press, 1965.
4. Comfort, A., *The Joy of Sex. A Cordon Bleu Guide to Love Making*. New York: Crown Publishers, 1972.
5. Conn, J. H., and L. Kanner, "Children's Awareness of Sex Differences," *Journal of Child Psychiatry*, vol. 1 (1947), pp. 3–57.
6. Coutu, W., "Role-Playing versus Role-Taking: An Appeal for Clarification," *American Sociological Review*, vol. 16 (1951), pp. 180–84.
7. Denzin, Norman K., *Socialization: Studies in the Development of Language, Social Behavior, and Identity*. San Francisco: Jossey-Bass, 1977.
8. ———, "The Genesis of Self in Early Childhood," *Sociological Quarterly*, vol. 13 (Summer 1972), pp. 291–314.
9. Durkin, Dolores, "Children's Acceptance of Reciprocity as a Justice Principle," *Child Development*, vol. 30 (1959) pp. 289–96.
10. ———, "Children's Concept of Justice: A Comparison with the Piaget Data," *Child Development*, vol. 30 (1959), pp. 58–67.
11. Edgerton, Robert B., "Pokot Intersexuality: An East African Example of the Resolution of Sexual Incongruity," *American Anthropologist*, vol. 66 (December 1964), pp. 1288–99.
12. Erikson, E. H., *Childhood and Society*. New York: W. W. Norton, 1950.
13. Flavell, John H., *The Developmental Psychology of Jean Piaget*. New York: Van Nostrand Reinhold, 1963.
14. Garfinkel, Harold, *Studies in Ethnomethodology*. Englewood Cliffs, N.J.: Prentice-Hall, 1967.
15. Gerth, H., and C. W. Mills, *Character and Social Structure*. New York: Harcourt Brace Jovanovich, 1963.
16. Hartley, E., M. Rosenbaum, and S. Schwartz, "Children's Perceptions of Ethnic Group Membership," *Journal of Psychology*, vol. 26 (1948), pp. 387–98.
17. Harvey, O., et al., *Conceptual Systems and Personality Organization*. New York: Wiley, 1961.

18. Henry, Jules, *Culture against Man*. New York: Random House, 1963.
19. Hoffman, H., "Child Rearing Practices and Moral Development: Generalizations from Empirical Research," *Child Development*, vol. 34 (1963), pp. 295–318.
20. Hurlock, E. B., *Child Development*. New York: McGraw-Hill, 1950.
21. Isaacs, S. S., *Social Development in Young Children*. London: Routledge & Kegan Paul, 1933.
22. Joffe, Carole, "Sex Role Socialization and the Nursery School: As the Twig Is Bent," *Journal of Marriage and the Family*, vol. 33 (August 1971), pp. 467–75.
23. Kinsey, A. C., et al., *Sexual Behavior in the Human Male*. Philadelphia: W. B. Saunders, 1948.
24. Klein, M., *The Psychoanalysis of Children*. London: Hogarth, 1932.
25. Kohlberg, L., "Cognitive Stages and Preschool Education," *Human Development*, vol. 9 (1966), pp. 5–7.
26. ———, "The Development of Children's Orientations toward a Moral Order: A Sequence in the Development of Moral Thought," *Vita Humana*, vol. 6. (1963), pp. 11–33.
27. ———, "Moral Development and Identification," in *National Society for the Study of Education* (62nd Yearbook). Chicago: University of Chicago Press, 1963.
28. Kuhn, M. H., and Thomas S. McPartland, "An Empirical Investigation of Self-Attitudes," *American Sociological Review*, vol. 19 (February 1954), pp. 68–78.
29. ———, "Self-Attitudes by Age, Sex, and Professional Training," *The Sociological Quarterly*, vol. 1 (1960), pp. 39–55.
30. Lerner, E., "The Problem of Perspective in Moral Reasoning," *American Journal of Sociology*, vol. 30 (1937), pp. 249–69.
31. Macaulay, E., and S. Watkins, "An Investigation into the Moral Conceptions of Children," *Educational Forum*, vol. 4 (1926), pp. 13–33, 92–108.
32. MacRae, E. R., "A Test of Piaget's Theories of Moral Development," *Journal of Abnormal and Social Psychology*, vol. 49 (1954), pp. 14–18.
33. Markey, James F., *The Symbolic Process and Its Integration in Children*. New York: Harcourt Brace Jovanovich, 1928.
34. Mead, G. H., *Mind, Self, and Society*. Chicago: University of Chicago Press, 1934.
35. Mead, Margaret, and Martha Wolfenstein (eds.), *Childhood in Contemporary Cultures*. Chicago: University of Chicago Press, 1955.
36. Mills, C. W., "Language, Logic, and Culture," *American Sociological Review*, vol. 4 (1939), pp. 670–75.
37. Murphy, G., L. Murphy, and T. Newcomb, *Experimental Social Psychology*. New York: Harper & Row, 1937.
38. Opie, Iona, and Peter Opie, *Children's Games in Street and Playground*. New York: Oxford University Press, 1969.
39. Parten, M. B., "Social Participation among Preschool Children," *Journal of Abnormal and Social Psychology*, vol. 27 (1932), pp. 263–69.
40. Piaget, J., *The Child's Conception of Number*. New York: Humanities Press, 1952.
41. ———, *The Child's Conception of Physical Causality*. Paterson, N.J.: Littlefield, Adams, 1960.
42. ———, *The Child's Conception of the World*. New York: Humanities Press, 1951.
43. ———, *The Construction of Reality in the Child*. New York: Basic Books, 1954.

44. ———, *Judgment and Reasoning in the Child*. New York: Humanities Press, 1952.
45. ———, *The Language and Thought of the Child*. New York: Humanities Press, 1959.
46. ———, *The Moral Judgment of the Child*. New York: The Free Press, 1948.
47. ———, *The Origins of Intelligence in Children*. New York: International Universities Press, 1952.
48. ———, *Play, Dreams, and Imitation in Childhood*. New York: W. W. Norton, 1951.
49. ———, "Principal Factors Determining Intellectual Evolution from Childhood to Adult Life," in *Factors Determining Human Behavior*. Cambridge, Mass.: Harvard University Press, 1937, pp. 32–48.
50. ———, and Bärbel Inhelder. *The Psychology of the Child*. New York: Basic Books, 1969.
51. Strauss, A. L., "The Development of Conceptions of Rules in Children," *Child Development*, vol. 23 (1954), pp. 193–208.
52. ———, "The Development and Transformation of Monetary Meanings in the Child," *American Sociological Review*, vol. 17 (1952), pp. 275–86.
53. Ushenko, A. P., "'Truth in Science and Philosophy," *Philosophy of Science*, vol. 21 (1954), pp. 101–17.
54. Vygotsky, L. S., *Thought and Language*. Cambridge, Mass.: M.I.T. Press, 1962.
55. Wallach, M. A., "Research on Children's Thinking," in *National Society for the Study of Education* (62nd Yearbook). Chicago: University of Chicago Press, 1963.
56. Whiting, Beatrice B. (ed.), *Six Cultures: Studies of Child Rearing*. New York: Wiley, 1963.
57. Wright, Richard, *Black Boy*. New York: Harper & Row, 1945.

Selected Readings

GARFINKEL, HAROLD, *Studies in Ethnomethodology*. Englewood Cliffs, N.J.: Prentice-Hall, 1967.
Contains an important study of an individual who attempted to alter his sex role identification.

HENRY, JULES, *Culture against Man*. New York: Random House, 1963.
A major study by an American anthropologist which probes the ways in which the family and educational systems mold the behavior of young children.

MEAD, MARGARET, AND MARTHA WOLFENSTEIN (eds.), *Childhood in Contemporary Cultures*. Chicago: University of Chicago Press, 1955.
Offers an informative set of studies and essays on children in various countries and at different points in history. Written largely from the anthropological and psychoanalytic points of view.

PIAGET, JEAN, AND BÄRBEL INHELDER, *The Psychology of the Child*. New York: Basic Books, 1969.
A summary of these psychologists' studies of early childhood.

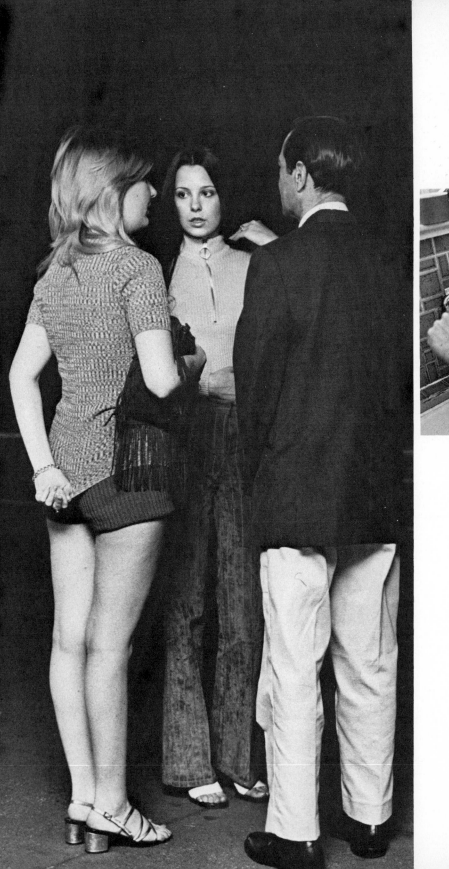

PART FOUR

Life Cycle: Adult Transformations

chapter 12

Self-Control, Social Control, and Identity Transformation

*T*he *self* is not a fixed product; it is not set at the conclusion of childhood, as Freud might have implied. In Part Four we examine the transformations of self which occur in later phases of the life cycle. Some have divided the life cycle, without great success, into the phases of *infancy, childhood, adulthood, middle age, old age,* and *death.* Chapters 12–16 take up the last four phases. We intend to demonstrate that the self changes as its social relationships and social worlds undergo transformation.

In earlier chapters we considered how the internal environment of the individual is categorized, perceived, and brought into systematic relation with the outside world. Central to this process is the development of self-awareness, the acquisition of language, and the ability to put the self in the perspective of another individual. Society, as Cooley (8) argued, exists inside the individual in the form of language and thought. Society and the individual are, to use his term, "two sides of the same coin." We wish to develop this point one step further by examining in greater detail the links between self-control, social control, and the transformations of self that emerge during the interaction process.

In Chapter 10 we noted that individuals act in ways to salvage and enhance their self-conceptions. In this chapter we shall examine those situations where individuals often find themselves denied the rights of esteem. Few individuals voluntarily submit to derogation, embarrassment, or self-mortification. Such activities do, however, occur, and with a patterned regularity that crosscuts small groups, total institutions, and intimate friendship circles. The circumstances that give rise to these interactional experiences will be examined.

We propose the following model of analysis. Individuals can *cede self-control,* that is, give up a degree of autonomy over their thoughts and actions, voluntarily—as in the case of hypnosis; involuntarily—as in the case of a mental hospital or a prison camp; or they can find, quite unexpectedly, that in the course of an emergent interactional episode that their fellow individuals have suddenly turned against them. Or they may find that the compounds they have ingested suddenly leave them with no immediate control over their own thoughts and actions.

If we examine the sources to which self-control can be ceded, the following distinctions are relevant. First, individuals may voluntarily give over control to another individual, perhaps a psychiatrist or a physician. Second, they can place themselves in the hands of a small group. Third, they may find that they are in the clutches of a complex organization, perhaps the military, or a mental hospital. Fourth, they may commit themselves to, or find that they are under the control of an ideology or an abstract cause, such as communism or a deviant cult. In a strict sense, commitment to a cause leads the individual into direct interactions with other individuals who may be caught up in organizations or small groups. This set of distinctions produces twelve possible relationships between the source of ceding control and the mode of ceding control. It is beyond the scope of this chapter to discuss these twelve ideal-type cases. We only note in passing that the relationship between who controls the individual and how that control has been gained is quite complex. Further, we must indicate that in some situations single individuals gain control over broad segments of the population, as politicians do. Finally, throughout this discussion the question of what is given up must be continually raised. Few individuals find themselves in situations where all aspects of their life have fallen under the complete control of another individual or group. Some slices of the self inevitably remain free from the control of others, even the decision to die. That is, coercion is seldom complete; only parts of the individuals' activities and self-conceptions come under the control of others. Even during instances of potentially total coercion (prison camps, solitary confinement), individuals attempt to keep control over the "deepest" and most sacred parts of their selves. They will fight to the bitter end to maintain segments of self-respect, to preserve control over their own thoughts, and to protect the sanctity, privacy, and inviolability of their physical bodies.

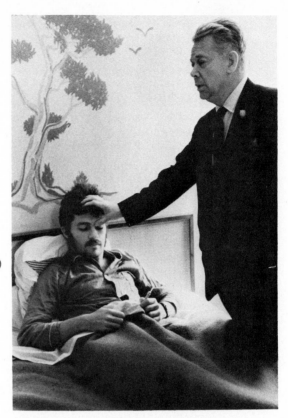

Voluntary ceded self-control? (*Magnum*)

Our discussion in this chapter is guided by two central questions: How is an individual's control of his or her own actions related to societal control of his or her actions? And, how can an individual's actions be controlled by another person or persons? To answer such questions, we shall discuss several topics that at first thought may seem quite unrelated. However, each bears on the issues of self-control and social control. We shall discuss the nature of voluntary behavior, the phenomenon of hypnosis, the loss of self-control, and the institutionally induced changes in individuals that cause them either to cede a measure of their own control to others or to change radically the social bases of their own self-control. Also, the circumstances of group commitment, embarrassment, degradation, and paranoia will be examined.

Voluntary Behavior

The popular conception of voluntary behavior is that it involves control of behavior by an internal psychological force called "will" or "will power." This force is not thought of as being dependent upon any specific biological or neurological structure and is usually believed to be "free" and, therefore, essentially unpredictable. Its most typical manifestation is in choosing among alternatives.

The discerning student will recognize in this commonly held but naïve view the same dualistic distinction that is generally made between thinking and language. Just as language supposedly expresses thinking and is its vehicle, so voluntary behavior is supposed to be merely an expression of the person's will.

A sounder and more scientific view is the conception of voluntary behavior as a type of activity that depends upon the internalization of language. We have noted that as one ascends the evolutionary scale from the simplest forms of life to humans, the central nervous system assumes greater and greater dominance. Internal cortical processes are not solely determined by stimuli from outside the nervous system, but depend also upon stimuli that originate within the system. Voluntary behavior, from this point of view, depends upon the ability of people to initiate responses within themselves which in turn inhibit or facilitate other responses. These controlling responses are verbal in nature or are derived from verbal behavior.

As a simple example, we may note that although persons ordinarily drop hot objects automatically, they can be prevented from doing so if they are warned in advance and thus conditioned not to drop them. If subjects are told that a painfully but not dangerously hot object will be placed in their hand for two seconds and that they will be given fifty dollars if they do not let go, they are likely to inhibit their ordinary reflexes.

Views of volitional behavior that are remarkably alike in some of their basic outlines have been developed by the following men: Clark Hull (from the study of hypnosis and suggestibility); A. R. Luria (through the experimental study of child psychology and of hypnotism); H. Head and K. Goldstein (from the study of aphasia, as discussed in Chapter 7); and C. V. Hudgins (from experiments on voluntary control of the pupillary reflex).

Hull (26) finds that there are two fairly distinct levels of human behavior: "an upper or symbolic level, and a lower nonsymbolic or instrumental level." Symbolic acts are described as "pure stimulus acts, acts that function purely as stimuli to evoke other acts." The most common form of symbolic behavior is speech. Hull applied this scheme to hypnotism and voluntary behavior. He indicated that in the hypnotic situation the symbolic stimulation is (1) produced by one individual, and (2) carried out on the instrumental level by another. In voluntary behavior, however, the same person performs both the symbolic act and its instrumental sequel. For example, a hypnotized man drinks a glass of water because he is told to do so by the hypnotist, whereas in ordinary life he drinks a glass of water because he tells himself to do so. The "will" is thus conceived by Hull as a symbolic process or as control of one's own behavior through self-stimulation (what he calls "pure stimulus acts").

Hudgins (25) has demonstrated experimentally that individuals' control of their own responses by verbal mechanisms can be extended even to some reflex activities that are ordinarily beyond voluntary control (for example, the pupillary reflex). The way in which the result was accomplished throws a great deal of light on what is sometimes called the "will." Subjects were first conditioned to produce the pupillary reflex when a bell was sounded through the simultaneous flashing of a light into their eyes. An electric circuit was then arranged so that when the subjects closed their hands at the vocal command of the investigator the light and bell circuits were closed, thereby causing the bell to ring and the light to go on. Finally, all other stimuli except the verbal command were eliminated and the subjects' pupils were observed to contract when the experimenter gave the command. The next step in developing voluntary control of this conditioned response was to require the subjects themselves to repeat the verbal cue. The commands were first repeated aloud, then in a whisper, and last subvocally. The subjects were finally able to cause the pupils of their own eyes to contract merely by thinking of the verbal command.

Luria (37), approaching the study of voluntary behavior from another perspective, also emphasizes that it involves the use by the individual of auxiliary verbal cues. He notes that people do not control their behavior directly by the exertion of "will power," but can do so only indirectly through the mediation of verbal self-stimulation. For example, if a despondent woman is urged to "buck up and be cheerful," she cannot do so merely by wishing it. However, if her attention can be directed to more cheerful subjects by talking with her or by inducing her to engage in some recreational activity such as a game of tennis, the desired result may be accomplished. Similarly, as Hudgins's experiment indicates, no one can cause the pupils of his or her eyes to contract merely by concentrating or exerting "will power." Intermediate steps, such as those used by Hudgins, must be included.

From this point of view, will power ceases to be conceived as a psychological force and becomes a number of complexly interrelated central processes deriving from the internalization of language and speech. Just as memory may be jogged by tying a string around one's finger, so do the culturally derived language mechanisms function as mediating and structuring devices through which self-regulation is achieved. *Self-control and voluntary behavior are thus conceived as products of external influences emanating from the cultural environment, rather than as the unfolding of vague, disembodied innate propensities of the organism.* Some sort of conception of this general nature seems to us to be required to make sense of the kinds of phenomena considered in this chapter.

The views of Hull and Luria, and the experimental results obtained by Hudgins and others, all point toward the same conclusion. Further corroborating evidence is found in the study of aphasics who loose a large part of their voluntary self-control and initiative when, because of the impairment of their language abilities, they are no longer able to stimulate themselves by means of verbal cues. That people stimulate themselves by their own verbal activities complicates the problem of controlled experiments with human subjects, as many psychologists have noted. (6)

Like the notion of will itself, the idea of "freedom of will" is based upon a false view of symbolic behavior. As a corrective we may note several points. To begin with, "free will" is not entirely free, for it is bounded, restricted, and limited by the culture of the actor. Thus, it does not occur to the readers of this book to make choices involving the values of the Bantu, Japanese, or Balinese, or to act like these people. This may appear to be a trite observation, but its truth is often ignored. It is, for example, commonplace to blame persons who, from an objective point of view, ought not to be blamed. Thus, children are often held responsible for stealing before they know what stealing really means. Our blaming rests upon the assumption that these persons know better and have a genuine choice of attitude and act. This assumption is often false. Whatever "will" may be, it cannot operate outside the confining limits of the actor's system of symbols.

Human social behavior is not mechanically determined by immediately given external events and situations. It is organized symbolically. Human freedom is thus a relative matter. Humans are not entirely bound by the physical conditions of space and time, but they are enclosed within symbolic systems. The thoughts of a prisoner in solitary confinement cannot be controlled by his jailers, but they are controlled and limited by the social groups that have imposed their standards, moral codes, and symbols upon him.

One of the authors once listened to a passionate plea for individual freedom addressed to a class of several hundred students by one of its members. The speaker argued that "the individual" should free him- or herself from all "herd" influences, from all groups and institutions; that he or she should think and act as a free individual. This view represents a logical consequence of the popular misconceptions of "freedom," "free will," and "individuality." Its essential absurdity will be clear to anyone who reflects upon it for a moment. In the first place, if this student desired to be free of all institutions, he obviously should not have learned English or any other language. He should not have attended a university or have spoken to a class as he did. The obvious implication of his view is that humans can be free only if they avoid all human contact and civilization.

Many years ago the French sociologist E. Durkheim opposed individualistic notions of freedom and autonomy by pointing to the body of moral and social rules that are chronologically antecedent to the birth of every individual. These group rules Durkheim saw as largely controlling the behavior of individual members, duty and voluntary behavior being closely linked. Durkheim stressed that concepts and categories are supraindividual, the product of collective activities, and that since individual thinking necessarily utilizes concepts, the idea of individual volition apart from norms is an illusory one. C. Blondel (3) has modified this position by arguing that it is not necessary to deny genuine individual autonomy merely because a person must always make choices within a framework provided by society. Freedom of the individual, he contends, is itself a social product. Human beings, in contrast to lower animals, are free precisely because they are social animals living primarily in a symbolic world. To this should be added a point which we have already made in another context, namely, that no two situations are ever completely identical; hence, all behavior possesses some degree of novelty, and some of it requires genuine decisions. The discovery of values and the consequent organization of behavior along new lines free humans from slavish obedience to tradition; at the same time, tradition enters into the organization of new as well as customary behavior.

Social control is often erroneously thought of as something that is achieved by formal governmental agencies and officially promulgated rules and regulations. Actually, most people do what they ought or have to do simply because they want to. It is only against this background of willing conformity that the formal agencies of control can be effective.

SOCIAL CONTROL AND COMMITMENT TO GROUPS

The above argument may be summarized by saying that social control and self-control are interlocked and interdependent processes. This interrelationship is brought about because people find self-fulfillment, self-expression, and a sense of identity and personal worth primarily through commitment to various kinds of groups and the standards of those groups. This point is well stated by Kanter, who, on the basis of her study of communes, remarks (28:65–66):

> For communal relations to be maintained, what a person is willing to give to the group, behaviorally and emotionally, and what it in turn expects from him, must be coordinated and mutually reinforcing. This reciprocal relationship, in which both what is given to the group and what is received from it are seen by the person as expressing his true nature and as supporting his concept of self, is the core commitment to a community.

In terms of the above statement, we may say that social control can be effective only when persons identify with the group and internalize its values so that it becomes essential to their own sense of self-esteem and personal worth to act so as to support the social order. They hold, in short, a sense of involvement and belonging; they think of the group as an extension or part of themselves and make its values and rules their own personal values and rules. They have lodged a portion of themselves in the group. The group has become a part of them. It exerts its influence over them in symbolic as well as in direct behavioral ways. Again quoting Kanter (28:66–67): "Commitment links self-interest to social requirements. . . . When a person is committed, what he wants to do is the same as what he has to do, and this gives to the group what it needs to maintain itself at the same time that he gets what he needs to nourish his own sense of self." As Kanter says (28:66): "A committed person is loyal and involved; he has a sense of belonging, a feeling that the group is an extension of himself and he is an extension of the group." That is, in social control there is always self-control, and in self-control there is always social control. By the same token, lack of self-control is often a reflection of an absence of social control. But without individuals committed to their maintenance, social groups would collapse. In this sense, persons create and contribute to the very situations that control their own lives, fates, and careers.

EMBRACEMENT AND DISTANCE

When individuals have committed themselves instrumentally, emotionally, and morally to a social group they may be said to have *embraced* that group's universe of discourse. Embracement produces both moral solidarity and a solidified group perspective. It is a mistake, however, to assume that all members of any group mutually and with equal enthusiasm commit themselves to the group's demands. In a different context, Goffman (16) has introduced the concept of *role distance* to describe those moments when individuals place a wedge between themselves and the role they are playing. Adults riding merry-go-rounds, for example, typically act as if they wish they were not seated on the wooden horse, while young children vigorously throw themselves into the activity of horse rider. In the present context we can propose that on occasion members of all groups place a wedge between themselves and the demands that their groups place on them. These "self-distancing" activities may include refusals to meet the requests of other group members or may be displayed in a progressive withdrawal from the group entirely. There is, then, a constant tension between the demands of the group and the demands individuals place on themselves. Total, complete, and continuous commitment and embracement to social groups is an infrequent occurrence. More typical are moments of heightened involvement, followed by periods of disinvolvement, disengagement, and self-distancing.

Role distance on the merry-go-round. (*Mimi Forsyth for Monkmeyer Press Photo Service*)

The problem we are concerned with below is the relationship between self-control and propaganda. For example, consider the man who implicitly believes what he reads in his favorite newspaper, what the latest government handout says, or what a particular television commentator announces. Is this person really a free agent? Or is the dupe of propaganda comparable to the hypnotized man who says, does, and apparently believes whatever he is told to say, do, or believe? If the latter answer is accepted, then it is probably necessary for most if not all of us to admit that we are almost continuously, in varying degrees, being manipulated by outside persons, agencies, and forces which shape our symbolic environments, our conceptions of the world. They do this in ways that often have little relationship to the real objective world—whatever that may be. Granting this situation, the important point really may be whether we are permitted to cherish the delusions of intellectual mastery of our environments and of being free and autonomous individuals. These, by the way, are delusions that the subject who acts out posthypnotic suggestions also ordinarily entertains.

PROPAGANDA

Persons who are relatively unaware of the pervasiveness of propaganda—having committed themselves to a general political or social philosophy—tend to select media sources that present them with views that they are predisposed to accept. They also tend to have friends and to belong to groups that reinforce their opinions and that rely on the same sources for support of their opinions. In this process of mutual reinforcement there is selective inattention to information and interpretations not in harmony with the person's basic social and political assumptions, which may be anywhere on the political spectrum from the extreme left to the extreme right. (5, 49) Some persons commonly have the comfortable illusion that they have valid and reliable information about, and are responding rationally to, their environment and have it under control in an intellectual sense.

On the other hand, there are people who develop a feeling that they are being manipulated by external forces that control events, social policy, and the flow of information. They tend to emphasize the unreliability of mass media reports and interpretations. They commonly assume the existence of extensive behind-the-scene news conspiracies by rich and powerful persons, corporations, or organizations to manipulate people, events, and information in their own interests for the sake of wealth, power, or other material advantage. Persons with such views are known to most of us; they tend to feel a sense of futility and helplessness with respect to the broad social and political issues and often simply ignore them and commit themselves only to small, restricted groups like the family. Others, who entertain the idea that things can be changed, may commit themselves to reform groups or "revolutionary" movements.

Interactional Loss of Self-Control

In the preceding section we discussed the situation where individuals cede self-control to a group or cause. Often voluntary and positive in consequence, these exercises in self-exchange involve planning and reciprocal commitments by the persons ceding control and by those who receive their goods, resources, and self-identities. They gain something positive for what they give. The tenuous, yet complex relationship between selves and others can be further elaborated by examining the situation of *interactional loss.* Such moments, which may be planned or unplanned, collusively based or emergent in tone, self-initiated or other-initiated, describe those occasions when individuals find their fellow interactants have either unexpectedly turned against them or now define them as less-than-competent selves. While on occasion planned—as when a person is a defendant in a divorce case—most typically these moments arise unexpectedly and catch them off guard. Incidents of this kind range from the deliberate embarrassment or harassment of individuals, to degradation ceremonies, self-mortification rituals, and collusively based conspiracies to drive someone from an organization. Then, people find that their ability to control and protect their valued self-identities have been denied, if not suddenly taken away.

In this section we examine the conditions that give rise to this in-

Life Cycle: Adult Transformations

teractional loss of self-control. For purposes of simplicity we focus on three forms of interactional loss: (1) emergent loss, as seen in embarrassment; (2) preplanned exclusion and self-loss, as witnessed in the degradation ceremony; and (3) emergent exclusion, which is common in instances of imputed paranoia or mental illness.

Any instance of emergent or planned self-loss requires time. Some moments are preceded by events which unfold in a serial fashion. That is, an individual is not just mortified, embarrassed, or degraded; a set of mutually held definitions of the situation must be brought into play if an instance of self-loss is to occur. In a certain sense individuals cooperate in their own mortification, and they act so as to sustain or justify definitions in which they have been judged as less than competent. It is a mistake to assume that when self-control is ceded over to others this ceding involves only one set of actors—those taking from the individual in question. It involves at least two parties: one to offer a definition, and another to accept or fight off that definition. Such moments are interactional productions.

EMBARRASSMENT: THE CASE OF EMERGENT SELF-LOSS

Consequently, we can see that it takes two parties to produce an instance of embarrassment—one party who acts in a less than propitious manner and another party who acts on those untoward actions. In this sense we agree with Gross and Stone, who argue that (18:1):

> Embarrassment exaggerates the core dimensions of social transaction, bringing them to the eye of the observer in an almost naked state. Embarrassment occurs whenever some *central* assumption in a transaction has been *unexpectedly* and unqualifiedly discredited for at least one participant. . . . Moreover embarrassment is infectious. It may spread, incapacitating others not previously incapacitated. It is a destructive disease. In the wreckage left by embarrassment lie the broken foundations of social transactions.

Embarrassment produces, according to Goffman's (16) formulations, moments of "flooding out." Individuals lose control over themselves, their occasions, and their respective involvements. Action stops, and attempts to smooth over the flawed episode only acknowledge that something untoward has occurred. In short, to act on an instance of embarrassment can be as embarrassing as the original episode itself. Hence, individuals employ elaborate avoidance or defensive techniques to act as if an instance of embarrassment had not occurred. But these strategies need not concern us at this point. More to the point are those actions that produce the interactional discomfort of embarrassment. Following Goffman and Gross and Stone, we can note that any of the following acts or activities can cause an embarrassing incident in the flow of interaction. First, individuals can display a lack of poise. They stumble, spill a drink, drop a cigarette, unaccountably touch another person, or perhaps give off an odor that discredits their claim of respectability. A person may also lose poise when he or she intrudes into the private settings of others, dresses improperly for a particular social occasion, or is the host of a cocktail party with no electricity or an inadequate supply of food and drink.

By failing to measure up to the demands of the occasion, the individual calls into question the actions of all those who have conformed to social expectations. To be in the company of an embarrassing actor not only challenges one's own credibility, but raises the question of why that individual's actions should be regarded as embarrassing; and if they are so judged, why are his or her actions so judged and not those of another person. In these instances, embarrassing actions provoke both sympathy and discomfort. All individuals can locate in their own biographies moments when they acted, or could have acted, in a similar fashion. For this reason, actors typically cooperate to pull one another through the embarrassing transaction. But for the individual in question, a sense of shame, of guilt, and a lack of self-respect are produced. Credible individuals ought not to embarrass others.

If loss of poise produces embarrassment, then it can be seen that presenting an inappropriate identity, or incorrect identification, can also disrupt the flow of interaction. Instances of misnaming, forgotten names, forgotten titles, and mistaken kinship affiliations are in this category. A divorced woman may be asked, innocently, how her former husband is doing. A college president may be misidentified by a member of the police. A faculty member may be taken to be a janitor, perhaps because he dressed like a janitor. Misidentifications intermingle with actions that disturb the sequential flow of sociable gatherings. Individuals may arrive at a cocktail party thinking they have been invited because they are friends of the host or hostess; however, they find they have been invited, not as guests, but as actors who might contribute to the status of the party givers. Having misread the character of the occasion, they may then act so as to quickly bring their role in it to conclusion. They may refuse to talk, talk to excess, exaggerate the effects of alcohol, or demand to be placed center stage. In these senses they juggle the career and development of the party. They actively intrude into the gathering so as to gain some control over their place in it. Feeling that they have been embarrassed because of their own misidentifications, they make no attempt to turn the tables.

DELIBERATE
EMBARRASSMENT
The foregoing examples of embarrassment were focused on unanticipated acts and actions that challenge the credibility of someone in a concrete situation. These accidental acts are less consequential than those that are deliberately produced; for if the individual does not anticipate such an activity, he or she is less accountable for its consequences. De-

liberate embarrassment (18) is more severe. Here members of a group plan in advance to discredit one of their members. They may do so to facilitate socialization into a role or a preferred activity or identity—for example, hazing in the military or in the college fraternity discourages one set of actions and rewards another set—or to halt the performance of an individual who is challenging the social group. Scapegoating, identity slurs, misrepresentations of integrity, and charges of malfeasance set the offended party off from other members of the group. Thus, embarrassment serves as a social control device for social groups. This suggests the third function of embarrassment: it reasserts and reaffirms power alignments, since only certain categories of individuals can legitimately embarrass others. Thus, embarrassment typically flows from the top down. It is bad form for a low-status actor to embarrass a superior, and he or she has less interactional power to command.

DEGRADATION CEREMONIES: PREPLANNED LOSS

With the exception of planned embarrassment, most embarrassing incidents emerge in an unpredictable manner. Neither their definers nor their actors anticipate their occurrence. These incidents are haphazardly, rather awkwardly accepted instances of status-forcing. The problematic individual is forced to accept an otherwise unacceptable definition of self. Degradation ceremonies describe planned and anticipated instances of status-forcing in which derelict individuals know in advance that they will lose self-credibility. Indeed, they may be shamed and openly required to plead guilty. Harold Garfinkel (14) has described the conditions that give rise to successful degradation ceremonies. Persons who are being degraded must be placed outside the everyday moral order and defined as a threat to that order. They may be defined as political criminals, "sex" fiends, child molesters, or murderers. Their actions must be cast in moral terms which threaten the existence of the social group, and their accuser must be defined as a person who is morally superior. The accuser will evoke higher moral values which witnesses accept, and he or she will be defined as a legitimate upholder of those values. If the accuser is successful in his or her attempts, the accused individuals have no options open. They must accept their new status. Degradation ceremonies force them to yield to the wishes of others. They give up control over their own moral career and find that their fate now lies in the hands of others.

PARANOIA: EMERGENT EXCLUSION AND SELF-LOSS

Planned exclusionary rituals are set up in advance and give the charged actor little control over his or her fate. They are to be contrasted with emergent exclusion. Often individuals begin to sense a wedge between themselves and others. They become uneasy, hypertensive; they overreact to the thoughts and actions of others. Such persons are often termed *paranoid*—their behavior is out of line with the realities of social interaction. Edwin Lemert (34), in a series of case studies of paranoid individuals, has come to different conclusions. He suggests that paranoid individuals may, indeed, be accurately reacting to the specifics of their social situation. His analysis is instructive and may be utilized as an instance of a situation in which neither the individual in doubt (a man, say) nor his fellow interactants wish to alter their social relationships. He has no desire to be excluded, and they have no desire to exclude. However, through a course of events, both parties come to reject one another. The person who loses the most is the actor defined as paranoid. He may have nowhere to turn and may be unable to pinpoint accurately the causes of his exclusion; nor can his fellows accurately recount exactly why it was they came to feel uncomfortable when in his presence. The emergence of exclusion rituals follows a relatively predictable career. First, there is an alteration in ongoing relationships. Persistent interpersonal difficulties between the individual and his interactive others lead to a collapse in trust and common understanding. The death of a relative, a threatened status loss, or a failure to be promoted produces a sense of uneasiness on the part of the "preparanoid" individual. This uneasiness, in turn, produces a series of overreactive behaviors toward superiors and close intimates. Arrogance, insults, and exploitations of the weaknesses of others may occur. Third, the individual begins to act in ways judged to be unreliable and dangerous to others. At this point he undergoes a set of redefinitions of both himself and others. He feels they are belittling him. A set of *spurious interactions* emerges. He avoids others and they avoid him. Conversation drops to a minimum, and he begins deliberately to exclude himself from their company. At the same time, they are gossiping behind his back and excluding him from their sociable interactions. Conspiratorial actions now develop. Others openly plot to remove the deviant from their presence and he, correspondingly, may plot to have them removed or seek relocation elsewhere. Delusion sets in. The individual is denied interactional feedback. He has no reliable "reality" check for his inferences and his hunches. No one will talk with or to him. Soon the individual moves into his own social world, and he may, as Goffman notes, produce an insanity of place both for himself and for others (17:390):

> The manic declines to restrict himself to the social game that brings order and sense to our lives. Through his antics he gives up "his" self-respect, this being the reward we would allow him to have for himself as a reward for keeping a social place that may contain no other satisfaction for him. The manic gives up everything a person can be, and gives up too, the everything we make out of jointly guarded dealings. His doing so, and doing so for any of a multitude of independent reasons, reminds us what our everything is, and then reminds us that this everything is not very much. A somewhat similar lesson is taught by other categories of troublemakers who do not keep their place.

In the end, what began as a minor disturbance in interpersonal relationships produces a massive realignment of self and others. A new deviant appears. He loses, as does everyone else. Emergent self-loss of the exclusionary variety vividly highlights the points made earlier, namely, the social order is a symbolic order that must, however tacitly, be jointly maintained by the actions of cooperating individuals.

Embarrassment, degradation, and the dynamics of organizational exclusion are descriptions of three situations where individuals lose more than they gain in their contracts with their outside social worlds. Whether fleeting, as with embarrassment, or preplanned, as in degradation, or emergent and long term, as with paranoia, agents of social control—who after all are fellow interactants—deliberately and unwittingly deny one another's claims of self-worth and self-esteem.

This is not to imply that all instances of self- and social control imply losses for one or more parties. Indeed, our earlier discussion of communes suggested that on many occasions individuals gain a great deal by giving themselves over to a social group, a cause, or an organization. Also, crowdlike collective behavior often produces serious alterations in the social structure. (5, 32, 33, 43, 49) In the next section we discuss the case of hypnosis, which describes a situation where the individual may enter into a relatively neutral relationship with an agent of social control, the hypnotist.

Hypnosis: The Ceding of Self-Control

The phenomenon of hypnosis provides striking examples of symbolic control over a wide range of human behavior. The hypnotized subject may be viewed as one who, in a peculiar sense, is relatively lacking in self-control, because behavior (ordinarily evoked by the person) is evoked by the hypnotist. A whole range of behavior may be elicited from a subject by simply ordering him or her to act and feel in certain ways.

The behavior elicited in hypnosis is in many respects unusual and puzzling. We shall therefore begin our discussion by describing some of it, turning then to the theories that have been proposed to account for it, and finally considering its implications in relation to less extreme behavior of a somewhat similar nature.

What is called the *hypnotic trance* is induced in subjects primarily by talking to them. A variety of specific devices may be used. A woman may be placed in a relaxed position and told that her eyelids are heavy and that she is becoming sleepy. She is also told that, as the hypnotist slowly counts to fifty, her sleepiness will increase until, on the count of fifty, she will be in a deep sleep. The subject may be asked initially to fix her eyes on a bright, rhythmically moving object to facilitate the process. Whatever the specific devices used, the essential factor is communication, usually verbal. Hypnotists cannot, however, induce the trance in anyone with whom they cannot communicate verbally. Lower animals, for example, cannot be hypnotized. Neither can retarded persons, the insane, or very young children.

SUSCEPTIBILITY.   Susceptibility to hypnosis, contrary to popular belief, is not correlated with lack of intelligence or lack of "will power." Persons who follow the commands of the hypnotist and who succeed in focusing on him or her to the exclusion of anything else may be hypnotized even though they do not wish to be and even though they believe that hypnotic phenomena do not exist or are merely "faked." Persons who are overcome by amusement, who think of other matters, or who react in opposition to the commands naturally do not make good subjects.

H. J. Eysenck tells of an experiment with a boastful and arrogant young man who came to the laboratory telling everyone that he did not believe in hypnotism and that no one could hypnotize him. (12:40–41) He continued to make such remarks while the hypnotic suggestions (for example, that he would fall into a deep sleep when the table was struck with a hammer) were being made to him. When the experimenter rapped the table the young man fell at once into a trance, leaving incompleted a sentence in which he had begun to say that he did not believe that a person with strong will power like his could be hypnotized. This subject remained under hypnosis for more than two hours. When he was awakened he completed the sentence that he had started more than two hours earlier and refused to believe that he had been hypnotized until he consulted his watch.

DISTORTION OF PERCEPTIONS.   When the subject, a woman, say, has been hypnotized, she can be induced to do, say, and apparently, believe many things that are contrary to her ordinary behavior and beliefs. She can be made to report seeing and hearing things that the hypnotist tells her she will see and hear, such as thirteen strokes of a nonexistent clock. She will squirm uncomfortably when told she is sitting on a warm radiator, and will reach out happily to gather in coins supposedly raining from the skies. She will eat make-believe fruit, carefully peeling a fictitious banana. Told that a lemon is an apple, she may agree that it tastes like one. J. N. Lewis and T. R. Sarbin (35) have shown that when a subject eats a make-believe meal under deep hypnosis, her gastric hunger contractions are apt to be inhibited as though she were eating real food. Actual perceptions can be "wiped out." Thus, the subject is told she cannot see a pack of cigarettes lying before her, and so will not reach for them when ordered to smoke. She can be told that some person in the room is absent, and when asked to count the people present will omit this person, although she will collide with the person if he or she walks about the room.

One of the most impressive features of hypnosis is the inhibition of pain reactions. As is well known, subjects under hypnosis who have been told that they will feel no pain neither report pain nor flinch when a pin is stuck into their hand or a flame is applied to their finger tips. Although rarely used since the development of anesthetics, hypnosis has been used in surgical operations, dentistry, and childbirth. For purposes of entertainment, hypnotists often demonstrate that hypnosis affects the memory. Some subjects can recite poetry once learned but apparently forgotten, or are able to recall events of early childhood. The subject may also be asked to reenact the first day at school or the tenth birthday, and may do so with seeming fidelity.

POSTHYPNOTIC SUGGESTION.   Posthypnotic action can be suggested during the actual trance. When the subject is being taken out of the trance, it is standard practice to suggest that she will remember nothing that occurred during the session; she will report that she does not remember, even when later urged to try to do so. The subject may be told that five minutes after waking she will feel intense thirst, but will not know why. Five minutes later she will get herself a glass of water. It was reported that one subject was told that when reading the even-numbered pages of a book he would breathe twice as fast as usual, and half as fast as usual when reading the odd-numbered pages. Several weeks later he was still doing this. Some persons have tried to break habits (such as smoking) by means of hypnosis, but this technique is not particularly successful, since the effects of hypnotic suggestion fade out unless they are renewed.

MORAL BEHAVIOR UNDER HYPNOSIS.   A controversial question is whether hypnotic subjects can be made to do anything that will harm them or that is counter to their moral ideas. Affirmative evidence is provided in a report of an investigation by L. W. Rowland. (12) He asked and eventually persuaded one of his subjects to reach out to touch a rubber rope (actually a coiled rattlesnake under glass). After hesitating, some subjects followed his command that they throw acid at him (he was protected by an invisible sheet of glass). It has been argued that the subjects knew they were in an experiment and that therefore the proof is inconclusive. However, of forty-two unhypnotized subjects, forty-one refused to follow instructions about reaching for the snake; the one person who complied did so because she thought it was an artificial snake, but she became frightened when told it was not. Experimentation to determine the limits of this kind of suggestion is beset by obvious difficulties.

Eysenck has made important contributions to the discussion of this aspect of hypnotic phenomena by citing instances that he believes demonstrate that serious infractions of rules, involving very severe punishment, can be produced by hypnosis. Thus, by posthypnotic suggestion a soldier assigned to military duty was induced to desert. (12) A private was hypnotized in the presence of a number of senior army officers and was told by a lieutenant colonel stationed about ten feet in front of him that when he opened his eyes he would see before him a "dirty Jap soldier" determined to bayonet him. The private was told that to save himself he would have to strangle his aggressor with his bare hands. The subject, when he opened his eyes, crept toward the lieutenant colonel, brought him down with a flying tackle, knocked him against the wall and began to strangle him. Three persons were needed to separate the two men. The victim of the attack reported that without immediate help he was sure he might have been killed or seriously injured. An assault upon an officer is, of course, a very serious offense in the army. (2)

CONCEPTUAL CONTROL IN HYPNOSIS.   Some writers have characterized hypnosis as a kind of enthusiastic faking. The argument is that subjects, although they appear not to experience pain or various sensations, or to see objects manifestly present, actually are merely reporting what they think they are supposed to report. This point has been explored in experiments by F. Pattee. (40) He designed a box with two openings (one on the left covered with red glass and one on the right with green glass). Inside the box were prisms that actually reversed the lines of vision. A hypnotized subject was told that he could not see with his left eye; he was then told to look through the box with both eyes open and to report the color that he saw. The subject thought that he saw green and denied seeing the red because he thought that it was his right eye that perceived the green; actually, because of the prisms, it was his left or "blind" eye. Other experiments along similar lines indicate the same sort of results for hearing. Other investigations on the capacity of hypnotized subjects to regress to childhood show conclusively that they do not actually regress, but merely reenact the gestures or simulate the performances that they believe to be appropriate. The performances on this kind of test (including writing, drawing, and IQ test performances) are about the same as those of nonhypnotized persons who are asked to playact. (26, 56, 57)

Skepticism about the actual perceptions of the hypnotized subject is warranted in the light of the aura of mysticism which surrounds the topic in everyday discourse; but in a sense, this skepticism misses the point. Since hypnotism involves control by the central nervous system (that is, through concepts) it is to be expected that the subject acts in terms of his or her own conceptions. An old demonstration will illustrate the point nicely. When he is told that his hand is numb up to the wrist, a subject reports that this line of numbness is there and responds accordingly. He reacts, in other words, according to the conceptions of neurology suggested by the hypnotist, and not in accordance with actual neural structure.

Hull found that although his subjects reported no pain when burned or stuck with pins, in fact automatic emergency reactions were occurring, because changes were observed in pulse rate, respiration, and galvanic skin response. The central problem of hypnosis then has to do not with whether the subject's conceptions or reports are accurate, but why he or she acts as though they were.

Hypnotic compliance with outside commands, requests, or "suggestions" carries an aura of the fantastic or mysterious. Yet conformance with commands, requests, or suggestions under normal waking conditions seems to most people an ordinary fact of life. This is so even when the suggestions and demands are fairly extreme. Even the phenomena of hypnosis find their parallels in normal behavior. To illustrate this to yourself, you might stretch out your arms before you, parallel to the ground, and then imagine that an iron bar runs through your right arm from shoulder to hand. Your right arm is likely to become, as it does in many people, rigid and heavy. Some people, if asked to clasp their hands tightly and imagine them to be stuck together, have momentary difficulty in wrenching them apart. All of us recognize that we can deliberately and imaginatively transport ourselves into certain social situations and so temporarily lose contact with reality. Much behavior is determined by what one believes, fantasizes, or imagines to be true. The mysteriousness of hypnosis arises largely from the fact that the source of control in hypnosis is another person.

Theories of Hypnosis

Theories of hypnosis center around explaining how the outsider gets control. Ordinarily, individuals who receive commands or suggestions make some evaluation of them before translating them into commands that they give themselves. Of course, if you are crossing the street and someone shouts "Look out!" you react without thinking it over; but usually self-stimulation is requisite to action, and involves the regulatory self-system described earlier.

THE CONDITIONED-RESPONSE VIEW.   Among the theoretical explanations of hypnosis is that it is a form of conditioned response. This theory is embodied, for example, in the writings of Hull. (26:397) The central idea is that words become linked with acts and tend to call forth these acts. Hence, "the withdrawal of the subject's symbolic activities would naturally leave his muscles relatively susceptible to the symbolic stimulation emanating continuously from the experimenter." Viewed as a conditioned response, the response to hypnotic suggestions, or indeed to any suggestion, involves no new principles. Pavlov makes this point when he says (41:407): "We can . . . regard 'suggestion' as the most simple form of the typical conditioned reflex in man." The verbal suggestion of the other person is but an external stimulus acting to arouse a conditioned response or a set of such responses. S. E. Asch (1:420) has pointed out that the older speculations on the nature of hypnosis were often very much like present-day conditioning theory.

The stimulus-response conception of hypnosis, like general conditioning theory, is subject to criticism for avoiding the issue of how self-control operates or fails to operate. It assumes that language behavior and all intellectual processes are reducible to stimulus-response mechanisms. By regarding hypnosis as merely another instance of conditioning, this view denies that the phenomenon of hypnosis raises any special problems or that it, in itself, requires any explanation at all.

FREUDIAN INTERPRETATION.   Although Freud used hypnosis in therapy in the early part of his career, he later abandoned it in favor of free association and other psychoanalytic techniques. However, hypnosis is still used in therapy to some extent. Freud viewed the hypnotic relation in terms of dominance and subjection. Other analysts, such as Ernest Jones and Paul Schilder, conceive of it as a kind of sexual response. Analysts generally do not pay much attention to hypnosis or propose specific theories to account for it.

A variant of the Freudian approach is represented by the view of H. Guze. (19) He notes that different hypnotic subjects respond differently to the same command. He interprets this as due to "their typical manner of dealing with their desires and drives." Hence, Guze hypothesizes that "all hypnotic commands become 'wishes' (that is, desires and drives) in the subject's thinking." Subjects handle them as they handle their other wishes; they may accept the wish enthusiastically, resist it but carry it out, reject it, carry it out and feel remorse, and so on. The point that individuals behave differently in response to the same stimulus, whether under hypnosis or not, is well taken. But Guze's account does not particularly advance our knowledge of what hypnotism itself is. Neither is his description of hypnosis as a heightened state of emotion illuminating.

A ROLE THEORY.   Another attempt to explain hypnosis is that it is goal-directed behavior, the object of which is to behave like a hypnotized person, "as this is continuously defined by the operator and as this is understood by the subject." (54:503) This conception implies complementary roles of hypnotizer and hypnotized, and T. R. Sarbin (44) has made this view more explicit. The subject, he says, attempts to enact the role of a hypnotized person, and the success of the attempt is a function of three factors: favorable motivation, role perception, and aptitude for role taking. The subject is likened to an actor on the stage, who also strives to act a fictional, or "as if," role. The hypnotizer is analogous to the stage director. Both actor and hypnotized subject may lose themselves in the excitement of the role, in the sense that they focus full attention on it and fail to notice many events that occur concurrently. Sarbin's account is designed to explain the differential ease with which persons can be hypnotized. Correlation of role-taking ability with susceptibility to hypnosis is not an easy matter to test, since the former ability is a fairly vague one. Sarbin's formulation, however, has the virtue of making the subject an active participant in the hypnotic process rather than a puppet, and it does point to an overall organization of behavior. On the other hand, calling hypnosis "role playing" does not explain it. Such a definition merely says that the behavior is organized much like other behavior and involves a process of interaction. In a sense, hypnosis is explained away by first noting how subjects act, and then suggesting that they act this way because they think they should.

Sarbin's role theory of hypnosis and the view that hypnotic phenomena are somehow fabrications have been satirized by H. J. Eysenck, a hard-nosed, empirically oriented British psychologist. He reports, for example, that when hpnotized subjects are successfully made to regress to earlier birthdays, a simple test of the validity of their experience is to ask them what the day of the week is. Of course, children are usually keenly aware of the day of the week on which their birthday falls, but hardly any adult can remember the day on which the tenth, seventh, or fourth birthday fell. Eysenck states that when regressed under hypnosis, 93 percent of the subjects correctly stated the day of the week of their tenth birthday, 82 percent were correct for their seventh birthday, and 69 percent for their fourth birthday. It is absurd to account for such results by saying that the subject was trying to enact the role of a hypnotized subject. (12:51) The same is true of the subject who goes on talking and does not bother to look at his or her hand when a needle is pushed through it by the hypnotist. Eysenck suggests that persons who think hypnotic phenomena can be imitated should try such experiments on themselves. A hypnotized subject will drink a glass of soapy water with every sign of enjoyment, Eysenck notes, if it has been suggested that he or she is drinking champagne. This is another self-experiment recommended for skeptics. (12:37, 1)

HYPNOSIS
AND SPEECH
MECHANISMS

While hypnosis has been employed primarily in therapy and as a source of entertainment, it is obvious that hypnotic phenomena have great theoretical significance and that hypnosis presents a potent research device. Eysenck suggests that perhaps 85 percent of the population can be hypnotized to some degree. If this potential exists so widely in human beings and is altogether absent in animals, this fact would seem to constitute a theoretical issue of top priority. This is all the more true because it is commonly stated that hypnotic phenomena resemble, or are at least related to, a considerable range of other common human behavioral phenomena, such as those discussed in psychology texts under the heading of suggestibility.

Nevertheless, as the psychologists who explore this area themselves say, there has been relatively little serious scientific effort expended in the attempt to formulate even provisional explanatory theories. Eysenck (12:65), in a brief review of current theories, characterizes the idea derived from Pavlov that hypnosis is like sleep, as "almost certainly false." The conditioned response view, he remarks, ". . . fails completely to account for many of the phenomena associated with hypnosis. . . . Certainly by itself it is not sufficient." Other theories are similarly characterized, and the role theory is called the "weirdest of all."

Since hypnotic behavior is triggered by the hypnotist's verbal cues and suggestions, it seems that a theoretical approach based on the analysis of speech mechanisms is indicated. It is logically impossible to explain behavior that occurs in humans and not in lower animals in terms of mechanisms and processes that are present in both. *The neglect of hypnosis by American psychology and social psychology is probably closely related to the fact that dominant current theories, especially those derived from the study of lower animals, do not handle the existing data.*

From the standpoint of experimental research, the potentials of hypnosis are great because the investigator can induce a wide variety of behavioral and organic manifestations, the sources of which the subject does not know. At the same time, although researchers may not know *how* the effects are produced or what brain mechanisms are involved, they do know that they were triggered by their own commands or suggestions. From the symbolic interactionist viewpoint, hypnotic phenomena point emphatically toward a general conception of humans as creatures in which the higher cortical functions associated with speech and language are dominant and pervasive influences throughout virtually the whole structure of behavior, so that, as Luria (37:428) has said, "we find them literally in every movement of the fingers."

One may perhaps speculate that there may be something like a command center within the neurological structure of the brain, from which emanates messages that stimulate or control other parts of the structure. Two pervasive complementary aspects of the functioning of the nervous system are *inhibitions* and *excitations*. The entire system cannot be equally excited all at once; when one part is in a state of excitement, certain cell assemblies become active, while others are inhibited. The phenomena of hypnotism and other forms of ceding or losing self-control may, on the neurological level, represent this balancing of excitation and inhibitions. Thus, while the command, or self-stimulating, part of the brain seems to be inhibited and inactive in a hypnotized subject, other central functions, such as memory, are apparently facilitated. In loss of control under the influence of alcohol, the inhibition is brought about by chemical influences which interact with self-perceptions and the definitions of others brought to bear upon the drinking individual. It has been observed with respect to alcohol that there is a patterning of effects as drinking proceeds, with the most complex and recently acquired controls being the first to deteriorate or weaken. Drinkers often begin to show this effect by becoming uninhibited in their speech, laughter, and actions and ending up in a state of general stupor.

Institutionally Induced Changes in Self-Control

CEDING CONTROL

People may also deliberately cede over a measure of their own self-control under quite regulated institutional conditions. In a sense this is what happens when students allow a psychologist to convert them into experimental hypnotic subjects. However, there are less equivocal and more ordinary instances of what is really a very complicated social process. We shall select one from a great many possible instances to clarify the point.

Under certain conditions people allow physicians and nurses to do things to their bodies that otherwise they would not permit. The physician says to a man: "I must operate on you." The patient then allows the physician to use drugs that render him temporarily insensible. He allows the physician to remove a bodily part. He also allows the hospital staff to control some other sectors of his life and behavior. They regulate his movements by confining him to his bed or room. They regulate his waking hours by taking away his control over when he will sleep (giving him drugs to induce sleep), or when he will eat (feeding him in accordance with a given schedule), or how he will eat (feeding him intravenously). All these events are fairly institutionalized, regularized, or routinized because the hospital is organized for this purpose. If the patient's condition warrants different kinds of control, he may be sent from one medical service to another within the same hospital.

If we observe closely we also note that the ceding of control from patient to hospital staff is not a static phenomenon. As the patient's condition worsens he may agree, explicitly or implicitly, to further loss of control over his own activities. As he gets better he is given, or requests, or demands that some of that control be ceded back to him. Disagreements occur daily between staff and patients in hospitals over just this matter, and a considerable amount of negotiation within hospitals pertains to setting these matters straight. A study of cardiac patients with "infarctions" has shown that after patients have been hospitalized they tend to judge their condition by the amount of pain they still experience. If there is considerable pain they will not wish to recover as much control as the staff wishes them to regain, and the staff may be annoyed at their over-anxiety. (24) More frequently the annoyance runs in the opposite direction, because the staff will not allow patients to act as they feel they have the right to act. Since most illnesses run a course (upward or downward), the negotiation over control between patient and staff is potentially, if not always actually, an explosive process.

This explosiveness is dramatic in situations in which patients are dying. (15) Suppose that a man thinks that he is quite sick, but the staff has informed his family that he is dying. Everyone controls his or her own responses so as to prevent the patient's coming "into awareness." When patients finally understand their real condition, they sometimes drastically change the conditions of control. Some give up and refuse to do anything to prolong their lives. Some escape all control by signing themselves out of the hospital or by committing suicide.

Continuing with medical examples, it is interesting to note what happens when sick patients return home from the hospital or from a clinic visit. The physician commonly gives the patient a set of directives that he or she is supposed to follow. The patient may or may not follow this regimen, depending on such conditions as whether he or she trusts or believes the physician, or whether he or she thinks the regimen is too difficult and can be altered without too much harm. More to the point of this chapter, however, are those instances in which patients think they are following the physician's directives but actually do not understand them. They act in accordance with the control ceded to the absent physician, but when the physician discovers what the patients have been doing, he or she may accuse them of departing from instructions because of laziness, insufficient trust, or some other unworthy motive. In virtually any clinic where patients of lower income groups are treated by middle-class nurses and physicians one can hear those accusations, either fired directly at the patients or merely noted among the staff itself.

In many instances, however, patients simply do not understand the orders. They act in accordance with the orders as they have heard them.

These relationships between patients and hospital staffs are not independent of group affiliations and positions in a nation's social structure. Middle-class Americans have learned to cede over to physicians, for instance, degrees of control that lower-class Americans have not yet learned to cede—a matter related to higher education, and meanings of health and body, as well as "health education." In some parts of the nation, as well as in a country like Greece, citizens still regard the hospital as a place to die and will not go there when sick. (4) Consequently, when Greek patients or their family discover that they are no longer regarded by the staff as dying, they will be whisked out of the hospital. They will cede nothing else to the medical people. Conversely—but illustrating the same point—when Malayans discover that one of their sick kinfolk is actually dying within a hospital they will take him or her home, disregarding all protestations of the hospital staff, because now a series of religious and other ritual actions must be performed both before and after the person's death. These would not be performed by the hospital staff, and thus great spiritual harm would be done to the dying person.

The preceding section dealt with institutionalized forms of ceding control. We now turn to a related phenomenon wherein a person retains self-control, but changes both behavior and the bases of controlling behavior under the guidance of others. Commonly, we recognize that any person who enters a new organization and who begins to believe in what it stands for may then begin to "conform" to its standards. Even skeptics may thus be converted after they have entered a group just to scoff at it. Naturally, there are many obstacles to these kinds of conversions, especially to well nigh total conversion, as when an Episcopalian joins a radically different religious group like Jehovah's Witnesses.

"BRAINWASHING" OR "THOUGHT REFORM"

Radical change requires that adult persons undergo turmoil. If some group or organization wishes them to change the bases of their self-control and thought in some given direction, they must be thrown into turmoil or self-doubt while simultaneously being led along to new ways of seeing themselves and the world. Thus, if their loyalties to colleagues, friends, and parents are to be loosened, these people must be impugned, attacked, shaken from pedestals, and questioned. A certain amount of self-doubt and doubt of others can be induced by verbal means, but it is also essential that crucial situations be established wherein the persons see themselves and the others, if possible, acting in ways that run counter to their cherished conceptions. Religious conversion, which is followed by a radical change in style of life, illustrates these processes.

Preaching, accusation, and rhetoric in general are important in bringing about conversion; but it is essential that people be put into situations in which they will feel guilt, feel and see their usual actions as strange, and be forced to review their past history and find themselves wanting.

Creation of a crisis provides the condition for changing the direction of the personal career, but in itself it is not enough. Crisis calls for self-appraisal and self-examination but does not automatically indicate direction. Some converts not only drop out or backslide, but move off in other directions—to alcohol, to other social movements, or to cynical manipulation of others. If the reformer is to make use of a crisis, he or she must help plot the course from there on in order to prepare the convert for difficulties and to help the rationale of the course become part of his or her thinking. This is done in religious conversions by various devices, such as predicting the harshness of parents and relations when the convert attempts to tell them about his or her revelations, and predicting that friends will abandon him or her because of the new beliefs. After the communist revolution in China, and intermittently since, so-called thought reform techniques were used all over the country as part of a mass conversion of the citizenry. The explicit or implicit aims, according to E. Schein and coauthors (46), were to create a new type of Chinese citizen, change attitudes, to produce an obedient and energetic party worker, to initiate into communist society those individuals who were not yet committed ideologically, and to develop ideological unanimity throughout the land. *Thought reform* is essentially an attempt to break old loyalties, principally to family and social class, and to develop new loyalties to country and party. The tactics used on citizens varied considerably, depending both on those in charge of reform and on the status of those to be reformed. Some of the same tactics were also used on foreigners in China, and later on captured prisoners during the Korean War. (36:25)

E. Hunter (27:25) has described the set of tactics used on students in the years immediately after the revolution. To begin with, propaganda and lectures unveiled a new terminology—that of the communists—that ran counter to familiar concepts in a great many ways. The meaning of the new terms could not be fully grasped at first, but they provided an initial vocabulary for the reinterpretation of events, persons, and groups. Students were sent to work in the fields so as to feel like the common people. They were sent to see village justice wreaked upon former landlords—often a harrowing experience for the onlooker, whose parents might also be landlords. Any who could not bear to watch were accused of sentimentality—a characteristic of the ruling class. A detailed biographical essay (called a "thought seduction essay") had to be written and turned in to the teacher, who, having read it, criticized it as revealing "deep-set contradictions" in their lives. The point of this criticism was to force the students to reveal publicly their former beliefs and actions, especially when they themselves wanted to forget them because they were not in harmony with party teachings. Students were then induced or compelled to confess their sins in class, such as admitting that they had helped the Japanese, and so on. Criticism of each student by every other was encouraged, and those who held back were prodded by name-calling ("lagging-behind particle") and other punishments.

Presumably, some persons were relieved by making their avowals and were supported by others' commentaries; but in general, public avowal and criticism are very destructive processes. Ordinarily, one is protected from certain kinds of adverse comment by the conspiracy of silence that governs polite intercourse. Selective inattention does not get much chance to operate effectively in such procedures as those we have described, because the individual's illusions about him- or herself are challenged directly. This challenge was increased by the mutual hostility engendered during these sessions. The right to privacy was invaded; not only did current acts and thoughts come under scrutiny, but the intimate details of past history were examined. The student was asked to explain the "why" of his or her acts, and then alternative motivations were pressed upon him or her.

The turning point in the brainwashing process appears to have been the genuine public confession when the student got down to rock bottom and accused him- or herself of having been a wastrel, an exploiter, a coward, and so forth. This amounted to a genuine public relinquishing of past identity. The anguish attending this process is suggested by the cutting off of contacts with parents, the renaming of one's family as "exploiters," and the sundering of relations with spouses. It was at this point that the more serious consequences of the new perspective began to come home to the convert; there was no turning back.

One of the final steps in the process was the writing of a "thought conclusion essay," an autobiography written to show how far one had come in the desired direction and in what ways. It included a ruthless renunciation of the past. This essay had to be read aloud to the class and was subjected to public criticism. When the candidate was finished with this ordeal, he or she was compelled to rewrite the essay along more acceptable lines. Not everyone, of course, went through to the final steps in the process. Some committed suicide, some ran away, and others were not deemed to require the full treatment. In 1956, the vigor of the criticism of Chinese intellectuals with regard to government action during the Hundred Flowers period apparently surprised even the high party officials. In 1967, it was apparent that large sections of the Chinese population were regarded by Mao Tse-tung as not entirely converted to the highest ideals of communist society.

There can be no doubt that thought reform is a technique of what one might call *forced conversion* or *coercive persuasion,* and that it sometimes brings about fundamental and permanent changes in outlook. In the testimony of Americans who have been temporarily subjected to the treatment there is often a note of profound respect for its potency. Ardent anti-communists, who remain so after a period of communist indoctrination, often unwittingly use the communist vocabulary or accept some of its assumptions. (27, 36) This is true even of the Chinese who fled the country after being subjected to thought reform. As for those who remained, R. J. Lifton has suggested with some accuracy that even the intellectuals who recanted under pressure after their harsh criticism during the Hundred Flowers episode "may also have felt some genuine repentance, for thought reform had applied to them its special techniques for reclaiming backsliders." It may have persuaded them "that their critical views were out of step with the march of history, and that they had helped their country's enemies and harmed a noble cause." Lifton saw signs of this "reclaiming power" in many of the Chinese he interviewed intensively in Hong Kong during 1954 and 1955, "the guilty sense of having been a betrayer, along with a paralyzing fear of the communists, persisting long after the escape from communist control." (36:414)

Lifton's extensive interviews with foreigners who had lived in China and who had been subjected to thought reform also suggest some of the operative mechanisms and personal strategies that allowed some persons to escape anything like full conversion. Lifton notes that the "first form of resistance is the acquisition of a sense of understanding, a theory about what is going on, an awareness of being manipulated." This awareness and these theories give a partial sense of control over the situation and help "to dispel the terrifying fear of the unknown and the sense of complete helplessness." A second important tactic is the avoidance of emotional participation, the prisoner remaining "as much as possible outside the communication system of thought reform." This is done by refusing to learn Chinese if one does not know it, and by keeping contacts with Chinese prison-mates to a minimum. The agents of thought reform were somewhat kept off balance also by a show of stoicism and displays of humor. A final and most important "resistance technique" was that of "identity reinforcement." Thus a Catholic bishop kept reminding himself that the communist remolding was really a test of his Catholic steadfastness. "He sought always to maintain himself as a priest struggling against his selfishness, rather than a stubborn imperialist spy. To do this, he needed a continuous awareness of his own world of prayer, Catholic ritual, missionary experience, and Western cultural heritage." Since nothing in the prison reminded him of these anchors of identity, he had to find them within himself. One prisoner reminded himself by secretly drawing pictures of scenes from his boyhood. But Lifton notes that none of these tactics was entirely successful, for thought reform had some impact on all of the foreign prisoners whom he studied.

In short, brainwashing, conversion, and other socially or institutionally induced changes illustrate how the bases of an individual's self-control may shift without any genuine loss of self-control except that which he or she may wish to cede some group or organization. It would be erroneous to assume that in these induced processes individuals simply are coerced to change their belief and behavior. If coerced, they may leave the organization or commit suicide; they may act conformingly as if they believed, but in fact they are controlling their behavior so as to pass muster in what might otherwise be situations dangerous to life itself. In such situations, even coerced behavior may have privately derisive meanings. This is a phenomenon we all recognize, even when we do not recognize particular evidences of it; for instance, army privates who mock their officers with salutes that are executed just properly enough so that the implied disrespect is not recognized.

When a number of coerced individuals recognize the existence of each other, they inevitably develop shared gestures—physical or verbal—to indicate to each other their true feelings and beliefs while seeming to conform to the new bases of self-control. It is commonly known that writers in totalitarian countries manage to slip the "true meaning" between the lines so that informed readers may share their ideas while the censors read the lines "straight." On the other hand, the general import of the available data seems to indicate that it is things which people are more or less forced to say and do that ultimately change the ways in which they think about themselves and about the external world.

The discussion to this point has placed the social effects that others may have on the self within a shifting context of self- and social control. The self and its variously implicated others are bound together in a variety of emergent and stabilized relationships which confer greater or lesser degrees of self-control. The effects of ceding control may be (1) positive, in the case of husbands and wives or members of communes; (2) neutral, as when a person submits to hypnotism; and (3) negative, as when a person is embarrassed, degraded, or formally excluded from a work organization.

If the temporal dimensions of the self-other relationship are considered, it can be seen that effects can be momentary and fleeting or long term and heavily consequential for the given individual—the paranoid, for instance. Finally, if we consider the spatial aspects of ceding control, we can see that the commitment of oneself to another (or the control of oneself by another) can lead to upward, downward, or lateral

CEDING CONTROL AS STATUS PASSAGE: BIOGRAPHICAL AND CAREER EFFECTS

social mobility. A person who becomes the protégé of a master cedes self-control or career control in return for the possibility of a high-status career. At the other extreme, we have individuals who, wittingly or unwittingly, give up self-control to others, or have it taken away, and in the end find that they are doomed to failure and demotion. In the middle are those who incur few career costs when they contract for a lateral transfer from one department to another within the same work organization. So, the status passage process which accompanies the act of ceding self-control to another individual, a group, an organization, or a cause can result in movements "in" or "out" of an interactional network, or "up" and "down" within that same context.

These remarks suggest that the commitments which an individual makes to others can carry significant biographical implications for his or her future career choices. For these and other reasons, persons take some care over the choices they make. Furthermore, they are often led to develop and adopt a set of "self-protective" strategies that enhance their abilities to mold and direct their own lives. These strategies are often referred to as *coping devices*. We conclude this chapter with a discussion of them.

Coping Mechanisms

It is commonly remarked how extraordinarily obtuse all of us are in situations in which our self-esteem is involved. People often embark upon and continue in relationships with other persons without much insight into the character of the relationship. Such blindness, it is generally understood, is explicable in terms of one's self-conceptions. Psychiatrists who deal with gross and persistent errors of this kind speak of them in such terms as "defense mechanisms," "security operations," and the like, the central idea being that the person meets supposed threats to self-regard with characteristic modes of defense. Defense modes include, among others, selective inattention, anxiety reduction, evasion of responsibility, rationalization, pretense, and the disowning of undesirable qualities in oneself.

The techniques of self-defense, or coping, which psychiatrists have characteristically stressed and which have often been picked up uncritically by sociologists, are those that emphasize self-deception, avoidance, and reduction of information. Such classic forms of ego defense as repression, denial, reaction formation, isolation, and rationalization lean heavily upon minimizing the recognition of potentially traumatic aspects of experience. These techniques are of the kind characteristically used by those who go to psychiatrists. These coping devices are frequently pathological in nature in the sense that they may themselves create other problems for the person. There are, however, many other techniques of

Life Cycle: Adult Transformations

adjustment that are perhaps more successful and that are used by people who do not seek professional help. To indicate the existence of more normal techniques, we have called them *coping mechanisms* rather than defense mechanisms, and we shall include a discussion of some of them along with others of the better-known classical variety.

COMMON DEFENSE MECHANISMS

The theoretical treatment of anxiety by the psychiatrist H. S. Sullivan (51) points up some of these conceptions. Even in the earliest months, according to Sullivan's theory, children encounter situations that arouse their anxiety and they learn to grade them in terms of the anxiety they provoke and to stay away from those that are most severe. Unavoidable anxiety situations come to be handled by a variety of means designed to minimize anxiety and to maximize satisfaction. Sullivan states that "the self-system comes into being, because of, and can be said to have as its goal, the securing of necessary satisfaction without incurring much anxiety."

A fundamental conceptual device that children utilize, according to Sullivan, is to classify experiences as pertaining to the *good me,* the *bad me,* and the *not me.* The first category is for acts that are approved; the second, for acts that are disapproved, and hence induce some anxiety; and the third, for acts that are so anxiety-provoking that they are more or less disavowed or "dissociated." Sullivan notes that the *not me* is tied up with emotions of dread, horror, and loathing, and is expressed obliquely with a lack of awareness (for example, in nightmares).

The *self-system* arises from the child's attempt to avoid anxieties arising in interpersonal relations with significant others, and especially with the mother. This system is not equivalent to an incorporation of the mother's perspective, but is based on the child's attempts to form a system of reaction that minimizes the anxiety that arises out of interactions with significant others. (51:159–61) Sullivan maintains that protection against the paralyzing effects of severe anxiety is a necessity, and that learning to protect oneself is part of one's educational experience.

The self-system tends to become stabilized in a generalized defense against anxiety. The person then, according to Sullivan, becomes "selectively inattentive" to happenings that could change him or her, since change itself leads to anxiety. Hence, awareness of one's own acts is greatly restricted, as is the understanding of the acts of others. One need not assume with Sullivan that anxiety avoidance is the central feature of behavioral organization, but certainly ideas of self do interfere with what is noticed and what is learned. People do strive to maintain self-esteem, and they raise defenses against threats to it.

A person with insight into his or her own deficiencies and weaknesses and the situations in which they become manifest to others may consciously maneuver to avoid competitive games, for example, and may choose as companions persons who will not shame him or her by their superior skills or attainments. Thus, the need to maintain self-regard often produces a vicious cycle; those very situations wherein a weakness could be overcome are avoided. A good part of social relations is unconsciously devoted to the search for companions and activities that allow weaknesses to remain hidden or relatively unnoticed while one's stronger points are exploited.

Characteristic defenses of self may occur without realization of their nature by the individual. Some of these have been given names. For instance, a person who has failed to reach certain goals may substitute less ambitious ones in a general lowering of his or her level of aspiration. Another well-known device is *rationalizing*, which we use in this context to mean explaining away or excusing one's failure. Another method characteristically used by some people is the shifting of one's own fault to another: this is called *scapegoating*, or *displacement*. Persons aware of undesirable qualities in themselves may bolster their self-esteem by *projecting* the same qualities to others, as when a selfish person says that it is a selfish world (that is, that everyone else is selfish too). In handling personal relations, it is common for attack to be met by counterattack, whether verbal or physical. Among the more complex forms of defense is *identification* with an aggressor, which permits a vicarious sharing of some of his or her strength.

The cultural patterning of defense and coping mechanisms is reflected in the existence of the conventions of politeness, which function, at least in part, to shield sensitive egos and to allow delicate relationships to exist. As with other forms of behavior, different mechanisms are stressed in different groups, and the standards of politeness and rudeness vary accordingly.

There are also conventionally sanctioned tactics for defending the self that are constantly used in a conscious manner. These include such ordinary devices as physical withdrawal, changing the subject, doing favors for one's opponent or using flattery, creating diversions, sparring for time, and exploiting the vulnerable points of the attacker. Human interaction is such that one's status is often challenged, feelings hurt, and reputation impugned by the acts, whether intentional or not, of others. Anyone who does not learn to cope with these occurrences is in a peculiarly helpless and vulnerable position. Orrin E. Klapp (30:159–61) has illustrated this point very vividly in his discussion of fool-making situations. As he says:

> Fool-making situations are so constantly presented to the average person that he may be unable to avoid occasionally falling into the role. Life is a continual process of fool-making . . . humor, derision, and belittlement are constantly assigning this role . . . social relations are continually ren-

dered unstable by fool-making. . . . Among the major routes of escape from the fool role are the following: . . . Avoidance of the imputation by "taking" a joke and "laughing it off" implies that there has been no injury, that the jibe is ineffectual or inapplicable. . . . A counterjoke or effective repartee "turns the tables" and makes the other a fool; "having the last word" or getting the best of a contest of wits has, in fact, the effect of defining the winner as a clever hero. . . . A similar strategy involves acceptance of the fool role and its use as a "ruse" or "trap" for a clever victory. . . . [And] by suffering or showing "human" traits which arouse sympathy, a person can escape from the fool role. Excessive persecution, for example, "carrying a joke too far," tends to make a martyr out of the fool.

Psychiatrists have worked out elaborate terminologies and explanations of individual and unconsciously used defense mechanisms, for neurotic and psychotic patients are notable for lack of insight into their own behavior. We may accept many of the psychiatric descriptions of normal devices for self-defense without necessarily agreeing with the explanations of them. Psychiatrists tend to overstress the unconscious nature of these defense and coping processes, both because of the importance of the unconscious in their theoretical systems and because of their concern with patients in whom this aspect of behavior is exaggerated. The relatively stable and secure person may discover these processes or recognize them when they are pointed out. One need not be altogether skeptical about the role of rationality at this point. Normal persons are able to assimilate a fair amount of criticism, direct or implied, without serious injury to self-esteem and without reversion to self-delusion. Retrospective analysis of one's past actions cannot help giving one new perspectives and further insight into one's characteristic ways of handling personal reactions. Techniques used by the young child do not necessarily survive the maturing effects of broader experience.

In some interesting recent research, psychiatrists have systematically looked into how ordinary nondisturbed persons may assimilate unfortunate, disastrous, or threatening experiences. One such study that we shall describe was concerned with parents whose children were discovered to have leukemia, an almost invariably fatal disease. The study included twenty-six mothers and twenty fathers from various socioeconomic levels, whose children were treated for their disease at the National Cancer Institute. The parents were systematically interviewed during the course of the illness, as well as after the deaths of their children. (13)

The parents were initially stunned at the diagnosis, and by the realistic explanation by the physicians of the limitations of chemotherapy and the eventual outcome of the disease. A few parents who were psychologically unstable expressed hostile and aggressive reactions at the

NORMAL COPING DEVICES

initial news, but most accepted it and expressed appreciation for having been told the worst so that they knew what to expect. At first, all of the parents experienced guilt because they had not paid attention to the earliest symptoms of the disease. They were reassured when it was explained that this would have made no essential difference. Some parents assuaged their feelings of guilt with respect to their earlier disciplining of their child by treating him or her overindulgently after the diagnosis.

The authors distinguished between pathological and socially desirable methods of coping with the problem. Among the latter, the following are of interest: (1) seeking information about leukemia, the doctors, and the hospital; (2) engaging in physical activity and assisting in the care of the child; (3) maintaining the normal routine of living; (4) talking with and observing other parents in the same situation; (5) looking for meaning in the events; (6) resorting to religious consolations; (7) anticipating mourning by crying at night, and ruminating concerning the death and funeral of the child; and (8) becoming or trying to become pregnant, or adopting a child shortly after the death of their own child. In addition to these forms of adaptive behavior, some parents and relatives of the children also responded in ways that aggravated the problem.

Similar types of responses were reported by a sociologist, Fred Davis (9), who studied how the families of polio-stricken children managed to live through and rally around each other during various phases of their "passage through crisis." The correspondence between the results reported by Davis and the psychiatrists noted above is all the more remarkable because the sociologist was interested in family functioning and not in the intimate details of coping responses.

As another illustration of normal coping devices, reference may be made to the ways in which persons succeed in reorganizing their lives after they have had a heart attack. One such person systematically read the scientific literature on heart disease, became intensely interested in the whole subject, and interviewed numerous researchers who were studying the relationships between cholesterol, fat intake, and other matters associated with heart disease. In addition to adopting a rigorous, low-cholesterol diet, he subsidized research in the field. Such heart patients often like to talk with other persons who have the same problem, and joke about themselves and their condition. (24)

It is a common observation that persons with a variety of problems seek to acquire an understanding of them both by talking to others and by reading books and articles. Thus, homosexuals, criminals, and other deviants may become concerned about trying to understand themselves and, in the process, either drop their deviance or adjust themselves to it. In Chapter 15 we refer to the techniques of neutralization that criminals and delinquents employ as symbolic adjustment devices. These permit them to continue in their deviant paths. Obviously this must be only a small part of the picture, since the great majority of delinquents abandon their delinquency and crime rates generally drop sharply with advancing age.

What this suggests may be not so much that law enforcement and punishment are effective, but that there are informal coping mechanisms at work pulling the individual back into the mainstream of normal, acceptable activity. Undoubtedly, one of these is represented by the person's family, relatives, and friends who often rally around him or her and more or less collectively devise schemes and techniques for giving encouragement and support. They may even more or less trick or trap him or her into lines of activity which, through a series of imperceptible stages, bring about commitment to acceptable norms. Conspicuous examples of this process are the manner in which an interest in the opposite sex or a hitch in the army may eliminate a boy's interest in gang membership.

In another psychiatric study (21), concerning the adjustment of severely burned persons, it is indicated that the reestablishment of a normal life is facilitated by such things as friendly interaction and banter with doctors, nurses, ward attendants, and visitors, and particularly by association with a group of other severely burned persons. Kidding and joking are important ways of avoiding self-pity and promoting acceptance of reality. As severely burned persons tentatively reestablish old relationships and activities, they are supported by recollections of past sources of pride, by their ability to take it, and even by active participation in speeding up their own recovery.

The crucial importance of significant others and social contexts is demonstrated graphically (in reverse) by a study (42) of the postoperative experiences of women who had been operated on for breast cancer. When interviewed at various intervals after they had left the hospital, they typically showed great anxiety or fear that they might die from cancer, whatever initial reassurance they may have received from their physicians. Commonly, these women attempted to discuss their fears with friends and relations, but discovered that nobody really wished to talk about the operation or its implications. Everyone preferred to assume that things were back to normal. The women thus tended to brood alone, often in an increasing cycle of depression and silent hysteria. The interviewers consequently found themselves acting as substitutes for the kinds of responsive audiences that most of the frightened women lacked.

COPING BY DETACHMENT

Transcendence of self is made possible by the fact that through using symbols and taking the roles of others one may take the view of an outsider (observer) with regard to one's self and one's own actions. This may lead either to concern over self and reputation, or to *detachment*. Probably relatively few persons achieve any large measure of disinterestedness in their view of themselves, but those who do are recognized and appreciated for it. It is thus one of the most effective ways of maintaining self-esteem.

One of the outstanding signs of the achievement of this detachment is a sense of humor, especially about one's own foibles, mistakes, and weaknesses. The person who can joke in the face of failure, danger, or death exhibits this detachment. The American officer in World War II who, in a critical phase of combat, asked his men: "What's the matter, do you want to live forever?" offered an example of it. "Gallows humor," like that of the conquered peoples of Europe who made bitter jokes at their own expense, is the expression of more than mere irony and resentment, since it indicates a realistic appreciation of an actual predicament. (See Chapter 5.)

PRIVACY AND THE SELF Privacy is also related to defense of self, as the expression "invasion of privacy" makes clear. Societies everywhere have unwritten rules that allow persons to withdraw from interaction in certain situations. The retreat to privacy may be used to escape from interaction which is troubling, embarrassing, or deflating. Some people who cannot successfully cope with certain kinds of social relations make a virtual fetish of privacy.

Privacy has positive values as well. It is perhaps an absolute necessity to withdraw to repair one's energies, to ruminate over the significance of past events, and to plan. It is only in moments in which one is not reacting to other people that communication with self can be at its best. Periods of privacy designed for this very purpose are institutionalized in all societies. An obvious example is the prescription by various religions of periods of meditation, fasting, and prayer.

When others try to get at secret thoughts and intimate biographical details which the individual wishes to reveal to no one or only to very special persons, barriers are erected. Inopportune revelation of self leaves one at the mercy of others. Privacy may be conceptualized as a series of concentric circles. The inner circle is forbidden to all trespassers. One's trusted intimates may enter into the second circle, and so on, as one moves to the outer circles that are accessible to all. This spatial symbolism is actually embodied in the architecture of dwellings, houses of worship, and public buildings, and in the rules permitting or forbidding entry into various rooms.

Allowing another person to enter into the ego's central core of privacy is a delicate process fraught with peril to both parties. It is attended by misgivings and release, and by hesitations and abrupt moments of confiding. Betrayal of this degree of confidence is destructive and corrosive. It has an effect like that of being turned over to the enemy after seeking refuge in the house of a blood relation. The recipients of con-

Coping by detachment: a private self?
(*E. Trina Lipton*)

fidence are also in a delicate position, because they may unwittingly betray the confidence or it may put them in a moral dilemma. Impersonal, institutionalized places of confession (such as the church and the doctor's office) are designed to protect both parties.

The individual maintains the integrity of his or her self-conception **TERRITORIALITY** through the use of an elaborate conception of *territoriality* and privacy. **AND THE SELF** Lyman and Scott (38:236–49) and Goffman (17:28–61) have offered typologies which link the individual's conceptions of self and social space. There are *public territories* where persons can come and go at will, and they are open to wide classes of the population. The sacred, private features of the self are likely to remain concealed in these settings. *Home territories* are those most sacred to the self, and they describe backstage regions for private, unobserved interaction. *Body territories* include the area immediately surrounding the physical body. More properly conceived as personal space, the individual is unlikely to permit other actors into that space.

Individuals develop territorial defenses which maintain the sanctity of those places most central to their self-conceptions. Through the use of markers, names, tags, labels, and addresses they communicate to outsiders what their spaces are, where those spaces end, and where the spaces of others take over. Spaces and their attached selves may be violated or challenged. Bodies may unexpectedly touch, glances may last too long, odors may be given off and communicate an untoward body state.

Individuals can challenge the credibility of their own self-conceptions by openly debasing themselves. Furthermore, they may befoul their own bodies, or in a more drastic fashion they may expose the private parts of their bodies. In each of these self-acts they cease to make the self a private and hence sacred object; thereby letting down their defenses and permitting others openly to defy or denigrate them. Hence they place others in the uncomfortable position of having to process the behaviors of a derelict self. Failures to maintain self-privacy and to keep up territorial defenses challenge the routine features of smooth, everyday interaction. (17:52–55)

REVELATIONS AND SELF-OTHER RELATIONS

It is interactionally useful to keep portions of oneself from others. In this sense an element of secrecy, as Simmel notes, surrounds each individual: his or her most private self-conceptions and fantasies may never be known by another individual (48:330–33) A *pretense awareness context*

Two friends on the road: pretense awareness? (*N. R. Farbman/Life Magazine* © *Time, Inc.*)

Life Cycle: Adult Transformations

exists in many relationships, even for those of the most intimate nature. The members agree not to challenge each other's moods and declarations, and they act as if they fully understand one another when, in fact, they are only "pretending." Thus, while they may suspect that the other is thinking something other than what he or she verbally declares, they are tactful enough not to ask. But, if the relationship is to take the turn toward deeper involvement, at some juncture they will be led to reveal the more private and hidden features of themselves. They move from the pretense and suspicion awareness context into the open context. This is not to say that their interactions will necessarily remain at the open level. A quasi-open context is more typical, and in time the relationship may slip back into more elaborate modes of secrecy and self-concealment.

Summary

Individuals can voluntarily, involuntarily, or unexpectedly cede self-control to another individual, to a group, to an organization, or to a cause. The loss of self-control under hypnosis indicates the extensive role of language mechanisms in voluntary behavior and suggests that the will should be conceived not as a psychic force or entity, but as a self-regulator by means of language cues. Behavior under hypnosis is a more extreme form of the type of influence constantly exerted by people over each other in ordinary social intercourse and designated by such terms as *suggestion* and *imitation*. Propaganda and media influences were compared to the *posthypnotic effects* hypnotists have on their subjects. Since social control also implies control of behavior by symbol manipulation, it is closely related to self-control. The behavior of the individual in the group situation illustrates the manner in which persons seem to lose self-control under the influences of social pressures. In certain institutionalized situations, such as when a person is hospitalized, it is expected that others will take over the control of some or much of his or her activities. The processes of *brainwashing* and other kinds of *coercive persuasion* may be considered as other instances of the partial loss of personal autonomy to outside forces, persons, or groups, as is the case for *embarrassment* and *degradation ceremonies*. Ceding control to others was compared to the phenomena of status passages. The *coping devices* persons use to salvage self-esteem were explored. Finally, it was noted that the privacy of the self is central to the maintenance of self-control.

References

1. Asch, S. E., *Social Psychology*. Englewood Cliffs, N.J.: Prentice-Hall, 1952.
2. Barber, T. X., "Antisocial and Criminal Acts Induced by 'Hypnosis,' " *Archives of General Psychiatry*, vol. 5 (September 1961), pp. 301–12.

3. Blondel, C., "Les Volitions," in G. Dumas (ed.), *Nouveau Traité de Psychologie*. Paris: Librairie Felix Alcan, 1939.
4. Blum, Richard, and Eva Blum, *Health and Healing in Rural Greece*. Stanford, Calif.: Stanford University Press, 1965.
5. Blumer, H., "Collective Behavior," in R. E. Park (ed.), *Outlines of the Principles of Sociology*. New York: Barnes & Noble, 1939.
6. Cason, H., "The Role of Verbal Activities in Conditioning Human Subjects," *Psychological Review*, vol. 41 (1934), pp. 563–71.
7. Cleveland, C. C., *The Great Revival in the West*. Chicago: University of Chicago Press, 1916.
8. Cooley, C. H., *Human Nature and the Social Order*. New York: Charles Scribner's Sons, 1902.
9. Davis, Fred, *Passage through Crisis*. Indianapolis: Bobbs-Merrill, 1963.
10. Erickson, H. M., "Experimental Demonstrations of the Psychopathology of Everyday Life," *Psychoanalytic Quarterly*, vol. 8 (1939), pp. 338–53.
11. ———, "Hypnotic Investigation of Psychosomatic Phenomena," *Psychosomatic Medicine*, vol. 5 (1943), pp. 51–58.
12. Eysenck, H. J., *Sense and Nonsense in Psychology*. Baltimore: Penguin Books, 1964.
13. Friedman, Stanford B., Paul Chodoff, John W. Mann, and David A. Hamburg, "Behavioral Observation on Parents Anticipating the Death of a Child," *Pediatrics*, vol. 20 (October 1963), pp. 610–24.
14. Garfinkel, Harold, "Conditions of Successful Degradation Ceremonies," *American Journal of Sociology*, vol. 61 (March 1956), pp. 420–24.
15. Glaser, B., and A. L. Strauss, *Awareness of Dying*. Chicago: Aldine, 1965.
16. Goffman, Erving, *Encounters*. Indianapolis: Bobbs-Merrill, 1961.
17. ———, *Relations in Public*. New York: Basic Books, 1971.
18. Gross, Edward, and Gregory P. Stone, "Embarrassment and the Analysis of Role Requirements," *American Journal of Sociology*, vol. 70 (July 1964), pp. 1–15.
19. Guze, H., "Hypnosis as Emotional Response: A Theoretical Approach," *Journal of Psychology*, vol. 35 (1953), pp. 313–28.
20. ———, "Hypnosis as Wish Fulfillment: A Projective Approach," *British Journal of Medical Hypnotism*, vol. 2 (1951), pp. 6–10.
21. Hamburg, David A. Beatrix Hamburg, and Sydney de Goza, "Adaptive Problems and Mechanisms in Severely Burned Persons," *Psychiatry*, vol. 16, no. 1 (February 1953), pp. 1–20.
22. Hebb, D. O., E. Heath, and E. Stuart, "Experimental Deafness," *Canadian Journal of Psychology*, vol. 8 (1954), pp. 152–56.
23. Hilgard, E. R., *Hypnotic Susceptibility*. New York: Harcourt Brace Jovanovich, 1966.
24. Hornoff, Mary C., Unpublished paper written under the direction of Anselm L. Strauss.
25. Hudgins, C. V., "Conditioning and the Voluntary Control of the Pupillary Light Reflex," *Journal of General Psychology*, vol. 8 (1933), pp. 3–51.
26. Hull, Clark L., *Hypnosis and Suggestibility*. New York: Appleton-Century-Crofts, 1933.
27. Hunter, E., *Brainwashing in Red China*. New York: Vanguard Press, 1951.
28. Kanter, Rosabeth, *Communities and Commitment*. Cambridge, Mass.: Harvard University Press, 1972.
29. Keir, J., "An Experiment in Mental Testing under Hypnosis," *Journal of Mental Science*, vol. 91 (1945), pp. 346–52.

30. Klapp, Orrin E., "The Fool as a Social Type," *American Journal of Sociology,* vol. 55 (1949), pp. 157–62.

31. Klein, Milton, Henry Guze, and Arthur Haggerty, "An Experimental Study of the Nature of Hypnotic Deafness," *Journal of Clinical and Experimental Hypnosis,* vol. 2 (1954), pp. 145–56.

32. Lang, K., and G. Lang, *Collective Dynamics.* New York: Macmillan, 1961.

33. Le Bon, G., *The Crowd.* London: Ernest Benn, 1916.

34. Lemert, Edwin M., "Paranoia and the Dynamics of Exclusion," *Sociometry,* vol. 25 (March 1962), pp. 2–20.

35. Lewis, J. N., and T. R. Sarbin, "Studies in Psychosomatics: The Influence of Hypnotic Stimulation on Gastric Hunger Contractions," *Psychosomatic Medicine,* vol. 5 (1943), pp. 125–31.

36. Lifton, R. J., *Thought Reform and the Psychology of Totalism.* New York: W. W. Norton, 1961.

37. Luria, A. R., *The Nature of Human Conflicts.* New York: Grove Press, 1960.

38. Lyman, Stanford M., and Marvin B. Scott, "Territoriality: A Neglected Sociological Dimension," *Social Problems,* vol. 15 (Fall 1967), pp. 236–49.

39. Pattee, F., "The Genuineness of Unilateral Deafness Produced by Hypnosis," *American Journal of Psychology,* vol. 63 (1940), pp. 84–86.

40. ———, "A Report of Attempts to Produce Uniocular Blindness by Hypnotic Suggestion," *British Journal of Medicine and Psychology,* vol. 15 (1935), pp. 230–41.

41. Pavlov, I., *Conditioned Reflexes.* New York: Oxford University Press, 1927.

42. Quint, Jeanne, "The Impact of Mastectomy," *American Journal of Nursing,* vol. 63 (November 1963), pp. 88–92.

43. Rude, George, *The Crowd in History.* New York: Wiley, 1964.

44. Sarbin, T. R., "Contributions to Role-Taking Theory, I: Hypnotic Behavior," *Psychological Review,* vol. 57 (1950), pp. 255–70.

45. ———, "Mental Changes in Experimental Regression," *Journal of Personality,* vol. 19 (1950), pp. 221–28.

46. Schein, E., I. Schucier, and J. Barker, *Coercive Persuasion.* New York: W. W. Norton, 1961.

47. Sherif, M., *An Outline of Social Psychology.* New York: Harper & Row, 1948.

48. Simmel, Georg, *The Sociology of Georg Simmel,* trans. by Kurt Wolff. New York: The Free Press, 1950.

49. Smelser, N., *Theory of Collective Behavior.* New York: The Free Press, 1963.

50. Strauss, Anselm L., *Mirrors and Masks.* San Francisco: Sociology Press, 1969.

51. Sullivan, H. S., *The Interpersonal Theory of Psychiatry.* New York: W. W. Norton, 1953.

52. Turner, R., and L. Killian, *Collective Behavior.* Englewood Cliffs, N.J.: Prentice-Hall, 1957.

53. Watkins, J. G., "Antisocial Compulsions Induced under Hypnotic Trance," *Journal of Abnormal and Social Psychology,* vol. 42 (1947), pp. 256–59.

54. Weitzenhoffer, A. M., *Hypnotism: An Objective Study in Suggestibility.* New York: Wiley, 1953.

55. White, R. W., "A Preface to the Theory of Hypnosis," *Journal of Abnormal and Social Psychology,* vol. 36 (1941), pp. 503–6.

56. Wolberg, Lewis, "Hypnotic Experiments in Psychosomatic Medicine," *Psychosomatic Medicine,* vol. 9 (1947), pp. 337–42.

57. Young, P. C., "Hypnotic Regression: Fact or Artefact?" *Journal of Abnormal and Social Psychology,* vol. 35 (1940), pp. 273–78.

Selected Readings

EYSENCK, H. J., *Sense and Nonsense in Psychology*. Baltimore: Penguin Books, 1964.
    A critical and skeptical review of the research on hypnosis.
GOFFMAN, ERVING, *Relations in Public*. New York: Basic Books, 1971.
    A probing and sensitive analysis of the rituals of face-to-face interaction that persons use to shield themselves from one another.
KANTER, ROSABETH, *Communities and Commitment*. Cambridge, Mass.: Harvard University Press, 1972.
    A thorough and systematic study of American communes which pointedly underscores the complex interrelationship between self-control and social control.
LIFTON, R. J., *Thought Reform and the Psychology of Totalism*. New York: W. W. Norton, 1961.
    A valuable account of persons who experienced *thought reform* and *brainwashing*. Indicates how individuals attempt to shield themselves from others when self-control over their own behavior is virtually denied.

Life Cycle: Adult Transformations

chapter 13

Selves, Careers, and Social Worlds

$\mathcal{W}_{e\ have}$ continually emphasized that the individual's self-conception arises out of his or her interpersonal relationships. In that regard, we shall now discuss the individual's moral careers in relation to membership in social worlds. We begin with a treatment of the concept of *career*, focusing on the varieties of careers (work, friendship, leisure, political, religious, intimate) that any given person can have. Then we move to the related concept of *social world*, indicating how individuals may move in and out of small-scale careers into more complex worlds of discourse. We conclude with a discussion of *alienation* and an analysis of how individuals mutually affect and alter one another's careers.

Careers

To say that an individual has a career involves three interrelated notions. (1, 2, 4, 15, 51) The concept designates objective movements that he or she may make through a social structure. Here we refer to status passages: movements in and out of the labor market, in and out of educational settings, in and out of marriages and friendships or groups. *Objective careers*—these movements through statuses and positions—produce a counterpart, termed the *subjective career*. In this category are the subtle and sometimes manifest changes in self-conception that accompany positional relocations. As Hughes (22, 23) noted, alterations in the objective career lead to changes in self-identity. The objective and subjective components of the career are especially important, since they set the stage for the larger redefinitions of self.

Goffman (15:127–28) has conveniently summarized the threefold nature (objective, subjective, self) of career:

> Traditionally the term *career* has been reserved for those who expect to enjoy the rises laid out within a respectable profession. The term is coming to be used, however, in a broadened sense to refer to any social strand of any person's course through life. . . . One value of the concept of career is its two-sidedness. One side is linked to internal matters held dearly and closely . . . the other side concerns public position, jural relations, and style of life. . . . The concept of career, then, allows one to move back and forth between the personal and the public, between the self and its significant society. . . . The main concern will be with the moral aspects of career—that is, the regular sequence of changes that career entails in the person's self and in his framework of imagery for judging himself and others.

The sacredness of the self-conception, as remarked by Goffman, needs to be underscored. He has written that it is important to see that (16:497): "The self is in part a ceremonial thing, a sacred object which must be treated with proper ritual care and in turn must be presented in a proper light to others . . . practices must be institutionalized so that the individual will be able to project a viable, sacred self." Any alteration in an individual's moral worth, then, alters his or her standing in a network of others. Goffman's remarks suggest that individuals go out of the way to protect one another's self-conceptions. In this sense each individual is the guardian of others' *moral careers* as well as of his or her own. It may be, as Goffman argues, that (16:499):

> This secular world is not so irreligious as we might think. Many gods have been done away with, but the individual himself stubbornly remains a deity of considerable importance. He walks with some dignity, and is the recipient of many little offerings. He is jealous of the worship due him, yet, approached in the right spirit, he is ready to forgive those who may have offended him. . . . Perhaps the individual is so viable a god because he can actually understand the ceremonial significance of the way he is treated, and quite on his own can respond dramatically to what is pro-offered him. In contracts between such deities there is no need for middlemen; each of these gods is able to serve as his own priest.

ASPECTS OF MORAL CAREERS Any moral career is a temporal process that flows through the strands of the individual's life. Individuals have multiple careers, each linked into distinct universes of discourse; that is, into unique social worlds. In this sense individuals have careers with all of their interactive fellows. Some of these careers are short term, as in a fleeting friendship or a short-term affair. Some are long term—marriage, or the work career of the individual who retires from the same university that hired him or her forty years earlier. Some careers have zigzag contours. A heroin user may, for instance, periodically "kick" the habit or move off hard drugs to soft drugs, and an alcoholic may move in and out of the drinking world. In this sense, careers have peak points of involvement, during which times the individual fully embraces the moral and subjective consequences of that involvement. At other times the involvement recedes into the background and may carry little if any implications for his or her other career commitments.

Careers are situated productions as well; that is, they are located in specific social situations. Careers are also "peopled productions." That is, they involve interactions with other individuals. These other persons, in turn, influence the directions that the individual's career will take in the future. Thus, careers are joint productions that are temporarily and situationally specific to each person. David L. Westby's study (57) of the career experiences of the symphony musician illustrates this point. He notes that images of conductors can significantly influence the career decisions of the musician. One violin player stated (57:224): "As far as symphonies are concerned I'm better off here. I could have gone to (name of a somewhat more prestigious orchestra) last year on viola. The salary is better there, but I couldn't stomach the conductor."

Other persons, then, positively and negatively influence the person's moral career. This is especially so for those careers which have an organizational locus. (4, 10) To have a career is to be involved in a set of commitments with other persons. Accordingly, it can be seen that trust and its imputation are central to the stability and shape of any career. An individual may overestimate or misrepresent, through selective inattention, the trustworthiness of another person. Or, that person may misrepresent him- or herself to the person. Such misreadings, deliberate or accidental, often result in betrayals and blocked or negative careers. Thus many persons find themselves in mental hospitals or jails, and only later learn that their wives or husbands were responsible for their commitment. A career is accomplished in the company of a set of *career others*—those individuals whose presence, commitment, and trust the individual comes to rely and depend on.

As individuals move through any specific career—say in the academic or work world—their set of career others will change as they move from one position to another. That is, as the career takes on new forms, or leads the individual into new areas, they find themselves in the presence of others who at an earlier time would not have been available to them. An individual has as many career others as he or she has ongoing careers. It should be clear, however, that these others may no longer be living, or they may have moved out of the person's immediate interactional world. Still, they continue to exert a symbolic influence over his or her behavior, and their imagined reactions may be assessed as the individual makes new decisions.

The multiple careers of any individual may be in harmony or in conflict with one another. Involvement in one social world—work, leisure, politics—may intrude into others—family, friends. As Simmel noted (49), the person is led to develop a set of strategies which keep these competing career demands in some kind of balance. In the company of one set of others, he or she simply does not talk about or act on the perspectives of other competing worlds. Husbands may leave the work at the office; children may not talk about their school experiences; and wives may not complain about their "bad days" with their work and the children when their husband comes home.

CAREER VISIBILITY.   While at any moment in time any individual is involved in multiple careers, some are more visible than others. The work career, for example, is highly prominent and visible and may go on display five or more days a week. Some careers are less visible: a person's interests in stamp collecting, or in a particular musician or artist, may never be known or may be made public only to a very small set of others. A related characteristic is that some careers are over and done once traversed. Thus, when medical students complete their residency, their formal relationships with the medical establishment may be terminated. Similarly, many persons terminate careers (divorces) or have them terminated (death, demotion, firing). Terminated careers are less visible than those that are ongoing, unless of course the previous career left the person with a set of markings that reveal his or her past. Abominations of the body—stigmata, like concentration camp markings, which are still visible—give away past involvements. Some careers are, however, simply buried; failures, broken love affairs, past criminal offenses may be kept secret or may be known only to a few other people. All of us, then, give off clues to our career involvements through our verbal or nonverbal gestures. Our clothing and other personal possessions may be the basic conveyors of information about what these commitments are.

CAREER ENTRANCE AND ACCESS.   Careers may be entered voluntarily (the dating market), involuntarily (the military), or by recruitment (medical schools). Depending on the mode of entry and on how the individual defines other career involvements, he or she may show great attachment of detachment or simple neutrality. Thus, someone just beginning to date may literally throw him- or herself into the pursuit of a sexual partner. In general, if the entry into the career has been voluntary, then perhaps the individual is more likely to commit and attach him- or herself to the identifications that follow from his or her location in that social world. (37, 38)

The topic of career entrance raises the related matter of career access. Some careers are closed off to many groups of individuals, while others are open for the taking. Becker and Strauss (3:255–56) observe:

> There are problems attending the systematic restriction of recruiting. Some kinds of persons for occupationally irrelevant reasons (formally, anyway), may not be considered for some positions at all. Medical schools restrict recruiting in this way: openly, on grounds of "personality assessments," and covertly on ethnicity. Italians, Jews, and Negroes who do become doctors face differential recruitment into the formal and informal hierarchies of influence, power, and prestige in the medical world. Similar mechanisms operate at the top and the bottom of industrial organizations.

CAREER CONTROL.   Career access suggests that people can have differing degrees of control over their own and others' careers. While ostensibly a person should have the greatest control over his or her own life chances, that may not be the case, as small children, the elderly, the stigmatized, and the impoverished know. Power and its influence, whether legitimate or illegitimate, surely are central to the shaping and molding of all careers. However, any assessment of power and its application must do more than assert that organizations or societies make certain classes of individuals act in certain ways. Power and influence are always filtered through interpersonal relationships, and in the final analysis involve one individual exerting his or her authority (however legitimate) over another. Thus negative power—the threat to kill or to punish, for example—often leads persons to act in ways they find repulsive and repugnant. But the main point is that, since careers involve others, power and influence and controlling strategies are intrinsic to careers.

Encounters, sometimes called *turning points* (52), describe those moments when individuals have a new and often drastically different set of self-identities thrust upon them. Mental patients who undergo mortification rites (where their identities may be challenged), military inductees who have their identity signs (like clothing) removed, and brides who take the final step to the wedding find that after the encounter they cannot return to the past in an unaltered form. In this sense, it can be seen that the career is continually being affected by matters not entirely under the control of the person.

CAREER PHASES.   In general, careers can be plotted in terms of a set of phases or substages. Thus the medical career may have at least four stages: (1) wishing to become a doctor; (2) gaining admission into medical school; (3) acquiring a clientele after graduation; (4) developing a set of informal relationships with medical colleagues. (23) Actually each

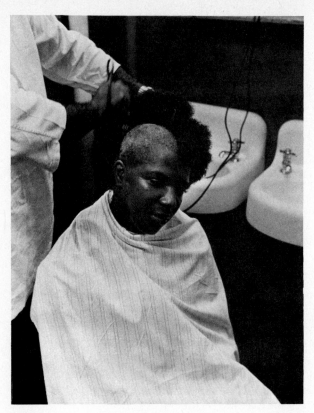

Self-control and a turning-point encounter. (*Richard Lawrence Stack from
Black Star*)

of these stages could be broken into subphases: making it through the
first, second, third, and fourth years; securing a place to practice; and so
on. Many careers have institutional markers that go with them. Thus
Goffman was led to observe (15) that the mental patient's career fell into
three phases: prepatient, inpatient, and postpatient. Location in or out of
the institution that controls the activities associated with the control will
place the person in career or out of career. In this sense, all persons who
have not yet been, but will be, hospitalized for mental illness are prepa-
tients. It would be misleading to assume that all careers are neatly patterned or phased; it is difficult, for example, to plot the marriage career
accurately. In this sense many careers are open-ended.

CAREER FLOW.   As these remarks on career phases suggest, careers are
temporal processes that flow through ongoing elements of social organization. (13, 14) Some carry the individual (the mental patient) into unwanted interactions. Others are more directly controlled by the person
(marriage). The temporal elements of the career can be charted—each has
a unique trajectory. Some trajectories are lingering. They speed up at certain points and then bog down, so to speak. Many deaths are of this
order. (53) Some trajectories are rapid—a person dies soon after an au-

tomobile accident. And then, some careers move along at an even and predictable rate. A college student, for example, may move smoothly through freshman year to graduation three years later. (3) In general, the flow, or temporal shape, of a career will reflect its organizational embeddedness, which, in turn, is influenced by the person's ability to control time's passage—that is, a person can find that other persons or organizations structure how he or she utilizes time; persons vary in the degrees of control they exercise over their own timetables. Organizational careers are more fixed and closed than are careers through marriages or friendships. Thus, the more open-ended the career the more likely it is that its temporal trajectory will be uneven, lingering, and emergent.

Whether they want to or not, all individuals have a personal moral career that encompasses all of their experiences and actions and commitments up to and including the present moment. Thus, while many careers are optional, the personal moral career is not optional. Every individual, accordingly, has a set of accounts or stories that he or she can tell which explain and justify the current status of his or her personal moral career. Sad tales are told by those who feel that their careers have gone astray. Happy tales are told by those who are relatively pleased with the progress of their lives. (15:150–54) In practice, most accounts fall somewhere between sad and happy; this is because a person's multiple identities are never at the same stage of completion, fulfillment, or accomplishment. So he or she will most likely develop a story which is specific to each ongoing career, as well as a master story which accounts for all of them.

MORAL CAREERS AND BIOGRAPHIES

The presumed existence of a personal career leads others to make biographical assumptions about us. If others have only a minimum amount of information about our age, status, education, or family, they will almost necessarily impute a set of biographical details to us. They will assume that we have a work history or a mental history. Thus, the possession of a personal moral career makes everyone vulnerable to attack. We are accountable for our own career, and occasionally may be called upon to elaborate just who we are and why we are as we are. (7) We turn now to the ways in which careers are linked with membership in social worlds.

Membership in Social Worlds

In Chapter 3 when discussing symbolic environments, we touched on the concept of *social worlds*—groupings of individuals bound together by networks of communication or universes of discourse. Whether the members are geographically proximate or not, they share important symbolizations, and hence also share perspectives on "reality." It is significant that the term *social world* is often used in common parlance to refer to such abstract collectivities as the worlds of theater, art, golf, skiing, stamp collecting, birdwatching, mountain climbing, and to occupational groupings like those of medicine and science. The concept, however, is equally applicable to almost any collectivity—including families, perhaps—if we emphasize communication and membership, for membership is not merely a matter of physical or official belonging but of shared symbolization, experiences, and interests. To emphasize this, someone has even written a book about divorced people titled *The World of the Formerly Married.* (24)

The idea of the social world implies that members may be scattered in space. A family does not disintegrate merely because the kinfolk no longer live together (20); and people who play chess and follow the competitions live all over the earth. These players can talk about and play chess with anyone, no matter where they may travel. When Bobby Fischer played Boris Spassky, fans everywhere followed the games with rapt attention. Stamp collectors also belong to an immensely scattered world; they can visit virtually any sizable city in the world and find a store that deals in stamps, where they can find other collectors with whom they can swap stamps and stories. Some social worlds, of course, are less than international in scope, and may even be quite localized, but the symbolic character of their membership is no less true.

Implied in the above examples is that the members can come from diverse backgrounds. Baseball fans discourse enthusiastically and heatedly across the boundaries of social class, region, or age. A cousin of one of the authors is the president of a large corporation and also an avid collector of Australian two-pence stamps; he corresponded for several months with a carpenter who was even more of a specialist. Once, at an airport, when he was traveling on business, he arranged to meet another collector. After two hours of conversation only about stamps, he discovered that the other collector was also a corporation official. Some social worlds, however, do not draw members from such a diversity of backgrounds; they are more closely linked with class, sex, occupation, and economic level. The world of labor union officials is closely linked with socioeconomic background; conversely, polo fans or the collectors of antique Chinese porcelain generally are not "working class." Fishing enthusiasts seem mostly to be men, while mostly women are involved with the world of fashion magazines.

COMMUNICATION AND ACTIVITY   Two key features of all these social worlds are *communication* and *activity.* Considering communication first, we note that all our examples involve conversation or some other form of communication. Typically, when people of a world come together they talk, sooner or later, about things of mutual interest that pertain to their shared world. For instance, golfers talk about their recent games, about their greatest victories and worst shots, about the fine points of technique, including "the latest" they have learned about the games of the experts; and, of course, they swap golf jokes and stories, some of which are about recognizable "social types" like duffers and experts. Any social world is likely to develop its legends and myths which are told and retold; it will also develop some special language, or lingo, for referring to events, objects, and activities that "matter." Many worlds also develop channels of written communication, which sometimes reach elaboration in a multitude of magazines: the world of sailing, for instance, has many magazines, some of them quite specialized to correspond to the different subworlds. At any rate, at the heart of interaction "within" any world is communication—whether written or spoken—when its members are very scattered. Then its media, supplemented by correspondence and by members who travel and speak, are vital to its existence and its membership.

Aside from communicative activity, the members also feel that they belong because they act in reference to these worlds. The members go places and do things: they ski; they buy skiing equipment; they buy and wear skiing clothes; they take trips to ski resorts; and they may "follow" actively the skiing activities of experts either by watching television or by actually going to meets. Even those who do not actually play a game but act the "passive spectator"—to use a term coined by critics of that kind of spectatorship—can be very actively and even passionately involved in watching the sport. This is as true of elderly women watching boxing as of earnest young men mooning over female stars of the theater. We shall say more about the careers and identities of members of these worlds; but it is necessary here to note that some members may be more "professionally" or commercially involved in the world's activities than are others. In evolving worlds, as in scuba diving during its early years, enthusiastic participants began to develop technology and later began to market scuba boards or other equipment. (Similar processes were prevalent in the "surfing" world. (28)) In more developed worlds there is an elaborate division of labor with built-in careers for many people, who profit either commercially or psychologically from their activities.

The more developed the world, the more *subcommunities* (or *segments* or *specialties*) it will have. This makes conceptualization—for the social psychologist—more difficult, since the more developed are these subcommunities the more differential perspectives are there likely to be toward SUBWORLDS the same broad spectrum of the "world" events. Surgeons, for instance, do not necessarily see eye to eye with internists on the question of what to do about ulcers, or a number of other potentially operable symptoms, and that example suggests what Bucher and Strauss (5) have noted—namely, that between the members of related subworlds there may be great antagonism. At the very least, as their activities and interests take them further from each other, some subcommunities tend to be indifferent to each other. A good example is that of young painters in the art world, who may first react with great antagonism to an older style of painting and then acquire their own audience, so that they are in social and work contact only with that audience and with other painters like themselves.

CENTRAL AND PERIPHERAL MEMBERS One more feature of social worlds is worth mentioning, since it is related both to the kinds of participation engaged in by members and the kinds of self-conception which they have. This feature is that these collectivities have members who are more *central,* as well as those who are more *peripheral,* to the world's functioning. Said another way, some persons invest more of their time, energy, money, and themselves into activities associated with the world. These latter include not only the spectators and the amateurs but a large percentage of the "pros"—whether they be managers, stars, coaches, salesmen, manufacturers, or what not. One need not argue whether, in the days of Hollywood's glory, the enthusiastic persons who ran the fan clubs were as central to Hollywood's success as the major investors in the industry; in any event, both were more involved in the movie world, albeit participating in it differently, than were the occasional movie-goers. (33) We shall turn to this aspect of social worlds later, when discussing what centrality and periphery mean to the participants themselves.

Ideologies and Social Worlds

To "belong" to a social world means to be affected, to a greater or lesser degree, by its *symbolic coordinates.* A technical term which is applicable to that phenomenon is *ideology.* (39) Social scientists use the term to refer to any body of systematically related and significant or basic beliefs held by a group. The term was invented during the eighteenth century and used within a political context by opponents who discredited each other's beliefs by finding their sources in selfish or class interests. However, *ideology* no longer conveys simply connotations of falseness and illusion. We shall discuss political and occupational ideologies as instances of how people's beliefs can be affected and sustained by participation in the communication networks of certain worlds.

The citizens of modern nations, when they consider matters pertaining to their governments and how they impinge on things of importance to them, tend to join conflicting ideological camps. These political ideologies are linked with—but also cut across—regional, religious, occupational, class, racial, and other worlds. The ideology is sustained by organizations of committed professionals who mobilize and direct various channels of communication. They produce their own literature, hold meetings, raise money, and compete with other similarly organized groups for access to the mass media. When one ideological camp takes control of the government, it may block or restrict the attempts of others to disseminate their ideologies through the media.

In newly formed nations ideological cleavages are readily apparent, often sharp and bitter, and may eventuate in violence. Even the minimum consensus necessary to form a nation does not exclude the resort to force or possibly civil war. In established, stable nations with long histories, sharp and bitter ideological divisions may exist for many decades. In 1954 a group of scholars (21) assessed the economic and political situation in France. They agreed that France was deeply divided along several ideological lines—class, regional, and religious especially—represented by a series of parties, organizations, newspapers, and other media. They pointed to this situation as the cause of France's inability to meet its grave economic, social, and international problems. The gravity of this political impasse in France eventually created a partial consensus among some of the more powerful groups who produced and supported the de Gaulle regime. Some of the old cleavages are undoubtedly still there behind the public scene.

The grass-roots basis of political ideology can, in a sense, be thought of as existing in the simplest forms of interaction between people. Individuals tend to have as their friends other people who have the same beliefs. (36) They exchange information and views and consequently validate and revalidate the interpretations they already hold, which are disseminated from power centers. Even in the case of the mass media, information and interpretation appear to exert their influence indirectly through the channels of personal communication between opinion leaders and the persons with whom the leaders talk. This latter phenomenon has been formally described in what has been called "the two-step theory of information flow." (30)

Selection pertains not only to choice of friends as communicators, but also to choice of newspapers, journals, and television and radio programs, all of which feed selective facts and interpretations to their audiences. If individuals are not "plugged in" to some extent to opposing channels of communication, there are no countering facts and interpretations. Hence persons who judge election results by polling their friends and associates are sometimes very surprised by the actual election results. Even when persons of a given political view receive the messages that circulate in other channels, they tend to perceive them selectively and to fit them into their own conceptual frameworks.

It is sometimes said that people adopt a political position in terms of self-interest—their own interest or that of their family, class, occupation, or religion. This is an erroneous idea, however, because it does not take into account that people interpret their own interests in different ways and are often uncertain of what their interests are. In the face of conflicting interpretations that are offered, they may be very confused about what their objectives are and can end up by voting against themselves.

Political ideas and convictions are formed, like other ideas, not on the basis of the way the world really is or on actual self-interest, but rather on the world as it is interpreted, and on what people are persuaded to believe to be their interests. The influence of the mass media is obviously great; but its effectiveness is limited by the influence of the smaller communication networks in which people are always involved. Interaction among friends, family members, and associates in work and recreational worlds provides a fund of detailed reports and interpretation of events directly observed or experienced. Such information is generally more persuasive than the more abstract, impersonal products of the mass media. It is perhaps for this reason that a unified propaganda "line," promulgated in nations in which only one official ideology is expressed in the mass media, is often far less effective than is popularly supposed. (34) This is pointed up by a joke reported from behind the iron curtain:

QUESTION: What is the difference between capitalism and communism?

ANSWER: In capitalism man exploits man; in communism it's just the opposite.

RACIAL IDEOLOGY Similar processes operate in the area of race and ethnic relations. The ideologies that groups develop to justify the discrimination process are often based on "definitions of the situation" that bear little relationship to "objective" social facts. Thus one team of researchers (50) noted that discrimination in Latin America, which is often based on the lightness of a person's skin, with a corresponding racial nomenclature to describe variations in skin color, commonly reflects a group's view of itself within the overall class structure. In Cartagena, Colombia, the team observed that when respondents were asked to place photographed Colombians in one of several racial groupings (based on skin color) (50:194):

> The elites showed a tendency to darken people; the middle class tended to darken blancos but to lighten the overall population; the working and lower classes lightened the population, particularly persons with high status, and were relatively imprecise in their definitions.

Whose work, whose career? (*Mimi Forsyth from Monkmeyer Press Photo Service*)

In this sense a person's definition of self as a member of a particular racial grouping, or category, is based on how far up the class ladder he or she has progressed. The Colombian elites and middle-class members were much more willing to discriminate against all other persons than were the working- and lower-class respondents.

In Western nations a chief source of ideology, for males at least, is their work. Everett C. Hughes has asserted and we concur that (23:594): "In our particular society, work organization looms so large as a separate and specialized system of things, and work experience is so fateful a part of every man's life, that we cannot make much headway as students of society and of social psychology without using work as one of our main laboratories." Work today rarely stands alone, for relatively little of it is done outside of organizational structures. Even professionals who have private practices are increasingly abandoning their offices for work within professional organizations, and private entrepreneurs belong increasingly to trade associations. Hence, when we talk about work as a source of ideology, it is necessary to think not only about the nature of a person's work but his or her occupation and position within a work organization. In general, the more rigorous the training demanded for a line of work, the more commitment an individual has to the work; and the more social activity is structured around friends drawn from the

OCCUPATIONAL IDEOLOGY

work world, the more the larger symbolic world is likely to be affected by work.

Countless studies have demonstrated that occupational affiliation or position in work organization or work world profoundly affect persons' views on various matters as well as their actual behavior. Thus, attitudes and behavior toward clients depend very much on the nature of the occupation. Undertakers, as R. W. Habenstein (18:242–44) observes, handle their client's family with suave control. Physicians typically handle their clients with firm authority. Janitors ordinarily can do neither, because they stand in a different relation to their clients. One study shows how their management is a compound of open respect and concealed disrespect. (17) Of course, not all people of the same occupation do the same types of work or meet others in the same types of relationships. Thus, some musicians play in large dance bands and play mostly for affluent dancers, while other musicians play for intently listening audiences who would sooner be caught dead than dancing. (1) Differential positions within work organizations and in different types of work organizations afford differential experiences with consequent impact on perspectives taken toward issues and audiences that may be far removed from the work itself. As M. Janowitz (29) suggests in his study of the American military, there are striking differences between officers who have come up through administrative routes and those who are experienced in front-line battle; likewise, there are considerable differences between officers who work in the three armed services. All these constitute work worlds.

Work, occupation, and organizational position can contribute to the formation of a person's occupational ideology in quite complex ways. We shall illustrate this from a study of Chicago psychiatrists. (54) In the United States there are two dominant ideologies held by psychiatrists. One ideology gives priority to biological etiology and physical treatment. The other gives priority to psychic processes and psychotherapeutic treatment. The first one, somatic ideology, receives continued support from the advances of biological science and from the biological orientation of most physicians. Nevertheless, the psychotherapeutic ideology has become the more influential during the past three decades.

In general, these two groups of psychiatrists live in entirely separate professional worlds. They may know some of the other variety, providing they use the same hospital, but they tend to belong to quite different sociability and communication networks. They go to different professional meetings, or if they go to national ones, they move in different circles when there. They read a rather different array of journals. In a large city like Chicago, they may have only the foggiest notions of psychiatrists of other ideological positions and what these individuals think of them. When interviewed about the nature of Chicago psychiatry, the psychiatrists who tended toward either ideological position differed a great deal in their conceptions of what psychiatry consisted of in their city. Some psychiatrists and some institutions were visible to some respondents, but they were invisible to other respondents. The psychotherapists all knew, and many were affiliated with, the local psychoanalytic institute, but were vague about other psychiatric institutions (54:42):

> Well, there are those people who identify—I'll start from what is most familiar to me—identify themselves as analysts . . . in terms of their training and the professional activity in which they engage. Then we go to the other end which is furthest away from that—something which I'm not particularly familiar with at first hand, I don't have contact with these people. These are people who do predominantly somatic-type therapy, coupled with some kind of psychotherapeutic orientation on the part of those who are not analysts. . . . My God, what do people do who have not had analytic training or at least analytically based training. . . . I mean what do those people do who purport to do psychotherapy?

The somatic psychiatrists were even more vague about local institutions, because in general there was less communication among them than among the psychotherapists, who had the institute as a central training, educational, and sociability locale.

An occupational ideology then is sustained through both formal and informal channels of communication. Once absorbed, it significantly influences how people regard and carry out their work, and how they form relationships to clients, assistants, and colleagues. It profoundly affects their perception so that they see symptoms selectively and interpretively. They diagnose and treat them accordingly. Their occupational convictions also deeply affect their self-conceptions; insofar as they regard certain kinds of work worth doing well, they also evaluate their own performances according to that standard. Thus, psychotherapists do not judge themselves in terms of pharmacological skills but in terms of success and failure with psychotherapeutic methods. Since their occupational convictions greatly affect the colleagues they see at work or socially, their self-conceptions are further affected.

In these respects, modern urban life can be viewed as a complex intermeshing of occupational, racial, political, and even residential ideologies. These ideologies come together inside the social worlds that urban inhabitants construct and destroy. (55, 56)

Reference Groups

There is a body of literature—now over thirty years old—which relates to the concept of *reference group*. Although this concept was not developed in terms of social worlds, except by T. Shibutani, to whom we refer below, it is useful to think of it that way. (47, 48) First, however, we shall present some standard materials bearing on this concept.

Reference group (25, 27, 32, 35, 42) is generally thought of as pertaining to the fact that people evaluate themselves and orient their behavior by reference to (1) the groups in which they hold official membership; (2) others to which they aspire or to which they hope to belong in the future; and (3) others which they reject and definitely do not wish to belong to. A reference group is thus any group with which persons psychologically identify themselves or in relation to which they think of themselves. Implicit in this idea is that their existing group memberships may be relatively meaningless to persons whose primary "ego anchorages" are established with reference to groups with which they are not formally or objectively linked. This type of anticipatory allegiance is especially noticeable in a mobile society in which the ambition to raise one's status is characteristically encouraged. (45, 46)

Reference groups are thus said to establish the individual's organizing conceptions or frames of reference for ordering experiences, perceptions, and ideas of self. M. Sherif has stated the matter as follows (45:214):

> The individual's directive attitudes, namely, ego-attitudes, which define and regulate his behavior to other persons, other groups, and to an important extent even to himself, are formed in relation to values and norms of his reference groups. They constitute an important basis of his self-identity, of his sense of belongingness, of the core of his social ties.

H. Hyman (25, 26) is credited with the first use of the term *reference groups,* analyzing the influence of such groups on college students' conceptions of their status. He found that they compared themselves with others in the following respects, listed in order of frequency: (1) economic, (2) intellectual, (3) social, (4) looks, (5) culture, (6) athletics, (7) prestige, (8) general, (9) character, (10) politics, (11) sexual qualities, (12) religion, and (13) esteem. Among the matters mentioned by students in connection with the ratings they gave themselves were family background, membership in special groups, breeding, people known, money, dates, ability to get along with the other sex, degrees, achievement, race, formal education, reasoning ability, intelligence, appreciation of the arts, reading, worldly experience, and academic background of the family. Hyman noted that the groups referred to in making comparisons differed among the subjects and were of crucial importance in self-conception. Thus, one subject whose income was $336 per year gave $900 per year as an amount that would make her "joyous," whereas another subject with an income of $4,000 per year said he would be content with no less than $25,000. Hyman found that, in general, small intimate groups were more important for reference in estimates of oneself than was the general population. Individuals chose the points on which they compared themselves with others so as to achieve the most satisfactory position possible.

L. Festinger's (11) experiments with voting behavior in relation to religious affiliation also shed light on the way in which reference groups influence behavior. Festinger compared the voting of Catholic and Jewish girls in several types of situations. In one, the girls knew nothing of each other's or the candidates' religious affiliations; in another, they knew the affiliation of the candidates but not each other's; and in the third situation, they knew each other's affiliations as well as those of the candidates. These experiments showed that the Catholic girls tended to vote for Catholic candidates when their own affiliation was known to the other voters, and that the Jewish girls voted for Jewish candidates mainly when their religious affiliations were not so known. Festinger supposed that Jewish girls felt free to vote as Jews when they were anonymous, whereas Catholic girls felt compelled to vote as Catholics only when they were openly identified as such.

Early studies like Hyman's and Festinger's were done by psychologists but for sociologists. R. K. Merton and A. S. Kitt (40) made the concept better known when they reinterpreted findings reported in *The American Soldier* in the light of the reference group concept. They showed, for example, how inexperienced troops were influenced by association with soldiers who had combat experience. Inexperienced troops, desiring to affiliate themselves with those who had experience in battle, tended to take over the latter's norms and values and to evaluate themselves by reference to them.

POSITIVE, NEGATIVE, AND MULTIPLE REFERENCE GROUPS

T. Newcomb (41:255–32) extended this concept in a study of the relationship of the attitudes of Bennington College students to the attitudes of *positive* and *negative reference groups*—the former being those in which one desires to be accepted and treated as a member, and the latter those to which one is opposed and in which one does not desire membership.

The idea of the negative reference group emphasizes that when one commits oneself to the viewpoint of values of one group, this fact automatically places one in a potentially hostile or competitive position with respect to other groups. Thus, for a Democrat the Republican party is a negative reference group, particularly at election time, while the Democratic party performs this function for Republicans. This illustration points to a pervasive aspect of human social relationships, namely, that some degree of conflict, hostility, avoidance, or antagonism is generally apparent or implicit in them, and these negative features constitute essential aspects of social structure. The two dominant political parties in the United States are in conflict, but they also depend upon each other and upon the conflict between them for their continued existence. To be *for* something implies being *against* something else. If one associates with certain people and groups, one must to some extent avoid other people and groups. There are satisfactions in opposing or fighting against something. The views of the atheist and the communist-hater are examples of the influence of negative reference groups, because they are distinguished by what they are against rather than by what they are for. Some persons find particular satisfaction in such hostile relationships; they may be said to be predominately influenced by their negative, rather than their positive, reference groups.

The concept of the reference group has also been elaborated in an effort to make it square with the complexity of identifications involving *multiple group memberships,* positive and negative relationships to the same group, multiple positive and negative group influences in the same situation, and shifting loyalties and relationships. The problem of what constitutes group membership is itself none too easy except when one deals with formal membership (the tokens of which are payment of dues, membership, and active participation), and these memberships are often of little or no significance for the person's behavior. Membership in a social class, for example, involves none of these. Does this mean that a person's class membership is to be judged by his or her way of life and by how he or she thinks, regardless of occupation and income? If we ask whether the undercover FBI agent in the communist party is really a member of the party, some of the problems of determining membership in groups are obvious. Most people would probably say that in this case, even though the FBI man pays dues to the communist party and carries a membership card, he is not really a member because he does not identify himself with the party, nor does he adopt its position. The party is, in short, not a reference group for him, although it might be called a negative reference group.

COMPARATIVE AND NORMATIVE REFERENCE GROUPS

Besides the ideas of positive, negative, and multiple reference groups, an early distinction was drawn, initially by Harold Kelley, between comparative and normative reference groups. (31, 32) *Comparative reference groups,* in the same sense as used in Hyman's study, pertained to the groups with which an individual compared him- or herself. *Normative reference groups* were those which were the sources of the individual's values. All these distinctions—not all of which are used or agreed upon by everyone who uses the term—have recently led Margaret Williams, a sympathetic critic, to remark that the term is "still not conceptually clarified. . . ." She also warned that "reference group theory is fair prey to falling into the mold of extreme group determinism. . . . 'Reference groups determine behavior.' " (59:550, 552) Bernard Cohen has ironically phrased the same criticism this way: "Your reference group is a group that you behave like and you behave like them because they're your reference group." (6:104)

Considerations like these led Manford Kuhn, a leading symbolic interactionist, to comment that the concept of reference group "represents a vast simplification of the idea of the other." (35:13) He attributed the concept's quick rise to popularity in part to that simplification, and went on to criticize the questionnaire studies done by reference group researchers: "There is always some mental relief associated with the implication in any operation that a broad and elliptical idea is 'nothing but' these marks on these pieces of paper." (35:11) He suggested (35:15) the complexity of who those others might be by noting "elementary distinctions" such as those based on time, continuity, physical and social space: "We can differentiate present others from absent others; proximal others from distal others; contemporary others from past others; continuous others from intermittent others; in-category others from out-category others; immediate, impulsive, passing others from considerable others." Kuhn then coined a term, *orientational other*, which refers to others to whom people are most fully committed, who have given them their most crucial concepts and categories, who have provided and continue to provide them with their categories of self and other and with meaningful roles to which such assignments refer, and to others with whom their self-conception is basically sustained or changed. (8)

Virtually identical with our own position is that of Shibutani (47, 48), who has suggested a redefinition of the reference group concept in terms of a conception of social worlds that squares with ours. Noting the salient characteristics of mass societies in which persons frequently internalize discordant values of different groups, Shibutani suggested that "much of the interest in reference groups arises out of concern with situations in which a person is confronted with the necessity of acting on the basis of alternative definitions, where he must make a choice between two or more organized perspectives." The key problem "in the study of reference groups . . . is that of ascertaining whose confirming responses are needed in order to sustain a given point of view." This leads to a consideration of which audiences—actual, imagined, or potential—the person is acting toward and with chief reference to. Shibutani, in a later paper on reference groups (48), goes on to relate these diverse audiences to diverse social worlds. In each world, "there develops a universe of discourse. Pertinent experiences are categorized in particular ways, and a special set of symbols is used to refer to them. . . . Each world is a universe of regularized mutual response, an arena in which there is some kind of organization that facilitates anticipating the behavior of others."

In short, the emphasis here is on interacting members of social worlds, where "membership" is linked with participation in communication networks, or in Shibutani's phrasing, within social worlds whose boundaries "are set neither by territory nor formal group membership, but by the limits of effective communication." (48:137)

Defined and used in this way, the concept of the reference group may do more than merely point to audiences otherwise unsuspected by the observer. In its present state the concept is chiefly useful for focusing attention on the more subtle nuances of identification and loyalty. The problem of accounting for individual behavior in terms of reference groups, therefore, centers around discovering which communication networks are operating, what information is being channeled to the person, and toward which audiences he addresses him- or herself and orients his or her behavior. The investigator's problem is thus rendered very complicated because he or she cannot rely on fixed external criteria like status, office, age, sex, or social class but must seek out a more subtle range of symbolic involvements in a multiplicity of social worlds.

Indeed, Raymond L. Schmitt (42), in the most extensive review of the reference group literature to date, concluded that there does not yet exist a viable or complete theory of the reference group. In his synthesis of this body of research, he argues that the concept refers to three interrelated notions: the reference other, the relationships between the individual and the reference other, and the individual in question. The reference other orientation, he proposes, must be placed more squarely within the symbolic interactionist framework. The present discussion of social worlds represents one way to make conceptual sense out of this tremendously vague and ill-defined concept.

Changing Worlds: Danger and Challenge

In modern societies, many social worlds are characterized by considerable rates of change, while others are even more highly volatile and unstable. If one thinks of activities like skiing, horse racing, or stock car racing, one can see that over the past two decades the associated worlds have expanded amazingly both in number of participants and in audience size. (44) They have become quite popular. Tennis, once the preserve of the more moneyed Americans, is now, according to a recent report, on the way to becoming a mass sport—complete with new types of clothing, a vast increase in the manufacture and sales of equipment, new kinds of celebrities and competitive matches, and an explosion of media reporting. Into many worlds there is built an inner dynamism—especially those worlds that are expanding—that is reflected in a kind of "budding" process, whereby "the" world becomes differentiated and, as already

Changing a social world: new dangers
and new challenges. (*Wide World*)

mentioned, subcommunities of interested persons begin to talk about
and do different things. Thus, while there is, in some sense, a general
world of scuba divers, some members are interested exclusively in un-
derwater photography, others are interested in exploration. In mountain
climbing, some individuals are expert at climbing steep but not inordi-
nately high ice mountains, while others organize expeditions to scale the
high Himalayas. Worlds and subworlds can also decline in popularity
and size and over time may even quite disappear. This phenomenon is
associated sometimes with generational differences: for instance, the
younger generations of mountain climbers use instruments that allow
them to cling to the surface of mountains which they climb vertically; the
generation that invented this mode of climbing looked with scorn upon
the older climbers who scaled mountains by foot, regarding this merely
as a species of hiking.

Whether the worlds are expanding or contracting, if they are changing at all they represent danger to some people and challenge to others.
An older tennis player can be overwhelmed not only by the sheer
number of newcomers, but by improvements in techniques, by new

jargon, and by the new perspectives toward the sport itself, for a mass sport cannot be a "gentleman's sport." Imagine what would happen if every talented ghetto youngster were given a tennis racket, training, and a chance to play freely at the most exclusive tennis clubs. We know how awkward it was for the first black tennis players when they were introduced into predominantly white, affluent American tennis competition—let alone the clubs. People can be wounded deeply—their self-conceptions battered, trampled on, wrenched—when their worlds are invaded by newcomers and leadership taken away. The history of politics is replete with the story of old leaders and elites who, when overwhelmed although not utterly vanquished by newcomers, mourned not merely the sharing of power but felt bitterly the ignominy of their loss: their world of political and governmental elitism was no longer only theirs. On the other hand, changes in social worlds can also represent great opportunity to those who stand to, or can manage to, profit from the changes. This point is more obvious for expanding worlds than for contracting ones, but even in the face of marked decline, some people are able to find satisfying substitute activities and careers. On the other hand, many social worlds trap their participants and limit their future career changes. (58, 28)

THE COLLAPSE OF SOCIAL WORLDS
The collapse or complete disappearance of a world, of course, seems more obviously to represent a threat. Its members may stand not only to lose fun or money but self-esteem. Ten years after the end of World War II, one of the authors visited Frankfurt, where he met a few surviving members of a once-thriving artistic community; they were still in a deep psychological depression and clinging to their memories of a glorious past. For such phenomena, sociologists have coined the term *collapse of social worlds*. However, what they have had in mind mostly is the rapid decline or disappearance of political, social class, or ethnic communities. During and directly after World War II, the social structures of European countries changed rapidly and extensively with a resultant widespread collapse of individual and social worlds. Countless Europeans lost their stable anchorage points. Families were broken up or disappeared, and when people displaced by the war returned to their communities, they found that the occupations, institutions, and even the physical landmarks around which their former ambitions and purposes had centered were gone. Under such circumstances individuals variously handle their loss of function, running the gamut from suicide to creating new functions for themselves within the emerging social structures of their nations. Also, new institutional devices may appear for helping the most unfortunate victims, since these people cannot return to old jobs,

occupations, and other social positions and may not by themselves find alternative paths.

An especially dramatic and poignant instance of a collectively shared collapse of a world is when a nation is conquered or experiences a radical social revolution. Some sense of what this was like when the Nazis forcibly occupied European countries is conveyed by G. E. Gedye, an English journalist who was in Austria when the Nazis took over that country. As in other countries, mass suicides were one response to the collapse of the normal world. Gedye wrote about the reaction of the Jews (12:305):

> It is quite impossible to convey to anyone outside Austria in how matter-of-fact a way the Jews of Austria today refer to this way out of their agony . . . Jewish friends spoke to one of their intention to commit suicide with no more emotion than they had formerly talked of making an hour's journey by train. . . . It is impossible . . . to imagine what it means for one-sixth of the population of Vienna to be made pariahs overnight, deprived of all civil rights, including the right to retain property large or small, the right to be employed or to give employment, to exercise a profession, to enter restaurants, cafes, bathing beaches, baths or public parks, to be faced daily and hourly, without hope of relief, with the foulest insults which ingenious and vicious minds can devise, to be liable always to be turned overnight out of house and home, and at any hour of every day and every night to arrest without the pretense of a charge or hope of a definite sentence, however heavy—and with all this to find every country in the world selfishly closing its frontiers to you when, after being plundered of your last farthing, you seek to escape. For most of the non-Jewish victims of the Nazis, many of whom are now sharing the punishment of the Jews, there is a hope that one day the nightmare may pass. For the Jews there is none while the Nazis rule.

At the close of World War II the counterpart of this phenomenon occurred as the Nazi leaders, in their turn, saw their world falling about them. E. Durkheim (9) has described this type of suicide as *anomic suicide*. He contrasted it with another type of suicide, which he called *altruistic*. Rather than representing despair and reflecting group disorganization, this *altruistic* kind of self-destruction indicates a high degree of social integration.

Suicides also accompany social revolution and other major social catastrophes. Obviously, this is not the only response that people can make. Sometimes they are able to emigrate to other countries, where they attempt to reconstruct something of their old social worlds. Societies of aristocratic Russian émigrés in Paris, and settlements of German emigrants who fled the Nazis and settled in American cities are notable for their communal adaptation to new circumstances. The adaptation is only partial, however, for the host country's ways are never thoroughly embraced, nor are those of the old country abandoned. After the Russian

Revolution and between the two world wars, Russian restaurants abounded in Paris, as the émigrés made the most of their heritage. The restaurants provided them with financial support and symbolic reinforcement. When whole communities suffer the loss of position and homeland, they are able to confront their common loss together and in some part create a new life. Inevitably, some of these individuals leave their huddled world and strike out into the larger society with various results. The sons and daughters of immigrants face an entirely different set of problems, and their behaviors and solutions must necessarily also be different.

One final comment might be made to indicate how the variable solutions to collective loss of world are linked with structural conditions. When the Chinese communists successfully took over China, many emigrants fled to Hong Kong and Taiwan. In both locations many of them have been successful in making an adaptation and not giving in to the collapse of their worlds. Hong Kong was and is thoroughly Chinese in character, and while many individuals have doubtless been permanently demoralized by migration, the immigrants, as a whole, seem to have made a successful adaptation. The merchants have been so successful that they are probably more affluent than they would be in China. In Taiwan, a different set of circumstances existed; the deposed Chinese government quite literally conquered the people of Taiwan, who had previously lived under Japanese control. The immigrants could not so easily reconstitute their worlds, because they were accustomed to ruling over a huge country. Although they rule over a considerable population, the island is tiny when compared with China; across a narrow body of water their successors rule without any apparent danger of being ousted. Any visitor to Taiwan who talks with the "mainland" Chinese soon becomes aware of some patterned forms of their discontent.

Alienation and Modern Society

A popular view of life in modern mass societies and the impersonal environment of urban centers stress alienation, frustration, and the sense of meaninglessness that contemporary mass societies sometimes or overwhelmingly generate. Mass media writers and social scientists, too, use terms like "our sick society" and think of industrialized nations as consisting of large undifferentiated masses of robotlike individuals, regimented in their daily activities and their leisure time pursuits. Some views of alienation include management and manipulation by powerful conspiratorial elites who possess the major share of the nation's wealth and who control its mass media. From this point of view, the average citizen is seen as a victim or dupe of social forces and pressures that he or she does not understand and is powerless to control. A specific ver-

Social worlds and urban disorganization? (*Robert Capa/Magnum*)

sion of this set of beliefs surfaced during the 1960s, when the universities, so swollen in size, were criticized and reacted to in terms of their impersonality and bureaucratization. In general, it is argued that in the "advanced" industrialized nations, the old values once represented by the family, the neighborhood, the church, and the small community have disintegrated, leaving people unattached, rootless, and disenchanted.

While this view of modern life will no doubt seem overdrawn to most, and while it often reflects the personal backgrounds and experiences of those who hold it, it does focus attention upon some conspicuous features and trends in contemporary nations. It is true, as the literature on anomie emphasizes, that people are encouraged to strive for goals while simultaneously denied access to the means of attaining them; that there are many persons who fall by the wayside or stand on the sidelines; and that there are marginal persons who belong to few groups, remain uncommitted, and are not caught up in significant and meaningful social enterprises. There are others who actively revolt against what they perceive as the emptiness and meaninglessness of their lives by joining with other like-minded persons to promote causes, to change the society, or to find means of escaping from its demands.

Selves, Careers, and Social Worlds

Anchored social relationships and alienation in public life. (*Bob Adelman*)

In contrast to those who deal with their marginality problems collectively, there are individual isolates who float about from one job to another, and who manage to find only peripheral and often fleeting positions on the edges of group structures. These persons are often troubled, dissatisfied, unattached to work or the opposite sex, and generally unanchored in the web of relationships from which most persons derive their satisfactions and their sense of identity and personal worth. Some of these unattached persons end up in mental hospitals, some spend time in jail or prison, but others stay out of "trouble." They join organizations, tending to drift through them, but rarely get committed in any deep sense to anything or anybody. These people are not just at odds with the government, the middle class, or some other feature of the nation; they are truly alienated. Yet they are not simply alienated from some vague entity known as "society," rather they have no genuine commitments to or identifications with any "meaningful" social world. Nor is it true that they never had such attachments—sometimes the worlds important to them have collapsed or disappeared or changed beyond endurance, but they have not had the flexibility or vitality to find others that "matter."

Life Cycle: Adult Transformations

The collapse of a world is the ultimate danger for the selves of those persons who are most deeply implicated in the realities of that world. Accordingly, one major aspect of self pertains to the matter of loyalty to one's social worlds. After participating in a social world, one develops deep obligations to what it stands for, as well as to fellow participants. To leave it, or to have it collapse, means more than a readjustment of one's activities; it means a foreclosing of obligations and perhaps even a smashing betrayal of the others' expectations. A classic instance is the upwardly mobile person who finds the requirements and satisfactions of his or her world of origin increasingly in conflict with the world of his or her aspirations. The sociological, as well as the fictional and biographical literature, reflect the various outcomes of this conflict. If roots in the old world are strong enough, mobility may be abandoned. The opposite may occur when roots are not deep or the mobile aspirant can find no ready compromise with family and friends; then all ties with the old world are cut. Among the most drastic examples of such severance is the abandonment of spouse and children; another is passing into a white or gentile or bohemian world. A type of modified passing, wherein the person occasionally returns home or keeps former connections surreptitiously, illustrates the range of possibilities open to those who experience this conflict between staying back home and moving out.

Such terrible strains can be engendered, however, by balancing allegiance and aspiration, so that when attempts at articulation finally fail, a person opts for one or another competing path. A vivid instance of actual and symbolic leaving home for a successful career is described by Moss Hart (19), who immediately after a big celebration following the initial performance of his first Broadway hit took a taxi to his home in Brooklyn. His family was asleep. He stood looking at the shabby apartment—he had for years hated his poverty—the "dust of countless black-hearted days clung to every crevice of the squalid ugly furniture" which he had known since childhood. "To walk out of it forever—not piecemeal, but completely—would give meaning to the wonder of what had happened to me, make success tangible, decisive. . . ." He woke his family, who in "stunned silence" listened while he told them they were all going to leave immediately for a hotel, without packing a thing. "We're walking out of here and starting fresh . . . with just what clothes you put on and tomorrow we'll get rid of those, too." An hour later, as they were leaving in a blinding rainstorm, Hart dashed back and threw the windows wide open so that the rain "whipped in through the windows like a broadside of artillery fire," flooding the furniture. He looked around "with satisfaction, feeling neither guilty nor foolish. . . . It was the hallmark, the final signature of defiance and liberation. Short of arson, I could do no more. I slammed the door behind me without looking back." As in many success stories, although the hero had cut his ties with a despised lower-class world, he had taken his family upwards with him.

Another aspect of the involved self pertains to "commitments," that is, the resources, time, energy, money, emotions, which one has invested in certain activities and relationships. Entrance into any world involves increasing commitment, for not only do other persons' demands on the self increase, but the person makes certain demands upon him- or herself as when he or she expends resources. (43)

In extreme cases, when drawn almost totally into a new world, individuals may drop their commitments to old ones; thus, converts to a religious sect may be required to quit their jobs, take up residence in a communal setting, and devote themselves wholly to sectarian activities. They must end all or most of their previous relationships, including leaving their spouses or converting them. Most of us, of course, do not face that kind of black-and-white situation but do juggle commitments to the multiple worlds in which we participate. Moreover, our commitments are not static, for we are likely simultaneously to be loosening some and tightening others.

This articulation of activities and resources can be a complex matter. Sometimes, of course, the requirements of worlds mesh pretty well, so that, for instance, a husband can devote evenings and weekends to his family but daytime hours to his work world. Or a businesswoman may get interested in the world of art and begin to collect paintings. Ordinarily she can, without undue strain, juggle the competing requirements of time, energy, and finances so that her avocational and vocational careers do not run grievously afoul of one another. However, those concerns not only may become slightly and occasionally competitive, but the collector's instinct may begin to run riot and begin to use up time, effort, and money previously allocated to the business and family side of her life. Some collectors have solved this conflict by leaving their jobs and work careers to become owners of art galleries, immersing themselves throroughly in the world of art. They continue to collect and yet stay comfortably and sometimes very profitably "in business." On the other hand, commitments to work and family may result in someone's sharply ending his or her participation in some other world; a friend of ours, for instance, eventually ended his commitment to the world of chess, because his wife's bitter complaints about his neglect of her began to affect their relationship.

Dropping out of worlds, with accompanying end of commitment, may also occur under less conflicting circumstances. In fact, probably most dropping out is more of a "dropping away." People's interests change over the life cycle, so that they are no longer so concerned with doing well or properly with regard to participation in certain worlds, whether they be vocational or familiar or avocational. Also, as noted earlier, most worlds are continually changing, so that people may no longer find themselves comfortable in a particular world or may simply be less interested in its affairs. So they drift out of it, cutting down on their associated activities, modifying the nature of their associated careers, loosening their ties with those with whom they have been more or less deeply involved, and resisting efforts to draw them back. The "subjective" side of this withdrawal is that they have begun to think differently about "things" than the world's members, including their former self. Much later they may even be unable to recapture or recall the former perspectives. At the very least, these will no longer make much sense to them. To grasp this point, the reader has only to watch adolescent children who take up and drop various activities—stamp collecting, bird watching, basketball. Years later they either cannot recollect what it was like to do those things or even remember that they did them.

We should not make the error of assuming that the end of the commitment means simply a cessation of the activities that normally accompany membership in that world. At the very least, a small "portion" of the self is no longer involved in those activities and in the associated relationships with other persons. At the other extreme—as represented by major conversions—the very nature of reality is changed. This means that the symbolic coordinates, as well as the accompanying social relationships which are closely associated with them, of a person's life get drastically changed. Most of us, most of the time, stand somewhere between those two extremes. Characteristically, we are engaged in a continuous process of allowing ourselves to be involved, while also seeking to extricate ourselves from involvement in one or another social world. The articulation of those involvements is surely a central practical problem for the citizens of modern nations, just as it is a central theoretical problem for social scientists who wish to understand life in those complex "societies."

Summary

Every action of the individual is potentially fateful or consequential. This is reflected in the fact that persons have moral careers which reflect their connections and commitments to other individuals. Persons are differentially able to control their own careers, but many times, when social worlds collapse, or when large-scale social disruptions occur, they find that their fates are determined by others or by events beyond their control. Any mass society can be studied from the standpoint of the social worlds that it encompasses. Some of these worlds are tight-knit; others are loose and scattered over large social spaces. Some demand a great deal from their members; others demand very little. The concept of reference group points up the fact that individuals relate themselves in various ways to different groups and that their group affiliations and commitments virtually shape their self-evaluation. We have argued also that when persons report feelings of alienation from their society, they are in fact expressing alienation from specific social worlds. Social life is an inherently moral concern, involving an articulation of actions that variously tie involved selves to one another.

References

1. Becker, Howard S., *Outsiders: Studies in the Sociology of Deviance* (rev. ed. with new Chap. 10). New York: The Free Press, 1973.
2. ———, and Anselm L. Strauss, "Careers, Personality and Adult Socialization," *American Journal of Sociology,* vol. 62 (November 1956), pp. 253–63.
3. ———, Blanche Geer, and Everett Hughes, *Making the Grade: The Academic Side of College Life.* New York: Wiley, 1968.
4. Blankenship, Ralph L., "Organizational Careers: An Interactionist Perspective," *Sociological Quarterly,* vol. 14 (Winter 1973), pp. 88–98.
5. Bucher, Rue, and Anselm L. Strauss, "Professions in Process," *American Journal of Sociology,* vol. 66 (January 1961), pp. 325–34.
6. Cohen, Bernard, "The Process of Choosing a Reference Group," in Joan Criswell, Herbert Solomon, and Patrick Suppes (eds.), *Mathematical Methods in Small Group Processes.* Stanford, Calif.: Stanford University Press, 1962, pp. 101–18.
7. Denzin, Norman K., "Children and Their Caretakers," *Transaction,* vol. 8 (July–August 1971), pp. 62–72.
8. ———, "The Significant Others of a College Population," *Sociological Quarterly,* vol. 7 (1966), pp. 298–310.
9. Durkheim, E., *Le Suicide.* Paris: Librairie Felix Alcan, 1897.
10. Faulkner, Robert R., "Orchestra Interaction: Some Features of Communication and Authority in an Artistic Organization," *Sociological Quarterly,* vol. 14 (Spring 1973), pp. 147–57.
11. Festinger, L., "The Role of Group Belongingness in a Voting Situation," *Human Relations,* vol. 2 (1947), pp. 154–80.
12. Gedye, G. E., *Fallen Bastions.* London: Victor Gollancz, 1939.
13. Glaser, Barney G., and Anselm L. Strauss, *Status Passage.* Chicago: Aldine, 1971.
14. ———, *Time for Dying.* Chicago: Aldine, 1968.
15. Goffman, Erving, "The Moral Career of the Mental Patient," in *Asylums: Essays on the Social Situation of Mental Patients and Other Inmates.* Garden City, N.Y.: Doubleday, 1961, pp. 128–69.
16. ———, "The Nature of Deference and Demeanor," *American Anthropologist,* vol. 58 (June 1956), pp. 473–502.
17. Gold, R., "Janitors versus Tenants: A Status-Income Dilemma," *American Journal of Sociology,* vol. 57 (1952), pp. 486–93.

18. Habenstein, R. W., "Sociology of Occupations: The Case of the American Funeral Director," in A. Rose (ed.), *Human Behavior and Social Processes*. Boston: Houghton Mifflin, 1962, pp. 225–46.
19. Hart, Moss, *Act One*. New York: Knopf, 1959.
20. Hess, Robert D., and Gerald Handel, *Family Worlds*. Chicago: University of Chicago Press, 1959.
21. Hoffman, S., et al., *In Search of France*. Cambridge, Mass.: Harvard University Press, 1963.
22. Hughes, Everett C., "Institutional Office and the Person," *American Journal of Sociology*, vol. 43 (1937), pp. 404–13.
23. ———, *Men and Their Work*. New York. The Free Press, 1958.
24. Hunt, Morton, *The World of the Formerly Married*. New York: McGraw-Hill, 1966.
25. Hyman, H., "The Psychology of Status," *Archives of Psychology*, vol. 269 (1942), pp. 1–94.
26. ———, "Reflections on Reference Groups," *Public Opinion Quarterly*, vol. 24 (1960), pp. 303–96.
27. ———, and E. Singer (eds.), *Readings in Reference Group Theory*. New York: The Free Press, 1968.
28. Irwin, John, *Scenes*. Beverley Hills, Calif.: Sage Publications, 1977.
29. Janowitz, M., *The Professional Soldier*. New York: The Free Press, 1962.
30. Katz, Elihu, "Communications Research and the Image of Society: Convergence of Two Traditions," in A. G. Smith (ed.), *Communication and Culture*. New York: Holt, Rinehart and Winston, 1966.
31. Kelley, Harold, "Two Functions of Reference Groups," in G. Swanson, T. Newcomb, and E. Hartley (eds.), *Readings in Social Psychology*. New York: Holt, Rinehart and Winston, 1952, pp. 410–14.
32. Kemper, Theodore D., "Reference Groups: Socialization and Achievement," *American Sociological Review*, vol. 33 (February 1968), pp. 31–45.
33. Klapp, Orrin, *Symbolic Leaders*. Chicago: Aldine, 1965.
34. Klapper, J., "What We Know about the Effects of Mass Communication: The Brink of Hope," in A. G. Smith (ed)., *Communication and Culture*. New York: Holt, Rinehart and Winston, 1966, pp. 535–51.
35. Kuhn, Manford H., "The Reference Group Reconsidered," *Sociological Quarterly*, vol. 5 (1964), pp. 5–21.
36. Lazarsfeld, P. F., B. Berelson, and H. Gaudet, *The People's Choice*. New York: Columbia University Press, 1948.
37. Lofland, John, *Doomsday Cult*. Englewood Cliffs, N.J.: Prentice-Hall, 1966.
38. ———, and Rodney Stark, "Conversion to a Deviant Perspective," *American Sociological Review*, vol. 30 (December 1965), pp. 862–75.
39. Mannheim, K., *Ideology and Utopia*. New York: Harcourt Brace Jovanovich, 1936.
40. Merton, R. K., and A. S. Kitt, "Contributions to the Theory of Reference Group Behavior," in R. K. Merton and P. F. Lazersfeld (eds.), *Studies in the Scope and Method of "The American Soldier."* New York: The Free Press, 1950, pp. 70–105.
41. Newcomb, T., *Social Psychology*. New York: Holt, Rinehart and Winston, 1950.
42. Schmitt, Raymond L., *The Reference Other Orientation: An Extension of the Reference Group Concept*. Carbondale, Ill.: Southern Illinois University Press, 1972.

43. Schwartz, Barry, "The Social Psychology of the Gift," *American Journal of Sociology,* vol. 73 (July 1967), pp. 1–11.

44. Scott, Marvin, *The Racing Game.* Chicago: Aldine, 1968.

45. Sherif, M., *Group Relations at the Crossroads.* New York: Harper & Row, 1953.

46. ———, J. O. Harvey, B. J. White, and R. Hood, *Theoretical and Experimental Studies in Interpersonal and Group Relations.* Norman, Okla.: University of Oklahoma Press, 1954.

47. Shibutani, Tamotsu, "Reference Groups as Perspectives," *American Journal of Sociology,* vol. 60 (1955), pp. 562–69.

48. ———, "Reference Groups and Social Control," in A. Rose (ed.), *Human Behavior and Social Processes.* Boston: Houghton Mifflin, 1962, pp. 128–47.

49. Simmel, Georg, *Conflict and the Web of Group Affiliations,* ed. and trans. by R. Bendix and E. C. Hughes. New York: The Free Press, 1953.

50. Solaun, Mauricio, and Sidney Kronus, *Discrimination without Violence: Miscegenation and Racial Conflict in Latin America.* New York: Wiley, 1973.

51. Stebbins, R. A., "Career: The Subjective Approach," *Sociological Quarterly,* vol. 11 (Winter 1970), pp. 32–49.

52. Strauss, Anselm L., *Mirrors and Masks.* San Francisco: Sociology Press, 1969.

53. ———, and Barney G. Glaser, *Anguish: A Case History of a Dying Trajectory.* San Francisco: Sociology Press, 1970.

54. ———, L Schatzman, R. Bucher, D. Ehrlich, and M. Sabshin, *Psychiatric Ideologies and Institutions.* New York: The Free Press, 1964.

55. Suttles, Gerald D., *The Social Construction of Communities.* Chicago: University of Chicago Press, 1972.

56. ———, *The Social Order of the Slum.* Chicago: University of Chicago Press, 1968.

57. Westby, David L., "The Career Experience of the Symphony Musician," *Social Forces,* vol. 38 (1960), pp. 223–30.

58. Wiley, Norbert, "The Ethnic Mobility Trap and Stratification Theory," *Social Problems,* vol. 15 (Fall 1967), pp. 147–59.

59. Williams, Margaret, "Reference Groups: A Review and Commentary," *Sociological Quarterly,* vol. 11 (1970), pp. 545–54.

Selected Readings

BECKER, HOWARD S., *Outsiders: Studies in the Sociology of Deviance* (rev. ed. with new Chap. 10.). New York: The Free Press, 1973.
This is a highly influential presentation of the related notions of careers and selves. It elaborates the symbolic interactionist view of deviance and deviant behavior and should be examined in the context of Chapter 15 in this book.

HUGHES, EVERETT C., *Men and Their Work.* New York: The Free Press, 1958.
Presents the main threads of Hughes's work and observations on careers, selves, and work.

KUHN, MANFORD H., "The Reference Group Reconsidered," *Sociological Quarterly,* vol. 5 (1964), pp. 5–21.
A major critique of the reference group concept and the concept of *other* within the symbolic interactionist tradition.

SCHMITT, RAYMOND L., *The Reference Other Orientation: An Extension of the Reference Group Concept.* Carbondale, Ill.: Southern Illinois Press, 1972.

Offers the most extensive and thorough review of the theoretical and research literature on the reference group concept.

STONE, GREGORY P., AND HARVEY P. FABERMAN (eds.), *Social Psychology through Symbolic Interaction*. Waltham, Mass.: Blaisdell Publishing Company, 1970. Contains a thorough and systematic collection of essays and articles articulating the interrelationship between selves, others, and social situations.

chapter *14*

Sexual
Activity and
Sexual
Identification

S*exual motivations* are often regarded as biological in origin. The fact that erotic activity involves specialized organs and is so obviously linked with biological maturation makes this seem self-evident to many scientists as well as laypersons. A closer examination will indicate, however, how inadequate and fallacious this conception is. Sexual activity, like virtually all other complex human behavior, is of primarily symbolic and interactional, rather than biological, significance. (26) The symbolic entanglements surrounding human sexual behavior make it extremely hazardous to apply to human beings the findings obtained from the study of lower animals. In this chapter we attempt to show concretely the great complexity of sexual activity and the enormous variety of modes of sexual expression. The social, symbolic, and interactional foundations of sexual conduct will be discussed.

The
Evolutionary
Picture

The general picture of subhuman sex behavior is described in terms appropriate to our purposes by Beach (2, 3), a psychologist who has surveyed the available literature and himself carried out extensive investigations of the sex behavior of the lower animals. His conclusions

Life Cycle: Adult Transformations

may be summarized as follows: (1) mating behavior in lower animal forms is controlled primarily by inherited mechanisms; specifically, by hormonal secretions and by the strength and aggressiveness of the animal; (2) the central nervous system plays a relatively minor part in the control of sex behavior in the simpler animal forms, its regulatory significance increasing as one ascends the evolutionary scale; (3) past experience, as opposed to hereditary mechanisms, increases in importance as one proceeds from the simpler forms, such as the rat and guinea pig, to the more complex apes and humans. A significant part of the sex behavior of male chimpanzees, for example, is learned.

In support of these general statements we may briefly note certain facts. In most lower forms receptivity of the female to sexual advances is determined by hormone balance and by other accompanying physiological changes occurring during the period of heat or estrus. With some exceptions, the female animal is receptive only when she is in heat. This is, of course, not true of the human female, who may actively desire or entirely reject sexual relations at any time during the menstrual cycle.

Removal or atrophy of the primary sex glands, the testes and the ovaries, produces relatively uniform results in the lower animals and highly variable, uncertain ones in human beings. Adult men who have been castrated, women who have had ovaries and uterus removed by surgery, and old people whose sex glands have ceased to function—all may and do continue to desire and enjoy coitus. Men who find themselves impotent sometimes have their potency restored either (1) by injection of an actual hormone; (2) by the injection of any substance which they believe to be a hormone; or (3) by psychiatric treatment. (39)

The characteristic and differentiating features of human sex behavior can be traced to the fact that humans talk about sex and other animals do not. The possibility of engaging in any sex behavior is, of course, contained in the biological structure of the individual. The intensity of "the sex drive" and certain other very general characteristics may be conditioned by biological factors. Isolated elements of the total pattern of sex activity are not learned; they are derived directly from man's biological structure. The orgasm, ejaculation, and nocturnal emission of men are examples. These relatively mechanical, nonvoluntary parts of sex behavior are natural biological acts.

Although one may designate various individual aspects of sex behavior as natural, unlearned, or inherited, the total organization and overall functioning of these aspects in given social situations cannot be so designated. The general pattern that an individual adopts cannot be explained biologically; it must be accounted for in terms of the standards or attitudes which individuals internalize toward themselves and their sexual activities. Social influences and expressions often shape sex behavior along lines that are contrary to what would be called "natural," or conventional, in the biological and social senses. Furthermore, social influences may lead to the complete elimination of some kinds of natural biological behavior.

Hormones, Homosexuality, and Inversion

One of the chief obstacles to a proper understanding of the nature of human sex behavior is the assumption, often made by relatively well-educated persons, that hormones or hormone balance accounts for the vagaries of sexual behavior. According to this view, heterosexuality is the consequence of a hormone balance, which in the male is weighted on the side of androgens and in the female on the side of the estrogens. (The *androgens* are the male hormones; the *estrogens*, the female hormones—both being found to some extent in both sexes.) The close connection between these hormones and the secondary sexual body characteristics has been scientifically demonstrated. Hence, many people think that when the female hormones are relatively prevalent in a male or the male hormones relatively prevalent in a female, the result is an effeminate male and a masculine female, respectively—that is, homosexuals. We shall indicate in the succeeding paragraphs that this conception is incorrect in almost every detail. (11, 20, 32)

Here it is necessary to distinguish among various aspects of sexual behavior and sexual characteristics and to note the difference between homosexuality and inversion. *Inversion* refers to the assumption of a female role by a male and, conversely, of a male role by a female. Inversion is a term descriptive of people and not of the sex act. Indeed, it is quite possible—though improbable—for an inverted male and female to engage in heterosexual relations. *Homosexuality*, on the other hand, means sexual or love relationships between members of the same sex. Since male and female counterroles are usually involved in the sex act, even homosexual partners often play opposite sex roles. Hence, in homosexual intercourse one partner can be characterized as inverted and the other cannot.

We must also bear in mind the distinctions between male and female secondary sexual characteristics: voice differences, distribution of hair, and so on. Moreover, the presence in a male of relatively female secondary physical characteristics does not imply either inversion or homosexuality. The distinction between homosexual and heterosexual behavior is based on the sex of the preferred partner. In short, the terms *homosexual, heterosexual,* and *inversion* refer to *behavior*, whereas *secondary sex traits* are structural, biological features of the organism—not forms of behavior.

In the light of these distinctions we may make several observations. (1) Inversion and homosexuality are not identical terms. (2) In experi-

Life Cycle: Adult Transformations

ments on animals, through the injection of hormones of the opposite sex, secondary physical traits of the opposite sex and partial inversion have both been produced, but homosexuality in the human sense of the term has not been brought about. (3) The injection of hormones in humans neither produces nor cures homosexuality, its main effect being to stimulate sex activity without influencing the choice of partners. (4) Homosexuality usually occurs along with heterosexuality in a mixed form; many persons are bisexual. (5) Many male homosexuals are not at all effeminate, and many female homosexuals are not masculine. (6) Probably most effeminate males and masculine women engage in exclusively heterosexual relations. (7) Many deviant forms of human sexual behavior have no parallel among the lower animals. Homosexuality is only one kind of deviation. If we account for it in terms of hormones, then we must ask what possible hormonal basis is involved when humans derive their sexual gratification from intercourse with lower animals and in many other ways, some of which are alluded to in the next section.

The crucial point in connection with the inversion of sex roles in humans is that a male or female identifies with the opposite sex. Thus, a female invert may assert and feel that she is a man, wear masculine clothes, act like a man, assume much of the masculine role in sexual relations, adopt a masculine name, and perhaps even apply the male terminology to her sexual organs, calling the clitoris a "penis" and the ovaries the "testes." This type of inversion is no doubt brought about by the fact that adult sexual patterns are conceptually organized and to a pervasive degree regulated by social definitions of one's behavior and sexual identity as well as shaped by personal experiences.

These factors point to the learned and socially defined nature of sex roles. Children at birth do not identify themselves with either sex, for they do not know that the sexes exist. They gradually learn this identification and, along with it, acquire the behavior deemed appropriate in their society. (22, 25) For example, the type of partner the male child will learn to prefer—blondes, or brunettes, women or men, white or black or brown women—is not determined by human biological structure, any more than religious, political, or ethical preferences are so determined. (7, 19) Moreover, various deflections in this learning process may occur. Later we will cite simple examples illustrating how this might come about through parental desire that a child be of a given sex, through anatomical peculiarities, and through mistakes in identifying the child's sex at birth.

Newborn children respond positively to pleasant stimuli, regardless of the source. They do not classify or discriminate among sources. The male child is as likely to have an erection when handled by his father as when handled by his mother. As the child matures and as he learns ways of classifying stimuli and of responding to them, his patterns of sexual expression gradually crystallize and become channelized. As H. S. Sullivan has observed (see Chapter 10), the patterning of sexual activity into a fixed set of identities occurs over a several-year period in the life cycle. The detailed description of this learning process and of the disorders that may occur is still a problem for the combined efforts of social scientists.

THE "POLYMORPHOUS PERVERSE" AND PATTERNS OF DEVIATION

Research findings concerning the biology of sexual differentiation and early sexual behavior suggest that the human organism at birth probably should be viewed as essentially indeterminate sexually, with the potential of adopting one or several of a large number of modes of expression. (18) As the fetus develops, in the early stages it is not sexually differentiated, but it becomes so before birth. The mechanisms involved in this parting of the ways, which determines whether the child is to be a boy or a girl, are not exactly understood. What the path of sexual development will be, presumably, is determined by early learning processes that are difficult to assess and have not been isolated. A term used by Freud, *the polymorphous perverse,* designates the child's potentiality for moving in any one of a number of directions. The term implies that knowledge of biological structures does not enable one to predict reliably how the individual will make use of these structures when he or she becomes an adult.

The modes of sexual expression engaged in by adults seem to present a picture of almost unlimited variability. In addition to the wide variety of relatively common heterosexual and homosexual patterns, there are many others. Thus, some persons obtain gratification not from engaging in the sex act, but by watching it performed by others (voyeurs), or by peeping activities, or by looking at pictures, or by reading pornographic material. "Masochists" obtain gratification from being whipped or being made to suffer pain, while those known as "sadists" enjoy inflicting pain or injury on others. "Pyromaniacs" find sexual pleasure in setting and watching fires. Another form of sexual expression is "fetishism," sexual interests being focused on objects that are endowed with erotic significance, such as, for men, high-heeled shoes or women's undergarments. Sexual interests may be directed toward almost any part or function of the body. Gratification may be achieved via different sense modalities—vision, sound, touch, smell, and taste.

"Transvestism," or the urge to dress up as a member of the opposite sex, is commonly misunderstood to be an aspect of homosexuality. (32) Most transvestites, however, are heterosexuals. An interesting example was provided to the authors by a member of the Institute for Sexual Research, established by Alfred C. Kinsey. A middle-aged man, happily married for many years, makes it a practice to serve breakfast to his wife as she lies in bed. Before doing so, he slips on a feminine wig and carefully and artfully attires himself in a feminine costume from a special wardrobe reserved for the purpose. His wife usually compliments him on his appearance on these occasions and does not reproach or harass him. One fear does trouble him—that some outsider may happen to appear at an inopportune time and thus create gossip or a scandal. To the outside world, he now appears simply as another older married man.

The unusual patterns of erotic expression to which allusion is made in this chapter should not be taken as an exhaustive description of the full range of human sexual possibilities. There are many others, including that of sexual acts with lower animals, which sometimes are forbidden in the criminal code. An Indiana farmer, for example, was sentenced to a long prison term for attempting intercourse with a chicken: he was charged under a sodomy statute which defined his offense as "the abominable crime against nature with man or beast." (His lawyer appealed the case on the grounds that a chicken was not a beast but a fowl.) Considering the immense variety of human sexual patterns, patterns that most probably have no counterparts among lower animals, it is difficult to imagine that any purely biological or hormonal explanation could possibly account for them. The common assumption that heterosexuality is simply "natural" or "instinctive" is naïve and grossly inadequate. Actually, there are a multiplicity of competing theories which attempt to explain one or more of these nonheterosexual patterns.

Social psychologists, quite apart from the unresolved etiological battle, need to be concerned with the social contexts within which the sexual patterns occur and the social consequences of the behaviors. Much useless theorizing goes on about why men frequent prostitutes, why they have mistresses while happily married, why they engage in "wife-swapping," why men and women engage in group intercourse or allow themselves to be observed while "loving" their boyfriends or girlfriends. They even theorize about how it is possible that married couples are still lustily engaging in sex although in their late eighties. (1, 6, 11, 31, 34, 43) In that consummately funny novel, *Lolita*, the author, Nabokov, wisely eschews any explanations as to why his hero is so enduringly attracted by young girls but sticks to telling us the story of what happens because of that compulsion. His book suggests the further point that whatever the ingenious social psychologist can possibly imagine in the way of sexual relations—heterosexual or otherwise—in terms of object, place, time, or manner, one can be certain that it has been tried, found satisfying, and is practiced somewhere by some persons.

Some individuals, viewed as sexual deviants, have organized themselves to protest public and legal discrimination. Homosexuals have had organizations of this kind for some time, and in recent years an aggressive "Gay Liberation Front" has attracted considerable public attention because of its attempts to reform the criminal code as that code affects homosexuals, and by its efforts to educate or inform the public and to bring the homosexuality issue into the open. (20) Transvestites also have organizations, and extremely interesting accounts have been published of transvestite conferences and gatherings. There are also, of course, various informal types of "swinger" groups that engage in unconventional sexual activity, including group sex among outwardly conventional wives and husbands. A variety of publications serve these groups. (43)

Transvestism suggests a number of points of special interest to social psychologists. For example, a male transvestite might well appear sexually attractive to an ordinary heterosexual male who mistakes him for a woman. One may ask whether such an attraction should be characterized as homosexual or heterosexual. Or suppose that two transvestites of opposite sex mistake each other's sexual identity and become erotically interested in each other: Would this be a heterosexual or a homosexual relationship? In view of these considerations, should not the usual definitions be revised to take account of the fact that a sexual attraction between two persons might be essentially homosexual for one of the pair and heterosexual for the other? The crucial elements appear to be beliefs that each holds concerning the sexual identity of the other, and that one or both members of a pair may hold erroneous beliefs—especially when assisted by the artifices of attire and cosmetics.

An especially extraordinary example of the complexity introduced by the above considerations is presented in the case of a male homosexual invert who had his male genitalia removed by surgery and an artificial vagina installed. Subsequently this person fell in love with and married a male member of the armed forces and lived with him as his wife. When the soldier was transferred to Europe and separated from his "wife," they exchanged love letters of the standard type that any newly married couple might write. We might add that the army authorities and the church got involved in this marriage, debating whether or not it could be legal or otherwise recognized as an actual union. In such matters, the judgment of the "outside world" may or may not be crucial; thus, a British male, after a similar transforming operation, married an American male. English people back home simply could not believe this person was no longer what he had been (an unmarried male), but his American acquaintances only knew him for what he now was (a married woman). On the other hand, after such operations, these persons often keep their biographies secret from anyone except spouses and very close friends. (15)

The sexual identity of practically all persons in any society is made obvious by a variety of external signs such as hair style, dress, and demeanor. It is of theoretical interest to a social psychologist to imagine

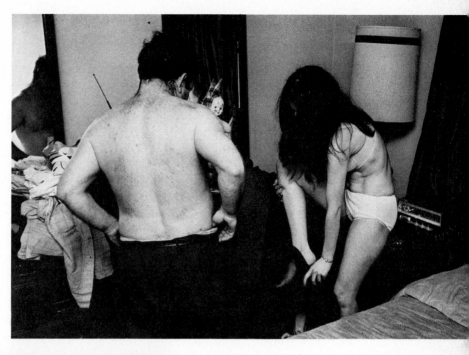

Above: The practice of prostitution may—for both persons involved—separate one's intimate behavior from one's sexual behavior. (*Bob Adelman*)

Left: "Lolita." Nymphets and the "polymorphous perverse" male? (*Culver Pictures*)

how sexual patterns and interrelationships might be altered if, instead of advertising sexual identity, every effort and artifice were utilized to make the sexes look exactly alike. Under such circumstances, budding romances might often come to an end with the discovery that the potential lover, sweetheart, husband, or wife was of the wrong sex. It is worth adding that in such societies as postrevolutionary Russia and China—or in certain social circles where signs of sexual identity are muted in favor of other characteristics and are unclear—men and women nevertheless do not ordinarily make mistakes in their identification of each other.

Sexual Identity and Self-Esteem

ADOLESCENCE

While childhood experiences may be of great significance in later sexual development (as we indicated in Chapter 11), establishing adult-type relationships, sexual and otherwise, with the opposite sex ordinarily begins after puberty. (37, 40) Commonly, there is considerable anxiety and uncertainty in the minds of young people as to how they appear to the opposite sex and as to whether they will be able to function as "real" men and women. In initial intersexual relationships, there is thus often a period of testing and self-exploration in which the primary focus may be on self-assertion and validation. The young man venturing into the sexual world for the first time may be less interested intrinsically in his partner than in asserting and establishing his own identity and masculinity, whether the partner is a prostitute or just a young acquaintance or friend. The young woman, during this period, is similarly concerned with proving to herself and her peers that she is attractive to the opposite sex. Harry Stack Sullivan has indicated that this is a phase of early adolescence. (40)

In late adolescence, once this period of concern with self is presumably resolved and maturing adolescents have acquired greater confidence in their own essential masculinity or femininity, they are ready for more serious and enduring sexual relations than the "puppy love" of early adolescence. They are now on the verge of maturity, which Sullivan describes as the capability of becoming as concerned (or more concerned) over the well-being of another as over one's own. In Freudian terms, they have passed from the phallic to the genital stages of development. (13) However, as the rest of this chapter indicates, there are many points at which this developmental schedule on the way to heterosexual maturity can be deflected. When it is, the consequences are, for obvious reasons, often serious both for the person's self-esteem and for his or her subsequent sexual career. We turn next to a more detailed statement about the development of sexual self-conceptions.

Through the process of socialization, everyone comes to acquire a distinct set of self-conceptions, or identities, specific to sexual conduct and activity. These *personifications,* or images of self as a male or female, cluster into three categories: (1) the "good" sexual me, (2) the "bad" sexual me, and (3) the "not" sexual me. The "good" sexual me refers to those identifications and actions that bring the individual pleasure, pride, and positive self-identification. The "bad" sexual me describes those misidentifications which challenge the individual's credibility and moral worth. Furthermore, the "bad" sexual me touches on those actions in the sexual arena which arouse guilt and anxiety on the part of the individual. The "not" sexual me refers to a small number of sexual acts and identifications the individual would never see him- or herself engaging in, or which, like erotic dreams and nocturnal emissions, are automatic. These often relate to sexual taboos and taking part in them produces shame and self-mortification. Women who have been raped, for example, disclaim any part in the sexual act and often view themselves afterward in tainted, morally repugnant terms.

THE
SEXUAL
SELF-CONCEPTION

Like the individual's other identities, or personifications, the sexual self-conception involves a number of interrelated dimensions. Three components of that identity have been noted—the "good," the "bad," and the "not" me. In addition we draw attention to the following: (1) the individual's sexual appetite, (2) his or her sexual prowess, (3) his or her knowledge about sexual activity, (4) his or her conception of self as an experienced or inexperienced sexual actor. These latter aspects suggest that persons view themselves as having particular levels of sexual desire—high, low, nonexistent. Furthermore, depending on their knowledge of sexual behaviors and the amount of their actual or fantasied sexual experience, they will see themselves as adept or inadept, powerful or impotent, interested or disinterested in sexual acts. The defined effect and outcome of first sexual experiences (whether autophilic, isophilic, or heterophilic) will shape the individual's conception of self as a sexual being. *Autophilic,* or masturbation, experiences may become the dominant focus of the individual's sexual behavior. *Isophilic,* or homosexual, experiences may predominate, and in this case the individual does not transfer his or her sexual appetite and self-conceptions to behaviors which lead to intercourse with members of the opposite sex, as in the case for *heterophilic* actors. (40:292)

DIMENSIONS
OF THE SEXUAL
SELF-CONCEPTION

Individuals may move through all three sexual cycles, alternating between autophilic and heterophilic acts, or their identity may focus solely on one of these three modes of sexual expression. Sometimes without observing behavior itself it is not easy to know which mode is dominant. In any case, the identity is potentially modified in each sexual encounter. Like their other identities, individuals' sexual self-conceptions are open to change.

Sexual self-conceptions are also differentially salient or prominent in the behavior repertoires of individuals. While Freud and the neo-Freudians made the sexual drive the predominant force in human behavior, the view presented in this chapter suggests that an individual may (1) never act out or act on the sexual identity—for example, priests who have taken the vows of celibacy; (2) engage in sexual behaviors only occasionally and then only on a fixed schedule—some Victorians; (3) frequently act in a sexual fashion—married partners in the honeymoon phase of the marriage. Thus, individuals can be studied in terms of the frequency with which they engage in sexual expression. The failure to act overtly in no way suggests that the individual may not be privately and covertly daydreaming about sexual matters.

In general, it can be argued, following Harry Stack Sullivan (40), that the sexual identity is most important within the confines of intimate relationships. It is there that intimacy and sexuality blend together in the tightly knit worlds of love and emotional attachment. Sexual identity finds its peak expression in those relationships. Accordingly, it can be seen that sexuality more or less lies dormant or at best is less prominent in the person's other interactive relationships. This is not to say that traces of flirtation and coquetry are not ubiquitous features of many other face-to-face encounters between the sexes. It simply suggests that sexual identity arises in predictable situations and circumstances within which it also finds its fullest expression. Sexual identity is molded and built up out of experiences with a relatively small number of individuals. Indeed, many people may have sexual experiences with only one other individual besides themselves.

SOURCES OF THE SEXUAL IDENTITY The identity of male or female, and the sexual connotations that surround "maleness" or "femaleness" arise out of the individual's network of interpersonal relationships. Grounded first in the intimate circles of the primary group, these identifications involve such matters as adornment and dress and the development of a set of covert, nonverbal gestures of a coquettish nature. The child learns to attach meanings to its sexual organs and learns "rules of privacy" concerning how these regions are clothed and shielded from the eyes of others. (10) The child's caretakers also instruct him or her in the ritual sacredness of certain behavior settings. Bathrooms and parental bedrooms take on moral significance in the daily domestic rhythms, and the child is taught to respect the rights of others when they occupy these settings. Body maintenance activities such as bathing, washing, and dressing also expand the child's awareness of its own and others' bodies. Sexuality is based on the body, and the body is displayed in concrete situations. In the moment of body display the child communicates (often unwittingly) a sexual sense of self.

The most direct source of sexual identity lies in the conversations and experiences the individual has with him- or herself and with others. Indirect sources, however, play a large role in the elaboration of one's sexual self-conception. Fantasies, reveries, and daydreams, often sparked by erotic or semierotic novels, paintings, movies, or magazines, also contribute to the individual's view of self as a sexual actor. Thus, with some certainty it can be assumed that by the middle years of childhood and early adulthood, all individuals will have developed, however unelaborated, a set of conceptions surrounding the sexual self. Research indicates, for example, that by the age of seventeen most males and females have had at least one sexual experience leading to coitus. Eleanore B. Luckey and Gilbert D. Nass's data from 2,230 male and female college students in the United States, Canada, England, Germany, and Norway revealed that the mean age of first coitus for males and females was as follows: United States 17.9, 18.7; Canada 18.5, 19.4; England 17.5, 17.5; Germany 19.0, 19.5; Norway 18.4, 18.8. (27:375)

John Gagnon and William Simon (14:20) have remarked:

THE SEXUAL DRAMA

> In general, the sexual dimension in our society comprises a limited biological capacity that is harnessed and amplified by varied social uses. . . . We have emphasized that the expression of the sexual component is the celebration of a social and psychological drama rather than a natural response. We have suggested that there may be substantial change in the social drama. In the past the drama has been a silent charade. Now we appear to be giving the drama a sound track and inviting the audience to participate.

As our society loosens the taboos surrounding the sexual act and as sexual identity becomes a more discussed topic, we may witness a greater openness concerning its various components. In the past, and we suspect the pattern will largely hold for the future, individuals have seldom "openly" talked about their sexual appetites, their conceptions of sexual prowess, nor have they fully taken their partners into confidence concerning their sexual fantasies. As a consequence, the sexual identity which is one of the individual's most ubiquitous elements of self-identification has remained one of the least talked about features of the self. Discussions of it are either confined to same-sex friendship and gossip circles, or they are played out in the private imaginations of the individual. Thus, like other taboos that surround discourse concerning the biological functions of the physical organism, the sexual self is seldom brought out in the open. It represents a private set of acts and activities.

One final topic remains to be treated. This is the locus of the sexual act. More specifically, what sexual identities do individuals bring into the sexual arena when they engage in sexual intercourse? The foregoing suggests that sexual identity is a complex mixture of positively and negatively defined elements. Accordingly, it can be seen that one person's "good" sexual me may be another person's "bad," or "not" sexual me. Thus any sexual encounter is likely to be a mixed and compromised expression of each individual's preferred and nonpreferred sexual desires. If someone finds that a stable sexual partner fails to conform with, or support and reward a preferred "good" me, he or she may take his or her sexual behavior elsewhere, thereby separating the intimate behavior from the sexual behavior. In this sense sexual partners are continually socializing one another, teaching one another new techniques and new modes of expression. The sexual identity, we conclude, is a dynamic, shifting set of self-indications that are grounded, as Gagnon and Simon argue, in the most intimate, yet biological of circumstances—the human body and its meetings with the bodies of others.

Falling in and Out of Love

Falling in love has been likened to getting hooked on drugs. (See Chapter 15.) The process commonly begins with "playing around" or as a "weekend habit." As it continues, it imperceptibly becomes continuous, more serious, often without the realization of the participants, who become progressively more psychologically dependent on each other as they learn more and more about each other and the relationship becomes more intimate and permeated by mutual trust. The lovers "turn each other on" and discover there is nobody else who gives them the same "high" that they have learned to enjoy and crave. Ultimately, they experience withdrawal distress when they are separated from each other. Despite difficulties and contrary arguments from parents and friends who urge them to break their compulsion, they tend to relapse repeatedly. Finally, there is nothing to be done but to accept the fact of their addiction to each other, and they either legalize it by marriage (methadone maintenance) or live together "in sin" (depend on the illicit market).

Like heroin addicts, lovers, when asked why they love each other, give varied, contradictory, and generally unilluminating answers. Like heroin users who praise the drug in exaggerated terms, lovers often extol the virtues of their partners in extremely unrealistic terms. Both love and drug addiction have their honeymoon periods when the habits are new, and before practical reality intrudes itself and brings the individual back to earth. Disillusionment sets in when the joys of the habits lose their novelty and when the persons discover that they have been trapped by delusions about themselves and the objects of their craving. Like addicts

The act of falling in love—the act of forming an intimate and close relationship—must be viewed processually and in dynamic terms. (*Lucia Woods/Photo Researchers, Inc.*)

who end up with "monkeys on their backs," lovers end up with "hostages to fortune" and with legal and financial obligations. When divorce occurs, the partners commonly tend to remarry (relapse), a tendency that has been described as "the triumph of hope over experience." When one has once been hooked on either love or drugs, he or she learns something new about the body and its potential, and it is inappropriate and futile to believe that he or she will ever forget it or be "cured" of it.

Both worlds of sex and drugs have their illicit markets and pushers, and in both worlds there are ways of obtaining highs without getting hooked or committed. Persons may avoid sexual commitments and marriage by going to prostitutes or by having episodic, temporary affairs with others who also are seeking to avoid commitment. (Men and women recently divorced, and wary of too hasty remarriage, are prime examples of people who engage in friendly sex without emotional commitment.) (21, 42) In much the same way, it is possible for the drug user to consume a variety of substances, switching from one to another so as to avoid becoming hooked on any of them.

As with drugs, young persons learn about sex primarily from their peer groups which exert pressure upon them to experiment, or, in conservative groups, not to experiment because to do so is wrong, dangerous, or sinful. Young Americans have learned not to trust "anyone over thirty" on either drug or sexual questions. Parental influence is often blocked either by inhibitions which prevent free communication between parents and children or by the dominance of peer group perspectives over those of an older generation. Parents of today, like those of past ages, are consequently being confronted by new sexual realities which they often have difficulty accepting. A whimsical example is provided by a loving mother of the authors' acquaintance who was concerned that her daughter was living with a man to whom she was not married. In response to the daughter's praise of her partner, the mother timidly suggested marriage. The daughter replied, "Oh, but mother, I don't know him nearly well enough for *that!*"

The process of falling in love may occur suddenly or gradually. Very little is known about why people fall in love with certain kinds of persons rather than others. It has been suggested that the falling in love process is something like the "imprinting" that has been observed in lower animals. It has also been suggested that it may actually be an instance of imprinting of very early childhood experiences with members of the opposite sex, perhaps even with one's parents. (6) One author has suggested that after puberty boys and girls tend to fall in love with the first potential love object that happens to come along at the critical period when the situation is right. It is also argued that one who becomes the first love object to the budding adolescent is usually a new person in town, someone not too familiar. However naïve, these remarks point to the relatively impoverished state of knowledge concerning the formation of close, intimate relationships. (30)

LOVE
AS PROCESS
These remarks suggest that the act of falling in love, or forming an intimate and close relationship, must be viewed processually and in dynamic terms. To love another individual, as Sullivan (40) remarked, "involves a situation where the person cares as deeply about another individual's fate and circumstances as they care about their own." A number of theories have been set forth to account for the formation of the love relationship. Goode (16) sets forth a structural theory of love which argues that societies control the origins and distribution of the love emotion. Arranged marriages, child marriages, chaperoned dates, sorority and fraternity dating systems, and long engagements—all display some attempt to regulate entry into the marriage market. Goode's argument rests on a simple assumption: "If societies did not control the marriage arrangement, their economic and prestige systems would collapse. Furthermore, their systems of social stratification would be thrown off balance." Goode's formulations are taken to a higher level by Ira L. Reiss (33), who argues for a "wheel theory" of love. His model proposes

that persons with like interests are thrown together by the stratification systems of societies. These interests, in turn, are reflective of common needs. Mating follows a process whereby persons with common interests and needs meet one another, reveal their selves to one another, and in that process learn that they are capable of meeting one another's basic needs. Reiss's theory elaborates the earlier work of Robert Winch who formulated the complementary theory of needs. (45)

We applaud Reiss's work on a processual model of relational formation. However, we reject the notion that societies somehow structure the love-making process so as to maintain their systems of wealth and prestige. People, not societies, fall in love and structure the formation of intimate relationships. Furthermore, we reject any theory which rests on some notion of needs, basic impulses, or drives. And, we must note that many persons fall in love more than once. Indeed, families are held together, in part, because of the "love rhetoric." Of course, remarriages assume a repetition of the falling in love process. (31) And members of the upper class often marry "down."

There are, then, very few studies or theories which adequately structure the process whereby intimate relationships are formed. We intend to suggest that persons symbolically and behaviorally commit themselves to other individuals in intimate and deeply emotional ways. These commitments lead to an embracement of the totality of that other person's selves and identities. This *embracement*, in turn, leads to interactions which reaffirm that person's uniqueness and sacred qualities. The other person comes to live an independent life in the fantasies and daydreams of the other individual. (4) Their selves become *lodged* in one another.

"Falling" out of love (42) involves a breaking away process. Often deeply emotional and agonizing, when lovers and intimates part they leave a portion of themselves behind. In this sense they are publicly exposed, and they may severely damage their self-conceptions in the process. This falling out process often involves name changes and entire changes in life style. New social worlds are entered, as old worlds are left behind. Just as falling in love involves the construction of new social worlds (42), falling out of love involves the destruction of existing worlds, along with the attendant building, or attempted rebuilding, of new or modified worlds.

Sexual Activities and Erotic Imagery

We turn next to sexual activities per se. Sexual intercourse requires that the overt behavior of the human male be accompanied and facilitated by an internal symbolic process or flow of thought, which is often called *erotic imagery*. Such a flow of erotic mental images and ideas is ordinarily, although not always, necessary before a man can achieve and maintain an erection, and it is certainly a requisite element in the desire to engage in sexual relations. The same is generally true of the human female. To be sure, a woman may engage in sexual relations without having any genuine erotic interest in such relations. However, if we conceive of the sex act as a relationship which is pleasurable and desirable to both parties, or which culminates in simultaneous or nearly simultaneous orgasms, then we may say that erotic imagery is equally necessary for both sexes. Erotic imagery may provide a common symbolic basis for the sexual act, and partners may come to share the same imagery. Social worlds differ in their vocabularies, or repertoires, of erotic imagery. Depending upon where persons are in their own sexual careers, their imagery of sexual activity will vary.

The term *erotic imagery* refers to a general process which we have already discussed in other connections as internalized language behavior, though it is not language in the narrow sense of the word. It is through this process that social influences and past experiences exercise their regulatory effects on human behavior in general, including sex behavior. Because they apply some voluntary control over this internal symbolic process, individuals are able in varying degrees to hasten, retard, or entirely inhibit their own sexual responses.

The individual may, as Sullivan (40) argues, have experiences at the prototaxic, parataxic, and syntaxic levels. A good deal of experience, he suggests, is not syntaxic. Such, we contend, is the case with sexual thought and behavior. The individual seldom dissects his or her sexual feelings, or reactions, or fantasies in a fully rational and logical fashion. Rather, he or she experiences these thoughts and behaviors at the more primitive prototaxic and parataxic levels. This is not to say that syntaxic thought cannot be employed, for it often is, as the research of Masters and Johnson reveals. (28, 29)

Most modern American books on sex techniques emphasize the failure of many middle- and upper-class wives to achieve a climax with a sufficient degree of regularity. A great deal of advice is proffered as to techniques which the husband may use to delay his own orgasm while, at the same time, he attempts to hasten his wife's. These procedures represent attempts to teach self-control and have to do with a question which apparently never arises in the rest of the animal world.

Masters and Johnson's study (28, 29) demonstrates clearly that this attitude toward husband control is very much a middle-class one. Their conclusion is worth quoting in detail, for it brings out nicely, in addition, the class-linked differences in meaning of sexual activity; it also suggests the class-linked relationships in generalized social relationships between the sexes. They assert (29:202):

Problems of premature ejaculation . . . disturbed the younger members of the study-subject population. These fears . . . were directed toward the culturally imposed fear of inability to control the ejaculatory process to a degree sufficient to satisfy the female partner. These expressed fears of performance were confined primarily to those . . . who had attained college or postgraduate levels of formal education. Only 7 of the total of 51 men whose formal education did not include college matriculation expressed the slightest concern with responsibility for coital-partner satisfaction. These men felt that it was the female's privilege to achieve satisfaction during active coition if she could, but certainly it was not the responsibility and really not the concern of the male partner to concentrate on satisfying the woman's sexual demands. Out of a total of 261 study-subjects with college matriculation, 214 men expressed concern with coital-partner satisfaction. With these men ejaculatory control sufficient to accomplish partner satisfaction was considered a coital technique that must be acquired before the personal security of coital effectiveness could be established.

A number of interesting human problems about human sexual behavior **MASTURBATION** arise in connection with the practice of *masturbation*. Masters and Johnson in the 1966 report (29) note that Kinsey (24) had calculated that 92 percent of males had "positive masturbatory" histories, and that this figure had since been supported in the United States and abroad by more recent reports. In the Masters-Johnson study, all the subjects of both sexes described a positive history of "masturbatory facility." (29:197–98)

There are those like Kinsey who seek to discuss sexual behavior largely in terms of overt behavior, excluding the accompanying internal symbolic processes. This approach leads to some curious contradictions. If we defined homosexual behavior in purely overt terms, as a positive sexual response to stimuli proceeding from the same sex, masturbation could be subsumed as a special case of homosexuality. Kinsey, of course, did not do this, he classified masturbation as either heterosexual, homosexual, or mixed—distinguishing among them in terms of the types of fantasy involved. That is, he distinguished in terms of criteria which he initially ruled out.

In line with our previous discussion, internal symbolic processes serve as integrative and organizing phenomena in human behavior. That they are cortical in nature and difficult to study in no way justifies us in disregarding or dismissing them. As we have repeatedly shown, it is through the mediation of such cortical or internal symbolic processes that the mores or ethical codes of a society exert their regulatory influences on human behavior.

The internal symbolic processes, or the erotic imagery usually accompanying the act of masturbation, do not differ in any essential detail from those attending the ordinary heterosexual act. Kinsey noted that before and during masturbation, erotic literature and pictures are occasionally used by Americans of the better-educated classes; and he adds that "nearly, but not quite, all males experience sexual fantasies during masturbation. . . . The fantasies are heterosexual when the primary interests of the individual are heterosexual, homosexual when the individual's overt experience or psychic reactions are homosexual." A person's experiences in a social milieu determine which specific excitatory ideas are likely to occur to that person in the course of the heterosexual act.

It is significant to note the change in attitude toward masturbation in our country. This practice used to be regarded as the cause of all sorts of harmful physical effects, including feeblemindedness and insanity. Research by competent investigators has failed to substantiate such a view. Today it is generally conceded that (1) masturbation is not known to have any necessarily deleterious physical consequences; and (2) the negative effects it does have are chiefly psychological in nature and arise from such feelings as guilt, fear, and shame, which are frequently associated with the practice. The effects of masturbation, in other words, are bound up with the way in which the act is defined within a given group or society.

INHIBITING AND FACILITATING STIMULI

People sometimes speak of human sexuality in animalistic terms, implying that human sex urges are aroused, repressed, and even expressed in ways essentially identical with those of other mammals. This view is incorrect, for human sexual responses are channeled in ways which have no parallel in the animal world.

Whole segments of a population may be ruled out as sexual or marital partners for social rather than biological reasons. This is true, for example, of the mutual exclusion of the white and black sections of the American population, the various castes of India, and the exogamous clans found among many preliterate peoples. Thus, if a native tribe is divided into four clans or subgroups, an unmarried male in one of them may be required to seek his sexual partners only among the women of one of the three other clans. In such cases, eligible and healthy persons of the opposite sex may not even be perceived as desirable sexual objects if they fall into forbidden categories. In our own society, such barriers as social class, age, religion, race, and marital status limit the choice of sexual partners.

Someone else's mother may become an exciting object, particularly if she is a widow and not too elderly; but sexual responses toward one's own mother are not permissible. Although a woman may be sexually attractive, to her own male children she is generally a sexual nonentity. This is but one instance of the operation of incest taboos. Human standards of incest vary considerably from society to society, applying sometimes only to the intimate family group and sometimes to a wide circle of persons, many of whom are biologically unrelated. (41) Incest taboos are found only among humans. They are social, not biological, phenomena.

We may cite other instances of classificatory elimination of sexual partners. Many white Americans find it difficult to be aroused by a dark-skinned black because of strong race prejudice against black people. Indeed some who are attracted by white-appearing persons undoubtedly feel repelled when these turn out to be mulatto. Black men and women have sometimes been repelled by the "washed-out" appearance of whites. Similar barriers may be created by religion, nationality, and age differences, and by a host of other matters connected with the individual's standards of beauty, cleanliness, and the like.

The arousal of inappropriate imagery may prevent or interrupt sexual activity. For example, laughter, accidentally caused, has been the ruination of many a love scene. Anger, irritation, disgust, and shock are other deterrents to sexual excitation. Conditions preventing or interrupting sexual activity may have nothing to do with relationships between the partners. Such external factors as too much noise, too much light, lack of privacy, and fear of possible interruption may interfere with intercourse. Internal factors having no direct connection with the overall relationship between the partners may also prove a hindrance—fear of pregnancy or disease, guilt feelings of any kind. As an example, one newly married couple was physically incapable of carrying out the sex act so long as they lived with the bridegroom's parents. Potency was restored when the couple moved to their own living quarters.

These two terms are used in a number of ways which are not altogether consistent or logical. *Impotence* is generally taken to refer to the inability of a male to achieve and maintain an erection sufficient to engage in intercourse, whereas *frigidity* refers to a general lack of interest or enjoyment of the sex act on the part of a woman. Both terms are highly relative. Every male would be impotent and every woman frigid in some conceivable type of situation. A woman who is exclusively homosexual would probably be frigid with respect to all men, and an exclusively homosexual man might be incapable of performing the sexual act with a woman. This statement needs qualification to allow for the fact that in many sexual relations one of the partners may be activated to positive response primarily by fantasies concerning someone other than the actual sexual partner. It is, perhaps, through the control of the fantasy process that certain individuals have been able to be homosexuals but be happily married and the parents of children. (11)

Since the anatomical and physiological bases of sex behavior constitute necessary, but not determining, conditions for the development of sexuality, it follows that impotence and frigidity may be the conse-

IMPOTENCE
AND FRIGIDITY

quence either of organic or of psychological conditions, the latter being the more common. In terms of the usual conception of frigidity, for example, it appears that American women of the urban middle classes are more likely to be sexually unresponsive than women of the lower classes. No biological explanation of these class differences is available, whereas divergent social backgrounds may sufficiently account for them. (23)

Although a decline in sexual interest and activity during old age is related to organic changes (17), the connection is not sufficiently close to be called a causal one. Hamilton, for example, notes that many men who came to his office with complaints of impotence were between the ages of thirty-seven and forty. Their ages were, in short, much less than the age at which the cessation of sex activity could be expected on purely biological grounds. Hamilton points out that, as one might anticipate, cases of this type often respond favorably to suggestions that there is nothing wrong with them. Seward (39), after surveying the research literature, has concluded that "impotence in the aging, to a surprising extent, is the product of psychological attitude."

Masters and Johnson's intensive study of a sample of aging men and women gives additional, strong evidence that despite organic changes, frequent sexual activity can be enjoyed well into old age. Decline of interest and gratification is related—unless there are organic reasons, including illness—to what Masters and Johnson term "psycho- and sociophysiological problems" attendant on the aging process. These include the widespread cultural attitudes toward aging as nonsexual or asexual, also the monotony of monogamous relations, mental or physical fatigue, overindulgence in food and drink, and fear of performance failure in the male. (28:238–70)

Thus, impotence and frigidity occur in individuals who are biologically sound. Conversely, sexual activity is engaged in by persons who lack what are often regarded as indispensable biological prerequisites. Women may continue to enjoy intercourse after passing through the menopause, up to and beyond the ages of sixty and seventy years, and Kinsey (24) cited the case of an eighty-eight-year-old man who enjoyed regular sex relations with his ninety-year-old wife. Males who are castrated when mature, as a consequence of war injuries for example, often continue to desire and enjoy sexual relations. Seward (39) cited the case of a fifty-three-year-old man, castrated at the age of twenty-four, whose sexual activities increased markedly after the operation. Prior to it, he had practiced coitus about once a month. Afterward, he had intercourse several times a week with his wife and sometimes with other women as well. His increased potency lasted for thirty years.

Impotence and frigidity, when not organic in origin, may be regarded as the consequences of the ways in which individuals think about themselves and about sexual matters. They are, in other words, learned ways of behaving. The central aspects of this problem have to do with the nature of the internal symbolic processes evoked by sexual stimulation. Thus, if a woman is so affected by her early training that sexual excitation sets up an internal symbolic response in terms of concepts like "evil," "sin," "danger," "fear," "dirty," "pain," and "immorality," then these ideas will prevent or inhibit the flow of facilitating and stimulating erotic imagery. Moreover, if the individual has been consistently brought up in the manner implied by these concepts, she is not even likely to possess an adequate repertory of sexually stimulating ideas. This means that even if she overcomes the ideas of evil, immorality, nastiness, and the like, she may still not be able to respond fully during sexual intercourse.

A similar point is made by Masters and Johnson concerning the problems of the impotent husband. (28) They remark that when an impotent husband goes to bed with his wife there may be more than one spectator who watches the episode. The wife who is attempting to stimulate and arouse him also is observing her own and her husband's behavior. "If he obviously isn't responding, what could she be doing that is wrong?" In her role as spectator, she may so distract herself, that when a sexual opportunity really presents itself, she may be, as the authors say, "psychologically caught in the corner observing the physical proceeding rather than physiologically tied to the bed totally involved with her own mating." Both partners may thus be so involved as observers and so worried about their own performances that sexual stimuli become relatively ineffective for both of them. Neither may realize that the other is, in a sense, detached from and not wholly involved in what's going on. These observations by Masters and Johnson point up a general aspect of human behavior that has been noted earlier, namely, that human beings are simultaneously subjects and objects; that they listen to themselves talk and observe their own actions, continuously monitoring both as interaction proceeds. We use this old and cynical proverb to make a related point: "When two divorced people marry, four people get into bed."

Impotence in the male also is closely bound up with the individual's conception of self and is often associated with increasing age. The middle-aged man begins to grow aware of his advancing age and sexual decline. Since many American males place a high value on potency as a test and proof of masculinity, many middle-aged and elderly men conceive of diminished potency as a reflection on themselves. Often they seek means of restoring their self-esteem by consulting physicians or by taking hormone pills. Some try to reassure themselves by seeking sexual adventures with women other than their wives. A substantial percentage of the sexual offenses committed against young girls are the acts of older men seeking means of bolstering their masculine self-esteem.

Sexual Politics: Meanings of the Sex Act

Younger Americans who are familiar with current mores and attitudes toward sex sometimes do not appreciate the degree to which women in the past and in other cultures have been, or are exploited by men, nor the degree of sexual animosity associated with that exploitation. (5, 12, 35) In an anthropological study of a Greek shepherd (Saramkatsan) community, in which men almost completely dominate the women, some of the attitudes of men and women are described. (9) The latter feel a strong sense of solidarity that is expressed among those related by kinship or marriage through frequent talk of how they are exploited. They have many jokes about the male genitalia and speak often of their dislike of sexual relations, saying they obtain no pleasure from them. When a bride is being prepared for the wedding, her young attendants commonly sympathize with her and say they will never leave their own homes for the sake of a strange man. The bride is likely to sympathize with their views and may say that she plans to take a knife with her into bed and castrate her husband when he tries to have intercourse with her. Women invariably regret they were born females and wish they had been born males.

The male attitudes are the counterparts of those of the women. Women, they say, need copulation and beating, but the men do not discuss the intimate details of their sexual lives with each other. When seduction occurs, the man always blames it on the woman. Women are not trusted to be alone. Sexual activity is viewed approximately as a necessary evil and as pollution for the person who engages in it. The division of physical labor is organized to assign certain hard labor to women and, in some instances, men will not help a woman at her work even though she may be ill. Outside the family itself, the social relations between the sexes are extremely restricted. While women are viewed as cunning, men think of themselves as courageous, strong, and proud. It is the cunning of women which is thought to attract men and to corrupt them by causing them to desire sexual relations. Cunning is also attributed to the Devil, who is believed to have a special hold over women. While the mens' views are in some respects the counterparts of feminine attitudes, many beliefs are shared by both sexes—such as the idea that sexual relations are inherently evil, something like "original sin." As Campbell describes the accepted view of sex: "Sexual intercourse, then, is not an unmixed good. It is something which is 'unseemly' or 'out of alignment'. . . . Sexual activity is necessary in that it produces children, who are God's children, but evil in that some sexuality is unavoidable." Campbell goes on to say that sexual intercourse among these people

Sex role expectations should not be confused with sexual identification. The persons above—though performing work typically assigned to the other sex—probably do not feel any less male or female for their "role reversals." (*Mimi Forsyth from Monkmeyer Press Photo Service*)

"must be performed in the utmost secrecy, without speech, and the woman must remain motionless and passive. It is thought shameful for a husband to gaze on his wife's body." (9:276–78)

Views similar to these were common in past generations within our own country and are still found today. The concept of original sin is often taken to refer to sexual intercourse, and many regard sex as a "dirty" subject that should be talked about as little as possible and certainly excluded from the school curriculum. Many difficulties that married couples experience in sexual adjustment are known to have their origins in the training of children which emphasizes this negative view.

Countless American women probably believe, like their Greek peasant counterparts, that men have stronger or at least less controllable sexual appetites than themselves. In a recent study of adolescents in Chicago, two anthropologists (37) report the girls saying about dating that it is the girl's "responsibility both to satisfy part of this inborn male desire for continued sexual satisfaction and to help the situation from getting out of hand." Although they admit to having "strong sexual feelings," they also believe that "they and not the boys are capable of rational control." (The researchers contrast this view, in passing, with its opposite: "The Ngulu, by way of contrast, are convinced that women are born sexually insatiable.") (37:467)

What these instances bring out is that sexual intercourse, like any other activity or object, can be viewed from a great variety of different perspectives and can have varied meanings to the participants. It can be fun or work, duty or a gift, sinful or unconnected with ideas of sin and vice. It may be seen as the lowest of human acts and as one of the finest. A pair of lovers may be "dead serious" in one session of lovemaking and at other times find it comic. The act may be performed routinely and almost mechanically as well as passionately. It may be an act of aggression or of affection, forgiveness or the reverse, betrayal or reconciliation, cooperation or competition. *In this sense, sexual politics intermingle with the politics of interpersonal relationships.* (36) Dominant moods are likely to vary with different partners; and when both members of a monogamous pair are in different moods, the session may be unsatisfactory to one or both. If mismatching becomes chronic, the partners constantly on different wave lengths or "out of phase," we may say that this form of marital communication has broken down. As Masters and Johnson remark, husbands and wives (and we might add, unmarried lovers, too) are commonly reluctant to "talk out" problems of this kind, and "when there is no security or mutual representation in sexual exchange, there rarely is freedom of other forms of marital communication." (28:15) Lovers caught in this sort of situation may relatively easily break their relationship, but obviously this is more difficult for wife and husband, especially when they have had children.

Mismatching in the bedroom commonly leads to inadequate sexual performance by one or the other of the spouses. To add to our previous discussion of genuine impotence, here is what Masters and Johnson say of inadequate performance (28:15): "The wife is afraid of embarrassing or angering her husband if she tries to discuss his sexually dysfunctional condition. The husband is concerned that his wife will dissolve in tears if he mentions her orgasmic inadequacy or asks for suggestions to improve his sexual approaches."

To return, however, to the theme of differential meanings given to sexual activity: the important point is not merely the enormous range of these meanings, but that they are engendered, emphasized, and often become customary and expected in different social worlds. (38) It is said, probably with some reason, that to become a female star on Broadway or in Hollywood, a woman must "cooperate" with many a male sponsor as she struggles up the ladder. Some circles, social groups, and societies simply take extramarital affairs for granted (31); others insist that the wife remain virtuous but permit the husband to take a mistress. Many very masculine social worlds—the world of auto racing, for instance— have their special sexual codes, complete with special terms ("old ladies," "groupies") for their associated females. Then there is the phenomenon of circles of middle-class "swingers," with their explicit codes of exchange of couples and their implicit expectations of such ordinarily taboo behavior as the playful stimulation of genitals by female couples and collectivities. (1, 43) The changing meanings of sex for each successive "younger generation" is another instance of evolving and declining social worlds—some younger people still adhering, nonetheless, to the standards and perspectives of their parents.

Abortion and Its Symbolism

Being human and thus able to anticipate the future, we are able both to anticipate that the outcome of a given act of sexual activity might be a pregnancy and able to evaluate that outcome, positively or negatively, in advance. Furthermore, the thoughts or fantasies that precede and are produced by a particular sexual encounter may engender feelings of guilt, shame, or exaltation. For centuries, methods of contraception have been practiced with greater or lesser success. During the last decade, at least in industrialized countries, contraceptive methods have become so effective and widely used that it is possible to separate sex almost completely from having children, just as the sex act can be separated from intimacy and love. That means not only effective family planning, but also a changing perspective about providing contraception for one's children at an appropriate age. ("Why not give them the pill?") And the implication of *that*, as well as the increasingly vocal and behavioral effectiveness of women's demands that they be given more to say about their own lives, has brought about a considerable debate about abortion.

Abortion, of course, is only one method of preventing the birth of unwanted children, but since it actually involves the destruction of a fetus, the definitional aspects of the public debate are particularly intriguing. Assuming there really is a fetus, at what point does it acquire the status of "human being," with rights and privileges and, for the religious, a soul? When does beginning human life become sacred? How does one accommodate the rights of the mother to those of the child she is carrying? It is around such issues that the current debate rages.

Conservative lawyers have argued that our constitution guarantees individuals the right to counsel even when they cannot speak up for themselves. The unborn child, they say, needs a lawyer to speak up for it, to point out that the Bill of Rights should apply, and that the unborn child should be granted the right to "life, liberty, and the pursuit of happiness" like other citizens. Deliberate abortion, therefore, is defined as criminal homicide or as murder. Others on the conservative side speak in religious terms of the sanctity of life, even arguing sometimes against all or most forms of birth control and certainly against abortion. The latter, they say, besides being a crime, is also a mortal sin. The Catholic Church in particular has been a leading force on the conservative side of the issue, although in the United States it has been far more effective in publicly opposing abortion than in preventing the use of contraceptives among lay Catholics. In accordance with a religious doctrine, which holds that only the baptized can be saved, members of the clergy sometimes perform the baptismal rites in the delivery rooms of hospitals in the case of a difficult birth or when it is feared the infant will not survive.

On the other side of the debate, there are the practical, no-nonsense views of those who regard it as absurd to talk of souls and of the sanctity of the life of an unborn child. The arguments on this side are of a secular, scientific, and rationalistic type, stressing the wishes and the welfare of the woman rather than those of her unborn child. (Although the latter's welfare can also be argued, if the mother does not really wish the child.) The law sometimes has declared abortion to be criminal even when performed to end a pregnancy resulting from rape or to avoid jeopardizing the health or life of the mother. From this standpoint the fetus, by implication or explicit relation, may not be considered a full-fledged autonomous human individual.

The debate over abortion is acrimonious and divisive, based as it is on assumptions and values that often are basically irrational and very deeply rooted. (8, 44) The issues are not such that they can be readily resolved by the accumulation of scientific evidence, by rational argument, or even by legislative action or decisions of the United States Supreme Court. Thus some nurses and doctors have rebelled against a recent court decision on the liberal side, simply by refusing categorically to do what the decision permitted them to do. Indeed, some hospitals have officially announced their refusal to change their policies on abortion despite the new law created by court decision. Even in abortion clinics, staff members have sometimes evidenced quite overt bias against their clients, particularly when they are "repeaters." This is all the more striking, since it is becoming apparent that increasing numbers of women are using early abortions as just another method of preventive contraception.

The combination of taboos, beliefs, and actions of individuals themselves is often strange and inconsistent. Members of religious groups opposed to abortion may support their church's position in public but find rationalizations for disregarding religious precepts in their private actions. It may also be observed that many abortions in the early stages of pregnancy are self-induced for varied private reasons. In the instance of medically performed abortions, most are, or were in the recent past, sought by married women: here reputation is not at stake.

Where very powerful taboos and a variety of conflicting ideologies and political lobbies exist, social change comes about relatively slowly and only after great public debate, and, in this instance, the emergence of new contraceptive techniques. Official policies ordinarily change only after a long preliminary period during which the actual practices of citizens depart further and further from the old standards and from the implications of old laws. Legislatures are extremely reluctant to introduce new legislation in such areas lest they lose the votes of conservative minorities that may be offended and accuse them of being on the side of the Devil, sin, and immorality. Presumably, it is with some relief that both married and unmarried lovers can increasingly escape the abortion debate simply because devices like the pill—and even more advanced methods seemingly soon possible—may make abortion virtually unnecessary. Some years ago, one of the authors listened to a mother talking in a shocked voice about the number of teen-age abortions in her daughter's school; the author suggested that soon we would have an injection that would "freeze" a child at the age of puberty only to be unfrozen to have children when she got married. The mother was horrified. Probably, now, she would no longer be, since that day seems to be rapidly approaching.

This public discussion of abortion, colored as it is with moral judgments and high passion about what are believed to be normal and abnormal practices, leads rather naturally to the topic of the next chapter: "deviancy."

Summary

Despite a widespread belief that sexual behavior and motivation are biologically determined, human sexual adjustments are primarily symbolic in nature and the patterning of human sexual responses is learned through social experience in group contexts. A comparison of human and subhuman sexual activities shows that hormonal control declines and is replaced by cortical control and learning mechanisms as one ascends the evolutionary scale from simpler mammalian forms to the great apes and then to man. The influence of symbolic processes and of learning in human beings is predominant; and many forms of deviant behavior, such as homosexuality, fetishism, and inversion are unique in the human species. There is an absence of evidence indicating that human sex preferences are determined by the sex hormones, and there is positive evidence that the masculine and feminine roles are, like other social roles, learned systems of behavior. The profound influence of symbolic processes on human sexual behavior is evident in masturbation, erotic imagery, the control or inhibition of the orgasm, and in different ways of defining or interpreting the significance of sexual activities. Sexual identities are conferred upon persons through the socialization process. Sexual self-conceptions arise out of intimate relationships. Falling in and out of love must be viewed processually. An individual's standing in the sexual arena often reflects his or her location in a society's or a group's stratification system. The profound symbolism that surrounds the sexual act and its consequences are expressed in the controversy surrounding the abortion issue.

References

1. Bartell, Gilbert, *Group Sex: A Scientist's Eyewitness Report on the Way of Swinging.* New York: Peter Wyden, 1972.
2. Beach, F. A., "Evolutionary Changes in the Physiological Control of Mating Behavior in Mammals," *Psychological Review,* vol. 54 (1947), pp. 297–315.
3. ———— (ed.), *Sex and Behavior:* New York: Wiley, 1965.
4. Berger, Peter I., and Hansfried Kellner, "Marriage and the Construction of Reality: An Exercise in the Microsociology of Knowledge," *Diogenes,* no. 46 (Summer 1964), pp. 1–23.
5. Bernard, Jessie, *Women and the Public Interest.* Chicago: Aldine, 1971.
6. Brecher, Edward M., *The Sex Researchers.* Boston: Little, Brown, 1969.
7. Broderick, C. B., "Social Heterosexual Relationships among Urban Negroes and Whites," *Journal of Marriage and the Family,* vol. 28 (1965), pp. 200–3.
8. Callahan, David, *Abortion: Law, Choice and Morality.* New York: Macmillan, 1970.
9. Campbell, J. K., *Honour, Family and Patronage.* New York: Oxford University Press, 1964.
10. Conn, J. H., and L. Kanner, "Children's Awareness of Sex Differences," *Journal of Child Psychiatry,* vol. 1 (1947), pp. 3–57.
11. Corey, D., *The Homosexual in America.* Philadelphia: Chilton Book Company, 1951.
12. Epstein, Cynthia Fuchs, *Woman's Place.* Berkeley, Calif.: University of California Press, 1971.
13. Freud, S., "The Psychology of Women," in *New Introductory Lectures on Psychoanalysis.* New York: W. W. Norton, 1933, pp. 153–83.
14. Gagnon, John, and William Simon, "Perspectives on the Sexual Scene," in John Gagnon and William Simon (eds.), *The Sexual Scene.* Chicago: Aldine, 1970, pp. 1–21.
15. Garfinkel, Harold, "Passing and the Managed Achievement of Sex Status in an Intersexed Person," part 1, in *Studies in Ethnomethodology.* Englewood Cliffs, N.J.: Prentice-Hall, 1967, pp. 116–85.

16. Goode, William, "The Theoretical Importance of Love," *American Sociological Review*, vol. 24 (February 1959), pp. 37–48.
17. Hamilton, G., "Changes in Personality and Psychosexuality with Age," in E. V. Cowdry (ed.), *Problems of Aging: Biological and Medical Aspects*. Baltimore: Williams and Wilkins, 1939, pp. 459–82.
18. Henslin, James (ed.), *The Sociology of Sex*. New York: Appleton-Century-Crofts, 1971.
19. Hill, Ruben, and Joan Aldous, "Socialization for Marriage and Parenthood," in D. Goslin (ed.), *Handbook of Socialization Theory and Research*. Chicago: McNally & Company, 1969, pp. 885–950.
20. Humphreys, Laud, *Out of the Closets: The Sociology of Homosexual Liberation*. Englewood Cliffs, N.J.: Prentice-Hall, 1972.
21. Hunt, Morton, *The World of the Formerly Married*. New York: McGraw-Hill, 1966.
22. Isaacs, S. S., *Social Development in Young Children*. London: Routledge & Kegan Paul, 1933.
23. Kinsey, A. C., et al, *Sexual Behavior in the Human Female*. Philadelphia: W. B. Saunders, 1954.
24. ———, *Sexual Behavior in the Human Male*. Philadelphia: W. B. Saunders, 1948.
25. Klein, M., *The Psychoanalysis of Children*. London: Hogarth Press, 1932.
26. Kuhn, Manford H., "Kinsey's View of Human Behavior," *Social Problems*, vol. 4 (1954), pp. 119–25.
27. Luckey, Eleanore B., and Gilbert D. Nass, "A Comparison of Sexual Attitudes and Behavior in an International Sample," *Journal of Marriage and the Family*, vol. 17 (May 1969), pp. 364–79.
28. Masters, W., and E. Johnson, *Human Sexual Inadequacy*. Boston: Little, Brown, 1968.
29. ———, *Human Sexual Response*. Boston: Little, Brown, 1966.
30. Murstein, Bernard (ed.), *Theories of Attraction and Love*. Berlin: Springer-Verlag, 1971.
31. Neubeck, Gerhard (ed.), *Extramarital Relations*. Englewood Cliffs, N.J.: Prentice-Hall, 1969.
32. Newton, Esther, *Mother Camp: Female Impersonators in America*. Englewood Cliffs, N.J.: Prentice-Hall, 1972.
33. Reiss, Ira L., *The Family System in America*. New York: Holt, Rinehart and Winston, 1971.
34. Ross, H. Lawrence, "Modes of Adjustment of Married Homosexuals," *Social Problems*, vol. 18 (1971), pp. 385–93.
35. Safilios-Rothchild, Constantina (ed.), *Toward a Sociology of Women*. Lexington, Mass.: Xerox College Publishing, 1972.
36. Scanzoni, John, *Sexual Bargaining: Power Politics in the American Marriage*. Englewood Cliffs, N.J.: Prentice-Hall, 1972.
37. Schwartz, G., and D. Merten, "The Language of Adolescence," *American Journal of Sociology*, vol. 72 (March 1967), pp. 453–68.
38. Scott, Marvin B., and Stanford M. Lyman, "Paranoia, Homosexuality, and Game Theory," in Stanford M. Lyman and Marvin B. Scott, *A Sociology of the Absurd*. New York: Appleton-Century-Crofts, 1970, pp. 71–88.
39. Seward, G. H., *Sex and the Social Order*. New York: McGraw-Hill, 1946.
40. Sullivan, Harry Stack, *The Interpersonal Theory of Psychiatry*. New York: W. W. Norton, 1953.
41. Thomas, W. I., *Primitive Behavior*. New York: McGraw-Hill, 1936.

42. Waller, Willard, *The Old Love and the New: Divorce and Readjustment.* New York: Liveright, 1930.
43. Walshok, Mary, "The Emergence of Middle-Class Deviant Subcultures: The Case of Swingers," *Social Problems,* vol. 18 (1971), pp. 488–95.
44. Westoff, C., E. Moore, and N. Ryder, "The Structure of Attitudes toward Abortion," *Milbank Memorial Fund Quarterly,* vol. 47 (1969), pp. 11–37.
45. Winch, Robert, *Mate-Selection: A Study of Complementary Needs.* New York: Harper & Row, 1967.

Selected Readings

BEACH, F. A. (ed.), *Sex and Behavior.* New York: Wiley, 1965.
An important collection of papers relevant to the topic of sex role socialization.

EPSTEIN, CYNTHIA FUCHS, *Woman's Place.* Berkeley, Calif.: University of California Press, 1971.
An impressive documentation of the secondary position women have been accorded in American society.

GAGNON, JOHN, AND WILLIAM SIMON (eds.), *The Sexual Scene.* Chicago: Aldine, 1970.
A useful set of readings stressing the social psychological nature of sexual behavior.

GARFINKEL, HAROLD, *Studies in Ethnomethodology.* Englewood Cliffs, N.J.: Prentice-Hall, 1967.
Contains a valuable study of a person who successfully carried off a sex role change and even managed to "fool" the researchers.

KINSEY, A. C., et al., *Sexual Behavior in the Human Male.* Philadelphia: W. B. Saunders, 1948.
Contains important base-line data on the sexual behavior of American males and was the first and most subjective of a series of studies by Kinsey and his associates.

KUHN, MANFORD H., "Kinsey's View of Human Behavior," *Social Problems,* vol. 4 (1954), pp. 119–25.
A devastating critique of Kinsey's conception of human sexual behavior.

WALLER, WILLARD, *The Old Love and the New: Divorce and Readjustment.* Philadelphia: Liveright, 1930.
This remains the most insightful analysis of marriage and divorce in the sociological literature. It has recently been republished by Southern Illinois Press (1967), with an introduction by Bernard Farber.

chapter 15

Deviance and Deviant Worlds

$\mathcal{S}$ociologists, *social* psychologists, psychiatrists, politicians, and everyday individuals hold widely differing conceptions concerning the nature and origins of what is commonly termed *deviant behavior.* Concepts such as *homosexual, prostitute, drug addict, paranoid, insane, eccentric, deviant, politically or morally corrupt,* and *revolutionary* cover a wide range of behaviors which defy classification under a single concept. Obviously these phenomena are not all of the same genre. All result, however, in negative actions from groups who define them as problems. Reaction may be spontaneous (as to a person with a stigma, perhaps a dwarf), or so highly institutionalized that an elaborate control apparatus is developed to contain it (as with crime). A group can react to one of these problems with irritation or mild displeasure, or it can regard the problem as genuinely threatening to the group's existence.

In this chapter we shall attempt to place the study of deviance within an expanded symbolic interactionist conception of social relationships and social worlds. Individuals, we have repeatedly suggested, occupy positions in interlocking and interconnected social worlds. These worlds commit them to certain lines of action and lead to the development of special self-conceptions; each can be viewed as a special universe of discourse and experience. They are uniquely bounded worlds of meaning and thought. Each world, from some perspective, can be seen as deviant. A variety of deviant social worlds, ranging from the professional criminal to the homosexual, the drug addict, and the political deviant, will be discussed.

Conceptions of Deviance

Deviance and its definitions arise out of the interactions of individuals who hold different degrees of power and authority over one another. In an ultimate sense the state and its government and its laws possess the final power to define what is and is not deviant or criminal behavior. The application of a deviant or criminal label to one individual or a group of individuals involves the political application of power. (7, 46, 53) Deviance and its study directly lead the sociologist into a consideration of power and its distribution within social groups and societies generally. There are, in any society, experts on conventional behavior, on normal behavior, on deviant behavior, and on criminal behavior. (5, 7, 34) In a complex society some things are deviant in some circles but not in others. Further, there are certain behaviors that simply go unnoticed, or if noticed, are passed off as uninteresting or as irrelevant. Whether one eats breakfast or not, or whether one has blue eyes, or brown eyes, or long hair, is basically irrelevant for one's biography and for one's relationships with others. Other behaviors, however, traditionally become so publicly real that professional interpreters of them emerge. Psychiatrists, sociologists, lawyers, educators, and physicians all offer differing theories to account for such actions as murder, rape, drug addiction, divorce, homosexuality, and insanity. Some of these formulations attain the status of scientific theories. Psychoanalysis, structural functionalism, and symbolic interactionism are examples of theories which purport to account for such actions as murder, rape, drug addiction, divorce, homosexuality, and insanity. Over time, as new issues become controversial—for example, civil rights, women's liberation, gay liberation, and urban riots—new theories emerge, or old theories are revised to explain what is occurring. (10) Inevitably clashes in perspective occur. Militant women's liberationists reject Freudian explanations of their behavior. Politicians treat as irrelevant the scientific utterances of social scientists, including political scientists. Deviance and its discovery involves inherently social processes, which at root rest on political debates over what will be termed conventional, acceptable behavior. (60, 61)

The Nature of Deviance

A basic preliminary point is that actions are not in themselves moral or immoral, deviant or nondeviant. It is the judgment that is passed on the behavior by others, and not the behavior itself, that determines and defines deviance. As Kai Erikson (38:6) remarks, "Deviance is not a property *inherent* in any particular kind of behavior; it is a property *conferred upon* that behavior by the people who come into direct or indirect contact with it. The only way an observer can tell whether a given style of behavior is deviant . . . is to learn something about the standards of the audience which responds to it." It is difficult, perhaps impossible, to think of any type of behavior outlawed in America today that has not been acceptable somewhere at some time.

There is nothing about many specific kinds of activity that automatically causes them to be regarded in the wider community as dangerous, queer, or perverted. Certain acts are sanctioned in some communities and negatively evaluated in others. Over a period of time definitions inevitably change as public orientation shifts. Addiction to opiates, for example, is regarded as a medical problem in most Western countries, and was so regarded in the United States until recent decades. Homosexuals are discriminated against in Western countries, but this particular bias is not universally shared even there. Indeed, when people meet homosexuals under predominantly normal conditions, as in some occupations, homosexuality is taken for granted and homosexuals are assumed to be much like other human beings.

Historical changes in definitions of deviancy are striking, and many illustrations could be cited. Thus, the treatment of religious sects is a highly variable matter, and in a given period depends upon whether the sect espouses practices that seem shocking or dangerous to its neighbors. During one period of its history a sect may be viewed as a menace to public morals, and at another it may be viewed as merely odd or peculiar. When politics get mixed into sectarianism, the sect may come to be regarded, at least for a time, as unpatriotic or even subversive. Of course a sect or any other group may engage in practices running counter to general moral standards and yet escape widespread attention. But if through some combination of circumstances the glare of publicity falls upon the group, influential groups of good citizens may demand that something be done about its degenerate or dangerous practices. When public furor dies down the group may continue its traditional practices more or less unmolested; but it remains vulnerable as long as the practices themselves fall within the definition of deviancy that is generally current.

It is a historic fact that when members of influential groups meet outsiders whose behavior is shocking and strange, they may not merely think the outsiders different but may believe them to be degenerate and inhuman. This has happened repeatedly when white Europeans spilled over into strange areas of the globe over the last five centuries. With domination comes a kind of tolerance; the superordinate group believes that it knows the people that it dominates and develops a rationale (in racial terms or otherwise) to explain the different behavior of the Asian or the African. It may, in fact, be hazarded that whenever people meet initially, whenever they discover each other's existence for the first time, strangeness and mutual ethnocentrism are likely to be accompanied by imputations of deviancy. Since conquering or superordinate groups generally have an advantage in making their definitions stick, only their definitions of deviancy may survive.

Deviance takes a number of forms and may be viewed at various levels. In *the group framework* it involves the public violation of group norms and the application of specialized procedures and sanctions to handle the deviant and control the volume of deviance. When the formal agencies of control lack jurisdiction over the behavior, it is dealt with by using informal control mechanisms, such as gossip or avoidance. On *the personal level,* deviance may be considered as behavior that violates the person's internalized norms and is believed to be controlled by internal psychic mechanisms, such as conscience.

Deviance may have its sources in the social structure or may be generated by causes within the individual. These causes may be consciously recognized and reported upon by the persons involved, or they may exist below the level of awareness as unnamed, unconscious, or subliminal influences. Since we have already touched on deviance in terms of self, generalized other, and conscience, we shall be concerned here with deviance at the group and interactional level. The upshot of these remarks is that an attempt to explain deviance must focus not on the act as such but on the social evaluation of the act that causes it to be regarded as deviant. (60)

SOURCES OF DEFINITIONS OF DEVIANCE The foregoing discussion can be summarized by noting that individuals may become tainted or "spoiled" interactants for any of the following four reasons. They may commit an illegal act and be apprehended, arrested, charged, and convicted. Then they find that their biographies have been significantly altered. They may be unable to return to their "normal" worlds of social interaction.

Second, they may, as Goffman (43) argues, belong to a work, ethnic, religious, or racial group that is viewed as less than desirable by the broader social order. Jews have suffered and died from being members of such a group, as have nearly all other major religious and ethnic groups in the world's history. Blacks, Italians, Irish, Japanese, Chinese, Germans, and Russians have, at different points in their collective world histories, been defined as political, economic, and moral threats to other sectors of humanity. (63) Whether or not group, economic, or political membership is viewed in undesirable terms depends in large part on a group's standing in the broader society. Those with power can legislate their own conceptions of moral desirability and acceptability. Those groups which are viewed as moral or economic threats, or those individuals who perform a country's "dirty work," often find themselves outside the mainstream of political processes. (6) As a consequence, they suffer economic as well as moral abuse from other citizens. It is this phenomenon that often leads such individuals to band together by living in common residential areas. In their respective ghettos they at least find some social support for their world views. Of course, processes of discrimination and segregation often make it impossible for these individuals to live their lives in morally, economically, and politically acceptable circumstances.

Third, individuals may be stigmatized because of physical deformity, or because they have acquired some disease or illness, or because they have deteriorated mentally or are mentally retarded. (56, 76) Fellow interactants assume that those they confront on a daily basis will "appear to be normal." They will walk normally, speak intelligently, not have sight or hearing impaired, have the usual level of physical stamina, and be able to follow the train of a normal conversation with relative ease. Any alteration in these attributes leads others to define these individuals in less than positive terms. They have not committed a deviant, or illegal act; they are spoiled, stigmatized actors by virtue of how they publicly present and display their bodies.

Fourth, persons can have character flaws, or stigmas, which, while not publicly visible, would if made known also brand that individual as stigmatized. Those who have been hospitalized for mental illness, those who are homosexual, or recently divorced, or unmarried parents, or former embezzlers, all share one common characteristic: their deviance is not publicly visible. For the deviance to have interactional effects, the individuals must make public these hidden facts in their biographies. Often it is to their advantage to do so, for a tainted past hovers over their life. If they refuse to tell, they may find that someone else will.

An individual may be stigmatized—especially those who belong to undesirable groups or have undesirable physical attributes—and never have committed a deviant or criminal act. (13) On the other hand, it is impossible for a person not to be stigmatized, if only for a short period of time, after he or she has broken a law, or engaged in a deviant act that evokes public outrage. There is an asymmetric relationship between stigma and deviance, and this asymmetry shifts over time as individuals move into new and different phases of their moral careers. What was deviant at one point in time may later be viewed as an attribute of excellence, bravery, or forward thinking.

THE ASYMMETRY OF SOCIAL REACTIONS

THE
BENEFITS OF
DEVIANCE
AND STIGMA

The theoretical and research literature often exhibits a rather grim, humorless view of the deviant. (82) It is assumed that those individuals who gain what are called "immoral" sexual pleasures, or engage in illicit drug practices, or make money illegally do so without reward, benefit, personal fulfillment, or professional advance. The sheer fact of the matter is that a good deal of what is stigmatized as deviant and illegal is pleasurable, profitable, and rewarding. This simple fact offers one explanation for why many individuals are drawn into those pursuits that social scientists, social workers, psychiatrists, and politicians find morally repugnant, deviant, and criminal.

DIMENSIONS
OF THE DEVIANT
ACT

Deviance and its attribution arise out of the definitions that individuals attach to themselves and to their own ongoing activity. Deviant acts can be assessed from a variety of perspectives. In this section we wish to stress the following elements of such activity. First, how frequently do they occur in the individual's activity cycle? Some, for example a murder, may only occur once. Others occur at a high frequency. Heroin users or prostitutes may engage in their particular forms of deviance on a daily basis. Other deviant acts may be more rigorously scheduled—for example, the weekend "chipping" of drugs.

Closely related to frequency is the dimension of biographical consequentiality. That is, how consequential for the individual is the deviant label? On the one hand, we have the convicted murderer who finds that his or her total life chances are drastically modified as a result of deviance. On the other extreme, individuals who privately engage in sexual fetishism may never be publicly labeled as deviant. Then the act itself does not influence the individual's other self-identities. The consequentiality issue touches on the matter of how "sticky" the deviant label is. In general, it can be predicted that those labels which have been applied by the social control agencies will be more sticky than those which arise out of friendship circles. The former produce files and dossiers on those individuals thay have apprehended for purposes of curing, incarcerating, or reeducating. These records become a permanent part of the individual's public identity and may even leak into media accounts. A related element of consequentiality describes the threat or harm component of the deviant act. Simply put: "How risky" is the act for the individual and for others? Some acts—murder, for example, or armed burglary—carry high elements of risk both for the person and his or her biography. Others carry low elements of risk but may be more consequential for the individual's biography. What Edwin M. Schur has termed "crimes without victims" fall in this category. Homosexuality, recreational drug use, and abortions describe potential deviant acts where there is no clear-cut victim. (58, 91) The individual willingly engages in the deviant act or goes to another individual for deviant, or illegal services.

A third feature of the deviant act refers to the circumstances under which it is performed. It may be done alone or in the company of a small group of others. Embezzlers (29) typically work alone, burglars and robbers do not. (37, 95) In general it appears that the more complex the network of others who are necessary to produce the deviant act, the more likely it is that individuals in that network will be apprehended. There are also situations of *double deviance,* where one deviant turns against another or simply botches an otherwise successful illegal act.

The circumstances of the act suggest the voluntary, coercive dimension: some deviant acts are forced on the individual—rape is an obvious example, as is armed robbery. The voluntary dimension also indicates that one person's deviant act may make another individual deviant in the process. The female who has been raped may now view herself in morally tainted terms, even though she had no choice in the matter. On the other hand, deviance may not produce new deviants, but simply lead others to view the individual as a fool, a dupe, or an easy mark. (44, 62) A good deal of public sympathy is likely to surround the individual who has been coerced into a deviant act; those who, because of stupidity or oversight, submit or are party to a deviant act are more likely to be viewed with scorn and ridicule.

The fourth dimension pertains to the range of accounts that individuals offer for their deviance. Their account, or "story," may stress the pleasurable effects of the act; it may stress its money-making features; or it may be grounded in highly emotional terms, perhaps matters of love, or hate, or extreme anger and frustration. Finally, individuals may employ a scientific theory to explain their deviance, or they may resort to some political or ideological cause or rhetoric. In any case, deviants are often asked to "account" for their deviance, and in this accounting process they are under some pressure to explain why they went astray. (73, 75)

Finally it must be asked: "Who does the labeling?" Individuals may label themselves as deviant, or they may be labeled by others as deviant. Furthermore, they may or may not accept the opinions of others. In any case, any analysis of the deviant act must record who the "labeler" of the act was.

It must be seen that what is deviant at one point in time may become normal acceptable behavior at another point in history. Thus, at one time it was considered deviant and immoral to drink alcoholic beverages, but such definitions have given way to a view of drinking behavior as fash-

FADS AND FASHIONS IN DEVIANCE

Marijuana use reflects the negotiated aspect of the deviance label. Rather than passively accepting the deviant label, many users have actively rejected and attempted to influence the assignation of it. (*Magnum*)

ionable. (11) Similarly, the marijuana laws which are now under revision and modification—moving toward greater leniency—reflect the fact that it has become fashionable for many sectors of society to have smoked marijuana; in the late 1960s, individuals refrained from reporting a marijuana experience.

As new issues come to the public's attention, public moral conscience is aroused and people become outraged over new forms of illegal or deviant behavior. In this sense a nation's social control agencies continually produce new side-effects of marijuana, heroin, and birth control pills. Nations are continually having or experiencing new epidemics of deviance. This keeps the social control agencies in business. It also clarifies ambiguous group boundaries and ambiguous conceptions of what is deviant and what is acceptable. (27, 38) Furthermore, each new form of deviance lays the groundwork for new behaviors which may eventually become fashionable and morally acceptable. (96)

A critical question concerning fads and fashions in deviance involves the original source or locus of the deviance. That is, from what sectors of society does it emanate, and who is defining it as deviant? It appears that unacceptable fashions that flow from those lacking political power will not become acceptable until more powerful and influential citizens experiment with and take up that new activity. Thus, marijuana laws were not modified until middle- and upper-class youths were apprehended for using it, and their parents began experimenting with the drug. So what is today's deviance may become tomorrow's fashion, and similarly, what is fashionable today may become outmoded and deviant in the future. These issues lead logically to the topic of "neutralization."

On the other hand, persons who violate norms that they themselves accept as valid and legitimate ordinarily feel guilty about their behavior. The term *techniques of neutralization* is a recently coined expression that refers to the symbolic devices used in this situation to permit the behavior to continue and to assuage pangs of conscience. Its meaning is closely akin to that of *rationalization.* It should be noted in passing that deviants do not necessarily feel guilty, and that this is especially true when they deny the validity of the public definition, as is the case with many marijuana smokers, political dissenters, homosexuals, and others. G. Sykes and D. Matza (107) enumerate techniques of neutralization as follows:

TECHNIQUES OF NEUTRALIZATION

1. Denial of harm—little or no real harm has been done.
2. Denial of the victim—the victim provoked the action and got what was coming to him.
3. Attacking the accusers—the police are corrupt, brutal, and unfair and the laws are unjust.
4. Invoking other and higher loyalties—that of loyalty to one's fellow gang members, for example.

The sense of guilt and the ideology used to neutralize it are indications that deviants are in a sense committed to the values they violate. They explain and excuse their behavior by means of concepts and ideas that are made available by the broader society. Thus, drug addicts and alcoholics account for and sometimes excuse their addiction to themselves and others in terms of neutralizing "motives" or excuses. The user of illicit drugs, for example, may utilize any or all of the techniques of neutralization by arguing that (1) no harm was done, (2) the laws are unjust, and (3) one's friends also use the drug.

Deviant Careers and Social Worlds

A good deal of the literature in criminology and the sociology of deviance assumes a relatively static view of the labeling, or defining process. To be termed a drug addict, a juvenile delinquent, a divorcee, or to be called homosexual or a radical, means different things for the individual at different points in his or her moral career. One is not just delinquent (39, 94) or addicted to a certain class of drugs, or mentally ill. Rather, over a period of time, one becomes delinquent, or addicted, or

Gamblers may become addicted not only to gambling but to a way of life. (*Ray Ellis/Photo Researchers, Inc.*)

mentally ill, or senile. In each phase of the deviant career, individuals see themselves differently. (7) The meanings that labels have for them and their significant others and for the public at large will vary in terms of how they act. (93) If they exacerbate their deviance, parade it, so to speak, then it may eventually become a permanent part of their identity kit, for they will now be viewed as homosexuals or drug addicts by their interactive fellows. On the other hand, they may choose to hide or conceal their deviance; then its relevance for their day-to-day interactions is minimal. (59) Some individuals assume a dramatic and emotional response in the first phases of their deviant careers and then with the passage of time normalize their deviant identification. (9, 56)

As we will show in this section, an actor's response to an ascription of deviance depends in large part on the public receptivity to his or her altered condition. Some forms of deviance have strong and massive institutional support—for example, organized crime. (16) Others emerge in the forms of social movements. Women's liberation, gay liberation, and the black power movement are three recent examples of how individuals have banded together in an attempt to have themselves collectively redefined by the broader social order. Many deviants fall heir to incipient, less well-defined social worlds. As our discussion of homosexuals will show, many individuals who are so defined can enter special bars, housing complexes, and public recreational areas where they will find other individuals who share their views of sexual behavior. Some deviants keep their deviant identities hidden altogether, or share it with only a small number of other individuals. What can be called *relational deviance* falls into this category. Marital partners may have their own private versions of the sexual act, which if made public would brand them deviant. They keep their deviance to themselves. Those who carry on affairs, embezzle, "shoot" drugs on the weekend, or keep hidden stocks of pornographic magazines also usually keep their deviances to themselves. Finally, there are those deviants, or "outsiders," who belong to no organized social world or social relationship. They furtively and secretly practice their deviant acts. Transvestites, "closet" homosexuals, and eccentrics fall into this category.

Depending on the individual's location in any of the above social worlds, his or her response to the label of deviant or criminal will vary. Consequently, any analysis of the deviant career must simultaneously assume a temporal and interactional, or organizational, stance. (31) Many students of deviance have ignored these temporal, moral, and interactional features of deviants and their careers. We turn now to the consideration of a variety of different deviant worlds.

Deviant Worlds and Individuals

In presenting a general framework for understanding deviant behavior, we noted that some forms of deviance are highly organized. Some shade off gradually and merge imperceptibly with conduct that is disapproved of or viewed as peculiar, yet is permitted and even protected when necessary by agents of the law. In this section we shall examine several instances of the more organized types of deviance and then certain of the less organized or unorganized types. All persons who label, or are labeled as, deviant are members of social worlds that differentially endorse those designations. All forms of deviant behavior find their locus in some social world, no matter how loosely organized. We shall illustrate this point by discussing political corruption and individual deviance, forms of behavior that have too often gone unnoticed by sociological students of deviance. (78, 79)

DEVIANT GROUPS AND THE WIDER SOCIETY

All deviant groups are related to and arise from the structure of the wider society. Some quite clearly perform functions for accepted groups. Respectable men of all social worlds take advantage of the availability of prostitutes, and quasi-criminal or quasi-underworld organizations capitalize on this patronage. It is not these organizations but the persistent market for prostitution that makes it difficult to suppress. The market for the prostitute's services presumably reflects the inadequacies of those legitimate institutions that regulate sexual and affectional behavior. (45)

Occasionally, zealous advocates of vice suppression may succeed in outlawing a particular form of activity, such as gambling, which happens to be an integral part of the way of life of some people. Illegal organization then flourishes around the otherwise unfulfilled demand for the banished activity or commodity. (84)

Some deviant groups may be said to constitute *deviant worlds* or *deviant communities* because, while they are located in space, they also tend to transcend particular locales. They are not tightly organized, but consist of loosely connected groups or circles of deviants, not all of which know or have direct communication with other circles. We shall discuss three of these worlds by way of illustration and in order to make additional theoretical points.

Criminal Worlds

As we have remarked, American emphasis on success, money, and competition, as well as the great proliferation of occupations and divisions of labor, have resulted in the development of illegal occupations that are integral parts of our commercial and occupational world. Students of criminology have classified crime and criminals in a great variety of ways. The criminal underworld is itself a complicated social structure with occupational diversity and status systems. For our purposes, we may classify criminals into three categories: (1) conventional criminals, (2) white-collar criminals, and (3) racketeers. (20)

THE CRIMINAL OCCUPATIONS

The conventional criminals may be either *professionals* or *amateurs*; *occupational* and *nonoccupational* would be equivalent terms. Most instances of murder, rape, and arson, for example, are not committed as occupational activities, and a great many persons from respectable society commit an occasional theft, murder, or other offense. The *conventional criminal occupations* probably number in the hundreds. An immense number of specific devices and skills may be employed, while new ones are constantly being invented and old ones improved. These skills may be roughly classified as (1) those involving violence or threats; (2) those involving manual or mechanical dexterity and skill (such as picking of pockets, shoplifting, safe cracking, and automobile stealing and stripping); and (3) those involving verbal dexterity and histrionic ability, frequently called swindling, fraud, and confidence games. In the last type, some mechanical or manual skill may be called for, as in the "shell game" or in "three-card monte." The specific types of fraud are legion.

Each of the various criminal occupations has its own specific rules and norms to guide and control the behavior of its practitioners.

Each has a hierarchy of status positions and possesses prestige relative to others, this prestige reflecting underworld public opinion. There are codes regulating standard performances: a "fingering job" ordinarily yields a regular 10 percent; "the nut" (expenses) is always subtracted from the money gained "at the top" (before dividing).

White-collar crime consists of offenses committed in legitimate occupations or business, for example, by corporations in the course of their regular business operations. (102) It is perhaps unnecessary at this point in time to note that there is considerable crime committed by politicians and public officials on behalf of the public interest. A businessman may break the law knowingly either for mercenary reasons or because he feels that he must because his competitors do likewise. Sometimes he may break a law because the law itself is vague and the boundaries of legality are not clear. Sometimes corporations challenge the legality of a statute by deliberately flouting it to see if the court decision will uphold their action. There is no world of white-collar crime as such.

The third general type of crime is *racketeering*. We are using the term here to designate underworld business activities. This means the provision of contraband goods or services for a market which usually includes clientele from the respectable world. Gambling, prostitution, and the bootlegging of liquor and drugs are examples. These businesses are organized like any other, with certain special features such as the prominence of bribery—involving collusion of public officials—and the inability of underworld businessmen to enforce contracts and settle disputes in the courts. As a substitute for court decision, racketeers have their own methods for settling disputes and for enforcing the fulfillment of contractual obligations. Racketeers, like conventional criminals, are part of the general criminal milieu.

Criminals of the first and third types have identifications with a somewhat vague but nonetheless real criminal world, a world that is somewhat wider than particular occupations or rackets. This world, much like that of the artist or the professional athlete, is *not* sharply set off from other worlds, but does command a certain loyalty and allegiance from its members. Criminal argot reflects something of the unity of the world when it designates all outsiders as "squares" and all insiders as "right." Marginal persons, such as lawyers who engage in dubious or dishonest practices, are called "kinky" to designate their separate status (102:164–66):

> The professional thief . . . has semilegitimate acquaintances among lawyers, fences, fixers, bondsmen, and politicians. These . . . are making money from the thief but are supposed to be members of legitimate society. He may call upon them, also, for assistance for the less legitimate purposes. . . . The thief is somewhat suspicious of all individuals in legitimate society other than those mentioned. He believes that whoever is not with him

is against him. Any noncriminal individual not personally known . . . is a possible danger and, as an individual, is somewhat disliked on that account. This feeling is reinforced by occasional trouble which results from perfectly proper acquaintances. . . . [There is considerable] danger that the thief may run into if he tries to make legitimate contacts with strangers. Because of this, the professional thief lives largely in a world of his own and is rather completely isolated from general society. The majority of them do not care to contact society except professionally.

The fact that all insiders are on the shady side of the law lends symbolic cohesion. The intense hatred felt for informers or stool pigeons is an index of this cohesion and of the need for secrecy in the face of the outside world. Of course all groups, occupational or otherwise, require for their very functioning that certain secrets be withheld from nonmembers. This is of special importance for criminal groups for obvious reasons. An important ingredient in the ideologies of the underworld is the preservation of trade secrets and the maintenance of a closed mouth before outsiders. Even the excriminal who writes a book about his experiences may feel uneasy about revealing current techniques, and may therefore write mainly of past history and of well-known crimes. The lines drawn between underworld and general society necessarily involve a certain suspicion and wariness (102:168–69):

One of the personal characteristics of the thief is extreme suspicion. This may be accounted for by the fact that he exists in a suspicious world. . . . The first thing in his mind in every touch is whether he is under suspicion. . . . He must decide whether there is an ulterior motive in any word or act of a prospect. He must often be courteous, kindly, and solicitous, and, because he has to play this role, he is naturally very sensitive to these characteristics in anyone else. Therefore, if someone would do or offer to do something for him which is unusually kindly, he immediately becomes suspicious.

LIFE STYLES OF CRIMINALS.   Although criminals of any country resemble the citizens of that country in many ways, cherishing and striving for many of the same ends, they also develop their own style of life. A professional thief cheerfully says that "the professional thief rejoices in the welfare of the public. He would like to see society enjoy continuous prosperity, for then his own touches will naturally be greater." (102:172)

Somewhat different styles within the criminal world arise from the different occupations; but existence within the criminal milieu lends certain general features to them. The professional criminal usually operates in terms of short-range goals. He or she becomes a liberal and unconcerned spender of money and worries only about the immediate future. Probably this is true even for the racketeer groups whose conspicuous consumption is a matter of public comment. In recent years racketeers have tended to move into middle-class suburban areas and to take over some middle-class manners and standards. High living with an emphasis on drinking, horse racing, and gambling is a feature of most criminal circles. *In fact, in an economic sense, many criminals partly live off other criminals;* the holdup man may spend his gains with a bookie or lose his money at gambling. There is a famous apocryphal story told about a criminal who found himself in a strange town, and who then asked an associate where they could gamble. He was told that there was only one "joint" but that it was "crooked." This information only led him to exclaim, as he prepared to be fleeced, "What are we going to do, there isn't any other."

Criminals often do not marry (but men may use the term "wife" to refer to the woman with whom they are currently living). Males associate with women of easy virtue who are part of, or marginal to, the criminal milieu. Professional criminals are aware of their somewhat different style of life and of the attitudes that respectable citizens have toward them. They know and often partly accept the values of respectable society toward crime, and hence show symptoms of uneasy conscience. They protect themselves against their conscience by means of rationalizations that are extremely varied and often ingenious. If they steal from someone who is rich they argue that the rich are themselves usually dishonest. If they steal from the poor they argue that they spend it on drink anyway. The confidence man likes to point out that victims have to be willing to cheat someone else before they themselves can be fleeced. (Incidentally, criminals invariably object to calling the victim a victim; they much prefer to call him or her "mark" or "sucker." As one thief said: "That makes it sound bad to call them 'victims.' ") Criminals also like to point out that many persons, such as the police, lawyers, prison staffs, and others from respectable society make money from them or have jobs dependent upon the existence of crime. They may point to the stimulating influence they have on the insurance business and the manufacture of safes, locks, keys, and burglar alarms.

Professional criminals often think of their activities as an occupation or a business and may not consider themselves enemies of society. They do not usually hate the police, lawyers, judges, and others who play a role in sending them to prison, unless they violate what seem to them to be the rules of the game and the standards of sportsmanship. As a famous "madam" complained (2:144):

> I didn't resent the honest cop and I was able to stay in business because of the dishonest variety. But the members of the gendarmerie who really started my adrenalin flowing like wine were the boys who believed in playing it both ways, and who wouldn't have turned a hair if their own mother happened to be the one caught in the middle.

RECRUITMENT.   Many criminals talk about "packing the racket" or going "legit." That they consider leaving the criminal life indicates its tensions and hazards. Criminals often feel a certain envy for those of their number who have managed to go straight. There is indeed a kind of folklore among them concerning instances of this kind. Nevertheless it is not easy to leave the underworld once people have become rooted in it and have an investment and involvement in it. Their friends are in the underworld, and they are accustomed to its routines, satisfactions, and excitements. Their loyalties tie them to it. When they try to abandon it they are not only drawn back, but are also pushed back because they are tagged by respectable society and cannot escape their past. When they try the good life they often find it dull and frustrating, and may discover that they do not have the requisite skills and knowledge to give them the standard of living to which they are accustomed. Not much is known about the drift out of the criminal world, but there is some evidence of a shift with increasing age to marginal, semilegitimate occupations. Individuals who make this change do not altogether renounce underworld associations, but do manage to avoid the worst risks.

There is an extensive literature on the causation of criminal behavior, and all sorts of theories from biological determinism to the strictly environmental have been proposed and defended. Two broad problems exist in this area. One is to account for the origin of criminal groups. This is a historical and sociological problem and does not deal with the behavior of individuals. The other is to explain how a given individual comes to join a criminal group and to accept its way of life. This is of interest to the social psychologist. (12)

The criminal underworld does not maintain itself biologically, for reproduction rates are low and criminals who do have children often try to keep them from following a life of crime. (This statement does not necessarily apply to other countries. In India, for example, criminal occupations, as well as prostitution and begging, have been matters of caste heritage and have been passed on from parents to children.) As a consequence, the criminal population is maintained by a process of recruitment about which relatively little is known. It is commonly assumed that adult criminals are recruited from juvenile delinquents, but this is only partly true and varies by types of crime. A substantial portion of adult offenders have no records of juvenile delinquency and evidently embark on criminal careers relatively late in life. A recent autobiographical account by a convict doing a life term in the Iowa State Penitentiary indicates that this man's first venture into crime was as a bank robber during the Depression when he was in his early twenties. (89) Statistical evidence indicates that close to one half of the apprehended criminals each year are officially first offenders.

Most juvenile delinquents come from the slums of large cities and

Perhaps no other institution contributes so much to criminal recruitment as does the prison. (*Sam Falk from Monkmeyer Press Photo Service*)

are brought up in homes characterized by poverty and ignorance. Such juvenile criminals, tough as they may sometimes be, are automatically disqualified from certain types of criminal occupations (such as the confidence game) that require the manners, dress, and speech of the better-educated classes. Tough urban juvenile delinquents, if they become adult criminals, are thus likely to become thugs or to enter some part of the occupational hierarchy of crime that makes demands that their slum training enables them to meet. In the higher branches of villainy and the more refined types of fraud, superior intelligence, command of language, histrionic ability, stable nerves, and other such qualities are required. Neuroticism, psychosis, and other abnormalities of character and personality are just as much obstacles to success in crime as elsewhere. This is why criminologists are, or ought to be, exceedingly cautious about drawing conclusions about criminals from the study of persons in prison. The more capable and successful criminals are probably not sent to prison so often as the defectives, the abnormal, and the unintelligent.

Virtually all criminal occupations offering reasonable returns without unreasonable risks require a certain amount of training or tutelage. Safecrackers, it is said, are recruited from persons in the mechanical trades. Receivers of stolen goods often come from the business world. For some years, the top American racketeers have had "heist" (holdup) backgrounds and have usually been of Italian origin. Confidence men, according to one criminal, usually come from small towns or the country.

Perhaps no other institution contributes so much to criminal recruitment as the prison. In it persons of all degrees of sophistication are thrown together for long periods of time. The stigma of the prison sentence prevents the exconvict from getting into noncriminal occupations, and imprisonment has provided him or her with information concerning a wide variety of illegal ways of making a living. Prison associates become contacts the amateur may use if he or she wishes to turn professional. (17)

Drug Addiction and the Addict's World

THE ADDICT'S SOCIAL WORLD It is well known from newspaper publicity that drug addicts constitute a submerged social group, albeit a loosely organized one, in the United States. This is a far from universal phenomenon.

Before the attempt at suppression of the drug trade that began in 1915, American drug addicts, for the most part, were scattered throughout respectable society and did not form a deviant subsociety or social world. When addicts are treated as medical cases, as they are in England and in most European countries, they are deviants in the same way as are people who take sleeping pills or insulin shots. *The social world of the drug addict is not called into being by the direct effects of the drug habit, but rather by the attitudes and actions of nonaddicts.* For example, it was reported that during World War II the Japanese failed to make provision for supplying a number of diabetics in Hong Kong with insulin. Consequently, a flourishing black market arose and the diabetics joined together in exchanging information and generally helping each other to maintain their supplies. If the situation had become permanent, there is no doubt that a diabetic subsociety would have been formed.

Similarly, American opiate addicts joined together in a loose group organization only when they were compelled to by the effects of antinarcotic legislation. When police enforcement of this legislation threatened to deprive addicts of their supplies, an informal organization arose to cope with the situation by furnishing smuggled drugs to the users. Marked as criminals and outcasts, addicts gravitated together for mutual protection, aid, and consolation. Addicts exchange information concerning matters vital to getting a steady drug supply; they discuss techniques of drug use and of avoiding the police, and generally talk about their common experiences.

No doubt some drug users in the United States are outside the addict's special world and have little or no contact with other users. Most addicts in this category of outsiders are probably either members of the medical or allied professions, or are well-to-do persons with steady and relatively unthreatened sources of drug supply. Some of these persons are not known to be addicts by any but a few intimate associates; others may be known as addicts in their local communities, yet participate fully in community life.

THE ADDICT'S ARGOT.   Out of the interaction within this subculture, a special language or argot has arisen that reflects the special concerns of the addict: for example, the peddler from whom he or she buys is a "connection"; a disruption of distribution channels by arrests is a "panic"; a person who is experimenting casually is a "joy popper" with an "ice cream habit"; full-fledged addicts have a "monkey on their backs"; a person who goes off drugs suddenly without medication "kicks the habit cold turkey"; one who sniffs the drug is a "snorter"; and one who uses it hypodermically "shoots it," and is either a "skin shooter" or a "main liner." It is a significant sociological fact that the American drug user early developed a rich and varied argot, whereas European addicts apparently did not until fairly recently. The American scene was especially favorable for the spawning of drug subcultures and cults which spread to other countries via the mass media or were carried by American visitors. British and Canadian observers, for example, sometimes comment on this cultural transmission.

THE UNDERWORLD ADDICT

Underworld addicts are set apart by public definition, and develop a way of life that is centered upon drugs as their dominant concern. Their lives are organized around the endeavor to keep themselves adequately supplied. Unlike the addict with a legitimate supply, the underworld user must depend upon the illegal peddler and must pay fantastic black-market prices. Patronage of the black market requires much time and effort and also usually leads to arrest and acquisition of a criminal record, making it difficult to hold a legitimate job. In any case, most legitimate jobs do not pay well enough to support a drug habit at black-market prices. All of this means that the American drug user must seek other, quicker means of making money. Theft, prostitution, and drug peddling are the most common means employed. *The fact that addicts often act as peddlers, or "pushers," is of considerable significance in the recruitment of new users, since this means that the tremendous drive of the habit is harnessed to the perpetuation of the drug problem.*

The underworld addict is unable to focus on long-range goals because he or she is constantly preoccupied with today's and tomorrow's

The interactions of the drug subculture have spawned special languages that sometimes wash into ordinary speech. Here two addicts prepare to "mainline." (*Bob Combs for* God's Turf)

supply. A pervasive feature of the life of this type of addict is the frantic need to keep one step ahead of a dwindling and constantly threatened supply—hence the argot term, "frantic junkie." The addict's time is broken up according to the demands of the habit, and days center on the times when he or she customarily "scores" with the "connection" or when he or she takes the shots. For the poorer addict these "connections" are erratic and irregular due either to difficulties in raising the necessary money or in locating the elusive and suspicious peddler. In addition to these hazards the addict must constantly be on the alert to avoid the police and the addicted "stool pigeons" who work for them. He or she must be ready to move at any moment, travel light, and if picked up he or she must be careful to have no incriminating evidence on his or her person. Addicts become exceedingly ingenious in all of these respects, so much so that even relatively unintelligent persons seem to have their dull wits sharpened by the need for dope. The drug user spends a good deal of his or her life inventing new devices and tricks and scheming and maneuvering to raise money to keep underworld connections and to evade detection.

Addicts become addicted not only to drugs but to a way of life. When they try to leave this way of life and to renounce their habits they find themselves drawn back to their old haunts and associates. They also find it difficult to adjust themselves to the normal routines and values of the ordinary world and to escape the stigma of their past. The failure of addicts to "kick the habit" permanently is doubtless tied up with their reluctance to abandon old associates and a familiar environment. The use of drugs thus is much more than a biological matter or a mere question of pharmacology.

The phenomenon of drug addiction illustrates this point. An outstanding characteristic of addictive drugs is that withdrawal from them after regular use over a period of a few weeks or more produces an automatic painful physical reaction. Opiate drugs (those derived from the opium poppy) and their synthetic equivalents are the most important drugs of this type. However, alcohol and the barbiturates also produce physical dependence and withdrawal distress. The barbiturates are widely prescribed by physicians for insomnia and other ailments. It is of incidental interest that barbiturate withdrawal is more severe and dangerous than opiate withdrawal. Addiction to this type of drug, however, requires that it be used in much larger quantities than those ordinarily prescribed by doctors. The withdrawal distress connected with opiates varies with individuals, and its intensity depends upon duration of use, amount used, and other factors. The symptoms of withdrawal form a characteristic pattern or syndrome, which in its severe form is unmistakable to those who are acquainted with it. These symptoms begin to appear about four or five hours after the last injection. If no further drugs are taken they increase in intensity for about seventy-two hours and the more noticeable ones disappear only gradually over a period of about two weeks. An injection of drugs during the withdrawal period causes all these symptoms to vanish in a matter of minutes. Withdrawal distress occurs in newborn infants whose mothers are addicts and in various animal species when drugs are regularly administered. This shows that the withdrawal reaction is biological in nature; and it is this fact that has led some students to declare that drug addiction is essentially an organic condition or disease.

THE FIXATION PROCESS

It is unnecessary, in view of the publicity given in recent years to teenage addiction, to describe addiction or withdrawal distress in detail. It should be noted, however, that much of the popular literature is motivated by the purpose of frightening or warning young persons. This has led to inaccurate and exaggerated descriptions of the alleged evil physical effects. The facts are that with the full establishment of addiction after several weeks of regular use, a bodily condition of tolerance or "drug balance" is acquired. When this has occurred the main effect of the drug is to maintain this balance, to prevent withdrawal symptoms, and to cause the addict to feel normal. The user may experience a physical "kick" when he or she "shoots up," especially if it is a "main liner" (an injection into the vein), but during the several hours between injections it is exceedingly difficult to determine with certainty whether the person is under the influence of a drug or not. Persons who take drugs by other means than hypodermic injection (for example, orally) may never have experienced physical pleasure from taking them. This is especially true when the initial use occurs during an illness.

During the initial period of use there occur several radical changes that amount almost to a reversal of the drug's effects. Thus, the original depressing effect on bodily functions tends to vanish and to be replaced by a stimulating one. Also, the euphoria or positive pleasure of beginning use vanishes and is replaced by the negative effect of relieving withdrawal distress and achieving approximate normality between the shots. Bodily functions originally disturbed by the regular injection of drugs generally return to an approximately normal level when tolerance has been built up. The long-continued use of such drugs as morphine or heroin, contrary to popular belief, does not lead to major tissue destruction or to insanity. Tooth decay, constipation, and sexual impotence, which are relatively frequent among drug addicts, are not invariable or necessary consequences of addiction, and some addicts, especially those who are well-to-do, do not experience them. The principal deleterious effects are psychological in nature and are connected with the tabooed and secret nature of the habit, with the extreme cost of obtaining a supply of drugs at black-market prices, and resulting changes in self-conception, occupation, and social relationships.

If we ask why people become addicted to the opiates, this question is the equivalent of asking what is the nature of the experience in which the craving for drugs is generated. It is not sufficient to say that it is the pleasurable sensations or inner experiences that occur when the drug is used. Marijuana, cocaine, and other substances produce such pleasure without having many of the unpleasant consequences associated with opiates, but they are nonaddicting.

Crucial elements in the fixation of addiction appears to be the users' understanding of what is going on. If, for example, they receive drugs without their knowledge, they will not develop a craving for them. Even if they know that they have been receiving morphine regularly, they will still evidently not get "hooked" if they do not grasp the nature of the withdrawal distress that occurs when they stop regular use.

It is the repetition of the experience of using drugs to alleviate withdrawal distress (when the latter is recognized and properly identified) that appears to lead rapidly to the changed orientation toward the drug and to the other behavior that constitutes addiction. Addicts do not get hooked on the pleasures of opium, but on the experience of relief that occurs immediately after a shot in a matter of five or ten minutes. This

New studies have stressed that the process of becoming physically addicted to a drug may be socially learned and involves cognitive factors. (*Jan Berry/Magnum*)

effect depends again on cognitive elements and is absent when the person does not understand the withdrawal distress from which he or she is suffering. Psychologists who rely on reinforcement explanations might describe the process as one in which a response pattern is established by negative reinforcement (that is, the removal of an unpleasant stimulus). What such a psychologist would ordinarily leave out would be the cognitive aspect of the situation which, from our point of view, seems of crucial importance as it probably accounts for a number of aspects of addiction that otherwise appear paradoxical.

To clarify the matter further let us assume that the beginner, on his or her way to addiction, takes a shot every four hours. The theory that we are presenting here is that addiction is established in the experiences that occur approximately ten minutes after each shot, and *not* by the way the user feels during the other 230 minutes. Those who think of drugs in terms of being "high" or "stoned" are likely to emphasize the 230 minutes rather than the ten, and to think of addiction in terms of an ecstatic pleasure that is often presumed to extend throughout the interval between shots and to be renewed by the next one. A major difficulty with this view is that addicts, who are after all the final and only real authorities on how they feel, uniformly deny it. Between injections they say they feel normal or, as a user remarked on a television program, the way one feels after a good breakfast.

Addiction to drugs is generally regarded as a medical, moral, or criminal problem. In the United States prior to 1915, it was regarded mainly as a medical matter. After the drug-suppression program began, it came to be viewed and treated as a criminal matter. Special interest groups played a part in developing this definition. This was accomplished relatively easily, since there existed a general public disapproval of addiction and a sense of mystery concerning the strange power of the habit and the transformation of character that it brought about. This negative imagery has now been elaborated and become more lurid. Lurid paperbound books tell of "gripping true adventures of a T-man's war against the dope menace" and portray heavy-lidded young women toying with hypodermic needles with the masculine hands of the law hovering in the background.

The prohibition method of dealing with vice is itself a peculiarly American method. Critics of the use of police suppression regard it as a manifestation of a Protestant "uplift" fervor. Whatever the explanation may be, in terms of its consequences police suppression has succeeded no better with addiction than it has with other forms of vice such as alcoholism, gambling, and prostitution.

The recruitment of new addicts seems to be closely tied up with the existence of illegal supply lines and with the underworld culture of the addict, which are direct consequences of prohibition methods of control. The effects produced by prohibition set up a vicious cycle leading to enhanced demands for more prohibitory legislation. Such legislation gets increasing support as public imagery of the addict assumes even more lurid and melodramatic aspects. An interesting peripheral question that is raised here concerns the limits of legal control of deviant behavior.

European observers have often commented upon what seems to be a peculiarly American legal philosophy. This philosophy places special emphasis upon the idea that the law should express the highest ideals and make no compromise with evil. European legal philosophy, in contrast, places relatively greater emphasis upon adapting laws to existing practices in order to avoid the consequences of driving underground certain types of behavior.

To maintain the illusion that vice is being eliminated and that virtue is protected, it is necessary that various myths and stereotypes be maintained. Ceremonial gestures are made from time to time to reassure the public. Among these are publicized "drives" against vice, exposés, stories of "ring busting," the glorification of the police, and reports of police accomplishments. (7)

Complete cynicism concerning the motives of policemen and newspaper publishers and other interested parties who stage cleanup campaigns is not warranted. Such drives do achieve temporary results, and are demanded and appreciated by the public. Basic reforms, however, usually come more slowly and in less spectacular ways. Most persons "in the know" recognize the ceremonial and strictly short-run significance of these spectacular battles with evil.

The Homosexual

In Chapter 12 we discussed the origins of homosexual behavior. Current consensus is that homosexual behavior, like heterosexual behavior, is probably always a learned form of behavior. Authorities do not agree, however, on just how such behaviors are learned. Presumably the basis for it is laid at a very early age when children form conceptions and attitudes on sexual matters from their experiences in the family group, and from experiences with their own bodies. We are interested here in the place accorded the homosexual in society. (54, 55, 113)

PUBLIC OPINION OF HOMOSEXUALS.   Like drug addicts, homosexuals may be so scattered as to have relatively little contact with others like themselves. Public censure, however, tends to cause them to congregate in places, especially cosmopolitan centers, where heterogeneity and size of the population makes for more anonymity and tolerance. There are laws that make homosexual behavior illegal and criminal.

As with other forms of behavior that are defined as deviant, there is divided or ambiguous public opinion concerning homosexuality. In general, homosexuality is recognized and tolerated with amusement, sympathy, compassion, and only mild disapproval. It is often accepted as a matter of fact in many segments of our society, particularly among people who have had close contact with it. The ambiguity of public opinion is reflected by the tendency of people to maintain a conspiracy of silence about known homosexuality until it comes to public attention. When this happens, all parties are embarrassed, but agree that something must be done to assuage that portion of the public that thinks of homosexuality as a dire evil to be sternly suppressed by police action. The police of large cities ordinarily tolerate or ignore homosexual activity as such, and only become concerned when it involves open scandal or is associated with other illegal activities.

Known male homosexuals are not allowed to hold certain types of positions, but may be tolerated or even expected in others, such as hairdressing, designing women's clothes, artistic pursuits, or ballet. It is an interesting question as to why concentration should occur in certain professions and populations. This may possibly be partly accounted for by a tendency of male inverts (effeminate males) to seek and prefer employment in activities generally regarded as somewhat feminine, and not quite appropriate for males. Concentration in an occupation also may be accounted for by the opportunities it provides for contacts of the desired kind with other males.

There are many misapprehensions about homosexuals and the lives they lead. It is sometimes thought that homosexuals are always effeminate (or masculine), detached, suicidal, or inclined to antisocial conduct stemming from their sexual deficiency. Actually, like other social deviants the homosexual shares most values dominant in his or her country, social class, and occupation. What homogeneity there is among these persons, apart from their sexual behavior, is largely brought about by the negative public evaluation of them (26:97):

Deviance is not inherent in any act. It is the judgment passed on the behavior by others that is the determining factor. Thus the application of the deviant label intimately involves the exercise of power. (*Eric Kroll/Taurus Photos*)

If there is any characteristic of homosexual life that has been instrumental in the development of homogeneous group traits, it is probably the pretense and the mask. Millions of people could not possibly live through each day of the year, concealing, pretending, deliberately lying, without reacting in similar manner.

Apart from the constant threat of blackmail and public disgrace, it may be embarrassing to the homosexual in relations with ordinary persons to have them know of his or her peculiarity. Hence he or she may become skillful at concealing the homosexual identity and at manipulating interaction to discover whether or not he or she may safely reveal that identity to a given individual. Many homosexuals become sensitized to the detection of homosexuality in others and develop techniques of communicating with each other. Occasionally the signals are misread (as is also true in heterosexual relations), and thus the homosexual leaves him- or herself open to unpleasantness or even danger. Like the criminal, he or she is wary of associations with outsiders unless he or she knows what to expect. As with other "minority groups," outsiders sometimes form friendships with insiders and so function as connecting links between respectable and nonrespectable worlds.

THE HOMOSEXUAL SUBCULTURE.   There is a loosely organized homosexual subculture, and typical forms of association exist within it. D. W. Corey (26:114–15) has described the world of the homosexual in general terms that fit the world of the criminal or the prostitute:

> One writer describes it as a *submerged world*, while another speaks of a *society on the fringe of society*. Both are correct, accurate, yet incomplete, for there is not one submerged world, one society on the fringe of society, but several, almost countless, different and disparate and dissimilar and almost disconnected, yet all having some relationship to one another, sometimes through an individual or two who travel in several of these submerged-island societies at once, or related on the other hand merely by the similarity of pursuits and personalities, or perhaps related primarily by the association that exists only in the imagination of the hostile world.

In this world homosexuals court, make love, have friends and acquaintances, engage in ordinary business with each other, and develop a common argot and a group philosophy. Warren (113:114) discusses the significance of argot in the homosexual community:

> Everyone [and every kind of sexuality] [can] be accounted for by some linguistic category of the gay world. Words . . . function to separate outsiders from insiders, to account for ambiguous persons within . . . sexual interaction and to describe the . . . relationships of insiders with one another. In such a way is a world set apart from other worlds.

Since they are under censure, they develop protective and operational rationales. One rationale is that homosexuality is a biological disorder, and hence other people should adopt a live-and-let-live attitude and not cast blame. Another is that homosexuals are superior to others in intelligence and sensitivity (artistic and other accomplishments by homosexuals are pointed to in evidence). Some will even argue that their forms of love-making are superior, and note with pride the complex domestic relations that grow up among them. Celebrations of homosexual romance in literature are used as support. Further powerful ideological support is gained by denigrating the general public (which misunderstands or discriminates) and by exaggerating the prevalence of homosexual practices. Kinsey's claim that some 40 percent of all males have had some homosexual experience was probably greeted with considerable satisfaction by many exclusively homosexual individuals. The "straight" world is often satirized in phrases such as "can heterosexuality be cured?" or "Heterosexuality is a dread disfunction . . . which infects a surprising percentage of American males." (113:129)

In a study of male homosexuals in Montreal, a sociologist, Maurice Leznoff (68), has indicated that the core of homosexual society consists of those homosexuals who are relatively unsecretive in their activities and inclinations. The danger of being exposed as deviants either is disregarded or does not exist for them. These overt homosexuals are the mainstay of the homosexual world. They are easily recognized by outsiders, and since they do not fear detection they congregate in fairly public places—certain bars, restaurants, and the like. Within the homosexual world studied by Warren, a variety of social types, ranging from "Nelly" queen, to mother, auntie, sister, and fag hag, are recognized. These labels designate specific identities within the gay community. (113:101–22) More numerous are those who practice homosexuality secretly or covertly. Those known in the lingo as "butches," are usually indistinguishable from ordinary heterosexual males because concealment is deemed vital. They hesitate to risk exposure by being seen in the company of known homosexuals or by appearing at homosexual parties and hangouts. However, as the homosexual's friendships, even among overt homosexuals, are not necessarily or even generally sexual in nature, the covert homosexual often has to seek a sexual partner. This often brings him into direct and even public contact with the overt homosexual at well-known hangouts. He thus risks discovery. Apparently there is some antagonism between overt and covert homosexuals, at least in Montreal: the covert homosexual, who generally is better educated and of higher occupational status, looks down on the other and is perhaps even hostile toward him because his very visibility calls public attention to the fact of homosexuality.

Other homosexual types include those who go further in their attempts to maintain secrecy and concealment. They confine their expressions of sexual interest to a single other person and never mingle in groups of their own kind. Undoubtedly there are others who, although they recognize their own homosexual impulses, do not reveal them overtly to anyone else.

RECRUITMENT.   The process of recruitment into the homosexual world is tied up with the public sanction against homosexuality and the discovery by individual deviants that such a world exists. People may even reach middle age without recognizing their homosexual tendencies for what they are. Discovery of identity may come in various ways, including contact with other homosexuals who may introduce them to the ways of "the gay society." The uninitiated may be inducted by chance contact or by being picked up. It is sometimes averred that hardened homosexuals pervert or seduce other persons. This is extremely doubtful. Whatever the cause of homosexuality may be, it is not so simple as this. An individual may ordinarily be seduced only if he or she cooperates and finds the experience to his or her taste.

The discovery by homosexual isolates of a "preformed" world is an event of great psychological importance known as "coming out." It shows them that they are not alone and provides them with a supporting milieu. Probably most pronounced or exclusive homosexuals recognize their deviance during adolescence, so that most movement into the homosexual world takes place during adolescence or early maturity. As he or she enters into homosexual associations, the novitiate acquires the knowledge essential to his or her participation in the deviant world. This includes knowledge of social skills, the signs of recognition and communication, and the more subtle modes of interacting with both homosexuals and normal people. The Montreal study suggests that initial sexual contacts often are accompanied by confusion and guilt, since the new activities run counter to general public sanction against such activities, a sanction previously internalized by the person him- or herself. The initial affair with an experienced homosexual not only inducts the neophyte into the strange new world, but affords him or her the rationales necessary for making the transition from the outside to the inside.

Homosexual experience of some of the trauma of aging is apparently similar to the experience of heterosexuals in our society. The Montreal homosexual world values youth. The aging homosexual seeks to avoid loneliness and isolation by means of a permanent union, or homosexual marriage. But these unions, because they lack the institutional supports given the heterosexual variety (and for a variety of other reasons), are usually unstable and temporary. As a consequence, loneliness is a common fate for the aging homosexual who finds himself unable to compete with younger persons.

Although we have hitherto been discussing homosexuality as something sharply set off from heterosexuality, the dividing line is actually not a clear one. Persons who are exclusively homosexual are far outnumbered by those who are in varying degrees capable of both kinds of attachments. Such persons sometimes move in and out of homosexual circles, but do not form groups of their own organized around their own catholicity of response. The subsociety of the exclusive homosexual is loosely organized and is thus able to absorb part-time homosexuals, homosexual isolates, and covert homosexuals, as well as those whose tastes and attachments are exclusively and overtly homosexual.

Subsequent to the report of M. Leznoff and W. A. Westley on Montreal homosexuals, Evelyn Hooker, as part of a long-range study of male homosexuals that has been underway for more than a decade, has described some of the salient aspects of homosexual life in Los Angeles. Her account generally confirms, parallels, and extends the Montreal study, but focuses on the "gay" or homosexual bar around which leisure time and recreational activities of many homosexuals are organized. These bars also serve to introduce newcomers into the homosexual world. Besides facilitating sexual contacts much as ordinary bars do, gay bars also function as communication centers that disseminate news and information that is of interest to the members of the subgroup. Like others who have studied homosexuals, Evelyn Hooker (51) indicates that it is undoubtedly only a small portion of the homosexual population that becomes publicly visible to the outsiders who visit "gay" bars or other gathering places frequented by homosexuals. The major portion of homosexual communities probably consist of a series of small and somewhat overlapping and very loosely interconnected cliques or friendship groups, the members of which may rarely or never show up at the public gathering places. (79)

The *neutralization* of the stigma associated with the homosexual identity is a complex matter (113:141) and often involves a celebration of the ritual solidarity gained by participation in the gay world. The theories which are offered as explanations for homosexuality are inverted and turned against "straight" society as the gay individual elevates the world of homosexuality to that of an aristocratic, secret, and stigmatized group. (113) In this instance the stigma is denied by the members of this social world.

Political Worlds, and Political Deviancy

Some years ago, a sociologist, John Landesco (64), remarked during a study of organized crime in Illinois that there were intimate and necessary relationships between American criminals and politicians; by this he meant both that criminals often required the services of politicians (including politically appointed judges and prosecutors), while some politicians profited from illegal payoffs. Politicians are faced not only with that kind of temptation but, because of the very exigencies of their offices, they almost necessarily tread a fine line between legal activities and those that vary from just a little illegal to those which are downright criminal.

In the words of George Washington Plunkitt (85), for many years a highly successful Tammany politician during the late nineteenth century, "Everybody's talkin' these days about Tammany men growin' rich on graft, but nobody thinks of drawin' the distinction between honest graft and dishonest graft. There's all the difference in the world between the two." Dishonest graft is "blackmailin', gamblers, saloonkeepers, disorderly people, etc." whereas honest graft, exemplified by his own career, he sums up "as I seen my opportunities and I took 'em." For example, his party is in power and is about to make many public improvements; he gets tipped off about a new park about to be laid out, so "I see my opportunity and I take it. I go to that place and I buy up all the land I can in the neighborhood." Only afterward is the park plan made public, so, when the others rush forward to buy it, he says: "Ain't it perfectly honest to charge a good price and make a profit on my investment and foresight?" (85:3) Another kind of honest graft was when Tammany raised many salaries, despite "an awful howl of the reformers," but Tammany garnered ten votes for every one it lost. And Plunkitt adds, criticizing Lincoln Steffens's famous muckraking book, *The Shame of the Cities,* that a reformer like Steffens cannot distinguish between the two kinds of graft and consequently "gets things mixed up." The politician is not a looter of the public treasury; rather, he looks after "his own interests, the organization's interests, and the city's interest at the same time."

Plunkitt added that he never "monkeyed" with the penal code. To do that would be corrupt, as some foolish or self-serving politicians occasionally are, he admits. Despite Plunkitt's nice distinction between honest and dishonest graft, some of a political machine's business—in the days when political machines more obviously ran our cities—involved frankly illegal operations or at least less than honest transactions in connection with perfectly legal political offices and legislative rulings. (78) Honest graft lies somewhere toward the middle of the entire range of political transactions—running from fully legitimate to quite illegitimate actions—which supports the organization's existence. Thus, one of Plunkitt's superiors, Boss Tweed, was later exposed as fabulously corrupt. All of New York City's financial affairs had become lucrative sources of graft, and the state and city legislation that Tweed's men influenced brought them handsome kickbacks from the businessmen who profited from this legislation. A species of extortion was used too, as when certain kinds of legislation were threatened unless the victims paid up. And Tweed's machine found that the best way to protect itself against newspaper action was to distribute city advertising as a token of peace—hush money which bound the press to silence. (14) Of course that was not the only kind of bribery that such a machine engaged in. However, all these kick-backs, trade offs, payments, and other negotiated covert agreements are essential to the smooth running of political machines.

Today it is claimed that such urban machines have been replaced by more modern kinds of organizations; but it can be safely said that old or new, urban or small-town, the American political organization skirts close to and often goes over the boundaries to clear illegality. Yet, seen from the side of the politician rather than the reformer or the mere lay-person, politics is a pragmatic matter—so much so, that idealism is either a chimera or hard to maintain in the face of "genuine reality." It is commonly said that crime does not pay. The assertion is probably not applicable to politicians.

Attempts are made periodically by reformers to firm up that fine line between political criminality and political legitimacy. Reformers see themselves as the defenders of the general welfare and speak of "cleaning up" and use other synonyms for civic purity and virtue, such as "public order," "getting things back to normal," and restoring states-manship to what otherwise is mere dirty politics. Reform movements bubble up eternally, resulting in exposés, trials, incarcerations, and occasionally in reform governments. Once in office, reformers face many of the same pragmatic considerations as their predecessors and eventually get involved in compromises and trade offs, but, it is hoped, more legitimate and legal. Eventually reformer officials become either relatively indistinguishable from the people they ousted or are voted out of office in preference for more professional types.

Whatever innocent citizens may think, there is also on the national and state levels the same ambiguity about legal and illegal actions. Our newspapers almost increasingly report on the indictment—and some-times the imprisonment—of state officials (at the time this book was being revised, former officials in more than a third of the states were in prison or under investigation); and in Washington, some congressmen are known for having far more probity than others; while the president himself may owe his election and his effectiveness somewhat, at least, to agreements made between his staff and influential state or city politi-cians who have less than saintly reputations. As for the executive agen-cies or the White House staff itself, occasionally someone is exposed, his or her corrupt action leading to resignation, sometimes to imprisonment. More rarely there is a full-fledged scandal touching on or located in the White House, resulting in such newsworthy events as the Teapot Dome investigation of 1923–1924 or the Watergate (variously termed "caper," "scandal," and so on which was brought to light in 1972).

Corruption aside, from the politician's viewpoint there is always important work to be done, and it can only be accomplished by effective political organization; this involves making deals and giving certain people "breaks," but the work does get done. Politicians should not be too greedy, of course (or obviously greedy, perhaps), and certainly not merely self-serving. The point is made clearly and with considerable justice by another famous Tammany politician, Richard Croker, who many years ago said, with what he doubtless considered straightforward realism (85:xix):

> Think what New York is and what the people of New York are. One half, more than one half, are of foreign birth. . . . They do not speak our language, they do not know our laws, they are the raw material with which we have to build up the state. . . . There is no denying the service which Tammany has rendered to the Republic. There is no such organization for taking hold of the untrained, friendless man and converting him into a citizen. Who else would do it if we did not? . . . although you may not like our motives or our methods, what other agency is there by which so long a row could have been hoed so quickly or so well.

If one accepts the generalized American system, he or she can only argue with Croker in terms of alternative organizational forms and their comparative potentials for more or less corruption. Of course if, like some religious sects or radical political groups, one renounces the political system and feels that the whole system is corrupt, then it can only be rectified by radical action, like a successful revolution, or perhaps by divine intervention.

In a more general sense, we can see that corruption and illegality are constant features of the world of politics for a variety of reasons. (41) First, politicians occupy positions of power that other individuals are denied. This means, in effect, that they have greater opportunities to stray from the boundaries of conformity. Second, access to situations of power and influence gives the politician resources ordinarily denied other individuals. These resources, in turn, open the avenues for exploitation, advantage, and self-enhancement. Third, those in political power are seldom scrutinized and policed and openly evaluated by the regular members of the nation's agencies of social control. This lack of open policing increases the likelihood that deviant behavior on the part of the politician, if it is not too flagrant, will go unnoticed and unchecked. Fourth, politicians are granted a range of privileges and given a set of "status symbols," ranging from chauffered cars, to free postal services, and unlimited resources to hire members of their own families as aides and secretaries and assistants. The sheer receipt of these status symbols sets the politician off from others and makes it possible that common citizens will feel a sense of alienation if not disrespect for those in power. Thus, the politician often finds him- or herself defined by some people in deviant if not unacceptable terms. As Horowitz and Mills (52, 80) have observed, a kind of "blunted immorality" characterizes today's politician.

The politician's "accounts" of his or her deviance are likely to differ from those offered by homosexuals, drug addicts, or underworld criminals. For unlike those who can lay no claim to political power, the politician shrouds the deviant acts around the dominant political ideology of the nation-state and its regional branches. Thus spying, espionage, blackmailing, murder, invasions of privacy, threats to freedom of speech, and election tampering are justified through recourse to a higher good or set of ideals which supposedly underpin the very workings of government. Political scientists, too, have often agreed that corruption is a necessary evil to get "things done," and even that it is a necessary accompaniment to the very development of industrialized nations.

The political deviant, then, utilizes the ideology of the state to justify illegal and corrupt acts. The ordinary deviant seldom utilizes accounts of this political nature. Instead, the homosexual, or drug addict, or burglar is likely to develop a "sad tale" that explains his or her deviance through a complex process of unraveling past biography. Somewhere in the past the individual will identify those forces that led him or her astray. These forces may be those stressed by a currently popular theory of personality development: thus many homosexuals explain their homosexual activity by making reference to Freud's theory of personality or to the presence of a weak father or mother in the family. Of course, the forces may be couched in other vocabularies: religious, environmental, or biological.

Yet, unlike other deviants (48), the politician can often control those forces that would define him or her as corrupt. Royko has observed the mayor of one large city (88:209–10):

> The limousine came that morning to take him to City Hall, but he sent it away. Reporters were told that he would spend the day at home with family and a few friends. The traditional birthday party was canceled. On his sixty-fifth birthday, in the city he had ruled for so long, he couldn't go to his own office because there would be questions for which he had no ready answers. The timing of the report seemed like a cruel act of fate. But it wasn't. As with most things that happened in his city, the timing of the report had been arranged by him. It gave him an excuse to stay home that day, and nobody could say he was hiding. In his Chicago, even a man's birthday could be put to political use. "Chicago ain't ready for reform yet," Alderman Bauler said when Daley was elected in 1955. And in 1970, ready or not, it wasn't getting it.

We turn next to the eccentric deviant. Such persons provide a convenient contrast to the "corrupt" politician.

Individual Deviance

By the term *individual deviance*, we refer to deviant behavior that does not have a cultural base—that is, it is not prescribed as customary by a deviant group or social world. Some forms of individual deviation are linked with biological causes and others with what may be called personal, or personal social, causes. The interaction between such individual deviants and others who regard them as in some way odd, strange, peculiar, different, or abnormal is of interest to social psychology. (43) Some of these forms of individual deviance are formally dealt with as crime; others are handled by specialized agencies and procedures, and still others are more or less officially ignored. (44) We now turn to some of the conspicuous types of such behavior.

In contrast with the amorphous and very complex deviant worlds there exists a variety of organized groups which, when they come to the attention of outsiders, tend to be regarded as queer, odd, peculiar, "crazy," "odd ball," or strange. *When all the patterned forms have been sorted out and named, there remains a residue of behavior that does not seem to fit well into the established categories. This kind of behavior may be called eccentric.* In the psychiatric vocabulary, persons who engage in such behavior may be called *psychopaths* or *sociopaths*—these words being used to indicate that while someone is not clearly or simply psychotic, neurotic, or criminal, there is nevertheless something out of the ordinary about him or her and his or her actions. The conduct so characterized is heterogeneous and extremely varied, ranging from that which might be called simply independent, unconventional, or original to that which is dangerously odd, menacing, or mysterious.

THE ECCENTRIC

The following may be considered forms of eccentricity: a prisoner in a state penitentiary spends his spare time in building a carefully constructed gallows on which he executes insects; a little old lady with a large fortune in securities begs for alms on the street corners and lives in a hovel; a gentle, elderly German immigrant who has difficulty meeting his simple needs makes ends meet by passing occasional counterfeit dollar bills, crudely manufactured solely for this purpose by himself; a man who lives in seclusion in the wilderness shoots at airplanes with a high-powered rifle because they disturb his solitude; a woman insists on dressing herself exclusively in bath towels carefully draped and pinned about her; an elderly millionaire gives away dimes, and another leaves a large fortune to his favorite dog or horse; other persons collect and hoard pieces of string, buttons, golf balls, old newspapers, ballpoint pens and a long list of other objects. It would be well not to confuse personal eccentricities with cultural differences. For example, an old lady who wears old-fashioned hats, or an Indian woman who wears a sari in the United States, should not be called eccentric. A Westernized native who returns to his tribal home in Africa in European clothes should also not be included in this category. However, although the logical distinction involved here is clear, it is often easier to make in theory than in practice.

On the other hand, eccentric behavior within certain limits may also be valued positively by a society: it may, for example, be regarded as colorful, humorous, enterprising, interesting, or exciting. Apart from furnishing entertainment and interest, eccentrics serve as innovators, producing new modes of behavior that may be taken up as fads or as permanent parts of the social heritage. In certain countries (including the United States) in which change and innovation are valued and in which individuality and independence are stressed, idiosyncratic behavior often attracts favorable publicity and attention. As is often observed a broad tolerance of variability promotes a sense of freedom and facilitates social change. This is quite evident in the areas of popular art, music, and current clothing fashion. The eccentric designer Coco Chanel, for example, left an indelible worldwide stamp on women's clothing styles.

The innovative function of eccentricity and its potential for arousing hostility or antagonism have been well brought out by M. M. Tumin (109) in an interesting study of a small Guatemalan community. He describes two of the principal deviants in the village. One was a hero and a successful curer of disease in a community where there is much anxiety over sickness. To his fellow Indian youth who are being alienated from traditional ways his behavior represents "one of the few imaginable future alternatives." (109:206) On the other hand, the second eccentric was wholly negativistic; he offered no alternatives for the norms that he too violated. He was a scapegoat, disliked intensely, and viewed as a threat. Tumin (109:210) notes that "in each case the deviant behavior appears to have its genesis in relatively unique and idiosyncratic facts of the individual life histories. Their deviations . . . are not understandable as *products* of the culture pattern in any determinate sense."

THE LONE CRIMINAL While some criminal activity is a group phenomenon, some of it in all areas is committed by persons who are not members of criminal groups. Even in those areas in which the influence of deviant subcultures is most pronounced, there are violators who act as individuals and who do not belong to the groups or do not even know of their existence. Although certain crimes are characteristically the work of what may be called "criminal isolates," there may be exceptional instances in which the offense in question is a group phenomenon. Most criminal homicide, for example, is committed on an individualistic basis by persons who do not belong to any group advocating or condoning murder. (116) However, some groups promote aggressive and militant policies or lesser forms of violence that may lead to murder; some are explicitly committed to assassination and murder. As an example within our own society we may refer to the hired killers of the organized, large-scale mobs referred to as the Syndicate, the Mafia, or in recent years, the Cosa Nostra. In the political area, assassination has frequently been used by dissident and militant revolutionary groups.

We have elsewhere discussed the professional thieves who make theft a means of livelihood, and there are many such occupations, including those of pick-pocketing and shop-lifting. While relatively little picking of pockets is done by amateurs from outside the criminal world, there is a great deal of shop-lifting by such persons. It is well known that large department stores, self-service stores, and all sorts of industrial and commercial enterprises expect to lose annually a certain percentage of their supplies or products to thieves. The latter are as a rule not professionals, but are either employees or ordinary "noncriminal" customers. Shop-lifters in grocery chains usually are housewives who are thrifty shoppers attempting to combat the high cost of living. (15) Embezzlers and white-collar criminals are generally also individualistic offenders. These offenses present quite different theoretical and practical problems from those posed by the crimes committed by members of criminal groups. The reaction of the offender to apprehension and punishment, his or her rationalizations and ways of reducing guilt feelings, the effectiveness of control measures, and the sources or causes of the behavior are markedly different. (29)

Because they are not members of a criminal organization or group criminal isolates, prior to their apprehension, have a position or status in the legitimate world. When they are processed by the apparatus of the criminal law this legitimate status is placed in jeopardy and is often lost or greatly reduced. If they are imprisoned, these offenders find themselves among a variety of persons who have little in common except that they are all prisoners or convicts; upon release, many of them will become exconvicts and share their recollections of having been "inside." This shared experience with the labeling, defining, and degrading ceremonies of the criminal law sometimes frightens the lone deviant and prevents him or her from repeating the offensive behavior. At other times it may cause him or her to try to work his or her way into the social structure of the criminal world. (67, 100)

Because lone criminals stand to lose whatever status they have in respectable society by being tagged as criminals, the trauma of formal punishment for them is likely to be roughly proportional to their status. While a short jail sentence may mean relatively little to casual workers and even less to professional criminals, it may represent a major personal tragedy to a corporation executive. Although the courts that impose punishment measure its severity in terms of time in prison and the amount of the fine, they cannot control loss of status.

Lacking the protective practical and symbolic devices the criminal societies invent to reduce the hazards of their activities and to assuage their consciences, and having no status in a criminal society, the lone or individualistic criminal is especially vulnerable to apprehension and punishment, as well as to psychological trauma. In dealing with the latter he or she must—if he or she does not move into a criminal society—rely on personal resources or on those provided by officials for the rehabilitation of offenders. For reasons of this nature, formal punishment is probably most effective for the individualistic criminal, and least effective for professional or subgroup crime.

Summary

Behavior and people are inherently neither deviant nor nondeviant, but come to be labeled one way or another by virtue of the reactions of others. These reactions cover the entire range from strong approval to violent disapproval. Negative reactions to disliked persons and acts may, on the one hand, result in the application of formal control measures such as prosecution and imprisonment or, on the other, be expressed informally through gossip, rebukes, or simple avoidance. Persons may be stigmatized as deviants because of what they do or they may be pushed into deviant social activities because of their appearance. They may drift into deviance, they may choose it, or they may become trapped in it through accident, ignorance, or unfortunate circumstances. Social psychologists have interested themselves in the ways in which behavior comes to be labeled as deviant, in the effects that this has on the deviants and their groups, and in the symbolic devices used to counteract or neutralize it. Measures designed to reduce or control deviance sometimes have the opposite of the intended effect. Deviance is a complex and pervasive phenomenon and occurs throughout the whole range of human relationships. It is found, for example, in the various agencies that are suppposed to enforce the rules, and also in deviant groups in which members violate the deviant norms.

Some forms of deviant behavior are governed by norms and values of subgroups within the broader society, for example, political deviance. Other forms do not have direct group support but are engaged in by persons as individuals rather than as group members. Criminals, drug addicts, and homosexuals form subsocieties within our culture, but by no means do all criminals, addicts, or homosexuals join these deviant social worlds. The lone deviant and the eccentric person present practical and theoretical problems that are very different from those posed by deviant groups.

References

1. Aberle, David, *The Peyote Religion among the Navaho.* Viking Fund Publications in Anthropology, no. 42. New York: Wenner-Gren Foundation for Anthropological Research, 1966.

2. Adler, Polly, *House Is Not a Home*. New York: Holt, Rinehart and Winston, 1953.
3. Aubert, Vilhelm, *The Hidden Society*. Totowa, N.J.: Bedminster Press, 1965.
4. Ball, Donald W., "The Problematics of Respectability," in Jack D. Douglas (ed.), *Deviance and Respectability*. New York: Basic Books, 1970, pp. 326–71.
5. ———, "White Collar Crime and Social Structure," *American Journal of Sociology*, vol. 58 (1953), pp. 263–71.
6. Beck, Bernard, "Bedbugs, Stench, Dampness, and Immorality: A Review Essay on Recent Literature about Poverty," *Social Problems*, vol. 15 (Summer 1967), pp. 101–14.
7. Becker, Howard S., *Outsiders: Studies in the Sociology of Deviance*. New York: The Free Press, 1963; rev. ed., 1973.
8. ——— (ed.), *The Other Side: Perspectives on Deviance*. New York: The Free Press, 1964.
9. Birenbaum, Arnold, "On Managing a Courtesy Stigma," *Journal of Health and Social Behavior*, vol. 11 (September 1970), pp. 196–206.
10. Blauner, Robert, "Internal Colonialism and Ghetto Revolt," *Social Problems*, vol. 16 (Spring 1969), pp. 393–408.
11. Blumer, Herbert, "Fashion: From Class Differentiation to Collective Selection," *Sociological Quarterly*, vol. 10 (Summer 1969), pp. 275–91.
12. Bordua, David, "Delinquent Subcultures: Sociological Interpretation of Group Delinquency," *Annals of the American Academy of Political and Social Science*, vol. 388 (1961), pp. 119–36.
13. Cahman, Werner J., "The Stigma of Obesity," *Sociological Quarterly*, vol. 9 (Summer 1968), pp. 283–99.
14. Callow, Alexander B., Jr., *The Tweed Ring*. New York: Oxford University Press, 1970.
15. Cameron, Mary O., *The Booster and the Snitch*. New York: The Free Press, 1964.
16. Chambliss, William J., *BOX MAN: A Professional Thief's Journal by Harry King* as told to and ed. by W. J. Chambliss. New York: Harper & Row, 1972.
17. Clemmer, D., *The Prison Community*. New York: Holt, Rinehart and Winston, 1958.
18. Clinard, Marshall B. (ed.), *Anomie and Deviant Behavior: A Discussion and Critique*. New York: The Free Press, 1964.
19. ———, *Sociology of Deviant Behavior* (rev. ed.). New York: Holt, Rinehart and Winston, 1963.
20. Clinard, M. B., and Richard Quinney, *Criminal Behavior Systems*. New York: Holt, Rinehart and Winston, 1967.
21. Cloward, Richard A., and Lloyd E. Ohlin, *Delinquency and Opportunity*. New York: The Free Press, 1960.
22. Cohen, Albert K., *Delinquent Boys: The Culture of the Gang*. New York: The Free Press, 1955.
23. ———, *Deviance and Control*. Englewood Cliffs, N.J.: Prentice-Hall, 1966.
24. ———, "The Sociology of the Deviant Act: Anomie Theory and Beyond," *American Sociological Review*, vol. 30 (1965), pp. 5–14.
25. ———, "The Study of Social Disorganization and Deviant Behavior," in Robert K. Merton, L. Broom, and Leonard S. Cottrell (eds.), *Sociology Today: Problems and Prospects*. New York: Basic Books, 1959, pp. 461–84.
26. Corey, D. W., *The Homosexual in America*. Philadelphia: Chilton Book Company, 1951.
27. Coser, Lewis A., "Some Functions of Deviant Behavior and Normative Flexibility," *American Journal of Sociology*, vol. 68 (1962), pp. 172–81.

28. Crawford, Gail, *Careers with Heroin.* Unpublished Ph.D. dissertation, University of Illinois, 1973.

29. Cressey, Donald, *Other People's Money.* New York: The Free Press, 1953. (Reissued, Belmont, Calif.: Wadsworth, 1971).

30. ——— (ed.), *The Prison: Studies in Institutional Organization and Change.* New York: Holt, Rinehart and Winston, 1961.

31. Davis, Fred, *Illness, Interaction and the Self.* Belmont, Calif. Wadsworth, 1972.

32. Davis, Kingsley, "The Sociology of Prostitution," *American Sociological Review,* vol. 2 (1937), pp. 744–55.

33. Davis, Nanette J., "Labeling Theory in Deviance Research," *Sociological Quarterly,* vol. 13 (Fall 1972), pp. 447–74.

34. Douglas, Jack D. (ed.), *Deviance and Respectability: The Social Construction of Moral Meanings.* New York: Basic Books, 1970.

35. Dubin, Robert, "Deviant Behavior and Social Structure," *American Sociological Review,* vol. 24 (1959), pp. 147–64.

36. Durkheim, Emile, *Suicide.* New York: The Free Press, 1951.

37. Einstadter, Werner, "The Social Organization of Armed Robbery," *Social Problems,* vol. 17 (1969), pp. 64–82.

38. Erikson, Kai, *Wayward Puritans.* New York: Wiley, 1965.

39. Finestone, Harold, "Cats, Kicks, and Color," *Social Problems,* vol. 5 (1957), 3–13.

40. Gagnon, John H., and W. Simon (eds.), *Sexual Deviance.* New York: Harper & Row, 1967.

41. Gardiner, J., *The Poltics of Corruption: Organized Crime in an American City.* New York: Russell Sage Foundation, 1970.

42. Garfinkel, Harold, "Conditions of Successful Degradation Ceremonies," *American Journal of Sociology,* vol. 61 (1956), pp. 420–24.

43. Goffman, E., *Stigma.* Englewood Cliffs, N.J.: Prentice-Hall, 1963.

44. ———, "On Cooling the Mark Out: Some Aspects of Failure," *Psychiatry,* vol. 15 (November 1952), pp. 451–63.

45. Gray, Diana, "Turning Out: A Study of Teenage Prostitution," *Urban Life and Culture,* vol. 1 (January 1972), pp. 401–25.

46. Gusfield, Joseph R., "Moral Passage: The Symbolic Process in Public Designations of Deviance," *Social Problems,* vol. 15 (Fall 1967), pp. 175–88.

47. Hagan, John, "Labelling and Deviance: A Case Study in the 'Sociology of the Interesting,' " *Social Problems,* vol. 24 (1973), pp. 217–27.

48. Hall, Peter M., "A Symbolic Interactionist Analysis of Politics," *Sociological Inquiry,* vol. 42 (1972), pp. 35–75.

49. Hirschi, Travis, *Causes of Delinquency.* Berkeley, Calif.: University of California Press, 1969.

50. ———, and Rodney Stark, "Hellfire and Delinquency," *Social Problems,* vol. 17 (Fall 1969), pp. 202–13.

51. Hooker, Evelyn, "The Homosexual Community," in J. H. Gagnon and W. Simon (eds.), *Sexual Deviance.* New York: Harper & Row, 1967, pp. 157–84.

52. Horowitz, Irving Louis, "The Pentagon Papers and Social Science," *Transaction,* vol. 8 (September 1971), pp. 37–46.

53. ———, and Martin Liebowitz, "Social Deviance and Political Marginality," *Social Problems,* vol. 15 (Winter 1968), pp. 280–96.

54. Humphreys, L., *Out of the Closets: The Sociology of Homosexual Liberation.* Englewood Cliffs, N.J.: Prentice-Hall, 1972.

55. ———, *Tearoom Trade,* Chicago: Aldine, 1970.

56. Jacobs, Jerry, *The Search for Help: A Study of the Retarded Child in the Community*. New York: Brunner Mazel, 1969.
57. Jaspan, N., and H. Black, *The Thief in the White Collar*. Philadelphia: Lippincott, 1960.
58. *Journal of Health and Social Behavior*, vol. 9 (June 1968). (Special issue on "Recreational Drug Use.")
59. Kando, Thomas J., "Passing and Stigma Management: The Case of the Transsexual," *Sociological Quarterly*, vol. 13 (Fall 1972), pp. 475–83.
60. Kitsuse, John K., "Societal Reaction to Deviant Behavior: Problems of Theory and Method," *Social Problems*, vol. 9 (1962), pp. 247–57.
61. ———, and Malcolm Spector, "Toward a Sociology of Social Problems; Value-Judgements, and Social Problems," *Social Problems*, vol. 20 (Spring 1973), pp. 407–19.
62. Klapp, O., *Heroes, Villains and Fools*. Englewood Cliffs, N.J.: Prentice-Hall, 1962.
63. Kronus, Sidney J., *The Black Middle Class*. Columbus, Ohio: Charles E. Merrill, 1971.
64. Landesco, John, *Organized Crime in Chicago: Part 3 of the Illinois Crime Survey, 1929*. Chicago: University of Chicago Press, 1968.
65. Lemert, Edwin, *Human Deviance, Social Problems and Social Control*, 2nd ed. Englewood Cliffs, N.J.: Prentice-Hall, 1972.
66. ———, *Social Pathology*. New York: McGraw-Hill, 1957.
67. ———, "The Behavior of the Systematic Check Forger," *Social Problems*, vol. 6 (1958), pp. 141–49.
68. Leznoff, Maurice, and W. A. Westley, "The Homosexual Community," *Social Problems*, vol. 3 (1956), pp. 257–63.
69. Lindesmith, A. R.., *The Addict and the Law*. Bloomington, Ind.: Indiana University Press, 1965.
70. ———, *Addiction and Opiates*. Chicago: Aldine, 1968.
71. ———, *Opiate Addiction*. Bloomington, Ind.: Principia Press, 1947.
72. Lofland, John, *Doomsday Cult*. Englewood Cliffs, N.J.: Prentice-Hall, 1966.
73. ——— (with the assistance of Lyn H. Lofland), *Deviance and Identity*. Englewood Cliffs, N.J.: Prentice-Hall, 1969.
74. Matza, David, *Becoming Deviant*. Englewood Cliffs, N.J.: Prentice-Hall, 1969.
75. ———, *Delinquency and Drift*. New York: Wiley, 1964.
76. Mercer, James R., *Labelling the Mentally Retarded*. Berkeley, Calif.: University of California Press, 1973.
77. Merton, Robert K., and R. A. Nisbet (eds.), *Contemporary Social Problems* (rev. ed.). New York: Harcourt Brace Jovanovich, 1966.
78. Merton, Robert K., *Social Theory and Social Structure* (rev. ed.). New York: The Free Press, 1957.
79. Mileski, Maureen, and Donald J. Black, "The Social Organization of Homosexuality," *Urban Life and Culture*, vol. 1 (July 1972), pp. 187–202.
80. Mills, C. Wright, *The Power Elite*. New York: Oxford University Press, 1959.
81. Mills, Theodore M., "Equilibrium and the Processes of Deviance and Control," *American Sociological Review*, vol. 24 (1959), pp. 671–79.
82. Mizruchi, E. M., and Robert Perrucci, "Norm Qualities and Differential Effects of Deviant Behavior," *American Sociological Review*, vol. 27 (1962), pp. 391–99.
83. Parsons, T., *The Social System*. New York: The Free Press, 1951.
84. Polsky, Ned, *Hustlers, Beats, and Others*. Chicago: Aldine, 1966.
85. Riordon, William, *Plunkitt of Tammany Hall*. New York: Dutton, 1966.

86. Roby, Pamela, "Politics and Criminal Law: Revision of the New York State Penal Law on Prostitution," *Social Problems,* vol. 17 (1969), pp. 83–109.

87. Rooney, Elizabeth, and Don C. Gibbons, "Social Reactions to 'Crimes without Victims,' " *Social Problems,* vol. 13 (1965), pp. 400–10.

88. Royko, Mike, *Boss: Richard J. Daley of Chicago.* New York: Dutton, 1971.

89. Runyon, Thomas, *In for Life.* New York: W. W. Norton, 1953.

90. Schervish, Paul G., "The Labeling Perspective: Its Bias and Potential in the Study of Political Deviance," *American Sociologist,* vol. 8 (May 1973), pp. 47–57.

91. Schur, Edwin M., *Crimes without Victims: Deviant Behavior and Public Policy.* Englewood Cliffs, N.J.: Prentice-Hall, 1965.

92. ———, *Labelling Deviant Behavior.* New York: Harper & Row, 1971.

93. Shibutani, T., *Society and Personality.* Englewood Cliffs, N.J.: Prentice-Hall, 1961.

94. Short, James F., and Fred L. Strodbeck, *Group Process and Gang Delinquency.* Chicago: University of Chicago Press, 1965.

95. Shover, Neal, "The Social Organization of Burglary," *Social Problems,* vol. 20 (Spring 1973), pp. 499–514.

96. Simmons, J. K., "Public Stereotypes of Deviants," *Social Problems,* vol. 13 (1965), pp. 220–26.

97. Skolnick, J., *Justice without Trial.* New York: Wiley, 1966.

98. Slotkin, J. S.,*The Peyote Religion.* New York: The Free Press, 1956.

99. Smelser, Neil J., "Stability, Instability and the Analysis of Political Corruption," in B. Barber and A. Inkeles (eds.), *Stability and Change: A Volume in Honor of Talcott Parsons.* Boston: Little, Brown, 1971, pp. 7–29.

100. Stonequist, E. V., *The Marginal Man.* New York: Charles Scribner's Sons, 1937.

101. Sutherland, E. H., *The Professional Thief.* Chicago: University of Chicago Press, 1937.

102. ———, *White-Collar Crime.* New York: Holt, Rinehart and Winston, 1949.

103. ———, and Donald Cressey, *Principles of Criminology,* 7th ed. Philadelphia: Lippincott, 1966.

104. Sutter, Alan G., "Playing a Cold Game: Phases of a Ghetto Career," *Urban Life and Culture,* vol. 1 (April 1972), pp. 77–91.

105. ———, "Worlds of Drug Use on the Street Scene," in D. Cressey and D. A. Ward (eds.), *Delinquency, Crime and Social Process.* New York: Harper & Row, 1969, pp. 802–29.

106. Sykes, G. M., *The Society of Captives.* Princeton, N.J.: Princeton University Press, 1958.

107. ———, and D. Matza, "Techniques of Neutralization: A Theory of Delinquency," *American Sociological Review,* vol. 22 (1959), pp. 664–70.

108. Tannenbaum, F., *Crime and the Community.* Boston: Ginn and Company, 1938.

109. Tumin, M. M., "The Hero and the Scapegoat in a Peasant Community," *Journal of Personality,* vol. 10 (1950), pp. 197–211.

110. Turner, Ralph, "Deviance Disavowal as Neutralization of Commitment," *Social Problems,* vol. 19 (1972), pp. 308–21.

111. ———, "The Public Perception of Protest," *American Sociological Review,* vol. 34 (1969), pp. 815–31.

112. Wallace, S. E., *Skid Row as a Way of Life.* New York: Bedminster Press, 1965.

113. Warren, Carol A. B., *Identity and Community in the Gay World.* New York: Wiley, 1974.

114. West, Ray B., Jr., *Kingdom of the Saints.* New York: Viking, 1957.
115. Wilkins, Leslie T., *Social Deviance: Social Policy, Action, and Research.* Englewood Cliffs, N.J.: Prentice-Hall, 1965.
116. Wolfgang, M.E., *Patterns in Criminal Homicide.* Philadelphia: University of Pennsylvania Press, 1957.

Selected Readings

BECKER, HOWARD S., *Outsiders: Studies in the Sociology of Deviance.* New York: The Free Press, 1973.
Chapter 10, "Labelling Theory Revisited," summarizes and criticizes the responses to the interactionist view of deviance set forth by Becker in 1963.

ERIKSON, KAI, *Wayward Puritans.* New York: Wiley, 1965.
A valuable analysis of deviance in Puritan society which stresses the positive functions deviant behavior performs for a group and a society.

LEMERT, EDWIN, *Human Deviance, Social Problems and Social Control,* 2nd ed. Englewood Cliffs, N.J.: Prentice-Hall, 1972.
An important set of essays by a theorist who anticipated the theories of deviance that emerged in the 1960s.

MATZA, DAVID, *Becoming Deviant.* Englewood Cliffs, N.J.: Prentice-Hall, 1969.
A provocative theoretical analysis that establishes similarities between the interactionist and the structural views of deviance.

POLSKY, NED, *Hustlers, Beats, and Others.* Chicago: Aldine, 1966.
Contains an intriguing set of essays on a variety of different types of deviants and the worlds they occupy.

SUTHERLAND, E. H., *The Professional Thief.* Chicago: University of Chicago Press, 1937.
A classic "insider" view of the social worlds of professional thieves.

WARREN, CAROL A. B., *Identity and Community in the Gay World.* New York: Wiley, 1974.
A very readable ethnographic, analytic account of stigma, identity, and community in a predominantly male homosexual world.

chapter 16

Illness, Aging, and Dying

*I*llness, aging, and death, along with the rituals that surround their social organization, constitute social and biological facts that affect every human society. *Illness,* whether painful, transitory, or terminal, dislodges persons from their ordinary rounds of activity. *Aging,* often associated with entry into the social worlds of the elderly, the retired, and the chronically ill, signals the movement into a final stage of the life cycle. *Death* disrupts and alters ongoing social relationships. All social groups and societies develop procedures, routines, rituals, institutions, and classes of experts to manage the disorganizing and disruptive effects of these three interrelated phenomena. They are of interest to the social psychologist for a number of reasons.

First, illness is painful and pain is rooted in the body. Like dying, illness and pain are not merely biological events; they involve the subjective interpretation of physiologically based events. Groups and social worlds develop their own vocabularies for interpreting pain, illness, and illness-related processes. These vocabularies transform purely physiological and biological events into socially defined events that can be consensually understood and, hence, acted on. They connect the internal environment of the person with the socially based "naming process."

Second, the definitions that surround the aging experience and the social worlds of the elderly constitute realities that bring new transformations to the self and to its social relationships. These transformations deserve study in their own right, for they mark significant developmental changes in the life cycle.

Third, dying is not a biological process that stands independent of social interpretation or social interaction. A death must be socially produced. The person must be defined as "dead," an increasingly problematic definition to make. Social arrangements must be made for disposing of the dead. These will involve rituals which signify the "passing on" of the dead (24), and may include the scheduling of funeral and interment services. (21) Periods of mourning and grief, however short or prolonged, may be observed. Ties to the dead must be severed at least partially, and the commitment of the living to their ongoing social life among the living must be reestablished.

Fourth, the very reality of death must somehow be conceptualized within any society, such that its existence does not overly disrupt ongoing social interactions. Death must be assigned some "meaning" which minimizes its effect upon the living. Societies and groups vary in the definitions which they bring to this experience. Indeed, it can be said that in many societies persons die socially before they die biologically. It may take such rituals as the funeral to affirm the finality of a physiological death.

Illness and Pain

In our earlier discussion of cognitive structures and the nature of the symbolic environment, we noted that individuals are simultaneously subjects and objects, that the parts of their bodies, and the processes that go on inside of them, are incorporated in their conceptualizations. This means that they become "objects" of thought and of the individual's self-reflection. Since the conceptual apparatus that individuals utilize in this process is largely presented to them ready-made by their society, this means that their inner life and responses to their own bodies are pervasively influenced by social factors. It also means that they go through a learning process as they acquire knowledge of themselves and learn the meanings of the signs that they constantly receive from their own insides.

A famous French physiologist, Claude Bernard, has said that the stability of the internal environment is an indispensable condition for a free life. This statement points up the fact that in the routine business of living we tend not to pay much attention to our bodies as long as they remain healthy and respond properly in their customary manner. Our attention is focused much more on the outside world and on external events. In certain situations, however, we receive from the body unusual types of messages to which we are not accustomed and which are not routine. Experiences of this kind include those of pain, great anxiety, and other types of problematic or extraordinary sensations, such as those involved in sexual activity or those experienced by a psychotic or a drug user. Experiences of this kind emanating from one's interior require that the person learn how to respond to them, how to cope with them, how to label them, and how to interpret what they signify. These labels come from one's social groups.

The above points are vividly attested to by that pervasive and seemingly quite physiological phenomenon known as pain. Most of us are likely to recognize, and even the experts note, that "pain is subjective"—despite its physiological sources. Pain is based in the body, of course, and in its internal malfunctioning or in the wounds received from the outside. People with different physical constitutions appear to have different capacities to withstand pain, as well as different thresholds for feeling pain. Also, persons from different ethnic group backgrounds reveal varying propensities to define and act on pain and illness. Nevertheless, there is no one-to-one relation between some physiological experience and the sensation of feeling a particular pain. In short, the messages coming from within the body, which we label "pain," are interpreted just as any other perception is. Like other perceptions, that of pain has a private coloration but its meanings are deeply social in nature; and as with other meanings, we act upon them. Thereby hangs the social psychological story.

Among the properties of pain are its (1) placement (where within or on the surface of the body); (2) frequency of appearance; (3) duration; (4) degree of intensity; and (5) quality—as described by such adjectives as burning, searing, flooding, annoying. Those properties seem "natural" to pain, but they are matters of definition and social experience. If knowledge of internal organs is imperfect or vague, or if pain vocabularies are inadequate, then pain will be attributed to "the stomach area," or "in there," or "down there" (pointing). Experience plays a part, too, as when sufferers from occasional backaches get to recognize the beginnings of a severe and lengthy "session" if they do not quickly correct their sitting position.

What the above discussion does not fully convey is that pain rarely is just pain; it is set within a context of meanings. Thus a new or unexpected pain brings about an etiological search—Why this pain? An expected and socially legitimate pain—for example, the experience of childbirth—needs no such search, for its interpretation is readily at hand. Evaluations as well as interpretations are placed on various pains. Some are legitimate (childbirth), some illegitimate (a bruised shinbone when one stumbles and clumsily falls). Some are expected, while many other pains arise accidentally.

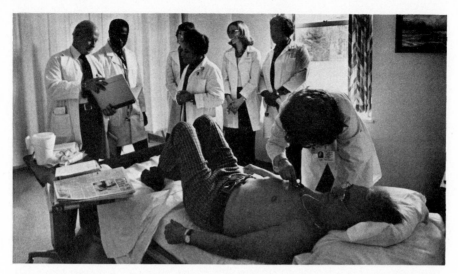

"Pain" is not an objective, psychological experience; rather, it is a matter of subjective experience and social definition. (*Mimi Forsyth for Monkmeyer Press Photo Service*)

On occasion, pain can be received joyfully because it stands for something valuable, as in circumcision rites or other rites of passage wherein the pain "proves manhood" as well as signaling passage into manhood. Pain can be endured, in a sense treated as neutral or as something that just has to be, as when someone needs an operation which he or she knows will be followed by a few days of postoperative pain. When a pain or illness becomes socially legitimated, and when it becomes apparent that it will not disappear, the person is under some obligation to seek out professional health care. In modern Western societies this involves a movement into the *sick role*. Sick persons must (1) receive treatment for their illness, (2) follow the instructions of their physician, and (3) not malinger in the sick role. That is, they are obligated to return to a normal state as soon as possible.

In terms of the complexities of "the naming process and the internal environment," the search for etiological meaning is among the most interesting. Ordinary pains get self-diagnosed. However, as we all recognize, extraordinary or persistent ones bring the sufferer to some presumably knowledgeable agent—a physician, faith healer, or a druggist. Through their experience, or through diagnostic procedures, the agents arrive at some decision about what in the body is causing the pain in question. If they cannot find a reasonable explanation, they have various options: to say so, to give a false answer, to refer the client to another agent, or to suggest a psychological rather than a physiological cause. Modern medicine, of course, frequently calls upon an elaborate technology and a complex division of labor to obtain a proper diagnostic answer—requiring the drawing and examination of blood, the taking and reading of x-rays, and examinations by specialists. It is worth adding that some diagnostic procedures themselves inflict pain, so that patients must undergo further pain in order, hopefully and eventually, to rid themselves of their major pains. Of course, procedural pain usually is of short duration, but sometimes, as with bone biopsies, it is exceedingly painful.

Because pain does not come with diagnostic labels attached, there is always the possibility of an erroneous interpretation. Physicians or other agents may misread or fail to read what the patient or the diagnostic tests tell them. They can also discount such evidence, thinking that the patient is simply a complainer or someone with psychiatric problems. When a wrong diagnosis occurs, treatments that fail to help the sufferer are commonly prescribed. Some diseases and ailments are so difficult to diagnose, or are so little recognized by many professionals, that the poor amateur may drag himself or herself to one presumed expert after the other, shopping around for relief. Some shoppers develop, quite literally, "pain biographies," in that much of their lives revolves around their search for a correct diagnosis.

If the feeling of and the diagnosis of pain have to do with the inner environment, we might also think about the "outer" aspects in terms of the expression of pain. Aside from involuntary expressions—like wincing or explosive crying—most expressions of pain are subject to self-control. This means that such expressions are greatly affected by the socialized experiences of the person. "Big boys don't cry" is a simple example. A more complex one is that in some Asian countries the women go through painful childbirths without even moaning because they are expected not to show pain. In America, there are such elaborate ideologies surrounding childbirth that many expectant mothers negotiate with their obstetricians, making them promise not to give drugs during childbirth. The natural childbirth ideology suggests that the so-called pains that precede birth are not inherently painful, but are merely "contractions" which become painful because of indoctrinated attitudes that arouse fear, anxiety, and tensions in the expectant mother.

Because pain has to be read by its expressions in order to be assessed, there is an assessment problem with which bystanders must cope. Is the person faking? Is he or she pretending to have more pain than he or she has in order to get our sympathy or to get out of a share of the work? In hospitals, problems of assessment are greatly magnified by the unfolding interaction which occurs between the patients and the caretakers. Does this stranger who lies in bed really hurt that much, or must we discount him because he is the kind of person who claims too much? Patients who are disliked, who do not act properly, tend to have their pain discounted in some degree. They are labeled as "complainers" or "overanxious" or even as "psychos." In such interactional dramas, the patient has the problem of legitimating the pain. If the patient's pain is unusual and unexpected, and if there are few overt physical signs, it is likely that he or she will have difficulty legitimating the condition, and his or her reputation as a good patient will be challenged by the medical staff. When pain is really expected—as after an operation—then the problems of legitimation are virtually nonexistent. If one wanted to write a script for maximizing the problems of assessment and legitimation, it would be this: unexpected pain, an inarticulate but obstreperous and seemingly not very sick patient, and a busy harrassed hospital staff. So, in social psychological terms, these are linked problems: others must properly interpret someone's internal environment, and the person must make his or her own interpretations acceptable to them.

These problems, of course, are not confined to the hospital; they also spill over into interaction within the family and among friends. People with occasional or acute pain may prefer to control their expressions of it, to "cover," so as not to disturb ongoing interaction. Chronic sufferers also learn to do this, or to withdraw, or stay out of interaction; often the consequence is social withdrawal. People whose pains are relatively unpredictable or who have experienced some radical transformation in their bodies, such as drastic weight loss, may withdraw from their normal rounds of social interaction. They become social isolates. They endure severe identity problems and may find that their social worlds are shrinking around them. Thus, in discussing a phenomenon like pain, the social psychologist moves from problems of "naming" internal body states to quite external considerations involving interaction, social relationships, and alterations in identity and self-image.

What arouses the emotional expression of pain is determined by social situations rather than by physiological processes. The physiology of a painful experience does not determine how it will be emotionally expressed. The arousal and expression of a pain-centered emotion may be analyzed in terms of three phases:

THE LINGUISTIC FOUNDATIONS OF PAIN-CENTERED EMOTIONS

1. A stimulus or situation that is defined or interpreted in certain ways; for instance, a contraction during childbirth.
2. An internal response to the defined situation, involving both physiological and symbolic processes. Here, the source of the pain must be located; its frequency of occurrence, duration, and intensity may also be noted.
3. An outward, conventionalized expression (by means of words, gestures, and facial expressions) that serves to indicate and hence convey the emotion and pain to others.

A given external situation or act does not call forth a pain-centered emotion until it has been interpreted in a certain way. The emotion is a response not to a raw stimulus as such, but to a defined, classified, and interpreted stimulus, to signs with meanings that vary according to situation, as shown in the accompanying tabulation. The physiological aspects of emotional response (such as a rise in blood pressure, a changed heartbeat, and increased activity of the ductless glands) are not learned forms of behavior. On the other hand, the symbolic processes involved in emotion are learned. The third phase of emotional behavior has sometimes been called the *mimicry* of emotion because persons may voluntarily utilize the conventional means of emotional expression without actually experiencing the genuine emotion. The actor does this constantly, but the same sort of mimicry is commonly used in ordinary life as people strive to conform to the polite usages of social intercourse and to evoke on the part of others their own felt sense of pain and discomfort.

Persons, of course, may pretend to be in pain when they are not, and others may suspect that they are pretending. In certain circumstances it is clear to all parties that excruciating pain is being experienced; no pretense is necessary when a young child suffers a broken finger as the result of a slammed car door. (See the discussion of *awareness contexts* below.)

THE TABOO OF PAIN In Western societies there appears to be a social taboo against the excessive *experiencing* of pain, just as there are taboos against the excessive or overly dramatic *expression* of pain. While ill persons are expected to experience and express pain, the experiencing of pain is regarded as evidence of medical neglect, just as the repeated assertion that one is suffering from unbearable pain is taken as evidence that the person is not being properly treated. Properly ill persons do feel pain, but their pain and their expression of pain should fall within socially prescribed dimensions. Modern health care systems, for example, are organized so as to minimize the importance of pain during one's stay in the hospital. Those who challenge social understandings about pain and its expression make medical nuisances out of themselves.

Persons who claim intense and worsening pain often find that the medical staff begins to ignore them. Strauss and Glaser (23:109) report on one such instance:

> Since Mrs. Abel . . . complained loudly for all to hear, the nursing staff found her an increasingly difficult cross to bear. . . . They reacted not only by spending less and less time within beckoning distance of the patient but by disengaging each other from her room when stuck there. They carefully

arranged staff rotation, so that nobody would have to spend much time with her.

If it is illegitimate or deviant to express excessive pain, it is also not appropriate to acknowledge the fact that certain persons, especially those who have just died, may have actually died in pain. Death, in contemporary Western cultures (1) is expected to be a peaceful event into which one slides without pain or discomfort. Sudnow (24:146) makes the following observation:

> The concern over whether or not the deceased experienced any pain before his death is typically voiced by the relative, who asks . . . "Did he have much pain before he died, Doctor?" . . . Universally, it seems, the doctor answers, "No," when asked if pain was experienced and in most instances provides a form of "elaboration" which the following recorded comment typified: "He was under heavy sedation right until the end and I can assure you that he experienced no discomfort at all."

Body Images, Disease, and Illness

As in other areas of symbolic behavior, one must distinguish carefully between the ideas that people have of their bodies and the more "scientific" conceptions of disease and illness held by students of anatomy and physiology. The two perspectives are often at variance with one another. In this section we examine some of the behavioral consequences that follow from these discrepancies.

It follows that conceptions of the body's insides and functions vary greatly from society to society. The Chinese practice of acupuncture and its recent adoption by Westerners are good examples of this point. In recent years some anthropologists studying underdeveloped countries have been concerned with the theoretical and practical consequences of native medical beliefs. Their research reveals how tremendously varied are conceptions of the body, its functioning, and the manner in which it should be treated when it does not function normally. The research also indicates that people believing these ideas tend to form conceptual systems that are related to other conceptual systems, such as those concerning the supernatural or those having to do with people. Popular medical ideologies also specify the persons who are viewed as capable of diagnosing and dealing with the disorder.

Among the Subanun of Mindanao, Charles Frake has reported that there are 186 names of diseases that classify specific illnesses, symptoms, or stages of illness. The diagnostic criteria that distinguish one disease from another are conceptually distinct. Every person is his or her own herbalist, as there is no separate status of diagnostician or curer. Each person diagnoses and names his or her own illness and then turns to appropriate remedies. (7) Elsewhere in the Philippines, another anthropologist reports, both natural and supernatural causes of illness are recognized, and one way of staying well is not to violate the mores. Five types of practitioners exist, each with individual qualifications, modes of treatment, and types of illness specialized in. (17) In still another Philippine community, where sorcery is recognized as a cause of some illnesses, the sorcerer is called upon to cure the supernaturally caused sickness, while other types of curers are called on to handle illnesses regarded as biological malfunctions. (14)

From the viewpoint of modern science, such systems of concepts and the therapies based on them are often erroneous. Indeed, one reason why research in medical anthropology is increasing is that in the under-developed countries of Asia, Africa, and South America various governments are endeavoring to effect some transfer of native allegiance to whatever Western medicine may exist within their countries. Even in the most technologically and scientifically advanced nations, however, ideas generally accepted by the scientific or medical community compete with many other systems of conceptualization. In certain areas of the United States, where the rural viewpoint still predominates, well-established popular ideational complexes coexist with rudimentary modern ideas. Carl Withers, an anthropologist who studied "Smalltown," a midwestern rural town of three hundred people, reported that (27:233):

> There are five historical layers of medical and pseudo-medical lore, all of which coexist and have coexisted in varying ratios for a long time. They are in a kind of rough-and-ready historical order of appearance: (1) early magical practice, including both "witchcraft" and divine healing; (2) an enormous body of "home remedies"; (3) rational or pseudo-rational medicine connected with the recognized medical profession; (4) patent medicines; and (5) a new and recent wave of curing by prayer and other religious techniques.

Lest we discount this report as "That happened many years ago" we must recognize that American physicians still compete—and are likely to do so for decades to come—with other types of practitioners. Studies have firmly established that persons of the lower socioeconomic classes, as well as those from rural areas, often prefer to go to chiropractors, homeopaths, osteopaths, and other types of practitioners not ethically or formally approved by the American Medical Association. These populations do this because they have more faith in those healers than in physicians, and because their own conceptions of bodily functioning are closer to those of the nonphysician healers. It is well known, for instance, that Christian Science is believed in by many well-educated people (even some who hold, or have held, positions of high political power). Indeed, Christian Scientists are mostly drawn from the middle classes. It is equally well known that even people who believe in "regular medicine" also frequent other types of practitioners, either when physicians fail or when they have certain types of ailments. Thus, arthritics in desperation at their discomfort and pain tend to shop around among physicians and other practitioners as well as try a variety of remedies (some illegal in many states) suggested by friends, relatives, and the mass media.

The Social Worlds of the Old

Aging is a social process that is subject to different definitions. The age sixty-five as a significant milestone in the aging process is supported by biological criteria, for the average life-expectancy for males in thirteen European countries of Western culture is sixty-five years (12). For females, the age is slightly higher. Chronological age is somewhat arbitrary, however, and some have proposed a social definition that stresses reductions in social competence. (12) Nonetheless, the age 65 is commonly utilized when enumerating the proportion of a population that is old or aging. Most Western societies, in fact, employ this definition, as evidence in their pension, health care, and social security programs (22), although some countries may vary from the standard of sixty-five years by a few years either way. By using the definition of aging as sixty-five years or older, we discover that approximately 10 percent of the total population of Americans is in the aging category. Western societies, for various reasons, vary in the proportion of their population which is age 65 or older. In Denmark, 12 percent of the population falls in this category; in Finland, 8 percent; in the German Democratic Republic, 15 percent; in Sweden, 13 percent; and in the U.S.S.R., 7 percent. These figures suggest that the social worlds of the old and the aging are sizable. In addition, we can expect these worlds to increase. When the post-World War II "baby boom" population becomes 65 and over, there will be a significant increase in the proportion of "aged" to "nonaged" people in American society. By the year 2030, the ratio of the retired population (over 65) to working population (20–64) in the United States will change from 18 to 26 percent. Many of the people reading this book now will be in that population.

It has been suggested that an old age "subculture" is emerging in the United States (13:24–25). This subculture, in part a reaction to the increasing stratification of American society along age-specific, work-related, and kinship lines, stresses a return to the values and ideologies of rural America at the turn of the century. The values of the small town, of an ethnically divided nation, and a fond memory of earlier historic times and customs are seen as characteristic of this "subculture." (13:7–9) The old have formed this social world perspective in response to (1)

ATTRIBUTES AND IMAGES OF THE OLD

The social worlds of the old are large and likely to grow still larger when the baby-boom of the 1950s reaches old age. (*Burk Uzzle/Magnum*)

pressures to retire by age 65; (2) increased leisure time as a result of early retirement or loss of family roles; and (3) a weakening of the family's functions, as social welfare and educational agencies take over the family's responsibilities in the areas of health care, child supervision, and extended family support in the forms of financial, moral, and social assistance.

The elderly, it is argued (4:14–23; 5:210–18), have been cut off from the mainstream of modern industrialized society. They may become social and psychological isolates who have *disengaged* themselves from society. Freed (or cut off) from the interactions and demands of family and work, the old are thrown together and often forced to live in age-segregated residences, which may range from retirement villages to care-centers, from rundown hotels to the back wards of mental hospitals for the senile. This isolation from the "youthful" and gainfully employed sectors of society reinforces the construction of an age-based subculture or social world and further isolates the elderly from their familiar worlds of discourse, thought, and remembrance.

DISENGAGEMENT THEORY

A popular theory of aging was set forth by Cumming and Henry (4) some years ago. Termed *disengagement theory*, it contains the following postulates:

1. Although individuals differ, the expectation of death is universal. . . . Therefore a mutual severing of ties will take place between the individual and those others in his society who belong to his social groups.

2. Disengagement becomes a self-perpetuating process, for once bonds have been cut, the freedom from other bonds is thereby increased.
3. Because males occupy instrumental roles in American society and females occupy affective roles, the process of disengagement will differ accordingly.
4. Disengagement may be initiated by the individual or by society, as when a male fails to adequately perform on the job.
5. When both the individual and society are ready for disengagement to occur, complete disengagement results. When society is ready and the individual is not, the result is usually disengagement.
6. Because disengagement results in the loss of central roles, personal crises will be produced for the individual if he cannot find new roles to fill.
7. Persons can ready themselves for disengagement if they perceive that death is near.

These postulates and a number of additional correlates suggest that elderly and aging individuals in American society often die socially before they die biologically.

Disengagement theory assumes that the growing isolation of the elderly person is a natural process, in part a consequence of the increasing "depersonalization" and industrialization of American society. Furthermore, it assumes that kinship ties cease to function as symbolic and

Disengagement theory appears not to apply to all elderly individuals, as the life of Pablo Casals attests. (© 1972 *Fritz Henle/Photo Researchers, Inc.*)

moral links to the common worlds of family life. The theory will not account for the "nondisengaging" behaviors of certain groups and of certain individuals. Elderly rural Americans, for example, are still commonly absorbed into the fabric of the extended family; those persons who do not leave the labor market at age 65 have often been observed to lead healthy, involved, and politically influential lives into their late eighties. Both Charles de Gaulle and Winston Churchill were in their mid-eighties when they died. Pablo Casals was 93 when he died, and Picasso was 86.

Disengagement theory, then, may apply only to special sectors or populations of the aged. In addition, it may apply only under very specific social circumstances.

THE FUNCTIONS OF DISENGAGEMENT It must be recognized, however, that the disengagement of the aged in modern society enhances, as Blauner (2:352) observes, "the continuous functioning of social institutions." It permits the changeover of personnel in an orderly manner, without the disruption that would occur if positions were filled only after persons worked to the end and died on the job. Blauner remarks on the chaos that followed the Kennedy assassination and suggests that most bureaucracies could not tolerate or function in the face of high mortality in the middle years of the adult work-cycle.

Consistent with our social psychological perspective, we are inclined to argue that persons' attitudes towards aging will directly reflect the definitions they hold toward themselves as an aging individual. A theory of aging which ignores personal and social identities will be devoid of insights into the subjective elements of the aging process. As presently stated, disengagement theory tends to neglect the *interpersonal context* in which aging occurs. There is also an apparent assumption that death represents an ugly and undesirable end to the life cycle. This view is contradicted by the beliefs of many individuals and social groups (1; 32).

If the interpersonal context of aging is considered, we would assume that like-situated persons who share similar world views and experiences would develop, over the course of time, a set of friendly, if not intimate, primary group relationships that would integrate each of them into a common community of discourse and interaction. If a newcomer finds him- or herself fitting into such a structure of social relationships, and if others accept that person, a niche for him or her will be found, if not created. If the identities, social relationships, and images of self offered to individuals fit their ongoing conceptions of themselves, then they will not experience isolation, or negative disengagement. In short,

Social-group relationships among the elderly offer an alternative to isolation and disengagement. (*Alex Webb/Magnum*)

as Rosow and Hochschild (20:32) have suggested, "old people living in a community of peers are much less likely to disengage, to isolate or cut themselves off from society, or to feel that they have been so cut off."

We turn now to a recent study of a community of the aged which was conducted by Hochschild among the residents of Merrill Court, a small apartment building for the elderly and the retired on the eastern side of the San Francisco Bay area.

The residents of Merrill Court were mostly rural-born, white, from the working class, Anglo-Saxon Protestant, widowed females in their sixties. Only five were men, three of whom were widowed. The widows' husbands had been carpenters, construction workers, farmers, grocery clerks, and salesmen. Three-fourths of them had come to California in the early 1940s. These residents of Merrill Court had developed their own community, based on close, "sibling" (almost "sisterly") bonds. The widows of Merrill Court exchanged cups of coffee, lunches, potted plants, kitchen utensils, and baked goods. They watched after one another's apartments, and they took phone calls for each other. They shared in common conversations, and their topics ranged over problems which confronted all of them: would Medicare pay for chiropractors, what were the visiting hours at various hospitals, which kinds of dentures were best, how much were TV repairs, and what was the latest development in daytime TV soap operas.

Merrill Court, Hochschild (13:38) reports, "was a beehive of activity." There were weekly meetings of the Service Club, bowling schedules to be met, Bible study classes to be attended, birthdays to organize for, crafts to be made out of discarded household items, and Christmas cards to be cut out for the Hillcrest Junior Women's Club.

AN
UNEXPECTED
COMMUNITY

The social arrangements of Merrill Court took on a life of their own. "They were designed, as if on purpose, to assure an *on-going* community." (13:47) The residents of Merrill Court felt that they were valued members of the local community. Della, a club president who, like past presidents, had come from a small town, expressed this sense of belonging as follows:

> Since I've been president here, I feel we are part of [the town] just like the VFW and the Eagles. "Why do they come to us [referring to other organizations]?" some of the women ask. They come and say they want 50 favors to be made for the Mayor's conference. They come to us because they think we can do the job; they wouldn't come to us if they didn't think that. It's an honor. (13:56)

The residents of Merrill Court had disengaged themselves from their earlier social worlds and social relationships. Within their own group, however, they produced an *unexpected community*, a social world unique in its customs, rituals, and routines. Hochschild's research provides an empirical challenge to disengagement theory and suggests that more ethnographies of the social worlds of the elderly are needed.

What, for example, do the aging worlds of the racial and ethnic minorities in the United States look like? How do American Indians, Japanese-Americans, Spanish-Americans, and the Eastern European Greeks, Poles, and Hungarians age and grow old in large metropolitan locales? How do the elderly ill and poor age and carve out lives in diners, sidewalks, parks, rundown apartment houses, and cheap hotels? If, as recent research suggests, the average income of couples over the age of 65 is $2,804, then clearly the average elderly person is living on or near the poverty level. The mental and physiological deteriorations of the body, which accompany aging, must be coupled in future ethnographies with studies of the elderly urban and rural poor. Such persons often lack access to proper medical care, thereby increasing the negative effects of aging.

Hochschild discovered a community of elderly people who were not isolated. It remains for future investigators to probe the worlds of such persons as the following elderly male (13:137–38):

> He lingers at the counter making talk with the waitress.
> "What'll it be today?"
> "Well, what do you have for me? You got some of that homemade potato soup? That's a good soup. We used to have that at home. Back in Michigan."
> "Anything else today?"
> "Coffee. My usual coffee. My mother won a prize at the county fair with her potato soup. She had a secret recipe."
> "And what else? Some dessert?"
> At a quarter of five, he is slowly eating his potato soup, his pie, and sipping his cup of coffee. He remarks:

"I used to be a very busy person. I used to have plenty of friends." He lives at the Executive Hotel at $2.00 a day. He plays solitaire in his room and watches television in the downstairs lobby.

"The Executive's alright," he says. "Now I just came here four years ago; but there are some older folks who *live* here."

Old age is a stage in the life cycle that nearly every individual enters. The social worlds of the old are diverse; they cross-cut income, racial, ethnic, religious, sexual, occupational, and kinship boundaries. Entry into this world signals a confrontation with dying and death, the topics of the next section.

Dying and Death

Every social structure must confront the biological and social realities that surround the eventual death of its members. Whether expected, accidental, or tragic, whether involuntary or deliberate, death is a "biological and existential fact of life that effects every human society." (2:346). Death, an approaching reality for the elderly, is an obdurate factor of everyone's reality, however frequently dismissed. Death produces serious organizational, moral, occupational, political, religious, and kinship problems for all human societies. The statuses held and the functions previously performed by the dead person must be filled and carried on. Orderly transitions of power and leadership from the dead to the living must be organized. Affective obligations and duties, previously met by the dead person, must be transferred to other members of the community. The symbolic and sacred moral worth of the dead person must be established and either affirmed or denied. The bonds that tie the dead individual to the living, whether these be fellow kin, citizens of a nation, or coworkers and friends from the past, must also be symbolically signified. In short, all social structures organize ritual acts which recognize and take note of death and of the dead.

In recognizing the "passing on" of the dead (24), societies and social groups establish a moral and symbolic distance between the living and the dead. As Blauner (2:357) suggests:

> The social distance between the living and the dead must be increased after death, so that the group first, and the most affected grievers later, can reestablish their normal activity without a paralyzing attachment to the corpse.

There are, however, efforts to maintain a symbolic link or social and historical relationship with the deceased person. Funerals and interment ceremonies, while formally disposing of the deceased body, symbolically announce that the living have properly cared for the body, the self, and the reputation of the person who has died. Grave markers, flowers placed on graves on Memorial Day, photographs of the deceased, printed announcements in newspapers commemorating the death of a father or mother, memorabilia such as treasured rings, watches, quilts, smoking pipes, tools, books, Bibles, coin and stamp collections, and other valued objects (often passed from generation to generation) all serve to record the fact that the dead person still occupies a place in the social worlds of the living.

But, before links to the dead can be established, their death must be a confirmed fact. A death, as was noted at the beginning of this chapter, must be socially produced.

DYING David Sudnow (24) recently investigated the place and production of death and dying in the social organization of hospitals. Such an investigation was warranted on at least two grounds. First, hospitals are the major setting for dying in our society, and second, little sociological attention has been given to the care and definition of the "terminally ill" or dying patient.

Sudnow's concern was with an identification of the events, cues, and symptoms physicians utilize when they define a patient as "termi-

Grave decorations, along with other forms of memorial, record the fact that the dead continue to occupy a place in the social worlds of the living. (*Paul Fusco/Magnum*)

Life Cycle: Adult Transformations

nal." His interest was processual, for persons must first be defined as dying before their deaths can be certified. He notes that (24:65):

> In certain medical circles there is considerable disagreement over the precise biological meaning of death; some argue that the cessation of cellular activity constitutes death, and others insist upon a more specific attention to properties of cellular multiplication. . . . Some persons argue that "dying" is a thing which becomes recognized once a deadly disease is located, i.e., that "dying" is a state wherein a person suffers from a disease which is nonreversible and is known to "produce death."

The location of a "death-causing disease" will not explain those deaths where no disease is discovered; for example, deaths from a gunshot wound. The cessation of cellular activity will also not explain the cause of death, for it is only a "sign" at best, an operational definition of the fact that a "death" is in process.

These remarks suggest that disease categories and measures of cellular multiplication are not, in and of themselves, causes of death in any biological sense. They are social categories, or linguistic labels, which members of the medical community utilize when they formulate a diagnosis and prognosis of a patient who appears to be "dying." Such categories are predictive indicators that serve to make the *dying trajectory* of the terminally ill patient understandable (in medical and lay terms) and, hence, controllable.

SOCIAL DEATH, CLINICAL DEATH, AND BIOLOGICAL DEATH

Considerations of this order are what led Sudnow (24:62) to propose that deaths occur within a social order that links the person not only to the medical order of the hospital, but also to the social worlds of kinship, work, aging, and illness. "Dying" provides a set of definitions that permit not only the patient but also the patient's kin and the hospital personnel to orient their actions to the future; that is, they can prepare for death's actual occurrence. By placing persons in the "dying" category, hospital personnel establish a way of attending to them (24:75). It places an interpretative frame around the experiences of dying persons such that these experiences can be processed within the medical order of the hospital.

In County Hospital, one of two medical settings studied by Sudnow, patients who were considered "dying" or "terminally ill" had their names posted on the "critical patients list." Morgue attendants would regularly consult this list so that they could make an estimate of the work load for the coming week. Physicians who were in need of special organs for research projects (e.g., eyes or kidneys) were alerted to up-coming deaths, and nurses were encouraged to speak with members of the patient's family concerning the chances of getting permission to relinquish the patient's eyes, liver, or other organs for research.

At County Hospital, the Catholic chaplain would regularly check the critical patients list to determine which patients should be administered their last rites. Many "posted patients" did not die, even after they had received their last rites. The priest reported that "such cleansing [was] not permanent . . . and that upon readmission to the hospital one must, before he dies, receive last rites again; the first administration is [was] no longer operative." (24:73)

In these senses, seriously ill "posted patients" can be regarded as candidates for an autopsy *before* their death; that is, their medical death actually precedes their biological death.

It is now possible to distinguish three categories of death: *clinical death*, which signals the appearance of "death signs" upon physical examination; *biological death*, which may be marked by the cessation of cellular activity; and *social death*, which occurs at that time when the patient is "treated essentially as a corpse, though perhaps still 'clinically' and 'biologically' alive." (24:74) Socially dead persons are, for all practical, moral, and symbolic purposes, treated "as if" they are dead. Once persons have socially died, they can then be treated as absent others whose affairs now become the sole concern of others. Their personal effects can be disposed of; funeral ceremonies can be scheduled; caskets can be picked out; and the final costs of a burial plot can be paid for. Insurance policies can be cashed, and retirement benefits can be applied for.

Sudnow (24:77) gives a typical instance of a "social death." A male patient was admitted to the emergency unit with a perforated duodenal ulcer. He was in critical condition for six days following his operation, and his wife was informed that his chances of survival were slim. She stopped visiting the hospital upon receipt of this information. The patient, however, began to show marked improvement and was released from the hospital after two weeks. He was readmitted the next day and died shortly thereafter of a severe coronary attack. Before he died, he told the following story concerning his experiences upon returning home. His wife had removed all of his clothing from the house, his personal effects were missing, and his wife had made arrangements for his burial. He found his wife with another man, and she was not wearing his wedding ring. The patient reported that he left his house, began to drink heavily, and suddenly suffered a heart attack.

If the *dying trajectory* of the terminally ill person were to be charted, it would appear that clinical death precedes (though not always) social death, followed then by actual biological death. However, a person may be defined as socially dead even before a clinical diagnosis is performed. Indeed, there are certain benefits to narrowing the temporal gap between clinical, social, and biological death, not the least of which involve the fact that an inevitable process is brought to rapid conclusion, thereby lessening social and psychological grief. A rapid death reduces the ambiguities—interactional and personal—that surround the relationships between the living and the dead, and it permits the living to return to the routine demands of their everyday worlds. (Morticians, furthermore, find that their best results are obtained "if the subject is embalmed before life is completely extinct—that is, before cellular death has occurred." [16:70]. In the average case this would mean within one hour after the heart ceased beating. Such haste raises fears of live burial, fears which are allayed by embalming itself. The removal of blood from the body, which "prevents" infection and discoloration, "has made the chances of a live burial quite remote." [16:70])

The dying career of a terminally ill person has a variable temporal shape (9:23). It may be short-term, long and lingering in duration, or it may vacillate between periods of recovery and periods of "near" death. The social, clinical, and biological definitions that surround one's dying career also shift and take on new meaning over time. If patients' biological death lingers, their social death may be hastened. On the other hand, if their biological death is unexpected and perhaps instant (as in an accident), it may take days or weeks before their social death is actually realized.

DYING TRAJECTORIES

A patient's dying career appears to involve a series of "critical junctures." (23:13) First, the patient is defined as dying. Second, staff and family make preparations for the death. Third, death is defined as inevitable. The fourth juncture is the final descent into death, which ends in the fifth (the last hours), the sixth (the death watch), and the seventh (the death itself). At some point in this career, announcements may be made that the patient is dying, or that he or she is leaving one phase and entering another. After death, legal pronouncements must be made, and then the death is made public.

As the patient moves through the dying trajectory, the awareness or knowledge of the impending death becomes problematic. Members of the medical staff may withhold critical knowledge about a patient's state of "dying" from kin as well as from the patient. Physicians may not inform members of the nursing staff that a patient is about to die. The information each person in the dying situation has about the identity of the other and his or her own identity in the eyes of the other refers to the *total awareness context of a social situation* (9:10). In the dying situation (as in all situations), four contexts of awareness can be identified. An *open* awareness context exists when each interactant is aware of the other's true identity; in this case, a patient and his or her family would

THE AWARENESS OF DYING

Mourning is not merely an individual expression of grief but also a ritual—with an etiquette detailing proper and improper actions—imposed by the social group. (*Carl Dotter/Magnum*)

both know that the patient is terminally ill and that death is near. A *closed* awareness context exists when neither party to the interaction knows the other's identities or intentions. In many dying situations, patients may not know that they are about to die, and they are thus unaware that their family is making plans for their death. A *suspicion* awareness context prevails when at least one party to the interaction suspects the true identity of the other. A wife may suspect that her husband is dying, yet neither the husband nor the hospital staff have informed her of his condition. A *pretense* awareness context is produced when both parties are fully aware of one another's identities, but act as if they are not. In many situations, for example, a husband and a wife will deny the fact that the husband is dying.

The Social Consequences of Death: Mourning

Death sets in motion a series of processes that serve to distinguish the living from the dead and thereby establish a continuity in the life cycle. Perhaps its major consequence is to disrupt the relational worlds of the living, in particular those intimates who mourn the passing of the deceased (11:112).

On the basis of extensive research in Great Britain, Gorer (11) proposed that most adult mourners pass through three stages: a short period of shock, which usually lasts between the occurrence of the death and the disposal of the body; a period of intense mourning accompanied by withdrawal from the external world, often linked with loss of weight and rest; and a final period of readjustment in which mourners return to their normal rounds of activity. Gorer (11:112) observes that:

> The first period of shock is . . . generally given social recognition. Kinsfolk gather around the mourners for the family gatherings, religious ceremonies and, often, ritual meals. . . . Once the funeral, and possibly the post-funeral meal, are finished, the ritual which might give support to the bereaved is finished too, and they are left to face the period of intense mourning without either support or guidance. . . . The customs of Britain . . . prescribe usually in great detail the costume and behavior appropriate to mourners in the period of intense mourning after the funeral; they also typically impose an etiquette on all those who come in contact with the mourners; and usually designate the number of days, weeks, months or years that this behavior should be followed.

Mourning, while a social process, and one which reflects each mourner's relationship to the deceased, is concomitantly a ritual act that is imposed upon the person by the social group. On this Durkheim (6:397) has argued:

> . . . mourning is not the spontaneous expression of individual emotions . . . mourning is not a natural movement of private feelings wounded by cruel loss; it is a duty imposed by the group. One weeps, not simply because he is sad, but because he is forced to weep. It is a ritual attitude which he is forced to adopt . . . but which is, in a large measure, independent of his affective state.

Among mourners in contemporary American society, the mourning debt is repaid, in part, through the purchase of floral arrangements, visits to the funeral home, and assistance in the preparation of post-funeral meals for the members of the immediate family. One's relationship to the deceased, and to the living members of the deceased's family, stands suspended until one or more of these ritual acts have been completed, or at least attempted. For the immediate family, the purchase of the casket (21) takes on some significance; not only must a casket (or some suitable substitute) be purchased, but its cost will define the moral worth of the deceased person (and perhaps of his or her remaining family). If a casket cannot be purchased, the funeral ceremony cannot be completed, and the mourners find themselves in the uneasy situation of still having to grieve. A recent strike involving four major vault manufacturers and Teamsters Union Local 786 in Cook County, Illinois (18) placed some 1500 families in a situation where their funerals could not be promptly completed because of the unavailability of caskets. One woman remarked (18:5):

> It is hard enough to lose your mother, but this kind of thing just leaves you hanging—knowing the funeral is not completed. . . . Now we'll have to go through all of that grief again when we bury her. . . . At the time of the fu-

neral, you are surrounded by relatives and friends. Now when we go out there [to the cemetery], it will just be us.

The obligatory, if not dramaturgical, character of mourning is well displayed in the death practices of the Kiowa Apache, reported on by Opler and Bittle (19:473):

> Among the Kiowa Apache the reaction to a death was immediate and violent. Close relatives wailed, tore their clothes, and exposed their bodies without shame; some shaved the head, lacerated the body, and cut off a finger joint. . . . A widower went to great lengths to show his grief. Sometimes he requested relatives of his wife to gash his forehead or to cut off all his hair, and gave presents to the one who performed the service.

The Meanings of Death

As an event which disrupts social structures, death represents an elaborate ritual occurrence that forces the living to define and reestablish their own relational ties to one another. The paradoxical consequence of death, then, is that the movement of a member out of a social group becomes the occasion for affirming the group's very foundation and basis of existence. For, without acknowledging—however ritualistically—the "passing on" of one of its members, the group as a collectivity runs the risk of having no one recognize its collective or individual death. The rituals of death, from this point of view, function in a self-serving manner for the group.

Death and its rituals reaffirm the social order. As a social process, death and dying represent the interplay, at the group level, of biological and social events. For, as we have shown, a biological death cannot occur until the occurrence of "social death" has been established. That social death often precedes biological death is a measure of humans' control over the termination of the life cycle of themselves and of their fellows. Peter Freuchen's discussion of the problem of the aged in Eskimo society makes this point rather forcefully. He describes the social and then biological death of an elderly woman named Naterk (8:178–81):

> [Old Naterk called her son Mala]. "I am tired and I am old. You must build me a snow house because I shall go on a very long journey all alone." . . . Thus Mala built a house. . . . Then she crawled into the house built for her and quietly stretched out on the old skin. Soon Mala came. . . . He now took his knife, cut a block of snow and walled up the entrance with it. . . . There, then, the old woman reposed, waiting for death. . . . How hard it was to play dead. But Old Naterk was no longer to be reckoned among the living. To the others she had passed on; she was gone. . . . Life, surely, was much more wearisome than death. But the most wearisome thing of all was this slow transition from life to death.

Illness, aging, dying, and *death* represent social and biological processes **Summary** that find their meanings and interpretations both in the human body and in the human social group. They are of concern to the social psychologist because they are recurring events that all social structures and all groups must confront. Their meanings are often lodged in disparate social groups, so that illness, aging, and dying vary from group to group. The social worlds of the elderly have assumed a subcultural flavor which emphasizes solidarity and mutual support of others. Death, whether clinical, biological, or social, is surrounded by a complex network of ritual acts that serve to establish the relationships between the living and the deceased.

References

1. Aries, Philippe, *Western Attitudes toward Death: From the Middle Ages to the Present.* Baltimore: Johns Hopkins University Press, 1974.
2. Blauner, Robert, "Death and Social Structure," in Marcello Truzzi (ed.), *Sociology and Everyday Life.* Englewood Cliffs, N.J.: Prentice-Hall, 1968, pp. 346–67.
3. Burgess, Ernest W. (ed.), *Aging in Western Societies.* Chicago: University of Chicago Press, 1960.
4. Cumming, Elaine, and William E. Henry, *Growing Old: The Process of Disengagement.* New York: Basic Books, 1961.
5. ———, William E. Henry, and Ernest Damianopoulos, "A Formal Statement of Disengagement Theory," in E. Cumming and W. E. Henry (eds.), *Growing Old: The Process of Disengagement.* New York: Basic Books, 1961, pp. 210–27.
6. Durkheim, Emile, *Elementary Forms of Religious Life.* New York: Free Press of Glencoe, 1947.
7. Frake, Charles O., "The Diagnosis of Disease among the Subanun of Mindanao," *American Anthropologist,* vol. 63 (1961), pp. 113–32.
8. Freuchen, Peter, "The Problem of the Aged in Eskimo Society," in R. C. Owen, James J. F. Deetz, and Anthony D. Fisher (eds.), *The North American Indians: A Sourcebook.* New York: Macmillan, 1967, pp. 175–83.
9. Glaser, Barney G., and Anselm L. Strauss, *Awareness of Dying.* Chicago: Aldine, 1965.
10. Goody, Jack, *Death, Property and the Ancestors.* Stanford, Calif.: Stanford University Press, 1962.
11. Gorer, Geoffrey, *Death, Grief, and Mourning in Contemporary Britain.* London: The Cressey Press, 1965.
12. Havighurst, R., *Psychological Aspects of Aging.* Washington, D.C.: American Psychological Association, 1956.
13. Hochschild, Arlie Russell. *The Unexpected Community.* Englewood Cliffs, N.J.: Prentice-Hall, 1973.
14. Lieban, Richard W., "Sorcery, Illness, and Social Control in a Philippine Municipality," in W. R. Scott and E. H. Volkart (eds.), *Medical Care: Readings in the Sociology of Medical Institutions.* New York: Wiley, 1966, pp. 222–32.

15. Lugo, James O., and Gerald L. Hershey, *Human Development*. New York: Macmillan, 1974.
16. Mitford, Jessica, *The American Way of Death*. New York: Simon & Schuster, 1963.
17. Nurge, Ethel, "Etiology of Illness in Guinhangdan," *American Anthropologist*, vol. 63 (1961), pp. 113–32.
18. O'Connor, Phillip J., "Burial Vault Strike: A Double Dose of Grief," *Chicago Daily News*, July 23–24 (1977), p. 5.
19. Opler, Morris E., and William E. Bittle, "The Death Practices of the Kiowa Apache," in R. C. Owen, James J. F. Deetz, and Anthony D. Fisher (eds.), *The North American Indians: A Sourcebook*. New York: Macmillan, 1967, pp. 472–82.
20. Rosow, Irving, *Social Integration of the Aged*. New York: The Free Press, 1967.
21. Salomone, Jerome J., "An Empirical Report on Some Controversial American Funeral Practices," *Sociological Symposium*, vol. 1 (1953), pp. 47–66.
22. Schultz, James, G. Carrin, H. Krupp, M. Peochke, E. Sclar, and J. Van Steenberge, *Providing Adequate Retirement Income*. Hanover, N.H.: Brandeis University Press, 1974.
23. Strauss, Anselm, and B. Glaser, *Anguish: A Case History of a Dying Trajectory*. Mill Valley, Calif.: The Sociology Press, 1970.
24. Sudnow, David, *Passing On: The Social Organization of Dying*. Englewood Cliffs, N.J.: Prentice-Hall, 1967.
25. Warner, W. Lloyd, *American Life: Dream and Reality*. Chicago: University of Chicago Press, 1953.
26. ———, *The Living and the Dead*. New Haven: Yale University Press, 1959.
27. Withers, Carl, "The Folklore of a Small Town," *Transactions of the New York Academy of Sciences*, vol. 8 (May 1946), pp. 234–51.

Selected Readings

MANNING, PETER K., AND HORACIO FABREGA, JR., "The Experience of Self and Body: Health and Illness in the Chiapas Highlands," pp. 251–301 in George Psathas, ed., *Phenomenological Sociology: Issues and Implications*. New York: Wiley, 1973.

A very useful ethnographic depiction of one social group's views on health, illness, and medical practices.

HOCHSCHILD, ARLIE RUSSELL. *The Unexpected Community*. Englewood Cliffs, N.J.: Prentice-Hall, 1973.

An important negative case for disengagement theory.

SUDNOW, DAVID. *Passing On: The Social Organization of Dying*. Englewood Cliffs, N.J.: Prentice-Hall, 1967.

An outstanding account of death and dying in the modern hospital.

Index

Abipone people, 110
abortion, 489-91, 492, 500
acupuncture, 545
Adler, Alfred, 258
Admiralty Islands, 124
adolescence, 346, 373
  Erickson on, 335-37
  friendship and, 342-43, 344
  sex and, 333, 339, 345, 472, 478, 523
adulthood, 339, 345, 347
  childhood and, 335, 353-54, 356, 362, 389
  social roles and, 364-66, 472
Africa, 124, 172
age, 329, 347, 364, 538-39, 560
  careers of, 435, 547-53
  childhood duration and, 314
  chronology and, 359, 547
  crime rates and, 423, 510
  motivation in, 253, 276
  sexual activity and, 465, 469, 475, 482, 484, 485, 523
  social change and, 451-52, 561
aggregates, 55, 56, 77-78, 108
  defined, 52
aggression, strategic, 420. See also crime; warfare
agriculture, 8, 9, 54, 145, 173
Ainu, 124
alcohol, 256, 262, 411, 414, 518
  addiction careers, 433, 501, 503, 515
  bootleg, 507
alienation, 431, 454-56, 460. See also isolation
Allee, W., quoted, 55-56
Allport, Gordon, cited, 263-64, 317; quoted, 257-58, 262
alphabet, the, 132, 144-45, 146, 170
American Medical Association, 546
American Philosophical Society, 18

American Sign Language, 70, 72, 132
  Keller and, 219-22
American Sociological Association, 41
Amish, 313
analogy, 161-64, 264
anal phase, 331, 332, 334, 336
animals, 32, 38, 53, 338, 375
  behavior levels of, 39-40, 56-58, 71-74, 75, 78, 79, 80, 83, 121-22, 126, 144, 149, 187, 211, 213, 230, 233, 247, 380
  conditioning in, 115-16, 117, 245
  domestication of, 54
  drugs and, 515
  humor in, 64-65, 66, 165
  hypnosis and, 404, 410
  imprinting phenomenon in, 478
  instinct and, 251, 252-53, 254
  memory in, 198-200
  perception in, 118, 119, 182, 192-95
  sex and, 66, 69, 75, 77, 464-65, 469, 482, 491-92
  societies of, 52, 55, 56, 58-66, 68-69, 70, 77-78, 108
  See also specific animals
anthropology, 172-73, 545-46
anthropomorphism, 56-58, 371, 379, 380
ants, 56, 58-61, 62
anxiety, 339
  pain and, 540, 542, 543
  paranoid, 391, 398, 399, 401-403, 417, 495
  poise failures and, 399-401
  reduction efforts, 258, 260, 338, 342, 347, 418, 419-21, 423
  self-awareness and, 319-20, 322, 324, 340, 419-20
  sexual attitudes and, 333, 343-44, 473, 485
  See also guilt

apes, see chimpanzees
aphasia, 53, 126, 151, 153, 218, 226-35, 238, 394
Arabic languages, 111, 113
Arabs, 6, 8, 9, 113, 145, 190
  handshakes, 124
  skin color and, 184
Aristarchus, 7, 21
Aristotle, 6, 7, 8, 21, 27
arson, 468, 506
art, 65, 76, 79, 168, 458, 520, 522
  cognitive dissonance and, 103
  perception and, 184, 186, 187-88, 195-96
  subcommunities, 440
  subjective reality and, 88, 99, 150
  thought and, 150-52
Asch, S. E., cited, 408; quoted, 327
aspiration levels, 325. See also motivation
atomism, 35, 36
attention, see perception
attitude consistency theory, 99-103, 104
Australia, 189-90
Austria, 453
authority figures, 342, 356, 357
  morality and, 367, 368

Babylonia, 54
baby talk, 111, 288-90, 291-92, 293
Bahima people, 124
balance theory, 100, 102
Bali, 186, 313
barbiturates, 515
Bastian, Jarvis, quoted, 78
bees, 56, 58, 59, 61-63
  life cycle, 254
  memory and, 199

behavior
  biological factors in, 268, 273, 325,
    346, 391-92, 544 (*See also* biologi-
    cal determinism; body)
  definitions and theories of, 3, 19,
    21, 23, 24-25, 31-40, 47-48,
    99-104, 211, 236, 246-80, 407-11,
    448-49, 450, 464, 466, 469, 496,
    510
  emotion and, *see specific emotion*,
    e.g., anxiety
  group, 372, 426-27, 445-50 (*See also*
    groups; individual, the)
  "healthy," 336, 348, 477-78, 542-
    43, 544-45 (*See also* deviance)
  human evolution and, 52-80, 83,
    139, 187, 213 (*See also* animals)
  humor as, 165-69
  inference from, in study, 28-29, 30,
    34, 46, 130-31, 189-90, 192-95,
    272-73, 362-63
  language as, 119-21, 132-33, 144,
    148-50, 164, 174-75, 286-88,
    293-95, 325-26, 360
  outside control of, 389-418, 427,
    459, 532
  self-accounts of, 41-43, 245, 276,
    328, 340, 419-20, 437, 528 (*See
    also* motivation)
  self-regulatory, 33, 40, 140, 296-97,
    312, 324-28, 333, 361, 363-64,
    367, 391-92, 393, 481 (*See also*
    morality)
  sexual, 344, 373, 379, 468-73 (*See
    also* sex)
  significant others and, 342-43, 347,
    351, 356-68, 382, 423, 432-33,
    449, 457-58 (*See also* social
    worlds)
  symbolic cues and, 84-85, 90-99,
    103, 133, 181-82, 192-95, 230-31,
    238, 284, 312-13, 320-21, 392-93,
    404-405, 407, 408, 410-11, 479-81
behaviorism, 33-35, 36-37
  Marxist materialism and, 268-69
belief, dissonance and, 99-104.
  See also commitment; conversion;
    stereotypes
Benedek, T., cited, 330, 332; quoted,
  331, 334
Benedict, Ruth, 328
Berger, Peter, cited, 41
  quoted, 89-90, 277
Bierens de Haan, J., quoted, 73-74,
  254
bilingualism, 185, 286
biological death, 557, 560, 561
  defined, 556

biological determinism, 31, 35,
    248-55, 267, 279-80, 464, 491
  Chomsky and, 294-95
  Freudian, 260, 261, 262, 329, 330,
    333, 334, 335-36, 339, 340, 345,
    468
  homosexuality and, 521-22
  need psychology and, 255-58
  of Piaget, 354
biosocial, defined, 60
birds, 192-93, 200, 469
Birdwhistle, Ray, 131
  quoted, 128, 129
bisexuality, 333, 373, 467, 524
Bittle, William E., quoted, 560
black-headed gulls, 192-93
Black Power movement, 504
blacks, 498
  "black English" of, 114, 225, 286
  civil rights of, 103, 207, 496, 504
  "in-jokes," 167-68
  IQ issue and, 224-25
  race prejudice and, 90-93, 162-63,
    165, 184, 198, 249, 298-301, 308,
    435, 452
  white sexual partners and, 91, 195,
    482, 483
Blauner, Robert, quoted, 550, 553
blindness, 180-81, 218-22, 223, 238,
    316, 499
blood, 90-91, 172
  circulation, 17
bodily movement
  aphasia and, 227, 231-32
  involuntary, 28-29, 115, 128-29,
    142, 392, 393-94, 404-405
  verbal conditioning of, 392, 393,
    408
  See also gesture
body, 85, 425, 545-47, 561
  handicaps, 499
  kinesthetic memory, 199-200
  needs of, 255-56, 266, 274-79, 339,
    515-17 (*See also specific needs*)
  pain and, 540, 543-44 (*See also*
    pain)
  psycho-sexual development and,
    330-33, 334, 335-37, 339, 343-45,
    348, 381, 467, 468, 469, 475, 476,
    484
  self-awareness and, 303-304, 314-
    16, 322, 323-24, 538, 539-40
  sexual differences and, 373, 374-
    75, 377, 378, 464, 465, 466, 467,
    468, 474-75, 480, 483
  See also brain; nervous system
brain, 86, 115, 143-44, 152
  evolution of, 53, 54, 78

brain (*cont.*)
  hypnosis and, 410-11
  injury, 226-27, 232
  language acquisition and, 294
brainwashing, 413-17, 427
Brazil, 90
breathing, 255, 405
Brown, R., cited, 190, 285, 306-307;
  quoted, 368
burglary, 500, 501, 509, 528
Burke, Kenneth, quoted, 163, 270

calendar, 8, 54
California, 551-53
Cameron, N., quoted, 237, 265, 327
Campbell, J. K., quoted, 486-87
Canada, 92, 475, 513
cancer, 12, 19, 22, 421-22, 423
career others, defined, 433-34
careers, 450-51, 452-53
  defined, 431-32
  of childhood, 312-14, 329, 434, 435
  of commitment, 433, 434-35, 456,
    457, 458-59, 476-77, 478
  deviant, 422-23, 503-505, 510-19,
    522-28, 532
  dying trajectory, 436-37, 556,
    557-58
  See also roles
Casals, Pablo, 550
Cassirer, E., quoted, 84
castration, 484, 486
  fear of, 332, 381
categorization, 93-98, 99, 103-104,
    283
  logic and, 15, 16-17, 19-20, 121,
    305, 306-307
  memory and, 200-202
  perception and, 161, 163-64,
    187-95
  racial, 90-93, 298-301
  sexual, 373-74
Catholics, 447, 490, 491, 556
causality, 12-23
  behavior and, 23, 33, 57, 253-54,
    262-63, 272-75, 277, 280, 510
  See also motivation
central nervous system, 35, 115, 392,
    407, 465
  See also nervous system
chain complexes in logic, 306-307
Chicago, Illinois, 444-45, 488, 528
child care experts, 548
  defined, 357
  sex roles and, 376-77
childhood, 66, 253, 356-68
  abstract thought and, 76, 97, 153,

childhood (*cont.*)
    187, 204, 223, 230-31, 236-37,
    283, 297-308, 367
  careers of, 312-14, 329, 434, 435
  conscience and, 328, 366-68, 419
  crime and, 510-11
  death in, 421-22
  dreams and, 155, 159, 317, 333
  drugs and, 515, 542
  egocentric thought in, 352-56,
    358-60, 366-67, 368, 382
  experience modes in, 338-39
  Freudian focus on, 263, 264, 334,
    335, 336, 337, 339, 389
  hypnosis and, 404
  language and, 40, 93, 111-12, 114,
    140-42, 144, 146-48, 153, 217-22,
    227, 238, 245, 283-307, 308, 317,
    318, 334, 339, 340, 351, 359,
    360
  memory in, 202-206, 265
  psychosexual development stages
    of, 330-33, 334, 335-37, 339-47,
    348, 374, 381, 467, 472, 475
  sexual attitudes in, 373, 374-77,
    378, 379-81, 382, 474
  stimuli interpretation in, 181, 182,
    191-92, 249-50, 251, 284, 303-304,
    315-16, 360
chimpanzees, 63-74, 77-78, 79, 126,
    165, 465, 491
  memory and, 199
  perception in, 193-95
China, 9, 33, 92, 414-17, 472, 498
  diet in, 248
  emigrants, 454
  medicine in, 545
  paper-making, 145
Chinese language, 169-70
Chomsky, Noam, 283, 294-95, 354
Christianity, 5-6, 7-8
  medicine and, 17, 490, 491, 556
  social world of, 89, 416, 447
Christian Science, 546
Churchill, Winston, 550
cities, 8, 54, 93-94, 144, 454, 519
  crime and, 510-11, 525-26, 527
Civil War, 206-207
classification, *see* categorization
clinical death, 556, 561
clitoris, 378, 467
codability, 190
coercion, 90, 327, 390, 427, 501
  in conversion, 414-17
cognitions, 99, 100. *See also* emo-
    tions; thought
cognitive dissonance, 21, 83, 99-104
  anxiety and, 258, 347

cognitive dissonance (*cont.*)
  emotional conflict and, 259, 330,
    331, 343, 457
  social control and, 326-27
coitus, 376, 377-78, 381, 465, 476, 505
  age at first, 475
  inhibition of, 480-81, 482-85,
    486-88
Coleridge, Samuel T., 174
Colombia, 442-43
color, 181, 185
  animal perception of, 119, 193-95
  skin colors, 184, 298-301, 442
"colored" (term), 298, 300
  See also blacks
commitment, 391, 395-98, 443-44,
    455, 460, 539, 558-60
  careers of, 433, 434-35, 456, 457,
    458-59, 476-77, 478
  conversion and, 413-17, 458, 459,
    510
  political, 337, 447-48
  reciprocal, 398-407, 417-18, 479,
    551-53
communes, 395, 403, 417
communication, 438-39
  channels of, 208-209, 439, 441-42,
    444-45, 450
  culture and, 76-77, 78, 79, 108,
    123-25, 208-10, 337
  insects and, 55, 56, 58, 59, 60-63
  by signs, 115-17, 142 (*See also* signs
    and signals)
  of subjective reality, 88, 338-39
  by symbols, 30-31, 73, 74, 89-90,
    95, 346 (*See also* symbols)
  See also art; language; speech
Communist Manifesto, 163
competition, 331, 334
componential analysis, 172-73
concept, defined, 94-95
  See also categorization; thought
conditioning, 37, 39, 115-17, 121-22,
    245
  human reflexes and, 392, 393, 408
  hypnosis as, 407-408
confidence men, 509, 511-12
conflict, *see* cognitive dissonance
congruity theory, 100-101
conscience, 76, 99, 314, 327-28,
    498
  defined, 33
  relativism and, 366, 367
  See also morality
consciousness, 33, 34
  of automatic functions, 231-32, 325
  dreams and, 158-61
  Freudian view of, 261, 262

consciousness (*cont.*)
  of self, 30, 83, 85-87, 315-24, 325,
    329
  sensorimotor, 303-304
  stream of, 155-56, 210
  symbols in extension of, 84-85,
    119, 153
  See also emotion; perception;
    thought
conspiracies, 398, 399, 400-401, 402
contraception, 489, 490, 491
conversation, 120, 133, 142-44, 402
  aphasia and, 229, 234-35
  in childhood, 141, 146-47, 285,
    296-97, 320, 354-55
  daydreams of, 156, 157
  memory and, 201-202
  metaphor and, 162
  modes of discourse, 173-75
  polite, 125-26, 415, 420
  preliterate cultures and, 144, 145,
    146
  in schizophrenia, 235-36, 237
  self-regulatory internal, 296-97,
    326, 361
  sexual, 475, 486, 488
  social worlds and, 438-39, 441
  trauma recovery and, 422, 423
conversion, 413-17, 427, 458, 459
  crime recruitment, 510-12, 518
Cooley, Charles H., 30, 295, 318, 329,
    348, 356
  quoted, 108, 319, 322
cooperation, 360-61, 367, 368, 372
  in careers, 432, 433-34
  of chimpanzees, 64-65, 66, 68-69,
    77
  commitment and, 395, 403
  in hypnosis, 403-404, 406-407,
    409-10
  language as, 120
  in medical care, 411-13
  in self-mortification, 399
Copernicus, 7
coping mechanisms, 418-27
  in pain, 543
Corey, D. W., quoted, 521
Cottrell, L., quoted, 346, 347
creativity, 149-52, 156, 229
crime, 25, 273, 394, 506-12, 521
  coercion into, 501
  criteria of, 490, 495, 496, 497,
    500-501, 512, 513, 518, 529
  Freudian studies of, 264
  hypnosis and, 405-406
  lone criminals and, 530-32
  neutralization technique and, 422-
    23, 503

crime (*cont.*)
  organizations and, 504, 505-506, 507, 508-509, 511, 513, 525-26, 530-31
  planning of, 212-13, 326
  political, 507, 509, 524-28
  sexual, 473, 485
  social status and, 401, 498, 499, 506, 507, 509, 510, 531-32
  See also deviance; prison
Croker, Richard, quoted, 527
culture, 4, 89, 345-46, 420
  defined, 76-77
  art and, 151
  biologic evolution and, 53-54, 78, 80, 83
  childhood status and, 313-14, 339
  conscience and, 327-28, 367
  death and, 538, 558-60
  eccentricity and, 529, 530
  free will and, 393, 394
  Freudian view of, 261, 262-63
  gesture codes and, 123-25, 128-29, 130-32
  humor and, 166
  language and, 41, 76-77, 78, 79, 85, 109-15, 121, 132-33, 140, 169-73, 174-75, 187-92, 224-25, 288-89
  memory and, 197, 209
  perceptions of order in, 42-43, 87-88, 247, 292, 346, 372-73, 402, 456
  perception selectivity in, 182-83, 184-85, 186, 195-96, 371
  writing and, 9, 144-46
  See also social worlds
Cumming, Elaine, quoted, 548-49
cuttlefish, 192

Daley, Richard, 528
Darwin, Charles, 185, 251, 372
daydreaming, 153-57, 161, 175
  sexual, 474, 475, 479-80, 481-82, 483
deafness, 132, 217-22, 223, 227, 238, 499
death, 402, 444, 538-39, 553-60, 561
  abortion debate and, 489-91
  in childhood, 421-22
  disengagement for, 548-50
  instinct concept, 260, 263
  pain and, 545
  self-imposed, 324, 390, 412, 415, 417, 453, 520
  trajectories, 413, 436-37, 556, 557-58
defense mechanisms (coping mecha-

defense mechanisms (*cont.*)
  nisms), 418-27. *See also specific mechanisms*, e.g., repression
definitional process, 19-20
degradation, 390, 398, 399, 401, 402-403, 427
  in brainwashing, 414-16, 417
  imprisonment as, 531
  self-debasement, 426
de Laguna, G. M., quoted, 290
Denmark, 547
Descartes, Réné, 6
detachment, 423-24, 485, 520
  See also isolation
determinism, *see* biological determinism
deviance, 47, 48, 279, 390, 394, 495-532
  classification and, 92, 495, 496-503, 532
  coping devices, 422-23
  dissonance and, 99, 100, 103
  linguistic, 111-12
  punishments of, 399-403, 423, 495, 498, 499-500, 509, 510, 511, 512, 513, 514, 516, 518-19, 527, 531-32
  sexual, 466-67, 468-72, 491-92, 495, 496, 500, 519-24
Dewey, John, 30, 164, 182
  cited, 9, 153, 181, 195
  quoted, 13, 150, 211-12
diabetes, 512
disease, *see* illness; *and see specific diseases*
disengagement theory, 548-50, 552
displacement (scapegoating), 401, 420, 530
Disraeli, Benjamin, 166
dissociation, 346, 419
dissonance theory, *see* cognitive dissonance
divorce, 477, 496, 499, 503
dogs, 121-22, 126, 144
  memory and, 199, 200
dolphin, 78
dreams, 154-61, 165, 317, 333, 419
  See also daydreaming
drives, *see* instinct
drugs, 390, 495, 496, 507, 540, 542
  addiction experience, 251, 256, 433, 476-77, 478, 500, 503, 512-13, 514-18, 528, 532
  attitudes toward, 251, 497, 500, 501-503, 504, 512, 513, 515, 518-19
dualism, 35, 40, 392
Durkheim, E., cited, 394-95, 453; quoted, 559

eccentricity, 528-30
  See also deviance
economics, 247, 267-69, 280
  crime and, 508-509, 531
  wealth standards, 446
education, *see* learning
ego, 331, 332, 333
  See also self, the
egocentrism, 352-56
  decline of, 358-60, 366-67, 368, 369, 371-72, 382
  of speech, 286-87
Egypt, 54, 145
Einstein, Albert, 23; quoted, 28
Ekman, Paul, quoted, 129, 130, 131, 132
Electra complex, 332
elimination, 252, 255, 331
  retentiveness, 332, 333
embarrassment, 390, 398, 399-401, 403, 417, 427
  coping devices and, 420-21, 424-25
embalming, 557
embezzlers, 499, 501, 531
emblematic gesture, 130-32
embracement, 396-98
emergence, *see* planning
emotion, 179, 219-21, 252, 328, 334
  in brainwashing, 415, 416
  chimpanzee expressions of, 63-64, 66, 68, 73, 74
  conflicting, 259, 330, 331, 343, 457
  coping devices and, 422
  dreams and, 154, 158, 165, 343, 419
  expressive language and, 125-26, 128, 142, 285, 559
  gesture patterns and, 123-25, 128, 130
  memory and, 198
  pain expression, 542-45
  in paranoia, 401-402
  racial stereotypes and, 92 (*See also* race)
  self-awareness and, 319-20, 322, 324, 329, 334
  in sexual repression, 332-33
  See also specific emotions
energy, psychoanalytic concept of, 259, 260, 261-62, 263, 264
England, 92, 124, 475, 512, 558
  humor in, 166
  Swazi visitors in, 197
English language, 111, 112, 113, 294
  "black," 114, 225, 286
  Chinese translation, 169-70
  colonialism and, 115
  Navaho compared, 171
environment, *see* experience; reality

Erikson, Erik H., 329, 335-37, 348
Erikson, Kai, quoted, 497
erotogenic zones, 330-33, 336
Ervin, S., quoted, 185
Eskimos, 113, 122-24, 190, 560
ethnography, 172-73, 552
ethnicity, *see* race
ethnomethodology, 40-46, 277
evolution, 52-80, 139
    language and, 40, 83, 139, 140, 187
    sex and, 465
    writing and, 144-46, 294-95
exchange theory, 32, 36-39, 258
exogamy, 482
experience, 25-26, 40, 41, 42, 47, 440
    classification of, 90-98, 103-104,
      163-64, 187-92, 291-93, 338
    collective memory, 206-10, 213
    conceptualizations of, 4-5, 32,
      83-104, 108, 150, 155, 172,
      206-10, 289, 292, 298, 329, 441
    consensus denied, 399-403, 444-
      45, 449 (*See also* deviance)
    dreams and, 158-59, 482
    logic and, 304, 354
    modes of, 338-39, 344, 346, 480
    objectivity and, 29-30, 368-73
    reconstruction-memory and, 265-
      66
    self and, 295, 325, 334, 338, 340-42,
      346, 354, 418, 419-20, 421, 538-39
    sensory, 116, 117-19, 178-79, 180-
      81, 221-22, 303-304, 368, 538, 539-
      40, 543-45
    sexual, 465, 473, 474-79, 480, 482,
      485
experimental methods, 7, 75-76
    on bee instincts, 254
    chimpanzee subjects, 64, 65-66,
      67, 68, 69-74
    developmental stages and, 345,
      348
    human subjects and, 26, 27, 32, 48,
      217-18, 393-94, 405-406
expressive (ritual) speech, 125-26,
    128
Eysenck, Hans J., cited, 404, 406,
    409-10

facial expressions, 128-29, 130, 142,
    295, 543
family, the, 108, 313, 329, 374, 438
    adolescence and, 333, 344, 373
    aging and, 253, 548, 549-50
    aphasia and, 229
    behavior codes and, 189-90, 321,
      328, 360, 361, 363-64, 366, 367,
      368, 423, 478

family, the (*cont.*)
    careers and, 434, 457-58
    conversion and, 413, 414, 415
    death and, 402, 413, 421-22, 444,
      545, 555, 556, 557-58, 559-60
    interrelationships in, 304, 318,
      340-41, 342, 347, 352, 356, 357,
      358, 363, 381, 419, 452, 479
    language learning and, 284,
      285-86, 288, 289-90, 291, 295,
      318, 320, 340, 351, 378
    mental retardation and, 219
    political ideology and, 442
    psychoanalysis and, 263, 335
    racial attitudes and, 299, 300, 301
    See also father-relationships; moth-
      ering
fantasy, *see* daydreaming; dreams;
    imagination
Faris, R., cited, 159; quoted, 156,
    265
father relationships, 332, 333, 340-41,
    364, 381
    homosexuality and, 528
feedback process, defined, 212
Ferguson, Charles A., quoted, 288
Festinger, Leon, cited, 99, 100, 101,
    102, 447; quoted, 258
fetishism, 468, 492, 500
field theory, of behavior, 36
Finland, 547
Ford, Henry, 168
form
    aphasia and, 232, 233
    perception of, 181, 187-88, 193
Fortune Magazine, quoted, 256
France, 92, 130, 441, 453
    children in, 313
French, Thomas, quoted, 159
French language, 111
fraud, 506, 528
Freuchen, Peter, quoted, 560
Freud, Sigmund, 149, 160, 161, 258,
    321, 329, 408; quoted, 158,
    159
    on development, 329, 330-35, 337,
      339, 340, 345, 348, 381, 389, 468,
      472, 474, 528
    motivation theories of, 258-66,
      267, 268, 269, 280, 496
friendship, 356, 423
    aging and, 550-53
    career flow of, 431, 433, 434, 512
    choice of, 397-98, 420, 441, 443,
      507-508, 521, 522
    conversion and, 413, 414, 510
    preadolescent, 342-43, 344
    privacy and, 424, 427

frigidity, 483-85
Frisch, K. von, 61-63

Gagnon, John, cited, 476; quoted,
    475
Galileo Galilei, 5-6, 21, 22
gambling, 506, 507, 509, 518
games, 351, 361, 438, 439
Gandhi, Mahatma, 264, 336
gangs, 343, 423, 503
Garfinkel, Harold, cited, 41-42, 45,
    401; quoted, 42-43, 44
Gaulle, Charles de, 441, 550
Gedye, G. E., quoted, 453
generalization
    abstract thought and, 95-98, 163,
      236
    science and, 14-16, 19-20, 46
generalized other, 173-74, 320, 322,
    351, 360-64, 366-68, 372-73
    defined, 361
    See also groups; society
genital phase, 331-32, 333, 336, 343,
    472
geocentrism, 371
German Democratic Republic, 547
German language, 111, 171
German people, 92, 475, 498
gestural markers, 129-32
gesture, 123-25, 126-32, 142, 197, 266
    children and, 129, 284-86, 295
    humor and, 165
    of insects, 60
    in pain, 543-44
    sexual, 474
    See also bodily movement
Gibson, J., quoted, 181, 187, 188-89
Gladstone, W. E., 166
Goffman, Erving, cited, 45, 132, 396,
    399, 436, 498; quoted, 402, 432
Goldstein, Kurt, cited, 228, 229, 230,
    236, 304, 392
Gorer, Geoffrey, quoted, 558-59
graft, 525-26
grammar, 285, 289, 340, 368
    innate language ability and,
      293-95
    pronouns, 318, 320, 322, 323, 355,
      356
Greece, 413, 486-87, 488
Greece, ancient, 208
    alphabet and, 144, 146
    dualism and, 35
    science and, 6, 7-8, 9, 17, 21, 35, 54
Gross, Edward, quoted, 399
groups, 4, 36, 47
    behavior levels in, 52, 55, 56,
      77-78, 80, 121-23, 213, 498-99

groups (*cont.*)
  career flow in, 431
  cognitive dissonance and, 103
  commitment to, 337, 391, 395-98, 447-48, 455, 456, 550-53, 560
  conversion forms, 413-17, 510-12
  deviant, 501, 504-505, 506-28, 529
  embarrassment response in, 399-401
  exclusion form, 401-403, 417, 548, 549
  intergroup attitudes, 90-93, 103, 112, 113, 150, 198, 289, 298-301, 366-67, 371-73, 435, 442-43, 497-98
  language and reality constructs, 85, 89, 108, 113-15, 117, 132-33, 163-64, 187, 217, 284, 292, 351
  memory and, 197-98, 201-202, 206-10
  motivation and, 247-48, 262-63, 267-69, 270-71, 273-74, 275-77, 278-79, 280, 337
  peer, 342 (*See also* peers)
  perceptual discriminations of, 184-85, 187-92, 197, 540
  primary, 108 (*See also* family, the)
  reference groups, 445-50, 453-54, 460
  See also culture; social worlds
Guatemala, 530
guilt, 327-28, 336, 401
  conversion and, 414, 415, 416
  drugs and, 516
  embarrassment and, 400
  neutralization, 422-23, 503, 509, 524, 531, 532
  sex and, 332, 473, 483, 485, 486, 489, 520-21, 523
Gutenberg, Johann, 145
Guze, H., quoted, 408

Hall, C., quoted, 159-60
Hammurabi Code, 54
hands, 53, 124
Hart, Moss, quoted, 457-58
Harvey, William, 6
Hayes, William, quoted, 151
Head, Henry, cited, 226, 227-28, 229-30, 232, 392
hearing, 182, 186, 226
  chimpanzee, 193
  hypnosis and, 404, 406
  lack or loss of, 132, 217-22, 223, 227, 238, 499
  memory and, 200
Hebrew, 114
hedonism, 246

Henry, William E., quoted, 548-49
herbalists, 545
heredity, 254, 268, 465
  of language ability, 294, 295
heroin, 500, 516
Hiller, E. T., quoted, 124, 125
Hindemith, Paul, cited, 151
Hindus, 92
Hippocrates, 9, 17, 275
history, 26-28, 48, 164, 267
  causation and, 272
  dreams and, 156
  individual careers and, 29, 431-37, 501
  language and, 75, 172, 200, 213
  oral tradition and, 144, 146
  reinterpretations of, 5, 206-10, 263, 271, 276, 277, 501
Hitler, Adolf, 274
Hothschild, Arlie R., quoted, 551-53
Hockett, Charles F., 74
  cited, 121
Homans, George, 37-38, 258
  quoted, 36
homeostasis, 260
homosexuality, 25, 466-67, 468, 473, 492, 528, 532
  attitudes toward, 422, 495, 497, 499, 503, 519-21, 522
  "closet," 504, 505, 521, 522-23, 524
  heterosexual behavior combined with, 333, 344, 373, 467, 483, 524
  masturbation and, 481, 482
  rights movement, 469-70, 496, 504
Hong Kong, 454, 512
Honigmann, J. J., quoted, 328
hormones, 465, 466, 467, 469, 485, 491, 492
Horowitz, Irving L., quoted 527-28
hospitals, 411-13, 427
  abortion and, 490
  death and, 413, 554-55, 556
  mental, 390, 433, 435, 436, 456, 499
  pain and, 423, 542-43, 544-45
Hudgins, C. V., cited, 392, 393, 394
Hughes, Everett, cited, 209, 432; quoted, 443
Hull, Clark L., quoted, 392-93, 408
humor, 139-40, 165-69, 175, 483, 488
  coercion and, 416, 417
  detachment and, 423, 424
  metaphor and, 162
  status and, 420-21
humors, theory of, 17
hunger, 247
  hypnosis and, 404-405
  as motive, 248-51, 255, 257, 259, 274-75, 279-80

hypnosis, 179, 390, 391, 392-93, 397, 403-407, 417
  theories of, 407-11, 427
hypochondriasis, 180

id, the, *see* unconscious, the
identification
  as deviant, 503-505
  with persecutors, 420
  See also self, the
identity crises, 336-37, 348
ideology
  political deviance and, 390, 413-17, 525, 527, 528
  social worlds and, 267-69, 440-45, 508, 520-22, 542
idiographic study methods, 262
ideographs, 170
illness, 530, 539-47, 552
  death and, 538, 555-56, 557, 561
  hypochondriac, 180
  See also specific diseases
illustrators, 130-32
imagery, 161-64
  in aphasia, 228, 230, 232
  daydream, 153, 154-55, 156-57
  dream, 157-61
  erotic, 479-82, 483-85, 492
  experience and, 221-22, 296
  of self, 314, 323, 418, 432, 434, 435, 437, 473-74, 550
  of social mobility, 164-65
  See also symbols
imagination, 34, 153, 305
  hypnosis and, 406-407
  planning and, 211, 230, 232
  of roles and viewpoints, 352-56, 359-60, 361, 362-63, 366-67, 368-73, 382, 434
  self-awareness and, 156-57, 318-20, 321, 322-23, 329
  sex and, 465, 470, 472, 473, 475, 476, 479-82, 483-85, 492
  symbols and, 76, 149, 173-74, 228-29, 237, 296 (*See also* imagery)
imitation, 360, 361
  in hypnosis, 406-407, 409-10
  verbal, 318, 320
  See also learning; roles
impotence (sexual), 465, 473, 483-85, 488, 516
imprinting, 478
incest, 482-83
India, 373, 482, 510
Indians (native Americans), 335
  history, 206
  See also specific groups

individual, the, 4, 15, 80, 286
  cognitive dissonance responses of, 99, 100-101, 102, 103, 326-27
  criminal isolates, 530-32
  drugs and, 515
  dying trajectory of, 556, 557-58
  eccentric, 528-30
  ethnomethodology and, 41, 43, 44, 45, 46, 277
  group commitment of, 395-98, 403, 550-51
  history and, 209-10, 213, 263, 267-68, 431-37
  identity crises of, 336-37, 348
  inferential processes in study of, 28-30, 32, 266, 272, 276, 542-43
  interaction and, 32, 230, 312-14, 338, 339 (See also society)
  loss of control in, 390, 391, 392-93, 394, 398-407, 408, 409, 410, 411-18, 454-56
  moral careers of, 431-37, 499, 501, 503-505, 510-12
  planning ability of, 210, 211
  social institutions and, 59, 262-63, 267-69, 275-77, 278, 279, 280, 287-88, 364, 365-66, 389, 391, 394-95, 424, 427, 431, 432, 435, 436, 504, 505-28
  social order concepts of, 42-43, 45, 87-88, 89-90, 173-75, 247-48, 284, 292, 320, 321, 322, 324-28, 346, 361, 370-71, 372-73, 394, 544-45
  statistical methods of study, 23, 47
  stimuli perception of, 181, 182, 183-84, 292-93 (See also perception)
  See also self, the
industrialization, 454, 455, 528
  aging and, 548, 549, 550
  medicine and, 546
infancy, 330-31, 339, 348, 389
  See also childhood
inhibition, 211, 296-97, 411
  sexual, 261, 480, 482-85, 486-88, 492
insanity, 495, 496, 504
  See also psychoses
insects, 55, 69, 79
  See also specific insects
instinct (drive), 33, 247, 251-55
  Freudian theory of, 259-62, 263, 264, 266, 280, 330-33, 334, 339, 340, 345, 348, 408
  need psychology and, 38, 255-58, 273, 479
insulin, 512
intelligence, 334

intelligence (cont.)
  defined, 213
  aphasia and, 234
  crime and, 511
  hypnosis and, 404
  isolation and, 217-25
  tests, 218-19, 223, 224-25
interaction, 32, 230, 312-14, 338, 339
  See also behavior; culture; social worlds; society
interviews, 24, 27, 32, 48
  psychoanalytic, 261, 262, 266
  rationalization and, 276-77
  triangulation and, 28-29, 30
inversion, 492, 520
  defined, 466, 467
Irish, the, 498
isolation, 217-22, 238, 295, 313, 315
  aging and, 548-50, 551
  aphasia and, 232
  chimpanzees and, 63-64, 68, 77
  as coping device, 418, 543
  crime and, 530-32
  homosexuals and, 523
  of prisoners, 223, 390, 394
  schizophrenia and, 235-37
  social alienation and, 456
  socioeconomic, 224-25, 499
Israel, 208-209
Italians, in America, 435, 498
Ittelson, W., quoted, 182

James, William, 30
  quoted, 210
Japan, 131, 197, 454, 498, 512
  shame-fearing culture of, 328
  suicide in, 252
Jericho, 54
Jews, 92, 114, 435, 447, 498
  in Nazi territories, 453
Johnson, E., cited, 480, 481, 484, 485; quoted, 488

Kanter, Rosabeth, quoted, 395, 396
Kazin, Alfred, quoted, 112
Keller, Helen, 218, 219-22
Kennedy, John F., 550
kinesics, defined, 128
  See also bodily movement; gesture
Kinsey, A. C., 468
  cited, 378, 481-82, 484, 522
Kiowa Apache, 560
Kirkman, Frederick B., 192-93
Klapp, Orrin E., quoted, 420-21
Klineberg, O., cited, 252; quoted, 113
Kluckhohn, C., quoted, 190, 323
Koch, Robert, 10

Kohlberg, Lawrence, quoted, 367-68
Kohler, Wolfgang, cited, 64-68; quoted, 69-70, 75
Korean War, 414
Kuhn, Manford H., cited, 313, 358, 364-65; quoted, 449
Kuhn, Thomas, quoted, 4-5, 16

labor, see work
Labov, William, 286; quoted, 225
Langer, S. K., quoted, 157, 162, 266
language
  animal signals compared, 39-40, 58, 60-61, 63, 70-78, 79, 83, 119, 121-22, 199-200
  brain function in, 24, 28, 53, 178-79, 187, 294
  "death" definitions, 555
  gesture and, 123-25, 126-32, 165, 284-85, 543-44
  group identity and, 107-15, 132, 245, 284, 298-301, 413, 414, 417, 439, 507, 509, 513, 514
  hypnosis and, 403-404, 408, 410-11
  lack or loss of, 217-38, 394
  learning, 111-12, 114-15, 121, 139-75, 178-79, 217-38, 283-308, 318, 340, 351
  listening and, 120, 142-44 (See also conversation)
  metaphoric, 161-64 (See also imagery; symbols)
  nature of, 34, 115-23, 140, 148-54, 294-95 (See also thought)
  reality and, 40, 43, 45, 83, 84-85, 89-90, 93-98, 99, 103-104, 163, 169-73, 180, 187-92, 269-72, 289, 317
  record-keeping and, 8, 9, 26-27, 73, 75, 144-46
  scientific, 19, 22, 30, 112
  self-account styles, 42-43, 269-72, 340
  self-awareness and, 83, 317, 318, 320, 321, 322, 323-24, 334, 389, 538, 540
  self-direction and, 392-93, 394
  sexual vocabularies, 378, 379, 380, 480, 489, 521
  See also speech
Lashley, K. S., cited, 274; quoted, 24
latency period, 332-33, 335, 336
Latin America, 442
laughter, 66, 165
law, the, 54, 59, 79, 270, 276
  court testimony, 200-201
  crime links with, 507-508, 509
  drugs and, 501-503, 512, 518-19

law, the (*cont.*)
 language of, 112
 politics and, 524-28
 sex and, 469, 470, 489-91, 519
 social control and, 327, 423, 505, 507, 518, 532
learning, 19
 abstract, in children, 97, 153, 297-308, 369
 in ants, 59-60
 in aphasia, 230-31, 234
 career flow, 431, 433, 434, 435-36, 437
 in chimpanzees, 64, 65-66, 67, 68, 69-74, 75, 77, 193, 194, 465
 conditioned control of reflexes, 393
 of coping devices, 419-20
 crime skills, 510-12, 531
 drug addiction, 516-17
 gesture codes, 132, 285, 295
 language, 111-12, 114-15, 121, 139-75, 178-79, 217-38, 283-308, 318, 340, 351
 to memorize, 202-203
 morals, 366-68, 510
 need perception and response, 248-51, 254-56, 266, 274, 276-77
 relativistic thought, 358-59, 362-63
 of the self, 204-206, 218-22, 263, 284, 286, 287-88, 298-301, 315-20, 329, 334, 346, 347, 418
 of self-control, 296-97, 312, 324-28, 331
 sex roles, 374-77, 379, 381, 382, 465-66, 467, 468, 476, 477-78, 480-81, 484-85, 487, 491, 492
 signals, 115-17
 of social worlds, 93-94, 191-92, 223-25, 249-50, 263, 277, 278, 280, 284, 292, 295, 298, 340-41, 344-45, 351-82, 413-17
 stimuli interpretation, 180-81, 182, 188-89, 191-92, 193-95, 284, 539, 544
Lee, D., quoted, 98
Leeuwenhoek, Antony van, 10
leisure, *see* play
Lewis, M. M., quoted, 114, 290
libido, 330-33, 380
 defined, 260, 263
limited inquiry principle, 23-24
Lippmann, Walter, quoted, 91
listening, 120, 142-44
Lister, Joseph, 10
literacy, 144-46
 aphasia and, 226, 234
literature, 6, 26-28, 29, 76, 79, 144-46
 on dreams, 157-58

literature (*cont.*)
 foreign, 39
 on instinct, 252
 sex and, 379, 522
logic, 6, 7, 9, 121, 146, 164
 causality and, 15-16
 cognitive dissonance and, 102
 development of, 304-308, 338, 352-53, 354, 358-59, 369, 382
 dreams and, 158, 161, 480
 social criteria of, 174
 statistical probability and, 22-23
 theory testing by, 21, 32
 See also reason
"looking-glass self," 318-20
Lorimer, F., quoted, 296
Los Angeles, Calif., 524
love, 247, 296, 474, 492
 adulthood and, 339, 472
 experience of, 476-79
 maternal, 253, 330-31, 340, 345, 482
Luckmann, Thomas, quoted, 89-90, 277
Luria, A. R., 268
 cited, 39, 191, 392, 393
 quoted, 40, 119, 152-53, 202-204, 233, 410

McDougall, William, 258
 cited, 252
machismo, 377
McNeill, D., quoted, 293-94
malaria, 3, 9-16, 21, 22, 24
 yellow fever and, 17-18
Malayans, 413
Mao Tse-tung, 415
Marceau, Marcel, 130
Margenau, Henry, quoted, 13
marijuana, 502-503, 516
Markey, James F., cited, 355; quoted, 352
marriage, 417
 career flow, 431, 433, 434, 435, 436, 476-77, 478
 homosexual, 523
 sex roles and, 468-69, 470, 474, 483, 484, 485, 486, 488
 society and, 478-79, 482, 499, 503, 509
Marx, Karl, 268
Marxism, 267-69, 280
masochism, 468
mass media, 357-58, 397-98, 427
 drugs and, 518, 519
 history and, 206, 277
 ideology and, 441-42, 454
 political corruption and, 525-26
 sexual codes and, 379

mass media (*cont.*)
 stereotypes and, 91-92
mastectomy, 423
Masters, W., cited, 480, 481, 484, 485; quoted, 488
masturbation, 332, 344, 377, 473, 481-82, 492
 in childhood, 380
mathematics, 46, 79
 acalculia, 226, 231
 animal "counting," 75-76
 language and, 8, 9, 22, 54, 121, 144, 146, 147-48, 149, 150, 191, 297
 money and, 301-303, 306
 quantitative counting, 202-203
Maxim, Hiram, 61
Mead, George Herbert, 30, 38, 39, 40, 44, 47, 346, 348, 356
 cited, 4, 35, 46, 316-17, 320, 329, 359, 370
 quoted, 84, 210, 322, 326, 360-61
meaning
 behavioral sense of, 98-99, 213, 283, 284, 346, 373
 cultural convention and, 120-32, 290, 292-93, 294, 456, 457
 of death, 539, 555, 560
 dreams and, 157, 158-61, 165
 formulation of, 143, 219-22, 289, 292, 539
 humor and, 168-69
 memory and, 198
 metaphor and, 162, 163, 169
 perception and, 142, 181, 182, 183-84, 187-89, 191-92, 193-95, 325, 540-41
 sexual words and acts, 126-27, 376, 377-78, 488-89, 492
medicine, 411-13, 421-22, 444, 545-47
 abortion and, 490, 491
 careers in, 434, 435-36
 death and, 413, 554-57
 drugs and, 512, 513, 515, 518
 illness roles and, 541-43, 544-45
 malaria control and, 3, 9-16, 17, 18, 21, 22, 24
 privacy and, 425
 "sex change" surgery, 470
 subcommunities, 440
 surgical trauma and, 423
Melanesia, 195
memory, 139, 153, 178, 179, 196-210, 234, 393
 of the dead, 553-54
 dreams and, 156, 158-59, 160, 161
 hypnosis and, 405, 406, 409, 411
 oral tradition and, 144, 145
 planning and, 210, 211

memory (*cont.*)
  perception and, 194, 196-97, 213
  reconstructive, 265-66, 271
  self-awareness and, 325, 416-17
mental hospitals, 390, 433, 435, 436, 456, 499
mentally retarded, 116, 218-19, 222-25, 295, 499
  hypnosis and, 404
Merrill Court community, 551-53
metaphor, 161-64
  See also imagery; symbols
Mexicans, 184
microbes, 84-85
microscopy, 10, 14
migration, 453-54
Mills, C. W., quoted, 46, 164, 246, 272, 275, 276, 527-28
mime, 130-31
misidentifications, 400
Mississippi River, 185, 197
money, 446
  aging and, 552
  children and, 204, 301-303, 306, 308, 362-63
  chimpanzees and, 66
Montreal, Canada, 522, 523
morale, 278-79
morality, 76, 79, 99, 284, 481
  careers, 422-23, 437, 503-505, 510
  degradation status, 401, 473
  drug addiction and, 516, 518
  generalized other and, 173-74, 320, 322, 329, 361, 363-64, 366-68, 485
  hypnosis and, 405-406
  instincts and, 252, 253, 332, 333, 339, 345
  perception and, 189-90, 378-79, 477-78, 486-91, 496-501
  self-control and, 296-97, 320, 321, 325-28, 332, 333, 396
Morgan's Canon, 56-58
morphine, 516
Morse code, 222
mosquitoes, 61
  malaria and, 9-16, 21, 24
  yellow fever and, 17-18
mothering, 289, 290, 364, 419, 482
  deprivation of, 77, 253, 313
  drug addiction and, 515
  homosexuality and, 528
  "instinctive," 252-53
  psychosexual development and, 330-31, 333, 338, 340, 345
motion, *see* bodily movement
motivation, 4, 245-80, 325
  anxiety as, 258, 260, 338, 340, 342, 347, 418, 419-21, 423

motivation (*cont.*)
  cognitive dissonance as, 100-101, 102
  daydreams and, 154-55, 156-57
  dreams, 158, 159-60, 161
  group commitment and, 337, 396, 413-17
  memory and, 197-98, 206-10, 263, 265-66, 271
  observation and, 28, 29, 272-73
  of perception, 181-83, 184, 187-88
  rewards as, 36-39, 258, 339
  self-knowledge and, 24, 25, 245, 246, 247-48, 259, 261, 264, 265, 266, 267, 269-73, 276-77, 320, 324, 503
motor aphasia, 227
mourning, 558-60, 561
murder, 264, 500, 506, 528, 530
Murngin people, 189-90
Murphy, G., cited, 198, 372; quoted, 366, 367
Murray, H. A., 258
  quoted, 323
music, 150, 151, 200
  perception of, 186, 226
  social worlds of, 433, 444
mutism, 218, 227
mysticism, 174, 175

Nabokov, Vladimir, 469
naming, 121
  identity and, 305, 317, 318, 320, 371, 400, 479
  memory and, 202
  perception and, 180, 187-89, 192, 289, 292-93, 538, 540
  privacy and, 425-26
narcissism, in infancy, 330
nationalism, 208-209
natural signs, 117-19
  See also sensation; signs and signaling
Navaho language, 170-71, 185
Nazis, 453
need psychology, 255-58, 280, 339, 343, 479
"Negro" (term), 298, 300, 301
  See also blacks
nervous system, 35, 39, 40, 88, 143
  autonomic, 115, 392, 407
  gesture and, 129
  hypnosis and, 392-93, 403-407, 410-11
  language learning and, 178-79
  sex and, 465, 481
Newcomb, Theodore, 372, 447
  quoted, 258, 315, 366, 367

New Guinea, 131, 185
Newton, Sir Isaac, 6, 20
New York City, 525-26, 527
New Zealand, 124-25
Ngulu people, 488
Niam-Niam people, 124
Nigeria, 124
Nixon, Richard, 166
nomothetic study methods, 262
Norwegians, 92, 475
number systems, 144

observation (scientific method), 5, 7, 10, 14, 22-23, 24-25, 28, 173
  ethnomethodological mode of, 42
  self-reflexive, 85-87, 88
  See also interviews; statistics
occupations, *see* work
Oedipal phase, 331-32, 333, 335, 340, 381
opiate drugs, 251, 515, 516-17
Opler, Morris E., quoted, 560
oral phase, 330, 332, 333, 336
oral tradition, 144, 145, 146
orientational other, defined, 449
ornamentation, chimpanzee, 65
oxygen deprivation, 255-56, 266, 274

pain, 538, 539-45
  cardiac, 412
  reflex inhibition, 392, 405, 407, 409
  sado-masochism and, 468
Palaung people, 124
paranoia, 391, 398, 399, 401-403, 417, 495
parataxic experience, 338, 480
Park, Robert, 30
Parsons, Talcott, 36
  cited, 337
Parten, M. B., quoted, 353
participant observation study technique, 25, 30, 32, 173
  ethnomethodology and, 42
  triangulation and, 29
Pasteur, Louis, 10
patriarchy, 381
Pavlov, Ivan P., 118, 152-53, 178, 268, 410
  quoted, 39-40, 408
Pawnee Indians, 190
peers, 342-43, 356-57, 360, 364
  aging and, 550-51
  morality and, 367, 368, 423, 477-78, 503
  See also friendship
Peirce, Charles, 30
penis envy, 332, 381

perception, 116, 178, 179-96
  agnosia, 226
  of drug withdrawal, 515-17, 540
  egocentric, 352-56, 368, 369, 371,
    382
  humor and, 165-66
  hypnosis and, 404-407, 409-10
  language and, 113-15, 119, 139,
    153, 161, 162, 163-64, 169-73,
    187-92, 289, 292-93, 538
  moral, 189-90, 496-501
  planning and, 181-82, 210, 211,
    212-13, 392, 405
  selectivity of, 92, 95-96, 150, 155,
    174, 180, 182-83, 194-95, 206,
    211, 265, 338, 346, 371, 398, 418,
    419, 441-42, 539
  the self and, 182, 211, 303-304,
    314-16, 323-24, 325, 445, 446,
    459, 539-40
  social class and, 307-308, 442-43
  social definition of, 539-41, 542-43,
    544
  See also sensation
personality, see self, the
phallic phase, 331-32, 333, 335, 472
phenomenology, 40, 45
Philadelphia, Pennsylvania, 17-18
Philippines, 173, 545-46
Phoenicians, 144
Piaget, Jean, 205, 283, 294, 304, 341
  quoted, 263, 303, 306, 316, 317,
    359-60
  on egocentrism, 230, 288, 352-56,
    358, 359-60, 366-67, 369
  Vygotsky and, 287-88, 306, 353-54
Picasso, Pablo, 195-96, 550
planning, 178, 179, 270, 424
  aphasia and, 226, 229, 230, 232
  in dreams, 156, 159
  of exclusion, 398, 399, 400-401,
    402-403
  perception and, 181-82, 210, 211,
    212-13, 392, 405
  preinterpretative, 270, 271-72
Plato, 54
play, 351, 353, 359-60, 361
  careers of leisure, 431, 434, 438,
    439, 450-51, 452
  friendship and, 342-43
  retirement and, 548, 551
Plunkitt, George W., quoted, 525
poetry, 169, 174
Poincaré, Henri, cited, 87-88
politics, 32-33, 54, 79
  analogical thinking and, 162-63
  behavior codes as, 496, 497,
    498-99, 502-503, 518-19

politics (cont.)
  career flow in, 431, 434
  crime in, 505, 507, 509, 524-28, 531,
    532
  humor and, 166, 417
  intelligence testing and, 224-25
  language and, 114-15, 125, 164
  memory and, 198, 208-10
  motivation and, 247, 267-69,
    278-79, 337, 390, 397-98, 413-17
  radical, 92, 278, 398, 491, 495, 503
  social worlds of, 440, 441-42,
    447-48, 452
  writing and, 144, 145
polyandry, 373
"polymorphous perverse," 468-73
porpoise, 78
Portuguese language, 115
posture, evolution of, 53
preadolescence epoch, 339, 342-43
Premack, David and Ann, 70-71, 72
press, the, 207-208
primates, 53, 58, 63-74, 77-78
  See also chimpanzees
printing, 145
prison, 433, 456, 509, 532
  brainwashing and, 416-17
  crime recruitment in, 510, 511, 512,
    531
  solitary confinement in, 223, 390,
    394
privacy, 415, 416, 417, 424-27
  political invasions of, 528
  sex and, 474, 475, 483
probability, 212-13
prohibition of vice, 518
projection mechanism, 277, 370, 371,
    379, 420
pronouns, 318, 320, 322, 323, 355, 356
propaganda, 397-98, 441, 442
  brainwashing, 413-17, 427
prostitution, 495, 500, 518, 521
  drugs and, 513
  market for, 469, 472, 477, 505, 507,
    509
prototaxic experience, 338, 480
protozoa, 55, 56
Proust, Marcel, 205
pseudo-communication, 125
psychiatric work worlds, 444-45
psychoanalysis, 48, 259-61
  dreams and, 158
  psychosexual development stages
    and, 321, 330, 334-35, 336-37,
    354, 381, 496
  psychotherapists and, 444-45
public place others, 358
punishment, see coercion; rewards

pupillary reflex, 392, 393
psychosis, 19, 237, 421, 511, 529, 540
  fantasy in, 154, 155, 157
Puritanical traditions, 187, 327, 380
  drugs and, 518
pyromania, 468

quantification, see statistical methods
quinine, 10, 11, 14

race, 90-93, 103, 208, 286, 540
  aging and, 552
  careers and, 435, 452
  intelligence and, 224-25
  intermarriage and, 482, 483
  "passing" and, 457
  perceptions of, 164-65, 167-68, 172,
    184, 195, 289, 298-301, 308, 371,
    497-98
  political ideology and, 441, 442-43
  race relations history, 206, 207,
    373, 453, 496, 497-98
  segregation by, 198, 300, 499
  See also specific groups
racketeers, 506, 507, 508, 511
Rank, Otto, 258
rape, 264, 473, 485, 496, 501, 506
  abortion law and, 490
rationalization, 269-73, 340
  defined, 269, 418, 420
  decision-making and, 398
  guilt feelings and, 422-23, 503, 509,
    521-22, 524, 528, 531, 532
  motive imputation and, 246, 264,
    266, 267-68, 269-70, 276-77
rats, 75-76, 252-53
reactance theory, 101
reaction formation, 418
reality
  conceptualizations of, 4-5, 16-20,
    21, 30, 83-104, 108, 118-19, 146,
    150, 155, 163-64, 172, 175,
    180-82, 187, 192-93, 303-304, 346,
    368-72, 438, 459, 539
  dreams and, 154-55, 341
  language and, 40, 43, 45, 83, 84-85,
    89-90, 93-98, 99, 103-104, 163,
    169-73, 180, 187-92, 269-72, 289,
    317
  paranoia and, 402
  planning and, 212-13
  See also experience; perception
reason, 80, 354
  behavior accounts and, 246, 264,
    270, 272 (See also rationalization)
  dreams and, 154, 155, 158-59
  schizophrenia and, 236-37

reason (*cont.*)
  sensorimotor, 303-304
  as symbolic activity, 33, 34, 76, 84,
    139, 213, 371
  See also logic
reductionism, 36, 38, 257-58, 260, 262
  defined, 35
reference group, 445-50, 460
regression, 158-59, 160, 333
  hypnosis and, 405, 406, 409
  Sullivan on, 340-41, 346
religion, 54, 79, 99, 197, 432
  career flow, 431
  conversion, 413-14, 416
  dreams and, 157
  humor and, 168
  language and, 76, 112, 284
  moral values and, 327-28, 490, 491
  motivation and, 247, 278, 422
  political ideology and, 441, 442,
    447, 497
  privacy and, 424, 425
  psychoanalysis and, 263
  science and, 5-6, 7-8, 17, 174,
    369-70, 546
  sex and, 482, 483, 486, 487
  See also Christianity
repression mechanism, 260-62, 265-
  66, 272, 418
  childhood memories and, 204
  dream imagery and, 158-59, 160
  latency period and, 332-33, 335
reward, 36-37, 116, 363, 402
  automatic responses and, 392
  in chimpanzee learning, 65-66, 68,
    70, 71, 193-94
  sublimation as, 261-62, 333, 335,
    339
ritual, 225, 247, 316, 317
  death and, 413, 490, 538, 539, 553,
    556, 558-60, 561
  of exclusion, 398, 399, 401, 402,
    417, 427
  function of, 157, 401
  pain and, 541, 542
  of political reform, 526
  of prohibitions, 518-19
  self-respect, 432
  sexual, 474
  speech, 125-26, 128
Roberts, H., quoted, 186
roles, 47, 367, 370, 399
  aging and, 548-50
  cognitive dissonance and, 102-103
  conversational, 120, 142-43
  death and, 557-58, 559-60, 561
  in hypnosis, 406-407, 409-10
  of illness, 541-43, 544-45

roles (*cont.*)
  imagination and, 156-57, 230,
    320-21, 359-60, 361, 362-63, 372
  self-concept and, 364-66, 372, 400,
    426-27, 432, 434, 437, 457-58,
    459, 503-505
  self-distancing in, 396-98
  sexual, 331, 333, 336, 341, 373-81,
    382, 465-66, 467, 468-72, 483,
    485, 486-89
  stereotypes, 91-92
Rome, ancient, 9
Ross, Ronald, 10
Royko, Mike, quoted, 528
rumor, memory and, 197, 201
Rush, Benjamin, 17-18
Russell, W. R., cited, 226-27, 233, 234
Russia, *see* Soviet Union
Russian Revolution, 453-54

sadism, 468
Sahlins, Marshall D., quoted, 78
Samoyedic language, 172
Sandburg, Carl, quoted, 183-84
Santo Domingo, 17, 18
Sapir, Edward, 337
  quoted, 109-10, 169, 172
Schambala language, 172
scapegoating, 401, 420, 530
schizophrenia, 218, 235-37, 337
Schneirla, T., cited, 57; quoted, 59,
  60-61
science, 3-48, 76
  biological disciplines of, 248
  cognitive dissonance and, 102
  language of, 19, 22, 30, 112, 172-73,
    174
  subjective reality and, 88, 99,
    368-70, 371, 372, 545-547
  symbols and, 84-85, 99, 144, 146
  See also experimental methods
sculpture, 150
self, the, 39, 312-48, 354, 358
  aphasia and, 234
  behavior accounts of, 245, 246,
    269-72, 276-77, 279-80, 328, 340,
    398, 500, 501, 503, 528
  control of, 389-427, 459, 481
  coping devices, 418-27
  death and, 538-39, 550
  dreams and, 156, 157, 158-59, 160,
    161, 419
  ego drives, 260, 263
  exchange theory and, 38
  language and, 30, 40, 76, 84, 85,
    140, 141, 153, 175, 217-38, 283,
    284, 286, 296-97, 318, 334, 389
  love and, 479

self, the (*cont.*)
  memory and, 197-98, 200-202,
    204-206, 207-208, 265-66, 325,
    416-17
  perception and, 182, 211, 303-304,
    314-15, 323-24, 371, 445, 538
  political ideology and, 442, 447-48
  privacy of, 415, 416, 417, 424-27
  psychosexual development stages,
    330-33, 334, 335-37, 338-47, 348,
    374, 472-75, 478, 492, 519, 520
  racial identification and, 298-301,
    442-43
  reference groups and, 445-50, 460
  reflexion, 85-87, 329, 351, 355, 361,
    485, 539
  roles of, 132, 364-66, 374, 396-98,
    399, 400, 402, 423, 426-27, 432,
    434, 457-58, 459, 472, 503-505,
    557-58
  schizophrenia and, 237
  separateness of, 316-17, 318-20,
    322, 329, 355, 370-71
self-interest, 247, 260
  group membership and, 278-79
self-preservation, 247, 252, 260
senility, 504
  isolation and, 223-24
sensation, 116, 392
  communication codes of, 126-28,
    142, 180-81
  hypnosis and, 404-405, 406, 407,
    409-10
  language and, 117-19, 121, 178-79,
    221-22, 297, 538, 543-45
  reason and, 211, 303-304, 371, 539
  sex modes and, 468
  See also perception; *and see specific
    senses*
sensorimotor intelligence, 303-304
Seward, G. H., quoted, 484
sex, 25, 195, 364, 373-81, 382, 464-92
  attitudes, 198, 276, 341, 343-44,
    374, 376, 377-79, 382, 476,
    477-78, 482, 484, 485, 486-89,
    496, 500
  careers and, 434, 476-77, 478
  childbearing and, 486, 489-91, 492
  chimpanzee, 66, 69, 75, 77, 465
  disengagement theory and, 549
  dreams and, 156, 160, 480
  as drive, 247, 255, 257, 260, 261-62,
    280, 330-33, 334, 335-36, 339,
    343-44, 345, 348, 465, 479, 491
  etiquette and, 124, 126-27, 189-90,
    301, 486, 487, 488, 542
  humor and, 166, 168, 483, 488
  hypnosis and, 408

sex (cont.)
  in insects, 60, 61
  trade in, 505, 507, 509
  See also homosexuality; women
shame, 327-28, 336, 400, 401
  See also guilt
Sherif, M., cited, 255; quoted, 301, 446
Shibutani, Tomatsu, cited, 445-46; quoted, 89, 449, 450
Shinn, M. W., quoted, 316
siblings, 352-53, 356, 374
significant others, 342-43, 347, 351, 356-68, 382, 423
  mobility and, 457-58
  reference groups and, 449
  See also social worlds
signs and signaling 28-29, 115-17
  chimpanzee, 63-64, 65, 66, 70-74, 193-95
  insect, 60-63
  memory and, 197, 199-200
  mental deficiency and, 222-23
  response inhibition, 211
  second system of, 39-40, 117-21, 152, 178-79 (See also language)
  sensory, 126-28, 178-79, 180 (See also sensation)
  symbols distinguished from, 119, 121-23, 126, 128, 133, 179
Simmel, Georg, cited, 4, 426, 434
Singelmann, Peter, 39
  quoted, 38
Singer, Charles, quoted, 7
slavery, science and, 7
sleep, 255
smoking, hypnosis and, 405
social class, 364, 438
  conscience and, 328
  drug use and, 503, 512
  ideology and, 414, 441, 442, 448, 454
  language and, 112, 113, 114-15, 142, 307-308
  mobility and, 457-58, 509, 511
  motivation and, 247, 248, 267-69, 276, 279, 280
  race and, 90-93, 164-65, 298, 299, 300-301, 442-43, 452
  science and, 7, 8, 412, 413
  sex and, 374, 378, 478, 479, 480-81, 482, 484, 489
  See also status
social death, 556-57, 560, 561
socialization, see learning; social worlds
social psychology
  methods of, 3-4, 9, 31-33, 40-47, 48, 80, 102, 262

social psychology (cont.)
  subhuman behavior studies of, 79-80
social worlds, 47, 431, 437-40
  defined, 89-90, 99, 351, 356-57, 449
  of the aging, 538, 539, 547-53
  career others and, 433-34
  centrality in, 440, 452, 548, 549
  of childhood, 351-82
  collapse of, 347, 450-56, 457, 459, 489-91
  conversion between, 413-17, 510-12
  of the deviant, 213, 505-28
  dropping out of, 457-59, 503-505, 510, 514-15, 548-50
  exclusion from, 230, 237, 401-403, 548
  humor and, 166, 167-68
  ideology and, 440-45, 509, 545-47
  intelligence and, 219, 223-25
  language and, 107-15, 119, 120-21, 122-23, 128, 141-42, 153, 164, 169-73, 175, 187, 245, 270-71, 284, 288, 290-91, 293, 300-301, 346, 378, 480
  memory and, 201-202, 206, 416-17
  perception and, 150, 155, 162, 164-65, 169, 174, 186-87, 189-90, 191-92, 195, 196, 206, 298, 372-73, 495-96, 540-41, 542-43, 544
  reference group, 445-50, 460
  subcommunities, 439-40, 451, 452
  See also culture; groups
society, 4, 32, 173-75, 287-88, 291, 292-93, 295
  agricultural, 54
  art and, 150-52, 169
  behavior codes of, 247, 248-49, 253, 275-79, 280, 300-301, 366-68, 496, 497-98, 504, 505, 542, 543-44, 559
  child care experts of, 357, 376-77, 548
  control mechanisms of, 390, 391, 394-96, 401, 402, 403, 413-17, 427, 432, 435, 436, 478-79, 496, 498, 500, 502, 509, 518-19, 525, 527, 532, 549, 550
  death and, 257, 452, 453, 538, 539, 549, 553, 554, 555, 556-57, 558-60, 561
  ethnomethodological view of, 41, 42-43, 44, 45
  exchange theory and, 38
  mass, 357-58, 449, 454-56, 459-60
  needs and, 255-58, 262-63, 267-69, 273-74, 278-79, 280

society (cont.)
  schizophrenia and, 235, 237
  science and, 5-7, 8-9, 33
  the self and, 139, 315, 320-28, 333, 348, 364-66, 389, 394-95, 396, 402, 424, 425-26, 432, 435, 437, 452, 500
  sexual repression by, 261-62, 333, 341-42, 344-45, 378-79, 381, 465-66, 475, 478-79, 519-24
  subhuman, 52, 55-56, 58-66, 68-69, 70, 77, 79, 254
  See also culture; groups; social worlds
sociolegal significant others, defined, 356, 357
Solomon Islanders, 114, 190
sorcery, 546
"sounding," 225
Southeast Asia, 124
Soviet Union, 39-40, 152, 198
  age ratios in, 547
  motivation theory in, 267-69, 280
  political language in, 125
space
  animals and, 67, 68, 75, 108
  gestural markers of, 129, 132
  language and, 119, 121, 172, 187-88
  perception of, 183, 193-94, 303, 304
  personal, 424, 425-26
special languages, 112-15, 162, 225
  baby talk, 111, 288-90, 291-92
specious present, defined, 210
speech, 120, 368
  aphasia and, 53, 126, 151, 153, 218, 226-35
  of children, 111, 283, 284, 285-90, 291-92, 293-94, 295, 308, 318, 334, 339, 360
  "expressive," 125-26, 128, 141, 284-85
  inner and outer, 141-42, 142-43, 146-48, 149, 173-74, 204, 232-33, 235, 286-87, 288, 296-97, 320, 354-55
  language properties of, 121
  in schizophrenia, 235
  written, 145-46, 295
Stalin, Joseph, 209
statistical methods, 22-23, 25, 26, 31, 45, 47
status, 347, 365
  of the aged, 547-48
  of children, 313-14, 339
  defenses of, 418-27
  degradation of, 401, 402, 414-16, 417, 426, 427, 531
  female, 486-89

Index

status (*cont.*)
  passages, 417-18, 431-32, 434-35, 437, 503-505, 553
  power hierarchies, 435, 496-501, 506, 507, 511, 527
  reference groups and, 446
  work ideology and, 443, 444
  See also roles; social class
Steffens, Lincoln, 525
stereotypes, 90-93, 95, 99, 103-104
  humor and, 167-68
  naming process and, 187, 301
  sexual, 92, 198, 343-44, 377, 486-89, 520
  "vicious," 518-19
stimulus-response psychology, 210-11, 314, 408, 517. *See also* conditioning
Stone, Gregory P., cited, 132, 317; quoted, 399
Strauss, Anselm L., cited, 317, 440; quoted, 435, 544-45
sublimation mechanism, 261-62, 333, 335, 339
Sudanese language, 172
Sudnow, David, 41
  quoted, 545, 554-55
suicide, 324, 412, 415, 417, 520
  anomic, 453
Sullivan, Anne Mansfield, 219-21
Sullivan, Harry Stack, 337-47, 348
  cited, 161, 265, 312, 329, 468, 472, 474, 480
  quoted, 29, 160, 182, 295, 419, 478
Sumeria, 54
superego, 332, 333, 335, 340
Swazi people, 197
swearing, 125-26
Sweden, 92, 547
symbolic coordinates, 99
  defined, 89-90
  classification process, 93-98
  dissonance among, 103-104
symbolic interactionism, 30-31, 32, 39, 40, 139
  ethnomethodology and, 44, 277
  hypnosis and, 410-11
  participant observation and, 25, 30
  research fields of, 46-47, 107, 496
  subject viewpoints and, 100, 277, 280
symbols, 34, 38, 47, 60, 63, 89-90, 93-98, 371
  analogy and, 161-64
  dreams and, 156, 157-58, 159-60, 161
  of emotion, 543-44
  food and, 249
  funeral, 553-54, 558-60, 561

symbols (*cont.*)
  gesture and, 123-25, 126-32, 284-85
  hypnosis and, 392-93, 403, 404-405, 407, 408, 410
  infant acquisition of, 287, 288, 291
  limitations of, 149-50, 169-73, 182, 209
  meaning (behavioral response) and, 98-99, 120-23, 125, 133, 188-89, 213, 219-22, 283, 292, 293, 296-97, 346, 373
  memory and, 198-206, 209
  natural signs and, 117-18, 119, 121-23, 126, 133
  primate learning and, 65-66, 69, 70-71, 73, 74, 75, 77-78
  of privacy, 424
  racial, 90-93
  self and, 30, 40, 76, 84, 85, 132, 139, 153, 211, 217-38, 321, 322, 324, 325, 329, 334, 338, 348, 394
  sexual roles and, 374-75, 464, 469, 470, 472, 474, 479-81, 491, 492
  social worlds and, 438, 440-45, 459 (*See also* social worlds)
  See also imagery; gesture; language
syntaxic experience, 338, 344, 346, 480

taboos, 186-87, 189-90, 195, 345
  changes in, 378-79, 490-91
  drugs and, 515, 516
  pain and, 542, 544-45
  sex and, 343, 381, 466-67, 468-72, 473, 474, 475, 482-83, 489
Taine, H., quoted, 291-93
Taiwan, 454
Tammany Hall, New York, 525, 527
taste, 186-87, 195
  hypnosis and, 404, 409-10
Teapot Dome scandal, 526
technology, 5, 7, 14, 28
  agricultural, 8, 9
  communication and, 77, 78, 145, 146
  imagery of, 179-80
television, 357-58
territoriality, 425-26
Thanatos, 263. *See also* death
theft, 273, 507-508, 509, 531
  children and, 394
  drugs and, 513
  recruitment into, 326, 510, 511
  thieves' slang, 114, 507, 509
theories, 102
  medical, 9-12, 14, 17-18
  testing methods, 21, 23, 24-25, 26, 46, 47, 48, 103

theories (*cont.*)
  See also experimental methods
thirst, 248, 255, 392, 405, 409-10
Thomas, W. I., 30, 257
thought, 23, 24, 26
  abstract, 75-76, 78, 83, 84-85, 95-96, 99, 121, 153, 162, 163, 187-95, 204, 223, 236-37, 283, 297-308, 367
  aphasic, 227-35, 394
  autistic, 154-61, 288, 341, 342, 352, 354
  behavior and, 29, 30, 31-33, 34, 35, 85-87, 88, 98-99, 148-50, 175, 286-87, 362
  drug addiction and, 516-17
  egocentric, 352-56, 358-60, 366-67, 368, 369, 371, 382
  experience modes and, 338
  language and, 30, 40, 75, 83-104, 119-21, 133, 139-75, 187-88, 213, 217-38, 283-308, 346, 354, 371, 392, 413-17, 427
  relativistic, 358-60, 362-63, 366-67, 368, 369-70
  writing and, 145-46, 203, 295, 296
Tierra del Fuego, 124
time, 297-98
  childhood duration and, 314
  chimpanzees and, 67, 68, 199
  gestural markers of, 129, 132
  language and, 75, 119, 121, 171-72
  meals and, 249
  memory, 197 (*See also* memory)
  motivation and, 272-73
  notation, 200
  perception and, 179, 181-82
  planning and, 179, 210-13
  self and, 325, 432-33, 434, 436-37, 449
Toda people, 373
toilet training, 331
Tolstoy, Leo, 258
tools, 64, 65-66, 67, 69-70, 75
touch, communication by, 126-28, 142, 187, 210-21
trade, 8-9, 54
  crime and, 505-506, 507, 508, 509, 512-13, 516
  exchange concepts and, 301-303, 308, 362-63
  writing and, 145
trance, in hypnosis, 403-406, 407, 409-10
translation, 169-70
transvestism, 468-69, 470, 505
Triandis, Henry, quoted, 182-83, 186
triangulation, 28-29, 30
Trobriand Islanders, 376

trust, 433, 476
Turks, 92, 125
Twain, Mark, 185
    quoted, 197
Tweed, William ("Boss"), 525-26

unconscious, the (id), 260-66, 421
    psychosexual development and,
        331, 334, 339, 340
    Soviet class theory and, 268, 280
    Sullivan's view of, 345, 346
United Nations, 170
United States, 169, 170, 188-89, 453
    aging in, 547
    children's status in, 253, 313, 317
    death in, 559
    drugs in, 497, 512, 513, 518
    food habits, 186-87, 248-49, 251
    gesture patterns in, 123, 130
    interest patterns in, 197-98, 209-
        10, 530
    medicine in, 542, 546-47
    political values in, 125, 164-65,
        166, 447-48, 490, 525-27
    prisons in, 223
    racial attitudes in, 90-93, 103,
        163-64, 184, 195, 206-207,
        298-301
    sex in, 343, 374, 475, 481, 482, 485,
        486, 488, 489
universals
    defined, 14, 15-16
    gestural, 129
    instincts as, 252
    of language usage, 283
    of self development, 314, 335

vision, 116, 179, 182, 184-85
    blindness, 180-81, 218-22, 223,
        238, 316, 499

vision (cont.)
    hypnosis and, 405-406
    naming and, 187-89, 190
    pupillary reflex and, 392, 393
    subhuman, 192-95
voyeurism, 468
Vygotsky, L., 268, 283
    cited, 39, 147, 148, 287-88, 306, 354
    quoted, 151-52, 296, 353

Wanyika people, 124
warfare, 8-9
    careers in, 434, 435, 444
    motivation in, 252, 273-74, 278, 447
    symbols and, 90, 222, 373, 441
Warren, Carol A. B., quoted, 521
Watergate scandal, 166, 526
Watson, James, 20, 175
Wegener, P., quoted, 162
Weiss, E., quoted, 259-61
Werner, H., 153, 223
white-collar criminals, 506, 507, 531
will, 334, 390-94, 403-404, 407
Withers, Carl, quoted, 546
Wolfenstein, Martha, cited, 313;
    quoted, 165
women, 91, 423, 434, 435
    aging and, 549
    childbirth pain and, 540, 542
    psychosexual development of,
        330, 331-32, 333, 374, 381, 472
    rights issues, 163, 253, 266, 379,
        489, 490, 496, 504
    sexual behavior patterns of, 195,
        378, 465, 466, 467, 473, 480-81,
        482, 483-85, 486-89, 501
    sexual symbolism and, 374-75,
        469, 470, 472, 474
    stereotypes of, 92, 198, 301, 343-44,
        377

work, 256
    aging and, 547-48, 550, 551, 552
    career flow, 347, 431, 433, 434, 437,
        458
    in crime, 505, 506-12, 513, 514
    division of labor in, 68-69, 77-78,
        254, 439, 486
    homosexuals and, 519-20, 522
    ideology and, 440, 441, 442, 443-
        45
    memory and, 197
    self-concept and, 364, 365, 445
    social class and, 268, 269, 276, 418,
        438, 457-58, 511
    strikes, 559
World War I, 227
World War II, 195, 227, 252, 512, 547
    Balkans in, 274
    blood banks, 91
    collapse of social worlds, 452, 453
    flyer training, 188-89
    humor in, 424
    Soviet Union and, 209
Wright, Richard, quoted, 376
writing, 140, 222
    agraphia, 218, 226
    evolution and, 73, 79, 144-46, 175,
        294-95
    idiographs, 170
    numbers and, 8, 9, 54, 203
    rules of, 295, 296

yellow fever, 17-18
Yerkes, R. M. and A. W., 69, 70
    quoted, 73, 193-94
Yoruba people, 197

Zuni people, 185